International Finance

Fourth edition

Maurice **D.** Levi

Routledge
Taylor & Francis Group

LONDON AND NEW YORK

First published 2005
by Routledge
2 Park Square, Milton Park, Abingdon, Oxon OX14 4RN

Simultaneously published in the USA and Canada
by Routledge
270 Madison Avenue, New York, NY 10016

Routledge is an imprint of the Taylor & Francis Group

© 2005 Maurice D. Levi

Typeset in Perpetua and Bell Gothic by Newgen Imaging Systems (P) Ltd, Chennai, India

Printed and bound in Great Britain by Bell & Bain Ltd, Glasgow

British Library Cataloguing in Publication Data
A catalogue record for this book is available from the British Library

Library of Congress Cataloging in Publication Data
A catalog record for this book has been requested

ISBN 0–415–30899–2 (hbk)
ISBN 0–415–30900–X (pbk)

To Kate

"As for foreign exchange, it is almost as romantic as young love, and quite as resistant to formulae."

H.L. Mencken

(As you shall see, it is not entirely resistant to formulae!)

About the author

Since receiving his PhD from the University of Chicago, Maurice D. Levi has taught and written research papers in a wide variety of areas of finance and economics. This broad range of research and teaching interests form the foundation for this book in international finance, a subject that he believes to be best treated as an application of financial and economic principles, rather than as a separate and isolated subject area.

Professor Levi has published research papers on financial market anomalies, the effectiveness of monetary and fiscal policy, the relationship between inflation and interest rates, the effect of taxes on international capital flows, and the link between inflationary expectations and unemployment, as well as in the numerous areas of international finance that are reflected in this book. He has also written in the areas of econometric methods, macroeconomics, labor economics, environmental economics, money and banking, and regional economics. His papers have appeared in just about every leading research journal in finance and economics including: *American Economic Review*; *Econometrica*; *Journal of Political Economy*; *Journal of Finance*; *Journal of Monetary Economics*; *Journal of Money, Credit and Banking*; *Journal of International Money and Finance*; *Journal of International Economics*; *Management Science*; *Ecological Economics*, and *Journal of Econometrics*. He is also the author of *Economics and the Modern World* (Heath, Lexington MA, 1994), *Economics Deciphered: A Layman's Survival Guide* (Basic Books, New York, 1981), and *Thinking Economically* (Basic Books, New York, 1985) and the coauthor, with M. Kupferman, of *Slowth* (Wiley, New York, 1980).

Since joining the Sauder School of Business of the University of British Columbia, Professor Levi has held visiting positions at the Hebrew University of Jerusalem, the University of California, Berkeley, MIT, the National Bureau of Economic Research, the University of Exeter, University of New South Wales, and the London Business School. He has received numerous academic prizes and awards including Killam and Nomura Fellowships and the Bronfman Award.

Contents

CONTENTS

Illustrations

FIGURES

TABLES

EXHIBITS

Preface

This book is intended for use in MBA and senior-level undergraduate business courses in international finance and international business. It is comprehensive, covering both the markets and management of multinational business. It is designed to be used in its entirety in courses that cover all areas of international finance, or to be used selectively in courses dealing only with international financial markets or only with international financial management. To the extent possible, the two major subdivisions of international finance are self contained, being delivered in separate segments.

The book is specifically designed for students who have taken introductory economics and finance, and who wish to build upon the basic financial and economic principles they have acquired. By assuming these prerequisites, this book is able to go further than competing textbooks in international finance. It is able to introduce the student to the new and exciting discoveries and developments in the dynamic and rapidly expanding field of international finance. These discoveries and developments, many of which have occurred during the last few years, are extensions of the principles of finance and economics.

Of course, it is necessary to recognize that business students, whether concentrating in finance or in international business, have a practical interest in the subjects they take. Consequently, a good textbook in international finance must cover real managerial topics such as how to evaluate foreign investment opportunities, where to borrow and invest, how exchange rates affect cash flows, what can be done to avoid foreign exchange exposure and risk, and the general financial management problems of doing business in the global environment. However, even these highly practical topics can be properly dealt with only by applying basic financial and economic principles that many other international finance textbooks appear reluctant to employ. As a result, despite adequate levels of preparation, generally including thorough introductions to economics and finance, the student often receives a rather descriptive treatment of these topics that fails to build on the foundations of previous courses. For this reason, many MBA students and undergraduate business majors with solid backgrounds in, for example, the consequences of arbitrage or the principles of capital budgeting feel they move sideways rather than forward into international finance.

The topics in this text are covered from the perspective of a person who wishes to learn about the financial management of an internationally oriented business. However, it is important that managers also understand international financial developments on a macroeconomic level. Such an understanding enables managers to anticipate economic changes and adjust to what they expect to occur. Because of this double level of interest in the forces behind events and the consequences of these events for the firm, this book includes several chapters on the international finance of the economy. However, these chapters are divided into two parts, with the essential material on the international financial environment limited to only two chapters in the early part of the book. This is to provide the book with a financial management focus, unlike the previous three editions that have given more priority to the wider picture of the global economy. The aspects of the international financial environment that are less essential to day-to-day international financial decisions are in a separate section at the end of the book. Nevertheless, even at this more aggregate level, a managerial perspective is taken, with the material linked to factors relevant to the handling of volatility that has its roots in global events.

This book represents a major revision and updating of the third edition of *International Finance* that go beyond moving less essential material on the international financial environment to later in the book. New topics have been included and topics previously covered have been considerably rearranged and reintegrated. In addition, additional examples have been provided. The guiding principle throughout this substantial revision has been to bring the book closer to the syllabus that is emerging in one-semester international finance courses in MBA and senior level undergraduate business programs. Most particularly, an attempt has been made to go beyond theory and into the vital and increasingly important real world of international finance.

As with previous editions, a substantial revision has been necessary because the international financial developments that are occurring are nothing short of spectacular. For example, new markets and instruments are emerging at a frantic pace, in part as a response to exchange rates that at times have been so volatile they have grabbed the headlines, not of the business section of the newspaper, but of the front page. The day-to-day lives of people have been affected by events such as the introduction of the euro, a common currency now shared by numerous countries in Europe. The euro represents an unprecedented experiment in international financial cooperation with huge implications for the traveler and the person in the street as well as corporate financial management. Great fortunes have been made and lost in foreign exchange. News reports have also been full of exchange rate crises in Asia, South and Central America, and Russia, and economic summits of world leaders dealing with these periodic crises. At the same time, there has been an explosion of research in international finance and international financial management. The revisions in this fourth edition of *International Finance* reflect the important recent developments and current research that have sharpened the insights from studying this dynamic subject.

This book has evolved over a number of years while teaching or doing research at the University of British Columbia and also at the Hebrew University, Jerusalem; the University of California, Berkeley; the Massachusetts Institute of Technology; the London Business School; the University of New South Wales; and the University of Exeter. I am indebted to all these institutions, especially the Sauder School of Business at the University of British Columbia, which has been my home base for over three decades.

An author's debts are a pleasure to acknowledge, and in the course of four editions of this book I have incurred many I would find difficult to repay. A huge debt is owed to Cynthia Ree who has spent endless days and weeks providing a usable electronic copy from which I could work, and to my colleague Ali Lazrak who has provided valuable comments. The help offered by reviewers has been immensely important in improving the final product. Only the anonymity of the individual reviews prevents me from apportioning the vast credit due to them. My wife, Kate, son Adam, and daughter Naomi have provided professional and indispensable help in preparing the manuscript. My son Jonathan also helped by asking questions that sharpened my understanding of difficult matters. Too numerous to mention individually but of great importance were the students in my MBA and undergraduate courses in international finance at the University of British Columbia, whose reactions have been a crucial ingredient in the revision of this text.

It is to my wife, Kate, and my daughter Naomi that I owe my greatest thanks. In addition to playing a vital role in preparing and checking the manuscript they have provided the moral support and encouragement that have made a fourth venture far less stressful than I had imagined.

Maurice D. Levi
Vancouver, BC

Chapter 1

The world of international finance

The globe is not a level playing field.

Anonymous

UNIQUE DIMENSIONS OF INTERNATIONAL FINANCE

While tradition dictates that we continue to refer to the subject matter in this book as *international* finance, the modifier "international" is becoming increasingly redundant: today, with fewer and fewer barriers to international trade and financial flows, and with communications technology directly linking every major financial center, all finance is becoming "international." Indeed, not only are domestic financial markets increasingly internationally integrated, but the problems faced by companies and individuals in different lands are remarkably similar.

Even though most if not all finance must be viewed at the international level, there are special problems that arise from financial and trading relations between nations. These are the problems addressed in this book. Many of these problems are due to the use of different currencies used in different countries and the consequent need to exchange them. The rates of exchange between currencies – the amount of a currency received for another – have been set by a variety of arrangements, with the rates of exchange as well as the arrangements themselves subject to change. Movements in exchange rates between currencies can have profound effects on sales, costs, profits, asset and liability values, and individual well-being.

Other special, uniquely international financial problems arise from the fact that there are political divisions as well as currency divisions between countries. In particular, the world is divided into nation-states that generally, but not always, correspond to the currency divisions: some nations share currencies, such as the **euro** that is the common currency for numerous European nations, and the Russian ruble that is still used by several former Soviet states. Political barriers provide additional opportunities and risks when engaging in overseas borrowing and investment. International finance has as its focus the problems managers face from these currency and country divisions and their associated opportunities and risks.

THE BENEFITS OF STUDYING INTERNATIONAL FINANCE

Knowledge of international finance can help a financial manager decide how international events will affect a firm and what steps can be taken to exploit positive developments and insulate the firm from harmful ones. Among the events that affect the firm and that must be managed are changes in exchange rates as well as interest rates, inflation rates, and asset values. These different changes are themselves related. For example, declining exchange rates tend to be associated with relatively high interest rates and inflation. Furthermore, some asset prices are positively affected by a declining currency, such as stock prices of export-oriented companies that are more profitable after devaluation. Other asset prices are negatively affected, such as stock prices of companies with foreign-currency denominated debt that lose when the company's home currency declines: the company's debt is increased in terms of domestic currency. These connections between exchange rates, asset and liability values, and so on mean that foreign exchange is not simply a risk that is added to other business risks. Instead, the amount of risk depends crucially on the way exchange rates and other financial prices are connected. For example, effects on investors when exchange rates change depend on whether asset values measured in foreign currency move in the same direction as the exchange rate, thereby reinforcing each other, or in opposite directions, thereby offsetting each other. Only by studying international finance can a manager understand matters such as these. International finance is not just finance with an extra cause of uncertainty. It is a legitimate subject of its own, with its own risks and ways of managing them.

There are other reasons to study international finance beyond learning about how exchange rates affect asset prices, profits, and other types of effects described earlier. Because of the integration of financial markets, events in distant lands, whether they involve changes in the prices of oil and gold, election results, the outbreak of war, or the establishment of peace, have effects that instantly reverberate around the Earth. The consequences of events in the stock markets and interest rates of one country immediately show up around the globe, which has become an increasingly integrated and interdependent financial environment. The links between money and capital markets have become so close as to make it futile to concentrate on any individual part.

In this book we are concerned with the problems faced by any firm whose performance is affected by the international environment. Our analysis is relevant to more than the giant multinational corporations (MNCs) that have received so much attention in the media. It is just as valid for a company with a domestic focus that happens to export a little of its output or to buy inputs from abroad. Indeed, even companies that operate only domestically but compete with firms producing abroad and selling in their local market are affected by international developments. For example, US clothing or appliance manufacturers with no overseas sales will find US sales and profit margins affected by exchange rates which influence the dollar prices of imported clothing and appliances. Similarly, bond investors holding their *own* government's bonds, denominated in their *own* currency, and spending all their money at *home,* are affected by changes in exchange rates if exchange rates prompt changes in interest rates. Specifically, if governments increase interest rates to defend their currencies when their currencies fall in value on the foreign exchange markets, holders of domestic bonds will find their assets falling in value along with their currencies: bond prices fall when interest rates increase. It is difficult to think of any firm or individual that is not affected in some way or other by the international financial environment. Jobs, bond and stock prices, food prices, government revenues, and other important financial variables are all tied to exchange rates and other developments in the increasingly global financial environment.

THE GROWING IMPORTANCE OF INTERNATIONAL FINANCE

While we shall emphasize the managerial issues of international finance in this book, it is important to emphasize that the international flows of goods and capital that are the source of supply of and demand for currencies, and hence essential to the subject of international finance, are fundamental to our well-being. A strong currency, for example, *ceteris paribus,* improves a country's standard of living: the currency buys more in world markets. Not only does a strong currency allow citizens to buy more imports, they can also buy more domestically produced products that are internationally traded because a country's citizens have to compete with foreigners for their own country's tradable products. The gain in standard of living from a rising currency is also evident when living standards are compared between nations. International rankings of living standards require conversions of local-currency incomes into a common measure, usually the US dollar. A rising currency moves a country up the ladder by making local incomes worth more dollars.

Citizens also gain from the efficient global allocation of capital: when capital is allocated to its best uses on a global scale, overall returns are higher and these extra returns can be shared among the global investors. Let us therefore pause to consider the evidence of the international movement of goods and capital. We shall also take a look at the sources of gains from the flows of goods and capital. We shall see that international finance is a subject of immense and growing importance.

The growth of international trade

International trade has a pervasive importance for our standard of living and our daily lives. In the department store we find cameras and electrical equipment from Japan and clothing from China and India. On the street we find automobiles from Germany, Japan, Korea, Sweden, and France using gasoline from Nigeria, Saudi Arabia, Great Britain, Mexico, and Kuwait. At home we drink tea from India, coffee from Brazil, whiskey from Scotland, beer from Germany, and wine from just about every country on Earth. We have become so used to enjoying these products from distant lands that it is easy to forget they are the result of complex international trading and financial linkages discussed in this book.

Record on the growth of trade

Peoples and nations have been trading from time immemorial. During the period since records have been kept the amount of this trade between nations has typically grown at a faster rate than has domestic commerce. For example, since 1950, world trade has grown by about 6 percent per annum, roughly twice that of world output over the same period. During the nineteenth century, international trade grew at such a tremendous rate that it increased by a factor of 25 times in the century leading up to the First World War. Even in the period since 1980, a mere moment in the long history of international trade, the value of trade between nations has tripled (see Table 1.1). Growth in the importance of trade in the form of the fraction of Gross Domestic Product (GDP) consisting of exports is shown for several countries in Figure 1.1.

Table 1.1 Aggregate international trade versus GDP

Year	World exports, billion US$	Exports/GDP%
1999	4945.9	16.0
1995	4531.7	15.7
1990	3070.0	14.2
1985	1610.8	13.7
1980	1541.3	14.7

Source: National Account Statistics: Analysis of Main Aggregates, United Nations, New York, 2003.

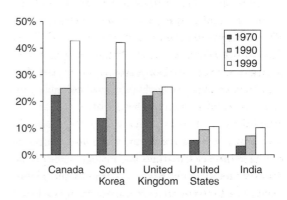

Figure 1.1 Percentage of GDP arising from exports

Note
Today, foreign markets represent a more important proportion of aggregate demand for the products of most countries than in the past. For example, the fraction of US GDP that is exported has almost doubled since 1970, while the fraction of South Korea's GDP that is exported has almost tripled.

Source: National Account Statistics: Analysis of Main Aggregates, United Nations, New York, 2003.

Indeed, if anything, the published export figures understate the growth of world trade. This is suggested by the fact that when the world's combined reported exports are compared to reported imports, global imports exceed exports. In the absence of extraterrestrial trade, this suggests a reporting error: when properly calculated, global imports must equal global exports. The mechanisms for reporting imports are generally better than those for reporting exports – governments keep track of imports for collection of duties and for safety and health reasons – and therefore it is likely that exports are understated rather than that imports are overstated. It is worth pausing to consider why international trade and the international financial activity associated with that trade have grown so rapidly in recent decades.

Reasons for the growing importance of international trade

There are two principal reasons why international trade has grown so rapidly:

1   A liberalization of trade and investment via reductions in tariffs, quotas, currency controls, and other impediments to the international flow of goods and capital.
2   An unprecedented shrinkage of "economic space" via rapid improvements in communication and transportation technologies, and consequent reductions in costs.

Much of the trade liberalization has come from the development of free-trade areas such as that of the **European Union (EU)** now consisting of more than two dozen countries from Sweden to Malta and Portugal to Greece, and that of the United States, Canada, and Mexico which signed the **North American Free Trade Agreement (NAFTA)** in 1993. Similarly, rapid growth of trade has occurred among the members of the **Association of South East Asian Nations (ASEAN)**. Indeed, more and more of global trade is occurring within trading blocks. This regionalization of trade has important

currency implications, making the trend of paramount importance to international finance. For example, the euro has become the common currency of many of the members of the EU, motivated by the desire to reduce the foreign exchange risks and currency conversion costs of doing business within this important **customs union**.[1] The previous currencies of this area have completely disappeared: no more German marks, Italian lira, and so on. The role of the US dollar within NAFTA has become a source of serious debate: should there be a North American common currency to reduce risks and costs in this important and possibly expanding region?

The second factor contributing to growing trade, namely the shrinkage of "economic space" caused by a lower cost of communication and transportation, has had a profound effect. For example, in real terms, long-distance telephone costs have been reduced by more than 90 percent since the 1920s. Connection times have been reduced even more dramatically: long-distance calls used to be connected manually by operators who would route calls through available lines.[2] The cost of international business travel by air has dropped so substantially that it can cost little more for a US executive to meet with an Asian or European client than another US executive in another US city. Air freight and ocean tanker costs for transporting goods have also fallen rapidly. This has resulted in a **globalization** of markets and consequent rapid

---

1   A customs union is different from a free-trade area. A customs union maintains common levels of tariffs and other trade restrictions against nonmembers while having free trade between the union members. A free-trade area allows countries to maintain different tariffs and other restrictions against nonmembers. This limits the ability of goods and services to move freely between members of a free-trade area: countries must check when products move across borders to see if they are produced by member countries or by nonmember countries.

2   See Ronald Abler, "Effect of Space-Adjusting Technologies on the Human Geography of the Future," in *Human Geography in a Shrinking World*, Ronald Abler, Donald Janelle, Allen Philbrick and John Sommer (eds), Duxbury Press, North Scituate, MA, 1975, pp. 35–56.

growth in international financial activity for settling transactions on the multinational scale.

Given the growing importance of international trade, it is worth briefly considering the rewards and risks that accompany it. This will allow us to briefly introduce some of the matters discussed at length later in this book.

The rewards of international trade

The principal reward of international trade is that it has brought about increased prosperity by allowing nations to specialize in producing those goods and services at which they are relatively efficient. The relative efficiency of a country in producing a particular product can be described in terms of the amounts of other, alternative products that could be produced by the same inputs. In other words, we can think of relative efficiencies in terms of the opportunity cost of one product in terms of another. When considered this way, relative efficiencies are described as **comparative advantages**. All nations can and do simultaneously gain from exploiting their comparative advantages, as well as from the larger scale production and broader choice of products that is made possible by international trade.[3]

In the last few years it has become increasingly recognized that there is more to successful international trade than comparative advantages based on productive efficiencies.[4] These particular advantages cannot explain distinct patterns of success, such as Singapore and Hong Kong's rapid growth with limited resources, versus Argentina's slow economic advance despite abundant natural advantages. Also, comparative advantages do not explain why some regions *within* countries, such as northern

Italy, grow faster than other regions, or why parts of industries expand while others contract. Dynamic factors, rather than static production efficiencies and "factor endowments," play a vital role in international trading success by offering countries **competitive advantages**. In particular, countries typically are successful internationally in products for which there are dynamic, discerning buyers at home. For example, the French success in wine and cheese, German success in beer and finely engineered automobiles, British success in cookies, Italian success in fashion and US success in entertainment, are all in part due to the presence of consumers in the respective countries whose sophisticated tastes have forced firms to produce first-class products to maintain their markets. Once successful at home, these firms have been able to succeed abroad.

A further factor affecting success in international trade is the presence of suppliers and firms in supportive industries in the vicinity of exporting firms. For example, in southern California the US entertainment industry can call on lighting and camera engineers, actors and screen designers, and even such "extras" as exotic animal trainers and explosives experts. Other so-called "**clusters**" of supportive activities are found in the northern German chemical industry, Mid-Western US automobile industry, northern Italian manufacturing industry and the Tokyo–Osaka-based consumer-electronics sector.

The risks of international trade

The rewards of trade do not come without accompanying risks. The most obvious additional risk of international versus domestic trade arises from uncertainty about exchange rates. Unexpected changes in exchange rates have important impacts on sales, prices and profits of exporters and importers. For example, if a Scottish whiskey exporter faces an unexpected increase in the value of the pound from $1.5/£ to $1.6/£, a bottle of whiskey sold for £10 will increase in price in the United States from $15 to $16. This will reduce sales, and since the Scottish exporter receives

---

3 For those who have not learned or have forgotten the principle of comparative advantage, a summary is given in Appendix A at the end of this chapter. The gains from exploitation of comparative advantage are no different from the gains from specialization *within* a country.

4 This recognition is in large part due to the influential book by Michael E. Porter, *The Competitive Advantage of Nations*, Harvard University Press, Cambridge, MA, 1989.

5

Table 1.2 *Selected foreign exchange gains, 2001: millions of US dollars*

Company	Country	Gain	Net Inc. (Loss)	Fx.Gain (%)	Industry
Citicorp	USA	2,383	9,642	25	Banking/Finance
Barclays	UK	1,470	3,585	41	Banking/Finance
Deutsche Bank	Germany	1,233	149	828	Banking/Finance
UBS	Swiss.	1,232	2,996	41	Banking/Finance
HSBC	UK/HK	600	5,406	11	Banking/Finance
Ford Motors	USA	283	(5,453)	n/d	Auto. Manuf.
IBM	USA	198	7,723	3	Computing
Chevron/Texaco	USA	191	3,288	6	Energy
Deutsche Telekom	Germany	178	(3,074)	n/d	Telecommunications
Telefonos De Mex.	Mexico	127	2,566	5	Telecommunications
Rio Tinto	UK	58	1,079	5	Mining
China Petroleum	China	45	1,936	2	Mining
Inco	Canada	39	305	13	Mining
Xerox	USA	29	(71)	n/d	Bus. Equip.
BHP Billiton	Australia	29	1,348	2	Mining
China Eastern	China	15	65	23	Airlines
Apple Comp.	USA	15	(25)	n/d	Computing
Can. Pacific	Canada	9	258	4	Railway
Nortel	Canada	9	(27,446)	n/d	Telecommunications

Source: COMPUSTAT, 2003. Information contained in this document is subject to change without notice. Standard and Poor's assumes no responsibility or liability for any errors or omissions or for results obtained by the use of such information.

£10 before and after the change in the exchange rate, it reduces the exporter's revenue and profit.[5] Similarly, prices, sales, revenue, and profits of importers are also affected by unexpected changes in exchange rates.

Tables 1.2 and 1.3 provide some examples of companies whose profits have been affected by changes in exchange rates. The examples indicate that effects can be substantial viewed both absolutely and relative to net income. Some companies, such as Ford Motor Company, have made foreign exchange gains while making losses overall. The power of exchange rates to affect the bottom line and even the survival of companies is also illustrated in Exhibit 1.1.

5 In our whiskey example, the dollar price might in reality increase by less than the change in the exchange rate. As is shown in Chapter 11, the amount of "pass through" of changes in exchange rates reaching the buyer depends on the elasticity of demand, use of tradable inputs, and so on.

Whether changes in exchange rates affect prices, sales, and profits of exporters and importers depends on whether changes in exchange rates really make a firm's goods cheaper or more expensive to buyers. For example, if a decrease in the value of the British pound from $1.5/£ to $1.4/£ occurs while the price of a bottle of whiskey for export from Scotland goes from £10 to £10.71, a bottle of whiskey will continue to cost $15 in the United States. This is because the pound price multiplied by the exchange rate, which gives the dollar price, is unchanged. Our example shows that in order to determine the effect of a change in exchange rates, we must examine inflation and how inflation and exchange rates are related. This requires that we study international finance at the level of the economy as well as at the level of the individual firm.

The risk faced by exporters and importers resulting from the impact of exchange rates on

Table 1.3 *Selected foreign exchange losses, 2001: millions of US dollars*

Company	Country	Loss	Net Inc. (Loss)	Industry
Telefonica	Spain	697	1,875	Telecommunications
Koninklijke	Holland	279	984	Publishing
Sony	Japan	239	115	Music/Electronics
United Pan Europe	Holland	153	(3,935)	Communications
Turkcell Iletisim	Turkey	151	(187)	Telecommunications
United Global Com.	USA	148	(4,494)	Communications
Exxon Mobil	USA	142	15,320	Energy
General Motors	USA	107	601	Transport Manuf.
Portugal Telecom	Portugal	106	273	Telecommunications
Alcatel	France	105	4,418	Telecommunications
Alberta Energy	Canada	71	517	Energy
Lucent	USA	58	(16,198)	Telecommunications
BASF	Germany	56	5,214	Chemical
Bell Canada	Canada	39	235	Telecommunications
Pfizer	USA	33	7,788	Pharmaceuticals
Monsanto	USA	32	5,462	Agricultural Supply
Abbot	USA	31	16,285	Health
Shell	UK/Holland	30	135,211	Energy
Dow Chemical	USA	24	27,805	Chemical

Source: COMPUSTAT, 2003. Information contained in this document is subject to change without notice. Standard and Poor's assumes no responsibility or liability for any errors or omissions or for results obtained by the use of such information.

prices, sales, and profits is only one, albeit probably the most important, of the additional risks of international trade versus domestic trade. Another risk of international trade is **country risk**. This includes the risk that, as a result of war, revolution, or other political or social events, a firm may not be paid for its exports: many exporters extend trade credit to buyers. Country risk applies to foreign investment as well as to credit granted in trade, and exists because it is difficult to use legal channels or reclaim assets when the investment is in another political jurisdiction. Furthermore, foreign companies may be willing but unable to pay because, for example, their government unexpectedly imposes currency exchange restrictions. Other country-related risks of doing business abroad include uncertainty about the possible imposition or change of import tariffs or quotas, possible changes in subsidization of local producers, and possible imposition of nontariff barriers such as quality requirements that are really designed to give domestic firms an advantage.

Practices have evolved and markets have developed which help firms cope with many of the added risks of doing business abroad. For example, special types of foreign exchange contracts have been designed to enable importers and exporters to **hedge**, or **cover**, some of the risks from unexpected changes in exchange rates. Similarly, **export credit insurance** and **letters of credit** have been developed to reduce risks of nonpayment when granting trade credit to foreign buyers. With international trade playing a growing role in just about every nation, it is increasingly important that we learn about the risk-reducing instruments and practices. We must also learn about the fundamental causes of the special risks of international trade. These are two important topics of this book.

EXHIBIT 1.1   CURRENCY MATTERS: CORPORATE EXPERIENCES

News reports over the years have been full of accounts of companies that have suffered huge losses or enjoyed great gains from exchange rate movements. The very fact that foreign exchange losses and gains frequently make the business headlines is proof in itself that companies have not hedged their foreign exchange exposure, or if they have hedged, that the hedges have been incorrectly designed.* Consider, for example, the following reports during just one short period of time:

■   In 1985, the same year that Volkswagen produced its 50 millionth car, the company found itself apparently defrauded to the tune of nearly half a billion Deutschmarks. At the time this was equivalent to approximately a quarter of a billion dollars. The problem was that the US dollar fell well below what it could have been sold for, and as required by company policy, by using an appropriate foreign exchange contract. The foreign exchange loss that ensued was enough to wipe out the profit from a calendar quarter of global operations.

■   In the case of BOC, a British producer of gases for industry, a foreign exchange gain of nearly seventeen million pounds was made by using a foreign exchange contract to sell the entire year's revenues for 1985 at a substantially higher price than would have been received by selling the foreign exchange as it was received.

■   The US photographic company, Eastman-Kodak, estimated that in the few years leading up to

1985, the strong US dollar cost the company $3.5 billion in before-tax earnings. Subsequent weakening of the dollar helped reverse the losses, showing that failure to fully hedge may or may not be harmful.

■   In 1986, Japan's largest camera producer reported a more than two-thirds reduction in profit attributed to a strong Japanese yen.

It is worth mentioning that in the case of Volkswagen, the apparent fraud was the result of a failure of managers in charge of reducing the company's foreign exchange risk – or more precisely its "exposure," a term we define later – to take the steps they were supposed to. Indeed, forged documents were used to hide the absence of the appropriate steps. The Volkswagen experience is a vivid example of how costly it can be not to apply some of the principles in this book, even though in Volkswagen's case top management knew very well what should be done. Indeed Volkswagen had very strict rules that all foreign exchange exposure be hedged. Unfortunately, those responsible for putting the rules into effect ignored top management's instructions.

*Hedging is action taken to reduce foreign exchange exposure, and is discussed later at length, especially in Chapters 12–15.

Source: Based on information in "Companies and Currencies: Payment by Lottery," *The Economist*, April 4, 1987, p. 8, and "Ex-VW Official is Arrested in Fraud Case," *The Wall Street Journal*, April 8, 1987, p. 27.

Increased globalization of financial and real-asset markets

Alongside the growing importance of international trade, there has been a parallel growth in the importance of foreign investment in the money market, the bond market, the stock market, the real-estate market, and the market for operating businesses (see Exhibit 1.2).[6] At times, the importance of overseas investments and investors has swelled to overshadow that of domestic investments and investors. For example, there have been periods when purchases of US bills and bonds by Japanese,

6 Some measures of globalization of financial markets are provided in Exhibit 1.2.

EXHIBIT 1.2 GETTING A GRIP ON GLOBALIZATION

A definition of globalization that many economists like is that "globalization is a shrinkage of economic space." In terms of economic arrangements, distance does not matter as much as it used to.

This book is an example of globalization. The author lives in Canada. The book is published by a British publisher. The copyediting was done in India. You, the reader, could be sitting down to learn international finance just about anywhere. Was all this difficult to achieve? The answer is "no, not at all!" With e-mail, fax, couriers and multinational publishing houses it is scarcely more difficult to do this across the globe than to try and do it all in a single country. Indeed, there are benefits from taking advantage of the forces of globalization.

If there is one industry where globalization can progress most easily, possibly even easier than in textbook publishing, it is in the area of banking and finance. This is because the costs of moving money from place to place can be inconsequential compared to transportation costs in, say, the oil or the automobile industry. The result is that returns offered to investors have to be just about the same in every country, at least after possible changes in exchange rates have been taken into account. Similarly, the cost of borrowing is similar everywhere, again after considering the role of changes in exchange rates. Sure, there are places with high interest rates facing investors and high financing costs facing borrowers, but these are typically countries where the currencies are widely anticipated to fall in value in the future. The high interest rates are the financial market's way of compensating for the expected exchange rate changes. One measure of globalization is, therefore, the extent to which real investment returns and borrowing costs differ from country to country. The more similar are interest rates, the greater the degree of globalization.

Another possible measure of globalization is the proportions of typical investment portfolios that are held in foreign securities. If people hold only their own countries' securities, this would be a sign that globalization has not come very far. However, if investors are internationally diversified, this is evidence that globalization has occurred. The actual holdings of foreign versus domestic securities would need to be compared to the importance of each country in the global financial market. For example, if a country is 10 percent of the world market, complete globalization would mean that only 10 percent of investments should be in domestic securities. The more domestic holdings exceed this proportion, the further globalization still has to go (as we shall see later in this book, on this measure globalization has scarcely begun).

There are yet further ways to measure the extent of globalization of financial markets. One way is to see if listing of a stock on a foreign stock exchange has any influence on its price. It should not if the world is truly global, because in such a world the security could be bought in its home country, wherever the investors reside. Similarly, if the world is really just one single, seamless global financial market as much of the rhetoric would suggest, central banks would have little or no effect on investment yields and borrowing costs in their countries. This would be especially the case for central banks of small countries, and is because in an open, competitive financial world each small country is a price taker, facing the returns and costs determined in the global financial marketplace. A measure of globalization is, therefore, the degree of influence a central bank has on domestic conditions.

There are other ways to measure globalization in financial markets. For example, does the pricing of securities depend on global factors affecting risk or is there room for domestic factors? To what extent do borrowers rely on lenders in their own country? These and other measures of globalization are explored in this book. As we shall see, while globalization has proceeded quite far already, there is still a long way that it can go.

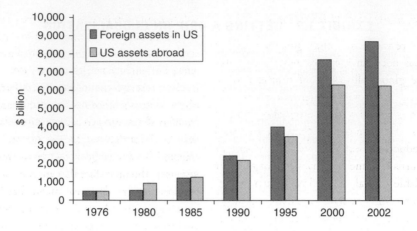

Figure 1.2 *International investment position of the United States*

Note
In the mid-1980s the United States switched from being an international net creditor nation to an international net debtor. By 2002 this net debt position had grown to over $2 trillion.
Source: Survey of Current Business, US Department of Commerce, Office of Business Economics, 2003.

Chinese, German, and other foreign investors have exceeded purchases of these instruments by Americans. Foreign buyers can be so crucial to the successful sale of securities that the US Treasury and private brokerage firms must watch overseas calendars to ensure they do not launch a major sale when, for example, Japanese or European financial institutions are closed for an official holiday. The horizons of investors and borrowers have clearly become global. In catering to the expanding horizons of investors and borrowers, there has been an explosion of internationally oriented financial products such as internationally diversified, global, and single foreign country mutual funds. The popularity of these products is a sign of the internationalization of financial markets.

Mutual funds that are called "international funds," are those with foreign but no US component. Global funds are those that include US as well as foreign assets. Funds referred to as "emerging country funds" hold assets from smaller economies such as Thailand, Turkey, Malaysia, the Philippines, and Indonesia. The buying of foreign securities directly by individuals without the use of mutual funds has also enjoyed rapid growth. Real estate and other markets have also experienced transformations from the phenomenal pace of globalization.

However, as with the expansion of international trade, the increased globalization of investment has brought with it both rewards and risks. The rewards and risks are evident in the large gains and large losses that have been made, depending on the timing and locations of investments.[7]

The growth in globalization of investment viewed from a US perspective can be seen in Figure 1.2. Since the mid-1970s Americans increased their investments abroad by more than ten times. During this same period, foreigners increased their investments in the United States by almost twenty times. As a consequence, the United States has gone from being the world's largest net creditor to the largest debtor in only a quarter of a century. Without access to foreign funds the United States would have had great difficulty funding its many financial needs, largely due to the low savings rate of Americans. The price, however, has been a need to make debt service payments that has reduced the fraction of the US national product enjoyed by Americans.

7 The dependence of returns on the timing and location of investment is graphically illustrated in Elroy Dimson, Paul Marsh, and Mike Staunton, *Triumph Of The Optimists: 101 Years Of Global Investment Returns*, Princeton University Press, Princeton, NJ, 2002.

Rewards of globalization of investment

Among the rewards of the globalization of investment has been an improvement in the efficiency of the global allocation of capital and an enhanced ability to diversify investment portfolios. The efficiency gain from the better allocation of capital arises from the fact that international investment reduces the extent to which investments with high returns in some countries are forgone for want of available capital, while low-return investments in other countries with abundant capital go ahead. The flow of capital between countries moves marginal rates of return in different locations closer together, thereby offering investors at home and abroad overall better returns. There is an additional gain from increased international capital flows enjoyed via an enhanced ability to smooth consumption over time by international lending and borrowing: countries can borrow abroad during bad years and pay back in good years. The analytical basis of the gain from consumption smoothing, along with the gain from a better international allocation of capital, are described in Appendix B.

Cost of globalization of investment

The benefits of the globalization of investment have not come without a price. The price is the addition of exchange-rate risk and country risk.

Unanticipated changes in exchange rates cause uncertainty in home-currency values of assets and liabilities. For example, if the exchange rate is $1.6 per British pound, that is, $1.6/£, a bank balance of £100 in London is worth $160 to a US investor. If the British pound unexpectedly falls in value to $1.5, the US investor's bank balance falls in value to $150. If instead of having an asset the US investor had a debt or liability of £100, the unexpected change in exchange rate from $1.6/£ to $1.5/£ means a reduction in the dollar value of what the American owes. The dollar value of the liability will decline from $160 to $150.

In the case of a foreign-currency-denominated bank balance or debt, exchange-rate risk is due

solely to uncertainty in the future exchange rates at which the asset or liability will be **translated** into dollars. In the case of many other assets and liabilities, exchange-rate risk is due both to uncertainty in the exchange rate to be used for translation, and also due to variations in local-currency values that may be affected by exchange rates: home-currency values of foreign stocks, bonds and property are affected by exchange rates. However, as we shall see later, the mere fact that an asset or liability is in a foreign country does not mean that it is subject to exchange-rate risk, and the mere fact that an asset or liability is at home does not mean that it is *not* subject to exchange-rate risk.[8]

Accompanying the increased exchange-rate risk associated with the globalization of investment is the risk from increasing interdependence between different countries' financial markets: by markets moving up and down together, diversification gains from global investment are diminished. There have been numerous examples of this interdependence in recent years. For example, the **Asian Crisis** of 1997–98 began in Thailand, but it quickly spread to South Korea, Malaysia, the Philippines, and Indonesia. Fear of the impact of massive drops in the values of Asian currencies on competitiveness of other trading nations spilled over to Argentina, Brazil, and eventually even to the markets of Europe and North America. The process of spreading crises through the interconnectedness of financial markets became widely referred to as **contagion**.

The globalization of investment has not only meant increased importance of foreign exchange risk but the increase in ownership of foreign assets has also meant that investors face increased country risk. As we have mentioned, country risk involves the possibility of expropriation or confiscation of property, or its destruction by war or revolution. It also involves the possibility of changes in taxes on foreign income and the imposition of restrictions on repatriating income from abroad. As in the case

---

8 The surprising fact that foreign assets may not be exposed to exchange-rate exposure while domestic assets are exposed is explained in Chapter 9.

Table 1.4 *The volatility of exchange rates*

Period	Volatility %						
	UK	FR	GER	ITALY	CAN	JAP	EURO, €
1999–2002	5	8[a]	8[a]	8[a]	3	7	8
1990–98	7	7	8	14	9	14	—
1980–89	18	22	19	21	6	24	—
1970–79	14	10	22	17	6	16	—
1960–69	7	3	2	0	3	0	—
1957–59	0	14	0	0	1	0	—

Note
a Coefficient of variation of euro.

Source: Standard deviation of month-end-to-month-end exchange rates, divided by the mean exchange rate over the period 1957–2002 (*International Financial Statistics*, International Monetary Fund, Washington, DC, 2003).

of foreign exchange risk, this book shows how practices and institutions have evolved to help investors reduce country risk.

Increased volatility of exchange rates

The more rapid growth of international trade versus domestic trade and the expanded international focus of investment that we have described offer more than adequate reason why it is increasingly important for students of business to study international finance. There is, however, an additional reason why knowledge of this exciting discipline has become imperative.

Exchange-rate risk has at times risen even more than the amount of foreign trade and overseas investment because of exchange-rate volatility. The volatility is described in Table 1.4 which shows the **coefficient of variation** of some major currencies.[9]

Exchange-rate volatility has been so substantial that at times the plight of the dollar, or the soaring or sinking value of some other major currency, has become headline material even outside of the business press. Prompted at times by tensions in Russia, the Middle East or some other politically

sensitive part of the world, and at other times by news on the economic health or malaise of some major country, exchange rates have jumped and dropped by startling amounts. Billions of dollars – and yen, euros, pounds, and francs – are made and lost in a day as a result of these currency swings. Rarely before have exchange rates darted around as much as they have in recent years, and therefore never before has exchange-rate risk been so important to measure and manage. If we add to the higher volatility the fact that international trade and investment are both far more important than they used to be, we can see why it has become so essential to understand the nature of exchange-rate risk and how to manage it.

There is no consensus as to why exchange rates have been so volatile. Some blame the switch to flexible exchange rates that occurred around 1973. However, others say the previous fixed-exchange-rate system could not have coped with the larger shocks that have occurred since that time: jumps and drops in oil prices, international conflicts, acts of terrorism, and so on. What is fairly certain is that the increased globalization of investment played a role by being associated with more **hot money** skipping from financial center to financial center in search of the highest return or to find safety. Another factor may have been the technology for moving money and transmitting information, which has allowed

---

9 The coefficient of variation is the standard deviation divided by the mean. It is a measure of volatility that can be compared over time and across counties.

both to move at the speed of light. Whatever the reason, a consequence of the greatly increased exchange-rate volatility has been a parallel increase in the importance of understanding the methods of managing foreign exchange risk, and the other topics covered in this book.

Increased importance of MNCs and transnational alliances

In addition to the growth of international trade and investment flows, and the riskiness of international trade and investment due to country risk and the volatility of exchange rates, interest in international finance has grown with the increased importance of **multinational corporations**. While the multi-nationalization of business is no easier to measure than globalization of financial markets, corporate investment across borders, which is the essence of corporations becoming multinational, has at times grown four times faster than global output and three times faster than international trade.[10] The United Nations estimates that there are more than 35,000 MNCs, with the largest 100 of these possibly being responsible for approximately 16 percent of the world's productive assets. The power held by these massive, effectively stateless enterprises has long been a source of governmental and public concern. The fear has been that by extending their activity they could influence governments and exploit workers and consumers, especially in smaller nations that might control fewer resources than the corporations themselves. Indeed, concern over the extension of control by foreign multinationals has been voiced even in the world's largest economy, the United States.

Concern has been expressed about the dominance of multinationals in international trade.[11] According to the US Bureau of Economic Analysis, US-based multinationals were associated with 80 percent of US exports and 40 percent of

imports. Because of their importance, we shall discuss multinationals both from the perspective of why they have grown in relative importance, and whether there really is any reason for concern. This is done in Chapter 17. We shall also discuss **transnational alliances**, which consist of separately owned corporations in different countries working in cooperation: MNCs are commonly owned business operations in different countries. Let us briefly review how the discussion of multinationals and transnationals fits with other topics in this book before beginning an exploration of the world of international finance.

TOPICS COVERED IN THIS BOOK

Part 1, consisting of Chapters 2–4, describes the organization of the foreign exchange markets. An introduction to the structure of the markets and the form in which currencies are exchanged is essential background to the study of international financial management. Chapter 2 explains the nature of the bank-note market and bank-draft market, the former involving the paper currency in our wallets and the latter involving checks, also known as **drafts**. It is shown, for example, that the ability to choose direct or indirect exchange between any pair of currencies allows us to compute all exchange rates from exchange rates of each currency vis-à-vis the US dollar. Transaction costs are shown to cloud the link between currencies. Chapter 3 turns to the so-called "forward exchange market" and explains how it works. This is the market in which it is possible to contract for future sale or purchase of a foreign currency so as to avoid being affected by unanticipated changes in exchange rates. Chapter 4 introduces two other instruments for reducing risk associated with exchange rates, namely currency futures and options. We explain their similarities and differences as well as the organization of the markets in which these instruments trade.

Part 2, consisting of Chapters 5 and 6, deals with the determination of exchange rates. The purpose of these two chapters is to give the reader an understanding of the fundamentals of why exchange

---

10 See "Multinationals: A Survey," in *The Economist*, March 27, 1993, p. 5.

11 See F. Steb Hipple, "The Measurement of International Trade Related to Multinational Companies," *American Economic Review*, December 1990, pp. 1263–70.

13

rates move up and down when they are free to change, as they are under the system of flexible exchange rates. Such an understanding is essential for successful financial management in today's international financial environment.

Chapter 5 looks at the structure and meaning of the balance-of-payments account, where the factors behind the supply of and demand for a country's currency are recorded. Indeed, the balance-of-payments account is viewed as a record of the causes of the supply and demand for a currency. Chapter 6 examines the supply and demand curves for currencies and the nature of the exchange-rate equilibrium they determine. It is shown that there is a real possibility that the exchange-rate equilibrium is unstable. This possibility is related to a phenomenon known as the J curve, whereby changes in exchange rates have unexpected effects. For example, it is shown that a depreciating currency – a currency with a falling foreign exchange value – can actually make a country's balance of trade worse. (Normally, one would think **depreciation** of a country's currency would improve its trade balance.)

In Part 3, consisting of Chapters 7 and 8, we describe two fundamental principles of international finance, the **purchasing-power-parity (PPP) principle**, and the **covered interest-parity principle**. The PPP principle states that exchange rates should reflect the relative local-currency prices of baskets of products in different countries, and that changes in exchange rates reflect differences in countries' inflation rates; according to PPP, countries with relatively rapid inflation should have depreciating currencies, and vice versa. Chapter 7 examines both the theory behind the PPP condition and its empirical validity. The principle used to explain the PPP condition in Chapter 7 is arbitrage, and it is shown that the conclusions in Chapter 6 based on currency supplies and demands can alternatively be reached by considering PPP.

Chapter 8 is devoted to the covered interest-parity condition. This condition says that when exchange-rate risk is avoided by using forward exchange contracts, investment yields and borrowing costs are the same in different currencies.

If there really were no differences in investment yields and borrowing costs between currencies, it would not matter how or where investment or borrowing occurred. However, there *are* differences in investment yields and borrowing costs, and the reasons they exist are explained in Chapter 8. It is important that we understand why these yield and borrowing cost differences occur, because they have implications for international cash management.

Part 4, consisting of Chapters 9–13, considers foreign exchange risk and exposure, and how exposure may be hedged by the use of forward, futures, and options contracts, as well as by borrowing or investing in the money market, so-called **swaps**. Chapter 9 is concerned with the definition and measurement of foreign exchange exposure, which is the amount which is at risk to changes in exchange rates. Different types of exposure and the factors determining the size of each type of exposure are described. In addition, exchange-rate *exposure* is carefully distinguished from exchange-rate *risk*. We explain that exposure is found virtually everywhere. For example, companies that do not export or import and have no foreign currency debts or assets may be exposed. This occurs if they compete at home with foreign firms whose share of a company's market depends on exchange rates.

Because the accounting conventions that are used can affect exposure as it appears in financial statements, Chapter 10 examines accounting procedures used for international transactions. This chapter, which can be omitted without loss of continuity, also explains the concept of real changes in exchange rates and its relation to exposure.

Most discussions of the effects of exchange rates emphasize the gains or losses on assets or liabilities, not the effects on a firm's ongoing profitability of its operations. However, as international trade grows and companies' competitors are increasingly foreign, exchange rates are having larger and larger effects on operations. Chapter 11 deals with the important matter of operating exposure by applying the standard tools of microeconomics. These tools are applied to discover the factors that influence how product prices, sales, production costs and profits of exporters and importers are affected by changes in exchange rates.

Chapter 12 then deals with the important question of whether managers should take steps to reduce the amount that is exposed to risk from unanticipated changes in exchange rates, or whether managers should leave hedging to individual share-holders. Several possible valid reasons for manage-rial hedging are discussed, and the consequences of different hedging techniques are described and compared. These include forward, futures, and options contracts, as well as swaps. The simple graphical technique of **payoff profiles** that has become commonplace in **financial engineering** is used to compare the consequences of different hedging techniques.

Chapter 13 considers the extent to which foreign exchange markets reflect available information, and the closely connected question of whether it is possible to profit from currency **speculation**. This leads into a discussion of exchange-rate forecasting and the record of attempts to forecast exchange rates and to profit from such forecasts.

Part 5 examines international investment and the financing of that investment. This begins with a discussion of short-term cash management in Chapter 14, and why an MNC might want to centralize the management of its working capital. It is shown that the same factors causing differences in investment yields and borrowing costs between currencies described in Chapter 8 are the factors which must be considered in cash man-agement. Chapter 15 deals with portfolio invest-ment, and explains how investors can choose between investments in different countries' stock and bond markets. Attention is paid to the benefits of an internationally diversified portfolio of secu-rities. It is shown that because economic condi-tions do not move in a perfectly parallel fashion in different countries, it pays to diversify inter-nationally. The theory and evidence on whether securities are priced in an internationally inte-grated or a segmented market setting are exam-ined within the context of the capital asset pricing model.

Chapters 16 and 17 focus on foreign direct investment, which is what occurs when, for example, a company builds a manufacturing plant in another country. Chapter 16 shows how to evaluate foreign direct investments, including the discount rate and tax rate to employ, the way to handle favorable financing terms offered to investing companies by foreign governments, restrictions on repatriating income, and so on. This involves the application of the principles of capital budgeting to the international context. Chapter 17 looks at the factors behind the growth of the giant MNCs which have been the result of foreign direct investment. It also considers problems caused by the growth of MNCs, and how costs and earnings can be allocated among divisions of an MNC by internal transfer prices for items exchanged between corporate divisions. Since a primary concern of MNCs is country risk of foreign facilities being seized and of taxes being imposed or changed on repatriated earnings, Chapter 17 looks at the measurement and avoidance of country risk. Associations between corporations in different countries, forming so-called transnational corporations, are one such means of reducing country risk and so transnational corporations are also discussed in Chapter 17.

Chapter 18 is concerned with financing of overseas investment. It covers equities, bonds, bank, and government lending, and the choices between them that result in alternative possible financial structures, including the question of whether overseas subsidiaries should follow parent company financing practices or those in the overseas desti-nation of investment.

Part 6 considers the institutional structure of international trade and finance. We begin with a discussion of the important role played by com-mercial banks. Today, large commercial banks offer deposits and make loans in a variety of cur-rencies other than the currency of the country in which they are located. Such deposits and loans are called **offshore currencies**, of which **Euro-dollars** are the best-known examples. Chapter 19 explains why the offshore-currency market has developed, and how it works. This leads naturally into a discussion of international banking. We explain the organizational structure of international banking, including the reasons why banks are among the largest MNCs that exist, sometimes having an office or other presence in a hundred countries.

As well as covering trade financing, Chapter 20 looks at the practical side of exporting and importing. It describes the documents that are involved in international trade, the methods of insuring trade, and so on. Among the matters discussed are letters of credit and bills of exchange. Because a substantial part of international trade takes a special form known as countertrade, which involves circumventing the normal use of currency in the exchange of goods and services, an account is also given of the nature of and possible reasons for this practice.

Part 7, consisting of Chapters 21–23, is devoted to further aspects of the global financial market beyond the fundamentals covered in Part 2. Chapter 21 presents several new theories of exchange rates when exchange rates are flexible, while Chapter 22 describes a variety of international financial systems based on fixed exchange rates – rates set and maintained by governments. The discussion of fixed rates involves descriptions of the now-defunct gold standard, the Bretton Woods system, **target zones** (which are bands within which governments try to keep exchange rates), the **European Monetary System (EMS)** and the advent of the new common currency of Europe, the euro. This leads us into a discussion of the automatic adjustment mechanisms which help to correct payments imbalances between countries, especially the mechanism involving the price level.

While it is less important to study fixed exchange rates today than when the exchange rates of almost all most major currencies were formally fixed, we should pay some attention to issues concerning fixed exchange rates because the international financial system has moved away from complete flexibility in exchange rates since 1985. Furthermore, fixed rates still exist in a number of countries. For example, the value of

the Hong Kong dollar has been pegged to the US dollar since the 1980s, and the Chinese RMB has also been pegged since the 1990s. It is also possible that the international financial system could return to fixed exchange rates. Systems of exchange rates have a history of change, with many different attempts to improve the way the financial system works.

Chapter 23 looks at the historical events which have shaped the international financial system, and some of the problems the system faces today. We consider many of the serious crises that have at times threatened the normal conduct of international business, including the Argentine Crisis and Asian Crisis. In the course of considering the possible future evolution of the international financial system, we consider the pros and cons of fixed and flexible exchange rates, and the international financial institutions charged with charting the course through trade imbalances, mounting debts, and fundamental shifts in global economic power.

The discussion in Part 7 is self-contained and can be covered at any point in the book. One possibility is that rather than leave this to the end, it can be inserted between Part 3 on the fundamental international parity conditions, and Part 4 on foreign exchange management. Furthermore, the material in Part 7 can be used in full or in part, depending on the extent to which the course covers the financial markets and environment of multinational business. Chapter 21, in particular, contains material which might be heavy going for students without an intermediate-level background in finance and economics.

The preceding overview of the contents of this book, along with the earlier parts of this chapter, indicate the broad range of increasingly important issues addressed in this most globalized of all subject areas of business, international finance. Having sketched the main features of the world we are to explore, let us begin our journey with a tour of the fascinating markets for foreign exchange.

SUMMARY

1 Every good or service reaching us from abroad has involved international finance. Knowledge of the subject can help managers avoid harmful effects of international events and possibly even to profit from these events.

2 International trade has grown approximately twice as fast as domestic trade. The increased relative importance of international trade has brought rewards and costs.

3 The principal reward from international trade is the gain in standard of living it has permitted. This gain comes from exploiting relative efficiencies of production in different countries and the exploitation of competitive advantages.

4 The costs of international trade are the introduction of exchange-rate and country risk. Methods and markets have evolved that allow firms to avoid or reduce these risks, and since international trade has become more important it has become more important to learn about these methods and markets.

5 International finance has also become a more important subject because of an increased globalization of financial markets. The benefits of the increased flow of capital between nations include a more efficient international allocation of capital and greater opportunities for countries and their citizens to diversify risk. However, globalization of investment has meant new risks and increased interdependence of financial and economic conditions in different countries.

6 Adding to the increase in relevance of exchange-rate risk from the growth in international trade and the globalization of financial markets has been an increase in the volatility of exchange rates and a growth in importance of MNCs. All of these factors combine to make it imperative that today's student of business study the factors behind the risks of international trade and investment, and the methods of reducing these risks.

REVIEW QUESTIONS

1 How might you measure growth in the relative importance of international trade in recent decades?

2 Why has international trade grown more rapidly than domestic trade?

3 What is a "comparative advantage?"

4 What helps provide a "competitive advantage?"

5 What is "country risk?"

6 What does it mean to "hedge?"

7 What are the principal benefits of international investment?

8 What are the principal costs of international investment?

9 What is "hot money?"

10 What is the difference between a multinational corporation and a transnational corporation?

ASSIGNMENT PROBLEMS

1   In what ways might the following be affected by sudden, unexpected changes in exchange rates?
    a   An American holder of US Treasury bonds
    b   An American holder of GM stock
    c   An American on vacation in Mexico
    d   An American holder of Honda stock
    e   A Canadian on vacation in the United States
2   What is meant by "shrinkage of economic space?"
3   What are the possible implications of adoption of a common currency such as the euro?
4   What competitive advantages may be behind the success of a particular industry in international trade?
5   Why have some governments been concerned with the growing importance of multinational corporations?

BIBLIOGRAPHY

Aliber, Robert Z., *The Handbook of International Financial Management*, Dow Jones-Irwin, Homewood, IL, 1989.
Aliber, Robert Z. and Reid W. Click, *Readings in International Business*, MIT Press, Cambridge, MA, 1993.
The Economist, "Multinationals: A Survey," March 27, 1993.
Eichengreen, Barry, Michael Mussa, Giovanni Dell'Ariccia, Enrica Detragiache, Gian Maria Milesi-Ferretti, and Andrew Tweedie, "Liberalizing Capital Movements: Some Analytical Issues," *Economic Issues*, 17, International Monetary Fund, Washington, DC, 1999.
Evans, John S., *International Finance: A Markets Approach*, Dryden Press, Fort Worth, TX, 1992.
Harris, Richard G., "Globalization, Trade and Income," *Canadian Journal of Economics*, November 1993, pp. 755–76.
Krugman, Paul A. and Maurice Obstfeld, *Geography and Trade*, MIT Press, Cambridge, MA, 1991.
—— *Currencies and Crises*, MIT Press, Cambridge, MA, 1991.
—— *International Economics: Theory and Policy*, 6th edn, Addison-Wesley, Boston, MA, 2002.
Ohmae, Keniche, *The Borderless World: Power and Strategy in the Interlinked Economy*, Harper-Collins, New York, 1990.
Porter, Michael E., *The Competitive Advantage of Nations*, Palgrave-Macmillan, New York, 1998.
Reich, Robert B., *The Work of Nations: Preparing Ourselves for the Twenty-First Century*, Alfred A. Knopf, New York, 1991.
Vernon, Raymond and Louis Wells, Jr, *Manager in the International Economy*, 5th edn, Prentice-Hall, Englewood Cliffs, NJ, 1986.

PARALLEL MATERIAL FOR CASE COURSES

Carlson, Robert S., H. Lee Remmers, Christine R. Hekman, David K. Eiteman, and Arthur Stonehill, *International Finance: Cases and Simulation,* Addison-Wesley, Reading, MA, 1980.

Dufey, Gunter and Ian H. Giddy, *Cases in International Finance,* 2nd edn, Addison-Wesley, Reading, MA, 1993.

Feiger, George and Bertrand Jacquillat, *International Finance: Text and Cases,* Allyn and Bacon, Boston, MA, 1982.

Moffett, Michael H., *Cases in International Finance,* Addison Wesley Longman, Reading, MA, 2001.

Poniachek, Harvey A., *Cases in International Finance*, Wiley, New York, 1993.

Rukstad, Michael G., *Corporate Decision Making in the World Economy*, Dryden, Fort Worth, TX, 1992.

APPENDIX A

The gains from trade in goods and services: the principle of comparative advantage

Comparative advantage is not the most intuitive concept in economics, and it can require a little thought to leave the reader convinced of why countries gain from exploiting their comparative advantages. Discovered by the English stockbroker-millionaire David Ricardo, an understanding of comparative advantage helps answer the following question:

> Suppose that China is much more efficient than the United States in producing steel and marginally more efficient than the United States in producing food, and that steel and food are the only items produced and required in both countries. Would both countries be better off from free trade between them than by prohibiting trade?

When faced with this question, some people might say that while China would be better off from free trade because it is more efficient producing both products, the United States would be worse off. The reasoning behind this view is the presumption that China would be able to undercut US prices for both products and thereby put Americans out of work. What the principle of comparative advantage shows is that in fact *both* countries are better off from free trade than no trade, and that it is *relative* efficiencies rather than *absolute* efficiencies of production that determine the pattern and benefits of trade. These relative efficiencies of production are referred to as **comparative advantages**. Let us explain this important principle of comparative advantage by an example. This example will also clarify what we mean by this concept.

Suppose that the amounts of labor needed to produce a ton of steel and food in the United States and China with the given stocks of land and capital devoted to these products are as shown on the top of Table 1A.1. These numbers assume that China can produce both products with less labor than the United States, which means that China has an **absolute advantage** in both products (of course, the assumption is made simply to provide an example).

If the United States were to produce one more ton of food by moving labor from producing steel, the forgone output of steel – that is, the opportunity cost of food in terms of steel – would be 2.5 tons of steel.[12] On the other hand, if the United States were to produce one more ton of steel by moving labor from producing food, the opportunity cost would be 0.4 tons of food. Similarly, in China the opportunity cost of one more ton of food is

---

12 Of course, it is individuals, not nations, who make production decisions. However, referring to countries as if they made production decisions is a convenient anthropomorphism.

Table 1A.1 The situation with no international trade

Output	United States	China
Number of people employed per ton of output		
Food	25	20
Steel	10	4
Opportunity cost per ton of output		
Food	2.5 tons steel	5.0 tons steel
Steel	0.4 tons food	0.2 tons food
Millions of people employed		
Food	75	40
Steel	75	40
Outputs, millions of tons		
Food	3	2
Steel	7.5	10

5.0 tons of steel, and the opportunity cost of one more ton of steel is 0.2 tons of food. These numbers are shown in Table 1A.1. We see that the United States has a lower opportunity cost of producing food, while China has a lower opportunity cost of producing steel. These relative opportunity costs are the basis of the definition of comparative advantage.

A comparative advantage in a particular product is said to exist if, in producing more of that product, a country has a lower opportunity cost in terms of alternative products than the opportunity cost of that product in other countries. Table 1A.1 shows that the United States has a comparative advantage in producing food and China has a comparative advantage in producing steel. It should be clear that as long as relative efficiencies differ, every country has some comparative advantage. This is the case even if a country has an absolute disadvantage in every product. What we will demonstrate next is that by producing the good for which the country has a comparative advantage (lower opportunity cost) and trading it for the products for which other countries have a comparative advantage (lower opportunity cost), *everybody* is better off.

Table 1A.1 shows the number of workers (available labor power) shared by the two industries in the United States and China. The table also gives the outputs of food and steel in each country, assuming half of the relevant working populations in each country is employed in each industry. For example, 75 million Americans can produce 3 million tons of food when 25 workers are required per ton, and the other 75 million who work can produce 7.5 million tons of steel. The total world output of food is 5 million tons, and the total world output of steel is 17.5 million tons.

Suppose now that 28 million Chinese workers are shifted from agriculture to steel, while at the same time 50 million American workers are shifted from steel to agriculture. The effect of this on the outputs of both countries is shown in Table 1A.2. We find that with China emphasizing steel production and with the United States emphasizing food, the outputs for the two countries combined are 5.6 million tons of food and 19.5 million tons of steel. The combined output of both items have increased by 10 percent or more merely by having China concentrate on its comparative advantage, steel, and the United States concentrate on its comparative advantage, food.

The United States and China can both be richer if they trade certain amounts between themselves. One such trading division would be for the United States to sell China 1.8 million tons of food and buy from China 5.5 million tons of steel, giving a **terms of trade** of approximately 3 tons of steel per ton of food (the terms of trade are the amount of imports a country receives per unit of exports). The United States and China would then end up

Table 1A.2 *Input/output under free trade*

Output	United States	China
Millions of people employed		
Food	125	12
Steel	25	68
Total output, millions of tons		
Food	5	0.6
Steel	2.5	17
Consumption amounts under trading division		
Food	3.2	2.4
Steel	8	11.5

consuming the amounts in the bottom rows of Table 1A.2, all of which exceed what they could consume under **autarky** as shown in Table 1A.1 (autarky means having no trade relations with other countries).

The gains shown by comparing Table 1A.2 with Table 1A.1 are due to specializing production according to the countries' comparative advantages. The benefit of specializing production is only one of the gains from trade.

Further gains from international trade

Given our assumption that China is relatively more efficient in producing steel than food, and the United States is relatively more efficient in producing food than steel, under autarky we can expect food to be cheap relative to steel in the United States and steel to be cheap relative to food in China. This suggests that by exporting food to China, where food is relatively expensive in the absence of trade, the United States can receive a relatively large amount of steel in return. Similarly, by exporting steel to the United States where steel is relatively expensive in the absence of trade, China can receive a relatively large amount of food. Therefore, via exchange of products through trade, both countries can be better off. The gain is a **pure exchange gain** and would be enjoyed even without any specialization of production. That is, there are two components to the gains from trade: the gain from adjusting the pattern of production (the gain from specialization) and the gain from adjusting the pattern of consumption (the pure exchange gain).[13]

The number of people required to produce the food and steel in our example is assumed to be the same whatever the output of these products. That is, we have implicitly assumed **constant returns to scale**. However, if there are **increasing returns to scale** it will take fewer people to produce a given quantity of the product for which the country has a comparative advantage as more of that product is produced. In this case of economies of scale there are yet further gains from international trade. Returns to scale can come in many forms, including pure technological gains, benefits of learning by doing, and so on. In addition, if there is monopoly power within a country that is removed by trade, consumers enjoy an additional benefit in terms of lower prices due to increased competition.[14] Yet a further gain from trade comes in the form of an increase in product variety. In addition, international

---

13 The pure exchange gain that comes from adjusting consumption cannot be shown in terms of our numerical example because demonstration of this gain requires measurement of relative satisfaction from the two products. This in turn requires the use of utility theory. Formal separation of the specialization gain from the pure exchange gain is generally presented in courses in the pure theory of international trade.

14 For evidence on this effect of trade, see James Levinsohn, "Testing the Imports-as-Market-Discipline Hypothesis," NBER Working Paper 3657, 1991.

trade can make a broader range of inputs and technology available and thereby increase economic growth.[15] Therefore, the gain from exploiting comparative advantages is only part of the total gain from free trade.[16]

Some costs of international trade

While most economists believe that international trade is beneficial, there are possible costs to be weighed against the gains. One possible cost of free international trade occurs when a country finds its own firms put out of business and thereby exposes itself to exploitation by a foreign monopoly. This is the flip side to the gain from competition described earlier, and is likely to occur only in oligopolistic markets with very few producers.[17] For example, it has been argued that it can be advantageous for governments to subsidize aircraft production in Europe so as to reduce prices faced on imported aircraft.[18] Another possible drawback of trade is the reduction in economic diversity a country might face. This is the flip side of the gain from specialization. Finally, some people have decried international trade because of the homogenization of culture and possible political domination it has brought to the planet, while others have questioned trade because of possible impacts on the environment.[19] It is clear that as in most things in economics, there is no free lunch.

APPENDIX B

The gains from the international flow of capital

In Appendix A we showed that everybody can simultaneously benefit from international trade in goods and services. In this appendix we show that everybody can also simultaneously gain from the international flow of financial capital. Between them, the international flow of goods and services and the international flow of capital constitute the sum total of reasons for the supply of and demand for foreign exchange. Indeed, as we shall show in Chapter 5, the two major subdivisions of the balance-of-payments account – the current account and the capital account – report respectively the demand for and supply of a country's currency due to trade in goods and services, and the supply of and demand for the currency due to the flow of capital. Therefore, what this and Appendix A do is show that the very bases of the study of international finance – transactions due to the flow of goods and services and the flow of capital – are both important contributors to our well-being. It is not, as is often thought, just the free international flow of goods and services from which we benefit.

15 See Gene M. Grossman and Elhanan Helpman, "Product Development and International Trade," *Journal of Political Economy*, December 1989, pp. 1261–83, and "Growth and Welfare in a Small Open Economy," *National Bureau of Economic Research*, Working Paper 2970, May 1989. For an alternative view, see Meir G. Kohn and Nancy P. Marion, "The Implications of Knowledge-Based Growth for the Optimality of Open Capital Markets," *Canadian Journal of Economics*, November 1992, pp. 865–83.

16 An account of the numerous sources of gains from trade can be found in Cletus C. Coughlin, K. Alec Chrystal, and Geoffrey E. Wood, "Protectionist Trade Policies: A Survey of Theory, Evidence and Rationale," *Review*, Federal Reserve Bank of St. Louis, January/February 1988, pp. 12–26.

17 See Elhanan Helpman and Paul R. Krugman, *Trade Policy and Market Structure*, MIT Press, Cambridge MA, 1989.

18 See James A. Brander and Barbara Spencer, "Export Subsidies and International Market Share Rivalry," *Journal of International Economics*, February 1985, pp. 83–100.

19 On the effects on culture and political domination, see J. J. Servain-Schreiber, *The American Challenge*, Hamish Hamilton, London, 1968. On trade and the environment, see Alison Butler, "Environmental Protection and Free Trade: Are They Mutually Exclusive?" *Review*, Federal Reserve Bank of St. Louis, May/June 1992, pp. 3–16.

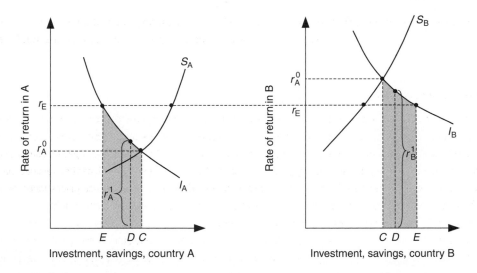

Figure 1B.1 *The gain from the better allocation of capital*

Notes

The heights of the curves I_A and I_B give the rates of return on an extra dollar's worth of investment in countries A and B. The curves S_A and S_B give savings at different returns on savings in the two countries. With no flow of capital between the countries, returns will be r_A^0 and r_B^0. Each dollar moving from A to B will result in a forgone return in A given by the height of I_A, and a return in B given by the height of I_B. For example, after CD dollars have left A for B, the added global return from *another* dollar is $r_B^1 - r_A^1$. The maximum gain from reallocating capital occurs at r_E and is given by the difference between the two shaded areas; the shaded area in B is the *total* return on investment between C and E, while the shaded area in A is the forgone *total* return on investment between C and E.

We have already noted in the text of this chapter that the international flow of capital means that a project with a very high yield in one country is not forgone for want of funds while a low-yield project in a country of abundant capital goes ahead. Capital flowing between the countries benefits everybody because the investors in the country with the low-yield projects can enjoy some of the high returns offered in the other country, while the country with the high-yield projects is able to fund projects that would otherwise be forgone. This is potentially a very important gain from the international flow of capital, and is illustrated graphically in Figure 1B.1.

The heights of the curves I_A and I_B in Figure 1B.1 give the rates of return on investment in countries A and B at different rates of investment. The curves slope downward because countries run out of good investment projects as their rates of investment increase: the more projects are pursued the lower the expected return from an incremental project[20] The curves labeled S_A and S_B give the amounts saved at different rates of return earned on peoples' savings. If there is no flow of capital between the countries, the equilibrium expected returns in A and B are r_A^0 and r_B^0.

The first dollar to flow from A to B means a forgone investment return in A of r_A^0 in return for a return in B from that dollar of r_B^0. This is a net gain of $(r_B^0 - r_A^0)$. After $\$CD$ of capital has moved from A to B, an additional dollar of capital flow produces a net gain of $(r_B^1 - r_A^1)$. It should be clear from the figure that there is a global gain in return from investment until enough capital has moved to equalize returns in the two countries. Indeed, if the interest rate in countries A and B is r_E, where by assumption the excess of investment over savings in B matches the excess of savings over investment in A, then the gain from a better capital flow is at a maximum. This maximum gain can be shown in the figure by recognizing that the *total* return from investment can be measured from the area under the investment curve for that amount of investment. For example, the return on the investment between C and E on

---

20 The height of I_A or I_B is referred to as the **marginal efficiency of investment**.

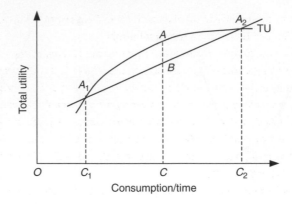

Figure 1B.2 *Utility from different consumption patterns*

Notes
If a country faces variable consumption, being with equal frequency C_1 and C_2, the average total utility level that it enjoys is distance BC. This is the average of distances $A_1 C_1$ and $A_2 C_2$. If the country borrows from abroad during bad times and lends abroad during good times, and thereby enjoys consumption at C every period, it enjoys a utility level given by a distance AC. The gain from smoothing consumption via borrowing from abroad and lending abroad is distance AB. This is a gain from the international flow of capital.

the right-hand-side of Figure 1B.1 is the shaded area: each *incremental* dollar of investment has a return given by the height of the investment curve, so adding all incremental gains between C and E gives the area beneath the curve. Against the return in B from imported capital is the forgone return in A from which capital is being exported. This lost return is given by the area beneath I_A between C and E on the left-hand-side of Figure 1B.1. The difference between the two areas is at a maximum at the equilibrium interest rate r_E. This is the rate that would occur in an integrated global capital market because it is the rate at which $S_A + S_B = I_A + I_B$ (note that at the equilibrium interest rate r_E the excess of savings over investment in country A is equal to the excess of investment over savings in country B).

There is a further benefit of the international flow of capital that comes from the smoothing of consumption that is permitted by lending and borrowing. This gain comes from the fact that if a nation were unable to borrow from abroad it would have limited scope to maintain consumption during temporary declines in national income.[21] Similarly, if the nation were unable to invest abroad, it would have limited scope for dampening temporary jumps in consumption during surges in national income.

It is frequently assumed that people are subject to diminishing marginal utility of income and consumption. Indeed, this is a basic rationale for the postulate of risk aversion which is essential to much of the theory of finance. Diminishing marginal utility of consumption means that a more even path of consumption over time is preferred to a more erratic path with the same average level of consumption. The reason for this preference for a smooth path of consumption over time is illustrated in Figure 1B.2.

The curve labeled TU shows the total utility derived from different rates of consumption. Because the curve slopes upward throughout its range, it shows that higher levels of consumption are preferred to lower levels; that is, total utility from consumption increases as consumption increases. However, the rate at which total utility increases with consumption diminishes as consumption expands. This is revealed by the lower slope of curve TU as

21 National income, which is roughly equivalent to the gross national product and usually denoted by Y, can be classified into consumption C, investment I, government spending G, and exports minus imports $(Ex - Im)$. This classification is met frequently in macroeconomics as the national income identity, $Y \equiv C + I + G + (Ex - Im)$. We see that for a decline in Y not to involve a decline in consumption it would be necessary to suffer a decline in investment, government spending, or exports minus imports. All these alternatives involve costs.

consumption increases, that is, as we move to the right along TU. The slope of TU gives the increase in total utility per unit of added consumption and is called the **marginal utility**.[22]

If a nation is forced to vary consumption from year to year because it cannot borrow and invest internationally and prefers not to vary other components of its national product, it may find itself consuming C_1 in one year when national income experiences a decline, and C_2 in the following year when national income experiences a favorable fluctuation. The total utility from consumption of C_1 is given by the distance A_1C_1, while the total utility from C_2 is given by A_2C_2. The average of A_1C_1 and A_2C_2, which is the average utility enjoyed in the two years, can be found by drawing a straight line between A_1 and A_2 and finding the height of this line at its center. This follows because the height of the line halfway between A_1 and A_2 is the average of A_1C_1 and A_2C_2. We find that the average utility from the two years of variable consumption is BC.

If the nation can borrow it might borrow the amount of C_1C during the economic downturn allowing it to consume OC. The nation might then lend amount CC_2 during the upturn and therefore also consume amount OC during this time.[23] With consumption of OC in both periods, and with total utility given by the distance AC in both periods, the average total utility is simply AC. It is clear by inspecting Figure 1B.2 that the utility when consumption is smoothed by international borrowing and lending is higher than when borrowing and lending does not occur. Intuitively, this outcome is because the added or marginal utility of income during the period of higher consumption is smaller than the marginal utility lost during the period of lower consumption.

The empirical relevance of the preceding argument has been examined by Michael Brennan and Bruno Solnik.[24] They start by calculating what consumption would have been without international capital flows. This is determined by subtracting private capital flows from actual consumption during years when there was a net capital inflow to the country, and adding private capital flows to actual consumption during years of net capital outflow. This tells us what would have had to happen to consumption if borrowing and lending had not occurred.[25] All consumption data are put in per capita terms and adjusted for inflation.

Brennan and Solnik compute the standard deviations of the growth rates of consumption adjusted for capital flows and compare these with the standard deviations of the growth rates of actual consumption. This comparison is made for the **Organization for Economic Cooperation and Development (OECD)** countries. They find that on average the standard deviations of actual consumption growth rates – which include international capital flows – are less than half the standard deviations of adjusted consumption growth rates – which exclude international capital flows. The reduction in standard deviation due to international capital flows is apparent in every country they examined, and for all measures of capital flows they considered.[26]

---

22 Most introductory finance textbooks deal with the notion of diminishing marginal utility of consumption and its role in risk aversion. See, for example, Richard Brealey and Stewart Myers, *Principles of Corporate Finance*, 7th edn, McGraw-Hill, New York, 2003.

23 Borrowing and lending involves paying and receiving interest. However, if the amount borrowed equals the amount subsequently lent, and if the periods are close together so that time value of money is unimportant, payments and receipts of interest cancel and can be ignored.

24 See Michael J. Brennan and Bruno Solnik, "International Risk Sharing and Capital Mobility," *Journal of International Money and Finance*, September 1989, pp. 359–73.

25 This assumes all borrowing and lending affects consumption and not the other components of national product. Of course, borrowing and lending do in reality affect government spending and investment. However, a smoother pattern of government spending and investment should contribute to smoother consumption. Furthermore, consumption is often considered as the end purpose of economic activity. This supports the case for concentrating on consumption.

26 The implications of consumption smoothing for welfare are overstated in Brennan and Solnik op. cit. See Maurice Obstfeld, "International Risk Sharing and Capital Mobility: Another Look," *Journal of International Money and Finance*, February 1992, pp. 115–21 and Michael J. Brennan and Bruno Solnik, "International Risk Sharing and Capital Mobility: Reply," *Journal of International Money and Finance*, February 1992, pp. 122–3.

Investment in new capital could, like consumption, be smoothed via international capital flows. The empirical evidence suggests, however, that relatively little investment smoothing occurs. This has been concluded from studies of the connection between saving and investment *within countries*. In completely integrated capital markets, a dollar increase in domestic saving would leave domestic investment unchanged and instead result in a dollar of exported capital. What has been shown, however, is that each dollar increase in domestic saving is, on average, associated with a 79 cent increase in net domestic investment.[27]

A benefit from international capital flows that is closely related to the gain from consumption smoothing is the gain from increased diversification of investment portfolios. This gain exists because the economic ups and downs in different countries are not perfectly synchronized. This allows internationally diversified investors to achieve a higher expected return for a given degree of risk, or a lower risk for a given expected return. We do not discuss this here as it is discussed extensively in Chapter 15. However, it should be clear that diversification gains depend on different countries having different economic conditions and experiences, just as do the other gains from the free movement of capital which we have described in this appendix.

27 See Martin Feldstein and Phillippe Bachetta, "National Saving and International Investment," *National Bureau of Economic Research*, Working Paper 3164, 1990.

Part I

The markets for foreign exchange

The foreign exchange market, which has several connected but nevertheless different parts, is the most active market on Earth, with daily turnover exceeding that of major stock markets. Along with the size of the market go massive profits and losses of unwary companies, opportunistic speculators, and central banks, as well as substantial income and employment in commercial and central banks, currency brokerages, and specialized futures and options exchanges.

Part I, which consists of three chapters, introduces the reader to the different components of the foreign exchange, or **forex**, market. Chapter 2 begins by considering the exchange of bank notes, such as the exchange of US Federal Reserve notes – the paper money Americans carry in their wallets – for euros or British pounds. Chapter 2 also explains how money in the form of bank deposits is exchanged in the **spot foreign exchange market**. An understanding of what actually happens when a person calls a bank to buy a foreign currency requires that we know how customers are debited and credited, and how the banks trade and settle transactions between themselves. This is all explained in Chapter 2. The chapter ends by showing why knowledge of exchange rates of each currency against the US dollar allows us to calculate all possible exchange rates. For example, it is shown why we can calculate the exchange rate between the euro and the British pound from the euro–US dollar exchange rate and the pound–US dollar exchange rate. It is also shown why this ability to compute so-called **cross exchange rates** is nevertheless limited in reality by the presence of foreign exchange transaction costs.

Chapter 3 describes another component of the foreign exchange market that plays an important role throughout the remainder of the book. This is the **forward** exchange market. Forward exchange involves a contractual arrangement to exchange currencies at an agreed exchange rate on a stated date in the future. The forward market plays an important role in avoiding foreign exchange risk (hedging) and in choosing to take risk (speculating). Chapter 3 provides the necessary background so that we can show in later chapters how forward exchange can be used for hedging and speculating.

After explaining the forward market we turn our attention to currency derivatives that, as their name suggests, *derive* their values from underlying values of currencies. The derivatives discussed in Chapter 4 are currency futures, currency options, and **swaps**. Currency futures are similar to forward exchange contracts in that they help fix the net cost of or receipts from foreign exchange involved in future transactions. However, currency futures trade on formal exchanges such as the Chicago International Money Market, have only a limited number of value dates, come in particular contract sizes, and can be sold back to the exchange. There are also a few other institutional differences that we describe. These differences make forward contracts and currency futures of slightly different value as vehicles for hedging and speculation.*

Chapter 4 also describes currency options and swaps. Unlike forward contracts and currency futures, options allow buyers of the contracts discretion over whether to exercise (complete) an exchange of currencies at a specified exchange rate. Different types of currency options are described, along with the factors that affect market prices, or premiums, on options. Currency swaps involve twinned transactions, specifically arranged to buy and to sell a currency, where the buying and selling are separated in time. For example, somebody buying a British Treasury bill might buy the British pound spot and at the same time sell it forward for the date of maturity of the Treasury bill.

The specifics of using futures, options, and swaps and their roles in hedging and speculating are only briefly covered in Chapter 4; we save the details for later chapters in which investment, borrowing, hedging, and speculation are covered in greater depth. In Part I the purpose of the discussion is primarily to introduce the reader to the institutional details of these fascinating and vital markets for foreign exchange.

* Most Importantly, forwards are used to settle transactions whereas futures and options are not. It is primarily for this reason that we treat forward exchange in a separate chapter.

Chapter 2

An introduction to exchange rates

The market in international capital ... is run by outlandishly well-paid specialists, back-room technicians and rows of computer screens. It deals in meaninglessly large sums of money. It seems to have little connection with the "real" world of factories and fast-food restaurants. Yet at times ... it seems to hold the fate of economies in its grasp. The capital market is a mystery and it is a threat.

The Economist, September 19, 1992

To the ordinary person, international finance is synonymous with exchange rates, and indeed, a large part of the study of international finance involves the study of exchange rates. What is not widely known is the variety of exchange rates that exist at the same moment between the same two currencies. There are exchange rates for **bank notes**, which are, for example, the Federal Reserve notes with pictures of former US presidents, and the equivalent notes issued by the European Central Bank. There are also exchange rates between checks stating dollar amounts and those stating amounts in euros or other currency units. Furthermore, the rates on these checks depend on whether they are issued by banks – **bank drafts** – or by corporations – **commercial drafts** – and on the amounts of money they involve, and on the dates on the checks.[1] Exchange rates also differ according to whether they are for the purchase or sale of a foreign currency. That is, there is a difference, for example, between the number of US dollars required in order to *purchase* a British pound, and the number of US dollars received when *selling* a pound.

We will begin by looking at exchange rates between bank notes. While the market for bank notes is only a small proportion of the overall foreign exchange market, it is a good place to begin because bank notes are the form of money with which people are most familiar.

THE FOREIGN BANK NOTE MARKET

The earliest experience that many of us have of dealing with foreign currency is on our first overseas vacation. When not traveling abroad, most of us have very little to do with foreign exchange, which is not used in the course of ordinary commerce, especially in the United States. The foreign exchange with which we deal when on vacation involves bank notes, or possibly foreign-currency-denominated travelers' checks. Table 2.1 gives the exchange rates on bank notes facing a traveler on October 22, 2002. Let us take a look at how these retail bank note rates are quoted.

The first column of Table 2.1 gives exchange rates in terms of the number of units of each foreign

---

1 A commercial draft is simply a check issued by a company.

Table 2.1 *Exchange rates on foreign bank notes (Traveler's dollar – October 22, 2002)*

	Foreign Currency per US dollar	
	Bank buys foreign currency (sells US$)	Bank sells foreign currency (buys US$)
Argentina (Peso)	3.82	3.55
Australia (Dollar)	1.84	1.73
Bahamas (Dollar)	1.04	0.96
Brazil (Real)	4.06	3.80
Canada (Dollar)	1.60	1.53
Chile (Peso)	758.00	720.00
China (Renminbi)	8.48	8.10
Colombia (Peso)	2,850.00	2,650.00
Denmark (Krone)	7.80	7.40
Europe (Euro)	1.05	0.99
Fiji Islands (Dollar)	2.22	2.05
Ghana (Cedi)	8,600.00	8,150.00
Great Britain (Pound)	0.66	0.62
Honduras (Lempira)	17.50	16.25
Hong Kong (Dollar)	8.00	7.50
Iceland (Krona)	91.00	85.50
India (Rupee)	50.00	46.50
Indonesia (Rupiah)	9,500.00	8,900.00
Israel (Shekel)	5.20	4.80
Japan (Yen)	129.00	121.00
Malaysia (Ringgit)	3.95	3.65
Mexico (New Peso)	10.40	9.60
Morocco (Dirham)	11.10	10.30
New Zealand (Dollar)	2.12	1.98
Norway (Krone)	7.85	7.35
Pakistan (Rupee)	61.00	57.00
Panama (Balboa)	0.97	1.03
Peru (New Sol)	3.75	3.48
Philippines (Peso)	55.00	51.25
Russia (Ruble)	33.00	30.50
Singapore (Dollar)	1.85	1.72
South Africa (Rand)	11.00	10.25
South Korea (Won)	1,290.00	1,200.00
Sri Lanka (Rupee)	100.00	93.00
Sweden (Krona)	9.60	9.00
Switzerland (Franc)	1.55	1.45
Taiwan (Dollar)	36.25	33.50
Thailand (Baht)	45.00	41.75
Trinidad/Tobago (Dollar)	6.30	5.90
Tunisia (Dinar)	1.44	1.34
Turkey (1 million Lira)	1.59	1.71
Venezuela (Bolivar)	1,480.00	1,370.00

Source: Compiled from various bank and currency exchange quotations, October 22, 2002.

currency that must be *paid to the bank* to buy a US dollar. The column is headed "Bank buys foreign currency (sells US $)" because when a bank buys foreign currency from a customer, it pays, or sells, the customer US dollars. Table 2.1 shows, for example, that it takes 3.82 Argentine pesos or 1.84 Australian dollars to buy a US dollar from the bank. The second column gives the number of units of each foreign currency that a customer will *receive from the bank* for each US dollar. For example, the traveler will receive Can$1.53 or £0.62 for each US dollar.

The rates of exchange posted for travelers in bank and currency exchange windows or international tourist centers are the most expensive or unfavorable that one finds. They are expensive in the sense that the buying and selling prices on individual currencies can differ by a large percentage – frequently more than 5 or 6 percent. The difference between buying and selling prices is called the **spread**. In Table 2.1 we see that, for example, the 0.11 (= 1.84 − 1.73) difference between the buying and selling exchange rates for the Australian dollar versus the US dollar is a spread of approximately 6 percent. Differences between the effective buying and selling rates on paper currency can be particularly large on very small transactions when there is a fixed charge for conversion as well as a spread on buying and selling rates.

Our experience changing currencies on vacation should not lead us to believe that large-scale international finance faces similar costs. The bank note market used by travelers involves large spreads because generally only small amounts are traded, which nevertheless require as much paperwork as bigger commercial trades. Another reason why the spreads are large is that each bank and currency exchange must hold many different currencies to be able to provide customers with the currencies they want, and these notes do not earn interest. This involves an opportunity cost of holding currency inventory, as well as risk from short-term changes in exchange rates. Furthermore, bank robbers specialize in bank notes; therefore, those who hold large amounts of them are forced to take costly security precautions – especially when moving bank notes from branch to branch or

country to country. A further risk faced in the exchange of bank notes is the acceptance of counterfeit bills which frequently show up outside their own country where they are less likely to be identified as forgeries.

It is worth noting that because banks face a lower risk of theft of travelers' checks, and because the companies that issue them – American Express, Visa, Thomas Cook, Master Card, and so on – will quickly credit the banks that accept their checks, many banks give a more favorable purchase exchange rate on checks than on bank notes. In addition, issuers of travelers' checks enjoy the use of the money paid for the checks before they are cashed. Furthermore, the banks selling the checks to customers do not face an inventory cost; payment to the check issuing company such as American Express by a check-selling bank is made only when the checks are being purchased by a customer. Travelers' checks also have the advantage of not having to be sent back to the country that uses the currency, unlike any surplus position of bank notes. They can be destroyed after the acceptor of the checks has been credited in their bank account. These benefits to the issuers and acceptors of travelers' checks keep down the buying–selling spread.

Credit card transactions share some of the advantages of travelers' checks. There is no need to physically move anything from country to country, no need to hold an inventory of noninterest earning notes, and so on.

While the exchange of bank notes between ordinary private customers and banks takes place in a retail market, commercial banks, and currency exchanges trade their surpluses of notes between themselves in a wholesale market. The wholesale market involves firms which specialize in buying and selling foreign bank notes with commercial banks and currency exchanges. These currency-trading firms are **bank-note wholesalers**.

As an example of the workings of the wholesale market – during the summer a British bank might receive large numbers of euros from Germans traveling in Britain. The same British bank may also be selling large numbers of Swiss francs to British tourists leaving for vacations in Switzerland. The British bank will sell its surplus euros to a bank-note wholesaler in London, who might then transport the euro notes back to a bank in continental Europe or to a bank outside Europe in need of euro notes for their citizens intending to travel to Europe. The British bank will buy Swiss francs from a wholesaler who may well have transported them from Switzerland, or brought them from banks which bought francs from vacationing Swiss. The spreads on the wholesale level are less than retail bank-note spreads, generally well below 2 percent, because larger amounts are generally involved.

THE SPOT FOREIGN EXCHANGE MARKET

Far larger than the bank note market is the **spot foreign exchange market**. This is involved with the exchange of currencies held in different currency denominated bank accounts. The **spot exchange rate**, which is determined in the spot market, is the number of units of one currency per unit of another currency, where both currencies are in the form of bank deposits. The deposits are transferred from sellers' to buyers' accounts, with instructions to exchange currencies taking the form of electronic messages, or of **bank drafts**, which are checks issued by banks. Delivery, or **value**, from the electronic instructions or bank drafts is "immediate" – usually in 1 or 2 days. This distinguishes the spot market from the forward market which is discussed in Chapter 3, and which involves the planned exchange of currencies for value at some date in the future – after a number of days or even years.

Spot exchange rates are determined by the supplies of and demands for currencies being exchanged in the gigantic, global interbank foreign exchange market.[2] This market is legendary for the frenetic pace at which it operates, and for the vast amount of money which is moved at lightning speed in response to minuscule differences in price quotations.

2 The supply and demand curves for currencies are derived and used to explain the economic factors behind exchange rates in Chapter 6.

ORGANIZATION OF THE INTERBANK SPOT MARKET

The interbank foreign exchange market is the largest financial market on Earth. After correcting for double-counting, so that a purchase by one bank and the corresponding sale by a second bank is counted only once, average turnover is over $1.2 trillion per day.[3] The largest part of trading, over 31 percent of the global total, occurs in the United Kingdom. Indeed, the amount of foreign currency trading conducted in London is so large that a larger share of currency trade in US dollars (26 percent) and euros (27 percent) occurs in the United Kingdom than in the United States (18 percent) or Germany (10 percent) respectively. Table 2.2 shows that the

Table 2.2 Geographical distribution of average daily foreign exchange turnover, April 2001

Country	Net turnover,[a] billion US$	Percentage share
United Kingdom	504	31.1
United States	254	15.7
Japan	147	9.1
Singapore	101	6.2
Germany	88	5.4
Switzerland	71	4.4
Hong Kong	67	4.1
Australia	52	3.2
France	48	3.0
Other	286	17.8
Total	1618	100.0

Note
a Net of double-counting; no adjustment for cross-border double-counting.

Source: Central Bank Survey of Foreign Exchange Market Activity in April 2001, Bank for International Settlements, Basle, Switzerland, December 2003, p. 8.

3 See *Triennial Central Bank Survey of Foreign Exchange and Derivatives Market Activity*, Bank for International Settlements, Basle, Switzerland, March 2002. After a period of phenomenal growth, the turnover on the market has declined, partly because of the advent of the euro, the new common currency of a dozen European countries: there is no longer need to exchange currencies when doing business between Germany, France, Italy, Spain, and so on.

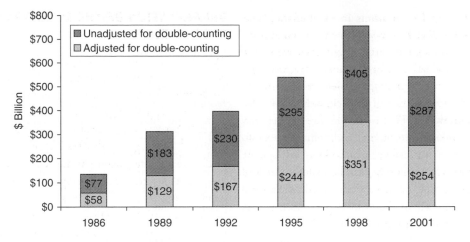

Figure 2.1 *Daily turnover in the US foreign exchange market, 1986–2001*

Notes
Daily trading volume in the US foreign exchange market averaged $254 billion in April 2001, down 28 percent from 1998. Introduction of euro, consolidation among financial institutions, increased trading through electronic brokers and shifting of trading from the United States have contributed to this decline.

Source: Summary of Results of the US Foreign Exchange Market Survey Conducted in April 2001, Federal Reserve Bank of New York, 2003, p. 3.

United States has the second largest foreign exchange market, followed by Japan, Singapore, and Germany. Figure 2.1 shows the size of the US foreign exchange market, indicating the recent decline due to the introduction of the euro and the new forms of electronic price discovery in the interbank market made possible by new electronic forms of market making.

The foreign exchange market is an informal arrangement of the larger commercial banks and a number of foreign exchange brokers. The banks and brokers are linked together by telephone, telex, and a satellite communications network called the **Society for Worldwide International Finan-cial Telecommunications (SWIFT)**. This computer-based communications system, based in Brussels, Belgium, links banks and brokers in just about every financial center. The banks and brokers are in almost constant contact, with activity in some financial center or other 24 hours a day.[4] Because of

the speed of communications, significant events have virtually instantaneous impacts everywhere in the world despite the huge distances separating market participants. This is what makes the foreign exchange market just as efficient as a conventional stock or commodity market housed under a single roof.

The efficiency of the foreign exchange market is revealed in the extremely narrow spreads between buying and selling prices. These spreads can be smaller than a tenth of a percent of the value of a currency exchange, and are therefore about one-fiftieth or less of the spread faced on cash by inter-national travelers. The efficiency of the market is also manifest in the electrifying speed with which exchange rates respond to the continuous flow of information that bombards financial markets. Participants cannot afford to miss a beat in the frantic pulse of this dynamic, global market. Indeed, the bankers and brokers that constitute the foreign exchange market can scarcely detach themselves from the video monitors that provide the latest news and prices as fast as the information can travel along the telephone wires and radio waves of business news wire services such as Dow Jones Telerate and Reuters.

4 Indeed, in the principal centers like New York, London, Tokyo, and Toronto, large banks maintain 24-hour operations to keep up with developments elsewhere and continue trading during other centers' normal working hours.

In the United States, as in most other markets, there are two levels on which the foreign exchange market operates, the direct interbank level, and an indirect level via foreign exchange brokers. In the case of interbank trading, banks trade directly with each other, and all participating banks are **market-makers**. That is, in the direct interbank market, banks quote buying and selling prices to each other. The calling bank does not specify whether they wish to buy or sell, or how much of the currency they wish to trade. Bank A can call Bank B for a quote of "their market" or Bank B can call Bank A. This is known as an open-bid double auction, "open" because the buy/sell intention and amount are not specified – it is left open – and "double auction" because banks can call each other for price quotations. Because there is no central location of the market and because price quotes are a continuous process – a quote of the bank's market to another bank is good only for seconds while the traders speak – the direct market can be characterized as a **decentralized, continuous, open-bid, double-auction market**.[5]

In the case of foreign exchange brokers, of which there are fewer than 20 versus over 100 commercial banks in the New York market, so-called **limit orders** are placed with brokers by some banks. For example, a commercial bank may place an order with a broker to purchase £10 million at $1.5550/£. The broker puts this on their "book," and attempts to match the purchase order with sell orders for pounds from other banks. While the market-making banks take positions on their own behalf and for customers, brokers deal for others, showing callers their best rates, and charging a commission to buying and selling banks. Because of its structure, the indirect broker-based market can be characterized as a **quasi-centralized, continuous, limit-book, single-auction market**.[6]

Figure 2.2, which depicts the US foreign exchange market, shows that currencies are also bought and sold by central banks. Central banks enter the market when they want to change exchange rates from those that would result only from private supplies and demands, and in order to transact on their own behalf; central banks buy and sell bonds and settle transactions for governments which involve foreign exchange payments and receipts. Exhibit 2.1 provides a succinct summary of the players in the foreign exchange market.

As we have mentioned, in the direct interbank market, which is the largest part of the foreign exchange market, bankers call foreign exchange dealers at other banks and "ask for the market." The caller might say, "Your market in sterling please." This means, "At what price are you willing to buy and at what price are you willing to sell British pounds for US dollars?" (British pounds are sometimes called sterling). In replying, a foreign exchange dealer must attempt to determine whether the caller really wants to buy or to sell, and must relate this to what his or her own preference is for sterling: do they want more or fewer pounds? This is a subtle and tricky game involving human judgment. Bluff and counterbluff are sometimes used. A good trader, with a substantial order for pounds, may ask for the market in Canadian dollars. After placing an order he or she might say, "By the way, what's your market in sterling?" Dealers are not averse to having their assistants place the really large and really small orders, just to hope for favorable quotes. A difference in quotation of the fourth decimal place can mean thousands of dollars on a large order. It is rather like massive-stakes poker.

If a trader who has been called wants to sell pounds, he or she will quote on the side that is felt to be cheap for pounds, given this trader's feel of the market. For example, if the trader feels that other banks are selling pounds at $1.6120/£, he or she might quote $1.6118/£ as the selling price, along with a buying price that is also correspondingly low. Having considered the two-way price, the caller will state whether he or she wishes to buy or sell, and the amount. Once the rate has been quoted, convention determines that it must be

5 See Mark D. Flood, "Microstructure Theory and the Foreign Exchange Market," *Review*, Federal Reserve Bank of St. Louis, November/December 1991, pp. 52–70.
6 See Mark D. Flood, op.cit., p. 57.

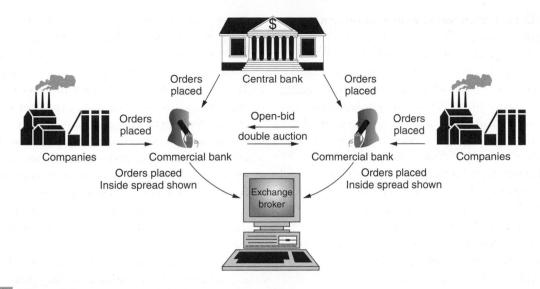

Figure 2.2 *Organization of the foreign exchange market*

Notes
The main foreign exchange market makers are large commercial banks who are in continuous contact with each other, quoting "bid" and "ask" exchange rates in the interbank market. The currency trading banks trade on their own account to affect the inventories of currencies they hold, as well as in response to large buy or sell orders of customers. In addition to interbank trading, limit book orders to buy and sell are placed with foreign exchange brokers who help match trades. Central banks also sometimes enter the market, buying and selling to influence exchange rates or performing transactions for the government.

honored whatever the decision of the caller, up to a predetermined limit. The standard-sized interbank trade is for $10 million (and the equivalent in the foreign currency). However, trades may be a multiple of the standard trade or less than the standard trade (although always more than $1 million). As mentioned, after being quoted the market the caller has only seconds to decide. Good judgment of the counterparty and good judgment of the direction of the market are essential in this multi-billion-dollar game. It is important to be accurate and constantly in touch with events.

Delivery dates and procedures for spot exchange

Whereas bank notes of the major Western countries are exchanged for each other instantaneously over the counter, when US dollars are exchanged in the New York interbank spot market with non-North American currencies, funds are not generally received until two business days after the initiation of the transaction. With the currencies of the North American

continent, the US and Canadian dollars and the Mexican peso, delivery is slightly quicker, with an exchange providing value after one business day. This means there is a distinction between the value date and the initiation date of a transaction, the trade date. The distinction can be illustrated by an example.[7]

Suppose that a financial executive of an American corporation, Amcorp, calls his or her bank, Ambank National, a large currency-dealing bank in New York City, to buy £2 million. Suppose that the call is placed on Thursday, May 18, and that the British pounds are to be used to settle Amcorp's debt to Britcorp. Ambank will quote an exchange rate at which it will sell Amcorp the £2 million. If Amcorp approves of this rate, then the foreign exchange department of Ambank will request details for making the payment in Britain. These details will include the bank at which Britcorp is to be paid and the account number.

7 It is possible to send money for value sooner than two days outside of North America and one day within North America. However, this is somewhat more expensive than the normal spot rate.

EXHIBIT 2.1 INSTITUTIONAL BASICS OF THE FOREIGN EXCHANGE MARKET

The following account of the foreign exchange market, which appeared in the *Review* of the Federal Reserve Bank of St. Louis, explains the dual tiers of the market: direct interbank trades plus trades through brokers:

> The foreign exchange market is the international market in which buyers and sellers of currencies "meet." It is largely decentralized: the participants (classified as market-makers, brokers and customers) are physically separated from one another; they communicate via telephone, telex and computer network. Trading volume is large, estimated at $254 billion for the US market in 2001.* Most of this trading was between bank market-makers.
>
> The market is dominated by the market-makers at commercial and investment banks, who trade currencies with each other both directly and through foreign exchange brokers. Market-makers, as the name suggests, "make a market" in one or more currencies by providing bid and ask prices upon demand. A broker arranges trades by keeping a "book" of market-maker's limit orders – that is, orders to buy (alternatively, to sell) a specified quantity of foreign currency at a specified price – from which he quotes the best bid and ask orders upon request. The best bid and ask quotes on a broker's book are together called the broker's "inside spread." The other participants in the market are the customers of the market-making banks, who generally use the market to complete transactions in international trade, and central banks, who may enter the market to move exchange rates or simply to complete their own international transactions.
>
> Market-makers may trade for their own account – that is, they may maintain a long or short position in a foreign currency – and require significant capitalization for that purpose. Brokers do not contact customers and do not deal on their own account; instead, they profit by charging a fee for the service of bringing foreign market-makers together.

* Number updated from original publication.

Source: Mark D. Flood, "Microstructure Theory and the Foreign Exchange Market," *Review*, Federal Reserve Bank of St. Louis, November/December 1991, pp. 52–70.

The details provided by Amcorp to Ambank will typically be conveyed to the designated bank in Britain, Britbank, by sending a message on the day of ordering the pounds, May 18, via SWIFT. The SWIFT network, which has been available since 1977, has grown so rapidly that it has virtually replaced the preexisting methods of conveying messages, namely the mail and telegraphic transfer. SWIFT uses satellite linkages, and transmits messages between banks in a standard format to minimize errors which can easily occur due to different languages and banking customs. SWIFT has been so successful that banks in just about every country, including Russia and other communist countries, have joined or applied to join.[8]

The spot exchange rate that is agreed by Ambank National on Thursday, May 18 will be binding and will not be changed even if market conditions subsequently change. A confirmation of the order for £2 million at the agreed exchange rate – for example, $1.6000/£ – will be sent out to Amcorp on Thursday, May 18. Because of the intervening weekend, the value date, which is two business days later, is Monday, May 22, and on this day Ambank will debit Amcorp's account at the bank by $3.2 million, the dollar price of the £2 million at $1.6000/£. On the same value date, May 22, Britbank will credit Britcorp's account by £2 million. The transaction is complete for the payer and payee, with the payee, Britcorp, being credited £2 million in Britain, and Amcorp, the payer, being debited the dollar equivalent, $3.2 million.

---

8 Since 1987, non-banking financial institutions such as brokerage firms have also been given access to SWIFT.

Our description of the transaction in the example is complete only for the payer and the payee. We have not yet described the settlement between the banks. Specifically, the bank that has purchased foreign currency will have to pay the bank that has sold the foreign currency. This payment generally takes place via a **clearing house**. A clearing house is an institution at which banks keep funds which can be moved from one bank's account to another to settle interbank transactions.

When foreign exchange is trading against the US dollar the clearing house that is used is called **CHIPS**, an acronym for **Clearing House Interbank Payments System**. CHIPS is located in New York and, as we shall explain later, transfers funds between member banks. Currencies are also traded directly for each other without involving the dollar – for example, euros for British pounds, or Danish crowns for Swiss francs. In these situations European clearing houses are used. However, because a substantial volume of transactions is settled in dollars, we consider how CHIPS works, although we can note that settlement between banks is similar in other financial centers. We will also explain a relatively new form of settlement between banks that has been spurred on by concern over the possible vulnerability of the international financial system to extreme outside events.

Bank settlement via CHIPS and CLS

CHIPS is a computerized mechanism through which banks hold US dollars to pay each other when buying or selling foreign exchange.[9] The system is owned by the large New York-based clearing banks; has over 150 members, including the US agencies and subsidiaries of many foreign banks; and handles hundreds of thousands of transactions a day, worth together hundreds of billions of dollars.

We can see how CHIPS works by extending the situation considered earlier, of Amcorp initiating payment to Britcorp on Thursday, May 18, with Britcorp being credited at Britbank two business days later, Monday, May 22, after the intervening weekend. The extension is to assume that immediately on agreeing to sell Amcorp £2 million, Ambank enters the interbank market to replenish its pound account at Britbank (Ambank has its sterling on deposit at Britbank).

Let us suppose that after placing a few telephone calls in the interbank market, Ambank finds the cheapest rate on pounds to be at UKbank (perhaps UKbank has just paid out US dollars for a client and wants to replenish its dollar holdings in exchange for pounds). On agreeing to buy £2 million from UKbank, Ambank gives instructions to deliver the pounds to its account at Britbank.[10] Ambank's payment to Britbank will be effected by Ambank entering into its CHIPS computer terminal its own code, that of UKbank, and the number of dollars to be paid. Similarly, UKbank enters its code, Ambank's code, and the number of dollars to be received. This is all done at the time the two banks agree on the purchase/sale, assumed to be the same day as Amcorp orders the pounds, May 18.

CHIPS records the information received from Ambank and UKbank, and keeps track of other amounts to be paid or received by these banks and the many other CHIPS members. On the value date of the transaction, May 22, settlement reports are sent to the banks for gross and net amounts to be paid or received on that day. Assuming Ambank and UKbank have no dispute over the reports they receive, the debtor bank, in our case Ambank, must send instructions to the Federal Reserve Bank of New York to debit Ambank's account there, called its **escrow account**, and to credit the escrow account of UKbank. The instruction from Ambank is sent via **Fedwire**, a system also used for settlement of domestic transactions.

Since September 2002 a new settlement system has been provided to the foreign exchange markets by New York-based CLS Bank, where CLS stands

---

9 For an account of the workings of CHIPS, see www.chips.org

10 The pounds will be moved from UKbank to Britbank as part of the normal settlement between banks provided by the clearing house in London.

for **Continuous Linked Settlement**.[11] The virtue of a continuous linked system is that it prevents situations where a bank pays for a currency before receiving it, and then finds out the bank that was to provide the currency has become bankrupt. This has been a fear since at least 1974 when Herstatt Bank, a small German bank, failed. By continuously linking payment and receipt so they occur at the same time, what is sometimes called "Herstatt risk" is avoided. The CLS Bank is owned by a consortium of banks and began settling just the major currencies and handling settlement only for banks, but is expanding to settle more currencies and to settle transactions for corporate members. The corporate members are referred to as "third parties," with their transactions going through banks, but with all transactions linked.

The informal, doubled-tiered structure of the US foreign exchange market, with direct interbank dealing coexisting with indirect brokered transactions, is similar to that of markets in Canada, Britain, and many other countries. In some continental European countries the procedure is more formal, with bank representatives, including a representative of the central bank, meeting daily face-to-face. Contracts are exchanged directly, although an informal market coexists in which many of the transactions occur. The formal meeting provides official settlement exchange rates that are used for certain transactions.

Exhibit 2.2 gives a lively and vivid account of a typical transaction in the US interbank market, and a transaction made indirectly via a broker. The example introduces some of the jargon that is involved in the parsimonious conversations.

Retail versus interbank spot rates

While it is only exchange rates between banks that are determined in the interbank market, exchange rates faced by banks' clients are based on these interbank rates. Banks charge their customers slightly more than the going interbank selling or **ask rate**, and pay their customers slightly less than the interbank buying or **bid rate**. That is, the retail spread is wider than the interbank spread. The extent of a bank's markup or markdown from the going interbank rate depends principally on the size of the retail transaction. Banks will not generally enter the interbank market, especially for small transactions, using instead currency they already own or adding to the amount they own. However, banks still base their retail spot rates on the interbank rates, telephoning the banks' own foreign exchange trading desks before quoting on large transactions. Larger banks have tellers' terminals linked to the foreign exchange trading room for continuous updating of retail rates.

Customer drafts and wire transfers

When a customer requests foreign exchange from a bank, with this to be paid to a creditor in a foreign country, the bank sells the customer a draft payable to the creditor. This draft will be drawn against an account the bank holds with a bank in the country in which the payment is to be made. For example, if an American needs to make a Canadian dollar payment to a Canadian, they can buy a draft from a US bank, where this draft is drawn against the US bank's Canadian dollar account at a Canadian bank. A speedier settlement can be made by buying a **wire transfer**, where instead of mailing a draft, the instructions are sent via SWIFT or some similar electronic means. The customer pays the US bank a charge for the draft or transfer, with wire transfers costing slightly more.

When one bank maintains an account at another bank the banks are called **correspondents**, where this term originates from the mail instructions that used to be sent between them. Commercial banks keep accounts at correspondents in all major countries to help their customers make payments in these countries, and to earn the fees charged for their services.

---

11 CLS is described in *Global Finance*, July 2003, pp. 1–3. See also www.cls-group.com

EXHIBIT 2.2   AN EXCHANGE ON THE EXCHANGE: A CONVERSATION BETWEEN MARKET-MAKERS IN THE FOREIGN EXCHANGE MARKET

The following account of an exchange between currency traders is an updated, slightly revised version of a description of a typical conversation that appeared in the *Review* of the Federal Reserve Bank of St. Louis: updating is required to reflect the fact that Germany has replaced the Deutschmark with the euro. In this account, Mongobank and Loans 'n Things are two market-making banks. Interpretations of jargon are given as the jargon is used. For example, we are told that "Two mine" means to purchase two million units of a currency. "One by two" means being willing to buy one million units of a currency and sell two million units of the same currency.

In the direct market, banks contact each other. The bank receiving a call acts as a market-maker for the currency in question, providing a two-way quote (bid and ask) for the bank placing the call. A direct deal might go as follows:

Mongobank: "*Mongobank with a dollar-euro please?*"
(Mongobank requests a spot market quote for the euro (EUR) against US dollars (USD).

Loans'n Things: "*20–30*"
(Loans'n Things will buy euros at 1.1520 USD/EUR and sell euros at 1.1530 USD/EUR – the 1.15 part of the quote is understood. The spread here is "10 points.")

Mongobank: "*Two mine.*"
(Mongobank buys EUR 2,000,000 for USD 2,306,000 at 1.1530 USD/EUR, for payment two business days later. The quantity traded is usually one of a handful of "customary amounts.")

Loans'n Things: "*My euros to Loans 'n Things Frankfurt.*"
(Loans n' Things requests that payment of euros be made to their account at their Frankfurt branch. Payment will likely be made via SWIFT.)[a]

Mongobank: "*My dollars to Mongobank New York.*"
(Mongobank requests that payment of dollars be made to them in New York. Payment might be made via CHIPS.)[b]

Spot transactions are made for "value date" (payment date) two business days later to allow settlement arrangements to be made with correspondents or branches in other time zones. This period is extended when a holiday intervenes in one of the countries involved. Payment occurs in a currency's home country.

The other method of inter-bank trading is brokered transactions. Brokers collect limit orders from bank market-makers. A limit order is an offer to buy (alternatively to sell) a specified quantity at a specified price. Limit orders remain with the broker until withdrawn by the market-maker.

The advantages of brokered trading include the rapid dissemination of orders to other market-makers, anonymity in quoting, and the freedom not to quote to other market-makers on a reciprocal basis, which can be required in the direct market. Anonymity allows the quoting bank to conceal its identity and thus its intentions; it also requires that the broker know who is an acceptable counterparty for whom. Limit orders are also provided in part as a courtesy to the brokers as part of an ongoing business relationship that makes the market more liquid . . .

A market-maker who calls a broker for a quote gets the broker's inside spread, along with the quantities of the limit orders. A typical call to a broker might proceed as follows:

Mongobank: "*What is sterling, please?*"
(Mongobank requests the spot quote for US dollars against British pounds (GBP).)

Fonmeister: "*I deal 40–42, one by two.*"
(Fonmeister Brokerage has quotes to buy £1,000,000 at 1.7440 USD/GBP, and to sell £2,000,000 at 1.7442 USD/GBP)

Mongobank: "*I sell one at 40, to whom?*"
(Mongobank hits the bid for the quantity stated. Mongobank could have requested a different amount, which would have required additional confirmation from the bidding bank.)

Fonmeister: [A pause while the deal is reported to and confirmed by Loans 'n Things]
"*Loans 'n Things London.*"
(Fonmeister confirms the deal and reports the counterparty to Mongobank. Payment arrangements will be made and confirmed separately by the respective back offices. The broker's back office will also confirm the trade with the banks.)

Value dates and payment arrangements are the same as in the direct dealing case. In addition to the payment to the counterparty bank, the banks involved share the brokerage fee. These fees are negotiable in the United States. They are also quite low: roughly $20 per million dollars transacted.

Notes
a The Society for Worldwide Interbank Financial Telecommunication (SWIFT) is an electronic message network. In this case, it conveys a standardized payment order to a German branch or correspondent bank, which, in turn, effects the payment as a local inter-bank transfer in Frankfurt.
b The Clearing House for Interbank Payments System (CHIPS) is a private inter-bank payments system in New York City.
Source: Mark D. Flood, "Microstructure Theory and the Foreign Exchange Market," *Review*, Federal Reserve Bank of St. Louis, November/December 1991, pp. 52–70.

Internet exchange

If one person has more, say, pounds than they need, and another person has fewer pounds than they need, they could, in principle, exchange the pounds between themselves. For example, the pound seller would receive dollars and the pound buyer would pay dollars. Both parties would gain relative to exchanging currency through a bank provided they kept the exchange rate among themselves between the bid and ask exchange rates of the banks. The reasons why this mutually beneficial arrangement rarely occurs are:

1   It is difficult for the parties to find each other.
2   Private transactions require trust in the other party because payment precedes receipt.

There are a growing number of alternatives for exchanging foreign currency through the Internet. The Internet provides a medium through which the parties can find each other. However, the need to have trust still necessitates an intermediary. This could be a well-known bank, but there are other institutions that are providing exchange services.

As confidence in the safety of such exchanges grows, it is likely that Internet-based currency exchange will grow in importance.

Conventions for spot exchange quotation

In virtually every professional enterprise, especially in the realm of finance and economics, there are special conventions and a particular jargon. This is certainly true in the foreign exchange market, where practices in the quotation of exchange rates make the quotes difficult to interpret unless the jargon and conventions are well understood.

Let us consider the spot exchange rates shown in the lower part of Figure 2.3 (the upper part of the table showing "Key Currency Cross Rates" is discussed later in the chapter). The figure quotes rates from *The Wall Street Journal* of May 23, 2003. These are the previous day's exchange rates, quoted at approximately 4:00 pm, Eastern Time in New York. As the table states, the rates are those on sales of more than $1 million by banks to other banks. That is, the rates are interbank rates.

Key Currency Cross Rates

Late New York Trading Thursday, May 22, 2003

	Dollar	Euro	Pound	SFranc	Peso	Yen	CdnDlr
Canada	1.3757	1.6087	2.2490	1.0618	.13406	.01173	...
Japan	117.23	137.09	191,65	90.481	11.424	...	85.217
Mexico	10.2617	12.0000	16.776	7.9200	...	.08753	7.4592
Switzerland	1.2957	1.5152	2.1182	...	.12626	.01105	.9418
U.K.	.61170	.7153	...	.4721	.05961	.00522	.44464
Euro	.85510	...	1.3980	.66000	.08333	.00729	.62160
U.S.	...	1.1694	1.6348	.77180	.09745	.00853	.72690

Source: Reuters

Exchange Rates

The foreign exchange mid-range rates below apply to trading among banks in amounts of $1 million and more, as quoted at 4 p.m. Eastern time by Reuters and other sources. Retail transactions provide fewer units of foreign currency per dollar.

	U.S. $ EQUIVALENT		CURRENCY PER U.S. $	
Country	Thu	Wed	Thu	Wed
Argentina (Peso)-y	.3472	.3518	2.8802	2.8425
Australia (Dollar)	.6581	.6561	1.5195	1.5242
Bahrain (Dinar)	2.6523	2.6524	.3770	.3770
Brazil (Real)	.3351	.3333	2.9842	3.0003
Canada (Dollar)	.7269	.7401	1.3757	1.3512
1-month forward	.7257	.7388	1.3780	1.3535
3-months forward	.7231	.7361	1.3829	1.3585
6-months forward	.7192	.7319	1.3904	1.3663
Chile (Peso)	.001414	.001406	707.21	711.24
China (Renminbi)	.1208	.1208	8.2781	8.2781
Colombia (Peso)	.0003461	.0003433	2889.34	2912.90
Czech. Rep. (Koruna)				
Commercial rate	.03729	.03718	26.817	26.896
Denmark (Krone)	.1575	.1573	6.3492	6.3573
Ecuador (US Dollar)	1.0000	1.0000	1.0000	1.0000
Egypt (Pound)-y	.1674	.1679	5.9751	5.9549
Hong Kong (Dollar)	.1282	.1282	7.8003	7.8003
Hungary (Forint)	.004753	.004747	210.39	210.66
India (Rupee)	.02134	.02134	46.860	46.860
Indonesia (Rupiah)	.0001200	.0001201	8333	8326
Israel (Shekel)	.2215	.2183	4.5147	4.5809
Japan (Yen)	.008530	.008527	117.23	117.27
1-month forward	.008539	.008536	117.11	117.15
3-months forward	.008557	.008555	116.86	116.89
6-months forward	.008581	.008580	116.54	116.55
Jordan (Dinar)	1.4104	1.4104	.7090	.7090
Kuwait (Dinar)	3.3490	3.3466	.2986	.2988
Lebanon (Pound)	.0006634	.0006634	1507.39	1507.39
Malaysia (Ringgit)-b	.2632	.2632	3.7994	3.7994
Malta (Lira)	2.7189	2.7167	.3678	.3681

	U.S. $ EQUIVALENT		CURRENCY PER U.S. $	
Country	Thu	Wed	Thu	Wed
Mexico (Peso)				
Floating rate	.0975	.0978	10.2617	10.2270
New Zealand (Dollar)	.5832	.5827	1.7147	1.7161
Norway (Krone)	.1490	.1485	6.7114	6.7340
Pakistan (Rupee)	.01732	.01732	57.737	57.737
Peru (new Sol)	.2864	.2866	3.4916	3.4892
Philippines (Peso)	.01893	.01900	52.826	52.632
Poland (Zloty)	.2692	.2677	3.7147	3.7355
Russia (Ruble)-a	.03249	.03238	30.779	30.883
Saudi Arabia (Riyal)	.2666	.2667	3.7509	3.7495
Singapore (Dollar)	.5805	.5799	1.7227	1.7244
Slovak Rep. (Koruna)	.02843	.02836	35.174	35.261
South Africa (Rand)	.1277	.1282	7.8309	7.8003
South Korea (Won)	.0008366	.0008373	1195.31	1194.32
Sweden (Krona)	.1277	.1274	7.8309	7.8493
Switzerland (Franc)	.7718	.7712	1.2957	1.2967
1-month forward	.7725	.7719	1.2945	1.2955
3-months forward	.7737	.7731	1.2925	1.2935
6-months forward	.7753	.7748	1.2898	1.2907
Taiwan (Dollar)	.02888	.02890	34.626	34.602
Thailand (Baht)	.02385	.02384	41.929	41.946
Turkey (Lira)	.00000068	.00000067	1470588	1492537
U.K. (Pound)	1.6348	1.6365	.6117	.6111
1-month forward	1.6316	1.6333	.6129	.6123
3-months forward	1.6253	1.6266	.6153	.6148
6-months forward	1.6160	1.6176	.6188	.6182
United Arab (Dirham)	.2723	.2723	3.6724	3.6724
Uruguay (Peso)				
Financial	.03420	.03420	29.240	29.240
Venezuela (Bolivar)	.000626	.000626	1597.44	1597.44
SDR	1.4175	1.4136	.7055	.7074
Euro	1.1694	1.1678	.8551	.8563

Special Drawing Rights (SDR) are based on exchange rates for the U.S., British, and Japanese currencies. Source: International Monetary Fund.

a-Russian Central Bank rate. b-Government rate. y-Floating rate.

Figure 2.3 *Interbank spot and selected forward exchange rates*

Notes
Exchange rates can be quoted either as US dollars per unit of foreign currency or as foreign currency per US dollar. The latter form, for example, SFr1.2957/$ is referred to as "European terms." This is the way most exchange rates are quoted in the interbank market. The exceptions are the euro and British pound which are quoted as "US dollar equivalent." For example, the pound would be quoted as $1.6348/£. Newspapers typically quote the mid-rate, which is half way between the bid and the ask rates, or selling rates, whereas interbank quotes involve both buying and selling rates.

Source: Reprinted by permission of *The Wall Street Journal*, ©2003 Dow Jones & Company Inc. All rights reserved.

As indicated in the figure, retail rates to bank clients will be less favorable than these interbank rates.

Figure 2.3 gives rates in two ways – as the number of US dollars per foreign currency unit, which is called **US dollar equivalent** – and as the number of units of foreign **currency per US dollar**. To a close approximation, the figures in the second two columns are merely the reciprocals of the figures in the first two columns. With the exception of the euro and UK pound for which the practice in the interbank market is to quote in US dollar equivalents, that is as US dollars per euro or per pound, other rates in the interbank market are quoted as foreign currency per US dollar. The quotation, (foreign) currency per US dollar, is known as **European terms**.[12] For example, on May 22, 2003 in the interbank market, the US dollar would have been quoted in European terms as 1.5195 Australian dollars (A\$1.5195/\$) or 8.2781 Chinese Renminbi (¥8.2781/\$).[13]

Figure 2.3 does not reveal whether the exchange rates are for selling or buying foreign currency. It is customary for newspapers to quote either mid-rates – rates half way between the buying and selling rates – or if only one side of the market is given, the rates are most likely the banks' selling rates. However, as we have seen, interbank traders when asked for the market give two-way quotations. The selling rates are called **offer rates** or ask rates. If the rates in the figure are the offer or ask rates, then in order to determine the buying or bid rates, the numbers in the table would have to be adjusted. We might guess that if banks are selling US dollars for 1.2957 Swiss francs (SFr 1.2957/\$), they might be buying US dollars for SFr1.2952/\$. Because the conventional form of quotation of Swiss franc and almost every other currency is in European terms, that is, foreign currency per US dollar, it is easier to think of exchange rates as the buying and selling prices of US dollars, rather than as the selling and buying prices of the foreign currency.

Note that the Swiss franc amount being paid for US dollars (the bank's Swiss franc buying or bid price on dollars, SFr1.2952/\$) is slightly lower than the amount being charged for US dollars (the bank's Swiss franc selling or ask price for dollars, SFr1.2957/\$). The difference between the two rates is the spread. More generally, the European terms exchange rates can all be thought of as bids and asks on the US dollar since they are in terms of amounts of foreign currency per US dollar. For example, the Can\$1.3757/\$ entry in Figure 2.3, can be thought of as the bid on a US dollar (ask on the Canadian dollar): the bank pays Can\$1.3757 for a US dollar. The ask for the US dollar (bid on the Canadian dollar) might be Can\$1.3762/\$.

In the case of the euro and pound, which unlike other currencies, are conventionally quoted as US dollar equivalents, it is easier to think of the \$1.1694/€ and \$1.6348/£ in Figure 2.3 as the US dollar selling prices of euros and pounds – the bank's ask or offer (selling) prices for euros and pounds. The bid or buying price of euros and pounds might be \$1.1690/€ and \$1.6343/£. Of course, an ask on the pound is a bid on the dollar, and a bid on the pound is an ask on the dollar. Because the convention is to quote the euro and sterling as US dollars per euro or pound, it is easier to think of their exchange rates as buying and selling prices of the euro or pound. That is, just as we can most easily think of European terms as buying and selling prices of US dollars – the rates are amounts of foreign currency per US dollar – in the case of the euro and pound we can most easily think of rates as buying and selling prices of euros and pounds.

In quotations between traders in the interbank market bids always precede asks. For example, in the case of quoting Swiss francs versus US dollars the rates would be quoted as SFr1.2957/62 per dollar. This means SFr1.2957 bid for a US dollar, and SFr1.2962 asked for a US dollar. Indeed, as Exhibit 2.2 indicates, the SFr1.29 part might be assumed to be understood, and the quote might be simply 57/62. The pound would be quoted as \$1.6343/48 per pound, or simply 43/48, the bid on the pound preceding the ask.

Whichever way rates are quoted, the last digit of the quotation is referred to as a **point**. For example,

---

12 This is a carry over of the fact that the practice on the European Continent was to quote in units of foreign currency per dollar, while the practice in the United Kingdom was to quote dollars per pound that is, US dollar equivalent.

13 Renminbi means "the peoples' money." The symbol ¥ follows the Chinese currency name, the "yuan."

the difference between the bid on the US dollar of SFr1.2957 and the ask for US dollars of SFr1.2962 is $1.2962 - 1.2957 = 0.0005$ or five points. Similarly the assumed bid on British pounds of $1.6343 differs from the ask of $1.6348 by five points. A point always refers to the last digit quoted. This is not always the fourth decimal. For example, with the Japanese yen the bid-ask spread quoted by a bank may be ¥110.20/25 per US dollar. Here, the point is the second digit after the decimal.

It is important that we distinguish between bid and ask exchange rates, even if it seems that the differences are so small as to be almost irrelevant. There are two reasons for this. First, the bid-ask spread provides banks with their incomes, earned by charging their customers, from dealing in foreign exchange. For example, even if the banks charge only 0.0002 ($= 2 \times 10^{-4}$) of the value of each transaction, the revenue to the market-making banks on their transactions of over $1.2 trillion ($= \$1.2 \times 10^{12}$) each day is $\$1.2 \times 10^{12} \times 2 \times 10^{-4} = \$240$ million. This is not all profit for banks because much of this revenue merely moves between banks doing interbank transactions, and also because banks themselves face operating costs. However, the amount does indicate the importance of spreads to banks, and to the banks' customers who face the spreads. Second, spreads may seem small but can have a substantial effect on yields when the spreads are faced on investments made for only a short period. For example, if a company invests abroad for 1 month and must therefore buy the foreign currency today and sell it after 1 month, a 0.1 percent spread on buying and on selling the foreign exchange is a 0.2 percent spread for the investment. When put on an annual basis by multiplying by 12, this involves an annualized cost of approximately 2.4 percent. If the extra interest available on foreign securities versus domestic securities is smaller than 2.4 percent, the spread will eliminate the advantage. The shorter the period for which funds are invested abroad, the more relevant bid-ask spreads on foreign exchange become.

DIRECT VERSUS INDIRECT EXCHANGE AND CROSS EXCHANGE RATES

Indirect exchange and the practice of quoting against the dollar

With more than 150 currencies in the world, there are more than $150 \times 149 = 22,350$ different exchange rates. This is because each of 150 different currencies has an exchange rate against the remaining 149 currencies. Fortunately for the people who work in the foreign exchange market, many of the more than twenty thousand possible exchange rates are redundant. The most obvious cause of redundancy is that once we know, for example, the price of dollars in terms of pounds, this immediately suggests knowing the price of pounds in terms of dollars. This reduces the number of relevant exchange rate quotations by one-half. However, there is another cause of redundancy because it is possible, for example, to compute the exchange rate between the euro and British pound from the exchange rate between the euro and the dollar and the pound and the dollar. Indeed, if there were no costs of transacting in foreign exchange, that is, no bid-ask spreads, with 150 currencies all 22,350 possible exchange rates could be precisely computed from the 149 exchange rates of each currency versus the US dollar. Let us show why by beginning with the simple situation in which the only currencies are the euro, the British pound, and the US dollar.

The procedure we are going to use is to consider people who either want to exchange euros for pounds or pounds for euros. These exchanges can be made directly between the euro and pound, or indirectly via the dollar. For example, it is possible to sell euros for dollars, and then sell these dollars for pounds. We will argue that for banks to attract business involving the direct exchange of euros and pounds, the exchange rate they offer cannot be inferior to the exchange rate implicit in indirect exchange via the US dollar.[14]

14 As we shall see, banks in the United Kingdom and the European Continent do indeed quote direct exchange rates between the euro and pound, and the pound and euro. Furthermore, these rates are at least as favorable as the implicit rates calculated from rates vis-à-vis the US dollar.

We will see that when there are no foreign exchange transaction costs, the constraint of competing with indirect exchange will force banks to quote a direct exchange rate between the euro and pound that is exactly equal to the implicit indirect exchange rate via the dollar. This means that, if there are no transaction costs, we can find all possible exchange rates by taking appropriate exchange rates versus the dollar. When there are transaction costs, we will see that direct exchange rates are not always precisely those that are implicit in rates against the dollar. However, we will see that in that case there are limits within which direct quotations can move, set by exchange rates versus the dollar.

Triangular arbitrage: zero foreign exchange transaction costs

Let us begin by defining the spot exchange rate between the dollar and pound as $S(\$/£)$. That is:

$S(\$/£)$ is the number of US dollars per British pound in the spot foreign exchange market. More generally, $S(i/j)$ is the number of units of currency i per unit of currency j in the spot exchange market.

First, consider a person who wants to go from euros to pounds. In terms of Figure 2.4, this is characterized by the darker arrow along the base of the triangle between € and £. If a bank is to attract business selling pounds for euros, the exchange rate it offers directly between the euro and pound must be no worse than could be achieved by going indirectly from the euro to the dollar and then from the dollar to the pound. In terms of Figure 2.4 the indirect route involves traveling from € to £ via $, that is, along the heavily shaded arrows from € to $, and then from $ to £.

If the person buys pounds directly for euros, the number of pounds received per euro is $S(£/€)$, the spot number of pounds per euro, as shown on the bottom of the triangle in Figure 2.4 with the dark arrow pointing from € to £. If instead the indirect route is taken from € to £ via $, then on the

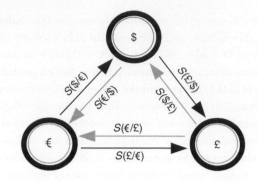

Figure 2.4 *Direct versus indirect exchange: zero transaction costs*

Notes
It is possible to buy pounds with euros directly or else to do this indirectly, using euros to buy dollars and then dollars to buy pounds. Similarly, it is possible to buy euros with pounds directly or to do this indirectly by buying and then selling dollars. The possibility of indirect exchange via dollars forces banks to quote a cross rate between euros and pounds given by the euro and pound rates vis-à-vis the dollar. With zero transaction costs, $S(€/£) = S(€/\$) \cdot S(\$/£)$, precisely.

first leg of the exchange, that from € to $, each euro buys $S(\$/€)$ dollars. Then, on the second leg, that from $ to £, each of these $S(\$/€)$ dollars buys $S(£/\$)$ pounds. Therefore, from the two legs $S(\$/€) \times S(£/\$)$ pounds are received for each euro. It is worth noting that the units of measurement follow the usual rules of algebra. That is, looking only at the currency units, $(\$/€) \times (£/\$) = (£/€)$, with the dollar signs canceling.

As we have said, a bank offering to exchange euros directly for pounds at $S(£/€)$ pounds per euro must offer at least as large a number of pounds as via the indirect route through exchanging into and out of the US dollar. That is, for the bank's exchange rate to be effective in attracting direct euro to pound business its quote must be such that

$$S(£/€) \geq S(\$/€) \cdot S(£/\$) \qquad (2.1)$$

That is, euros will be exchanged for pounds directly rather than via the dollar only if at least as many pounds are received directly.

Let us next consider a person who, instead of wanting to convert euros into pounds, wants to convert pounds into euros. This person can go from

£ to € directly along the lighter leftward pointing arrow in Figure 2.4. This would result in $S(€/£)$ euros for each pound. Alternatively the person can go from £ to € indirectly along the other two lighter arrows, going from £ to $, and then from $ to €. This route gives $S($/£)$ dollars for each pound, and then each of these dollars buys $S(€/$)$ euros. Therefore, the number of euros received per pound from the indirect route is $S($/£) \times S(€/$)$.

A bank quoting an exchange rate for directly converting pounds into euros must offer at least as many euros as would be obtained by using the indirect route via the US dollar. That is, for the bank to attract business, the exchange rate must satisfy

$$S(€/£) \geq S($/£) \cdot S(€/$) \qquad (2.2)$$

We can compare the inequality (2.2) with the inequality (2.1) by noting that in the absence of transaction costs, by definition,

$$S(£/€) \equiv \frac{1}{S(€/£)}$$

$$S($/€) \equiv \frac{1}{S(€/$)} \qquad (2.3)$$

$$S(£/$) \equiv \frac{1}{S($/£)}$$

That is, for example, if there are £0.7153/€, there are $(1/0.7153) = €1.3980/£$. Using equations (2.3) in inequality (2.1) gives

$$\frac{1}{S(€/£)} \geq \frac{1}{S(€/$)} \cdot \frac{1}{S($/£)} \qquad (2.4)$$

Inverting both sides of the inequality (2.4), and therefore necessarily reversing the inequality, gives

$$S(€/£) \leq S(€/$) \cdot S($/£) \qquad (2.5)$$

The inequality (2.5) is consistent with (2.2) only if the equalities rather than the inequalities hold. That is, the ability to choose the better of the two ways to go from euros to pounds and from pounds to euros ensures that

$$S(€/£) = S(€/$) \cdot S($/£) \qquad (2.6)$$

Equation (2.6) tells us we can compute the exchange rate between euros and pounds from the euro–dollar and dollar–pound exchange rates. For example, if there are $1.5/£ and €0.9/$, there are €1.35/£. What we have shown in deriving equation (2.6) is why this is so. In summary, the reason is that there is always the possibility of indirect exchange via the dollar in going from euros to pounds or from pounds to euros. However, we recall that so far we have assumed zero transaction costs.

The exchange rate $S(€/£)$ is a **cross rate**. More generally, cross rates such as those given at the top of Figure 2.3 are exchange rates directly between currencies when neither of the two currencies is the US dollar. For example, $S(Can$/£)$, $S(¥/Can$)$, $S(¥/€)$, $S(€/SFr)$ are all cross rates. What we have derived in equation (2.6) generalizes for any cross rate as

$$S(i/j) = S(i/$) \cdot S($/j) \qquad (2.7)$$

Of course, since $S($/j) = 1/S(j/$)$, we can also compute the cross rate $S(i/j)$ from

$$S(i/j) = \frac{S(i/$)}{S(j/$)} \qquad (2.8)$$

The cross rate formula in equation (2.8) uses exchange rates in European terms, that is, as units of currency per US dollar. For example, if we know $S(Can$/$) = 1.40$ and $S(SFr/$) = 1.30$, we can calculate the Canadian dollar per Swiss franc rate as

$$S(Can$/SFr) = \frac{S(Can$/$)}{S(SFr/$)} = \frac{1.40}{1.30}$$
$$= 1.0769$$

If instead of exchange rates being in European terms as in equation (2.8) they are in US dollar equivalent terms, that is, dollars per unit of foreign currency, then we can write

$$S(i/j) = \frac{S($/j)}{S($/i)} \qquad (2.9)$$

45

More generally, we can write the cross rate in four possible ways

$$S(i/j) = \frac{S(i/\$)}{S(j/\$)}$$

$$S(i/j) = \frac{S(\$/j)}{S(\$/i)}$$

$$S(i/j) = S(i/\$) \cdot S(\$/j)$$

$$S(i/j) = \frac{1}{S(\$/i)} \cdot \frac{1}{S(j/\$)}$$

In the case of the euro and the pound, both are normally quoted in US dollar equivalent terms, that is, as US dollars per euro or per pound. Therefore, instead of equation (2.6) we should write

$$S(€/£) = \frac{S(\$/£)}{S(\$/€)}$$

Traditionally, the rule for calculating cross rates has been based on **round-trip triangular arbitrage**, which involves a different line of argument than is employed earlier. We can use Figure 2.4 to explain the difference between round-trip triangular arbitrage and the argument we have employed.

Round-trip triangular arbitrage is based upon the notion that if you started with $1, and went clockwise from $ to £ to € and then back to $ in Figure 2.4, you could not end up with more than $1 from this triangular journey or there would be an **arbitrage profit**. Similarly, you would not be able to take the reverse, counterclockwise route, and go from $ to € to £ and back to $, and end up with more than $1 if you started with $1. Indeed, it should not be possible to profit from starting at any point of the triangle and going around in either direction, ending up where you started. This argument, based on going along all three sides of the triangle and ending up where you started, gives the correct result when there are no transaction costs. However, it gives an inaccurate answer when there are transaction costs, for the following reason.

The choice of direct versus indirect exchange of currencies that we employed above in deriving equation (2.6) involves selecting between one (direct) transaction and the alternative of two (indirect) transactions. This means just one extra transaction cost when taking the indirect route rather than the direct route. On the other hand, round-trip triangular arbitrage is based on three transactions, and hence three transaction costs, for example, for converting $ to £, for converting £ to €, and converting € to $. When there are transaction costs, the approach we have taken, which may be called **one-way arbitrage**, gives a narrower permissible bid-ask spread for a cross-rate transaction than is found by triangular arbitrage: the term "one-way" comes from starting with one currency and ending up with another. In a market where a few points may translate into thousands of dollars, it is important that we derive the correct permissible spread, and this requires one-way arbitrage, not the more circuitous round-trip triangular arbitrage.[15]

Triangular arbitrage: nonzero foreign exchange transaction costs

Defining the costs of transacting

As we have already noted, in reality the price that must be paid to buy a foreign currency is different from the price at which the currency can be sold. For example, the US dollar price a person must pay a bank for a euro will exceed the US dollar amount received from the sale of a euro. In addition, the buyer or seller of a currency might have to pay a lump-sum fee or commission on each transaction. Economists have identified advantages of "two-part tariffs" such as a lump-sum and a per-unit charge, but for our purpose, we can think of both the bid-ask spread and the exchange dealer's fee as two parts of the total spread. They both provide revenue for dealers in foreign currencies and cause those

---

15 Transaction costs become especially important in the context of **interest arbitrage**, which is covered in Chapter 8.

who need to exchange currencies to lose in going back and forth. Let us define buy and sell rates:

$S(\$/\text{ask}£)$ is the price that must be *paid to the bank* to buy one pound with dollars. It is the bank's offer or ask rate on pounds. $S(\$/\text{bid}£)$ is the number of dollars *received from the bank* for the sale of pounds for dollars. It is the bank's bid rate on pounds.

Instead of writing $S(\$/\text{ask}£)$ we could write $S(\text{bid}\$/\text{ask}£)$, because if a bank is offering to sell pounds for dollars, it is offering to buy dollars for pounds; these are just two perspectives of the same transaction. Similarly, instead of writing $S(\$/\text{bid}£)$ we could write $S(\text{ask}\$/\text{bid}£)$. However, we need label only one currency because, for example, if we are talking of the bank's ask rate for pounds in terms of dollars, $S(\$/\text{ask}£)$, we know this is also the bank's bid rate on dollars. That is, when we have stated what is done with one currency – a purchase or a sale – stating what is done with the other is redundant. We choose to label only the second currency in the expression, showing whether this is the bank's ask (selling) or bid (buying) price, because the exchange rate is most easily thought of as the price of the second currency.

Because of transaction costs, we must be careful when taking the inverse of an exchange rate. When there are transaction costs, instead of writing

$$S(\$/£) \equiv \frac{1}{S(£/\$)}$$

as in equations (2.3), we must write

$$S(\$/\text{ask}£) \equiv \frac{1}{S(£/\text{bid}\$)} \quad \text{and}$$

$$S(\$/\text{bid}£) \equiv \frac{1}{S(£/\text{ask}\$)}$$

More generally,

$$S(i/\text{ask}j) \equiv \frac{1}{S(j/\text{bid}i)} \quad \text{and}$$

$$S(i/\text{bid}j) \equiv \frac{1}{S(j/\text{ask}i)} \tag{2.10}$$

These rules follow immediately from the extended notation described above.

Cross-rate spreads and transaction costs

Figure 2.5 shows exchange rates when going between pairs of currencies when transaction costs are included. If a person were to buy pounds directly with euros they would receive $S(£/\text{bid}€)$ of pounds from the bank; this is what the bank bids for euros in terms of pounds, as is shown along the darker horizontal arrow in Figure 2.5. If instead the person goes indirectly from € to $ and then from $ to £ along the darker arrows, on the first leg each euro buys $S(\$/\text{bid}€)$ of dollars; this is the bank's buying or bid rate for euros in term of dollars. On the second leg, each dollar buys $S(£/\text{bid}\$)$ pounds – the bank's buying or bid rate on dollars for pounds. Therefore, the indirect route gives $S(\$/\text{bid}€) \times S(£/\text{bid}\$)$ pounds per euro.

The bank's direct quote for $S(£/\text{bid}€)$ – pounds paid for a euro – will not be accepted by customers if it gives less pounds than the indirect route. Therefore, for direct exchange to occur we

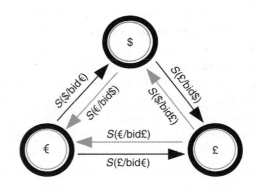

Figure 2.5 *Direct versus indirect exchange: nonzero transaction costs*

Notes
One-way arbitrage ensures that the number of euros received for each pound sold directly for euros, $S(€/\text{bid}£)$, must be no less than the number of euros received indirectly via the dollar, which is $S(\$/\text{bid}£) \cdot S(€/\text{bid}\$)$. Similarly, the number of pounds received for each euro sold directly for pounds, $S(£/\text{bid}€)$, must be no less than the number of pounds received indirectly, which is $S(\$/\text{bid}€) \cdot S(£/\text{bid}\$)$. In this way, one-way arbitrage imposes a trading range on the possible cross rates between euros and pounds.

require

$$S(\pounds/\text{bid}\euro) \geq S(\$/\text{bid}\euro) \cdot S(\pounds/\text{bid}\$)$$

or using US dollar equivalent quotations for the euro *and* pound

$$S(\pounds/\text{bid}\euro) \geq \frac{S(\$/\text{bid}\euro)}{S(\$/\text{ask}\pounds)} \qquad (2.11)$$

Next, consider a person wanting to exchange pounds into euros, the reverse of the previous situation. They can exchange directly along the lighter arrow in Figure 2.5, receiving $S(\euro/\text{bid}\pounds)$ euros per pound – the rate in euros the bank pays for, or bids on, pounds. Alternatively, they can exchange via the dollar receiving $S(\$/\text{bid}\pounds) \times S(\euro/\text{bid}\$)$ euros per pound; this is seen from the two lighter arrows from £ to $ and from $ to € in Figure 2.5. The direct euro–pound rate will attract business only if it gives at least as many euros per pound as buying euros indirectly. Therefore, for the direct exchange rate to attract business it is required that

$$S(\euro/\text{bid}\pounds) \geq S(\$/\text{bid}\pounds) \cdot S(\euro/\text{bid}\$)$$

or using equation (2.10) to have US equivalent quotation for the euro as well as the pound

$$S(\euro/\text{bid}\pounds) \geq \frac{S(\$/\text{bid}\pounds)}{S(\$/\text{ask}\euro)} \qquad (2.12)$$

Inverting the left-hand-side of equation (2.12) gives

$$\frac{1}{S(\pounds/\text{ask}\euro)} \geq \frac{S(\$/\text{bid}\pounds)}{S(\$/\text{ask}\euro)} \qquad (2.13)$$

Taking reciprocals, and therefore reversing the inequality in (2.13), gives

$$S(\pounds/\text{ask}\euro) \leq \frac{S(\$/\text{ask}\euro)}{S(\$/\text{bid}\pounds)} \qquad (2.14)$$

By comparing the inequalities (2.11) and (2.14), we find what we do and do not know about cross rates when there are transaction costs. We no longer

know exactly what the cross rates are from rates against the dollar. Instead, we know the smallest number of pounds a bank can offer on euros – given by inequality (2.11). We also know the maximum number of pounds it can ask per euro – given by inequality (2.14). Indeed, if we assume spreads on the cross rate assure

$$S(\pounds/\text{bid}\euro) \leq S(\pounds/\text{ask}\euro)$$

then from equations (2.11) and (2.14)

$$\frac{S(\$/\text{bid}\euro)}{S(\$/\text{ask}\pounds)} \leq S(\pounds/\text{bid}\euro) \leq S(\pounds/\text{ask}\euro)$$
$$\leq \frac{S(\$/\text{ask}\euro)}{S(\$/\text{bid}\pounds)}$$

What we learn is that, while the extreme points of the cross rate are set by arbitrage, we do not know where in between these limits the actual direct cross exchange rate will be.

The exact bid and ask cross rates depend on the competition between banks for direct exchange between currencies. If there is a lot of competition because there is a lot of business, the spread in the cross rate between euros and pounds will be small, perhaps on the order of the size of the bid-ask spread between the dollar and one of these foreign currencies. If there is little competition, the spread could be quite large, perhaps as much as double the size of the bid-ask spread in the euro rate or pound rate vis-à-vis the dollar.

For example, suppose that rates on the euro and pound vis-à-vis the US dollar are quoted as:

$S(\$/\text{bid}\euro)$	$S(\$/\text{ask}\euro)$	$S(\$/\text{bid}\pounds)$	$S(\$/\text{ask}\pounds)$
1.1020	1.1050	1.5775	1.5810

Then, for cross transactions to occur between euros and pounds we know from inequality (2.11) that

$$S(\pounds/\text{bid}\euro) \geq \frac{S(\$/\text{bid}\euro)}{S(\$/\text{ask}\pounds)} = \frac{1.1020}{1.5810}$$
$$= 0.6970 \qquad (2.15)$$

and from inequality (2.14) that

$$S(\pounds/\mathrm{ask}\text{€}) \leq \frac{S(\$/\mathrm{ask}\text{€})}{S(\$/\mathrm{bid}\pounds)} = \frac{1.1050}{1.5775}$$
$$= 0.7005 \qquad (2.16)$$

The point spread on the dollar–euro rate is 30 points, equivalent to approximately 0.29 percent of the spot rate. The point spread on the dollar–pound rate is 35 points, or approximately 0.22 percent of the spot rate. On the other hand, the maximum possible point spread on the cross rate between euro and pounds, given from inequalities (2.15) and (2.16), is 35 points or 0.050 percent of the cross spot rate. This is a larger percent spread than for either of the spreads of rates versus the dollar. Indeed, it is approximately the sum of the two spreads versus the dollar. However, there is a large volume of direct exchange between euros and pounds, and therefore spreads in quoted cross-rates are likely to be less than 0.50 percent. With the pound–euro market being very active, the cross-rate spread might be similar to that between the euro and the dollar or pound and the dollar.

What do we conclude from the above? We learn that when going from one foreign currency to another, for example, from Chinese RMB to pounds or from Mexican pesos to Japanese yen, it pays to call a number of banks. The worst you could find are exchange rates as unfavorable as on two separate transactions, going into and out of the US dollar. Generally you will find a better situation. Different banks may have quite different direct quotes according to whether or not they are market makers in the direct exchange you are considering, and you might as well find the best deal.

Another thing we have discovered is that, if there were no transaction costs, we could find all the possible exchange rates between n currencies from $(n-1)$ exchange rates, those against the US dollar. However, since in reality there *are* transaction costs, the situation is very different. Not only are there $2(n-1)$ rates against the US dollar, that is,

a bid and an ask for each rate, but there are also a number of bid and ask rates for cross exchanges. The major currencies of OECD countries trade directly against each other with, for example, quotations in Britain for direct purchase or sale of Canadian dollars, Swiss francs, and so on. In Tokyo there are quotes in yen against British pounds, Canadian dollars, and so on. There are consequently far more than $2(n-1)$ different quoted exchange rates.

It is worth pointing out that there is no rule that exchange rates must always be expressed only against the US dollar. Any currency would do from a conceptual point of view. However, as a practical matter, it is important that the currency of quotation be one that is widely traded and held. The amount of trading and familiarity create the needed liquidity. At the beginning of the twentieth century, the pound sterling was widely used as the quotation currency, but after the 1944 Bretton Woods Agreement (which is described in Chapter 22), the US dollar emerged as the standard for stating other currencies' values.[16] We might also note that it is possible to find all exchange rates even without knowing the values of currencies against an nth currency. Instead, we can use the values of all currencies against a commodity such as gold, or even against a currency "basket" such as Special Drawing Rights (SDRs), which are described in Chapter 18.

The conditions we have derived are valid not only for conventional or spot exchange rates, but also for forward exchange rates, which are explained in Chapter 3. That is, if we replaced the $S(i/j)$'s in this chapter with forward exchange rates, everything would still be valid.

16 There is some evidence that the attractiveness of quoting in the US dollar is diminishing, especially in the European and Asian trading blocs. See Stanley W. Black, "Transaction Costs and Vehicle Currencies," *Journal of International Money and Finance*, December 1991, pp. 512–26, and Jeffrey Frankel and Shang-Jin Wei, "Trade Blocs and Currency Blocs," *National Bureau of Economic Research*, Paper 4335, 1991.

SUMMARY

1   The bid-ask spread on foreign bank notes is high because of inventory costs and the costs and risks of note handling. Bank notes are exchanged at a retail and at a wholesale level.

2   The spot foreign exchange market is the market in which currencies in the form of bank deposits are exchanged. In this market, currencies are received one or two business days after an exchange of currencies is agreed.

3   The interbank foreign exchange market is the largest market on Earth. It consists of a complex, international network of informal linkages between banks and foreign exchange brokers. When banks are dealing with each other, they quote two-way exchange rates. The interbank market can be characterized as a decentralized, continuous, open-bid double-auction market. When banks or companies deal with a foreign exchange broker, they state their intentions. The broker quotes the inside spread to prospective counterparties.

4   Banks settle between themselves on the same day their customers receive and pay for foreign exchange. Messages between banks are sent via SWIFT.

5   Banks use clearing houses like CHIPS to clear balances between themselves. Banks also maintain correspondent accounts with each other for settling customers' accounts in foreign currencies. System-wide risk has helped spur the growth of Continuous Linked Settlement, (CLS). Under this system, credits and debits are simultaneous.

6   Exchange rates are generally quoted in European terms, that is, in units of foreign currency per US dollar. Newspapers generally quote selling or middle rates. When exchange rates are quoted in European terms, it is easier to think of rates as bids and asks on the US dollar. The British pound and the euro are quoted in US dollar equivalent. The dollar–pound and dollar–euro rates are best thought of as bids and asks on the pound or euro. In the interbank market, bid rates are typically quoted before ask rates.

7   Transaction costs in the form of bid-ask spreads on exchange rates are important because they can greatly influence returns on short-term foreign investments. They also provide large revenues for banks and represent a cost to businesses.

8   A cross rate is an exchange rate which does not involve the US dollar, for example, Malaysian ringgits per British pound. In the absence of transaction costs, cross exchange rates between currencies other than the US dollar can be obtained from exchange rates vis-à-vis the US dollar.

9   In the absence of transaction costs, the many possible cross exchange rates between n different currencies can be obtained by just knowing the $n-1$ values of the currencies against the remaining nth currency. In principle, any standard will do for measurement.

10   In the presence of transaction costs, we cannot compute cross rates precisely from rates versus the dollar. Instead, we can compute only a range within which cross rates must be quoted.

REVIEW QUESTIONS

1 What is a "bank draft"?
2 What is an exchange rate "spread?"
3 What does a bank-note wholesaler do?
4 What is a "spot exchange rate?"
5 What is the "interbank spot market?"
6 What is SWIFT and what does it do?
7 What is Continuous Linked Settlement?
8 What is CHIPS and what does it do?
9 How does the interbank spot market differ from the brokered market?
10 What do we mean by the "bid" rate and "ask" rate on a foreign currency?
11 What is the difference between the US $ equivalent and European terms methods of quoting exchange rates?
12 What do we mean by a "point" in quotation of exchange rates?
13 What is triangular arbitrage, and how does it differ from one-way arbitrage?
14 What is a cross rate?

ASSIGNMENT PROBLEMS

1 Do you think that because of the costs of moving bank notes back to their country of circulation, buying foreign currency bank notes could sometimes be cheaper than buying bank drafts? Could there be a seasonal pattern in exchange rates for bank notes? (*Hint*: Think of what is involved in shipping US dollars arising from Americans spending summers in Europe versus Europeans vacationing in America.)
2 How can companies that issue and sell traveler's checks charge a relatively low fee? How do they profit?
3 Compute the percentage spread on South African rands and Canadian dollars from Table 2.1. Why do you think the spread on Canadian dollars is lower?
4 What steps are involved in settling a purchase made in Britain with a credit card issued by a US bank? Why do you think the spread between buy and sell rates used in credit-card payments is smaller than those applying to foreign bank notes?
5 Does the use of US dollars as the principal currency of quotation put US banks at an advantage for making profits? Why do you think the US dollar has become a principal currency of quotation?
6 Why do you think that banks give bid and ask rates when dealing with each other? Why don't they state their intentions as they do when dealing with foreign exchange brokers?
7 Check a recent business newspaper or the business page for spot exchange rates. Form an $n \times n$ exchange-rate matrix by computing the cross rates, and check whether $S(\$/£) = 1/S(£/\$)$ and so on.

8   Complete the following exchange-rate matrix. Assume that there are no transaction costs.

Currency sold	Currency purchased				
	$	£	SFr	€	¥
$	1	1.5	0.8	1.2	0.009
£		1			
SFr			1		
€				1	
¥					1

BIBLIOGRAPHY

Aliber, Robert Z. (ed.), *The Handbook of International Financial Management*, Dow Jones Irwin, Homewood, IL, 1989.

Bank of England, *The Foreign Exchange Market*, Fact Sheet, Bank of England, London, 1999.

Chebucto Community Net, *The Tobin Tax: An International Tax on Foreign Currency Transfers*, http://www.chebucto.ns.ca//Current/P7/bwi/ccctobon.html, 2004.

Deardorff, Alan V., "One-Way Arbitrage and Its Implications for the Foreign Exchange Markets," *Journal of Political Economy*, April 1979, pp. 351–64.

Einzig, Paul *A., Textbook on Foreign Exchange*, St. Martins, London, 1969.

Flood, Marc D., "Microstructure Theory and the Foreign Exchange Market," *Review*, Federal Reserve Bank of St. Louis, November/December 1991, pp. 52–70.

Frankel, Jeffrey A., Giampaolo Galli, and Alberto Giovannini, *The Microstructure of Foreign Exchange Markets*, Conference Report, National Bureau of Economic Research, Cambridge, MA, 1996.

Krugman, Paul, "Vehicle Currencies and the Structure of International Exchange," *Journal of Money, Credit and Banking*, August 1980, pp. 513–26.

Kubarych, Roger M., *Foreign Exchange Markets in the United States*, Federal Reserve Bank of New York, 1978.

Lothian, James R., "Exchange Rates," *The Oxford Encyclopedia of Economic History*, Joel Mokyr (ed.), Oxford University Press, Oxford, 2003.

Miller, Paul and Carol Ann Northcott, "CLS Bank: Managing Foreign Exchange Settlement Risk," *Bank of Canada Review*, Autumn 2002, pp. 13–25.

Reihl, Heinz and Rita M. Rodriguez, *Foreign Exchange Markets*, McGraw-Hill, New York, 1977.

Syrett, William W., *A Manual of Foreign Exchange*, 6th edn, Sir Isaac Pitman, London, 1966.

Chapter 3

Forward exchange

The future is not what it used to be.

Paul Valéry

It would be difficult to overstate the importance of the forward market for foreign exchange. Indeed, a financial manager of a firm with overseas interests may find herself as much involved with this market as with the spot market. This is confirmed in the aggregate turnover statistics in Table 3.1 which show that the market share of forward exchange is even larger than the share for spot exchange. Table 3.1 also makes it clear that the majority of forward contracts are part of swaps (swaps are a combination of spot purchase/sale and forward sale/purchase and are discussed later in this chapter). The forward market is valuable for reducing risks arising from changes in exchange rates when importing, exporting, borrowing, and investing. Forwards are also used by speculators. This chapter explains the nature of this extremely important market, while a later chapter, Chapter 12, describes the role forward exchange plays in foreign exchange management.

WHAT IS FORWARD FOREIGN EXCHANGE?

The 1- or 2-day delivery period for spot transactions is so short that when comparing spot rates with forward exchange rates we can usefully think of spot rates as exchange rates for un-delayed transactions. On the other hand, forward exchange rates involve an arrangement to delay the exchange of currencies until some future date. A useful working definition is:

> The **forward exchange rate** is the rate that is contracted today for the exchange of currencies at a specified date in the future.

If we look back at Figure 2.3 in Chapter 2, we note that for Canada, Japan, Switzerland, and United Kingdom we are given exchange rates for 1-, 3-, and 6-month forwards. Although they are not quoted in the table, forward rates are also available for other currencies and for other maturities. Forward exchange contracts are drawn up between banks and their clients or between two banks. The market does not have a central location but instead is similar to the spot market, being

Table 3.1 *Foreign exchange net turnover by market segment: daily averages, April 2001*

Market segment	Turnover in billions of US dollars		Percentage share	
Spot market		387		33.0
Forwards		787		66.6
Outright	131		11.0	
Swaps	656		55.6	
Options (OTC)		60		0.4
Total turnover		1234		100

Source: Central Bank Survey of Foreign Exchange Market and Derivative Market Activity in April 2001, Bank for International Settlements, Basle, Switzerland, October 2001.

a decentralized arrangement of banks and brokers linked by telephone, SWIFT, and similar networks. Furthermore, the interbank component of the forward market involves continuous two-way open bidding between participants, that is, a so-called "continuous open-bid double auction": each bank, on request, quotes a "bid" and "ask" rate to other banks, valid for that moment. Foreign exchange brokers play a similar role as in the spot market, serving to match buy and sell orders between potential counterparties.

Figure 2.3 tells us that on Thursday, May 22, 2003 a bank dealing in over $1 million could have purchased spot US dollars with Japanese yen for approximately ¥117.23/$.[1] This would have meant delivery of the yen to the dollar-selling bank's designated account on Monday, May 26, 2003, 2 business days after the agreement was reached: Saturdays and Sundays are not business days. Dollars would be received on the same day by the dollar-buying bank. If, however, the purchaser wanted to have the dollar in 6 months rather than "immediately," then the rate would have been ¥116.54/$, or 0.69 (116.54 versus 117.23) fewer ¥/$ than the rate for spot delivery. That is, the US dollar is cheaper for forward than for spot purchase. Figure 2.3 gives the exchange rate for buying the US dollar with the UK pound in 6 months as £0.6188/$. In the case of the dollar in terms of pounds, the forward price of the dollar is 71 points (0.6188 versus 0.6117) more expensive than for spot delivery. Hence, while the forward dollar is cheaper than the spot dollar in terms of Japanese yen, the forward dollar is more expensive than the spot dollar in terms of pounds.

FORWARD EXCHANGE PREMIUMS AND DISCOUNTS

When it is necessary to pay more for forward delivery than for spot delivery of a currency, as

is the case for the US dollar in terms of pounds in Figure 2.3, we say that the currency is at a **forward premium**. When a currency costs less for forward delivery than for spot delivery, as is the case for the dollar in terms of Japanese yen in Figure 2.3, we say that the currency is at a **forward discount**. In the figure the dollar is at a forward premium against the pound, and at a forward discount against the yen.

In order to show how to calculate forward premiums and discounts, let us first express the forward exchange rate in terms similar to those used for the spot rate:

$F_n(¥/\$)$ is the n-year forward exchange rate of Japanese yen per dollar. More generally, $F_n(i/j)$ is the n-year forward exchange rate of currency i to currency j.

For example, in Figure 2.3, $F_{1/4}(¥/\$) = ¥116.86/\$$ and $F_{1/2}(¥/\$) = ¥116.54/\$$ With the help of the definition of the forward rate we can define the n-year forward exchange premium or discount of US dollar versus the Japanese yen, on a per annum basis, as approximately[2]

$$\text{Premium/discount } (\$ \text{ versus } ¥)$$
$$= \frac{F_n(¥/\$) - S(¥/\$)}{nS(¥/\$)} \quad (3.1)$$

When the value of expression (3.1) is positive, the dollar is at a forward premium vis-à-vis the Japanese yen. This is because in this case the dollar costs more yen for forward delivery than for spot delivery. When expression (3.1) is negative, the dollar is at a forward discount vis-à-vis the Japanese yen. In this case the dollar is cheaper to buy forward than to buy spot. In the event that the forward rate and spot rate are equal, we say that the forward currency is **flat**. In Figure 2.3 the dollar is at a forward

---

1 We say approximately because the quoted rates are for currency trades that have already occurred (at or just before 4 pm Eastern time). The exchange rate on new transactions at which banks can transact will depend on the market that is continually changing.

2 We simplify the annualized premium or discount by taking a simple arithmetic average. If we want the exact premium or discount at a compound rate we would compute $\sqrt[n]{F_n(¥/\$)/S(¥/\$)} - 1$.

Table 3.2 *Per annum percentage premium (+) or discount (−) on forward foreign exchange vis-à-vis the US dollar*

Currency	Premium or discount	Forward period		
		1-month	3-month	6-month
UK pound	£ discount	−2.34	−2.33	−2.30
	US$ premium	+2.35	+2.35	+2.32
Can dollar	Can$ discount	−1.98	−2.09	−2.12
	US$ premium	+2.01	+2.09	+2.14
Swiss franc	SFr premium	+1.09	+0.99	+0.91
	US$ discount	−1.11	+0.99	+0.91
Japanese yen	¥ premium	+1.27	+1.27	+1.20
	US$ discount	−1.23	−1.26	−1.18

Notes
This table is derived from Figure 2.3 in Chapter 2 using the formula, Premium/Discount (i versus j) = {[$F_n(j/i)$ − $S(j/i)$]/$nS(j/i)$} × 100, where n is the number of years forward. The discounts/premiums on the US dollar versus the foreign currencies (bottom row of each pair) do not precisely equal the negatives of the forward exchange premiums/discounts of the foreign currencies versus the US dollar (top row) because of the base-selection problem in computing percentage differences and because of bid-ask spreads.

discount. More generally, the per annum n-year premium/discount of currency i versus currency j is

Premium/discount(i versus j)

$$= \frac{F_n(j/i) - S(j/i)}{nS(j/i)}$$

Forward premiums and discounts are put into annual terms by dividing by n because interest rates are quoted in per annum terms, and it is useful to be able to compare interest rates and forward premiums in these same terms. Often, forward premiums and discounts are put in percentage terms by multiplying by 100. Using the values in Figure 2.3, we find that for the 6-month forward dollar versus the Japanese yen, expression (3.1) is negative and equal to

Premium/discount($ versus ¥)

$$= \frac{116.54 - 117.23}{0.5 \times 117.23} \times 100\% = -1.18\%$$

This is a forward discount on the dollar versus the yen of 1.18 percent per annum; the dollar costs 1.18 percent per annum less for forward delivery than for spot delivery. Table 3.2 gives the forward premiums and discounts for all forward currencies quoted in Figure 2.3.

When the dollar is at a forward discount vis-à-vis the Japanese yen, the yen is at a forward premium vis-à-vis the dollar. This follows because when dollars cost less yen for forward delivery than for spot delivery, the yen must cost more dollars for forward delivery than for spot delivery. Indeed, the n-year annualized forward premium of the yen versus the dollar is

Premium/discount (¥ versus $)

$$= \frac{0.008581 - 0.008530}{0.5 \times 0.008530} \times 100\% = 1.20\%$$

This is an annualized premium on the yen (since the value is positive) of 1.20 percent per annum.[3]

The definition of forward premium or discount does not depend on whether exchange rates are quoted in US dollar equivalent or in European terms. A currency is at a forward premium if the forward price of that currency in terms of a second currency is higher than the spot price. This applies to cross rates as well as to rates involving the US

3 There is a small difference between the numerical value of the dollar-versus-yen discount and the numerical value of the yen-versus-dollar premium, that is, 1.18 percent versus 1.20 percent. This is because of the base-selection problem in taking percentage differences.

dollar. For example, if the euro costs more pounds for forward than for spot delivery, the euro is at a forward premium against the pound, and the pound is therefore at a forward discount against the euro.

FORWARD RATES VERSUS EXPECTED FUTURE SPOT RATES

As is explained in more detail in Chapter 13, if we assume that speculators are risk-neutral, that is, speculators do not care about risk, and if we ignore transaction costs in exchanging currencies, then forward exchange rates equal the market's expected future spot rates. That is, if we write the market's expected spot price of currency j in terms of currency i as $S_n^*(i/j)$ where the $*$ refers to "expected" and n refers to the number of years ahead, then

$$F_n(i/j) = S_n^*(i/j) \qquad (3.2)$$

Equation (3.2) follows because if, for example, the market in general expected the euro to be trading at $1.1600/€ in 1-year's time, and the forward rate for 1 year were only $1.1500/€, speculators would buy the euro forward for $1.1500/€, and expect to make $0.0100 $(= \$1.1600 - \$1.1500)$ on each euro when the euros are sold at their expected price of $1.1600 each. In the course of buying the euro forward, speculators would drive up the forward price of the euro until it was no longer lower than the expected future spot rate. That is, forward buying would continue until the forward price of the euro was no longer below the expected spot rate. This can be written as

$$F_n(\$/€) \geq S_n^*(\$/€) \qquad (3.3)$$

where inequality (3.3) means that the forward price of the dollar cannot be below the expected spot price for the date of forward maturity: it must be greater than or at most equal to.

Similarly, if the market expected the euro to be trading at $1.1600/€ in 1-year's time and the forward rate for 1-year were $1.1700/€, speculators would sell euros forward. They do this even though

they have no euros and are not expecting any euros. They would expect to profit from subsequently buying euros for delivery on the forward contract at their expected price of $1.1600/€ which is $0.0100 less than the price at which they have sold euros forward. In the course of selling euros forward speculators would drive down the forward euro price until it were no longer above the expected spot price. This can be written as

$$F_n(\$/€) \leq S_n^*(\$/€) \qquad (3.4)$$

where inequality (3.4) means that the forward price of the euro cannot be above the expected spot price for the date of forward maturity: it is either less than or equal to.

Inequalities (3.3) and (3.4) are consistent only if the equalities of both relationships hold, that is,

$$F_n(\$/€) = S_n^*(\$/€) \qquad (3.5)$$

More generally, we have the condition in equation (3.2), recalling again that we are at this stage assuming risk neutrality and zero transaction costs – assumptions we relax later in the book.

PAYOFF PROFILES ON FORWARD EXCHANGE

While the price paid for a forward currency equals the future spot rate expected by the market at the time of purchase, when the forward contract matures its value is determined by the realized spot rate at that time. The greater the extent to which the eventually *realized* spot rate differs from the spot rate that was *expected* at the time of buying the contract, the larger is the change in the value of the forward contract vis-à-vis the purchase price. Stated differently, the larger is the unexpected change in the spot exchange rate, the greater is the change in the value of a forward contract between purchase and maturity. If the spot rate is as was expected, there is no gain or loss on the forward contract. However, if the spot rate is higher or lower than expected, there is a gain or loss.

It is possible to plot the gain or loss on a forward contract against the unanticipated change in the spot rate, where the unexpected change in the spot rate is the difference between the anticipated spot rate that influenced the forward rate and the eventually realized spot rate. Such a plot is called a **payoff profile**, and is useful for comparing the consequences of buying different instruments – forwards versus futures versus options – and for the management of foreign exchange risk which we discuss in later chapters. Let us develop a payoff profile by considering an example. Suppose that the expected spot rate between the dollar and euro for 1-year's time is $1.15/€ at the time of buying a 1-year forward contract to purchase €1 million with US dollars. With the forward rate equal to the expected future spot rate, the forward contract will be priced at $1.15 million: the contract buyer is to pay $1.15 million in one year's time in exchange for €1 million received at that time. Let us now consider the gain or loss on the forward contract when the eventually realized spot rate is different from the originally expected rate.

As Table 3.3 shows, if the realized future dollar value of the euro is $1.14/€ instead of the originally expected $1.15/€ the unanticipated decline in the euro by $0.01/€ causes a decline in the value of the contracted €1 million by ($0.01/€) × (€1 million), or $10,000 (note the € signs cancel in the multiplication to give a dollar amount). On the other hand, if the eventually realized US dollar value of the euro is $1.16/€ the dollar value of the contracted €1 million increases by ($0.01/€) × €1 million = $10,000. Similarly, at a realized spot rate of $1.18/€ the value of the €1 million to be received under the forward contract provides a gain of $30,000 (= $0.03/€ × €1million). These and other values for different realized spot rates are shown in Table 3.3.

We plot the unanticipated change in the spot rate along the horizontal axis of Figure 3.1, and the gain or loss on the forward contract to purchase €1 million at $1.15/€ on the vertical axis. The unanticipated change in the expected spot rate is written symbolically as $\Delta S^u(\$/€)$ where Δ is the Greek "delta" for "difference," and the "u" superscript represents "unanticipated." The gain (+) or loss (−) on the contract is written as $\Delta V(\$)$, where the $ sign in parentheses indicates it is a US dollar gain or loss. We see from the figure that the payoff profile is an upward-sloping straight line. To the right of the vertical axis where $\Delta S^u(\$/€)$ is positive, that is, the euro has unexpectedly gone up in value, or **appreciated**, there is a gain on the forward contract to buy euros. To the left of the vertical axis where $\Delta S^u(\$/€)$ is negative, that is, the euro has unexpectedly declined, or **depreciated**, there is a loss on the forward contract to buy euros.

A forward contract to *sell* €1 million at $1.15/€ has a payoff profile that is opposite to that in Figure 3.1. In order to construct the profile, we again plot the gains or losses on the contract against the unanticipated change in the spot exchange rate. These gains and losses, and the associated unexpected changes in the spot exchange rate, are shown in Table 3.4. For example, selling €1 million for the contracted $1.15 million when the realized exchange rate at maturity is $1.14/€ means having a gain of $10,000: the forward contract provides $1.15 million for €1 million at the contract rate, whereas €1 million would provide only $1.14 million if sold at the realized spot exchange rate. However, if, for example, the realized spot rate became $1.16/€ the forward sale of €1 million at

Table 3.3 *Unanticipated changes in the spot exchange rate and gains or losses on forward purchase of €1 million at $1.15/€*

Realized spot rate	Unanticipated change in spot rate	Gain (+) or loss (−) on contract
$1.12/€	−$0.03/€	−$30,000
$1.13/€	−$0.02/€	−$20,000
$1.14/€	−$0.01/€	−$10,000
$1.15/€	$0	$0
$1.16/€	$0.01/€	$10,000
$1.17/€	$0.02/€	$20,000
$1.18/€	$0.03/€	$30,000

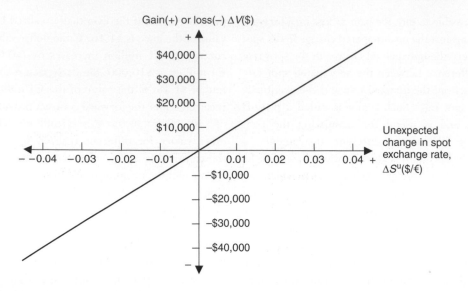

Figure 3.1 *Payoff profile on forward contract to buy €1 million*

Notes
We assume the forward rate is the expected future spot rate. When the realized spot value of the foreign currency exceeds the expected value and hence the forward rate, there is a gain from buying the forward currency. The figure plots the gains and losses on a forward purchase of €1 million for different values of the difference between the expected (and hence forward) exchange rate and the realized rate. These values are shown in Table 3.3. We observe an upward-sloping payoff profile.

Table 3.4 *Unanticipated changes in the spot exchange rate and gains or losses on forward sale of €1 million at $1.15/€*

Realized spot rate	Unanticipated change in spot rate	Gain (+) or loss (−) on contract
$1.12/€	−$0.03/€	$30,000
$1.13/€	−$0.02/€	$20,000
$1.14/€	−$0.01/€	$10,000
$1.15/€	$0	$0
$1.16/€	$0.01/€	−$10,000
$1.17/€	$0.02/€	−$20,000
$1.18/€	$0.03/€	−$30,000

$1.15/€ means having a loss of $10,000: at $1.16/€ the €1 million is worth $1.16 million versus the $1.15 million for which the euros were sold. When these and the other values in Table 3.4 are plotted as they are in Figure 3.2 we obtain a downward-sloping profile.

The payoff profiles are useful for comparing the consequences of different foreign exchange management techniques. Before we turn in the next

chapter to the profiles from other instruments, specifically futures and options, let us consider a few other aspects of the forward exchange market.

OUTRIGHT FORWARD EXCHANGE AND SWAPS

Outright and swap transactions

As Table 3.1 shows, the largest part of average daily turnover on the foreign exchange market takes the form of **swaps**.[4] The balance consists of **outright forward contracts**. As the name suggests, an outright forward exchange contract consists simply of an agreement to exchange currencies at an agreed price at a future date. For example, an agreement to buy Canadian dollars in 180 days at Can$1.3988/$ is an outright forward exchange contract. A swap, on the other hand, has

4 The term "swap" is also used in the context of exchange of interest payments involved in debt responsibilities rather than the exchange of principal as in the context here. This other context is discussed in Chapter 18.

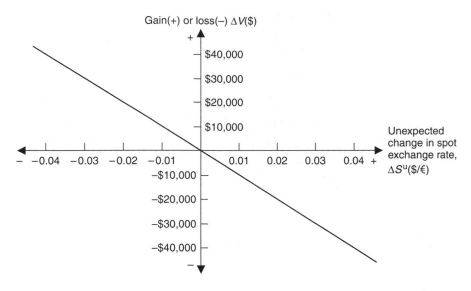

Figure 3.2 *Payoff profile on forward contract to sell €1 million*

Notes
We assume the forward rate is the expected future spot rate. When the realized spot value of the foreign currency exceeds the expected value and hence the forward rate, there is a loss from selling the foreign currency forward: it has been sold for less than it has become worth. When the realized spot value of the currency is lower than expected there is a gain to the seller of the forward currency; it has been sold for more than it has become worth. The figure plots the gains and losses on a forward contract to sell €1 million for different values of the difference between the expected (and hence forward) exchange rate and the realized rate. These values are shown in Table 3.4. We observe a downward-sloping payoff profile.

two components, usually a spot transaction plus a forward transaction in the reverse direction, although a swap could involve two forward transactions in opposite directions. For example, a **swap-in** Canadian consists of an agreement to buy Canadian dollars spot, and also an agreement to sell Canadian dollars forward. A **swap-out** Canadian consists of an agreement to sell Canadian dollars spot and to buy Canadian dollars forward. An example of a swap involving two forward transactions would be a contract to buy Canadian dollars for 1-month forward and sell Canadian dollars for 2-months forward. This is a **forward–forward swap**. When the purchase and sale are separated by only one day the swap is called a **rollover**. A definition of swaps that covers all these forms is:

A foreign exchange swap is an agreement to buy and sell foreign exchange at pre-specified exchange rates, where the buying and selling are separated in time.

The uses of swaps

Swaps are valuable to those who are investing or borrowing in foreign currency. For example, a person who invests in a foreign treasury bill can use a spot-forward swap to avoid foreign exchange risk. The investor sells forward the foreign currency maturity value of the treasury bill at the same time as the spot foreign exchange is purchased to pay for the bill. Since a known amount of the investor's home currency will be received according to the forward component of the swap, no uncertainty from exchange rates is faced. In a similar way, those who borrow in foreign currency can buy forward the foreign currency needed for repayment of the foreign currency loan at the same time that they convert the borrowed foreign funds into their own currency on the spot market. The value of swaps to international investors and borrowers helps explain their substantial popularity.

While valuable to investors and borrowers, swaps are not very useful to importers and exporters.

Payments and receipts in international trade are frequently delayed. However, it is an outright forward purchase of foreign exchange that is valuable to the importer, not a swap. Similarly, the exporter needs to make an outright forward sale of foreign exchange to ensure the amount received in its own currency. This is not, however, the place to present the details of these uses of forward exchange or the details of the value of forward exchange to borrowers and investors. That must wait until Part 4.

Swaps are popular with banks because it is difficult to avoid risk when making a market for many future dates and currencies. For some dates and currencies a bank will be **long** in foreign exchange by having agreed to purchase more of the foreign currency than it has agreed to sell. For other dates and currencies, a bank will be **short**, having agreed to sell more of these currencies than it has agreed to buy. Swaps help the bank to economically reduce risk. For example, if bank A is long on spot British pounds and short on 30-day forward pounds it will try to find another bank, bank B, in the opposite situation. Bank A will sell pounds spot and buy pounds forward – a swap-out of sterling – with bank B. In this manner, both banks balance their spot versus forward positions while economizing on the number of transactions that achieves this. The use of only standard length, or so-called **even-dated contracts**, leaves some exposure to remaining long and short positions from day to day. These are then covered with **rollover swaps**. In this way swaps allow banks to exchange their surpluses and shortages of individual currencies to offset spot and forward trades with their customers and with each other. It should be no surprise that matching customer trades with appropriate swaps is a complex and dynamic problem.[5]

Exhibits 3.1 and 3.2 summarize the different uses of swaps and outrights and some of the characteristics of the forward market.

THE FLEXIBILITY OF FORWARD EXCHANGE

The forward market offers more flexibility than Figure 2.3 in the previous chapter might indicate. For example, as Table 3.5 shows, while the majority of contracts involve the US dollar versus the major currencies, there are contracts against less important currencies and also "cross forwards" between other major currencies.[6] Furthermore, while Figure 2.3 suggests only a few specific and rather short maturities of forward contracts – 1, 3, and 6 months – contracts can be arranged for any period from a couple of days up to several years. Since for most currencies the spot market value date is already 2 business days in the future, the shortest forward contracts are for 3 days (forwards can be for 2 days ahead – rollovers – in North America where settlement takes only 1 business day).

Sometimes buyers and sellers of forward exchange are not precisely sure when they will need their foreign currency or when they will receive it. For example, a US importer may know that he or she must pay a British producer 30 days after delivery of the goods, but the exact day of delivery may not be known because of possible shipping delays. To take care of this, banks also sell forward exchange with some flexibility, allowing buyers to take delivery of foreign exchange on any day during the last 10 days of the contract period, or according to some other flexible scheme. Flexibility will cost the buyer a little more, the exchange rate being, for example, the most unfavorable for the customer during the period of possible delivery. However, it can relieve the buyer of considerable worry.

Some banks offer **nondeliverable forward contracts** alongside conventional contracts. These are similar to the traditional form of forward

---

5 The reader is referred to the many accounts of this dynamic market. *Foreign Exchange Markets in the United States*, by Roger Kubarych, Federal Reserve Bank of New York, 1978, is an excellent account of the New York foreign exchange market. Other valuable sources include Paul Einzig, *A Dynamic Theory of Forward Exchange*, Macmillan, London, 1966; Raymond G. Connix, *Foreign Exchange Today*, revised edn, Wiley, New York, 1980.

6 Table 3.5 also shows currency pairs for futures and options which are discussed in Chapter 4.

EXHIBIT 3.1   STRUCTURE OF THE FORWARD MARKET

The following excerpt from the *Review* of the Federal Reserve Bank of St. Louis explains the difference between outright forwards and swaps as well as the different users of these "products."

> Participants in the foreign exchange market also deal for future value dates. Such dealing composes the forward markets. Active forward markets exist for a few heavily traded currencies and for several time intervals corresponding to actively dealt maturities in the money market. Markets can also be requested and made for other maturities, however. Since the foreign exchange market is unregulated, standard contract specifications are matters of tradition and convenience, and they can be modified by the transacting agents.

> Forward transactions generally occur in two different ways: outright and swap. An outright forward transaction is what the name implies, a contract for an exchange of currencies at some future value date. "Outrights" generally occur only between market-making banks and their commercial clients. The interbank market for outrights is very small.

> A swap is simply a combination of two simultaneous trades: an outright forward contract and an opposing spot deal. For example, a bank might "swap in" six-month yen by simultaneously buying spot yen and selling six-month forward yen...

> In practice, the vast majority of foreign exchange transactions involve the U.S. dollar and some other currency. The magnitude of U.S. foreign trade and investment flows implies that, for almost any other currency, the bilateral dollar exchange markets will have the largest volume.

Source: Mark D. Flood, "Microstructure Theory and the Foreign Exchange Market," *Review*, Federal Reserve Bank of St. Louis, November/December 1991, pp. 52–70.

---

contract in that they specify an exchange rate and a future settlement date. However, on the settlement date, the foreign currency is not paid for and delivered. Rather, the difference between the agreed settlement rate and the current spot rate is paid by the party losing, and received by the party gaining. The amount would be that shown on the relevant payoff profile, with this being on the maturity date. The settlement is in US dollars. These types of contracts are particularly popular with emerging market currencies where physical delivery is difficult. This type of contact is in some ways like a currency futures contract, which is a topic in Chapter 4.

FORWARD QUOTATIONS

Swap points and outright forwards

Even though some forward contracts are outright, the convention in the interbank market is to quote all forward rates in terms of the spot rate and the number of **swap points** for the forward maturity in question. For example, the 6-month forward Canadian rate would conventionally be quoted as

Spot	6-month swap
1.3965–70	23–27

The swap quote is the way spot transactions themselves are quoted, and is in Canadian dollars per US dollar. The spot rate means that the bid on US dollars is Can$1.3965 — the quoting bank is willing to pay Can$1.3965/$ — and the ask on US dollars is Can$1.3970 — the quoting bank will sell US dollars for Can$1.3970/$. The swap points, 23–27 in this example, must be added to or subtracted from the spot bid and ask rates. The need to add or subtract depends on whether the two numbers in the swap points are ascending

EXHIBIT 3.2 DIFFERENCES BETWEEN OUTRIGHT FORWARDS AND SWAPS

The following excerpt from a biannual survey of foreign exchange markets by the Basle-based Bank of International Settlements highlights the important differences between outright forwards and swaps. For example, it explains how much more "international" are swaps.

The forward market comprises two distinct segments, the outright forward market and the swap market. Outright forward deals are similar to spot transactions except that they are for settlement more than two days hence. Swap deals on the other hand have two separate legs. The two counterparties agree to exchange two currencies at a particular rate at one date and to reverse the transaction, generally at a different rate, at some future date. Most swaps have a spot and a forward leg but forward/forward transactions also take place. Swap transactions in the exchange market involve the exchange of principal. In this they differ from other currency swaps (for example interest rate swaps) which entail the exchange of cash flows ...

The maturity of most forward business is quite short. Nearly two thirds of all transactions have a maturity of seven days or less, and only 1% have a maturity of more than one year. There is some variation across countries, with shorter maturities tending to account for a larger share of business in the countries with the most active markets ....

The outright forward market is strikingly different from other market segments. Firstly, a far larger share of this type of business is with "customers", particularly in countries which do not host major trading centers. In the market as a whole, almost half of all outright forward deals are with customers.... Many of the deals are undertaken to hedge exposures arising from foreign trade rather than to manage financial risks arising from funding and portfolio decisions.

A second notable feature of the outright forward market is that trading is less international than in other market segments. Almost 56% of all deals are concluded with counterparties located in the same country, with the share of local deals being higher, sometimes much higher, in countries with small markets. The domestic orientation of the outright forward market owes much to the importance of business with customers, which tends to be more local in character.

The swap market is ... capable of being used to a considerable degree for the purpose of hedging financial risk – in contrast to the use of outright forwards mainly for commercial risk hedging.... The swap market is heavily concentrated on the U.S. dollar. This currency is involved on one side in 95% of all transactions.... Swap business is quite international, with about 57% of transactions being concluded with counterparties located abroad. The pattern of cross-border trading is not much different from that of the market as a whole. Dealers tend to do more of their business with counterparties located abroad while customers conclude the bulk (71%) of their deals with local counterparties.

Source: Central Bank Survey of Foreign Exchange Market Activity in April 1992, Bank for International Settlements, Basle, Switzerland, March 1993, pp. 18–20.

(the second being higher than the first) or descending. Let us consider our example.

When the swap points are ascending, as they are in the example, the swap points are added to the spot rates so that the implied bid on US dollars for 6 months ahead is

$$Can\$1.3965/\$ + Can\$0.0023/\$$$
$$= Can\$1.3988/\$$$

That is, the quotation "Spot 1.3965–70; 6-month swap 23–27" means the quoting bank is bidding Can\$1.3988 on the US dollar for 6-months forward.

Table 3.5 *Foreign exchange derivative turnover by currency pair: daily turnover in April 2001, in billions of US dollars*

Currency pair	Currency swaps	Options
US dollar/Euro	1	17
US dollar/Japanese yen	2	17
US dollar/British pound	1	3
Euro/Japanese yen	—	6
Euro/British pound	—	2
All other	3	15

Source: Central Bank Survey of Market Activity in April 2001, Bank for International Settlement, Basle, December 2003.

In other words, the quoting bank is willing to buy 6-month forward US dollars – sell Canadian – at Can$1.3988/$. This is the 6-month outright forward rate. Similarly, the above quote, "Spot 1.3965–70; 6-month swap 23–27" is an implied outright ask on US dollars for 6 months of

$$Can\$1.3970/\$ + Can\$0.0027/\$$$
$$= Can\$1.3997/\$$$

This means the quoting bank is willing to sell forward US dollars – buy Canadian – for Can$1.3997/$.

The need to add the swap points in this case is due to the ascending order of the swap points: 27 is larger than 23. If the numbers had been reversed the points would have to be subtracted. For example, suppose the Canadian dollar had been quoted as

Spot	6-month swap
1.3965–70	27–23

The bid and ask on the US spot are the same as before: the market-maker bids Can$1.3965 on the US dollar and asks Can$1.3970. However, the implied outright bid on the US dollar for 6-months forward is

$$Can\$1.3965/\$ - Can\$0.0027/\$$$
$$= Can\$1.3938/\$$$

That is, the market-maker is willing to buy US dollars for delivery in 6 months for Can$1.3938/$. Similarly, the implied ask on the US dollar for 6-months forward is

$$Can\$1.3970/\$ - Can\$0.0023/\$$$
$$= Can\$1.3947/\$$$

The need to add or subtract points based simply on the order of the swap points – ascending or descending – is a matter of convention. There is, however, a simple way of checking whether the arithmetic has been done correctly. Specifically, we note in the first case where we had

Spot	6-month swap
1.3965–70	23–27

that there are 5 basis points in the spot spread – Can$1.3965/$ versus Can$1.3970/$. However, the implied 6-months forward spread is larger because we calculated the forward bid on the US dollar as Can$1.3988/$ and the ask on the US dollar as Can$1.3997/$. This is a spread of 9 points (1.3997 − 1.3988). Similarly, in the second case where we had

Spot	6-month swap
1.3965–70	27–23

The spot has the same 5-point spread. The implied 6-month outright forwards are in this case a 6-month bid on the US dollar of Can$1.3938/$ and an ask of Can$1.3947/$. The spread on the 6-month forward rate is larger than on the spot rate, again being 9 points (1.3947 − 1.3938) on the forward versus 5 points on the spot. The simple test of the outright calculation arithmetic is whether spreads widen with maturity as they should.

The same rule of adding swap points when the order of swap points is ascending, and subtracting swap points when they are descending, applies whether exchange rates are quoted in foreign currency per US dollar, as are all currencies except the euro and pound, or as US dollars per foreign currency. For example, suppose a market-making bank is quoting British pounds as

Spot	1-month	3-month	6-month
1.5780–85	19–17	55–50	95–85

that is, with the forward swap points being descending in magnitude. In this case the swap points must be subtracted, giving the implied forward outrights quoted in Table 3.6.

While the rule for adding or subtracting points depending on whether they are ascending or descending is the same whether rates are quoted in currency per US dollar – European terms – or as US dollar per unit of foreign currency – US dollar equivalent – the interpretation of whether the foreign currency is at a forward premium or discount is different. In the case of the foreign currency per US dollar quotation used for currencies other than the euro and pound, adding points means that the foreign currency is at a forward discount; there is more foreign currency per US dollar for forward than for spot delivery. This means that with quotation as foreign currency per US dollar, an ascending order of swap points means the foreign currency is at a forward discount, and a descending order means the foreign currency is at a forward premium. This is the opposite to the situation with

Table 3.6 *Bids and asks on pounds*

Type of exchange	Bank buys sterling (bids)	Bank sells sterling (asks)	Spread (points)
	(US dollars/£ sterling)		
Spot	1.5780	1.5785	5
1-month	1.5761	1.5768	7
3-month	1.5725	1.5735	10
6-month	1.5685	1.5700	15

US dollar equivalent quotation with the euro and pound. Clearly, it is necessary for foreign currency traders to think quickly and accurately.

Bid-ask spreads and forward maturity

The check that we have suggested, of seeing whether implied outright rates have wider spreads with increasing forward maturities, is based on spreads observed in the market. The reason banks quote larger spreads on longer maturity contracts is not, as some people seem to think, that longer maturity contracts are riskier to the banks because there is more time during which the spot exchange rates might change. As we have seen, banks tend to balance their forward positions by the use of swaps and rollovers, and since they can simultaneously buy and sell forward for each maturity, they can avoid losses from changes in exchange rates during the terms of forward contracts; what a bank gains (loses) on a forward contract to *sell* it loses (gains) on an offsetting forward contract to *buy*. Rather, the reason spreads increase with maturity is the increasing **thinness** of the forward market as maturity increases.

By increasing thinness we mean a smaller trading volume of longer maturity forwards, which in turn means greater difficulty offsetting positions in the interbank forward market after taking orders to buy or sell; since banks state their market and are then obligated if their bid or ask is accepted, they may want to enter the market immediately themselves to help offset the position they have just taken. The market-makers cannot count on receiving offsetting bids and asks and simply enjoying their spreads. The longer the maturity, the less likely are unsolicited offsetting orders, and therefore the more likely the market-maker is to face other market-makers' spreads. The difficulty of offsetting longer maturity forward contracts makes them riskier than shorter maturity contracts, but the extra risk involves uncertainty about the price of an offsetting forward contract when reentering the market, rather than uncertainty about the path of the spot exchange rate during the maturity of the forward contract. That is, the concern is for uncertainty between rates when buying and selling offsetting contracts.

Maturity dates and value dates

Contracts traded on the interbank forward market are mostly for even dates – "1 month," "6 months," and so on. The value date of an even-dated contract such as, for example, a 1-month forward, is the same day in the next month as the value date for a currently agreed spot transaction. For example, if a forward contract is written on Monday, May 18, a day for which spot transactions are for value on Wednesday, May 20, the value date for a 1-month forward is June 20, the value date for a 2-month forward is July 20, and so on. A 1-year forward contract agreed to on May 18 is for value on May 20 in the following year. However, if the future date is not a business day, the value date is moved to the next business day. For example, if a 1-month forward contract is agreed on Tuesday, May 19, a day for which spot value is May 21, the 1-month forward value date would not be Sunday, June 21, but rather the following business day, Monday, June 22. The exception to this rule is that when the next business day means jumping to the following month, the forward value date is moved to the *preceding* business day rather than the *next* business day. In this way, a 1-month forward always settles in the following month, a 2-month forward always settles 2 months later, and so on.[7]

It makes no difference whether the terminology "1 month," "2 months," and so on is used, or whether the terminology is 30 days, 60 days, and so on. The same rules for determining the value dates for forward contracts apply whichever way we refer to even-dated contracts.

SUMMARY

1   A forward exchange contract is an agreement to exchange currencies at a future date at a pre-contracted exchange rate. Forward contracts are written by banks and trade between banks in the interbank market and are sold to bank's clients.

2   As with the spot market, the forward market is a decentralized, continuous open-bid double-auction market. Forward exchange trades in both outright and swap form, where the latter involves the purchase/sale and subsequent sale/purchase of a currency.

3   A forward premium on a foreign currency means that the forward value of the foreign currency exceeds the currency's spot value. A forward discount means the forward value is less than the spot value.

4   If speculators are risk neutral and we ignore transaction costs, the forward exchange rate equals the market's expected future spot rate.

5   Payoff profiles show the change in value of an asset or liability that is associated with unanticipated changes in exchange rates. For forward contracts, payoff profiles are upward- or downward-sloping straight lines.

6   Swaps, which involve a double exchange – usually a spot exchange subsequently reversed by a forward exchange – are traded between banks so that individual banks can efficiently manage their foreign exchange risk.

7 When holiday dates differ between countries so that the value date in one country is a business day, but not in the other, the value date is determined by the business days of the bank making the market, that is, the bank which was called to quote its market.

7 Swaps are also valuable to international investors and borrowers, whereas outright forwards are valuable to importers and exporters.

8 In the interbank market forward exchange rates are quoted as the spot rate plus or minus swap points. The swap points are added to or subtracted from the spot rate depending respectively on the ascending or descending order of the swap points.

9 It is possible to tell from the order of swap points whether a currency is at a forward premium or discount.

10 Forward bid and ask spreads widen with increased maturity because of the increasing thinness of markets as maturity increases. It is harder to keep buy and sell orders balanced simply by changing the bid-ask rates in markets with fewer transactions.

REVIEW QUESTIONS

1 What is a forward rate?
2 What is a forward premium?
3 What is a forward discount?
4 Why and under what conditions is the forward rate equal to the expected future spot rate?
5 What goes on the axes of a payoff profile for a forward exchange contract?
6 How does an "outright" forward contract differ from a "swap?"
7 What does it mean to be "long" in a currency?
8 What does it mean to be "short" in a currency?
9 What is the meaning of the "maturity date" on a forward contract?
10 What is the meaning of the "value date" on a forward contract?

ASSIGNMENT PROBLEMS

1 Why are forward spreads on less-traded currencies larger than on heavily traded currencies?

2 Why do banks quote mainly even-dated forward rates, for example, 1-month rates and 3-month rates, rather than uneven-dated rates? How would you prorate the rates of uneven-dated maturities?

3 Compute the outright forward quotations from the following swap quotations of Canadian dollars in European terms:

Spot	1-month	3-month	6-month
1.3910–15	10–9	12–10	15–12

4 When would spreads widen quickly as we move forward in the forward market? Consider two sets of quotations, from a volatile time and from a stable time.

5 Could a bank that trades forward currency ever hope to balance the buys and sells of forward currencies for each and every future date? How do swap contracts help?
6 Why do banks operate a forward exchange market in only a limited number of currencies? Does it have to do with the ability to balance buy orders with sell orders, and is it the same reason why they rarely offer contracts of over 5 years?
7 Why is risk neutrality relevant for the conclusion that forward exchange rates equal the market's expected future spot exchange rates?
8 Why is it necessary to assume zero spreads when concluding that forward exchange rates equal expected future spot rates?
9 Plot the payoff profile for a forward contract to buy $1 million US at Can$1.3900/$.
10 Plot the payoff profile for a forward contract to sell $1 million US at ¥120/$.

BIBLIOGRAPHY

Burnham, James B., "Current Structure and Recent Developments in Foreign Exchange Markets," in Sarkis J. Khoury (ed.), *Recent Developments in International Banking and Finance*, Volume IV, Elsevier, Amsterdam, 1991, pp. 123–53.

Chrystal, K. Alec, "A Guide to Foreign Exchange Markets," *Review*, Federal Reserve Bank of St. Louis, March 1984, pp. 5–18.

Einzig, Paul A., *The Dynamic Theory of Forward Exchange*, 2nd edn, Macmillan, London, 1967.

Flood, Mark D., "Microstructure Theory and the Foreign Exchange Market," *Review*, Federal Reserve Bank of St. Louis, November/December 1991, pp. 52–70.

Glassman, Debra, "Exchange Rate Risk and Transaction Costs: Evidence from Bid-Ask Spreads," *Journal of International Money and Finance*, December 1987, pp. 479–90.

Kubarych, Roger M., *Foreign Exchange Markets in the United States*, Federal Reserve Bank of New York, New York, 1983.

Riehl, Heinz and Rita M. Rodriguez, *Foreign Exchange and Money Markets*: *Managing Foreign and Domestic Currency Operations*, McGraw-Hill, New York, 1983.

Chapter 4

Currency futures and options markets

Futures and options on futures are derivative assets; that is, their values are derived from underlying asset values. Futures derive their value from the underlying currency, and options on currency futures derive their values from the underlying futures contracts. . . .

Chicago Fed Letter, November 1989

CURRENCY FUTURES

What is a currency future?

Currency futures are standardized contracts that trade like conventional commodity futures on the floor of a futures exchange. Orders to buy or sell a fixed amount of foreign currency are received by brokers or exchange members. These orders, from companies, individuals, and even market-making commercial banks, are communicated to the floor of the futures exchange. At the exchange, orders to buy a currency – **long positions** – are matched with orders to sell – **short positions**. The exchange, or more precisely, its **clearing corporation**, guarantees both sides of each two-sided contract, that is, the contract to buy and the contract to sell. The willingness to buy versus the willingness to sell moves futures prices up and down to maintain a balance between the number of buy and sell orders. The market-clearing price is reached in the vibrant, somewhat chaotic appearing **trading pit** of the futures exchange. Currency futures began trading in the International Money Market (IMM) of the Chicago Mercantile Exchange (CME) in 1972. Since then many other markets

have opened, including the COMEX commodities exchange in New York, the Chicago Board of Trade, and the London International Financial Futures Exchange (LIFFE).

In order for a market to be made in currency futures contracts, it is necessary to have only a few value dates. At the CME, there are four value dates of contracts per year – the third Wednesday in the months March, June, September, and December. In the rare event that contracts are held to maturity, delivery of the underlying foreign currency occurs two business days after the contract maturity date to allow for the normal two-day delivery of spot currency. Contracts are traded in specific sizes: ¥12,500,000; Can$100,000; £62,500; €125,000; and so on. This keeps the contracts sufficiently homogeneous and few in number that there is enough depth for a market to be made. The major currencies that are traded, along with their contract sizes and other information, are shown in Figure 4.1.

Figure 4.1 shows that in the CME, prices of futures on foreign currencies are quoted as US dollar equivalents, that is, as the number of US dollars per unit of the foreign currency. On the

Currency Futures

	OPEN	HIGH	LOW	SETTLE	CHG	LIFETIME HIGH	LIFETIME LOW	OPEN INT
Japanese Yen (CME)-¥12,500,000; $ per ¥ ·								
Dec	.8643	.8745	.8632	.8695	.0065	.8915	.8318	129,461
Est vol 28,466; vol Wed 17,264; open int 129,572, −28,271.								
Canadian Dollar (CME)-CAD 100,000; $ per CAD								
Dec	.7290	.7327	.7278	.7315	.0016	.7432	.6160	56,865
Mr04	.7285	.7295	.7262	.7289	.0016	.7395	.6150	2,637
June	.7250	.7265	.7243	.7263	.0016	.7350	.6201	997
Sept	.7220	.7235	.7220	.7237	.0016	.7315	.6505	577
Est vol 12,855; vol Wed 10,086; open int 61,291, −20,340.								
British Pound (CME)-£62,500; $ per £								
Dec	1.6002	1.6122	1.5974	1.6042	.0044	1.6690	1.5000	28,683
Est vol 7,508; vol Wed 10,969; open int 28,939, −15,625.								
Swiss Franc (CME)-CHF 125,000; $ per CHF								
Dec	.7274	.7292	.7222	.7229	−.0059	.7835	.6773	40,897
Ju04	...	...	...	.7258	−.0059	.7550	.7117	109
Est vol 7,930; vol Wed 10,955; open int 41,231, −31,515.								
Australian Dollar (CME)-AUD 100,000; $ per AUD								
Dec	.6589	.6638	.6582	.6606	.0008	.6740	.5025	36,175
Mr04	.6557	.6570	.6557	.6544	.0007	.6570	.5193	418
Est vol 2,702; vol Wed 3,875; open int 36,688, −12,274.								
Mexican Peso (CME)-MXN 500,000; $ per MXN								
Dec	.09070	.09095	.08970	.09070	.00010	.09590	.08330	30,882
Mr04	...	...	...	.08952	.00010	.09330	.08770	422
Est vol 5,659; vol Wed 8,942; open int 31,427, −17,536.								
Euro/US Dollar (CME)-€125,000; $ per €								
Dec	1.1256	1.1318	1.1200	1.1215	−.0056	1.1860	.9551	79,126
Mr04	1.1233	1.1280	1.1180	1.1188	−.0056	1.1795	1.0425	767
Est vol 42,755; vol Wed 43,474; open int 80,039, −36,660.								
Euro/US. Dollar (FINEX)-€200,000; $ per €								
Dec	...	...	...	1.1212	−.0056	1.1785	1.1132	252
Est vol 306; vol Wed 274; open int 252, +31.								
Euro/Japanese Yen (FINEX)-€100,000; ¥ per €								
Dec	129.88	129.88	128.90	128.97	−1.63	132.05	126.12	6,424
Est vol 301; vol Wed 2,684; open·int 6,424, −296.								
Euro/British Pound (FINEX)-€100,000; £ per €								
Dec	.7011	.7011	.7011	.6992	−.0051	.7065	.6915	1,483
Est vol 89; vol Wed 226; open int 1,483, +199.								

Figure 4.1 *Prices of principal CME currency futures: September 18, 2003*

Notes

Futures prices of foreign currencies against the dollar are quoted in US dollar equivalent terms. The table shows the US dollar cost per unit of foreign currency. The price of a contract is the per unit value in the table multiplied by the contract size. In the case of the Japanese yen, it is necessary to put 0.00 in front of the unit price. The cross rates between the euro and yen and euro and pound are prices of the euro in terms of yen and pounds (reprinted by permission of *The Wall Street Journal* © 2003 Dow Jones & Company Inc. All rights reserved).

other hand, forward rates, except for the euro and British pound, are quoted in European terms, that is, as foreign currency per US dollar. In the case of the Japanese yen the first two zeros in the US dollar price of the yen are omitted. For example, the

contract maturing in December has an actual settle price of $0.008695 per Japanese yen (this is equivalent to ¥115.01/$ in European terms).

The prices in Figure 4.1 are US dollar prices *per unit* of foreign currency. To convert these *per-unit* prices into futures *contract* prices it is necessary to multiply the prices in the figure by the contract amounts. For example, the Japanese yen contract is for ¥12.5 million. With the settle price per yen for December delivery of $0.008695, the price of one Japanese yen contract is

$$\$0.008695/\yen \times \yen12,500,000 = \$108,687$$

Note that as always, the currency symbols can be canceled, so that ¥ disappears leaving a price in US dollars. Similarly, a September 2004 Canadian dollar contract has a settle price of

$$\$0.7237/Can\$ \times Can\$100,000 = \$72,370$$

As with forward exchange contracts, if we assume risk neutrality, the per unit price of futures equals the expected future spot exchange rate of the foreign currency. Otherwise, if, for example, the expected September 2004 spot rate of the Canadian dollar were above $0.7237/Can$, speculators would buy Canadian dollar futures, pushing the futures price up to the expected future spot level. Similarly, if the expected September 2004 spot rate were below the futures price of $0.7237/Can$, speculators would sell Canadian dollar futures until they had forced the futures price back to the expected future spot rate. With futures prices equal to expected future spot exchange rates, it follows that it is changes in expected spot exchange rates that drive futures contract prices up and down.

Both buyers and sellers of currency futures must post a **margin** and pay a transaction fee. The margin is posted in a margin account at a brokerage house, which in turn posts margin at the clearing house of the exchange. The clearing house of the exchange, in turn, pairs buy and sell orders, that is, matches each buy order with a sell order. As we have said, all buy and sell orders are guaranteed by the clearing corporation which operates the clearing house. Margins must be supplemented by contract holders and brokerage houses if the amount in a margin account falls below a certain level, called the **maintenance level**. For example, the CME's standard required margin on British pounds is $2,000 per contract, and the maintenance level is $1,500.[1] This means that if the market value of the contract valued at the settle price has a cumulative fall of more than $500, the full amount of the decline in value from the standard margin must be added to the clients' and the brokers' margin accounts. Declines in contract values which are small enough to leave more than $1,500 of equity do not require action. Increases in the values of contracts are added to margin accounts and can be withdrawn or used as margin on further futures contracts. Margin adjustment is done on a daily basis and is called **marking to market**. Let us consider an example of marking to market.

Marking to market: an example

Suppose that on Day 1 (which for Figure 4.1 is September 18, 2003), a British pound December futures contract is purchased at the opening of the market at the opening per unit price of $1.6002/£. This means that one contract for £62,500 costs the buyer

$$\$1.6002/£ \times £62,500 = \$100,012$$

The settle price, which is the price at the end of the day used for calculating settlement in the buyers' and sellers' accounts, is $1.6042/£; this per unit futures price is the market's expected future spot price for the third Wednesday in December at the end of trading on Day 1, September 18. At this price, the December contract to buy £62,500 is worth

$$\$1.6042/£ \times £62,500 = \$100,262$$

The purchase of the pound futures contract has earned the contract buyer

$$\$100,262 - \$100,012 = \$250$$

This is placed in the contract purchaser's margin account, being added to the $2,000 originally placed in the account. This is shown in Table 4.1.

Suppose that by the end of Day 2 the December pound futures price falls to $1.5980/£. The contract is now worth

$$\$1.5980/£ \times £62,500 = \$99,875$$

Compared to the previous settle contract price of $100,262 there is a loss of

$$\$100,262 - \$99,875 = \$387$$

When this is deducted from the $2,250 in the margin account the total is $1,863 ($2,250 − $387). The margin remains above the maintenance level of $1,500 so nothing needs to be done.

Suppose that by the close of Day 3, because of a decline in the expected future spot rate, the settle price on December pounds falls to $1.5920. The contract is now valued at

$$\$1.5920/£ \times £62,500 = \$99,500$$

The loss from the previous day is

$$\$99,875 - \$99,500 = \$375$$

This brings the margin account to $1,488 ($1,863 − $375) which is below the maintenance level of $1,500. The contract buyer is asked to bring the account up to $2,000, requiring that at least $512 be put in the buyer's account.

If on Day 4 the December pound futures rate settles at $1.6010/£ the contract is worth

$$\$1.6010/£ \times £62,500 = \$100,062$$

This is a gain over the previous settlement of

$$\$100,062 - \$99,500 = \$562$$

This is added to the margin account and can be withdrawn or used towards the margin on another

---

1 Brokers who trade on the CME set the Exchange's margin and maintenance level for clients, but may require more from small clients and less from large clients. Brokers face the minimum levels of margin. All futures trading in the United States is regulated by the Commodities Futures Trading Commission (CFTC).

Table 4.1 Settlements on a pound futures contract

Day	Opening or settle price	Contract price	Margin adjustment	Margin contribution (+) or withdrawal (−)	Margin account
1 Opening	$1.6002/£	$100,012	0	+$2,000	$2,000
1 Settle	$1.6042/£	$100,262	+$250	$0	$2,250
2 Settle	$1.5980/£	$99,875	−$387	$0	$1,863
3 Settle	$1.5920/£	$99,500	−$375	+$512	$2,000
4 Settle	$1.6010/£	$100,062	+$562	−$562	$2,000

futures contract. We assume it is withdrawn. All this is summarized in Table 4.1.

We have seen that with risk neutrality, the futures price equals the expected future spot exchange rate. Therefore, the example indicates that futures can be thought of as daily bets on the value of the expected future spot exchange rate, where the bets are settled each day: futures traders are trying to guess what will happen tomorrow to the market's view of what the spot rate will be on the date of contract maturity.[2] On the other side of the margin adjustments to the futures *buyer's* account described earlier and in Table 4.1, are the adjustments to the margin account of the futures *seller*. When the buyer's account is adjusted up, the seller's account is adjusted down the same amount. That is, what buyers gain, sellers lose, and vice versa. The two sides are taking bets against each other in a zero-sum game. The fee for playing the game is the brokerage charge.

Futures contracts versus forward contracts

The daily settlement of bets on futures means that a futures contract is equivalent to entering a forward contract each day and settling each forward contract before opening another one, where the forwards and futures are for the same future delivery date.[3] The daily marking to market on futures means that any losses or gains are realized as they occur, on a daily cycle. With the loser supplementing the margin daily and in relatively modest amounts, the risk of default is minimal. Of course, with the clearing corporation of the exchange guaranteeing all contracts, the risk of default is faced by the clearing corporation. Were the clearing corporation not to guarantee all contracts, the party on the side of winning the daily bets would be at risk if the other party could not pay. Let us consider how these institutional arrangements in the futures market differ from the forward market.

In the forward market there is no formal and universal arrangement for settling up as the expected future spot rate and consequent forward contract value move up and down. Indeed, there is no formal and universal margin requirement.

Generally, in the case of interbank transactions and transactions with large corporate clients, banks require no margin, make no adjustment for day-to-day movements in exchange rates, and simply wait to settle up at the originally contracted rate. A bank will, however, generally reduce a client's remaining line of credit. For example, if a bank has granted a client a $1 million line of credit and the customer trades $5 million forward, the bank is likely to reduce the credit line by, perhaps $500,000, or 10 percent of the contract. For a customer without a credit line, the bank will require that a margin deposit be established. The procedure for maintaining the margin on a forward contract depends on the bank's relationship with the customer. Margin may be **called**, that is, requested,

2 Therefore, as in all financial markets, successful trading involves beliefs about what other peoples' beliefs will be, those of the market in general.

3 See Fischer Black, "The Pricing of Commodity Contracts," *Journal of Financial Economics*, January/March 1976, pp. 167–9.

from customers without credit lines, requiring supplementary funds to be deposited in the margin account, if from the customer's perspective, an unfavorable movement in the exchange rate occurs. In deciding whether to call for supplementing of margin accounts, banks consider the likelihood of their customers honoring forward contracts. The banks exercise considerable discretion, which is in sharp contrast to the formal daily marking to market of the futures market.

Many banks are also very flexible about what they will accept as margin. For example, stocks, bonds, and other instruments may be accepted in order to ensure that customers honor contracts, although it may be necessary to post more than 10 percent of the value of a forward contract if the instruments that are posted are risky. In the case of futures-exchange brokers' margins at the futures exchange, a substantial part of initial margins may be accepted in the form of securities, such as treasury bills, but subsequent maintenance payments are typically in cash. This means that while with forward contracts there is no opportunity cost of margin requirements, there may be such an opportunity cost with futures contracts, especially when contract prices have fallen and substantial cash payments have consequently been made into the margin account.

Unlike the case for forward contracts, when the buyer of a futures contract wants to take delivery of the foreign currency, the currency is bought at the going spot exchange rate at the time delivery is taken. What happens can be described by considering an example.

Suppose a futures contract buyer needs British pounds in August, and buys a September pound futures contract.[4] In August, when the pounds are needed, the contract is sold on the exchange, and the pounds are bought on the spot exchange market at whatever exchange rate exists on the day in August when the pounds are wanted. Most of the foreign exchange risk is still removed in this situation because if, for example, the pound has unexpectedly increased in value from the time of buying the futures contract, there will be a gain in the margin account. This gain will compensate for the higher than expected spot exchange rate in August. However, not all exchange rate risk is removed because the margin account will not in general *exactly* compensate for the unexpected movement in the spot exchange rate. The remaining risk is due to variations in interest rates and margin account balances which leave uncertainty in the amount in the account or in the cost of maintaining the account. Specifically, the amount in the margin account or paid to maintain it depends on the entire path of the futures price from initial purchase, and on interest rates earned in the account or forgone on cash contributions to the account; daily cash settlements generally do not earn interest. The risk due to variability in the amount in the account and in the interest rate is called **marking-to-market risk**, and makes futures contracts riskier than forward contracts for which there is no marking to market.[5] Even in the very rare circumstance that delivery is taken on the maturity date of a futures contract, there is still marking-to-market risk because the margin account does not provide exact compensation for any unexpected change in the spot exchange rate.[6] This is again due to variations in the time path of amounts in the margin account and in interest rates. We see that a problem with futures in comparison with forwards is that futures contracts leave some risk whereas forwards do not.

Another problem with using futures contracts to reduce foreign exchange risk is that the contract size is unlikely to correspond exactly to a firm's needs. For example, if a firm needs £50,000, the closest it can come is to buy one £62,500 contract. On the other hand, forward contracts with banks

---

4 Alternatively, a June contract might be purchased and delivery of the pounds taken. The pounds could then be held, earning interest until needed.

5 While marking to market adds risk vis-à-vis forwards, the guarantee of the futures exchange to honor all contracts reduces risk.

6 Statistics from the CME show that fewer than 1 percent of futures contracts result in delivery. See *Currency Trading for Financial Institutions*, International Monetary Market, Chicago, 1982.

can be written for any desired amount. The flexibility in values of forward contracts and in margin maintenance, and absence of marking-to-market risk, make forwards preferable to futures for importers, exporters, borrowers, and lenders who wish to precisely hedge foreign exchange exposure. Currency futures are more likely to be preferred by speculators because gains on futures contracts can be taken as cash, and because the transactions costs are small.[7] As we have mentioned, with forward contracts it is necessary to buy an offsetting contract for the same maturity to lock in a profit, and then to wait for maturity before settling the contracts and taking the gain. For example, if pounds are bought forward in May for delivery in December, and by August the buyer wants to take a gain, in August it is necessary to sell pounds forward for December, and then wait for the two contracts to mature in December to collect the gain.[8] The extent to which futures are used to speculate rather than to hedge is indicated, albeit imperfectly, by the statistics on **open interest**. Open interest refers to the number of outstanding two-sided contracts at any given time. (Recall that orders to buy are matched with orders to sell so each contract has two sides.) The statistics on open interest in the last column of Figure 4.1 indicate that most of the activity is in the nearest maturity contracts. While not apparent from Figure 4.1, open interest also falls off substantially just prior to maturity, with delivery rarely being taken. This does not necessarily mean that futures are not generally used to reduce risk, but is suggestive of this.[9]

Payoff profiles on currency futures

It should come as little surprise that because currency futures are similar to forward contracts, the payoff profiles are also similar. The similarities between the profiles, as well as the minor differences that exist, can be clarified by considering an example similar to that used in Chapter 3 for a forward contract. The situation is summarized in Table 4.2 and in the associated payoff profile in Figure 4.2. Both the table and the figure describe the consequences of unanticipated changes in the spot exchange rate on the contract value and margin account of a purchaser of euro futures.

We assume that at the time of buying the futures contract the market's expected future spot rate for the maturity date of the contract is $1.12/€. At this expected spot rate a futures contract for €125,000 has a market price of

$$\$1.12/€ \times €125,000 = \$140,000$$

The purchaser is betting on the outcome vis-à-vis this price. Let us compare this contracted price with the value of €125,000 at realized spot rates to find the outcome of the bet.

If the eventually realized spot exchange rate is $1.13/€, the contract price at maturity will be

---

7 A spread of just 10 points on a forward contract for $100,000 translates into $100, compared to a typical combined cost of a comparably valued futures purchase and subsequent sale of typically $20–$40.

8 Banks will sometimes offer to pay gains out early by discounting what is to be received. This is done to make forward contracts more competitive with futures as a speculative vehicle.

9 See James Tobin, "On the Efficiency of the Financial System," *Lloyds Bank Review*, July 1984, pp. 1–15.

Table 4.2 *Realized spot rates and gains/losses on futures to buy euros*

Realized spot rate	Realized rate versus futures price	Maturity value of contract	Accumulated marking-to-market gain (+) or loss (−)
$1.15/€	+$0.03/€	$143,750	+$3,750±
$1.14/€	+$0.02/€	$142,500	+$2,500±
$1.13/€	+$0.01/€	$141,250	+$1,250±
$1.12/€	$0	$140,000	$0±
$1.11/€	−$0.01/€	$138,750	−$1,250±
$1.10/€	−$0.02/€	$137,500	−$2,500±
$1.09/€	−$0.03/€	$136,250	−$3,750±

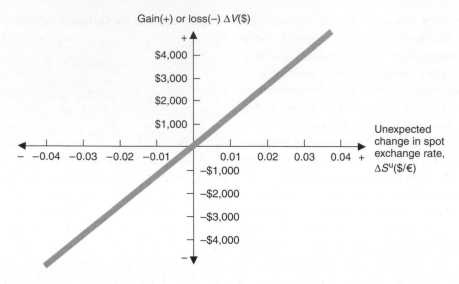

Figure 4.2 *Payoff profile for purchase of euro futures contract*

Notes
The futures contract is for the purchase of €125,000. If the spot price of the euro unexpectedly increases by $0.01/€ there is a gain on the contract of $0.01/€ × €125,000 = $1,250 which is added to the buyer's margin account. If the spot price of the euro unexpectedly decreases by $0.01/€ there is a loss on the contract of $1,250 which is subtracted from the buyer's margin account. However, the exact gain or loss also depends on the path of interest rates which affect earnings on margin accounts and the cost of maintaining margin. This makes the actual gain or loss associated with any change in the exchange rate somewhat uncertain, represented by the broad line. The payoff profile for the seller of a euro futures contract is a downward-sloping line of the same absolute slope.

worth $1.13/€ × €125,000 = $141,250.[10] This represents a gain over the initially contracted price of $1,250. That is, the futures contract buyer has won $1,250 on the bet. However, depending on the actual time path of the expected future spot rate between the initial purchase of the contract at $1.12/€ and the contract's maturity, the gain, properly calculated, might not be *exactly* $1,250. For example, if it has been necessary to make many cash contributions to the margin account which will involve an opportunity cost, the true gain, including this cost, would be less than $1,250. Alternatively, if money has been withdrawn and invested, there

10 A minimum change in price per unit of currency – or **tick** – for the euro is $0.0001/€, which for a contract of €125,000 is worth $0.0001/€ × €125,000 = $12.50. For the other currencies traded on the IMM the minimum price changes per unit and associated contract price changes are Japanese yen ($0.000001/¥; $12.50); Canadian dollar ($0.0001/Can$; $10); British pound ($0.00002/£; $12.50); Swiss franc ($0.0001/SFr; $12.50); Australian dollar ($0.0001/A$; $10).

might be more than $1,250 from the margin, including the interest earnings. The uncertainty is the result of marking-to-market risk and is shown in Table 4.2 by the ± in the last column.

Table 4.2 also shows that if the realized spot rate is $1.11/€ the futures contract is worth $138,750 ($1.11/€ × €125,000). This is a loss vis-à-vis the contracted price of $140,000. The bet has resulted in a loss of $1,250 ($140,000 − $138,750). However, because of daily marking-to-market, the properly calculated loss might differ slightly from this amount. Other values in Table 4.2 are calculated in similar fashion. The table shows that as the eventually realized spot value of the euro increases – reading up the table from bottom to top – there is a larger and larger gain on the futures contract to buy euros. The exact gain depends on the time path of the future's price from buying the contract to the contract's maturity, and on interest rates along this time path.

The gain or loss on the contract at different realized spot rates, that represent unexpected changes in the spot rate, are plotted in Figure 4.2 (recall that the unexpected change in the spot rate from purchase to maturity is the realized spot rate at maturity, minus the expected spot rate at the time of buying the futures contract, $1.12/€). We see an upward-sloping line, akin to that plotted for a forward purchase of euros in Chapter 3 – see Figure 3.1. However, the upward-sloping line here is made purposely "fuzzy" because of uncertainty in precise payoffs from marking-to-market risk.

The opposite side of the purchase of euro futures is the sale of euro futures. The payoffs for this are those in the final column of Table 4.2 with the signs reversed, and the consequent payoff profile is a downward-sloping line, but one sharing the same absolute value of slope as the line in Figure 4.2.

The link between the futures and forward markets

As mentioned in Chapter 3, the market for currency futures is small compared with the market for forwards. However, despite the large difference in the sizes of the two markets, there is a mutual interdependence between them; each one is able to affect the other. This interdependence is the result of the action of arbitragers who can take offsetting positions in the two markets when prices differ. The most straightforward type of arbitrage involves offsetting outright forward and futures positions.[11]

If, for example, the 3-month forward price for buying euros were $1.1200/€ while the selling price on the same date on the CME were $1.1210/€, an arbitrager could buy euros forward from a bank and sell futures on the CME. The arbitrager would make $0.0010/€, so that on each contract for €125,000, he or she could make a profit of $125. Action to profit from this arbitrage opportunity would quickly bring the forward price up to the futures price. Similarly, arbitrage would bring the futures price up to the forward price if the futures price were lower. However, we should remember that since the futures market requires daily maintenance, or marking-to-market, the arbitrage involves risk which can allow the futures and forward rates to differ a little. It should also be clear that the degree to which middle exchange rates on the two markets can deviate will depend very much on the spreads between buying and selling prices. Arbitrage will ensure that the bid price of forward currency does not exceed the effective ask price of currency futures, and vice versa. However, the prices can differ a little beyond this due to marking-to-market risk. We should also note that the direction of influence is not invariably from the rate set on the larger forward market to the smaller futures market. When there is a move on the futures markets that results in a very large number of margins being called, the scramble to close positions with sudden buying or selling can spill over into the forward market.

CURRENCY OPTIONS

What is a currency option?

Forward exchange and currency futures contracts must be exercised. It is true that currency futures can be sold and margin balances can be withdrawn. It is also true that forward contracts can be offset by a second contract that is the reverse of the original contract. However, all forward contracts and currency futures must be honored by both parties. That is, the banks and their counterparties, or those holding outstanding futures, must settle. There is no option allowing a party to settle only if it is to that party's advantage.

Unlike forward and futures contracts, **currency options** give the buyer the opportunity, but not the obligation, to buy or sell at a pre-agreed price – the **strike price** or **exercise price** – in the future. That is, as the name suggests, the buyer of an option

---

11 We can note that even without any arbitrage via offsetting outright forward and futures positions, the rates for forward contracts and currency futures will be kept in line by users of these markets choosing between them if the rates differ. This is analogous to one-way arbitrage in the case of cross rates in Chapter 2.

contract purchases the option or right to trade at the rate or price stated in the contract if this is to the option buyer's advantage, but to allow the option to expire unexercised if that would be better. That is, options have a throw-away feature.

Exchange-traded options

Futures options versus spot options

At the CME, the currency options that trade are options on currency futures. Such options give the buyers the right but not the obligation to buy or sell currency futures contracts at a pre-agreed price. Options on futures derive their value from the prices of the underlying futures. The futures, in turn, derive their value, as we have seen, from the expected future spot value of the currency. Therefore, *indirectly*, options on futures derive their value from the expected future spot value of the underlying currency.

Currency options also trade on the Philadelphia Exchange. Unlike the CME options which are on currency futures, the Philadelphia options are on spot currency. These options give the buyers the right to buy or sell the currency itself at a pre-agreed price. Therefore, options on spot currency derive their value *directly* from the expected future spot value of the currency, not indirectly via the price of futures. However, ultimately, all currency options derive their value from movements in the underlying currency. Indeed, as they approach maturity, futures options become more and more like spot options.[12]

Characteristics of currency options

We can illustrate the features of currency options by considering the quotations in Figure 4.3. The figure shows the major currency options trading on the

12 As we have seen, if delivery on futures is taken, the currency is purchased at the spot rate. This means that at maturity of the futures contract, an option on currency futures is an option on the spot currency.

Currency

STRIKE	CALLS-SETTLE			PUTS-SETTLE		

Japanese Yen (CME)
12,500,000 yen; cents per 100 yen

Price	Oct	Nov	Dec	Oct	Nov	Dec
8600	1.30	1.78	2.06	0.35	0.83	1.11
8650	1.00	1.51	1.80	0.55	1.06	1.35
8700	0.77	1.27	1.56	0.82	1.32	1.61
8750	0.59	1.08	1.36	...	...	...
8800	0.45	0.94	1.18	...	...	2.23
8850	0.32	0.79	1.03	...	...	...

Est vol 2,587 Wd 752 calls 607 puts
Op int Wed 29,287 calls 32,274 puts

Canadian Dollar (CME)
100,000 Can.$; cents per Can.$

Price	Oct	Nov	Dec	Oct	Nov	Dec
7200	1.31	1.83	...	0.16	0.68	...
7250	0.92	1.51	...	0.27	0.86	...
7300	0.61	1.22	...	0.46	1.07	...
7350	0.39	0.99	...	0.74	1.34	...
7400	0.23	0.80	...	...	1.65	...
7450	...	0.64	...	...	...	...

Est vol 731 Wd 261 calls 75 puts
Op int Wed 11,585 calls 5,717 puts

British Pound (CME)
62,500 pounds; cents per pound

Price	Oct	Nov	Dec	Oct	Nov	Dec
1580	2.78	...	3.80	0.36	1.10	1.38
1590	2.00	2.88	3.26	0.58	...	1.84
1600	1.38	2.32	2.72	0.96	...	2.30
1610	0.90	...	2.18	1.48	...	2.76
1620	0.56	1.42	1.72	...	...	3.30
1630	0.26	...	1.38	...	...	...

Est vol 302 Wd 132 calls 104 puts
Op int Wed 3,598 calls 3,858 puts

Swiss Franc (CME)
125,000 francs; cents per franc

Price	Oct	Nov	Dec	Oct	Nov	Dec
7150	1.16	...	1.93	0.37	...	1.14
7200	0.85	...	1.66	0.56	1.08	1.37
7250	0.59	1.12	1.42	0.80	1.33	1.63
7300	0.41	0.92	1.21	1.12	...	1.92
7350	0.29	...	1.03	...	...	2.24
7400	0.20	...	0.87	1.91	...	2.57

Est vol 75 Wd 535 calls 74 puts
Op int Wed 2,721 calls 1,440 puts

Euro Fx (CME)
125,000 euros; cents per euro

Price	Oct	Nov	Dec	Oct	Nov	Dec
11100	1.69	2.44	2.85	0.54	1.29	1.70
11150	1.37	2.16	2.57	0.72	1.51	1.92
11200	1.09	1.89	2.31	0.94	1.74	2.16
11250	0.86	1.66	2.08	1.21	2.01	2.43
11300	0.66	1.44	1.86	1.51	2.29	2.71
11350	0.50	1.25	1.67	1.85	...	3.01

Est vol 1,909 Wd 1,172 calls 673 puts
Op int Wed 27,707 calls 20,189 puts

Figure 4.3 Premiums on principal CME options on currency futures: September 18, 2003

Notes
Currency options trading on the CME are options on futures contracts that trade on the same exchange. Prices quoted are US cents per unit of foreign currency. Contract prices are therefore the prices quoted multiplied by contract sizes (reprinted by permission of *The Wall Street Journal* © 2003 Dow Jones & Company Inc. All rights reserved).

CME, on September 18, 2003 (options also exist on other currencies including the Australian dollar, Brazilian real, and Mexican peso).

The first thing we notice in Figure 4.3 is that the sizes of CME contracts are the same as on currency futures. This is to allow options to be used in conjunction with futures. The options are **American options**. American options offer buyers flexibility in that they can be exercised on any date up to and including the maturity date of the option. **European options**, on the other hand, can be exercised only on the maturity date of the option contract and not before (the Philadelphia Stock Exchange trades European options as well as American options). Buyers would pay no more for a European option of a given kind than for a more flexible American option of the same kind.

The expiry months for options are March, June, September, and December plus two near-term months (hence the October and November quotes in Figure 4.3).[13] CME options expire on the Saturday before the third Wednesday of the expiry month. This makes them essentially mid-month options. The Philadelphia Exchange also trades end-of-month options which expire on the last Friday of the nearest 3-month maturing contract.

The numbers in the first column of each currency in Figure 4.3 give strike prices in US dollar equivalent terms. As we have stated, the strike price gives the exchange rate at which the option buyer has the right to buy or sell the foreign currency, and is also known as the exercise price. We can see that on each currency there are options at numerous strike prices with gaps of 0.5 cents on the Canadian dollar, one cent on the British pound, and so on (in interpreting the strike prices, 7300 for the Canadian dollar means US$0.73/Can$, 1600 means US$1.60/£, etc). When a new set of options is introduced, which occurs as an old set expires, the new options are written at the rounded-off value of the going spot exchange rate, and at a slightly higher and slightly lower exchange rate. New strike prices are introduced if the spot rate changes by a large amount.

Whether the option gives the buyer the right to buy or sell the foreign currency is identified by whether the option is listed in one of the columns headed "Calls" or one of the columns headed "Puts." A **call option** gives the buyer the right to buy the foreign currency at the strike price or exchange rate on the option, and a **put option** gives the buyer the right to sell the foreign currency at the strike price.

We can illustrate the concepts so far introduced, and at the same time explain how options work, by considering a couple of options on euros in Figure 4.3 showing option prices on September 18, 2003. Let us consider the euro call option for October with a strike price of $1.1200/€. This option gives the buyer the right to purchase a euro futures contract for €125,000 at a price per euro of $1.1200 until and including the expiry date in October: all CME options are American options. The price of the option, 1.09 US cents per euro, means that for the contract to buy a €125,000 futures contract the option buyer must pay.[14]

$$\$0.0109/€ \times €125,000 = \$1,362.50$$

This means that by paying $1,362.50, the option buyer acquires the right to buy the €125,000 futures contract for $1.12/€ until and including the expiry date of the option. The option will not be exercised if the futures price of the euro is below $1.1200/€ because in these circumstances it would be better to buy the contract directly. Since the futures contract maturity date is only one month away the futures price will be very close to the spot rate. Therefore, we can think of the call option on the euro at $1.1200/€ as having exercise value if the spot rate is above $1.1200/€.[15] If the

---

13 The Philadelphia Exchange also trades longer term options with maturity up to 36 months.

14 As always, the currency symbols can be canceled.

15 In actual fact, rather than exercise the option, the buyer is likely to accept the difference between the exercise price and the going futures price from the option **writer**. The writer is the person selling the call option, and who received the $1,362.50 from the sale of the option.

spot rate is below $1.1200/€ the option has no value for immediate exercise because it gives the holder the right to pay more than the euro's current value.

Consider next the October put option on the euro, also at the strike price $1.1200/€. This option has a price per euro of 0.94 US cents, or $0.00940/€. Therefore, the option to sell €125,000 up to and including the maturity date in October costs

$$\$0.00940/€ \times €125,000 = \$1,175$$

If the futures price of the euro is above $1.1200 the option will have no immediate exercise value; it would be better to sell the euro on the futures market than at the exercise price. It is thrown away, with the loss of $1,175. On the other hand, if the euro futures price is below $1.1200 then the put option gives the buyer the right to sell €125,000 at the higher exercise price, $1.1200. The $1,175 paid for the put option can be thought of as an insurance premium against the risk that the euro futures price might fall below $1.1200. In the event that this does not occur, the insurance simply expires.

Because of the way new options are introduced, with strike prices at, above and below the current futures price, there are options with higher and lower strike exchange rates than the futures exchange rate. A call option that gives the buyer the right to buy currency futures at a strike exchange rate that is below the current futures price is said to be **in the money**. This is because the option holder has the right to buy the futures contract for less than it would cost in the futures market. For example, the euro call option at $1.1200 is in the money if the current futures price is above $1.1200. A call option with a strike price that is above the current futures exchange rate is said to be **out of the money**; the option holder would find it cheaper to buy the foreign currency on the futures market than to exercise the option. The fact that a call option might be out of the money does not mean the option has no value. As long as there is a possibility that the futures price might move above the strike price

during the maturity of the option, people will be willing to pay for the option contract.

A put option that gives the buyer the right to sell the foreign currency is said to be in the money when the strike exchange rate is higher than the current futures exchange rate. This is because the option holder has the right to sell the currency contract for more than it could be sold on the futures market. A put option is out of the money when the strike exchange rate is lower than the current futures exchange rate. This is because the option holder wanting to sell the futures contract would be better off not to exercise the option, but rather to sell at the futures price. As with call options, the fact that a put option is out of the money does not mean it has no value. It has value as long as there is a possibility that the futures rate might move below the strike exchange rate during the life of the option.

The extent to which an option is in the money is called its **intrinsic value**. For example, if the futures exchange rate is $1.1300 per euro the $1.1200 call has an intrinsic value of one US cent per dollar. That is, the intrinsic value is how much per euro would be gained by exercising the option immediately. The actual market price of the option will exceed the intrinsic value. This is because there is always the possibility of an even larger gain from exercising the option during the remainder of its maturity. While call options have intrinsic value when the strike price is *below* the futures exchange rate, put options have intrinsic value when the strike price *exceeds* the futures exchange rate. The impact of different variables on option premiums is summarized in Table 4.3.

The amount paid for the option on each unit of foreign currency – for each British pound or each euro etc. – is called the **option premium**. This premium can be considered to consist of two parts, the intrinsic value if there is any, and the **time value** of the option. The time value is the part of the premium that comes from the possibility that, at some point in the future, the option might have higher intrinsic value than at that moment. When an option is **at the money**, which occurs when the strike price exactly equals the current futures

Table 4.3 *Impact of variables affecting currency call and put option premiums*

Variable that is increasing	Effect on price of call	Effect on price of put
Spot price of foreign currency	Increase	Decrease
Exercise price	Decrease	Increase
Exchange rate volatility	Increase	Increase
Domestic interest rate	Increase	Decrease
Forward premium	Increase	Decrease
Time to maturity	Uncertain[a]	Uncertain[a]

Note

a Time to maturity increases the chance the option will move into the money, increasing the option premium. On the other hand, longer time to maturity involves greater opportunity cost of money invested.

rate, the option premium is equal to the option's time value.

Quotation conventions and market organization

Option dealers quote a bid and an ask premium on each contract, with the bid being what buyers are willing to pay, and the ask being what sellers want to be paid. After the buyer has paid for an option contract, he or she has no financial obligation. Therefore, there is no need to talk about margins for option *buyers*. The person selling the option is called the **writer**. The writer of a call option must stand ready, when required, to sell the currency to the option buyer at the stated strike price. Similarly, the writer of a put option must stand ready to buy the currency from the option buyer at the strike price. The commitment of the writer is open throughout the life of the option for American options, and on the maturity date of the option for European options. The option exchange guarantees that option sellers honor their obligations to option buyers, and therefore requires option *sellers* to post a margin.

As in the case of futures contracts, an exchange can make a market in currency options sufficiently deep only by standardizing the contracts. This is why option contracts are written for specific amounts of foreign currency, for a limited number of maturity dates, and for a limited number of strike exchange rates. The standardization allows buyers to resell contracts prior to maturity. It also allows writers to offset their risks more readily because, for example, the writer of a call option can enter the market as a buyer of a call option to limit losses or to lock in gains.[16]

Determinants of the market values of currency options

The factors that influence the price of an option are:

1 *Intrinsic value* As we have said, the premium on an option can be considered to be made up of the time value and the intrinsic value. (We recall that the intrinsic value is the extent to which the current futures price exceeds the strike price on a call option, and the extent to which the strike price exceeds the current futures price on a put option. Alternatively, it is what the option would be worth if it had to be exercised immediately.) Therefore, the more the option is in the money (i.e. the higher is the intrinsic value) the higher is the option premium.

2 *Volatility of the underlying exchange rate* *Ceteris paribus*, the more volatile is the underlying rate, the greater the chance that an option will be exercised to the benefit of the buyer and to the cost of the seller.[17] That is,

16 The ways that options can be used for hedging and speculating are described in Chapter 13.
17 The effects of volatility and the other influences listed here on *stock* options were first described by Fischer Black and Myron Scholes, "The Pricing of Options and Corporate Liabilities," *Journal of Political Economy*, May/June 1973, pp. 637–59. The effects of volatility and other factors on *currency* options have been described by Mark B. Garman and Steven W. Kohlhagen, "Foreign Currency Option Values," *Journal of International Money and Finance*, December 1983, pp. 231–7, and by J. Orlin Grabbe, "The Pricing of Call and Put Options on Foreign Exchange," *Journal of International Money and Finance*, December 1983, pp. 239–53.

the higher the volatility of the underlying exchange rate, the greater the possibility that it will at some time exceed the strike exchange rate of a call, or be below the strike exchange rate of a put. Consequently, buyers will pay more for an option, and sellers will demand more, if the volatility of the exchange rate is higher.

Since Philadelphia options give the buyer the option to buy or sell spot foreign exchange, it is the volatility of the spot exchange rate that determines the value of Philadelphia options. With CME options being on currency futures contracts rather than on spot exchange, it is the price and volatility of CME futures contracts that determines the value of CME currency options. However, because the spot exchange rate is the principal factor affecting futures contract prices, it is still the volatility of the spot rate that matters.

3 *American or European option type* The greater flexibility of American than European options means buyers will not pay more for a European option than for an American option of the same strike price and maturity (recall that American options can be exercised at any time before the expiry date, while European options can be exercised only on the expiry date). Indeed, for a given strike price, exchange rate volatility and period to expiration, American options are typically more valuable than European options.

4 *Interest rate on currency of purchase* The higher the interest rate on the currency paid for an option, the lower is the present value of the exercise price. A higher interest rate consequently has the same effect on an option as does a lower exercise price, namely, it increases the market value of a call and reduces the market value of a put.[18]

5 *The forward premium/discount or interest differential* Because of very different rates of inflation, imbalances of trade, and so on, there can be trends in exchange rates that are to an extent predictable. For example, the foreign exchange values of currencies of countries with very rapid inflation tend to decline vis-à-vis those with slow inflation. *Ceteris paribus*, the greater the expected decline in the foreign exchange value of a currency, the higher is the value of a put option on that currency because there is a greater chance the put option will be exercised, and the larger the possible intrinsic value when it is exercised. Similarly, the more a currency is expected to increase in value – because of low inflation, consistently good international trade performance, and so on – the higher is the value of a call option on that currency. Again, this is because, *ceteris paribus*, the more the currency is expected to increase in value, the more likely it is that a call option will be worth exercising and the bigger the possible intrinsic value.

Because the forward rate, under the assumption of risk neutrality, equals the expected future spot rate, currencies that are expected to decline in value tend to trade at a forward discount, while currencies expected to increase in value tend to trade at a premium.[19] Indeed, the more a currency is expected to decline/increase in value, the larger the forward discount/premium tends to be. It follows that *ceteris paribus*, the greater is the forward discount on a currency, the higher the value of a put option and the lower the value of a call option on that currency. Similarly, the greater is the forward premium, the higher the value of a call option and the lower the value of a put option on the currency.[20]

---

18 This is because other things are assumed constant as the interest rate changes. See John C. Cox and Mark Rubenstein, *Options Markets*, Prentice-Hall, Englewood Cliffs, NJ, 1985, p. 35.

19 This was explained in Chapter 3.

20 There is an arbitrage relation between option prices and the forward exchange rate that can be used to describe the effects we have described. This is discussed in the appendix to this chapter. See also Cox and Rubinstein, op. cit., pp. 59–61.

An alternative way of stating the effect of expected decreases or increases in exchange rates on the value of options is in terms of interest rates. Countries with currencies that are expected to decline in value tend to have high interest rates relative to other countries. (such high rates are necessary to compensate investors for the expected decline in exchange rates). Therefore, put options tend to be worth more when interest rates are higher than elsewhere; the relatively high interest rates suggest an expected decline in the value of the currency, and a consequently increased chance that a put will be exercised. Similarly, call options tend to be worth more when interest rates are lower than elsewhere because relatively low interest rates suggest an expected increase in the currency's value, and consequently an increased chance the call will be exercised.

6   *Length of period to expiration* Ceteris paribus, the longer the maturity period of the option, the greater is the chance that at some time the exchange rate will move above the strike price of a call or below the strike price of a put. That is, the longer the maturity, the greater the chance the option will move into the money. This particular effect of time means that the longer the period to expiration, the higher the option premium a buyer is prepared to pay, and the higher the option premium a seller will require. However, there is another force of time working in the other direction. Specifically, the longer the maturity, the higher is the opportunity cost of funds used to buy the option. This effect lowers the option premium: buyers pay less when the money paid for an option could earn more if invested in something else. As it turns out, the empirical evidence shows what seems intuitively reasonable, namely that option premiums increase with maturity. That is, the chance of moving into the money has a larger effect than the opportunity cost.

The effects of different variables on call and put option premiums described earlier are summarized

in Table 4.3. They are also illustrated in the appendix to this chapter.[21]

Over-the-counter (OTC) options

Well before options began trading on formal exchanges in 1981, there had been an active **over-the-counter option** market in Europe, the options being written by large banks.[22] Indeed, the over-the-counter option market continues to exist alongside the formal option exchanges. Amounts traded tend to be large, generally over $1 million. The banks that write over-the-counter options often use formal exchange options to hedge their own positions.

Many over-the-counter options written by banks are contingent upon such outcomes as whether a corporate takeover or bid on a foreign project is accepted[23] (see Exhibit 4.1). That is, the buyer of the option purchases the opportunity to buy a foreign currency at a given strike exchange rate if, for example, a particular takeover occurs. An example of such an over-the-counter option is the option on sterling purchased by US insurance broker, Marsh and McLennan Company. Marsh and McLennan made a cash and share offer for C.T. Bowring and Company, a member of Lloyds of London, which required Marsh and McLennan to pay £130 million if the offer was accepted. Rather than take a chance on the exchange rate that might prevail on the takeover settlement date, Marsh and McLennan wanted to buy a call option for £130 million that it could exercise only if its takeover effort succeeded.[24] Bankers Trust agreed to provide an option which could be exercised up to 6 months after the original

21 The appendix considers arbitrage conditions referred to as **put-call parity** and **put-call forward parity**.

22 Currency options had also been traded in an unorganized fashion in the United States until this was ruled illegal. See David Babbel, "The Rise and Decline of Currency Options," *Euromoney*, September 1980, pp. 141–9.

23 As Exhibit 4.1 explains, there are many other possible ways of designing options.

24 This interesting case is described in "Marsh and McLennan Insures Takeover Exposure with Call Provision," *Money Report*, Business International, June 13, 1980.

EXHIBIT 4.1   THE SCOPE FOR WRITING OPTIONS

It is possible to write options based on more than just the eventually realized spot exchange rate. Among the various currency options that are used are the following:

Path-dependent or "Asian" Options These pay out according to the average spot rate that has prevailed over a stated previous period of time. For example, an Asian option might have an exercise price equal to the average end-of-day spot rate for the previous year. Such an option is useful for hedging risk when a company is converting its foreign currency income into domestic currency continuously throughout the year. For example, to avoid making foreign exchange losses, an exporter can buy Asian puts on each of the foreign currencies it earns. Then, if a foreign currency, on average, falls in value over the year, the option holder makes a gain on that option equal to its loss on foreign exchange earnings in that currency.

Look-back Options These options give buyers the right to enjoy the best exchange rate that has occurred during a preceding period of time. For example, a 3-month look-back call on the Japanese yen gives the option buyer the right to buy yen at the lowest price of the yen in the previous quarter of a year. Similarly, a look-back yen put gives the owner the right to receive the best selling price of the yen in a given previous period of time. Of course, the premiums charged by writers of such options are higher than for regular options; in a sense the option provides discretion over whether to exercise, and over the exercise price within the range it has traveled.

Option-linked Loans An option can be written to repay a loan in the currency of the borrower's choice, where the different amounts of the alternative currencies which can be paid are stated in the contract. Multinational companies earning various foreign currencies find these useful since they can pay back with the less valuable currencies. The cost of the loans does, however, reflect the option the borrower enjoys. Alternatively, the option over currency of repayment can be given to the lender. In this case the cost of the loan – the interest rate – is low to reflect the lender's option.

Option-linked Bonds An extension of the option-linked loan is a bond for which the buyer has the choice of currency for paying coupons, and possibly, also for repayment of principal. As with option-linked loans, the amounts of alternative currencies required on the coupons or principal are stated on the bond, with the borrower deciding what to pay based on spot exchange rates when payments occur. Payments will be in the least valuable currency at the time. This makes the bond yields high to compensate the lender. Alternatively, the option over currency of receipt of coupons or principal can be given to the lender. This reduces yields as the lender stands to benefit, and the borrower stands to lose.

Source: "The Look-back and the Linkage," *Euromoney,* special supplement, *Risk Management; Taming the Demon,* April 1989, p. 51.

---

takeover offer. The takeover bid did succeed and the option was duly exercised.

The reason why the over-the-counter market coexists alongside the formal options market is that options that trade on option exchanges are not perfectly suited for contingencies such as whether a takeover bid is accepted, whether an export contract is signed, and so on. Exchange-traded options are imperfectly suited for such contingencies because, even though the option buyer can choose whether to exercise, the value of exchange-traded options is contingent upon what happens to exchange rates rather than on whether a deal is consummated.[25] An option that is contingent upon completion of a takeover might be cheaper than a

25 See Nalin Kulatilaka and Alan J. Marcus, "Hedging Foreign Project Risk," Working Paper, Boston University School of Management, April 1991.

traditional exchange-traded option. This is because the writer of a call contingent on completion of a takeover or a bid on a foreign project does not deliver foreign exchange if the foreign currency increases in value but the deal is not completed. That is, there are outcomes where the deal-completion-contingent option writer does not lose, but where the writer of an exchange option would lose; an exchange call option will be exercised if the option has value on the options exchange, even if the deal is not completed. Banks that write over-the-counter customized options frequently "reinsure" on an options exchange, so it is the bank rather than the option buyer that gains when the foreign currency increases in value but, for example, the takeover offer is rejected. The bank gains because it reinsures by buying an exchange-issued call option to cover the call it has written, and the exchange call increases in value without the need to deliver the foreign currency if the takeover offer is rejected.

Payoff profiles for currency options

By plotting the payoff profiles for currency options we can graphically compare the consequences of using options for hedging and speculation with the alternative methods involving forward and futures contracts. Let us begin by considering a call option.

Payoff profiles for call option buyers/writers

Let us consider a call option on €125,000 with a strike or exercise price of $1.1200/€. If at the date of expiry the spot (and hence also the futures) rate is $1.1200/€, so that the option expires exactly at the money, the option buyer will lose what he or she had paid for the option. Let us suppose this was $1,000. The option buyer will also lose the amount paid for the option if it expires out of the money, that is at a spot exchange rate of less than $1.1200/€. This is shown in Table 4.4 with zero exercise value at the strike price of the euro and below. It is also illustrated by the horizontal line at $1,000 in Figure 4.4.

If the realized spot price of the euro at maturity is more than $1.1200/€ the call option ends up in the money and has exercise value. For example, at $1.1280/€ the intrinsic value of the call option at $1.1200/€ is:

$$\$0.0080/€ \times €125,000 = \$1,000$$

Table 4.4 *Payoffs on purchase of euro call option*

Realized spot rate	Realized rate minus strike rate	Gain (+) or loss(−) on contract	Cost (−) of option	Overall gain (+) or loss (−)
1.1500	+$0.0300/€	+$4,000	−$1,000	+$3,000
1.1420	+$0.0240/€	+$3,000	−$1,000	+$2,000
1.1360	+$0.0160/€	+$2,000	−$1,000	+$1,000
1.1280	+$0.0080/€	+$1,000	−$1,000	—
1.1200	—	—	−$1,000	−$1,000
1.1120	−$0.0080/€	—	−$1,000	−$1,000
1.1040	−$0.0160/€	—	−$1,000	−$1,000
1.0960	−$0.0240/€	—	−$1,000	−$1,000
1.0880	−$0.0300/€	—	−$1,000	−$1,000

Notes
We assume the option is a call to buy €125,000 with a strike price, $X(\$/€)$, of $1.1200/€, and that the price paid for the option is $1,000. At $1.1200/€ and exchange rates below this at maturity the option has no exercise value. At realized spot rates above $1.1200/€ the call option expires in the money. At $1.1280/€, for example, the option has exercise value of €125,000 × $0.0080/€ = $1,000. This gain on the option is offset by the amount paid. Above $1.1280/€ there is an overall gain on the option for the option buyer. The option writer gains what the option buyer loses and loses what the buyer gains.

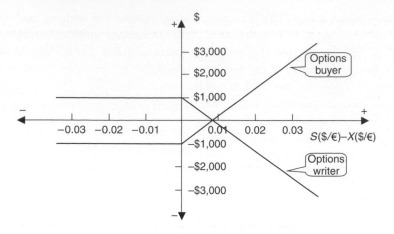

Figure 4.4 *Payoff profiles of buyer and writer of euro call option for €125,000*

Notes
The euro call buyer is assumed to pay $1,000 for an option to buy €125,000 at strike exchange rate, $X(\$/€)$. If the realized spot exchange rate $S(\$/€)$, is at or below the strike rate the option has no exercise value. Then, the buyer loses $1,000 and the writer gains $1,000. At realized spot rates above $X(\$/€)$ the call option has exercise value. For example, at $S(\$/€) - X(\$/€) = \$0.0080/€$ the exercise value is $1,000, so buyer and writer both break even overall. At $S(\$/€) - X(\$/€) > \$0.0080/€$, the buyer gains overall and the writer loses. The greater is $S(\$/€) - X(\$/€)$ the greater the buyer's gain and writer's loss. The figure plots the values shown in Table 4.4.

This is the same as the amount paid for the option contract and so the option buyer breaks even. At realized spot exchange rates at maturity above $1.1280/€ the option buyer enjoys a profit, and the higher the value of the euro the greater the gain from having purchased the option contract. This is shown in Table 4.4 and plotted in Figure 4.4. The payoff profile for the euro call option buyer is shown to be − $1,000 at all exchange rates where the realized spot value of the euro is no greater than the strike price, that is, to the left of the vertical axis. At realized spot rates above the strike price there is positive exercise value, with this increasing linearly with the spot rate.

Figure 4.4 also shows the payoff profile of the writer, that is, the seller, of the option. What the buyer pays the writer receives, and what the buyer receives, the writer pays.[26] Therefore, the writer has a gain of $1,000 when the option ends up out-of-the-money, that is, to the left of the vertical axis. When the realized spot rate ends up above the strike

price, that is, to the right of the vertical axis, the writer loses what the buyer gains, so the slope of the payoff profile is the negative of the buyer's profile.

Payoff profiles for put option buyers/writers

The gains or losses of buyers of euro put options are shown in Table 4.5 and plotted in Figure 4.5. When the realized spot price of the euro ends up at or above $1.1200/€ the put has no exercise value. The writer receives the price the buyer pays for the option, assumed to be $1,000, and so the writer gains $1,000 and the buyer loses $1,000. At realized spot rates below $1.1200/€ the put on the euro moves into-the-money. For example, at $1.1120/€ the option to sell €125,000 at $1.1200/€ has exercise value of

$$\$0.0080/€ \times €125,000 = \$1,000$$

This just offsets the amount paid for the option so the writer and the buyer break even. At realized spot rates below $1.1120/€ the option buyer begins to have an overall gain and the buyer an equal overall loss. The more the realized rate is below $1.1120/€ the more the put buyer gains and the writer loses.

26 We are ignoring transactions costs. Under this assumption the option market, like the futures market, is a zero-sum game.

Table 4.5 Payoffs on purchase of euro put option

Realized spot rate	Realized rate minus strike rate	Gain (+) or loss(−) on contract	Cost (−) of option	Overall gain (+) or loss (−)
1.1500	+$0.0300/€	—	−$1,000	−$1,000
1.1420	+$0.0240/€	—	−$1,000	−$1,000
1.1360	+$0.0160/€	—	−$1,000	−$1,000
1.1280	+$0.0080/€	—	−$1,000	−$1,000
1.1200	—	—	−$1,000	−$1,000
1.1120	−$0.0080/€	+$1,000	−$1,000	—
1.1040	−$0.0160/€	+$2,000	−$1,000	+$1,000
1.0960	−$0.0240/€	+$3,000	−$1,000	+$2,000
1.0880	−$0.0300/€	+$4,000	−$1,000	+$3,000

Notes
We assume the option is a put to sell €125,000 with a strike price, $X(\$/€)$, of $1.1200/€, and that the price paid for the option is $1,000. At $1.1200/€ and exchange rates above this at maturity the option has no exercise value. At realized spot rates below $1.1200/€ the put option expires in the money. At $1.1120/€, for example, the option has exercise value of €125,000 × $0.0080/€ = $1,000. This gain on the option is offset by the amount paid. Below $1.1280/€ there is an overall gain for the option buyer.

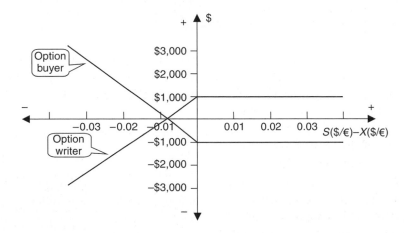

Figure 4.5 Payoff profiles of buyer and writer of euro put option for €125,000

Notes
The buyer of the €125,000 euro put at strike price $X(\$/€)$ is assumed to pay $1,000 to the option writer. If the realized spot exchange rate ends up at or above the strike rate, that is, $S(\$/€) - X(\$/€) \geq 0$, the put option ends up out of money, and the writer earns $1,000 and the buyer has a loss of $1,000. At spot rates below $X(\$/€)$ the option has exercise value. For example, at $S(\$/€) - X(\$/€) = -0.0080/€$ the put option has exercise value of $1,000. The buyer and writer then both break even. When $S(\$/€) - X(\$/€) < -\$0.0080/€$ the buyer makes an overall gain and the writer loses. The values plotted are shown in Table 4.5.

FORWARDS, FUTURES, AND OPTIONS COMPARED: A SUMMARY

While forwards, futures, and options can all be used to both reduce foreign exchange risk – that is, to hedge – and purposely to take foreign exchange risk – that is, to speculate – the differences between forwards, futures, and options make them suitable for different purposes. An explanation of which type of contract would be most appropriate in different circumstances must wait until we have dealt with many other matters, including further ways of hedging and

Table 4.6 *Forwards, futures, and options compared*

	Forward contracts	Currency futures[a]	Currency options[b]
Delivery discretion	None	None	Buyer's discretion. Seller must honor if buyer exercises.
Maturity date	Any date	Third Wednesday of March, June, Sept., or Dec.	Friday before third Wednesday of March, June, Sept., or Dec. on regular options. Last Friday of month on end-of-month options.
Maximum length	Several years	12 months	36 months
Contracted amount	Any value	£62,500, Can$100,000, etc.	£31,250, Can$50,000, etc.
Secondary market	Must offset with bank	Can sell via exchange	Can sell via exchange
Margin requirement	Informal, often line of credit or 5–10% on account	Formal fixed sum per contract, for example, $2,000. Daily marking to market.	No margin for buyer who pays for contract. Seller posts 130% of premium plus lump sum varying with intrinsic value.
Contract variety	Swap or outright form	Outright	Outright
Guarantor	None	Futures clearing corporation	Options clearing corporation.
Major users	Primarily hedgers	Primarily speculators	Hedgers and speculators

Notes
a Based on Chicago IMM Contracts.
b Based on Philadelphia Stock Exchange contracts which are on spot foreign exchange. IMM options are on futures, and contracted amounts equal those on futures contracts.

speculating, so that at this point we can do little more than list the differences between forwards, futures, and options. This is done in Table 4.6. The table notes the primary users of the markets as well as the institutional difference between forwards, futures, and options. The reasons the different markets have different primary users can be explained with the payoff profiles we have constructed, and are covered more fully in Chapter 13.

SUMMARY

1   Currency futures are bets on what will happen to the spot exchange rate, settled every day.
2   Futures are traded in specialized markets in standard contract sizes, such as €125,000. There are relatively few maturity dates.
3   Because of their low transaction costs and easy settlement, currency futures appeal to speculators.

4 The payoff profiles for futures are similar to those for forward contracts, except that futures outcomes are a little uncertain because of marking-to-market risk.

5 Marking-to-market risk is the result of uncertainty in the path of the future's contract value between purchase and sale and the volatility of interest rates.

6 Futures and forward exchange rates are linked by arbitrage.

7 Currency options give buyers the right or opportunity, but not the obligation, to buy or sell foreign exchange at a pre-agreed exchange rate, the strike exchange rate. Call options give the buyer the right to purchase the foreign currency at the strike exchange rate, and put options give the buyer the right to sell the foreign currency at the strike exchange rate.

8 American options allow the buyer to exercise at any time prior to the expiry of the option, while European options allow the buyer to exercise only on the expiry date of the option.

9 The value of an option depends on the extent to which it is in the money, that is, the extent to which the option has intrinsic value, and also on the volatility of the underlying exchange rate, the interest rate on the currency paid for the option, the forward exchange premium or discount and the length of time to expiration. The value of the option can also be considered to depend on the interest rate differential, which, like the forward premium or discount, reflects the expected path of the exchange rate.

10 An over-the-counter customized options market coexists with the exchange-based currency options. Over-the-counter options are written by banks.

11 Options allow their owners to gain from favorable outcomes, but to lose only the price paid for the option when outcomes are unfavorable. Buying an option is like buying insurance against an unfavorable change in the exchange rate.

12 Payoff profiles for options have sloped segments like those of forwards and futures, but also have horizontal segments. The horizontal segments represent the limit of any loss to the amount paid for an option contract.

REVIEW QUESTIONS

1 What is a currency futures contract?
2 How are futures contracts "cleared?"
3 What is the meaning of "margin" on a futures contract?
4 What is a meant by a margin's "maintenance level?"
5 What is "marking-to-market?"
6 What causes marking-to-market risk?
7 What is meant by the "strike" or "exercise" price of an option?
8 How do American options differ from European options?
9 What is a "put option" on a currency?
10 What is a "call option" on a currency?
11 What is an options "writer?"
12 What does it mean to be "in the money?"

13   What does it mean to be "out of the money?"

14   What is an "option premium?"

15   What is the "time value" on an option?

16   What factors influence options prices?

17   What is an "over-the-counter option?"

18   What goes on the axes of a payoff profile for a currency option?

ASSIGNMENT PROBLEMS

1   Why do you think that futures markets were developed when banks already offered forward contracts? What might currency futures offer which forward contracts do not?

2   To what extent do margin requirements on futures represent an opportunity cost?

3   How does the payoff profile of a futures sale of a currency compare to the profile of a purchase of the same currency?

4   Why is a futures contract similar to a string of bets on the exchange rate, settled every day?

5   Do you think that a limit on daily price movements for currency futures would make these contracts more or less risky or liquid? Would a limitation on price movement make the futures contracts difficult to sell during highly turbulent times?

6   How could arbitrage take place between forward exchange contracts and currency futures? Would this arbitrage be unprofitable only if the futures and forward rates were exactly the same?

7   Does the need to hold a margin make forward and futures deals less desirable than if there were no margin requirements? Does your answer depend on the interest paid on margins?

8   How does a currency option differ from a forward contract? How does an option differ from a currency future?

9   Suppose a bank sells a call option to a company making a takeover offer where the option is contingent on the offer being accepted. Suppose the bank reinsures the option on an options exchange by buying a call for the same amount of foreign currency. Consider the consequences of the following four outcomes or "states:"

a   The foreign currency increases in value, and the takeover offer is accepted.

b   The foreign currency increases in value, and the takeover offer is rejected.

c   The foreign currency decreases in value, and the takeover offer is accepted.

d   The foreign currency decreases in value, and the takeover offer is rejected.

Consider who gains and who loses in each state, and the source of gain or loss. Satisfy yourself why a bank that reinsures on an options exchange might charge less for writing the takeover-contingent option than the bank itself pays for the call option on the exchange. Does this example help explain why a bank-based over-the-counter market coexists with a formal options exchange market?

10   What is the payoff profile from buying *and* writing a call option? Ignore the transaction costs.

11   What type of option(s) would speculators buy if they thought the euro would increase more than the market believed?

12 What type of option would speculators write if they thought the Swiss franc would increase more than the market believed?

BIBLIOGRAPHY

Borensztein, Eduardo R. and Michael P. Cooley, "Options on Foreign Exchange and Exchange Rate Expectations," *IMF Staff Papers*, December 1987, pp. 643–80.

Einzig, Paul A., *The Dynamic Theory of Forward Exchange*, 2nd edn, Macmillan, London, 1967.

Garman, Mark B. and Steven W. Kohlhagen, "Foreign Currency Option Values," *Journal of International Money and Finance*, December 1983, No. 3, pp. 231–7.

Giddy, Ian H., "Foreign Exchange Options," *The Journal of Futures Markets*, Summer 1983, No. 2, pp. 143–66.

Grabbe, J. Orlin, "The Pricing of Call and Put Options on Foreign Exchange," *Journal of International Money and Finance*, December 1983, No. 3, pp. 239–53.

International Monetary Market of the Chicago Mercantile Exchange, *The Futures Market in Foreign Currencies*, Chicago Mercantile Exchange, Chicago, undated.

——, *Trading in International Currency Futures*, Chicago Mercantile Exchange, Chicago, undated.

——, Understanding Futures in Foreign Exchange, Chicago Mercantile Exchange, Chicago, undated.

Kolb, Robert W., *Futures, Options and Swaps*, 4th edn, Blackwell, Malden, MA, 2002.

Kubarych, Roger M., *Foreign Exchange Markets in the United States*, Federal Reserve Bank of New York, 1978.

Levy, Edmond, "Pricing European Average Rate Currency Options," *Journal of International Money and Finance*, October 1992, pp. 474–91.

Philadelphia Stock Exchange: *Understanding Foreign Currency Options: The Third Dimension to Foreign Exchange*, Philadelphia Stock Exchange, undated.

Smith, Clifford W. Jr., Charles W. Smithson, and D. Sykes Wilford, *Managing Financial Risk*, Harper and Row, New York, 1990.

APPENDIX A: PUT-CALL FORWARD PARITY FOR EUROPEAN OPTIONS

Put-call forward parity: a graphical view

When there are alternative financial arrangements that can achieve the same goal, arbitrage ensures the prices of the alternatives and/or returns on the alternatives are equal.[27] When it comes to options, equivalent outcomes can be achieved by buying a European call and selling a European put on the one hand, and a forward purchase of the foreign currency at the strike exchange rate on the other hand.[28] Similarly, selling a European call and buying a put is equivalent to selling the foreign currency forward at the same exchange rate. The equivalence of the payoffs for these situations is illustrated in Figures 4A.1 and 4A.2.

Figure 4A.1 shows the payoff profile for the buyer of a spot call option for €125,000 at a strike price of $X(\$/\euro)$ for different realized spot rates. At realized spot rates at maturity that are less than or equal to the strike price, that

---

27 The choice between alternatives can be thought of as one-way arbitrage. We ignore transaction costs.
28 The maturities of options and forwards must also be the same.

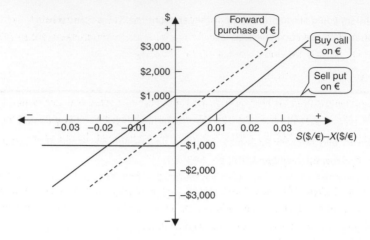

Figure 4A.1 *Equivalence of buying foreign currency European call and selling put, versus buying the foreign currency forward*

Notes
The payoff profiles are drawn for options and forwards for €125,000 with an assumed option contract price of $1,000. The call is seen to increase in value with the dollar price of the euro, $S(\$/€)$, versus the strike price, $X(\$/€)$, breaking even when the euro ends up in the money by $0.0080/€. The sale of the euro put provides $1,000 when the euro call ends up in the money, and loses money otherwise. The vertical sum of payoffs for the call purchase and put sale is the same as the payoffs for a forward purchase of the euro at the same price and for the same maturity date. Note, however, that this put-call forward parity applies only to European options.

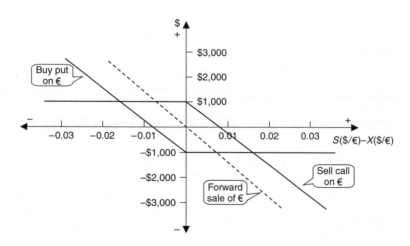

Figure 4A.2 *Equivalence of selling foreign currency European call and buying put, versus selling the foreign currency forward*

Notes
The payoff profiles are drawn for options and forwards for €125,000 with an assumed option contract price of $1,000. The put is seen to increase in value as the spot price of the euro falls below the strike price, breaking even when the option is in the money by $0.0080/€. The sale of the euro call provides $1,000 when the euro put is in-the-money, and loses money otherwise. The vertical sum of payoffs for the purchase of the euro put and sale of the euro call is the same as for the sale of the euro forward at the same price and for the same maturity date. Note, however, that this put-call forward parity applies only to European options.

is, $[S(\$/€) - X(\$/€)] \leq 0$, the buyer loses the price paid for the contract, assumed to be $1,000. At realized spot rates above the strike price the call moves into the money and the option has exercise value. For example, at $S(\$/€) - X(\$/€) = \$0.0080/€$ the exercise value of the option is

$$\$0.0080/€ \times €125,000 = \$1,000$$

This amount is the same as the price we assume was paid for the option so the buyer and writer do not gain or lose. At realized values of $S(\$/€) - X(\$/€)$ above $0.0080/€ the option buyer has a net gain and the writer an equal net loss.[29] For example, at $S(\$/€) - X(\$/€) = \$0.0160$ the exercise value of the option is

$$\$0.0160/€ \times €125,000 = \$2,000$$

After allowing for the $1,000 paid for the option by the buyer and received by the writer, the buyer gains $1,000 and the writer loses $1,000. Other payoffs to the option buyer are shown by the line that is horizontal to the left of the vertical axis and upward sloping to the right of the vertical axis.

Writing a put on €125,000 provides $1,000 to the option writer if the option ends up at or out of the money, that is, if the spot price of the euro is not below the exercise price. This is illustrated in Figure 4A.1 by the horizontal line to the right of the vertical axis at height $1,000. Sale of the put is a break-even proposition at a spot rate where the put is in the money by $0.0080/€, that is, $S(\$/€) - X(\$/€) = -\$0.0080/€$, and when the option ends up more in the money the put seller loses. This is illustrated in Figure 4A.1 by the upward-sloping line to the left of the vertical axis.

If the two option profiles, those for buying a call and writing a put, are combined, the result is an upward-sloping line through the origin as in Figure 4A.1. This is the same payoff profile as for a forward contract to buy €125,000 at $X(\$/€)$.[30] For example, when $S(\$/€) - X(\$/€) = \$0.0080/€$ a forward contract for €125,000 at $X(\$/€)$ gains $1,000, when $S(\$/€) - X(\$/€) = -0.0080/€$ the forward contract loses $1,000, and so on. Figure 4A.1 shows that the forward profile is identical to the combination of buying the euro call and selling the euro put at the same price and for the same maturity. We recall, however, that these results hold only for European options.

Factors influencing currency option prices

The equivalence of the option combination and forward contract described earlier can also be illustrated by considering the payoffs in Table 4A.1. The table can also be used to identify the factors influencing option premiums summarized in Table 4.3.

The top line of Table 4A.1 shows the payoffs from buying a call at price C. If the realized spot price of the euro, $S_T(\$/€)$, ends up less than or equal to the strike price, $X(\$/€)$, the euro call option has no exercise value. If, on the other hand, the spot rate is higher than the strike price, the option buyer's gain on each euro is equal to the excess of the spot rate over the strike rate, that is, $S_T(\$/€) - X(\$/€)$.

The second row of Table 4A.1 shows the payoffs from selling a put on the euro and being paid P. This has zero value if the realized spot rate is above the strike rate, and causes the writer a loss of the difference between the spot and strike rate, $S_T(\$/€) - X(\$/€)$, if the spot rate1 is below the strike rate. The combination of the call purchase and put sale are shown in the third line of the table. We see that for a net outlay of $(P - C)$ the option combination provides the difference between the spot rate and the forward rate, whether this is positive or negative.

The bottom part of Table 4A.1 considers the payoffs from what we later call a "synthetic" forward contract.[31] As we shall show, a forward purchase of the euro for dollars is equivalent to borrowing dollars, buying euros spot

29 We ignore any transactions costs.
30 Profiles for forward contracts are shown in Chapter 3.
31 This is covered in Chapter 12.

Table 4A.1 *European option put-call forward parity*

Position taken	$ cash flow/€ period 0	$ cash flow/€, $S_T(\$/€) \leq X(\$/€)$	Period T $S_T(\$/€) > X(\$/€)$
Option position			
Buy call	$-C$	0	$S_T(\$/€) - X(\$/€)$
Sell put	$+P$	$S_T(\$/€) - X(\$/€)$	0
Combination	$P - C$	$S_T(\$/€) - X(\$/€)$	$S_T(\$/€) - X(\$/€)$
"Forward" position			
Borrow dollar	$+X(\$/€)/(1 + r_\$)^T$	$-X(\$/€)$	$-X(\$/€)$
Invest euro	$-S_0(\$/€)/(1 + r_€)^T$	$+S_T(\$/€)$	$+S_T(\$/€)$
Combination	$X(\$/€)/(1 + r_\$)^T - S_0(\$/€)/(1 + r_€)^T$	$S_T(\$/€) - X(\$/€)$	$S_T(\$/€) - X(\$/€)$

with the borrowed dollars, and the investing the euros. If the borrowing and investing is for the same maturity as the forward contract, the payments and receipts on the borrowing-investment combination results in the same payments and receipts as with the forward exchange contract. Specifically, from the forward purchase of euros, euros are received at maturity and dollars are paid. The same occurs from borrowing dollars, buying euros with the dollars and investing the euros: euros are received at maturity and dollars are paid.[32]

Table 4A.1 shows a "synthetic" forward contract to buy a euro at exchange rate $X(\$/€)$. This is the number of dollars paid per euro received at maturity and is shown in the second column. There is a minus sign in front of $X(\$/€)$ because the cash flow in T years is a dollar payment for the euro. The realized value of each euro at maturity is $S_T(\$/€)$. This is the amount received and is hence positive. The amount of dollars paid for the euro and the realized value of the euro do not depend on whether $X(\$/€)$ is larger or smaller than $S_T(\$/€)$, as shown in the table.

In order to owe $X(\$/€)$ dollars T years in the future means borrowing $X(\$/€)/(1 + r_\$)^T$ dollars today: if you borrow this amount today you will owe $X(\$/€)$ in T years time.[33] The borrowed dollars are a cash inflow.

In order to receive $S_T(\$/€)$ dollars from investing in euros for T years it is necessary to invest today, $S_0(\$/€)/(1 + r_€)^{T}$.[34] Since this is invested, it is a cash outflow which is shown by the minus sign in Table 4A.1. The bottom half of the table shows the effect of the combination of borrowing dollars and investing in euros. We see that the cash flows in period zero and period T are the same as with the option position, buying the call and selling the put. Therefore, the option combination, buying a call and selling a put is equivalent to buying euros forward for the same maturity date.

The option combination has a net cost of $(P - C)$, as shown in the first column. The forward purchase of euros has a net cost of $[X(\$/€)/(1 + r_\$)^T] - [S_0(\$/€)/(1 + r_€)^T]$. These are equivalent as shown by comparing the option position and forward contract payoffs. Arbitrage therefore ensures:

$$P - C = \frac{X(\$/€)}{(1 + r_\$)^T} - \frac{S_0(\$/€)}{(1 + r_€)^T}$$

32 We ignore costs of transacting.
33 If we allow for borrowing-investment spreads, then $r_\$$ is the borrowing rate, not the investment rate.
34 If we allow for interest rate spreads, $r_€$ is the investment rate. $S_0(\$/€)$ is the current spot rate.

Alternatively:

$$C = P + \frac{S_0(\$/€)}{(1 + r_€)^T} - \frac{X(\$/€)}{(1 + r_\$)^T} \tag{4A.1}$$

The expression in (4A.1) is the put-call forward parity relationship. This can be used to describe the factors influencing option premiums.

We see from put-call forward parity relationship in equation (4A.1) that for a given value of P, the call on the euro is worth more the greater the extent that the euro is in the money, that is, the greater is $S_0(\$/€)$ relative to $X(\$/€)$. Also, the call premium is higher the larger is $r_\$$ relative to $r_€$. The intuition for the prediction about interest rates is that the higher are dollar versus euro interest rates, the more the market believes the euro will be increasing in value. Indeed, the higher dollar interest rates are the way the market is compensating for the expected decline in the dollar versus the euro.[35] The impact of time to maturity, T, is seen to be ambiguous.

The put-call forward parity relationship can also be used to explain the factors influencing the premiums on currency put options. To do this, we can rewrite equation (4A.1) as:

$$P = C + \frac{X(\$/€)}{(1 + r_\$)^T} - \frac{S_0(\$/€)}{(1 + r_€)^T} \tag{4A.2}$$

From equation (4A.2) we can see that for a given value of the call premium, C, the put is worth more, the greater is the strike price relative to the spot price of the euro, that is, the greater the put is in the money. The put premium also depends on the two interest rates. In this case, the lower the euro interest rate, $r_€$, relative to the dollar interest rate, $r_\$$, the less the put option is worth. The intuition here is that a low euro interest rate versus the dollar rate reflects a market expectation that the euro will appreciate. This lowers the value of an option to sell the euro: it is less likely to be exercised. As with the call option, the effect of time to maturity is ambiguous.

---

35 This is explained more fully in Chapter 8 which explains the interest rate parity theory.

Part II

The determination of exchange rates

An exchange rate can be thought of as the price of one country's money in terms of another country's money. With exchange rates being a price, it should come as little surprise that they are the result of supply and demand. As with traditional supply and demand, we can construct curves which describe how quantities supplied or demanded depend on the price, in this case the price of the currency. We can then determine the equilibrium price, or exchange rate. After the equilibrium is explained we can identify how different factors such as inflation, interest rates, economic growth, foreign debt, political uncertainty, and so on can cause exchange rates to change.

In this chapter we consider the system of flexible exchange rates, which is the predominant exchange rate system in operation today. We also limit ourselves to consideration of "flow" supplies of and demands for currencies – the amount demanded or supplied *per period of time* – rather than stocks of currencies, which are the amounts that exist at a *given point in time*. Later in the book, in Chapters 21, 22, and 23, we deal with fixed exchange rates, and with exchange rate theories involving stocks rather than flows of currencies. These later chapters can be inserted after Chapter 6 in courses that focus on international financial markets and the international financial environment. The two chapters that we do include in Part II contain the essential material on why exchange rates change that is needed in courses that focus on international financial management.

Chapter 5 begins by describing why the balance-of-payments account can be considered as a listing of the reasons for a currency being supplied and demanded. The chapter explains that all positive or credit items

listed in the account give rise to a demand for the country's currency, and all negative or debit items give rise to a supply of the currency. After explaining the basic principles of balance-of-payments accounting, each major entry in the account is examined to provide an understanding of what factors can make it increase or decrease, and thereby change the equilibrium exchange rate. The purpose of the chapter is to provide an understanding of the forces behind movements in currency values which is an essential input into the measurement and management of foreign exchange risk later in the book.

Chapter 5 includes a brief account of the different interpretations of the balance of payments with fixed and flexible exchange rates. It is shown that with flexible exchange rates, the balance of payments is achieved without any official buying or selling of currencies by governments, whereas with fixed exchange rates there are changes in official foreign exchange reserves. The chapter also shows how to interpret imbalances in the current- and capital-account components of the balance of payments. This is illustrated by comparing a country's balance-of-payments account to the income statement of a firm. The chapter concludes with a discussion of a country's net indebtedness, and a brief account of recent developments in the balance of payments and indebtedness of the United States.

Chapter 6 builds the supply-and-demand picture of exchange rates that is suggested by the balance-of-payments account. This involves deriving the supply curve for a country's currency from that country's demand curve for imports, and the demand curve for a country's currency from that country's supply curve of exports. Using the knowledge about balance-of-payment entries developed in Chapter 5, it is shown how inflation and other factors can shift the currency supply and demand curves, and therefore result in a change in exchange rates. It is also shown, however, that a currency supply curve can slope downward rather than upward as might normally be expected, and that if this happens, exchange rates may be unstable. The chapter explains that the conditions resulting in an unstable foreign exchange market are the same conditions that result in the so-called "J curve." (A J curve occurs, for example, when a depreciation makes a country's balance of trade worse, rather than better as would normally be expected.)

Chapter 5

The balance of payments

Money is just something to make bookkeeping convenient.

H.L. Hunt

INFLUENCES ON CURRENCY SUPPLY AND DEMAND

The price of a country's currency depends on the quantity supplied relative to the quantity demanded, at least when exchange rates are determined in a free, unregulated market.[1] It follows that if we know the factors influencing the supply of and demand for a currency, we also know what factors influence exchange rates. Any factor increasing the demand for the currency will, *ceteris paribus*, increase the foreign exchange value of the currency, that is, cause the currency to **appreciate**. Similarly, any factor increasing the supply of the currency will, *ceteris paribus*, reduce its foreign exchange value, that is, cause the currency to **depreciate**.[2] Clearly then, there is considerable interest in maintaining a record of the factors affecting the supply of and demand for a country's currency. That record is maintained in the balance-of-payments account. Indeed, we can think of the balance-of-payments account as an itemization of the reasons for demand for and supply of a currency.

The motivation for publishing the balance-of-payments account is not simply a desire to maintain a record of the reasons for a currency being supplied or demanded. Rather, the account is primarily to report the country's international performance in trading with other nations, and to maintain a record of capital flowing into and out of the country. However, reporting on a country's international trading performance and capital flows involves measurement of all the reasons why a currency is supplied and demanded. This is what makes the balance-of-payments account such a handy way of thinking about exchange rates. This chapter shows why the balance-of-payments account can be thought of as a list of items behind the supply of and demand for a currency. We begin by examining the principles guiding the structure of the balance-of-payments account and the interpretation of the items that are included. We then consider the different ways that balance can be achieved between quantities supplied and quantities demanded. As we shall see, the balance-of-payments account is designed to always balance, but the price at which balance is achieved depends on the magnitudes of items in the account.

1 When exchange rates are fixed, they are still determined by supply and demand, but there is an official supply or demand that is adjusted to keep rates from changing. Fixed exchange rates are discussed briefly later in this chapter, and in greater detail in Chapter 22.
2 When an exchange rate is fixed at a lower value, the currency is said to have been **devalued**. When an exchange rate is fixed at a higher value, the currency is said to have been **revalued**. These terms replace "depreciate" and "appreciate," which are the terms used with flexible rates.

PRINCIPLES OF BALANCE-OF-PAYMENTS ACCOUNTING

The guiding principles of balance-of-payments accounting come from the purpose of the account, namely to record the flow of payments between the residents of a country and the rest of the world during a given time period. The fact that the balance of payments records the flow of payments makes the account dimensionally the same as the national-income account – so many dollars per year or per calendar quarter. Indeed, the part of the balance-of-payments account that records the values of exports and imports also appears in the national-income account.

Balance-of-payments accounting uses the system of **double-entry bookkeeping**, which means that every debit or credit in the account is also represented as a credit or debit somewhere else. To see how this works we can take a couple of examples.

Suppose that an American corporation sells $2 million worth of US-manufactured jeans to Britain, and that the British buyer pays from a US dollar account that is kept in a US bank. We will then have the following double entry in the US balance of payments:

	(credits +; debits −) Millions dollars
Export (of jeans)	+2
Foreign assets in the US: US bank liabilities	−2

We can think of the export of the American jeans as resulting in a demand for US dollars, and the payments with dollars at the US bank as resulting in a supply of dollars. The payment reduces the liability of the US bank, which is an asset of the British jeans buyer. We see that the balance-of-payments account shows both the flow of jeans and the flow of payments, and the entries sum to zero.

As a second example, suppose that an American corporation purchases $5 million worth of denim cloth from a British manufacturer, and that the British company puts the $5 million it receives into a bank account in the United States. We then have the double entry in the US account:

	(credits +; debits−) Millions dollars
Imports (of cloth)	−5
Foreign assets in the US: US bank liabilities	+5

We can think of the US import of cloth as resulting in a supply of US dollars, and the deposit of money by the British company as resulting in a demand for dollars. The deposit of money increases US bank liabilities and the assets of the British company. In a similar way, every entry in the balance of payments appears twice.

The balance-of-payments account records *all* transactions that affect the supply of or demand for a currency in the foreign exchange markets. There is just as much demand for US dollars when non-Americans buy US jeans as there is when they buy US stocks, bonds, real estate, bank balances, or operating businesses, and all of these transactions must be recorded. Since all sources of potential demand for dollars by foreigners or supply of dollars to foreigners are included, there are many types of balance-of-payments account entries. We need a rule for determining which entries are credits and which entries are debits. The rule is that any international transaction that gives rise to a demand for US dollars in the foreign exchange market is recorded as a credit in the US balance of payments, and the entry takes a positive sign. Any transaction that gives rise to a supply of dollars is recorded as a debit, and the entry takes a negative sign. A more precise way of expressing this rule is with the following definition:

Credit transactions represent demands for US dollars, and result from purchases by foreigners of goods, services, goodwill, financial and real assets, gold, or foreign exchange from US residents. Credits are recorded with a plus sign. Debit transactions represent supplies of US dollars, and result from purchases by US residents of goods, services, goodwill, financial, and real assets, gold, or foreign exchange from foreigners. Debits are recorded with a minus sign.[3]

The full meaning of our definition will become clear as we study the US balance of payments in Table 5.1. Let us consider each item and the factors that influence them.

BALANCE-OF-PAYMENTS ENTRIES AND THE FACTORS THAT INFLUENCE THEM

Exports of goods, services, and income receipts

In order for overseas buyers to pay for US goods and services which are invoiced in dollars, the overseas buyers must purchase dollars. In the rarer event that US exports of goods and services are invoiced in foreign currency, it is the American exporter that will purchase dollars when selling the foreign currency it receives. In either case US exports give rise to a demand for US dollars in the foreign exchange market, and are recorded with a plus sign. (If the foreign buyer of a US good or service pays with foreign currency which the US exporter chooses to hold rather than sell for US dollars, the balance-of-payments account records the value of the export, and an increase in US assets abroad. In this case the US export is considered, as always, to give rise to a demand for US dollars, and the increase in US assets abroad is considered to give rise to an equal increase in the supply of US dollars.)

US exports of goods, which are sometimes referred to as **merchandise exports**, include wheat and other agricultural commodities, aircraft, computers, automobiles, and so on. The factors affecting these exports, and hence the demand for US dollars, include:

1   *The foreign exchange value of the US dollar*   For a particular level of domestic and foreign prices of internationally traded goods, the higher the foreign exchange value of the dollar, the higher are US export prices facing foreigners, and the lower is the quantity of US exports. Normally, we single out the exchange rate as the principal factor of interest and put this on the vertical axis of a supply and demand figure. Then, all other factors listed below *shift* the currency demand curve. Changes in the exchange rate cause movements *along* the demand curve.

2   *US prices versus the prices of foreign competitors*   If inflation in the United States exceeds inflation elsewhere then, *ceteris paribus*, US goods become less competitive, and the quantity of US exports will decline. US inflation therefore tends to reduce the demand for US dollars at each given exchange rate.[4] This is a leftward shift in the demand curve for dollars.

3   *Worldwide prices of products that the US exports*   Changes in the worldwide prices of what the US exports shift the demand curve for dollars. Higher world prices shift the demand curve to the right, and vice versa. This is a different effect to that in point 2 mentioned earlier. Here, we refer to **terms of trade** effects; an increase in US export prices versus US import prices – where imports are *different* goods than exports – is an improvement in the US terms

---

3   The item with the least obvious meaning in this definition is "goodwill." As we shall explain later, goodwill consists of gifts and foreign aid. In keeping with the double-entry bookkeeping system, the balance-of-payments account assumes gifts and aid buy goodwill for the donor.

4   The *value* of exports could increase if the reduced *quantity* of exports comes as a result of higher prices. As we shall show in chapter 6, values increase from higher prices when demand is inelastic so that the quantity of exports falls less than export prices increase. However, profit maximizing exporters do not choose an inelastic part of the demand curve.

Table 5.1 *Summary format of the US balance of payments, 3rd quarter, 2002*

Line# (credits, +; debits, −)			Billions of US dollars
1	Exports of goods, services, and income receipts		+313
2	Goods	+176	
3	Services, including travel, royalties, and license fees	+74	
4	Income receipts on US assets abroad	+63	
5	Imports of goods, services, and income payments		−427
6	Goods	−299	
7	Services, including travel, royalties, and license fees	−61	
8	Income payments on foreign assets in United Status	−67	
9	Unilateral transfers, net, increase/financial outflow (−)		−13
10	US-owned assets abroad, net		+24
11	US official reserve assets, incl. gold reserves at IMF, net	−1	
12	US Govt. assets other than official reserves, net	0	
13	US private assets, net	+25	
14	Direct investment	−27	
15	Foreign securities	+18	
16	US claims on foreigners reported by non-banks	−12	
17	US claims reported by US banks	+46	
18	Foreign owned assets in the US net, increase/financial inflow (+)		+149
19	Foreign official assets in US	+9	
20	Other foreign assets in US	+139	
21	Direct investment	+11	
22	US Treasury securities	+55	
23	US securities other than Treasury securities	+47	
24	US currency	+2	
25	US liabilities reported by non-banks	+16	
26	US liabilities reported by US banks	+8	
27	Statistical discrepancy (sum of above, sign reversed)		−46
	Memoranda:		
28	Balance on goods (lines 2+6)		−123
29	Balance on services (lines 3+7)		+12
30	Balance on goods and services (lines 28+29)		−111
31	Balance on investment income (lines 4+8)		−3
32	Unilateral current transfers (net) (line 9)		−13
33	Balance on current account (lines 1+5+9, or lines 30, 31, and 32)		−127

Source: US Department of Commerce, *Survey of Current Business,* December 2002.

of trade. On the other hand, in point 2 we refer to prices of US goods versus *competitors'* goods abroad, that is, prices of the same goods supplied by Americans or by foreigners.

4   *Foreign incomes*   When foreign buyers experience an increase in their real incomes, the result is an improvement in the export market for American raw materials and manufactured goods. *Ceteris paribus*, this increases US exports, and therefore also increases the demand for dollars.

5   *Foreign import duties and quotas*   Higher foreign import tariffs – taxes on imported goods – and lower foreign import **quotas** – the quantity of imports permitted into a country during a period of time – as well as higher foreign **nontariff trade barriers** such as quality requirements and red tape, reduce US exports.

Alongside exports of goods are exports of services. These service exports are sometimes called **invisibles**. US service exports include spending by foreign tourists in the United States. Service exports also include overseas earnings of US banks and insurance companies, engineering, consulting, and accounting firms; overseas earnings of US holders of patents; overseas earnings of royalties on books, music, and movies; overseas earnings of US airlines and shipping, courier, and freight services; and similar items. These service exports give rise to a demand for US dollars when the foreign tourists buy US currency, when the US banks repatriate their earnings, and so on. US earnings on these "performed service" exports respond to the same factors as affect exports of goods – exchange rates, US prices versus foreign competitors' prices, worldwide prices of US exports, incomes abroad, foreign import tariffs and quotas, and so on.

The final category covered by "exports of goods, services, and income receipts," namely "income receipts," is the earnings US residents receive from past investments made abroad. These earnings can come in the form of interest on bills and bonds, dividends on stocks, rent on property, and profits of businesses. Sometimes these various sources of

investment income are, for convenience, simply referred to as **debt-service exports**. These export earnings are derived from past foreign investments and therefore depend principally on the amount Americans have invested abroad in the past. Debt-service exports also depend on the rates of interest and sizes of dividends, rents, and profits earned on these past foreign investments. Unlike the situation with goods and services exports, the exchange rate plays only a minor role in the income received from abroad. Exchange rate changes affect only the **translated value** of foreign currency denominated income.

Imports of goods, services, and income payments

US imports of goods include such items as oil, automobiles, consumer electronics, computers, clothing, wine, coffee, and so on. US imports respond to the same factors that affect exports, the direction of response being reversed. *Ceteris paribus*, the quantity of US imports of goods increases when the US dollar is worth more in the foreign exchange markets: a more valuable dollar makes imports cheaper. US imports are also higher when US prices are higher relative to competitors' prices of the same goods, when world prices of US imports increase, when US tariffs are reduced, and when US import quotas are increased.[5] US imports of performed services (such as American tourists' spending abroad, Americans' use of the services of foreign banks and consulting firms, Americans' use of foreign patents, airlines, and shipping, and purchases of foreign movies and books) also depend on exchange rates, relative prices, US incomes, and US import restrictions. In the case of income payments, which are payments by Americans of

---

5 As with the effects of exchange rates and inflation on exports, we should really distinguish between the *quantity* and *value* of imports. For example, an appreciation of the US dollar could reduce the *value* of US imports even if it increases the *quantity* of US imports. This occurs if the demand for imports is inelastic. We discuss this possibility in Chapter 6.

interest, dividends, profit and rent abroad, the principal relevant factor is past foreign investment in the United States; US income payments are higher the higher have been foreign investments in US government bonds, corporate bonds, stocks, and past foreign investments in US real estate and operating businesses. Income imports also depend on the rates of return foreigners earn on their investments in the United States.

Until 1986, the United States earned more on its investments abroad than foreigners earned on US investments. That is, US investment income from abroad – income receipts – exceeded US investment income paid abroad – income payments. This was because until 1986, the value of US investments abroad exceeded the value of foreign investments in the United States. Because of considerable borrowing by the US government from overseas lenders, and because of considerable foreign private investment in the United States, in 1986 the country went from being a net creditor nation to a net debtor nation. Indeed, in a matter of only a few years after 1986, the United States became the largest debtor nation. This has meant that the US has become a net payer of investment income abroad.

Table 5.1 shows that the United States ran a large goods deficit in the third quarter of 2002. US exports of goods amounted to $176 billion during the quarter, while US goods imports amounted to $299 billion. This is a **balance-of-trade deficit** during the quarter of $123 billion. This is shown on line 28 of Table 5.1.

On the service side, US exports of performed services were $13 billion ($74 billion−$61 billion) larger than US imports. However, there is a $4 billion ($67 billion−$63 billion) deficit on income. This is a result of US indebtedness.[6] Services, including debt service, therefore had a $9 billion surplus, offsetting a little the balance-of-trade deficit.

Unilateral transfers (net)

Unilateral transfers include such items as foreign aid, nonmilitary economic development grants, and private gifts or donations. These items are called *unilateral* transfers because, unlike the case of other items in the balance of payments, where the item being traded goes in one direction and the payment goes in the other direction, in the case of gifts and aid there is a flow in only one direction, the direction of payment. However, unilateral transfers must be included somewhere in the account because the receipt of a gift or of foreign aid gives rise to a demand for the country's currency in the same way as the export of goods and services.[7] Similarly, gifts or aid to foreigners give rise to a supply of the country's currency in the same way as the import of goods and services. What the balance-of-payments accountant therefore does is include unilateral transfers as if the donor were buying goodwill from the beneficiary. That is, the granting of aid is considered as a purchase or import of goodwill, a debit entry under unilateral transfers, and the receipt of aid is considered a sale or export of goodwill, a credit entry. By including transfers as a trade in goodwill, we preserve double-entry bookkeeping, since the payment for or receipt from the transfer, which will appear elsewhere in the account, is matched by the transfer entry itself.

The value of unilateral transfers depends both on a country's own generosity and on the generosity of its friends. It also depends on the number of expatriates who send money to relatives or receive money from relatives. Poorer countries, from which large numbers leave for job opportunities elsewhere, receive net earnings on unilateral transfers. India and Pakistan, for example, receive net inflows on transfers. Richer countries – such as the United States, Canada, Britain, and Australia – which have foreign

---

6 Indebtedness is difficult to measure accurately because US overseas investments are generally older than foreign investments in the US, and may therefore be undervalued.

7 If the gift or aid must be spent in the donor country, so that the money never leaves the country, the gift or aid appears elsewhere in the account. In this case it is as if the donor country had an export that automatically matched the transfer.

aid programs and many recent immigrants, generally have net outflows on transfers.

When we compute the subtotal up to and including unilateral transfers we obtain the **balance of payments on current account**. That is, the balance of payments on current account consists of exports and imports of goods, services, and income, plus net unilateral transfers: lines 1, 5, and 9 in Table 5.1. The current account is in deficit by $127 billion, as shown on line 33. The balance of payments on current account shows how much the country will have to borrow or **divest** – sell off its past investments – to finance the current-account deficit, or how much the country must lend or invest if it has a current account surplus. Borrowing or divesting is necessary if a country has a deficit in its current account, because it is necessary to pay for the extent to which its imports exceed its exports or to which it gives away more than it earns or receives from abroad. Similarly, lending or investing must occur if the country has a current-account surplus, since what the country earns and does not spend or give away is not destroyed, but is loaned or invested in other countries. In summary:

> The current account of the balance of payments is the result of the export and import of goods, services, income and goodwill (or unilateral transfers). A deficit in the current account must be financed by borrowing from abroad or by divestment of foreign assets, while a surplus must be loaned abroad or invested in foreign assets.

A country can finance a current-account deficit by selling to foreigners the country's bills, bonds, stocks, real estate, or operating businesses. A country can also finance its current account deficit by selling off its previous investments in foreign bills, bonds, stocks, real estate, and operating businesses, that is, via divestment. Before we examine how the US financed its $127 billion current-account deficit in Table 5.1, we should recall that there is nothing to distinguish the demand for a country's currency when foreigners buy its financial

and real assets from when foreigners buy its goods and services; a check or draft for the country's currency must be purchased whatever is being bought. Similarly, a country's currency is supplied in the same way whether residents of a country are buying foreign financial or real assets or are importing goods and services. Of course, different factors influence the purchase and sale of financial and real assets than influence the purchase and sale of goods and services. As we shall see, there are different long-run implications of trade in assets than of trade in goods and services; today's trade in stocks, bonds, real estate, and businesses affects *future* flows of dividends, interest, rents, and profits.

US-owned assets abroad (net)

There are several components to this item which can be considered separately. We see from Table 5.1, line 10, that collectively, the items under this heading satisfied $24 billion of the US borrowing requirement: the US reduced by $24 billion its foreign assets, meaning a divestment and associated net additional demand for $24 billion US dollars.

The first subcomponent of US assets abroad is **US official reserve assets**. Official reserves are liquid assets held by the US Federal Reserve and the Department of the Treasury; the Federal Reserve Bank of New York buys and sells foreign exchange on behalf of the Federal Reserve System and the US Treasury. These liquid assets include gold, foreign currency in foreign banks, and balances at the International Monetary Fund (IMF).[8] We see in line 11 of Table 5.1 that there is an entry of $1 billion for changes in official reserves. The negative sign means a supply of US dollars because the US Federal Reserve or Treasury bought gold, foreign currency, or balances held at the IMF. Whatever is bought, the US is accumulating foreign assets and is supplying US dollars: recall that US dollar supply is a debit and hence negative item in the account. The Federal

8 The IMF is an organization in which many countries hold funds for financing balance-of-payments deficits. We discuss this institution in Chapter 22.

Reserve sells dollars when it is trying to prevent an appreciation of the dollar vis-à-vis other currencies: adding to the supply of dollars tends to push the price of the dollar down. On the other hand, the US government buys dollars – reducing foreign assets – when it wishes to prop up the dollar in the foreign exchange market. The main influence on the size of the official reserve entry is the extent to which the US Government wishes to influence exchange rates. The harder the Government is trying to support the dollar, the larger is the positive entry.

The next item under the heading US assets abroad (net) is "U.S. government assets other than official reserves," line 12 of Table 5.1. This item shows new loans and loan repayments involving the US Government. When the US Government makes a foreign loan or repays a loan, this item shows a negative entry because there is a supply of dollars. When the US Government borrows from foreign governments, there is a positive entry and a demand for dollars. In the third quarter of 2003, the net demand for dollars under this heading is approximately zero, indicating the US Government made no new net loans during this period. As with the US official reserve assets entry, a major factor influencing the size of this item is US Government efforts to influence the foreign exchange value of the US dollar.

After the two entries reflecting US Government activity are four items which together constitute "U.S. private assets abroad." These entries show the extent to which US private firms and individuals have made investments in foreign companies, bills, bonds, stocks, real estate, and so on, or have divested themselves of such investments by selling assets purchased in the past.

The first subcategory of US private assets is **direct investment**. By definition, direct investment by Americans occurs when US ownership of a foreign operating business is sufficiently extensive to give Americans a measure of control. Government statisticians have chosen the level of 10 percent or more ownership of a company's voting shares to constitute control. New flows of investment during the measurement period, where 10 or more percent ownership has been reached, are considered

direct investment (or divestment when funds are brought home). A typical example of direct investment would be the building of a factory in a foreign country by a US multinational corporation. Line 14 of Table 5.1 shows a supply of $27 billion of US currency to the foreign exchange market due to US direct investment during the period. This supply of US dollars adds to the supply of dollars from the deficit in the current account and the dollar sales of the US Government. This means that further down the balance-of-payments account there must be entries showing the US borrowing and/or divestment that is financing the current-account deficit, the US Government sales of dollars, and the US direct investment abroad.

Direct investment depends on the after-tax, expected return from investing in plant and equipment, real estate, and so on in foreign countries relative to the opportunity cost of shareholder capital. The expected return must be sufficient to compensate for the unavoidable risk of the direct investment.[9] Expected after-tax returns abroad may be high if foreign real wage rates are low, if raw materials are cheap, if corporate taxes are low, if borrowing rates are low – perhaps because of subsidized loans – and so on. The risks of foreign direct investment include both business and political risks.

The next private investment item is titled "foreign securities." This shows the supply of or demand for US dollars from the purchase or sale by US residents of foreign stocks and bonds.[10] When US residents add to their holdings of these assets, there is a supply of dollars and a negative entry in the balance-of-payments account: it is a capital outflow from the United States. When US residents

9 Because the opportunity cost of capital includes the chance of investing at home rather than abroad, direct investment can also be considered to depend on expected returns abroad versus expected returns at home. The details of factors affecting direct investment are described in Chapters 16 and 17.
10 Of course, when a US resident holds 10 percent or more of the voting stock of a foreign company, the flow of US dollars for the foreign stock appears as a direct investment.

sell these assets and repatriate the proceeds, there is a demand for dollars and a positive entry. Line 15 shows that during the third quarter of 2003 US residents divested themselves, that is, sold, $18 billion of foreign stocks and bonds. This is a demand of dollars, partially offsetting the supply of dollars from direct investment, US Government dollar sales, and the deficit in the current account.

The amount of foreign security investment depends on the difference in expected returns between foreign stocks and bonds and domestic stocks and bonds, and on relative risks of investments at home versus abroad. The expected return on a foreign security depends on the expected dividend on the stock or interest on the bill or bond, the expected change in the security's local currency market value, and the expected change in the exchange rate. Because funds flow between countries until the risk-adjusted expected returns in different locations are equal, the advantage that exists for investing in a particular location will be more obvious from statistics in the balance-of-payments account on the amounts flowing, than from statistics on yields.[11] In addition to the difference between expected returns abroad and expected returns at home, US residents' purchases of foreign securities depend on diversification benefits from foreign investment. We shall discuss these benefits in Chapter 15.

The next two items, shown in lines 16 and 17, give the supply of and demand for US dollars due to investments by businesses and banks. Line 16 gives lending by non-bank firms, including credits extended by US firms in commercial transactions, where the receivables on the credits are assets of US firms. A negative entry means an increase in outstanding loans and credits during the reporting period, and a consequent supply of dollars. A positive entry means a reduction in outstanding loans and credits, and a demand for dollars from repayment. US firms extended $12 billion of credits and loans during the reporting period.

Line 17 shows the change in the amount loaned to foreign borrowers by US banks. The large positive entry for this item tells us that US banks reduced their lending abroad during the reporting period. This can occur because US banks' dollar claims on their own offices abroad decline, and because of loan repayments by foreign borrowers. A reduction of US bank claims on their own offices abroad occurs when the banks find it more profitable to make dollar loans in the US than to make dollar loans in the **Eurodollar market**.[12] The main reason why banks find it more profitable to lend in the US than abroad is higher interest rates in the US than in the Eurodollar market. Even a small interest-rate advantage can move a vast amount of money between nations. The speed with which the money can move is so rapid that funds moved between banks and bank offices has been called **hot money**. This money needs only an internal bank reallocation, or an order sent via the SWIFT network if the money is moving between unrelated banks. The effect on exchange rates can be as fast as the money itself can move, which in turn is as fast as a satellite signal. For this reason, changes in interest rates can cause very large, sudden changes in exchange rates.

Foreign owned assets in the United States (net)

The next set of items in the balance of payments, those on lines 18 to 26, are comparable to those described earlier and shown in lines 10 to 17, but give the supply of and demand for US dollars due to borrowing, lending, investment, and divestment by foreigners rather than US residents. The entry "foreign official assets in U.S." on line 19 gives the

11 This point is made, for example, by Fischer Black in "The Ins and Outs of Foreign Investment," *Financial Analysts Journal*, May–June 1978, pp. 1–7.

12 Eurodollars are US-dollar-denominated bank deposits in banks located outside the United States. The US-dollar loans that appear in line 17 are made out of Eurodollar deposits. The reasons for the emergence of the Eurodollar market are given in Chapter 22.

increase or decrease in US dollar assets held by foreign governments in the Unites States. The positive entry shows that there was a demand for US dollars due to dollar buying by foreign governments. This occurs when there are efforts by foreign governments to support the US dollar or depreciate their own currency. The principal factor determining the size of this item is the extent to which foreign governments are trying to influence exchange rates.

When exchange rates are fixed, central banks buy/sell whatever amount of dollars is necessary to prevent the dollar from falling/rising. When exchange rates are flexible, or floating, governments do not buy or sell foreign currencies, instead leaving exchange rates to be determined by the market forces of supply and demand. What then do we make of the positive entry on line 19? The answer is that exchange rates were not completely flexible in 2003. Rather, there was an effort to support the US dollar even though officially exchange rates were flexible, a so-called **dirty float**. If exchange rates had been truly flexible, there would have been no buying or selling of US dollars by foreign governments, and line 19 would have been zero.

Line 21 shows the amount of direct investment made by foreigners in the United States. As with US direct investment abroad, this is determined by the after-tax expected rate of return on the direct investment relative to the shareholders' opportunity cost of capital, and the amount of unavoidable risk on the investment. The expected rate of return is a function of market opportunities in the United States, including the possibility of facing quotas and other forms of protectionism if the direct investment is not made. We find a demand for US dollars from direct investment by foreigners in the United States during the reporting period. This helps finance the current account deficit, but means profit repatriation within the income payments component of *future* US current accounts.

Line 22 shows substantial purchases of US Treasury securities by overseas investors; the entry is positive when foreigners increase their holdings of

US Treasury securities, and negative when they reduce them. Similarly, in line 23 we see a substantial increase in foreign holdings of US stocks and bonds during the reporting period, augmenting the demand for dollars by foreign governments and for direct investment. The principal factors influencing foreign investment in US Treasury securities, as well as stocks, bonds, and other securities, are US versus foreign yields, and expected future changes in exchange rates. *Ceteris paribus*, the higher are US versus foreign yields, and the more the dollar is expected to increase in value, the greater is the demand for US securities and dollars. Expected changes in exchange rates tend to be reflected in forward exchange premiums or discounts. Therefore, we can also think of the demand for US securities in lines 22 and 23 as depending on yield advantages, plus the forward premium or discount on the US dollar. At times, the need to issue Treasury bills and bonds to finance the US fiscal deficit helps to fuel the demand for dollars: paradoxically, large US fiscal deficits contribute to a strong US dollar by increased dollar demand by foreigners. Line 24 shows foreign demand for US currency, specifically Federal Reserve notes people carry in their wallets. The wide acceptability of dollars around the world contributes to this.

Line 25 shows the non-bank trade credits (deferred payment when buying goods) granted by foreign firms to US firms. These are liabilities of the firms granted the credits. As well as the $16 billion of US dollar demand for this reason, line 26 shows a further $8 billion demand for dollars due to US bank liabilities. US bank liabilities consist of deposits by foreigners in US banks. This could have occurred because of an expected appreciation of the US dollar, or because foreign investors preferred to shift their dollars into US bank accounts from US securities. However, this does not seem likely in light of the positive entry in line 23.

Statistical discrepancy

Until 1976 the **statistical discrepancy** was called "errors and omissions," which gives a better idea of

EXHIBIT 5.1 EXTRATERRESTRIAL TRADE OR THE ETHER? DATA DIFFICULTIES IN THE BALANCE OF PAYMENTS

While we remain Earthbound, the balances of payments of all the countries in the world should themselves balance. That is, surpluses in some countries should exactly match deficits in others, with the sum of positive and negative balances being zero. So much for the theory. As the following excerpt from the *Review* of the Federal Reserve Bank of St. Louis explains, in practice, balance-of-payments accounting does not quite fit the theory. It turns out that the underreporting of service exports is probably the principal culprit.

> In late 1987, the U.S. Commerce Department announced that in its monthly trade reports, exports to Canada would henceforth use Canadian customs data on imports from the United States rather than U.S. export data. The rationale for this procedure is the documented inaccuracy since 1970 of U.S. customs data for exports to Canada. The discrepancies between the U.S. and Canadian data have become substantial both in absolute terms – nearly $11 billion in 1986 – and in terms of their effect on the U.S. trade balance – a 42 percent reduction in the 1986 U.S. trade deficit with Canada. While these errors are corrected in the annual reconciliation of U.S.-Canadian trade data, their persistence raises a broader question: Are U.S. exports to other countries similarly understated?
>
> This possibility raises some important political and economic issues. In recent years, the trade balance has been the focus of much economic policy debate, rivaling or complementing such traditional domestic issues as employment, inflation and growth. In this context, isolating large understatements in U.S. merchandise export data

is clearly a topic with important policy implications. . . . Any exported good from the country of origin is an imported good for the country of destination. As a consequence, if the data are complete and accurate, the world can have neither a trade deficit nor surplus; it must have a balance. Yet, the world trade data do not yield a balance on current account.

Throughout the first half of the 1980s, world merchandise trade was in "surplus," substantially so in 1980 and 1981, and negligibly so since then. More broadly throughout the 1980s, the current account – the sum of merchandise and service trade minus transfers – has been in substantial deficit with no clear trend toward balance. The implication of these statistical discrepancies is that substantial export income is not being reported; that is, exports of services are understated.

The world current account balance discrepancy can be accounted for by a negative service account balance, with unreported shipping income, unreported direct investment income and unreported portfolio investment income the largest contributors. Shipping income is irrelevant for the United States; the IMF working party found it attributable to "several economies with large maritime interests (notably those of Greece, Hong Kong and Eastern Europe)." The other two discrepancy items, direct and portfolio investment income, were found to be attributable in large part to U.S. investors' unreported or misreported foreign income.

Source: Mack Ott, "Have U.S. Exports been Larger than Reported?," *Review*, Federal Reserve Bank of St. Louis, September/October 1988, pp. 3–23.

its meaning. A discrepancy can exist because of errors in estimating many of the items in Table 5.1. Errors might appear because of differences between the time that current-account entries are made and

the time that the associated payments appear elsewhere in the balance-of-payments account. It is customary for the US Department of Commerce and similar foreign agencies to collect data on exports and imports of goods and services from customs agents; the data on these current account items are reported as the goods cross the border or as the services are rendered. The payments for these goods or services, which are financial flows, appear only afterward, possibly in a subsequent report of the balance-of-payments statistics. The trade credits that allow payments to occur after goods or services are delivered should be in the accounts – in line 16 or line 25 – but they are often missed.

Another reason for errors is that many entries are estimates. For example, data on travel expenditures are estimated from questionnaire surveys of a limited number of travelers. The average expenditure discovered in a survey is multiplied by the number of travelers. A further reason for measurement error is that illegal transactions, which affect foreign exchange supply and demand despite their illegality, do not explicitly enter the accounts. We can therefore have flows of funds without any associated measured flows of goods or services. As Exhibit 5.1 explains, error also arises from unreported or misreported income on investment and shipping, although the latter is not a problem in the US account. Finally, we can have unreported flows of capital.

An obvious question is how the balance-of-payments accountant knows the size of the statistical discrepancy, since by definition, it is due to missing or inaccurate data. The answer is that due to the use of double-entry accounting principles, all the entries in the account must add to zero (we saw this earlier in this chapter where we explained that every positive entry is matched by a negative entry). If the balance-of-payments entries do not sum to zero, errors must have been made equal to the extent to which the sum of entries differs from zero. If you check by adding the numbers in the far-right column of Table 5.1 you will see they add to +$46 billion. Therefore a supply of $46 billion must have been missed and is included to reconcile the account.

The fact that the balance of payments must sum to zero means that it is subtotals such as the balance on current account that are of interest. Furthermore, as we shall explain later, the fact that the overall balance is zero can provide useful insights

into, for example, *why* a country has a current-account deficit.

IMPLICATIONS OF THE BALANCE-OF-PAYMENTS ACCOUNTING IDENTITY

Interpreting the accounts with fixed and flexible rates

We can offer an interesting explanation of why a country can run a current-account deficit if we consider the following accounting identity:

$$B_c + \Delta R + B_k + \varepsilon \equiv 0 \qquad (5.1)$$

Here B_c is the balance of payments on current account, which is the sum of lines 1, 5, and 9 in Table 5.1. The next term ΔR is the change in official reserves of both the United States and foreign governments, that is, the sum of lines 11 and 19. The next term, B_k, is the result of private investments of US residents overseas, titled "U.S. private assets, net," and foreign private investments in the United States, titled "Other foreign assets in U.S." B_k is the sum of lines 13 and 20, and is called the **balance of payments on capital account.** The balance of payments on capital account, B_k, is the net result of all the borrowing, lending, investment, and divestment of non-bank firms, banks, and individuals. The final term, ε, is the statistical discrepancy shown in line 27. In summary:

$$B_c = \text{balance on current account}$$
$$\Delta R = \text{changes in official reserves}$$
$$B_k = \text{balance on capital account}$$
$$\varepsilon = \text{statistical discrepancy}$$

Equation (5.1) is a fundamental balance-of-payments identity. It is useful to consider the implications of this identity separately for fixed and flexible exchange rates.

Flexible rates

We have said that if exchange rates are truly flexible, there cannot be any changes in official reserves because central banks do not buy or sell currencies and gold. This means that if exchange rates are truly flexible,

$$B_c + B_k + \varepsilon = 0$$

Assuming that we can calculate balances without error, this means

$$B_c + B_k = 0 \qquad (5.2)$$

Equation (5.2) says that with flexible exchange rates, the correctly measured current-account deficit/surplus is exactly equal to the correctly measured capital-account surplus/deficit. It is equation (5.2) that is behind the view of many economists that the large US current-account deficits of the 1980s were the result of too much foreign borrowing, which in turn was the result of the low US savings rate. Let us consider this view.

Some people tend to think that the direction of causation runs from the current account to the capital account. They would argue that having a deficit in the current account from spending more abroad than is earned from abroad causes a country to have to borrow abroad or divest itself of assets. This suggests a direction of causation from B_c to B_k. However, an equally valid way to view the situation is that an inflow of capital, such as occurs when the US Government sells its bills and bonds to foreign lenders to finance the US fiscal deficit, forces the country to run a deficit in the current account equal to the net import of capital. What happens is that the demand for dollars that foreigners must buy in order to be able to purchase the US bills and bonds increases the value of the dollar, thereby reducing US exports and increasing US imports, causing a current-account deficit. Indeed, flexible exchange rates are the mechanism that ensures a current-account deficit results from the capital imports. A need to borrow from abroad can arise when a country is investing more in new plant, equipment, R&D, and so on, than is being saved in that country. More generally, borrowing arises when domestic savings are insufficient to fund

business, government, and consumer needs for financing.

Fixed rates

When exchange rates are fixed, there is no simple link between the correctly measured current and capital accounts as in equation (5.2). However, we can still use the fundamental accounting identity in equation (5.1) to reach some important conclusions.

If we again assume the current- and capital-account balances are correctly measured, we can rearrange equation (5.1) to state

$$\Delta R = -(B_c + B_k)$$

This tells us that when exchange rates are fixed, as they were for the major currencies during the so-called Bretton Woods era from 1944 to 1973, the increase/decrease in official reserves equals the combined surplus/deficit in the current and capital accounts.[13] Indeed, the mechanism for fixing exchange rates ensured that this happened. If a country had a combined deficit on its current and capital accounts, the net excess supply of the country's currency would have forced down its exchange rate if the government did nothing.[14] Only by buying an amount of its currency equal to the excess supply could the country keep its exchange rate from falling. That is, governments had to demand whatever excess amounts of their currencies were supplied if they were to prevent their exchange rates from falling. Similarly, governments had to supply whatever excess amounts of their currencies were demanded if they were to prevent their exchange rates from increasing. Therefore, ΔR had to be equal and opposite in sign to the combined balance on current and capital account, $B_c + B_k$.

13 The Bretton Woods fixed-exchange-rate system is described in more detail in Chapters 22 and 23.
14 Current- and capital-account deficits mean residents are selling more of their own currency to buy foreign goods and assets than foreigners are demanding to pay for American goods and assets. Hence the net excess supply.

Long-run versus short-run implications of payments imbalances

Flexible rates

If $B_c + B_k = 0$, but B_c is large and negative and B_k is large and positive, the country is likely to run into trouble eventually. This is because with B_c negative and B_k positive a country is paying for its excess of imports over exports of goods, services, income, and goodwill by borrowing abroad or divesting itself of investments made in the past. This is sustainable in the short run, but not in the long run, because B_c includes income payments and receipts. If the country is borrowing or divesting, the size of income payments will grow faster than its income receipts, and so therefore will future deficits on current account. That is, if B_c is negative and B_k is positive, then B_c will become more negative in the future via the additional net payments of interest, dividends, rents, and profits. This will make it necessary to borrow or divest more, thereby making B_c even more negative in the future, and so on. As we explain in Chapter 23 when discussing international debt crises, such patterns have occurred in the past with nearly catastrophic consequences.

Fixed rates

If $B_c + \Delta R + B_k = 0$ with $B_c + B_k$ negative and ΔR positive, this means the government is buying up its own currency to offset the net excess supply due to the current- plus capital-account deficits. The government buys its own currency by selling gold and foreign exchange reserves. This can occur in the short run if the government has a large stock of reserves. However, eventually reserves will run out. Official reserves can sometimes be borrowed from foreign governments, but the income payments to official foreign lenders due to borrowing causes higher future current-account deficits, requiring even more borrowing, still higher future current-account deficits, and so on. Eventually the country is likely to run out of credit.

What we discover is that a country must not allow anything but temporary deficits in the current account, or it is likely to fall deeper and deeper into debt. With fixed exchange rates, it is possible to have a deficit in the combined current and capital accounts, but again, if this is not temporary, the country will run out of reserves, fall into debt, and eventually run out of credit.

The firm versus the economy: an analogy

We can illustrate the importance of correcting imbalances of payments by considering an analogous situation of imbalances in the current and capital accounts of an individual firm. This analogy also helps us push our understanding of the balance of payments a little further.

The analogous account to the balance of payments on current account for the firm is the firm's income statement. In the case of the firm, the credit entries are revenues from sales and earnings on past investment such as interest received on bank accounts. The debit entries are the firm's payments for wages, salaries, rent, raw materials, equipment, and entertainment/advertising – the buying of goodwill – plus interest and dividend payments. If the firm has a surplus on its income statement, it can add to its investments or build up a reserve in the bank against possible losses in the future. If the firm has a deficit in its income statement, it must borrow, raise more equity, or divest itself of assets purchased in the past.

In the case of a surplus, the addition to investments means higher future income and, *ceteris paribus*, ever larger future surpluses in its income statements. In the case of borrowing or divesting to cover losses, the extra debt or reduced income base of assets suggests even larger future losses. However, when we consider an individual firm, we recognize that having payments that exceed receipts is acceptable when it occurs because the firm is expanding or otherwise enhancing its capital stock. This situation is acceptable because the firm is increasing its potential to generate future revenue or reducing its future costs of production. Indeed, provided the investment is a good investment, the extra revenue or saving in production costs will service any added debt incurred in making the investment. Therefore, having a deficit in the income statement, the analogous account to the current account of the balance of payments, is not necessarily a matter of concern. It depends on whether the deficit is the result of *current* operating and debt costs exceeding current revenue, or whether the deficit results from *capital* investment.

It follows from what we have just said that it is not necessarily bad for a country to have a current-account deficit and a capital-account surplus. If the country is borrowing from abroad to finance the building of important infrastructure, the development of natural resources such as oil reserves, the purchase of state-of-the-art production robots, construction equipment, and so on, then an excess of imports over exports in the current account is due to the import of capital equipment. This is far healthier than a trade balance from importing consumer goods such as VCRs, expensive wine, clothing, and automobiles. Indeed, if the imported capital offers a return in excess of future interest or dividend payments incurred in financing the capital, this is a very healthy and sustainable situation. We see that we need to know the composition of the current-account deficit as well as whether the account is in deficit.[15] Unfortunately, no accounting distinction is made between the import of capital goods and the import of consumer goods. Both appear in the current account and contribute to a deficit even though they have different implications for future living standards and financial viability.

THE NET INTERNATIONAL INVESTMENT POSITION

The capital account of the balance of payments presents the record of the *flows* of funds into and out

of a country. Capital inflows result from the sale of financial and real assets, gold, and foreign exchange to foreigners. Outflows result from the purchase of these assets from foreigners. The inflows and outflows are added to and subtracted from *stocks* of outstanding international assets and liabilities. The account that shows the stocks of assets and liabilities is called the **international-investment-position** account. This account is analogous to a firm's balance sheet. Table 5.2 gives the international investment position of the United States at the end of 2001.

When capital leaves the United States for investment overseas, it is added to US assets abroad. The debit that appears in the balance of payments therefore corresponds to an increase in the value of US assets in Table 5.2. Similarly, when capital flows into the United States, the credit that appears in the balance of payments corresponds to an increase in foreign assets in the United States as shown in Table 5.2.

The inflows and outflows of investments are categorized into official/government and private components, with further divisions within these major categories. The listed items correspond to those in the balance-of-payments account and indeed, in principle, an outflow of capital in the balance of payments should increase the corresponding "U.S. asset abroad" item in the international investment-position account. Similarly, an inflow of capital should increase the corresponding "foreign assets in the U.S." item in the investment-position account. However, while there is a close correspondence between the balance-of-payments account and the net-international-investment-position account, that correspondence is imperfect. One of the main problems arises from changes in market values of existing assets. Such changes in values do not appear in the balance of payments but should be reflected in a country's investment position. An attempt is made to deal with changes in values of existing assets for direct investment but not for stocks, bonds and other investment items. We see in Table 5.2 that the market value of US direct investments abroad exceeds their "current cost" – the value at the time of the investment – by

15 This point has been made by K. Alec Chrystal and Geoffrey E. Wood, "Are Trade Deficits a Problem?," *Review*, Federal Reserve Bank of St. Louis, January/February 1988, pp. 3–11.

111

Table 5.2 *International investment position of the United States year-end 2001, billions of US dollars*

US Govt. assets abroad		216	Foreign official assets in US			1,022
US official reserves	130		Foreign private assets in US with FDI at current cost			7,123
Other US Govt. assets	86		(Foreign private assets in US with FDI at market value)			8,150
US private assets abroad with FDI at current cost		5,981	FDI at current cost		1,499	
(US private assets abroad with FDI at market value)		(6,647)	(FDI at market value)		(2,527)	
FDI at current cost	1,623		US Securities		3,246	
(FDI at market value)	(2,291)		Treasury securities	389		
			Bonds	1,394		
Foreign securities	2,111		Stocks	1,464		
Bonds	1046		US Currency	276		
Stocks	1065					
			Liabilities of US non-banks		804	
US non-bank assets	830		Liabilities of US banks		1,298	
US bank assets	1,417		Foreign owned assets in US, FDI at current cost			8,145
Total US assets with FDI at current cost		6,197	(Foreign owned asset in US, FDI at market value)			(9,172)
(Total US assets with FDI at market value)		(6,863)	Net international position of US, with FDI at current cost			−1,948
			(Net international position of US, with FDI at market value)			(−2,309)

Source: US Department of Commerce, Bureau of Economic Analysis, June 2002.

$666 billion ($6,647–$5,981 billion). In the case of foreign direct investment in the United States the discrepancy is a somewhat larger at $1,028 billion ($2,527–$1,499 billion). The use of these two measures of direct investment means there are two different measures of national net indebtedness, where for the United States, net indebtedness is foreign assets in the United States minus US assets abroad. Table 5.2 shows that the United States is a net debtor by approximately $2 trillion. This represents approximately 20 percent of the US GDP. Therefore, while substantial, the US foreign debt problem is not as serious as the debt problems that have been faced by many Latin American and Eastern European nations which have often had debts equal to more than a year of the debtors' GDPs.[16]

One of the most important items in the net international investment position is the official reserve position of the government. This position is very important during times of fixed exchange rates or dirty floats for judging how long a country can influence exchange rates. A government can defend its currency only as long as it has sufficient reserves. If, for example, a government can afford many years of substantial deficits with its stock of

16 International debt problem are discussed in Chapter 23.

reserves, a devaluation – an official reduction in the fixed exchange rate – can be considered unlikely. On the other hand, if reserves will meet existing deficits for only a few months, a devaluation is quite possible.

OBJECTIVES OF ECONOMIC POLICY

Even when it is pointed out that a trade deficit can be healthy if it is due to importing capital equipment that increases future output and exports, it is difficult for many people to avoid thinking that it is still better to try to achieve trade surpluses than trade deficits. This presumption that trade surpluses are an appropriate policy objective has a long history, being the opinion of a diverse group of writers of the sixteenth, seventeenth, and eighteenth centuries known as **mercantilists**. The mercantilists believed that trade surpluses were the objective of trade because, during the time that this view of trade prevailed, surpluses resulted in increased holdings of gold, the medium of exchange against which internationally traded products were exchanged. Today, a version of mercantilism is that trade surpluses are an appropriate objective because they result in accumulations of foreign assets, as reflected in the net international investment position. This seems so eminently reasonable that it is worth asking why indefinitely running trade surpluses is not a good policy objective.

Consider what it means to have a trade surplus, with merchandise exports exceeding imports, and to have this surplus continue indefinitely. It means that a country is producing more goods for foreigners to enjoy than foreign countries produce for the country's own residents. But why should one country manufacture goods for the pleasure of another in excess of what it receives in return? Indefinite trade surpluses mean a country is living below its means. The country could enjoy more of its own production and still keep trade in balance.

One of the most direct ways of exposing the modern-day mercantilist fallacy is by considering the **national-income accounting identity** which is met in macroeconomics. This identity is written as

$$Y \equiv C + I + G + (Ex - Im) \tag{5.3}$$

where

$Y =$ Gross domestic product (GDP)[17]

$C =$ Consumption

$I =$ Gross investment

$G =$ Government expenditures

$Ex =$ Exports of goods and services

$Im =$ Imports of goods and services

By rearranging equation (5.3) we can state the balance of payments on goods and services as

$$Ex - Im \equiv Y - (C + I + G) \tag{5.4}$$

Equation (5.4) makes it clear that to have a surplus in trade, that is, to have $(Ex-Im)$ positive, means producing, Y, more than is "used" or "absorbed" by the economy, $(C+I+G)$, in the form of consumption, business investment or the provision of services by the government. Interpretation of the balance of trade as expressed in equation (5.4) has been called the **absorption approach** to the balance of payments.

Just as surpluses mean a country is living below its means, deficits mean a country is living above its means. In terms of equation (5.4), a deficit means producing less than the country absorbs, that is, $Y < (C+I+G)$. A deficit means enjoying the products and resources of other nations in excess of the products the country in turn provides for other countries. This is marvelous as long as a country can get away with it, but as with individuals or firms that live beyond their means, a day of reckoning eventually comes when the credit runs out. This makes

---

17 Gross domestic product, is the value of goods and services produced *within a nation*. Gross national product (GNP) is the value of goods and services produced by factors of production *owned by residents of a nation*. GNP includes net income earned by residents from abroad via having made investments, working abroad, and so on. If we write Y as GDP, then we exclude income earned abroad or paid to foreigners in Ex and Im in equation (5.3).

continuous deficits as undesirable as continuous surpluses. Indeed, in the case of deficits the situation is not easily sustainable.

In order to live within its means, a country does not need to balance its trade each and every year. Rather, it can have temporary surpluses and temporary deficits that on average leave its trade balanced.

Temporary trade surpluses followed by temporary trade deficits, or temporary deficits followed by temporary surpluses, are a very different matter than continuous surpluses or deficits. During temporary trade surpluses, the country increases its holdings of foreign assets such as stocks, bonds, real estate, operating businesses, and so on. The income on these foreign assets allows the country to run trade deficits in the future without the country slipping into debt; interest, dividend, and other earnings in the current account can offset the trade deficit. Even if there is an overall current account deficit because interest, dividends, and other "invisibles" do not fully offset the trade deficit, a country can sell off some of its past investments without becoming a debtor nation.

When a country has a trade surplus, it is saving, that is, acquiring foreign assets which can add to future income or which can be sold to finance future spending. It follows that indefinitely running trade surpluses is analogous to a family saving, and neither themselves nor their descendants ever dissaving.

Saving is a reasonable choice for people who are patient, but only if it means that at some point in the future they or their descendants enjoy the benefits of past saving by consuming more than they earn. That is, it is appropriate to save sometimes, and dissave sometimes, as long as on average over a long interval of time the savings are approximately equal to the dissavings. Similarly, it is appropriate to sometimes have trade deficits and sometimes have trade surpluses. The objective of economic policy should be to aim to have balanced trade over a long period, perhaps as long as a decade or more.[18]

What we have said is important because people tend to look at relatively short periods of trade statistics and become seriously alarmed without considering the trade pattern of earlier years, or the likely trade pattern of future years. Such alarm was voiced, for example, in the 1990s at the large Japanese trade surpluses. More recently worries have been expressed about the trade surpluses of the Peoples Republic of China. Few people stop to recall that in the 1970s Japan ran trade deficits from importing expensive oil and other resources. Similarly, China, which has run trade deficits in the past as capital investments were occurring, may again run deficits as consumers express their tastes for imports, as they can now more easily do since admission to the **World Trade Organization, (WTO)** in 2002.

SUMMARY

1   The balance-of-payments account is a record of the flow of payments between the residents of one country and the rest of the world in a given period. Entries in the account that give rise to a demand for the country's currency – such as exports and asset sales – are identified by a plus sign. Entries giving rise to a supply of the country's currency are identified by a minus sign. Therefore, we can think of the balance-of-payments account as a record of the supply of and demand for a country's currency.

18 The conclusion that an appropriate objective of policy is to balance the current account on average by borrowing sometimes and lending at other times is supported by the gain from consumption smoothing that is described in Appendix B, Chapter 1. In that appendix, it is shown that there is a gain in expected utility from borrowing and lending.

2   The balance-of-payment account is based on double-entry bookkeeping. Therefore, every entry has a counterpart entry elsewhere in the account, and the account must balance. What is important, however, is *how* it balances. Anything tending to increase the size of positive entries, such as higher exports or increased sales of bonds to foreigners, will cause the account to balance at a higher exchange rate.

3   Credit entries in the balance of payments result from purchases by foreigners of a country's goods, services, goodwill, financial and real assets, gold and foreign exchange. Debit entries result from purchases by a country's residents of goods, services, goodwill, financial and real assets, gold and foreign exchange from foreigners.

4   The current account includes trade in goods and services, income and unilateral transfers. The goods or merchandise component alone gives the balance of trade as the excess of exports over imports. If exports exceed imports, the balance of trade is in surplus, and if imports exceed exports, it is in deficit. Income includes the flow of interest and dividend receipts and payments. Unilateral transfers are flows of money not matched by any other physical flow, and double-entry bookkeeping requires that we have an offsetting flow that can be marked down as goodwill.

5   A current-account deficit can be financed by selling a country's bills, bonds, stocks, real estate, or businesses. It can also be financed by selling off previous investments in foreign bills, bonds, stocks, real estate, or businesses. A current-account surplus can be invested in foreign bills, bonds, stocks, real estate, or businesses. The principal factors influencing investments in foreign financial and real assets are rates of return in the foreign country versus rates of return at home, and the riskiness of the investments.

6   Purchases and sales of financial and real assets result in a supply of or demand for a country's currency in the same way as purchases and sales of goods and services.

7   Changes in official reserves occur when governments intervene in the foreign exchange markets to influence exchange rates. When exchange rates are truly flexible, changes in official reserves are zero.

8   Since all entries in the balance of payments should collectively sum to zero, the balance-of-payments accountant can determine the errors that were made. This is called the statistical discrepancy.

9   With flexible exchange rates, the correctly measured deficit/surplus in the current account equals the correctly measured surplus/deficit in the capital account. With fixed exchange rates, the combined increase/decrease in official reserves of the domestic and foreign governments is equal to the combined surplus/deficit of the correctly measured current and capital accounts.

10 It is equally valid to consider a current-account deficit/surplus to be the cause of, or to be caused by, a capital-account surplus/deficit.

11 The balance-of-payments account is analogous to a firm's income statement. Deficits are equivalent to corporate losses and can be financed by selling bonds or new equity, or by divesting assets. If there is a net outflow from a firm or country due to acquiring new productive capital, this might not be unhealthy. Unfortunately, the balance-of-payments account does not distinguish imports of capital goods from imports of consumption goods.

12 The international investment position is a record of the stock of foreign assets and liabilities. The size of official reserves is relevant for determining the likelihood of devaluation.

13 It is not a good idea to run persistent deficits or persistent surpluses in the balance of trade. Rather, a country should balance its trade on average over the long run.

REVIEW QUESTIONS

1   Does the balance-of-payments account record stocks or flows?
2   Are transactions giving rise to the demand for a country's currency recorded as debits or credits in the balance of payments?
3   What economic variables might affect the value of a country's merchandise (goods) exports?
4   What are a country's "terms of trade?"
5   What are "invisibles" in the balance of payments?
6   What are "debt service exports?"
7   How are interest earnings from foreign investments included in the balance of payments?
8   What is a "balance of trade deficit?"
9   What is a "unilateral transfer?"
10 What are "official reserve assets?"
11 What is "direct investment?"
12 What is a "current account surplus?"
13 What is a "capital account deficit?"
14 What is the identity linking the current account, capital account, change in official reserves, and statistical discrepancy?
15 What does the net international-investment-position account show?
16 What did the "Merchantilists" think?
17 What is the chief characteristic of the absorption approach to the balance of payments?
18 If a country is living beyond its means, does it have persistent trade surpluses or deficits?

ASSIGNMENT PROBLEMS

1   Since gold is a part of official reserves, how would the balance-of-payments statistics show the sale of domestically mined gold to the country's central bank? What happens if the mining company sells the gold to foreign private buyers?
2   Can all countries collectively enjoy a surplus, or must all surpluses and deficits cancel against each other? What does gold mining mean for the world's balance?
3   Under what conditions would inflation increase the value of exports?
4   Even if inflation did increase the value of exports, would the balance of trade and the exchange rate necessarily improve from inflation that is higher than in other countries?

5   How do we know that an exogenous increase in exports will cause a currency to appreciate even though the balance of payments is always zero? How does your answer relate to the law of supply and demand whereby supply equals demand even after demand has increased?

6   What is the difference between the immediate and the long-run effect of the sale of bonds to foreign investors?

7   What is the difference between the immediate and the long-run effect of direct investment by foreigners when the direct investment is in a heavily export-oriented activity such as oil exploration and development? Would it make any difference if the industry into which direct investment occurred were involved in the production of a good the country previously had been importing?

8   If the balance of payments of Alaska were prepared, what do you think it would look like? How about the balance of payments of New York City? What do you think the net investment position of these locations will be? Should we worry if Alaska is in debt?

9   If the overall level of interest rates in all countries went up, how would this affect the balance of payments of the United States as a net debtor nation?

10 Which item(s) in the balance-of-payments account, Table 5.1, would be most affected by an expected appreciation of the US dollar, and how would the item(s) and the current spot value of the dollar be affected by the expected appreciation? Do you believe that the higher expected future value of the US dollar could increase the spot value immediately?

BIBLIOGRAPHY

Baldwin, Robert E., "Determinants of Trade and Foreign Investment: Further Evidence," *Review of Economics and Statistics*, Fall 1979, pp. 40–8.

Bame, Jack J., "Analyzing U.S. International Transactions," *Columbia Journal of World Business*, Fall 1976, pp. 72–84.

Caves, Richard E. and Ronald W. Jones, *World Trade and Payments: An Introduction*, 4th edn, Little Brown and Company, Boston, 1984, Chapter 5.

Chrystal, K. Alec and Geoffrey E. Wood, "Are Trade Deficits a Problem?," *Review*, Federal Reserve Bank of St. Louis, January/February 1988, pp. 3–11.

Cooper, Richard N., "The Balance of Payments in Review," *Journal of Political Economy*, August 1966, pp. 379–95.

Grubel, Herbert G., *International Economics*, Richard D. Irwin, Inc., Homewood, IL, 1977, Chapter 13.

Heller, H. Robert, *International Monetary Economics*, Prentice-Hall, Inc., Englewood Cliffs, NJ, 1974, Chapter 4.

Kemp, Donald S., "Balance of Payments Concepts: What Do They Really Mean?," *Review*, Federal Reserve Bank of St. Louis, July 1975, pp. 14–23.

Miller, Merton H., "Financial Markets and Economic Growth," *Journal of Applied Corporate Finance*, Fall 1998, pp. 8–15.

Mundell, Robert A., "The Balance of Payments," in David Sills (ed.), *International Encyclopedia of the Social Sciences*, Crowell-Collier and Macmillan, Inc., New York, 1968. Reprinted as Chapter 10 in Robert Mundell, *International Economics*, The Macmillan Company, New York, 1968.

Ohmae, Kenichi, "'Lies, Damned Lies, and Statistics': Why the Trade Deficit Doesn't Matter in a Borderless World," *Journal of Applied Corporate Finance*, Winter 1991, pp. 98–106.

"Report of the Advisory Committee on the Presentation of the Balance of Payments Statistics," in US Department of Commerce, *Survey of Current Business*, June 1976, pp. 18–25.

Salop, Joanne and Erich Spitaller, "Why Does the Current Account Matter?," *Staff Papers*, International Monetary Fund, March 1980, pp. 101–34.

Stern, Robert M., *The Balance of Payments: Theory and Economic Policy*, Aldine Publishing Company, Chicago, 1973, Chapter 1.

Stern, Robert M. *et al.*, "*The Presentation of the U.S. Balance of Payments: A Symposium*," Essays in International Finance, Number 123, International Finance Section, Princeton University, Princeton, NJ, August 1977.

Wilson, John F., "*The Foreign Sector in the U.S. Flow of Funds Account*," International Finance Discussion Papers, Board of Governors of the Federal Reserve System, Number 239 (undated).

Chapter 6

Supply-and-demand view of exchange rates

According to the laws of supply and demand, when buyers don't fall for prices, prices must fall for buyers.

Anonymous

In Chapter 5 we explained that when exchange rates are flexible, they are determined by the forces of supply and demand.[1] In this chapter we consider these forces of supply and demand by deriving the supply and demand curves for a currency and using them to explain what makes exchange rates change. As we might expect, this involves consideration of the effects of items listed in the balance-of-payments account on the supply and demand curves. With the balance-of-payments account recording flows of payments into and out of a country, the explanation of exchange rates based on the account emphasizes *flow* demands and supplies of a currency.[2] However, as we shall see, in the case of currencies there is no assurance that the supply-and-demand situation will

have the form that is familiar from the applications of supply and demand in other markets. In particular, there is no assurance that the supply curve of a currency will be upward-sloping.

The possibility that a currency supply curve slopes downwards rather than upwards is not a mere curiosity with little practical relevance. Rather, it is a realistic possibility that is critical to explaining why foreign exchange markets may be unstable. This possibility has attracted substantial interest because of the extreme volatility of exchange rates during certain times. It is also of interest because the condition for exchange-rate instability helps explain the so-called "J curve" whereby, for example, a depreciation of a currency worsens rather than improves a country's trade balance. The cause of the J curve and of exchange-rate instability can be understood by applying the central economic paradigm of supply and demand.

The traditional approach to supply and demand is to begin by explaining why supply and demand curves slope the way they do, and then to consider the effects of shifts of the curves. Our approach here is the same. Of course, in the case of exchange rates we write the exchange rate (the price of a country's currency expressed in terms of some other currency) on the vertical axis. In order to

1 When exchange rates are fixed, as they were under the gold standard and the Bretton Woods standard, they are also determined by supply and demand. The difference between fixed and flexible rates is that with fixed rates there is official demand or supply at the fixed rate, and this is adjusted to ensure that the exchange rate stays at or near the chosen rate. The determination of fixed exchange rates under a variety of fixed-rate systems is explained in Chapter 22.

2 In Chapter 21 we describe theories of exchange rates which emphasize *stock* demands and supplies, specifically, the amount of currency versus the amount of currency people want to hold.

establish the slopes of the supply and demand curves for currencies, we consider the effects of exchange rates on the values of imports and exports. This is similar to considering the effect of price on quantity supplied and demanded.[3] We then show that all other factors in the balance-of-payments account can be considered as shifting the supply or demand curves, with effects on exchange rates that depend on the slopes of the curves.

IMPORTS, EXPORTS, AND EXCHANGE RATES

Deriving a currency's supply curve

As you would expect, the supply curve of a currency shows the amount of that currency being supplied on the horizontal axis, and the price of the currency, given by the exchange rate, on the vertical axis. However, when we draw the supply curve of a currency, we do not plot *quantities* on the horizontal axis as we do with normal supply curves – so many bushels of wheat or automobiles produced per month. Rather, we plot monetary *values* on the horizontal axis – the number of British pounds or euros that are being spent on imports. Values involve the multiplication of prices and quantities, and respond differently than do quantities. Indeed, as we shall show, the fact that values rather than physical quantities are on the horizontal axis explains why the currency supply curve can easily slope downward rather than upward with respect to the price of the currency.

The supply curve of a currency derives, at least in part, from a country's demand for imports. This is because when paying for imports that are invoiced in foreign currency, the importing country's residents must sell their currency for the needed foreign exchange, and when imports are invoiced in domestic currency, the foreign recipient of the

currency sells it. In either case, imports result in the country's currency being supplied.[4] The amount of the currency supplied is equal to the value of imports. Let us see how to plot the value of currency supplied against the exchange rate by considering British imports of wheat which, for simplicity, we assume is the only import.

The quantity of pounds supplied equals the value of British wheat imports. This involves multiplying the pound price of wheat by the quantity of wheat imported. The multiplication gives the number of pounds Britain spends on wheat imports, and therefore also gives the number of pounds supplied to the foreign exchange market. Let us suppose that the world price of wheat is $3/bushel, that wheat is traded without tariffs or other restrictions, and that Britain buys such a small proportion of global wheat output that the world price of wheat is not influenced by Britain's imports.

At an exchange rate of $1.5/£ the pound price of wheat is $3 \div ($1.5/£) = £2/bushel. Figure 6.1a, which shows the British import demand curve for wheat, reveals that at £2/bushel the quantity of wheat imports is zero, point A. That is, at £2/bushel Britain's production of wheat equals Britain's consumption of wheat so that Britain is precisely self-sufficient at this price. With zero imports the number of pounds supplied is therefore zero at the exchange rate $1.5/£. This is shown by point A' on the supply curve of pounds, $S_£$, in Figure 6.1b. If the exchange rate is $1.7/£, the pound price of wheat is $3 \div ($1.7/£) = £1.76/bushel. Point B on the import demand curve in Figure 6.1a shows that at this price, wheat imports are approximately 0.75 billion bushels. The number of pounds supplied per year at exchange rate $1.7/£ is therefore £1.76 × 0.75 billion = £1.32 billion per year. This quantity of pounds supplied is plotted against the exchange rate $1.7/£, point B' on $S_£$ in

---

3 The pattern is similar, but different in that currencies involve *values* of exports and imports, not *quantities* of goods or services as in traditional supply and demand. We have far more to say about this later.

4 If imports are invoiced in the importer's currency, and the foreign recipient of the currency chooses *not* to sell it, we still consider that the currency is supplied to pay for imports. This is matched, however, by a foreign demand for the currency in the capital account.

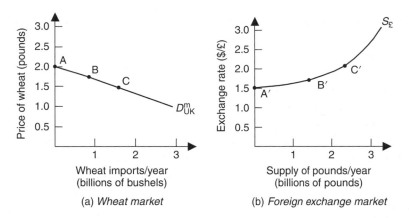

Figure 6.1 *Deriving the supply of pounds*

Notes
A currency is supplied in the course of paying for imports. If we limit consideration to goods and services, the supply of a currency equals the value of imports. We find the currency supply curve by taking each possible exchange rate and finding the price of imports at that exchange rate. We then determine the quantity of imports at that price from the demand curve for imports and calculate the value of imports by multiplying the price and the quantity of imports. We then plot the value of imports against the exchange rate at which it occurs.

Figure 6.1b.[5] Similarly, at the exchange rate $2/£ the pound price of wheat is $3 \div ($2/£) = $ £1.5/bushel. Figure 6.1a shows import demand of 1.5 billion bushels at this price, point C, which involves an annual expenditure of £1.5 × 1.5 billion = £2.25 billion. This gives point C′ on $S_£$ in Figure 6.1b. By continuing in this way we can construct the supply curve of pounds, which in this case happens to slope upward (we consider the condition for a downward-sloping currency supply curve, and the implications of such a curve, later in the chapter).

Deriving a currency's demand curve

The demand curve for a currency shows the value of the currency that is demanded at each exchange rate. Because the need to buy a country's currency stems from the need to pay for the country's exports, the currency's demand curve is derived from the country's export supply curve, which shows the quantity of exports at each price of exports. The value of exports is then the price multiplied by the quantity.

5 We see that we are calculating the *area* under D_{UK}^m in Figure 6.1a, and plotting this as the *distance* along the horizontal axis in Figure 6.1b.

Figure 6.2a shows the supply curve of British exports. For simplicity of reference we assume that Britain exports only oil. The demand for pounds to pay for Britain's oil exports is equal to the value of these exports. Therefore, in order to construct the demand curve for pounds we must calculate the value of oil exports at each exchange rate. Let us suppose that the world price of oil is $25/barrel and that Britain has no effect on this price when it changes its oil exports.

If we begin with an exchange rate of $2/£, the pound price of oil is $25 \div $2/£ = $ £12.5/barrel. Figure 6.2a shows that at £12.5/barrel oil exports are zero, point D. That is, at £12.5/barrel Britain's production of oil equals Britain's consumption of oil, so that the country is exactly self-sufficient. With zero oil exports, the quantity of pounds demanded to pay for Britain's oil exports is therefore also zero at $2/£. This is shown by point D′ on the demand curve of pounds, $D_£$, in Figure 6.2b. If the exchange rate is $1.8/£ the pound price of oil is $25 \div $1.8/£ = £13.89 and oil exports are approximately 0.1 billion barrels per year, point E in Figure 6.2a. The value of oil exports and quantity of pounds demanded per year at $1.8/£ is therefore £13.89 × 0.1 billion = £1.389 billion. This is

121

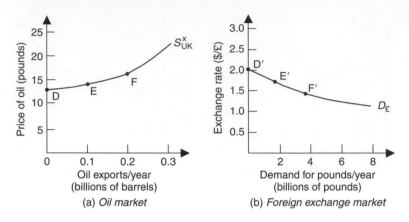

Figure 6.2 *Deriving the demand for pounds*

Notes
A country's currency is demanded in the course of foreigners buying that country's exports. If we limit consideration to goods and services, the demand for a currency equals the value of exports. We find the currency demand curve by taking each possible exchange rate and finding the price of exports at that exchange rate. We then determine the quantity of exports at that price from the supply curve for exports and calculate the value of exports by multiplying the price by the quantity of exports. We then plot the value of exports against the exchange rate at which it occurs.

shown by point E′ on $D_£$ in Figure 6.2b. Finally, at $1.50/£ the price of oil is $25 ÷ $1.5/£ = £16.67/barrel, and exports are approximately 0.2 billion barrels – point F in Figure 6.2a. Therefore, the number of pounds demanded at $1.5/£ is £16.67 × 0.2 billion = £3.33 billion per year – point F′ in Figure 6.2b.

THE FACTORS AFFECTING EXCHANGE RATES

Terms of trade and the amount of trade

If we plot the supply and demand curves for pounds in the same figure, as in Figure 6.3, we can find the exchange rate that equates the value of exports and imports, and hence that equates the supply of and demand for the country's currency resulting from these activities. We see that equality of supply and demand occurs at an exchange rate of approximately $1.75/£.

It is clear from Figure 6.3 that *ceteris paribus*, an exogenous increase in the value of exports at each exchange rate, which shifts the demand curve for pounds, $D_£$, to the right, will, with the slopes of curves shown, result in an increase in the value of

the pound. Such an increase in the value of exports could occur as a result of a higher world price of oil, or from an increase in the quantity of oil exported at each oil price. It is also clear from the figure that *ceteris paribus*, an exogenous increase in the value of imports at each exchange rate, which shifts the supply curve of pounds, $S_£$, to the right, will result in a decrease in the value of the pound. This could result from a higher world price of wheat or an increase in the quantity of wheat imported at each price. The price of a country's exports relative to the price of its imports is called the country's terms of trade. A country's terms of trade are said to improve when the price of its exports increases relative to the price of its imports. Our description of Figure 6.3 makes it clear that the pound will appreciate in value as a result of an improvement of Britain's terms of trade. That is, the pound will appreciate if, *ceteris paribus*, oil prices increase relative to wheat prices. The pound will also appreciate if the quantity of exports increases relative to the quantity of imports. This could happen, for example, if Britain steps up production and exports of oil at each oil price. It could also happen if Britain has a good wheat harvest and therefore imports less wheat at each exchange rate.

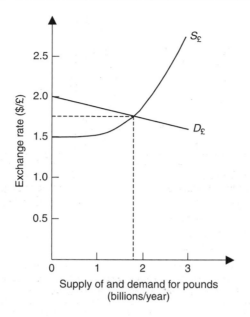

Figure 6.3 *The exchange rate from imports and exports*

Notes
The equilibrium exchange rate is that at which the quantity of currency supplied equals the quantity demanded. Factors other than the exchange rate which affect the value of imports and exports shift the currency supply and demand curves and thereby change the equilibrium exchange rate.

Inflation

Terms of trade effects concern export versus import prices, where the exports and imports are *different* products. Exchange rates are also influenced by inflation which affects the competitiveness of one country's products versus the *same* products from another country. In order to show the effects of inflation it is necessary to describe the derivation of the import demand and export supply curves. These curves were taken to be exogenous in Figures 6.1a and 6.2a. That is, we have not yet shown what is behind the import demand curve, D^m_{UK}, in Figure 6.1a, and the export supply curve, S^x_{UK} in Figure 6.2a.

Deriving the import demand curve

Figure 6.4a shows the demand for wheat in Britain, D^w_{UK}, and the quantity of wheat British farmers supply at each price, S^w_{UK}. If Britain can take the world price of wheat as given, whether Britain is an importer or exporter of wheat depends on the world price of wheat translated into pounds. For example, if the world price of wheat is equivalent to £1.5/bushel, Britain produces 2.5 billion bushels per year and consumes 4 billion bushels per year, so that imports are 1.5 billion bushels per year. At £2.0/bushel Britain is self-sufficient, producing and consuming 3.5 billion bushels per year, and at prices above £2.0/bushel Britain is a wheat exporter.

If we consider only pound prices of wheat below £2/bushel, where Britain is a wheat importer, we can plot the British demand curve for imports by selecting different pound prices and measuring the distance between D^w_{UK} and S^w_{UK} at each price. These distances, which are the quantities of wheat imported at each price, are plotted against the prices at which they occur. By doing this we obtain the British wheat import demand curve D^m_{UK} shown in Figure 6.4b. This is the import demand curve that we took as our starting point in Figure 6.1a. As we saw earlier, by assuming that the world price of wheat is $3/bushel, we can construct the supply curve of pounds, $S_£$, in Figure 6.1b.

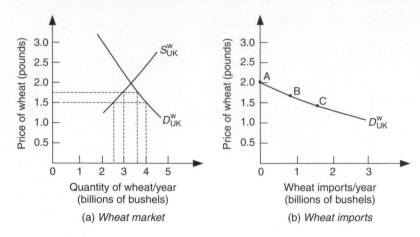

Figure 6.4 *Deriving the demand for imports*

Notes
The quantity of imports demanded at each price is the excess of the quantity of the product that is demanded over the quantity of the product produced in the country. That is, it is the horizontal distance between the country's demand curve for the product and its supply curve.

Deriving the export supply curve

Curves D^o_{UK} and S^o_{UK} in Figure 6.5a show, respectively, British oil demand and supply at different oil prices. We can construct the export supply curve from D^o_{UK} and S^o_{UK} by considering different pound prices of oil, and computing the excess of quantity supplied over quantity demanded at each price. For example, at £12.50/barrel oil consumption equals oil production, so that exports are zero. This is point D on the export supply curve, S^x_{UK}, shown in Figure 6.5b and Figure 6.2a. Proceeding in this way, we obtain the supply curve of exports, S^x_{UK}, that we merely assumed in Figure 6.2a. As we saw earlier, by assuming that the world price of oil is $25/barrel and considering different exchange rates, we can derive the demand curve for pounds, $D_£$, in Figure 6.2b.

When we plot the supply and demand curves for pounds in the same figure as in Figure 6.3, we find that the exchange rate that equates the supply of and demand for pounds before any inflation has occurred. Let us now consider what happens when there is inflation.

Inflation, import demand, and export supply

Let us assume that Britain experiences inflation of 25 percent. If all prices and wages in Britain increase

25 percent during a year, the British demand curves for wheat and oil at the end of the year will be 25 percent higher than at the beginning of the year. That is, they are shifted vertically upward by 25 percent. This is because with all prices and wages higher by the same amount, real incomes and relative prices are unchanged. Therefore, after the 25 percent inflation the same quantities of goods are purchased at prices 25 percent higher than before the inflation as were purchased before the inflation: nothing real has changed.

At the same time as the British demand curves for wheat and for oil shift upward, so do the supply curves. The easiest way of thinking about why this occurs is to note that the supply curves for competitive firms are their marginal cost (MC) curves. Indeed, the individual competitive firm's short-run supply curve is that firm's MC curve, and the competitive industry's short-run supply curve is the horizontal sum of all existing firms' MC curves. Long-run supply curves which consider newly entering firms also shift up by the rate of inflation, because inflation also increases the marginal costs of new firms. Hence, if all wages and prices increase by 25 percent, the marginal costs become 25 percent higher, and therefore so are the supply curves. We can reach the same conclusion if we think of

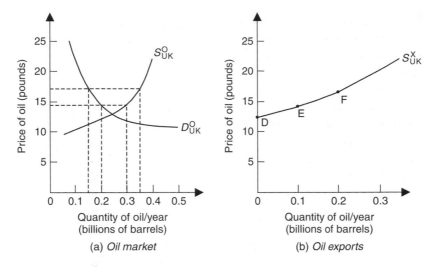

Figure 6.5 *Deriving the export supply curve*

Notes
The quantity of exports supplied at each price is the excess of the quantity of the product that is supplied over the quantity demanded in the country. That is, it is the horizontal distance between the country's supply curve of the product and its demand curve.

supply as being set to equate marginal cost and marginal revenue. At any given output the marginal cost is 25 percent higher after inflation, and therefore if the marginal revenue is also 25 percent higher from the demand curve shifting up 25 percent, there is no reason to change output; marginal cost remains equal to marginal revenue.

The left-hand diagrams in Figure 6.6 show the supply and demand curves for wheat and oil before and after 25 percent inflation. The supply and demand curves before inflation are identified by P_0, the price level at the beginning of the year, and those after inflation are identified by P_1, the price level at the end of the year.

The right-hand diagrams in Figure 6.6 show the demand for imports and the supply of exports before and after 25 percent inflation. As before, P_0 signifies the curve before inflation, and P_1 after inflation. We recall that the demand for imports and supply of exports are obtained by selecting different prices and calculating the difference between domestic supply and demand at each price. For example, before inflation, the demand for imports of wheat was zero at £2/bushel. After inflation, it is zero at £2.50/bushel. That is, the intercept of

$D_{UK}^m(P_1)$ with the price axis is 25 percent higher than the intercept of $D_{UK}^m(P_0)$. Since the slopes of the supply and demand curves for wheat are the same before and after inflation, the slope of the demand curve for wheat imports is the same before and after inflation. Therefore, we find that $D_{UK}^m(P_1)$ is above $D_{UK}^m(P_0)$ by 25 percent, not only at the intercept with the price axis, but at every other quantity of imports. Similarly, the supply curve of oil exports intercepts the price axis at £12.50 before inflation, because this is where quantity of domestic oil supplied equals the quantity demanded. After inflation the intercept is at a price 25 percent higher. Because the slopes of the supply and demand curves for oil are the same before and after inflation, the slope of the export supply curve is the same before and after inflation. Therefore, as in the case of the demand curve for imports, the supply curve of exports shifts upwards 25 percent at every quantity.

We can employ Figure 6.6 to show how inflation affects currency supply and demand curves and hence the exchange rate. There are different effects according to whether inflation occurs only in Britain alone, or in Britain and elsewhere, and so we consider these situations in turn.

125

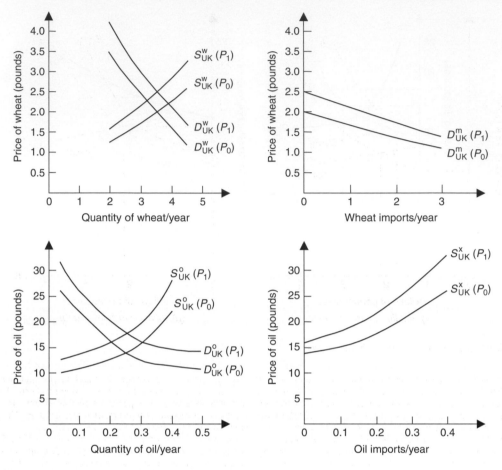

Figure 6.6 *Inflation in relation to supply and demand*

Notes
Curves identified with P_0 represent the situation before inflation. Curves identified with P_1 represent the situation after inflation. We see that inflation in all prices and incomes shifts demand and supply curves vertically upward by the amount of inflation. Thus the demand curve for imports and supply curve of exports also shift vertically upward by the amount of inflation.

Inflation in only one country

Figure 6.7a shows the supply and demand curves for pounds that are implied by the demand curve for imports and supply curve of exports when inflation of 25 percent occurs in Britain but not in the United States. The curves labeled $S_£(P_0)$ and $D_£(P_0)$ are those before inflation, and are the same supply and demand curves for pounds used in Figure 6.3. The curves labeled $S_£(P_1)$ and $D_£(P_1)$ are the supply and demand curves for pounds after 25 percent inflation in Britain but not in the United States. The derivation of $S_£(P_1)$ and $D_£(P_1)$ is based on the following reasoning.

Because inflation occurs only in Britain, we can take the US dollar prices of wheat and oil as unchanged. Consider, first, the supply curve of pounds. We know from Figure 6.6 that the same quantity of wheat is imported after inflation as before inflation if the pound price of wheat is increased by 25 percent; this follows immediately from the fact that $D_{UK}^m(P_1)$ is 25 percent higher than $D_{UK}^m(P_0)$. When the same quantity of wheat is imported at a price that is 25 percent higher, the supply of pounds, which is the pound price of imports multiplied by the quantity of imports, is also 25 percent higher (recall that the quantity of

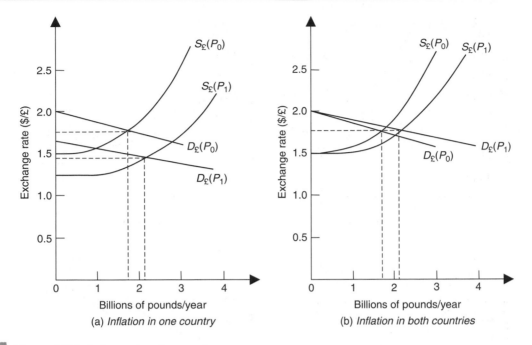

Figure 6.7 *Inflation and exchange rates*

Notes

Curves labeled with P_0 represent the situation before inflation. Curves labeled with P_1 represent the situation after inflation. With inflation in one country only (a), the same quantity of exports is sold after a depreciation that is approximately equal to the country's rate of inflation. The same *quantity* sold at the higher prices means the *value* of exports is higher by the rate of inflation. This means the currency demand curve shifts down and to the right approximately in proportion to inflation. The same argument applies to the currency supply curve. Therefore, the exchange rate of the inflating country depreciates by approximately its rate of inflation as in (a), and the quantity of currency traded increases by the rate of inflation. When inflation also occurs in the other country (b), the same *quantities* are imported and exported at the same exchange rates at the post-inflation prices. Therefore, the *values* of imports and exports are higher by the rate of inflation at each exchange rate. That is, the currency supply and demand curves shift to the right in proportion to the rate of inflation, and the exchange rate is unaffected.

pounds supplied is the pound *value* of imports, which is the pound price times the quantity). The change in exchange rate that will achieve a 25 percent higher pound price and a corresponding 25 percent higher supply of pounds is a 25 percent depreciation of the pound. This follows because the dollar price of wheat is unchanged. That is, at an exchange rate that is 25 percent lower, the pound price of wheat is 25 percent higher and the quantity of imports is unchanged. Therefore, at an exchange rate that is 25 percent lower there is a 25 percent higher quantity of pounds supplied. This means that inflation of 25 percent shifts the supply curve for pounds downward by 25 percent and to the right by 25 percent, so that points on $S_£(P_1)$ in Figure 6.7a are 25 percent below and 25 percent to the right of corresponding points on $S_£(P_0)$.

The reasoning behind the effect of inflation on the demand for pounds is similar to the reasoning behind its effect on the supply of pounds described earlier. Figure 6.6 shows that the same quantity of oil is exported after inflation as before inflation if the pound price of oil increases by 25 percent; $S_{UK}^x(P_1)$ is 25 percent above $S_{UK}^x(P_0)$. Because the dollar price of oil is unchanged, to achieve a 25 percent higher pound oil price we need a 25 percent pound depreciation. Therefore, at a 25 percent lower exchange rate in Figure 6.7a we have a 25 percent higher pound price of oil and the same quantity of oil exports. This represents a 25 percent increase in the *value* of exports, which is price times quantity, and hence in the demand for pounds. Therefore, the effect of inflation is to shift each point on the demand curve for pounds downward by 25 percent

127

and to the right by 25 percent; at a 25 percent lower exchange rate the demand for pounds is 25 percent higher after inflation than before.

Figure 6.7a shows the supply and demand curves for pounds shifted downward by 25 percent and to the right by 25 percent. If we compare the equilibrium where $S_£(P_1)$ intersects $D_£(P_1)$ with the equilibrium where $S_£(P_0)$ intersects $D_£(P_0)$, we see that the pound depreciates by 25 percent. That is, inflation in one country reduces the exchange rate of that country's currency by the same percentage as the country's inflation. We also can see from comparing equilibria in Figure 6.7a that the quantity of pounds traded also increases by 25 percent.[6] We should recall that in order to reach these conclusions we considered only exports and imports, and assumed that *all* prices and wages in Britain increased by the same amount.

Inflation also in other countries

The difference between having inflation only in Britain, and having inflation in Britain and the United States, is that in the latter case we must allow for increases in the *dollar* prices of the imported and exported products. Let us assume US inflation is also 25 percent, so that the dollar prices of wheat and oil increase by 25 percent, that is, from $3/bushel and $25/barrel, to $3.75/bushel and $31.25/barrel.

Let us consider first the supply curve of pounds. We know from our earlier discussion and from Figure 6.6 that the quantity of wheat imports after inflation is the same as before inflation if the pound price of wheat increases by the amount of inflation, that is, 25 percent. Therefore, at the same exchange rate as before there is a 25 percent increase in the pound price of wheat and the same quantity of wheat imports. It follows that at the same exchange rate the supply of pounds is 25 percent higher after inflation than before inflation. This is due to an unchanged quantity of imports and a 25 percent higher price. That is, the supply curve of pounds is shifted 25 percent to the right at every exchange rate. This is shown in Figure 6.7b, where $S_£(P_1)$ is at a 25 percent higher quantity of pounds at each exchange rate.

Considering the demand for pounds, we note that, as before, oil exports are the same after inflation as before inflation if the pound price of oil is 25 percent higher. This was seen in Figure 6.6. With the dollar price of oil increasing 25 percent, the pound price of oil increases 25 percent with an unchanged exchange rate. That is, at the same exchange rate the pound price of oil is 25 percent higher and the quantity of oil exported is unchanged. This means that at the same exchange rate the quantity of pounds demanded to pay for oil is 25 percent higher after inflation than before. We discover that inflation in Britain and the United States shifts $D_£$ to the right by the rate of inflation. That is, at each exchange rate in Figure 6.7b, $D_£(P_1)$, the demand curve for pounds after inflation, is at a 25 percent higher quantity of pounds than $D_£(P_0)$, the demand curve for pounds before inflation.

Comparing the two equilibria in Figure 6.7b, we see that when inflation occurs at the same rate in Britain and the United States, the exchange rate remains unchanged. This contrasts with the conclusion in Figure 6.7a where inflation in Britain alone causes the pound to depreciate by the rate of inflation. What is similar in the two equilibria is that the quantity of currency traded is the same. That is, whether it is just Britain with 25 percent inflation, or Britain plus the United States with 25 percent inflation, the quantity of pounds exchanged grows by 25 percent.[7]

6 The conclusion that 25 percent inflation, with other countries having zero inflation, causes 25 percent depreciation is also reached by considering the PPP principle presented later in the book. However, PPP, which is based on arbitrage arguments, does not imply an increase in the quantity of currencies traded, whereas our discussion here does.

7 The conclusion, that with both countries having the same inflation the exchange rate does not change, also follows from PPP. However, PPP does not make predictions about the quantity of currency that is exchanged.

More generally, the above analysis can be extended to show that a country's exchange rate depreciates by the extent that the country's inflation exceeds that of other countries. Of course, this assumes all other factors affecting exchange rates are unchanged.

We know from the description of the balance-of-payments account in Chapter 5 that there are many factors behind the supply and demand curves for a country's currency in addition to terms of trade, inflation and the other factors which affect the value of merchandise imports and exports. Let us consider how these other factors influence exchange rates by examining how they shift the supply and demand curves for pounds in Figure 6.3.

Service trade, income flows, and transfers

Imports and exports of services such as tourism, banking, consulting, engineering, and so on, respond to exchange rates in the same way as imports and exports of merchandise. Therefore, the currency supply and demand curves derived from international trade in these services look like those in Figure 6.3. The currency supply curve from importing services can be added to that due to importing merchandise, and the currency demand curve from exporting services can be added to that from exporting merchandise. This has the effect of shifting both $S_£$ and $D_£$ in Figure 6.3 to the right. We can think of the currency supply and demand curves for imports and exports of services as being "horizontally added" to the currency supply and demand curves from imports and exports of merchandise. Horizontal addition involves the addition of quantities demanded and supplied at each price, and the plotting of the resulting quantities against the prices at which they occur. With supply and demand curves for currencies from services sloping the same way as currency supply and demand curves from merchandise, the horizontally added curves slope the same direction as the component curves.

If exports of services exceed imports of services, then the currency demand curve, $D_£$, is shifted to the right more than the currency supply curve, $S_£$, from the inclusion of services. Therefore, the exchange rate is higher than in Figure 6.3. On the other hand, if imports of services exceed exports of services, then the currency supply curve is shifted to the right more than the demand curve. Therefore, the exchange rate is lower than in Figure 6.3.

The supply and demand for a currency from payments and receipts of interest, dividends, rents, and profits do not respond to exchange rates or to other influences in the same manner as the currency supply and demand from merchandise or services. Income payments and receipts are largely determined by past investments and the rates of return on these investments. Therefore, we might consider income payments and receipts as being independent of exchange rates.[8] However, as in the case of considering the effect of services, we can simply add the value of income from investments to the currency demand curve, and the value of debt service and similar payments to the supply curve. If the values of investment income and payments are independent of the exchange rate, the addition of these items to the currency supply and demand curves involves simple parallel rightward shifts of the curves. It should be apparent that the higher is foreign investment income relative to payments, the higher is the exchange rate. It follows that *ceteris paribus*, the more a country's residents have invested abroad in the past and the less they have borrowed, the higher is the country's exchange rate. Countries that have incurred lots of debt, *ceteris paribus*, have lower exchange rates. In addition, high global interest rates are good for net creditor countries — those with more overseas investments than debts.

---

8 Exchange rates do affect the domestic-currency value of a given amount of foreign-currency receipts or foreign-currency payments. However, this is an effect of *translating* foreign currency into domestic currency, and is different from the effects of exchange rates on merchandise and services which result from changes in amounts bought and sold.

High global interest rates are bad for net debtor countries.[9]

Transfers can easily be accommodated in the supply-and-demand model of exchange rates. We add the amount of transfers received from abroad to a currency's demand curve and the amount sent abroad to the supply curve. Clearly, *ceteris paribus*, net inflows of transfers tend to increase the value of a currency and net outflows tend to reduce it. Transfers depend on a country's need for help or its ability to help others. Transfers also depend on the number of residents sending funds to relatives abroad or receiving funds from relatives abroad.

Foreign investment

Foreign investment in a country represents a demand for the country's currency when that investment occurs.[10] Therefore, foreign investment in a country, whether it be direct investment, portfolio investment, or additions to bank deposits of nonresidents, shifts the demand curve for the country's currency to the right. Similarly, investment abroad by a country's residents represents a supply of the country's currency and shifts the currency supply curve to the right. Therefore, *ceteris paribus*, net inflows of investment tend to increase the foreign exchange value of a country's currency, and net outflows tend to reduce it. The amount of investment flowing into or out of a country depends on rates of return in the country relative to rates of return elsewhere, as well as on relative risks. *Ceteris paribus*, increases in a country's interest rates or expected dividends cause an increase in demand for that country's currency from increased foreign investment, and a decrease in supply of that country's currency from a decrease

in residents' investment abroad. Consequently, increases in interest rates or expected dividends tend to cause a currency to appreciate, and vice versa. Similarly, for given interest rates and expected dividends, an expected appreciation of a country's currency increases the attractiveness of investments in that country and thereby causes the country's currency to appreciate. That is, expected future appreciation of a currency causes the currency to increase in value, just as with other assets: expectations are generally self-fulfilling.

All the conclusions we have reached have assumed that the demand curve for a currency slopes downward and the supply curve slopes upward. It is time to show why this assumption may not be valid. In particular, it is time to see why the supply curve of a currency may slope downward, and what this implies for exchange rates. We shall focus on the implications for stability of exchange rates.

THE STABILITY OF EXCHANGE RATES

The conditions required for instability

The supply curve for pounds, $S_£$, is derived from the British demand for imports. Figure 6.8a shows two demand curves for imports. The import demand curve labeled D_{UK}^m ($\eta_m > 1$) is the same import demand curve drawn in Figure 6.1a. It is labeled with $\eta_m > 1$ in parentheses because it is an elastic import demand curve. That is, when the price of imports falls, the quantity of imports increases by a greater percentage than the price declines; the demand elasticity exceeds 1.0. The currency supply curve derived from D_{UK}^m ($\eta_m > 1$) is $S_£$ ($\eta_m > 1$). This is the same supply curve of pounds as in Figure 6.1b. The currency supply curve obtained from an elastic demand for imports is seen to slope upward.

Figure 6.8a shows an inelastic demand curve for imports, D_{UK}^m ($\eta_m < 1$). It is inelastic because a reduction in the price of imports causes a smaller percentage increase in the quantity of imports demanded than the percentage reduction in price. We can derive the supply curve of pounds that is associated with the inelastic import demand curve

---

9 By high or low global interest rates we are referring to rates around the world, not to interest rates in one country versus another. As we explain in the next section, relative interest rates affect exchange rates by affecting the flows of financial capital between countries.

10 In all future periods when interest or dividends are paid, or profits and rents are repatriated, there is a supply of the country's currency.

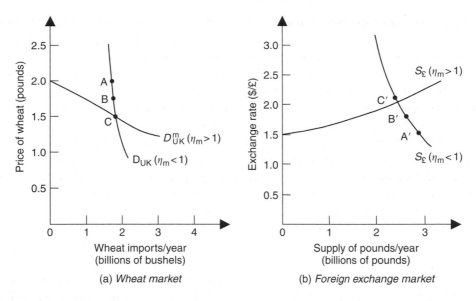

Figure 6.8 *Currency supply and import elasticity*

Notes
When the demand for imports is elastic, that is, $|\eta_m| > 1$, the supply curve of the currency is upward sloping. When the demand is inelastic, that is, $|\eta_m| < 1$, the supply curve of the currency is downward sloping. The downward slope occurs because depreciation raises import prices and reduces the quantity of imports, but the *value* of imports increases. This occurs when the percentage reduction in quantity imported is less than the percentage increase in the price of imports.

by doing the same as before. That is, we consider a number of possible exchange rates, compute the price and quantity of imports at each of these exchange rates, and then plot the values of imports (which is price multiplied by quantity) against the associated exchange rates; recall that it is the *value* of imports that is the *quantity* of currency supplied. Let us do this, and again assume that the given world price of wheat is $3/bushel.

At an exchange rate of $1.5/£ the pound price of wheat is $3 \div \$1.5/£ = £2.0/bushel$, and according to the inelastic demand curve D^m_{UK} ($\eta_m < 1$), Britain imports 1.5 billion bushels at this price, point A in Figure 6.8a. The quantity of pounds supplied, which equals the value of imports, is therefore £3 billion (£2/bushel × 1.5 billion bushels) at the exchange rate $1.5/£. This gives point A′ in Figure 6.8b. At $1.7/£ wheat costs $3 \div \$1.7/£ = £1.76$ and Britain imports 1.6 billion bushels, point B in Figure 6.8a. Therefore, the quantity of pounds supplied per year at the exchange rate $1.7/£ is £2.82 billion (£1.76/bushel × 1.6 billion bushels), point B′ in Figure 6.8b. Similarly, at $2/£ wheat costs

$3 \div \$2/£ = £1.5/bushel$. At this price Britain imports 1.7 billion bushels per year, point C in Figure 6.8a. Therefore, the quantity of pounds supplied per year at the exchange rate $2/£ is £2.55 billion (£1.5/ bushel × 1.7 billion bushels). This gives point C′ in Figure 6.8b. We find that when the demand for imports is inelastic, the supply curve of the country's currency slopes downward. Yes, it is possible to have a downward-sloping supply curve for a currency, something we are not likely to encounter anywhere else.[11] What happens is that when demand is inelastic the amount spent on a product decreases with decreases in the price of the product. The price of imports decreases with increases in the foreign exchange value of the importer's currency. Therefore, when the demand for imports is inelastic, the higher is the foreign exchange value of a country's currency, the lower is the price of imports, the less is spent on imports, and so the lower is the quantity of

11 The reason we can have downward-sloping supply curves for currencies and not for other things is that for currencies we plot values (price × quantity) on the horizontal axis, whereas we normally plot just the quantity.

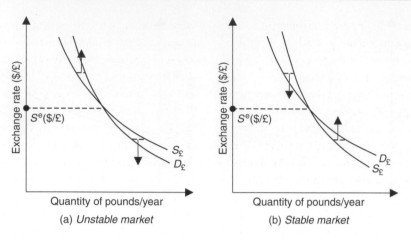

Figure 6.9 *Stability of foreign exchange markets*

Notes
When the currency supply curve slopes downward, foreign exchange markets may be unstable. They are unstable if the currency demand curve is steeper than the supply curve, that is, the demand curve cuts the supply curve from above when going down along the demand curve.

the country's currency supplied. We discover that all we need for a downward-sloping currency supply curve is inelastic import demand. This could easily occur. For example, it is generally felt that when the price of oil falls due to an appreciation of a country's currency, the quantity of oil demanded and imported increases less than the percent decline in the price, that is, the demand for oil is inelastic. Let us now consider the consequences of an inelastic demand for imports and the associated downward-sloping currency supply curve for the stability of exchange rates.

Figure 6.9 shows two situations in which the currency supply curve slopes downward. In the situation in Figure 6.9a the demand curve for pounds is steeper than the supply curve, but in Figure 6.9b the situation is the reverse. Let us consider the stability of the exchange rate in Figures 6.9a and b by allowing the exchange rate to deviate slightly from its equilibrium $S^e(\$/£)$ where the supply and demand curves intersect. In particular, let us consider whether market forces are likely to push the exchange rate back to equilibrium when it is disturbed from equilibrium.

In Figure 6.9a a small decline in the exchange rate below equilibrium will result in an excess supply of pounds: at rates below $S^e(\$/£)$ the quantity of pounds supplied exceeds the quantity

demanded. This will push the value of the pound even lower. This will cause an even larger excess supply, and so on. Similarly, in Figure 6.9a a small increase in the exchange rate above equilibrium will result in an excess demand for pounds. This will push the value of the pound even higher, cause an even larger excess demand, and so on. We find that the equilibrium exchange rate in Figure 6.9a is unstable. Small shocks to exchange rates can result in substantial movements in exchange rates from equilibrium when the demand and supply curves for a currency have the configuration in Figure 6.9a.

Figure 6.9b has a downward-sloping supply curve of pounds just as in Figure 6.9a, but here the demand curve for pounds is flatter than the supply curve. In this case a small decline in the value of the pound below the equilibrium exchange rate $S^e(\$/£)$ causes an excess demand for pounds: at rates below $S^e(\$/£)$ the quantity of pounds demanded exceeds the quantity supplied. This pushes the exchange rate back up to equilibrium. Similarly, a small increase in the exchange rate above the equilibrium causes an excess supply of pounds. This pushes the exchange rate back down to equilibrium. The equilibrium in Figure 6.9b is therefore stable.

Consideration of Figures 6.9a and b allows us to conclude that having a downward-sloping currency supply curve is necessary but not sufficient to cause an unstable foreign exchange market. A relatively flat or elastic currency demand curve can offset the destabilizing nature of a downward-sloping supply curve. For an unstable market it is necessary to have a downward-sloping currency supply curve – which we recall requires inelastic demand for imports – *and* a relatively steep or inelastic currency demand curve. A sufficient condition for instability is that the supply curve slopes downward and the demand curve is steeper at equilibrium than the supply curve. A more precise statement of the condition for stability of the foreign exchange market is derived in Appendix A. This condition is known as the **Marshall–Lerner condition** and is stated directly in terms of the import and export elasticities of demand, which are determinants of the slopes of the currency supply and demand curves.

Unstable exchange rates and the balance of trade

Because there have been times when exchange rates have been extremely volatile, the conditions for an unstable foreign exchange market are of considerable interest. Therefore, we should not leave the matter until we have an intuitive understanding of these conditions. Such an understanding can be obtained by examining how exchange rates affect the balance of trade.

A depreciation of a country's currency increases the price of imports in terms of domestic currency. This reduces the *quantity* of imports, but does not necessarily reduce the *value* of imports. If import demand is inelastic, the higher price of imports more than offsets the lower quantity, so that the value of imports is higher. This means that if import demand is inelastic, depreciation can worsen the balance of trade (recall that the balance of trade is the *value* of exports minus the *value* of imports). However, even when more is spent on imports after depreciation, the balance of trade is not *necessarily* worsened. This is because depreciation makes exports cheaper in terms of *foreign* currency, and this increases the quantity exported. The value of exports unambiguously

increases along with the quantity of exports because exports are not made cheaper in *domestic* currency. Indeed, if anything the stronger demand for exports after depreciation can cause an increase in domestic-currency prices of exports. It follows that even if depreciation increases the value of imports, the balance of trade is worsened only if the value of exports increases less than the value of imports.

The preceding argument can be directly related to Figure 6.9. If import demand is inelastic, a depreciation of the pound, which is a movement down the vertical axis, causes an increase in the value of British imports and hence in the quantity of pounds supplied; the pound supply curve slopes downward. This on its own does not cause instability, for the same reason it does not necessarily worsen the balance of trade, namely, that the depreciation also increases the value of exports and hence the quantity of pounds demanded. The foreign exchange market is unstable only if the value of exports does not increase sufficiently to compensate for inelastic import demand, just as depreciation worsens the balance of trade only if the value of exports does not sufficiently increase to compensate for the increase in the value of imports.

SHORT-RUN VERSUS LONG-RUN TRADE ELASTICITIES AND THE J CURVE

A worsening of the balance of trade following a depreciation of a currency may be temporary. Similarly, instability in exchange rates may be only a short-run problem. Because the consequences of the trade balance worsening with depreciation and of exchange-rate instability are more serious if they persist, it is worthwhile considering why they may be temporary problems. Our consideration leads us to the **J curve**. The J curve has taken on such importance since the second half of the 1980s that it has moved out of the textbooks into the columns of the popular press.

It takes time for people to adjust their preferences towards substitutes. Therefore, it is generally believed that demand is more inelastic in the short run than in the long run. This belief is particularly strong for the

133

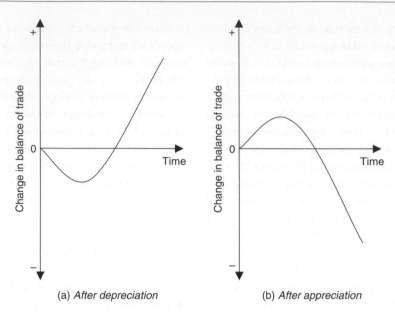

(a) *After depreciation*   (b) *After appreciation*

Figure 6.10 *The J curve*

Notes
The J curve describes the balance of trade after a depreciation or appreciation. The time path of the trade balance looks like a J if the elasticities of demand for imports and supply of exports are smaller in the short run than the long run.

elasticity of demand for imports, because the demand curve for imports is derived from the difference between the demand curve for a product in a country and the domestic supply curve of the product; with both supply and demand more inelastic in the short run than the long run, the difference between supply and demand is *a fortiori* more inelastic in the short run. That is, after a depreciation and consequent increase in import prices, a country's residents might continue to buy imports both because they have not adjusted their preferences towards domestically produced substitutes (an inelastic demand curve) and because the domestic substitutes have not yet been produced (an inelastic domestic supply curve). Only after producers begin to supply what was previously imported and after consumers decide to buy **import substitutes** can import demand fully decline after a depreciation. Similarly, exports expand from a depreciation only after suppliers are able to produce more for export and after foreign consumers switch to these products.

If import demand and export supply are more inelastic in the short run than the long run, we may find a depreciation worsening the balance of trade in

the short run, but subsequently improving it. That is, the time path of changes in the balance of trade might look like that shown in Figure 6.10a.[12] The figure assumes that depreciation occurs at time 0, and that because people temporarily spend more on imports, and because exports do not sufficiently increase, the trade balance worsens immediately after the depreciation. Only later, when import and export elasticities increase, does the balance of trade turn around and eventually improve. Because of the shape of the time path followed by the trade balance in Figure 6.10a, the phenomenon of an initial worsening and subsequent improvement of the trade balance after a depreciation is known as the **J-curve effect**.

12 For a further discussion of the time path see Michael H. Moffett, "The J-Curve Revisited: An Empirical Examination for the United States," *Journal of International Money and Finance*, September 1989, pp. 425–44, and David K. Backus, Patrick J. Kehoe, and Finn E. Kydland, "Dynamics of the Trade Balance and the Terms of Trade: The J-Curve?," *American Economic Review*, March 1994, pp. 84–103.

Figure 6.10b shows what might happen after an *appreciation* of the exchange rate if imports and exports are more inelastic in the short run than in the long run. The figure shows that after an appreciation at time 0, the associated decline in import prices could reduce spending on imports. If the value of exports does not decrease as much as the value of imports declines, the balance of trade will improve from the currency appreciation – not what one would normally expect. However, over time, as import and export demand become more elastic, the quantity of imports increases more than the price declines, and/or exports decrease sufficiently for the balance of trade to worsen. In the case of an appreciation we find that the balance of trade follows the path of an inverted J. What we have shown is that the J curve occurs under the same conditions as instability of exchange rates in the short run but stability in the long run. When imports and exports are sufficiently inelastic in the short run, we have both unstable exchange rates and a temporary worsening/improvement of the

balance of trade after a currency depreciation/appreciation, and when the trade balance turns around, stability returns to foreign exchange markets.

Before leaving the question of the J curve and instability of exchange rates, we should make it clear that foreign exchange markets can be stable even if imports and exports are extremely inelastic. This is because there are numerous other reasons for supplying or demanding a currency. For example, currency speculators might buy a currency during the downward-sloping period of the J curve if they think the currency will eventually move back up again as the trade balance improves. This demand from speculators makes the demand curve for a currency flatter (more elastic) than from considering the demand for the currency only by the buyers of the country's exports.[13] On the other hand, the J-curve effect which relates to the balance of trade, is not obviated by currency speculators, so that we can have stable foreign exchange markets coexisting with a J curve.

SUMMARY

1   Flexible exchange rates are determined by the forces of currency supply and demand.

2   We can construct the supply curve of a currency from a country's demand curve for imports, and the demand curve for a currency from the country's supply curve of exports.

3   The effect of any item in the balance-of-payments account on the exchange rate can be determined by identifying how it shifts the currency supply or currency demand curve.

4   *Ceteris paribus*, an improvement in a country's terms of trade causes the country's currency to appreciate.

5   Inflation that is higher than in other countries causes a country's currency to depreciate. If inflation in different countries is equal, *ceteris paribus*, exchange rates do not change.

6   If import demand is inelastic the currency supply curve slopes downward. This is because depreciation raises the price of imports in domestic currency more than it reduces the quantity of imports. In this way depreciation increases the *value* of imports, meaning a downward-sloping supply curve of the currency.

7   When the supply curve slopes downward the foreign exchange market may be unstable. Instability occurs when the currency demand curve is steeper than the downward-sloping supply curve.

13 The question of whether speculators are likely to stabilize or destabilize exchange rates is addressed in Chapter 23.

8   Because import demand elasticities are smaller in the short run than in the long run, instability is more likely in the short run than the long run.

9   The same conditions that cause short-run instability and long-run stability result in a J curve. The J curve shows that a depreciation can temporarily worsen the balance of trade, while an appreciation can temporarily improve the balance of trade.

REVIEW QUESTIONS

1   Does currency supply depend on the quantity or on the value of imports?

2   Under what condition does the value of imports vary in the opposite direction to the quantity of imports when exchange rates change?

3   Does currency demand depend on the quantity or on the value of exports?

4   Why does the value of exports *always* vary in the same directions as the quantity of exports when exchange rates change?

5   Why does inflation shift up a country's supply curve of a product in proportion to inflation? Does the explanation have to do with the fact that a firm's supply curve is the firm's marginal cost, MC, curve?

6   Why does inflation shift up a country's demand curve for a product in proportion to inflation? Does the explanation have to do with inflation raising all prices and incomes, leaving relative prices and real incomes unchanged?

7   How does a country's demand curve for imports relate to the country's demand curve for the good and its supply curve of the good?

8   Is a downward-sloping currency supply curve a necessary or sufficient condition for unstable exchange rates?

9   What is the J curve?

10 How does the J curve depend on short-run versus long-run elasticities of import demand?

ASSIGNMENT PROBLEMS

1   Assume that the foreign-currency amount of interest and dividend earnings from abroad is fixed. Show how the horizontal addition of interest and dividend earnings to a currency's demand curve will appear when consideration is given to the effect of exchange rates on the translated values of these earnings.

2   Are debt-service imports as likely to be affected by exchange rates as are debt-service exports? (*Hint*: It depends on the currency of denomination of debt-service earnings and payments.)

3   What is the slope of the currency supply curve when the demand for imports is unit-elastic, that is, equal to 1.0?

4   What is the intuitive explanation for the fact that a decrease in demand for a currency can cause it to appreciate if import and export demand are sufficiently inelastic?

5   How can speculators cause the foreign exchange market to be stable even when the economy is moving along the downward-sloping part of a J curve?

6   Why is the import demand curve likely to be more elastic in the long run than in the short run?

7   Why are exports likely to be more elastic in the long run than in the short run?

8   Does only the equilibrium exchange rate change with inflation, or is the quantity of currency traded also affected, and if so, why?

BIBLIOGRAPHY

Alexander, Sidney S., "The Effects of a Devaluation on the Trade Balance," IMF *Staff Papers*, April 1952, pp. 263–78. Reprinted in Richard E. Caves and Harry G. Johnson (eds), *AEA Readings in International Economics*, Richard D. Irwin, Homewood, IL, 1968.

Haberler, Gottfried, "The Market for Foreign Exchange and the Stability of the Balance of Payments: A Theoretical Analysis," *Kyklos*, Fasc. 3, 1949, pp. 193–218. Reprinted in Richard N. Cooper (ed.), *International Finance*, Penguin, Baltimore, 1969.

Heller, H. Robert, *International Monetary Economics*, Prentice-Hall, Englewood Cliffs, NJ, 1974, Chapter 6.

McKinnon, Ronald I., "*Money in International Exchange: The Convertible Currency System*," Oxford University Press, 1979.

Mundell, Robert A., *International Economics*, Macmillan, New York, 1968, Chapter 1.

Pippenger, John E., *Fundamentals of International Finance*, Prentice-Hall, Englewood Cliffs, NJ, 1984, Chapter 5.

APPENDIX A

Stability in foreign exchange markets

Let us consider the stability of $S(\$/\pounds)$, assuming for simplicity that the only two countries in the world are the United States and the United Kingdom, and that there are no capital flows. Under these assumptions, the quantity of pounds demanded is equal to the value of British exports. We can write this as $p_x \cdot Q_x(S \cdot p_x)$ where p_x is the pound price of British exports and $Q_x(S \cdot p_x)$ is the quantity of British exports. That is, the value of pounds demanded is the price of exports multiplied by the quantity of exports. [We put $(S \cdot p_x)$ in the parentheses to signify that Q_x depends on $(S \cdot p_x)$, which is the dollar price of British exports; S is short for the spot rate, $S(\$/\pounds)$. It is the dollar price that is relevant to the US buyer of British exports.]

The quantity of pounds supplied is equal to the value of British imports. We can write this as $(p_m/S) \cdot Q_m(p_m/S)$ where p_m is the US dollar price of British imports and $Q_m(p_m/S)$ is the quantity of British imports. That is, the value of pounds supplied is the pound price of imports (p_m/S) multiplied by the quantity of British imports, where the term in parentheses in $Q_m(p_m/S)$ signifies that the quantity of imports depends on p_m/S [Recall that since S is the exchange rate $S(\$/\pounds)$, dividing by S puts the dollar price of imports into British pounds. It is the pound price of British imports, p_m/S, that is relevant to the British buyer, and which hence determines the quantity of imports into Britain.].

We can write the excess demand for pounds, E, as

$$E = p_x \cdot Q_x(S \cdot p_x) - \frac{p_m}{S} \cdot Q_m\left(\frac{p_m}{S}\right) \tag{6A.1}$$

That is, the excess demand for pounds is the value of pounds demanded minus the value supplied. If we assume a perfectly elastic supply of exports and imports then we can assume that p_x and p_m remain unchanged as

137

the quantities of exports and imports vary with the exchange rate.[14] With this assumption we can differentiate equation (6A.1) to obtain

$$\frac{dE}{dS} = p_x \cdot \frac{dQ_x}{d(Sp_x)} \cdot \frac{d(Sp_x)}{dS} - \frac{p_m}{S} \cdot \frac{dQ_m}{d(p_m/S)} \cdot \frac{d(p_m/S)}{dS} - Q_m \cdot \frac{d(p_m/S)}{dS}$$

or

$$\frac{dE}{dS} = p_x \cdot \frac{dQ_x}{d(Sp_x)} \cdot p_x + \frac{p_m}{S} \cdot \frac{dQ_m}{d(p_m/S)} \cdot \frac{p_m}{S^2} + \frac{p_m Q_m}{S^2} \tag{6A.2}$$

Multiplying and dividing the first two terms on the right-hand side of equation (6A.2) to form elasticities, we have

$$\frac{dE}{dS} = \left(\frac{Sp_x}{Q_x} \cdot \frac{dQ_x}{d(Sp_x)} \right) \cdot \frac{p_x Q_x}{S} + \left(\frac{p_m/S}{Q_m} \cdot \frac{dQ_m}{d(p_m/S)} \right) \cdot \frac{p_m Q_m}{S^2} + \frac{p_m Q_m}{S^2} \tag{6A.3}$$

We can define the elasticity of demand for exports, η_x, and the elasticity of demand for imports, η_m, as follows:[15]

$$\eta_x = -\left(\frac{Sp_x}{Q_x} \cdot \frac{dQ_x}{d(Sp_x)} \right) \quad \text{and} \quad \eta_m = -\left(\frac{p_m/S}{Q_m} \cdot \frac{dQ_m}{d(p_m/S)} \right)$$

We note that these elasticities are defined in terms of the currencies in which buyers are paying for their purchases, that is, exports from Britain are defined in terms of dollar prices, $S \cdot p_x$, and imports into Britain are defined in terms of pound prices p_m/S. Using these definitions in equation (6A.3) gives

$$\frac{dE}{dS} = -\eta_x \cdot \frac{p_x Q_x}{S} - \eta_m \cdot \frac{p_m Q_m}{S^2} + \frac{p_m Q_m}{S^2}$$

where we have defined the elasticities as positive. If the foreign exchange market started from a position of balance, then

$$p_x Q_x = \frac{p_m Q_m}{S}$$

That is, the pound value of British exports equals the pound value of British imports. This enables us to write

$$\frac{dE}{dS} = -(\eta_x + \eta_m - 1) \cdot \frac{p_x Q_x}{S} \tag{6A.4}$$

The stability of the foreign exchange market requires that as the value of the pound goes up (S increases), the excess demand for pounds must fall (E falls). Similarly, it requires that as the pound falls in value (S goes down), the excess demand for pounds must rise (E goes up). This means that for stability, E and S must move in opposite directions ($dE/dS < 0$). That is, for stability:

$$\frac{dE}{dS} = -(\eta_x + \eta_m - 1) \cdot \frac{p_x Q_x}{S} < 0 \tag{6A.5}$$

14 Stability conditions can be derived without assuming perfectly elastic supply of exports and imports, but only at the expense of considerable additional complexity. See Miltiades Chacholiades, *Principles of International Economics*, McGraw-Hill, New York, 1981, pp. 386–7, or Joan Robinson, "The Foreign Exchanges," in Joan Robinson, *Essays in the Theory of Employment*, Macmillan, London, 1939.

15 In this appendix we use the foreign elasticity of *demand* for exports, whereas in the main text we use the domestic elasticity of *supply* of exports. We can use the foreign elasticity of demand here because we are assuming only two countries. We could have assumed two countries in the text and then used the two elasticities of demand as we do here. However, the approach in the text is more general, because it uses the demand for the currency irrespective of who buys the country's exports.

We know that $p_x \cdot Q_x / S$ is positive. Therefore, stability of the foreign exchange market requires that

$$\eta_x + \eta_m - 1 > 0$$

or

$$\eta_x + \eta_m > 1 \qquad\qquad\qquad (6A.6)$$

We discover that for stability, the average elasticity of demand must exceed 0.5. For exchange-rate instability,

$$\eta_x + \eta_m < 1$$

When $\eta_x + \eta_m = 1$, the market is metastable, staying wherever it is. The condition (6A.6) is generally known as the Marshall-Lerner condition, after Alfred Marshall and Abba Lerner, who independently discovered it.

Because demand elasticities are generally smaller in the short run than in the long run, foreign exchange markets might be unstable in the short run, but eventually return to stability. However, if there are speculators who realize that stability occurs in the long run, the foreign exchange market may be stable in the short run even if the Marshall-Lerner condition does not hold.

Part III

The fundamental international parity conditions

Part III explains the nature of, and limitations of, two fundamental international financial relationships that between them tie together interest rates, inflation rates, and expected changes in exchange rates. The first of these relationships is the purchasing-power-parity (PPP) principle which occurs in the product markets. It states that, when measured in the same currency, baskets of freely traded goods and services should cost the same everywhere. The second relationship occurs in the money markets, and states that, after allowance for exchange rates, investment yields and borrowing costs should be the same whatever the currency of investment or loan. This relationship is known as the interest-parity principle.

Chapter 7 begins by explaining the law of one price as it applies to an individual commodity such as gold or wheat. In this context the law of one price states that the dollar cost of a particular commodity should be equal everywhere. This means that when prices are measured in local currency, the ratio of, for example, the dollar price of wheat in the United States and the pound price of wheat in Britain should be the exchange rate of dollars for pounds. If not, commodity arbitrage would occur. We show, however, that shipping costs, tariffs, and quotas can result in deviations from the law of one price.

Chapter 7 also explains the extension of the law of one price from an individual commodity to goods and services in general. The extension gives rise to the PPP principle, which states that the ratio of the dollar price of a *basket* of goods and services in the United States to the pound price of the same *basket* in Britain should be the exchange rate of the dollar for the pound.

When considered as a relationship over time rather than at a point in time, PPP becomes a link between changes in exchange rates and differences between inflation rates: currencies of countries with rapid inflation will depreciate vis-à-vis currencies of countries with slow inflation. Chapter 7 explains the nature of this link, and why it might be and, indeed frequently is, broken. It is also shown that another version of PPP that involves expectations of exchange rates and inflation can be derived by considering speculation.

In the context of the money market, which is the market in which short-term securities are traded, the law of one price states that covered (i.e. hedged) dollar rates of return and dollar costs of borrowing will be the same whatever the currency of denomination of the investment or loan. If this were not so, there would be interest arbitrage. This involves borrowing in one currency and lending in another currency, with foreign exchange risk hedged on the forward exchange market. The relationship between interest rates and exchange rates whereby it is irrelevant in which currency a person invests or borrows is called the covered interest-parity condition. This condition is explained in Chapter 8, along with the way that the forward exchange market can be used to eliminate exchange-rate risk and exposure when engaging in interest arbitrage.

The covered interest-parity condition is derived with the assumptions that there are no transaction costs, political risks of investing abroad, taxes which depend on the currency of investment or borrowing, or concerns over the liquidity of investments. Chapter 8 describes the effects of dropping these assumptions which, as we shall see in later chapters, have bearing on corporate financing decisions and international cash management.

Chapter 7

The purchasing-power-parity principle

It would be too ridiculous to go about seriously to prove that wealth does not consist in money, or in gold and silver; but in what money purchases, and is valuable only for purchasing.

Adam Smith

Of the many influences on exchange rates mentioned in Chapter 6, one factor is considered to be particularly important for explaining currency movements over the long run. That factor is inflation. In this chapter we examine the theory and the evidence for a long-run connection between inflation and exchange rates. This connection has become known as the **purchasing-power-parity (PPP) principle**. An entire chapter is devoted to the exploration of this principle because it plays an important role in foreign exchange risk and exposure, and many other topics covered in the remainder of this book.

The PPP principle, which was popularized by Gustav Cassell in the 1920s, is most easily explained if we begin by considering the connection between exchange rates and the local-currency price of an individual commodity in different countries.[1] This connection between exchange rates and commodity prices is known as the **law of one price**.

THE LAW OF ONE PRICE

Virtually every opportunity for profit will catch the attention of an attentive individual somewhere in the world. One type of opportunity that will rarely be missed is the chance to buy an item in one place and sell it in another for a profit. For example, if gold or copper was priced at a particular US dollar price in London and the dollar price was simultaneously higher in New York, people would buy the metal in London and ship it to New York for sale. Of course, it takes time to ship physical commodities, and so at any precise moment, dollar prices might differ a little between markets. Transportation costs are also involved in attempts to profit from price differences. However, if there is enough of a price difference between locations, people will take advantage of it by buying commodities in the cheaper market and then sell them in the more expensive market.[2]

People who buy in one market and sell in another are **commodity arbitragers**. Through their

---

1 Gustav Cassell, *Money and Foreign Exchange after 1914*, Macmillan, London, 1923, and Gustav Cassell, "Abnormal Deviations in International Exchange," *Economic Journal*, December 1918, pp. 413–15.

2 As we shall mention later, one-way arbitrage arguments would mitigate the wedge between prices in different locations caused by transportation costs. If a buyer faced the same transportation costs of sourcing a product from two markets the prices in the two source locations would be driven together.

actions commodity arbitragers remove any profitable opportunities that may exist. They force up prices in low-cost countries and reduce prices where they are high. Normally, arbitragers cease their activities only when all profitable opportunities have been exhausted, which means that except for the costs of moving goods from place to place, including any tariffs that might be involved, prices of the same product in different markets are equal.[3]

In fact, prices of commodities should be the same in different countries even if there is no direct commodity arbitrage between countries themselves. This is because *outside* buyers will select the lowest price. For example, even if it is extremely costly to arbitrage wheat between Canada and Australia, the two countries' prices would need to be the same; otherwise, outside buyers would buy everything from the cheaper and none from the more expensive supplier. In other words, shipping costs between Canada and Australia set only a maximum on the possible price difference between the countries; the actual price difference is generally smaller than this maximum. For example, if Canadian and Australian ports used to export wheat are at the same distance from Chinese receiving ports so that shipping costs to China from Australia and Canada are the same, shipping costs *between* Canada and Australia will not result in different selling prices. Similarly, even when there are tariffs, if they apply equally to potential sources, they cannot cause price differences. In the terminology of Chapter 2, one-way arbitrage creates a tighter link between prices in different countries than does two-way arbitrage.

When prices in different countries are expressed in the *same* currency, the outcome of commodity market arbitrage – that particular commodity prices are everywhere equal – is easily seen. For example, the dollar prices of an ounce of gold in London, Paris, Frankfurt, Zurich, and New York, certainly if observed at the same time with all markets open, are very similar. But what does it mean for arbitrage to ensure that prices are the same when they are in

different foreign currencies? The answer follows from the **law of one price**, which states that in the absence of frictions such as shipping costs and tariffs, the price of a product when converted into a common currency such as the US dollar, using the spot exchange rate, is the same in every country.[4] For example, because the dollar equivalent of the price of wheat in Britain is $S(\$/£)p_{UK}^{w}$, where p_{UK}^{w} is the pound price of wheat in Britain, the law of one price states that

$$p_{US}^{w} = S(\$/£)p_{UK}^{w} \qquad (7.1)$$

When the law of one price does not hold, buying decisions help restore the equality.

For example, if $p_{US}^{w} = \$4/\text{bushel}$, $p_{UK}^{w} = £2.5/\text{bushel}$, and $S(\$/£) = 1.70$, then the dollar price of wheat in Britain is $\$1.70/£ \times £2.5/\text{bushel} = \$4.25/\text{bushel}$. With the US price of $4/bushel, wheat buyers will buy from the US and not from Britain, forcing up the US price and forcing down the British price until they satisfy equation (7.1).

ABSOLUTE (OR STATIC) FORM OF THE PPP CONDITION

If equation (7.1) were to hold for each and every good and service, and we computed the cost of the same basket of goods and services in Britain and the United States, we would expect to find that

$$P_{US} = S(\$/£)P_{UK} \qquad (7.2)$$

P_{US} and P_{UK} are respectively the costs of the basket of goods and services in the US measured in dollars and in Britain in pounds. Equation (7.2) is the **absolute (or static) form of the PPP condition**. The condition in this form can be rearranged to give the spot exchange rate in terms of the relative costs of the basket in the two countries, namely,

$$S(\$/£) = \frac{P_{US}}{P_{UK}} \qquad (7.3)$$

---

3 We exclude local sales taxes from the price.

4 As we have just said, even in the *presence* of shipping costs and tariffs, the law of one price might still hold as a result of one-way arbitrage.

For example, if the basket costs $1,000 in the United States and £600 in Britain, the exchange rate according to equation (7.3) should be $1.67/£.

The PPP condition in the absolute form in equation (7.2) or (7.3) offers a very simple explanation for the level of exchange rates. However, it is difficult to test the validity of PPP in the form of equation (7.2) or (7.3), because different baskets of goods are used in different countries for computing price indexes. Different baskets are used because tastes and needs differ between countries, affecting what people buy. For example, people in cold, northern countries consume more heating oil and less olive oil than people in more temperate countries. This means that even if the law of one price holds for each individual good, price indexes, which depend on the weights attached to each good, will not conform to the law of one price. For example, if heating oil prices increased more than olive oil prices, the country with a bigger weight in its price index for heating oil would have a larger price index increase than the olive-oil-consuming country, even though heating oil and olive oil prices increased the same amount in both countries. Partly for this reason, an alternative form of the PPP condition which is stated in terms of rates of inflation can be very useful. This form is called the **relative (or dynamic) form of PPP**.

THE RELATIVE (OR DYNAMIC) FORM OF PPP

In order to state PPP in its relative (or dynamic) form let us define the following:

$\dot{S}(\$/£)$ is the percentage change in the spot exchange rate over a year, and $\dot{P}_{US}$ and $\dot{P}_{UK}$ are respectively the percentage annual rates of change in the price levels in the United States and Britain. That is, $\dot{P}_{US}$ and $\dot{P}_{UK}$ are the US and British annual rates of inflation.

If the PPP condition holds in its absolute form at some moment in time, that is,

$$P_{US} = S(\$/£)P_{UK} \qquad (7.2)$$

then at the end of 1 year, for PPP to continue to hold it is necessary that

$$P_{US}(1 + \dot{P}_{US}) = S(\$/£)[1 + \dot{S}(\$/£)]$$
$$\times \; P_{UK}(1 + \dot{P}_{UK}) \qquad (7.4)$$

The left-hand side of equation (7.4) is the price level in the United States after 1 year, written as the US price level at the beginning of the year, multiplied by 1 plus the US annual rate of inflation. Similarly, the right-hand side of equation (7.4) shows the spot exchange rate at the end of 1 year as the rate at the beginning of the year multiplied by 1 plus the rate of change in the spot exchange rate. This is multiplied by the price level in Britain after 1 year, written as the price level at the beginning of the year multiplied by 1 plus the British annual rate of inflation. Equation (7.2) is therefore the PPP condition at one point in time and equation (7.4) is the PPP condition a year later.

Taking the ratio of equation (7.4) to equation (7.2) by taking the ratios of the left-hand sides and of the right-hand sides gives by cancelation

$$(1 + \dot{P}_{US}) = [1 + \dot{S}(\$/£)](1 + \dot{P}_{UK}) \qquad (7.5)$$

Equation (7.5) can be rearranged into

$$1 + \dot{S}(\$/£) = \frac{1 + \dot{P}_{US}}{1 + \dot{P}_{UK}}$$

or

$$\dot{S}(\$/£) = \frac{1 + \dot{P}_{US}}{1 + \dot{P}_{UK}} - 1 \qquad (7.6)$$

Alternatively, equation (7.6) can be written as

$$\dot{S}(\$/£) = \frac{\dot{P}_{US} - \dot{P}_{UK}}{1 + \dot{P}_{UK}} \qquad (7.7)$$

Equation (7.7) is the PPP condition in its relative (or dynamic) form.

To take an example, if the United States experiences inflation of 5 percent ($\dot{P}_{US} = 0.05$) and Britain 10 percent ($\dot{P}_{UK} = 0.10$), then the dollar price of pounds should fall, that is, the pound should

145

depreciate at a rate of 4.5 percent, because

$$\dot{S}(\$/£) = \frac{\dot{P}_{US} - \dot{P}_{UK}}{1 + \dot{P}_{UK}} = \frac{0.05 - 0.10}{1.10}$$
$$= -0.045, \text{ or } -4.5\%$$

If the reverse conditions hold, with the United States having 10 percent inflation versus 5 percent inflation in Britain, then $\dot{S}(\$/£)$ is positive, and the pound appreciates in value against the dollar by 4.8 percent:

$$\dot{S}(\$/£) = \frac{0.10 - 0.05}{1.05} = 0.048, \text{ or } 4.8\%$$

Both values are close to the 5 percent obtained from taking an approximation of equation (7.7) and writing instead

$$\dot{S}(\$/£) \cong \dot{P}_{US} - \dot{P}_{UK} \qquad (7.8)$$

What the PPP condition in this approximate form says is that the rate of change in the exchange rate is equal to the difference between the inflation rates.

Equation (7.8) is a good approximation of equation (7.7) when inflation is low. However, when inflation is high, equation (7.8) may be a poor approximation of equation (7.7). For example, suppose we are interested in the rate of change in the number of US dollars per British pound when British inflation is 25 percent and US inflation is 5 percent. Equation (7.7), the exact PPP formula, implies that

$$\dot{S}(\$/£) = \frac{\dot{P}_{US} - \dot{P}_{UK}}{1 + \dot{P}_{UK}} = \frac{0.05 - 0.25}{1.25}$$
$$= -0.16, \text{ or } -16\%$$

However, from the approximation based on equation (7.8)

$$\dot{S}(\$/£) = \dot{P}_{US} - \dot{P}_{UK} = 0.05 - 0.25$$
$$= -0.20, \text{ or } -20\%$$

Higher inflation makes the approximation even worse. For example, if British inflation was 50 percent; and US inflation 5 percent, then from the

precise PPP condition in equation (7.7)

$$\dot{S}(\$/£) = \frac{\dot{P}_{US} - \dot{P}_{UK}}{1 + \dot{P}_{UK}} = \frac{0.05 - 0.50}{1.5}$$
$$= -0.30, \text{ or } -30\%$$

However, from the approximation

$$\dot{S}(\$/£) = \dot{P}_{US} - \dot{P}_{UK} = 0.05 - 0.50$$
$$= -0.45, \text{ or } -45\%$$

The approximation of the dynamic PPP implies a depreciation of the pound much larger than does the exact PPP condition.

The relative or dynamic form of PPP in equation (7.7), and its approximation in equation (7.8), are not necessarily violated by sales taxes or shipping costs that make prices higher than static-form PPP levels. For example, suppose that because of a British value-added tax (VAT) or because of higher shipping costs of principal commodity imports to Britain than to the United States, US prices are consistently lower by the proportion τ than British prices as given by equation (7.2). That is

$$P_{US} = S(\$/£)P_{UK}(1 - \tau) \qquad (7.9)$$

Equation (7.9) means that for a given exchange rate and price level in Britain, US prices are only $(1 - \tau)$ of the British level. If the same connection exists 1 year later after inflation has occurred and the exchange rate has changed, we have

$$P_{US}(1 + \dot{P}_{US}) = S(\$/£)[1 + \dot{S}(\$/£)]$$
$$\times P_{UK}(1 + \dot{P}_{UK})(1 - \tau) \qquad (7.10)$$

Taking the ratio of equation (7.10) to equation (7.9) gives

$$(1 + \dot{P}_{US}) = [1 + \dot{S}(\$/£)](1 + \dot{P}_{UK}) \qquad (7.11)$$

which is exactly the same as equation (7.5). It follows that equations (7.7) and (7.8), the exact and approximate forms of relative PPP, are unaffected by τ. The relative (or dynamic) form of PPP can hold even if the absolute (or static) form of PPP is (consistently) violated.

EFFICIENT MARKETS (OR SPECULATIVE) FORM OF PPP

The PPP condition, which we have derived from arbitrage considerations, can also be derived by considering market efficiency arguments involving the behavior of speculators.[5] In order to do this let us define the *expected* level and rate of change of the spot exchange rate, and expected inflation in the United States and Britain, as follows:

$S_1^*(\$/\pounds)$ is the expected spot exchange rate in 1 year, and $\dot{S}^*(\$/\pounds)$ is the expected annual percent change in the spot exchange rate. $\dot{P}_{US}^*$ and $\dot{P}_{UK}^*$ are respectively the expected annual rates of inflation in the United States and Britain.

Consider a speculator deciding whether to buy and hold the US basket or the British basket.[6]

After 1 year, each dollar invested in the US basket will be expected to be worth

$$\$(1 + \dot{P}_{US}^*) \qquad (7.12)$$

where the dollar sign shows this is a dollar amount. This value will be compared to the expected value of the British basket if it is alternatively bought and held for 1 year. To calculate this, note that each dollar invested in the British basket must first be used to buy pounds, providing[7]

$$\pounds \frac{1}{S(\$/\pounds)}$$

The expected value of this basket in pounds at the end of 1 year is

$$\pounds \frac{1}{S(\$/\pounds)} (1 + \dot{P}_{UK}^*)$$

The expected dollar value of this is

$$\$ \frac{S_1^*(\$/\pounds)}{S(\$/\pounds)} (1 + \dot{P}_{UK}^*) \qquad (7.13)$$

We can write the identity $S_1^*(\$/\pounds) \equiv S(\$/\pounds)[1 + \dot{S}^*(\$/\pounds)]$, and using this in (7.13) allows us to rewrite this as

$$\$[1 + \dot{S}^*(\$/\pounds)](1 + \dot{P}_{UK}^*) \qquad (7.14)$$

In an efficient market, and assuming equal risk of speculating in the two baskets, the expected dollar payoffs from holding the British and American baskets must be the same. That is

$$(1 + \dot{P}_{US}^*) = [1 + \dot{S}^*(\$/\pounds)](1 + \dot{P}_{UK}^*) \qquad (7.15)$$

Rearranging equation (7.15) to place $\dot{S}^*(\$/\pounds)$ on the left-hand side

$$\dot{S}^*(\$/\pounds) = \frac{(1 + \dot{P}_{US}^*)}{(1 + \dot{P}_{UK}^*)} - 1 = \frac{\dot{P}_{US}^* - \dot{P}_{UK}^*}{(1 + \dot{P}_{UK}^*)} \qquad (7.16)$$

Equation (7.16) can be approximated by

$$\dot{S}^*(\$/\pounds) \cong \dot{P}_{US}^* - \dot{P}_{UK}^* \qquad (7.17)$$

provided that expected inflation in Britain is not high.

Equation (7.16), and the approximate version in equation (7.17), represent the **efficient markets (or speculative) form of PPP**. While the relative and the efficient markets form of PPP look very similar, they are in fact different. Realized inflation and realized exchange rates may not fit the relative form of PPP at any particular time, but the efficient markets form of PPP should nevertheless still hold. This is because with rational expectations, expected values of variables should on average be equal to realized values. That is, there should be no

---

5 This approach has been suggested by Richard Roll, "Violations of PPP and their Implications for Efficient Commodity Markets," in Marshall Sarnat and George Szegö (eds), *International Finance and Trade*, Ballinger, Cambridge, MA, 1979.

6 We assume the basket of goods is nonperishable in this version of PPP, or that an index of price levels exists which can be traded.

7 Again, here and in what follows we put the currency symbol in front of magnitudes to show what they are.

persistent biases.[8] This means that if expectations are rational, then on average $\dot{S}^*(\$/£)$, $\dot{P}_{US}^*$ and $\dot{P}_{UK}^*$ should equal the actual rates of change in these variables, so that if equations (7.16) and (7.17) hold, then equations (7.7) and (7.8) also hold, *on average*. Sometimes the change in exchange rates will exceed the values predicted by realized inflation in the countries, and sometimes the change in exchange rate will be less than predicted. On average over a long period of time the over- and under-predictions of exchange rate changes should cancel. We see that speculation, in conjunction with the assumption that expectations are rational, means the relative form of PPP holds on average.

Unfortunately, PPP does not fit the data very well, particularly over short intervals of time. This is because, as we saw in Part II, there are many factors other than commodity prices which influence exchange rates, and these other factors can dominate inflation, at least in the short run. However, rather than simply dismiss the PPP condition as an explanation of exchange rates, let us consider the evidence in more detail to see whether there are circumstances under which PPP gives useful predictions.

THE EMPIRICAL EVIDENCE ON PPP

A major problem in testing the validity of the PPP condition is the need to use accurate price indexes for the inflation rates for the countries being studied. Price indexes cover many items, and what is happening to relative prices within an index is not revealed.

In an effort to use as specific a set of prices as can be obtained and to avoid index-number problems, J. David Richardson considered data on prices of narrowly classified industrial items in the United States and Canada.[9] The classifications are as specific as "cement," "animal feeds," "bakery products," "chewing gum," and "fertilizers." That is, Richardson examined the law of one price rather than the PPP condition. Clearly, if the law of one price does not hold between the United States and Canada, there is not much hope for the PPP condition, especially between countries further apart and more different in the contents of price indexes than are these two neighboring countries.

Richardson estimated an equation similar to that in equation (7.7) for several commodity groups, and found that it did not fit the data well in most commodity categories. Richardson's results suggest that even the law of one price is violated, at least during the time period of his study.

A possible explanation of Richardson's results on the law of one price is the differential pricing of the same object in different countries by multinational firms. Such differential pricing, with higher prices charged where demand is more inelastic, is predicted by the theory of discriminating monopoly.[10] Firms with monopoly power may be able to prevent arbitragers from taking advantage of price differences by withholding supply from any company which handles the monopolists' product and cooperates with arbitragers.[11] This possibility is supported by the observation that where there is little or no opportunity for price discrimination, as in the case of commodity markets, the law of one price does appear to hold in the long run although not in the short run.[12]

Irving B. Kravis and Richard E. Lipsey extensively studied the relationship between inflation rates and exchange rates using different price

8 The lack of bias in expectations if expectations are rational is one of the conditions of rationality described by John F. Muth, "Rational Expectations and the Theory of Price Movements," *Econometrica*, July 1961, pp. 315–35.

9 J. David Richardson, "Some Empirical Evidence on Commodity Arbitrage and the Law of One Price," *Journal of International Economics*, May 1978, pp. 341–51.

10 A monopolist that can segment markets charges a higher price to customers whose demand is relatively price insensitive.

11 Substantial evidence supports the discriminating monopoly argument. See Peter Isard, "How Far Can We Push the 'Law of One Price'?" *American Economic Review*, December 1977, pp. 942–8.

12 See Aris A. Protopapadakis and Hans R. Stoll, "The Law of One Price in International Commodity Markets: A Reformulation and Some Formal Tests," *Journal of International Money and Finance*, September 1986, pp. 335–60.

indexes.[13] They used the GNP implicit deflator (which includes prices of all goods and services in the GNP), the consumer price index, and the producer price index. They also took care to distinguish between goods that enter into international trade (tradable goods) and those that do not (nontradable goods). They discovered, using these many prices and price indexes, that there were departures from PPP. They concluded, "As a matter of general judgment we express our opinion that the results do not support the notion of a tightly integrated international price structure. The record . . . shows that price levels can move apart sharply without rapid correction through arbitrage."[14] They did find that PPP holds more closely for tradable goods than for nontradable goods, but the departures from PPP even over relatively long periods were substantial even for traded goods.

Hans Genberg concentrated on testing to see whether PPP holds more precisely when exchange rates are flexible rather than fixed.[15] The most important aspects of his conclusion can be seen by comparing the two columns in Table 7.1. The table gives the average deviations, in percentages, from an estimated PPP condition. The estimates show departures from PPP for each country with its combined trading partners. The importance of each partner is judged by the share of that partner in the country's export trade. The PPP condition is then statistically fitted between the country, for example, Belgium, and the weighted average of its trading partners. The table shows, for example, that for the United States from 1957 to 1976, the actual difference between the US inflation rate and the inflation rate in its (weighted) trading partners differed from the exchange rate change by, on average, 3.8 percent per annum.

Table 7.1 *Average absolute deviations from PPP, in percent*

	1957–66	1957–76
United States	1.2	3.8
United Kingdom	0.5	3.8
Austria	1.3	2.0
Belgium	1.4	2.1
Denmark	1.3	2.0
France	2.5	3.0
Germany	1.3	2.7
Italy	1.2	5.8
Netherlands	0.5	1.7
Norway	0.9	2.9
Sweden	0.7	1.4
Switzerland	0.7	5.8
Canada	2.0	3.3
Japan	1.9	3.8
Average	1.2	3.2

Notes
There are larger departures from PPP for the years 1957–76, which include a period of flexible exchange rate. However, this could be because conditions were more volatile during the more recent period.

Source: Hans Genberg, "Purchasing Power Parity under Fixed and Flexible Exchange Rates," *Journal of International Economics*, North-Holland Publishing Company, May 1978, p. 260.

The second column of Table 7.1 includes the flexible-exchange-rate period which began in 1973. We find from the average deviations from PPP given at the bottom of the table that the addition of the flexible period makes the deviations increase. The implication is that there were greater violations during the flexible years, 1973–76.[16]

Evidence that considers only years of flexible exchange rates and that is not in agreement with Genberg's conclusion has been provided by Maurice

---

13 Irving B. Kravis and Richard E. Lipsey, "Price Behavior in the Light of Balance of Payments Theories," *Journal of International Economics*, May 1978, pp. 193–246.

14 Ibid., p. 216.

15 Hans Genberg, "Purchasing Power Parity under Fixed and Flexible Exchange Rates," *Journal of International Economics*, May 1978, pp. 247–67.

16 Genberg also discovered that most of the departures from PPP resulted from movements in exchange rates rather than from changes in price levels. This supports Richardson's conclusion. See also Mario Blejer and Hans Genberg, "Permanent and Transitory Shocks to Exchange Rates: Measurement and Implications for Purchasing Power Parity," unpublished manuscript, International Monetary Fund, 1981.

Obstfeld.[17] Using data for the OECD countries over the 20-year period 1973–93, Obstfeld finds strong evidence for the relative form of PPP. Similar support for the principle in this form, but from a very different data set, is obtained in the study of German hyperinflation by Jacob Frenkel.[18] Indeed, Frenkel finds that in general, every 1 percent difference in inflation is associated with a 1 percent change in the exchange rate, as predicted by PPP. It would be surprising in the extreme circumstances experienced during hyperinflation if we did not find agreement with PPP.

Niels Thygesen has summarized the results of a study by the Commission of the European Communities, which set out to discover how long it takes for inflation rates to restore PPP after exchange rates have been artificially changed by the government to gain competitiveness for exports.[19] The idea is that devaluation should raise the rate of inflation until PPP is restored. This could come about via higher import prices and consequent wage demands setting off reactions elsewhere in the economy. Using economic models of Britain and Italy, the study concluded that it took 5–6 years for inflation differentials to restore the PPP condition. However, Thygesen also observed that 75 percent of the return to PPP was achieved within 2 years.

The question of whether and how long it takes for exchange rates to return to PPP levels after departing from them concerns **reversion to the mean**. Niso Abuaf and Philippe Jorion directly studied this issue of reversion using 80 years of data, a period long enough to offer the prospects of seeing if there is a long-run tendency towards parity.[20]

They find that in the event of a 50 percent overvaluation of exchange rates relative to PPP, it takes 3–5 years for the departure to be halved.

Another study that examined how long it takes for PPP to be restored after being disturbed is that of John Hodgson and Patricia Phelps.[21] They used a statistical model that allows lags and discovered that differential inflation rates precede the change in exchange rates with a lag of up to 18 months. A similar conclusion was reached by William Folks, Jr, and Stanley Stansell.[22] Their purpose was to forecast changes in exchange rates, and they discovered that exchange rates do adjust to relative inflation rates, but with a long lag.

A conclusion that differs from that of Hodgson and Phelps and Folks and Stansell was reached by Richard Rogalski and Joseph Vinso.[23] They chose a flexible-exchange-rate period, 1920–24, and studied relative inflation for six countries.[24] Rogalski and Vinso concluded that there is no lag. This, they claim, is what is expected in an efficient market, because relative inflation rates are publicly available information and should therefore be reflected in market prices such as exchange rates. This question of efficiency in the spot exchange rate has been tackled by Jacob Frenkel and Michael Mussa, who argue that even if we do observe departures from PPP, this does not imply that foreign exchange

17 Maurice Obstfeld, "International Currency Experience: New Lessons and Lessons Relearned," *Brookings Papers on Economic Activity*, No. 1, 1995, pp. 119–220.

18 Jacob A. Frenkel, "Exchange Rates, Prices and Money: Lessons from the 1920s," *American Economic Review*, March 1980, pp. 235–42.

19 Niels Thygesen, "Inflation and Exchange Rates: Evidence and Policy Guidelines for the European Community," *Journal of International Economics*, May 1978, pp. 301–17.

20 Niso Abuaf and Philippe Jorion, "Purchasing Power Parity in the Long Run," *Journal of Finance*, March 1990, pp. 157–74.

21 John A. Hodgson and Patricia Phelps, "The Distributed Impact of Price-Level Variation on Floating Exchange Rates," *Review of Economics and Statistics*, February 1975, pp. 58–64.

22 William R. Folks, Jr. and Stanley R. Stansell, "The Use of Discriminant Analysis in Forecasting Exchange Rate Movements," *Journal of International Business Studies*, Spring 1975, pp. 33–50.

23 Richard J. Rogalski and Joseph D. Vinso, "Price Level Variations as Predictors of Flexible Exchange Rates," *Journal of International Business Studies*, Spring 1977, pp. 71–81.

24 This period was also studied by Jacob A. Frenkel, not because exchange rates were flexible but because the inflationary experience was so extreme. See Jacob A. Frenkel, "Purchasing Power Parity: Doctrinal Perspective and Evidence from the 1920s," *Journal of International Economics*, May 1978, pp. 169–91.

markets are inefficient. Exchange rates, they show, move like stock and bond prices. Indeed, Frenkel and Mussa find average monthly variations in exchange rates to be more pronounced than the variation of stock prices.[25]

As we have mentioned, a possible reason for departures from PPP is the use of different weights in different countries' baskets of goods. This possibility is considered in the careful work of Irving Kravis et al. (1975).[26] To overcome the problem of different weights they recalculated foreign inflation using US weights for all countries' price indexes, rather than own-country weights. They also separated data according to whether the items were traded or nontraded. Far stronger support for the PPP condition was found in the common-weight inflation data, especially for traded goods. However, since the usefulness of PPP for explaining exchange rates hinges largely on it applying to broad baskets of goods and using available price indexes based on local consumption patterns, we are left to conclude that PPP provides a rather limited description of exchange-rate levels and changes.

Our conclusion to the empirical evidence, that PPP violations do occur, should come as little surprise. Those who travel extensively often observe that PPP does not occur. There are countries that travelers view as expensive and others that are viewed as cheap. For example, Switzerland and Japan are generally viewed as expensive, while India and China are viewed as relatively cheap. This indicates, without any formal empirical evidence, that there are departures from PPP, at least in the absolute or static form. There are two major reasons we can offer as to why this occurs.

25 Jacob Frenkel and Michael Mussa, "Efficiency of Foreign Exchange Markets and Measures of Turbulence," *National Bureau of Economic Research*, Working Paper 476, Cambridge, MA, 1981.

26 Irving Kravis, Zoltan Kenessey, Alan Heston and Robert Summers, *A System of International Comparisons of Gross Product and Purchasing Power*, Johns Hopkins University, Baltimore, 1975.

REASONS FOR DEPARTURES FROM PPP

Restrictions on movement of goods

The possibility of two-way arbitrage allows prices to differ between markets by up to the cost of transportation. For example, if it costs $0.50/bushel to ship wheat between the United States and Canada, the price difference must exceed $0.50 in either direction before two-way arbitrage occurs. This means a possible deviation from the absolute form of PPP for wheat that spans $1. In reality, however, competitive pressures for similar prices to buyers in other countries will keep prices in a narrower range than would result from two-way arbitrage between Canada and the United States. This is the one-way arbitrage referred to earlier in this chapter.

Import tariffs can also cause PPP violations. If one country has, for example, a 15-percent import tariff, prices within the country will have to move more than 15 percent above those in the other before it pays to ship and cover the tariffs that are involved. The effect of tariffs is different from the effect of transportation costs. Tariffs do not have a symmetric effect. As a result of tariffs, price levels can move higher only in the country which has the import tariffs.

Whether it be transportation costs or tariffs, these factors explain departures from PPP only in its absolute or static form. As indicated earlier in the derivation of equation (7.11), when the maximum price difference from shipping costs and import tariffs has been reached, the PPP principle in its relative or dynamic form should explain movements through time that push against the maximum price difference. For example, suppose that prices at existing exchange rates are already 25 percent higher in one country because of import tariffs or transportation costs. If that country has an inflation rate that is 10 percent higher than the inflation rate in another country, its exchange rate will have to fall, on the average, by 10 percent to prevent commodity arbitrage.

Quotas, which are limits on the amounts of different commodities that can be imported, generally mean that price differences can become quite sizable, because commodity arbitragers are limited in their ability to narrow the gaps. Like import tariffs, they provide a reason for persistent departures from PPP.

Price indexes and nontraded outputs

We have already observed in describing the research of Irving Kravis and Richard E. Lipsey that many of the items that are included in the commonly used price indexes do not enter into international trade. We cannot, therefore, invoke the notion of commodity arbitrage to create an equivalent of equation (7.1) for these items. Most difficult to arbitrage between countries are immovable items such as land and buildings; highly perishable commodities such as fresh milk, vegetables, eggs, and some fruits; and also services such as hotel accommodations and repairs. These "nontraded" items can allow departures from PPP to persist when we measure inflation from conventional market-basket price indexes.

To some extent, a tendency towards parity even in nontraded items can be maintained by the movement of the buyers instead of the movement of the items themselves. For example, factories and office complexes can be located where land and rent are cheap. Vacationers can travel to places where holidays are less expensive. The movement of *buyers* tends to keep prices in different countries in line with each other.

The relative prices of traded versus nontraded outputs will not differ greatly between countries if *producers* within each country can move into the production of the nontraded outputs when their relative prices increase. Consequently, if comparative advantages do not differ significantly between nations, the relative prices of traded versus nontraded items will be kept similar between countries by the prospective movement of domestic producers. Therefore, if the prices of traded goods satisfy PPP, then so should the prices of nontraded items. However, we do require that the producers can move between traded and nontraded goods, and that comparative advantage differences are small.

And even when producers can move, price adjustment can take a very long time, during which departures from PPP can persist.[27]

STATISTICAL PROBLEMS OF EVALUATING PPP

It has been suggested that the difficulty finding empirical support for PPP may be due to the statistical procedures that have been used.[28] We can indicate the problems with the statistical procedures by examining the bases for judging empirical support for PPP.

Most tests of PPP are based on estimates of a regression equation that in the context of the dollar–pound exchange rate can be written

$$\dot{S}(\$/\pounds)_t = \alpha + \beta \left[\frac{\dot{P}_{US} - \dot{P}_{UK}}{1 + \dot{P}_{UK}} \right]_t + \varepsilon_t \qquad (7.18)$$

where ε is the *ex ante* regression error and the subscripts t refer to the time period of observation of the variables. It is argued that if PPP is valid, then in estimates of equation (7.18), α should be close to zero, β should be close to 1.0, and the *ex post* regression errors should be small.[29] This is because

27 Mario Blejer and Ayre Hillman have provided a formal model with the costs of commodity arbitrage allowing temporary departures from PPP. See their article "A Proposition on Short-Run Departures from the Law of One Price: Unanticipated Inflation, Relative Price Dispersion, and Commodity Arbitrage," *European Economic Review*, January 1982, pp. 51–60.

28 The statistical problems have been surveyed by John Pippenger, "Arbitrage and Efficient Markets Interpretations of Purchasing Power Parity: Theory and Evidence," *Economic Review*, Federal Reserve Bank of San Francisco, Winter 1986, pp. 31–48. See also Sandra Betton, Maurice D. Levi, and Raman Uppal, "Index-Induced Errors and Purchasing Power Parity: Bounding the Possible Bias," *Journal of International Financial Markets, Institutions and Money*, 2/3, 1995, pp. 165–179.

29 Small errors mean that the equation fits well. The "goodness of fit" measure that is usually used is the R^2 statistic, which gives the fraction of the variation in the dependent variable, $\dot{S}(\$/\pounds)$, that is explained by the explanatory variable(s), in this case, $(\dot{P}_{US} - \dot{P}_{UK})/(1 + \dot{P}_{UK})$.

in such a case the regression equation reduces to equation (7.7). The statistical problems that can result in incorrect rejection of PPP are:

1 *Errors in measuring the inflation differential* A characteristic of the regression methodology is that errors in the measurement of explanatory (i.e. right-hand) variables bias regression coefficients towards zero.[30] This means that if the inflation differential is poorly measured because different baskets are used in each country, then we could find the estimated β to be smaller than 1.0 even if the true β is exactly equal to 1.0. Generally, when the slope co-efficient is biased downwards towards zero, the intercept, α, is made positive even if it is really zero.

2 *Simultaneous determination of inflation and exchange rates* It is another characteristic of the regression methodology that if the direction of causation goes from inflation to exchange rates and vice versa, then failure to use simultaneous-equation methods biases coefficients such as β, again usually towards zero.[31] In the case of PPP, causation does go both ways because changes in exchange rates affect inflation and inflation affects exchange rates. Neither side of the regression equation is predetermined, an essential characteristic required to avoid coefficient bias.

As mentioned, researchers who have tried to overcome the statistical problems, and who have considered inflation versus exchange rates over long time periods, have tended to support PPP. For example, by considering only the long-term trends which remain after removing "noise" in the data, Mark Rush and Steven Husted have shown that PPP holds for the US dollar versus other currencies.[32] The Rush and Husted results indirectly support the view that departures from PPP are due to poor measurement of inflation: long-term trends should reduce or remove the unsystematic errors in calculating inflation because the errors should average out and become relatively less important as the interval of measurement increases. Further support for the view that data errors are responsible for rejection of PPP is provided by Craig Hakkio who reduced the possible problem of poor inflation measurement by considering many countries concurrently over many periods.[33] This reduces the role of measurement errors by reducing the role of any one variable containing unsystematic errors. Hakkio is unable to reject PPP.

Further indication that errors in the inflation variable may be responsible for poor support for PPP is found in tests using **cointegration techniques**, which involve studying the differences between two variables versus the variables themselves. The basic intuition behind the cointegration method is that if two economic variables move together, then differences between them should be more stable than the original series. This means that if the spot exchange rate and the inflation differential do move together according to long-run PPP, then even though the two series may temporarily move apart, they must move back eventually through their cointegration. The cointegrating coefficient, which is the equivalent to β in equation (7.18), should equal unity if PPP holds.

Yoonbai Kim has applied cointegration methods to the PPP relationship of the US dollar versus the

30 See Maurice D. Levi, "Errors in the Variables Bias in the Presence of Correctly Measured Variables," *Econometrica*, September 1973, pp. 985–6, and Maurice D. Levi, "Measurement Errors and Bounded OLS Estimates," *Journal of Econometrics*, September 1977, pp. 165–71.

31 This bias exists if common factors affect $(\dot{P}_{US} - \dot{P}_{UK})/(1 + \dot{P}_{UK})$ and $S(\$/\pounds)$. See Maurice D. Levi, "World-Wide Effects and Import Elasticities," *Journal of International Economics*, May 1976, pp. 203–14.

32 See Mark Rush and Steven Husted, "Purchasing Power Parity in the Long Run," *Canadian Journal of Economics*, February 1985, pp. 137–45.

33 Craig S. Hakkio, "A Re-examination of Purchasing Power Parity: A Multi-Country and Multi-Period Study," *Journal of International Economics*, November 1984, pp. 265–77. See also Yoonbai Kim, "Purchasing Power Parity in the Long-Run: A Cointegration Approach," *Journal of Money, Credit and Banking*, November, 1990, pp. 491–503.

153

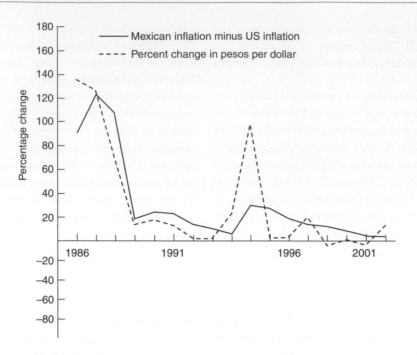

Figure 7.1 *US–Mexican inflation and the peso–dollar exchange rate*

Notes
The dotted line plots the percentage change in the spot rate of pesos per dollar, while the solid line shows Mexican inflation minus US inflation. The ups and downs of these series show that while the two series are different, they move closely enough together to provide casual support for PPP.

Source: International Financial Statistics, International Monetary Fund, Washington, DC.

currencies of Britain, France, Italy, Japan, and Canada.[34] He used annual data and found support for PPP using both consumer price indexes and wholesale price indexes in all cases except for Canada. Robert McNown and Myles Wallace have also applied cointegration techniques, focusing on the situation for countries with very high inflation rates.[35] This is a potentially fruitful context because the extreme values of changes in exchange rates and inflation differentials should minimize statistical problems such as the use of incorrectly constructed indexes. McNown and Wallace studied Israel, Argentina, Brazil, and Chile, all of which have had periods of very high inflation as well as periods of

modest inflation. The estimates of cointegration coefficients were not significantly different from unity as hypothesized according to long-run PPP.

Casual support for PPP involving a country which has had periods of high inflation is provided by a simple plot of the spot rate between the Mexican peso and the US dollar versus the inflation differential between these countries. This is shown in Figure 7.1 for a period when Mexican inflation and the peso–dollar exchange rate varied widely. While the time paths of the two series do not track each other exactly from year to year, the overall correspondence is quite clear.

34 See Yoonbai Kim, op. cit.
35 See Robert McNown and Myles S. Wallace, "National Price Levels, Purchasing Power Parity and Cointegration: A Test of Four High Inflation Economies," *Journal of International Money and Finance*, December 1989, pp. 533–46.

THE PRACTICAL IMPORTANCE OF PPP

It might seem that failure of PPP to hold would reduce its practical relevance. After all, it would then be of little use in helping to forecast exchange rates. In fact, the very opposite is true about PPP deviations. Knowing whether PPP holds, and knowing whether it holds more-or-less continuously or only on average over many years, is important in international managerial decisions. For example, if it is known that PPP is systematically violated and that these violations are unlikely to be corrected for a long or indefinite period of time, this knowledge can direct production decisions. Plants can be located where costs are lowest as well as on the basis of comparative advantage. This involves studying the costs in different locations to determine which currency is undervalued most relative to its PPP value, and where reversion is likely to be the slowest. On the other hand, if PPP holds more-or-less continuously, the only reason for choosing one production location over another is comparative advantage.

If PPP departures occur, but these are corrected over time, knowledge of how long such corrections might take is useful for determining whether it is worthwhile exploiting the temporary departures. Companies for which start-up and shut-down of activities is easiest will have the most to gain from paying attention to the behavior of PPP.

SUMMARY

1   The law of one price states that a commodity will have the same price in terms of a common currency in every country. The law follows from commodity arbitrage, which involves buying in the cheapest country if prices are different.

2   It follows from the law of one price that the dollar price of a commodity in the United States equals the pound price of the commodity in Britain multiplied by the spot exchange rate of dollars per British pound. Deviations from this relationship can be caused by transportation costs and import tariffs.

3   The principle of PPP is the extension of the law of one price to prices of a basket of goods. In its absolute form, PPP says that the dollar price of a basket of goods in the United States is the pound price of the basket in Britain, multiplied by the exchange rate of dollars per pound.

4   In its relative form, PPP says that the rate of change of the exchange rate is approximately equal to the difference between inflation rates.

5   Speculation and efficient markets also produce the relative form of the PPP condition in terms of expected values.

6   Empirical support for the PPP condition is weak, although there is some evidence it may hold in the long run.

7   The reasons the law of one price and PPP do not hold include transportation costs, tariffs, quotas, and the fact that there are goods and services that are nontradable. PPP may not hold even if the law of one price holds for every item because of different weights for different items in different countries' price indexes.

8   The fact that empirical evidence does not support PPP may be due to statistical difficulties in evaluating the principle.

REVIEW QUESTIONS

1   What is the "law of one price?"
2   How does the law of one price relate to PPP?
3   Explain what a commodity arbitrager does.
4   Write down the absolute form of PPP and interpret it.
5   Write down the relative form of PPP and interpret it.
6   Write down the efficient markets (or expectations) form of PPP and interpret it.
7   Why might the efficient markets (or expectations) form hold exactly even though the relative form of PPP does not?
8   What statistical problems are associated with empirical tests of PPP?

ASSIGNMENT PROBLEMS

1   Why might the law of one price hold even in the presence of import tariffs?
2   Assume that the prices of a standard basket of goods and services in different countries are as follows

United States	$400
Canada	C$550
United Kingdom	£280
Japan	¥60,000

   a   What are the implied PPP exchange rates?

   b   How would the presence of a high sales tax in Britain, such as the VAT, influence your guess of where the actual value of $S(\$/£)$ would be vis à vis the PPP value of $S(\$/£)$?

3   Why might there be departures from PPP even if the law of one price holds for every commodity?

4   a   Assume $\dot{P}_{Mex} = 50$ percent and $\dot{P}_{US} = 2$ percent. Calculate $\dot{S}(P_S/\$)$ and $\dot{S}(\$/P_S)$ according to the precise and approximate dynamic PPP conditions.

   b   Assume that Mexican inflation increases to 100 percent, while US inflation remains at 2 percent. Calculate $\dot{S}(P_S/\$)$ and $\dot{S}(\$/P_S)$ according to the precise and approximate PPP conditions.

   c   How does the error in the approximate condition depend on whether you are measuring $\dot{S}(P_S/\$)$ or $\dot{S}(\$/P_S)$?

   d   How would a constant percentage sales tax in Mexico affect your answers above?

5   If speculators are risk-averse, could this affect the accuracy of the link between the expected change in the exchange rate and the difference between expected inflation rates?

6   Is the accuracy of the approximate PPP condition negatively affected by the level of inflation?

7   Why might the relative form of PPP hold even though the absolute form does not hold?

8   Assume inflation in Brazil is 15 percent and in China 2 percent. What is the percent change in the exchange rate of Brazilian reals per Chinese RMB, and Chinese RMB per Brazilian real, and why do these two percent changes differ?

9   What is required for price discrimination between markets to cause departures from the law of one price?

10 What is the relevance of a "goodness of fit" measure such as the R^2 statistic, for judging PPP?

11 What is one-way versus two-way arbitrage in the context of PPP, and how do the implications of the two types of arbitrage differ?

12 Specialization, which has accompanied freer trade, has caused countries to produce larger amounts of each of a narrower range of products, trading these for the wider range of products that people consume. How might this have affected PPP?

13 What characteristics of a Big Mac® led *The Economist* to choose it as a basis for their alternative PPP exchange-rate measure? Can you suggest any other items which might be used?

14 Several possibilities, both theoretical and empirical, have been raised to explain the apparent failure of PPP. List and explain at least three of these. Comment on the validity of the explanation.

15 Does empirical evidence suggest PPP may be more likely to hold in the short-run or the long-run? Can you suggest an explanation for why this might be true?

BIBLIOGRAPHY

Abuaf, Niso and Philippe Jorion, "Purchasing Power Parity in the Long Run," *Journal of Finance*, March 1990, pp. 157–74.

Balassa, Bela, "The Purchasing-Power Parity Doctrine: A Re-Appraisal," *Journal of Political Economy*, December 1964, pp. 584–96. Reprinted in Richard N. Cooper (ed.), *International Finance: Selected Readings*, Penguin Books, Middlesex, UK, 1969.

Dornbusch, Rudiger and Dwight Jaffee, "Purchasing Power Parity and Exchange Rate Problems: Introduction" and the papers included in "Purchasing Power Parity: A Symposium," *Journal of International Economics*, May 1978, pp. 157–351.

Frenkel, Jacob A., "Exchange Rates, Prices and Money: Lessons from the 1920s," *American Economic Review*, March 1980, pp. 235–42.

Gaillot, Henry J., "Purchasing Power Parity as an Explanation of Long-Term Changes in Exchange Rates," *Journal of Money, Credit and Banking*, August 1970, pp. 348–57.

Hakkio, Craig, "A Re-examination of Purchasing Power Parity: A Multi-Country and Multi-period Study," *Journal of International Economics*, November 1984, pp. 265–77.

Huang, Roger, "Expectations of Exchange Rates and Differential Inflation Rates: Further Evidence on Purchasing Power Parity in Efficient Markets," *Journal of Finance*, March 1987, pp. 69–79.

——, "Risk and Parity in Purchasing Power," *Journal of Money, Credit and Banking*, August 1990, pp. 338–56.

Kim, Yoonbai, "Purchasing Power Parity in the Long Run: A Cointegration Approach," *Journal of Money, Credit and Banking*, November 1990, pp. 491–503.

Lee, Moon H., *Purchasing Power Parity*, Marcel Decker, New York, 1976.

Manzur, Meher, "An International Comparison of Prices and Exchange Rates: A New Test of Purchasing Power Parity," *Journal of International Money and Finance*, March 1990, pp. 75–91.

Meese, Richard, "Currency Fluctuations in the Post-Bretton Woods Era," *Journal of Economic Perspectives*, Winter 1990, pp. 117–34.

Obstfeld, Maurice, "Currency Experience: New Lessons and Lessons Relearned," *Brookings Papers on Economic Activity*, No. 1, 1995, pp. 119–220.

Officer, Lawrence H., "The Purchasing Power Theory of Exchange Rates: A Review Article," *Staff Papers*, International Monetary Fund, March 1976, pp. 1–60.

Peel, David A., "Further Evidence on PPP Adjustment Speeds: the Case of Effective Real Exchange Rates and the EMS," *Oxford Bulletin of Economics and Statistics*, September 2003, pp. 421–37.

Pippenger, John, "Arbitrage and Efficient Market Interpretations of Purchasing Power Parity: Theory and Evidence," *Economic Review*, Federal Reserve Bank of San Francisco, Winter 1986, pp. 31–48.

Roll, Richard, "Violations of PPP and their Implications for Efficient Commodity Markets," in Marshall Sarnat and George Szegö (eds), *International Finance and Trade*, Ballinger, Cambridge, MA, 1979.

Rush, Mark and Steven L. Husted, "Purchasing Power Parity in the Long Run," *Canadian Journal of Economics*, February 1985, pp. 137–45.

Viner, Jacob, *Studies in the Theory of International Trade*, Harper and Row, New York, 1937.

Chapter 8

Interest parity

International finance is the art of borrowing on the strength of what you already owe.

Evan Esar

The purchasing-power-parity (PPP) condition considered in Chapter 8, applies to product markets. There is another important, parallel parity condition that applies to financial markets. This is the **covered interest-parity condition**. It states that when steps have been taken to avoid foreign exchange risk by use of forward contracts, rates of return on investments, and costs of borrowing, will be equal irrespective of the currency of denomination of the investment or the currency borrowed.

In this chapter we derive the covered interest-parity condition and show its connection to the PPP principle. We also consider the "frictions" that must be absent for the covered interest-parity condition to hold. The frictions that must be absent include legal restrictions on the movement of capital, transaction costs, and taxes. These frictions play an analogous role to the frictions that must be absent for PPP to hold, namely, restrictions on the movement of goods between markets, transportation costs, and tariffs.

Our approach to deriving the covered interest-parity condition begins by explaining how to make short term investment and borrowing decisions in the international context. We then show how shopping around for the highest investment yield or lowest borrowing cost pushes yields and costs in different currencies towards equality, thereby

resulting in covered interest parity. Our focus is on investment yields and borrowing costs in different *currencies,* and not different *countries,* because as we shall see, securities are often denominated in different currencies within a single country. For most purposes in this book the *currency* of denomination is more important than the *country* in which a security is issued. Currency of denomination introduces foreign exchange risk while country of issue introduces political risk, and for most countries and time periods, foreign exchange risk is a far larger concern than political risk.

As we proceed in this and later chapters, it will be useful at a number of points to develop and illustrate concepts by referring to an example. For this purpose, we shall consider a manufacturing company that makes denim clothing, primarily jeans. The company is called Aviva Corporation. Aviva is headquartered in the United States but has sales, and purchases its denim, in many different countries. For this chapter, the important characteristic about Aviva is that it has uneven cash flows; therefore, on some occasions it has surplus funds to invest, and on other occasions it needs to borrow.

Short-term borrowing and investment take place in the **money market**. This is the market in which short-term securities such as treasury bills and commercial paper are traded. Because there are actively traded forward contracts with relatively short-term money-market maturities, the money market deserves special treatment. Forward contracts allow money-market borrowers and investors to avoid foreign exchange risk and exposure. Foreign exchange risk and exposure are discussed in some detail in Chapter 9. For the time being we note that they are the result of sensitivity and uncertainty in asset or liability values due to unexpected changes in exchange rates.[1] Let us start by asking in which currency Aviva should invest.

THE INVESTMENT AND BORROWING CRITERIA

Determining the currency of investment

Suppose that a firm like Aviva Corporation has some funds to place in the money market for 3 months. Perhaps it has received a major payment but can wait before paying for a large investment in new equipment. The firm could place these funds in securities denominated in its own domestic currency at an interest rate that can be discovered simply by calling around for the going rates on, for example, locally traded commercial paper or treasury bills. Alternatively, it could invest in foreign currency-denominated securities. Should it buy money market securities denominated in domestic or in foreign currency?

Many countries have money markets in which financial securities denominated in the countries' own currencies are actively traded. For example, there is a well-developed market in Canadian dollar securities in Canada, of pound securities in Britain, and of yen securities in Japan. Furthermore, in large international financial centers such as London and New York, there are active markets in securities denominated in a variety of different foreign currencies. For example, in London there are active markets in US dollar securities, euro securities, yen securities, Swiss franc securities and other currency-denominated instruments, as well, of course, as securities denominated in British pounds. By glancing at quoted interest rates it might sometimes seem possible to obtain higher yields on some foreign currency-denominated securities than on others. However, realized yields on foreign-currency securities depend on what happens to exchange rates as well as on interest rates. If, for example, the value of the foreign currency in which Aviva's investments are denominated happens to fall unexpectedly before maturity, then there will be a foreign exchange loss when the investments are converted back into dollars. As we shall see, the existence of the forward exchange market allows us to compute yields which include the effects of exchange rates. However, we shall also see that when the forward market is used to remove foreign exchange risk, yield differences on different currency-denominated securities are likely to be very small.

Let us see how an exchange-risk-free investment decision is made. We will select for our example Aviva's choice between alternative 3-month rather than full-year securities to make clear the need to keep exchange-rate movements and interest rates in comparable annualized terms.

Aviva knows that if it puts its funds in a US-dollar investment such as a bank deposit for 3 months, at maturity each dollar will provide

$$\$\left(1 + \frac{r_\$}{4}\right)$$

where $r_\$$ is the annualized US dollar interest rate, and division by 4 gives the 3-month return.[2] The interest rate is measured in decimal form, so a 5-percent rate is expressed as $r_\$ = 0.05$.

---

1 Risk can exist even if values of assets and liabilities, are not uncertain. Risk also exists if there is uncertainty in the prices of what people buy, so-called **inflation risk**, due to uncertainty in the buying power of given amounts of money.

2 Later, we allow for compound interest in computing returns. However, division by 4 is expositionally more convenient than taking the fourth root to find the 3-month return.

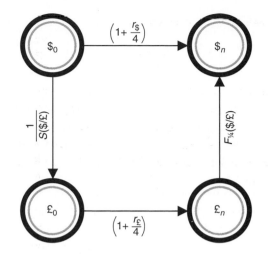

Figure 8.1 *Dollar versus hedged pound investments*

Notes
A US investor with funds to invest for 3 months can simply invest in domestic-currency denominated 3-month securities. After 3 months, the payout per dollar invested is as shown on the top horizontal arrow pointing from time zero to maturity, one-quarter of a year later. Alternatively, the investor can buy pounds spot, shown by the left, downward-pointing arrow, and invest in pound-denominated securities, shown by the lower rightward-pointing arrow. The pound investment can be hedged by selling the pounds forward for dollars, shown by the right upward-pointing arrow. The payout from hedged pound investment is given by the multiplication of the relevant amounts on the three sides of the figure, left, bottom, and right.

This alternative is illustrated in Figure 8.1 with the horizontal arrow from $\$_0$ to $\$_n$. The rightward pointing arrow indicates an investment, moving money from the current period, time zero, to a later period, n, in this case a quarter of a year.

Suppose that Aviva considers investing in a pound-denominated bank deposit, and that the spot dollar/sterling exchange rate, in the conventional US terms of quotation, is $S(\$/£)$. The exchange rate $S(\$/£)$ gives the number of dollars per pound sterling, and so for \$1 Aviva will obtain $1/S(\$/£)$ in British pounds, assuming that there are no transaction costs. This is illustrated in Figure 8.1 with the downward-pointing arrow from $\$_0$ to $£_0$.

If the annualized interest rate on 3-month British pound bank deposits is $r_£$, then for every dollar invested, Aviva will receive after 3 months the number of pounds that was invested (the principal),

$1/S(\$/£)$, plus the 3-month interest on this, which is the principal multiplied by $r_£/4$. This is illustrated in Figure 8.1 with the rightward-pointing arrow from $£_0$ to $£_n$ where in this case $n = \frac{1}{4}$. That is, Aviva will receive

$$£ \frac{1}{S(\$/£)} \left(1 + \frac{r_£}{4}\right) \qquad (8.1)$$

For example, if $S(\$/£) = 1.5000$ and $r_£ = 0.06$, then each dollar invested in pound-denominated bank deposits will provide after 3 months:[3]

$$£ \frac{1}{1.5000} \left(1 + \frac{0.06}{4}\right) = £0.6767$$

This certain number of pounds represents an uncertain number of dollars, but a forward contract can offer a complete hedge and guarantee the number of dollars that will be received for the pounds at the maturity of the security.

If, at the time of buying the 3-month pound-denominated deposit, Aviva sells forward the amount of pounds to be received at maturity, that is, the amount in equation (8.1) or £0.6767 in our example, then the number of dollars that will be obtained is set by the forward contract. After 3 months, Aviva delivers the British pounds and receives the number of dollars stated in the forward contract. This is illustrated in Figure 8.1 with the upward-pointing arrow from $£_n$ to $\$_n$.

If, for example, the 3-month forward rate at the time of investment is $F_{1/4}(\$/£)$, then we multiply the amount in equation (8.1) by this exchange rate to find the number of dollars received at maturity for each original dollar invested in the pound-denominated bank deposit. We obtain

$$\$ \frac{F_{1/4}(\$/£)}{S(\$/£)} \left(1 + \frac{r_£}{4}\right) \qquad (8.2)$$

For example, if $F_{1/4}(\$/£) = 1.4950$, then the number of pounds from equation (8.1), approximately £0.6767, will provide $(\$1.4950/£) \times £0.6767 = \$1.0116$ when sold forward for dollars.

3 We round to the fourth decimal.

This is the number of dollars received after 3 months, or $\frac{1}{4}$ of a year, for each original dollar in the pound-denominated bank deposit. This implies an annual rate of return of approximately,

$$4\left(\frac{1.0116 - 1.0000}{1.0000}\right) = 0.04647, \text{ or } 4.65\%$$

It is important to remember that the number of dollars given in equation (8.2) is a certain amount that is known at the time of investment. The purchase of the spot pounds, the investment in the pound-denominated deposit, and the forward sale of pounds all take place at the same time, and so if the security itself is risk-free there is no doubt about the number of dollars that will be received. If the spot exchange rate changes before the deposit matures, that will make no difference. The exchange rate to be used in converting the dollars into pounds at maturity is already set in the forward contract, which is part of the swap of dollars for pounds (recall from Chapter 3 that a swap is any exchange of currencies that is reversed, in this case dollars into pounds in the spot market and back to dollars in the forward market). In terms of our example, it is guaranteed that $1.0116 will be received.

It is now a simple matter to express the rule for deciding the currency in which to invest. The investor should choose a 3-month US-dollar deposit, rather than a pound deposit whenever[4]

$$\left(1 + \frac{r_\$}{4}\right) > \frac{F_{1/4}(\$/£)}{S(\$/£)}\left(1 + \frac{r_£}{4}\right)$$

The investor should select the pound deposit rather than the US-dollar deposit whenever the reverse inequality holds, that is

$$\left(1 + \frac{r_\$}{4}\right) < \frac{F_{1/4}(\$/£)}{S(\$/£)}\left(1 + \frac{r_£}{4}\right)$$

Only if

$$\left(1 + \frac{r_\$}{4}\right) = \frac{F_{1/4}(\$/£)}{S(\$/£)}\left(1 + \frac{r_£}{4}\right) \qquad (8.3)$$

should the investor be indifferent, since the same amount will be received from a dollar invested in securities denominated in either currency.[5]

We can convert equation (8.3) into a more meaningful equality if we subtract $(1 + r_£ / 4)$ from both sides:

$$\left(1 + \frac{r_\$}{4}\right) - \left(1 + \frac{r_£}{4}\right) = \frac{F_{1/4}(\$/£)}{S(\$/£)}\left(1 + \frac{r_£}{4}\right) - \left(1 + \frac{r_£}{4}\right)$$

With cancellation and rearrangement we obtain

$$r_\$ = r_£ + 4\left[\frac{F_{1/4}(\$/£) - S(\$/£)}{S(\$/£)}\right] \times \left(1 + \frac{r_£}{4}\right) \qquad (8.4)$$

We interpret this equation below, but before we do, we can note that part of the second right-hand term in equation (8.4) involves the multiplication of two small numbers, the forward pound premium and $r_£/4$. This product is very small. For example, if the forward premium is 4 percent and British interest rates are 8 percent per annum, the cross-product term from equation (8.4) will be 0.0008 (0.04×0.02), which is less than one-tenth of 1 percent. In order to interpret equation (8.4), we might therefore temporarily drop the term formed from this product (which means dropping the $r_£/4$) and write it as:

$$r_\$ = r_£ + 4\left[\frac{F_{1/4}(\$/£) - S(\$/£)}{S(\$/£)}\right] \qquad (8.5)$$

---

4 When exchange rates are in European terms, the forward and spot rates must be inverted. This is left as an exercise at the end of the chapter.

5 In more general terms, equation (8.3) can be written as

$$\frac{F_n}{S} = \frac{(1 + r)^n}{(1 + r_f)^n}$$

where the form of the exchange-rate quotation and the annualization are assumed to be understood. Here, r is the domestic interest rate and r_f is the foreign currency interest rate.

The first term on the right of equation (8.5) is the annualized pound interest rate. The second right-hand term is the annualized (because of the 4) forward premium/discount on pounds. Therefore, we can interpret equation (8.5) as saying that investors should be indifferent between home- and foreign-currency denominated securities if the home-currency interest rate equals the foreign-currency rate plus the annualized forward exchange premium/discount on the foreign currency. Investors should invest in the home currency when the domestic-currency interest rate exceeds the sum of the foreign-currency rate plus the foreign exchange premium/discount, and invest abroad when the domestic-currency rate is less than this sum. We discover that a mere comparison of interest rates is not sufficient for making investment choices. In order to determine in which currency-denominated securities to invest, we must add the foreign-currency interest rate to the forward premium or discount. Using the terminology of Chapter 3, we must add the foreign-currency interest rate to the spot-forward swap of pounds for dollars, where this swap is put in annualized terms.

The difference between equation (8.4) and equation (8.5) is that in equation (8.4) we include the forward exchange premium/discount on the principal invested in pound securities *and* the forward exchange premium/discount on the interest earned. In the approximate form equation (8.5) we consider the forward premium/discount earned on the principal, but not the premium/discount on the interest.

An example: comparing investments

Suppose Aviva Corporation faces the exchange rate and interest rate situation shown in Table 8.1 and has $10 million to invest for 3 months. Into which currency-denominated bank deposit should it place its funds?

The yield on pound-denominated deposits when the proceeds are sold forward, called the **covered** or **hedged yield**, can be calculated from

$$r_£ + 4\left[\frac{F_{1/4}(\$/£) - S(\$/£)}{S(\$/£)}\right]\left(1 + \frac{r_£}{4}\right)$$

where the first element is the pound interest rate and the second element is the premium/discount on the pound vis-à-vis the dollar, including the premium/discount on both the principal and interest. Substituting the values in Table 8.1

British pound covered yield

$$= 0.05125 + 4\left(\frac{1.5121 - 1.5140}{1.5140}\right)$$
$$\times \left(1 + \frac{0.05125}{4}\right) = 0.046167, \text{ or } 4.6167\%$$

This yield, which involves no foreign exchange risk because the pounds are sold forward, is slightly higher than the yield on US-dollar deposits.

Similarly, the covered yields on the euro is

Euro covered yield

$$= 0.07430 + 4\left(\frac{1.1175 - 1.1258}{1.1258}\right)$$
$$\times \left(1 + \frac{0.07430}{4}\right) = 0.044262, \text{ or } 4.4262\%$$

Table 8.1 *Exchange rates and interest rates on different currency-denominated 3-month bank deposits*

	US dollar	British pound	Euro	Swiss franc	Japanese yen
Interest rate[a]	4.4375%	5.1250%	7.4300%	3.9375%	1.125%
Spot rate (US equivalent)	1.0	$1.5140/£	$1.1258/€	SFr 1.4065/$ ($0.710985/SFr)	¥114.12/$ ($0.0087627/¥)
Forward rate[b] (US equivalent)	1.0	$1.5121/$	$1.1175/€	SFr 1.4052/$ ($0.711642/SFr)	¥113.20/$ ($0.0088339/¥)
Covered yield	4.4375%	4.6167%	4.4262%	4.3112%	4.3843%

Notes
a Interest rates on 3-month time deposits.
b 3-month forward rate.

For the covered yield on the Swiss franc and Japanese yen hedged against the US dollar we use the exchange rates in US-dollar terms shown in parentheses below the European-terms quotations. For example, for the covered yield on Swiss franc deposits we compute

Swiss franc covered yield

$$= 0.039375 + 4 \left(\frac{0.711642 - 0.710985}{0.710985} \right)$$
$$\times \left(1 + \frac{1.039375}{4} \right)$$

$$= 0.043108, \text{ or } 4.3108\%$$

The *covered* yields in Table 8.1 are much closer in value than the yields in the local currencies. An inspection of the spot versus forward exchange rates shows why. The British pound and euro which have higher interest rates than are available on US dollar securities, are both at a forward discount. The discounts offset the higher foreign currency interest rates. On the other hand, the Swiss franc and Japanese yen, the currencies with lower interest rates than on the US-dollar deposits, are both at a forward premium. The premiums help make up for the lower interest rates.

If Aviva were to invest its $10 million for 3 months in the British pound deposits, covered in the forward market, it would receive back,

$$\$10,000,000 \left(1 + \frac{0.046167}{4} \right)$$
$$= \$10,115,415$$

However, if Aviva had chosen US-dollar deposits it would have received back:

$$\$10,000,000 \left(1 + \frac{0.044375}{4} \right) = \$10,109,375$$

The difference between the two paybacks is $6,040. This is the reward for Aviva doing its homework and finding the covered yield on different currency-denominated investments.

Determining the currency in which to borrow

Imagine that Aviva Corporation needs to borrow for 3 months. If the annualized interest rate for domestic-currency borrowing is $r_\$$, then the required repayment after 3 months is the principal plus interest, or

$$\$ \left(1 + \frac{r_\$}{4} \right) \qquad (8.6)$$

for each dollar borrowed. This is illustrated by the upper leftward-pointing horizontal arrow in Figure 8.2, showing borrowing as bringing funds to the current time period.

Suppose that instead of borrowing dollars directly, Aviva considers obtaining dollars indirectly by using a pound-denominated loan, and converting the borrowed pounds into the dollars it needs. If the spot exchange rate is $S(\$/£)$, then borrowing $1 requires borrowing $1/S(\$/£)$ in pounds. This is illustrated by the left-hand, upward-pointing arrow in Figure 8.2. For example, at the exchange rate $S(\$/£) = 1.5140$, borrowing

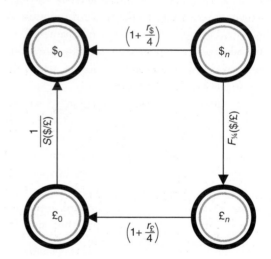

Figure 8.2 *Dollar versus hedged pound borrowing*

Notes
A US borrower seeking funds for 3 months can simply borrow dollars. The repayment at the end of the 3 months is shown on the top horizontal arrow pointing leftwards from maturity of the loan to time zero. Alternatively, the borrower can borrow pounds – the bottom leftward-pointing arrow – and use these to buy dollars spot – the left upward-pointing arrow. In this way the borrower has use of dollars. The pound loan can be hedged by buying the pounds forward, shown by the right downward-pointing arrow. The repayment for hedged pound borrowing is given by the multiplication of the relevant amounts on the three sides of the figure, left, bottom, and right.

$1 means borrowing £0.6605. If the annualized interest rate is $r_£$, then for each dollar borrowed via pounds, Aviva must repay

$$£\frac{1}{S(\$/£)}\left(1+\frac{r_£}{4}\right) \tag{8.7}$$

This is illustrated in Figure 8.2 by multiplication of the amount on the lower leftward-pointing horizontal arrow and the amount on the left-hand, upward-pointing arrow. For example, if $r_£ = 0.06$ (the 3-month *annualized* borrowing rate), Aviva must repay £0.6605 × 1.015 = £0.6704. Without a forward exchange contract the number of dollars this would represent when Aviva repays its pound debt is uncertain. However, with a forward exchange contract the risk is eliminated.

Suppose that Aviva buys forward the amount of pounds in equation (8.7) at $F_{1/4}(\$/£)$. When the debt is repaid, Aviva will receive the required number of pounds on the forward contract for which it must pay

$$\$\frac{F_{1/4}(\$/£)}{S(\$/£)}\left(1+\frac{r_£}{4}\right) \tag{8.8}$$

The forward hedging is illustrated by the right-hand downward-pointing arrow in Figure 8.2. For example, if $F_{1/4}(\$/£) = 1.5121$, repaying £0.6704 involves paying $1.0137 ($1.5121/£ × £0.6704). On the other hand, if Aviva borrowed dollars for 3 months at $r_\$ = 0.05$, or 5 percent per annum, it would have to repay $1.0125 on each dollar. In this case of dollar borrowing, it is cheaper to borrow dollars directly than incur a hedged loan in pounds. In general, a firm should borrow pounds via a swap whenever the amount in equation (8.8) is less than that in equation (8.6), that is, when

$$\frac{F_{1/4}(\$/£)}{S(\$/£)}\left(1+\frac{r_£}{4}\right) < \left(1+\frac{r_\$}{4}\right)$$

A firm should borrow dollars when the reverse inequality holds. In our particular example Aviva should borrow in dollars: the amount to be repaid is lower from a direct dollar loan. The borrowing decision criterion is seen to be the same as the

investment criterion with, of course, the inequality reversed.

Borrowing and investing for arbitrage profit

Imagine a firm that can borrow its own currency and/or a foreign currency, as can a large corporation or bank. Suppose that it can borrow dollars for 3 months at an annualized interest rate of $r_\$$. Thus, for each dollar it borrows, it must repay $(1 + r_\$/4)$ dollars. This is illustrated by the leftward-pointing upper arrow in Figure 8.3. The firm can take each borrowed dollar and buy $1/S(\$/£)$ pounds, illustrated by the left, downward-pointing arrow in Figure 8.3. If these pounds are invested for 3 months at $r_£$ per annum, and if the resulting receipts are sold forward, the firm will receive

$$\$\frac{F_{1/4}(\$/£)}{S(\$/£)}\left(1+\frac{r_£}{4}\right)$$

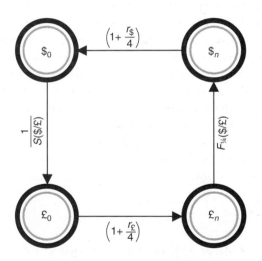

Figure 8.3 Covered interest arbitrage: dollar borrowing and pound investing

Notes
An interest arbitrager may begin by borrowing dollars – the upper leftward-pointing arrow. These borrowed dollars can be used to buy pounds spot – the left downward-pointing arrow. The pounds can then be invested for the same maturity as the dollar loan. With pounds maturing from the investment and dollars to be repaid on the loan there is exchange rate exposure and risk. The exposure and risk can be avoided by selling pounds forward for dollars – the right upward-pointing arrow. Exchange rates and interest rates adjust so that interest arbitrage opportunities do not persist.

The pound investment and forward sale of pounds are illustrated by the lower rightward-pointing and right-hand upper pointing arrows in Figure 8.3. Note that the company has begun with no funds of its own, and has taken no risk. Borrowing in dollars and simultaneously investing in pounds will result in a profit if the number of dollars received from the hedged pound investment exceeds the repayment on the dollar loan, that is, if

$$\left(1 + \frac{r_\$}{4}\right) < \frac{F_{1/4}(\$/£)}{S(\$/£)} \left(1 + \frac{r_£}{4}\right)$$

The reverse activity, borrowing in pounds and investing in dollars, will be profitable if the reverse inequality holds. As long as either inequality holds, it pays to borrow in one currency and lend, or invest, in the other. Borrowing and investing in this way with exchange rate risk hedged in the forward market is known as **covered interest arbitrage**. In terms of Figure 8.3, covered interest arbitrage borrowing of dollars and investing in pounds is seen to be a complete circuit around the figure in a counter-clockwise direction. The alternative covered interest arbitrage of borrowing pounds and investing in dollars would be a clockwise circuit around the figure.

It should be no surprise that the potential for covered interest arbitrage helps guarantee that little opportunity for profit remains, and that investors and borrowers will be relatively indifferent with regard to choosing a currency. This is clear, for example, from the similarity of covered yields in Table 8.1.

THE COVERED INTEREST-PARITY CONDITION

Mathematical statement of interest parity

We have determined that 3-month investors and borrowers would be indifferent between dollar and pound denominations of investment or debt if

$$\left(1 + \frac{r_\$}{4}\right) = \frac{F_{1/4}(\$/£)}{S(\$/£)} \left(1 + \frac{r_£}{4}\right) \qquad (8.9)$$

More precisely, if we allow for compound interest, as we should for long-term investing and borrowing, investors and borrowers will be indifferent between the dollar and pound for investing and borrowing when

$$(1 + r_\$)^n = \frac{F_n(\$/£)}{S(\$/£)} (1 + r_£)^n \qquad (8.10)$$

When equation (8.10) holds, no covered interest arbitrage is profitable. Equation (8.10) is the **covered interest-parity condition**. When this condition holds, there is no advantage to covered borrowing or investing in any particular currency, and no profit from any covered interest arbitrage.

The covered interest-parity condition is the financial-market equivalent of the law of one price from the commodity market, and follows from financial-market efficiency. The market forces leading to covered interest parity, as well as the factors which might result in small deviations from the parity condition, can be illustrated graphically.

Market forces resulting in covered interest-parity: a graphical presentation

We can represent covered interest parity by using the framework of Figure 8.4. The annualized 3-month forward premium on the pound – on principal plus interest – is drawn on the vertical axis, and the annualized interest rate difference between the dollar and the pound is drawn along the horizontal axis. The area above the horizontal axis represents a pound forward premium, and the area below this axis represents a pound forward discount. To the right of the vertical axis there is a dollar interest advantage, and to the left there is a dollar interest disadvantage.

Covered interest parity, as expressed in equation (8.4), can be written as

$$r_\$ - r_£ = 4\left[\frac{F_{1/4}(\$/£) - S(\$/£)}{S(\$/£)}\right]$$
$$\times \left(1 + \frac{r_£}{4}\right) \qquad (8.11)$$

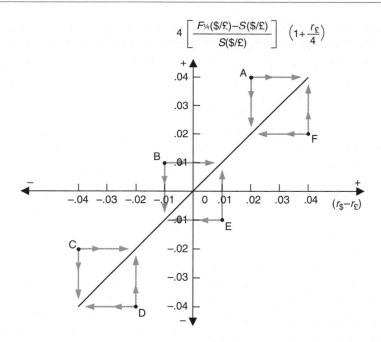

Figure 8.4 *The covered interest-parity diagram*

Notes
The diagonal is the line of covered interest parity. On the line, investors and borrowers are indifferent between dollar and pound investing/borrowing. Above and to the left of the line there is an incentive to invest in pounds and borrow dollars.
Below and to the right of the line there is an incentive to invest in dollars and borrow pounds. In situations off the interest parity line, forces are at work pushing us back towards it.

If the same scale is used on the two axes in Figure 8.4, this parity condition is represented by a 45-degree line. This line traces the points where the two sides of our equation are indeed equal.

Suppose that instead of having equality as in equation (8.11), we have the following inequality:

$$r_\$ - r_£ < 4\left[\frac{F_{1/4}(\$/£) - S(\$/£)}{S(\$/£)}\right] \times \left(1 + \frac{r_£}{4}\right) \qquad (8.12)$$

This condition means for example, that any pound forward premium more than compensates for any dollar interest advantage. Thus:

1   Covered investment in pounds yields more than in dollars.
2   Borrowing in dollars is cheaper than covered borrowing in pounds.

It also means that it is profitable for an interest arbitrager to borrow dollars and make a covered investment in pounds. Because this act of covered interest arbitrage involves borrowing in the cheaper currency, *and* investing in the higher yielding currency, we can concentrate on the consequences of interest arbitrage rather than the separate activities of borrowing and investing.

The incentive in equation (8.12) to borrow dollars and make a covered investment in pounds means an incentive to:

1   Borrow dollars, perhaps by issuing and selling a security – thus tending to increase $r_\$$.
2   Buy spot pounds with the borrowed dollars – thus tending to increase $S(\$/£)$.
3   Buy a pound security – thus tending to reduce $r_£$.
4   Sell the pound investment proceeds forward for US dollars – thus tending to reduce $F_{1/4}(\$/£)$.

Table 8.2 Points off the interest-parity line[a]

	Point					
	A	B	C	D	E	F
Interest differential	+.02	−.01	−.04	−.02	+.01	+.04
Forward premium[b]	−.04	−.01	+.02	+.04	+.01	−.02
Covered margin	−.02	−.02	−.02	+.02	+.02	+.02

Notes
a dollar advantage = +; dollar disadvantage = −.
b Forward premium (+) or discount (!) on the US dollar.

The inequality in equation (8.12) can be represented in Figure 8.4 by points such as A, B, and C that are above and to the left of the 45-degree line. The character of these points is summarized in Table 8.2. At point B, for example, dollar interest rates are 1 percent lower than pound interest rates, and at the same time the dollar is at a 1 percent forward discount. For both reasons there is an advantage to covered borrowing of dollars and investing in pounds. The **covered margin** or advantage of doing this is the interest differential $(r_£ − r_$)$, plus the forward pound premium − on principal plus interest − for a total of 2 percent. In terms of equation (8.12), the inequality holds because the left-hand side is negative ($− 0.01$) and the right-hand side is positive ($+ 0.01$). As we shall explain later, the covered interest arbitrage involving each of the four steps we have distinguished, will tend to restore covered interest parity by pushing the situation at B back towards the parity line. The same thing will occur at every other point off the interest-parity line. For example, consider the situation at point A, where there is an incentive to borrow dollars and invest in pounds, covered. The extra borrowing in dollars to profit from the arbitrage opportunity will put upward pressure on dollar interest rates. If the borrowing is through selling dollar money-market instruments, efforts to sell them will reduce their prices. For given coupons or maturity values, this will raise their yields. Thus, we will find $r_$ increasing. The increase in $r_$ can be represented in Figure 8.4 as a force pushing to the right of A, towards the interest-parity line.

The second step in covered interest arbitrage requires the spot sale of US dollars for British pounds. This will help bid up the spot price of the pound; that is, $S(\$/£)$ will increase. For any given $F_{1/4}(\$/£)$, the higher value of $S(\$/£)$ will reduce the numerator and increase the denominator and thereby reduce the value of the forward pound premium

$$\frac{F_{1/4}(\$/£) − S(\$/£)}{S(\$/£)}$$

This is shown in Figure 8.4 by an arrow pointing downward from A, towards the interest-parity line.

The pounds that were purchased will be used to invest in pound securities. Extra pound-security buyers will, *ceteris paribus,* cause the price of pound securities to increase, and therefore cause pound yields to decrease, that is, $r_£$ will fall. This means an increase in $(r_$ − r_£)$, which is shown by an arrow pointing to the right from A. Again, the movement is back towards the covered interest-parity line.

Covering the pound proceeds of the investment by the forward sale of pounds will lower $F_{1/4}(\$/£)$. For every given value of $S(\$/£)$, there will be a lower value of the pound premium, $[F_{1/4}(\$/£) − S(\$/£)]/S(\$/£)$. Thus, there is a second force that will also push downward from A towards the parity line.[6] We can observe, of course, that since all four steps of arbitrage occur simultaneously, all the forces shown by the arrows occur simultaneously.

Points B and C in Figure 8.4, like point A, indicate profitable opportunities for covered borrowing in dollars and investment in pounds, and so there will be changes in interest and exchange rates also at these points as shown by the arrows. For example, at

6 There is an additional force pointing downward from A due to the lower pound interest rate. However, this is the effect of the reduced premium on the pound interest and is very small.

point C the dollar-interest rate is 4 percent lower than the pound rate. This is only partially offset by a 2-percent annual forward discount on pounds. This will encourage covered arbitrage flows towards pound investments. As before, there will be borrowing in dollars, and hence an increase in r_S; spot purchases of pounds, which will raise $S(\$/£)$; investment in pound securities which will lower $r_£$; and forward sales of pounds, which will lower $F_{1/4}(\$/£)$. All these changes are forces back to the interest-parity line. Indeed, at any point above the interest-parity line the forces shown by the arrows emanating from A, B, and C in Figure 8.4 are at work. We find that if we are off the covered interest-parity line and above it, market forces force us back down towards the line.

Below the interest-parity line, forces push us back up. At points such as D, E, and F, covered interest arbitragers will wish to borrow in pounds and invest in dollars. For example, at point E, dollar interest rates are 1 percent higher than pound rates, *and* the dollar is at a 1-percent forward premium. Thus dollar investments have a 2-percent advantage. This will cause arbitragers to sell pound securities, lowering their prices and raising $r_£$. This is shown in Figure 8.4 by an arrow that points to the left. The interest arbitragers then sell pounds for dollars, lowering $S(\$/£)$ and causing a movement upward, towards the parity line. They also purchase dollar securities, lowering r_S and causing a second movement towards the left. Hedging by buying pounds forward for dollars increases $F_{1/4}(\$/£)$, thereby raising the forward premium on sterling, $4[F_{1/4}(\$/£) - S(\$/£)]/S(\$/£)$. This means that again there will be movement towards the line, since the forward premium is the primary component on the vertical axis. (The other component, $r_£$, also causes movement, albeit small, back up towards the parity line.)

We find that above the covered interest-parity line, dollar borrowing and pound investment, with the associated spot and forward transactions, push us back towards the line. Below the line, pound borrowing and dollar investment with associated currency transactions also push us back towards the line. The amount of adjustment in interest rates

versus spot and/or forward exchange rates depends on the "thinness" of the markets. For example, if a large part of the adjustment towards covered interest parity occurs in the forward rate, the paths followed from points such as A or E back towards the parity line will lie closer to the vertical arrows than to the horizontal ones. In such a case we can think of the forward premium/discount as being determined by the interest differential, rather than vice versa.[7]

COMBINING PPP AND INTEREST PARITY

The uncovered interest-parity condition

Equation (8.10) is the condition for *hedged* or *covered* interest-parity because it involves the use of the forward market. It can be argued that a similar *unhedged* interest-parity condition should also hold. This follows because, as we explained in Chapter 3 and shall confirm later, speculation will make the forward exchange rate approximately equal to the expected future spot rate. That is, if we define $S_n^*(\$/£)$ as in Chapter 3, namely

$S_n^*(\$/£)$ is the expected spot exchange rate between the dollar and the pound in n years' time,

then it follows that to a close approximation

$$S_n^*(\$/£) = F_n(\$/£) \qquad (8.13)$$

Recall that the reason equation (8.13) holds is that if

$$S_n^*(\$/£) > F_n(\$/£)$$

speculators will buy pounds n-years forward; they can buy pounds forward for less than they expect to be able to sell them. This will force up the forward rate, $F_n(\$/£)$, until it is no longer less than the expected future spot rate. Similarly, if

$$S_n^*(\$/£) < F_n(\$/£)$$

---

7 Indeed, foreign exchange traders and brokers frequently compute forward premiums and discounts from interest differentials.

speculators will sell pounds n-years forward; they can sell forward pounds for more than they expect to be able to buy them when they honor their forward contract. Selling pounds forward pushes the forward rate down until it is no longer more than the expected future spot rate. Only when equation (8.13) holds is the forward rate in equilibrium in the sense that speculative pressures are not forcing the forward rate up or down.

Substituting equation (8.13) into equation (8.10) allows us to say that, to a close approximation, **uncovered interest parity** should hold in the form

$$(1 + r_\$)^n = \frac{S_n^*(\$/£)}{S(\$/£)}(1 + r_£)^n \qquad (8.14)$$

This is only an approximate condition because *uncovered* interest parity involves risk: we assume $S_n^*(\$/£) = F_n(\$/£)$ and as we shall see in Chapter 13, this assumption is invalid if there is a risk premium in the forward market.

Equation (8.14) can be put in a different form by noting that by definition

$$S_n^*(\$/£) \equiv S(\$/£)(1 + \dot{S}^*)^n \qquad (8.15)$$

where $\dot{S}^*$ is the average annual expected rate of change of the exchange rate. Substituting equation (8.15) into equation (8.14) gives

$$(1 + r_\$)^n = (1 + \dot{S}^*)^n(1 + r_£)^n \qquad (8.16)$$

Taking the nth root of both sides gives

$$1 + r_\$ = 1 + \dot{S}^* + r_£ + \dot{S}^* \cdot r_£ \qquad (8.17)$$

Assuming $\dot{S}^*$ and $r_£$ are small compared to 1, the "interaction term" $\dot{S}^* \cdot r_£$ will be very small, allowing us to write to a close approximation

$$r_\$ - r_£ = \dot{S}^* \qquad (8.18)$$

That is, the interest differential should approximately equal the expected rate of change of the spot exchange rate.

The expectations form of PPP

We recall from Chapter 7 that the expected dollar return from holding commodities in the

United States is $\dot{P}_{US}^*$, that is, the expected US rate of inflation. Similarly, we recall that the expected dollar return from holding commodities in Britain is $P_{UK}^* + S^*$ because there are expected changes both in the pound prices of commodities and in the dollar value of the pound. We have seen that if we ignore risk, the rates of return from holding commodities in the two countries will be driven to equality by speculators until[8]

$$\dot{P}_{US}^* - \dot{P}_{UK}^* = \dot{S}^* \qquad (7.17)$$

where $\dot{S}^*$ is the expected rate of change of the spot rate, $S(\$/£)$. Equation (7.17) is the PPP condition in terms of expectations. It is known variously as the **expectations**, **speculative**, and **efficient markets PPP**.

The interrelationship of the parity conditions

If we take the PPP condition in its expectations form equation (7.17), and compare it with the uncovered interest-parity condition in equation (8.18), we note a clear similarity. We have

$$\dot{P}_{US}^* - \dot{P}_{UK}^* = \dot{S}^* \qquad (7.17)$$

$$r_\$ - r_£ = \dot{S}^* \qquad (8.18)$$

The right-hand sides of these two equations are equal. It follows that the left-hand sides must likewise be equal. This means that

$$r_\$ - r_£ = \dot{P}_{US}^* - \dot{P}_{UK}^* \qquad (8.19)$$

By rearranging, we have

$$r_\$ - \dot{P}_{US}^* = r_£ - \dot{P}_{UK}^* \qquad (8.20)$$

The two sides of this equation are the two currencies' interest rates less the expected rates of inflation in the associated two countries. The interest rate minus expected inflation is the expected **real**

---

8 As before, we assume no holding costs, or that holding costs are equal in the two countries.

interest rate, popularized principally by Irving Fisher.[9] As a result, equation (8.20) is called the **Fisher-open condition**.[10] The Fisher-open condition states that the expected real rates of interest are equal in different countries. From purchasing-power-parity and uncovered interest parity we have been able to derive an equality relationship between expected real returns in different countries.[11]

The equality of expected real interest rates can be considered as having an independent existence, one that does not have to be derived from PPP and interest parity. It follows from investors allocating their funds to where expected real returns are highest. Investing according to the highest expected real yield will tend to reduce returns in the countries with high returns where funds are sent – because of the greater supply of funds. It will also tend to increase expected returns in countries from which the funds are taken – because of the reduced supply of funds. The flow of funds will continue until the expected real returns in different countries are equalized.[12]

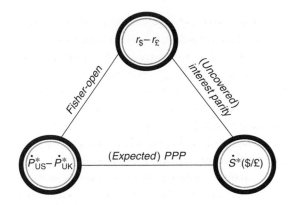

Figure 8.5 *The interdependence of exchange rates, interest rates, and inflation rates*

Notes
Interest parity, PPP, and the Fisher-open condition are related. Any one of these conditions can be derived from the other two.

If we write the uncovered interest parity, expected purchasing-power-parity, and Fisher-open conditions all together, that is,

interest parity: $r_\$ - r_£ = \dot{S}^*(\$/£)$

PPP: $\dot{P}^*_{US} - \dot{P}^*_{UK} = \dot{S}^*(\$/£)$

Fisher-open: $r_\$ - \dot{P}^*_{US} = r_£ - \dot{P}^*_{UK}$

we find that we can derive any one from the other two. This is left as an end-of-chapter problem for the reader. The conditions are shown in Figure 8.5. Each side of the triangle in Figure 8.5 represents a condition. The figure helps clarify why satisfying any two conditions implies that the remaining condition is satisfied.

Because each of the three parity conditions along the sides of Figure 8.5 can be derived from the other two, any one condition must be correct if the other two are correct. For example, if we believe expected real returns are equal in different countries and that uncovered interest parity holds precisely, we are implicitly accepting that PPP in its expectations form also holds precisely.

WHY COVERED INTEREST DIFFERENCES PERSIST

In reality, covered interest parity holds very closely, but it does not hold precisely. This is

9 See Irving Fisher, *The Theory of Interest*, A. M. Kelley, New York, 1965.

10 Generally, economists refer to equation (8.18), not equation (8.20), as the Fisher-open condition. However, since Fisher spoke of real interest rates as actual rates minus the expected inflation rate, equation (8.20) would be more appropriately referred to by his name. Equation (8.18) should perhaps be called the "interest-open" condition, where "open" means "open economy."

11 We state this in terms of countries rather than currencies because inflation refers to countries. Of course, returns within countries are in the countries' currencies.

12 The relationship between security yields in different countries can be extremely complex because of taxes, regulations, currency risks, citizens' tastes, and so on. The problem has been tackled by F. L. A. Grauer, R. H. Litzenberger, and R. E. Stehle, "Sharing Rules and Equilibrium in an International Capital Market under Uncertainty," *Journal of Financial Economics*, June 1976, pp. 233–56, and Fischer Black, "International Capital Market Equilibrium with Investment Barriers," *Journal of Financial Economics*, December 1974, pp. 337–52. Few data exist on real rates in different countries. See, however, Robert Z. Aliber, "Real Interest Rates in a Multicurrency World," unpublished paper, University of Chicago.

apparent from, for example, the covered interest differentials in Table 8.1. The failure to achieve exact covered interest parity could occur because in actual financial markets there are

1   transaction costs;
2   political risks;
3   potential tax advantages to foreign exchange gains versus interest earnings; and
4   liquidity differences between foreign securities and domestic securities.

In addition, uncovered interest parity may not hold because of risk aversion: recall that uncovered parity is based on spot rate expectations, not on forward rates which eliminate foreign exchange risk.

In this chapter we explain how the four factors listed above contribute to departures from covered interest-parity. Later, in Chapter 14, we show that these are the same factors that influence cash management.

Transaction costs and interest parity

The cost of transacting in foreign exchange is reflected in the bid-ask spread in exchange rates. The bid-ask spread represents the cost of two foreign exchange transactions, a purchase and a sale of foreign currency. That is, if a person buys and then immediately sells a foreign currency, the cost of these two transactions is the difference between the buying and selling prices of the currency, which is the bid-ask spread. Covered investment or borrowing involve two foreign exchange transaction costs – one on the spot market and the other on the forward market. These two transaction costs discourage foreign-currency denominated investment and borrowing. Interest arbitrage also involves two foreign exchange transaction costs, since the borrowed currency is sold spot and then bought forward. However, there are additional transaction costs of interest arbitrage due to interest-rate spreads. This is because the borrowing

interest rate is likely to exceed the investment interest rate.[13]

It might seem that the extra cost of investing in foreign currency-denominated securities vis-à-vis domestic-currency securities would require covered foreign-currency yields to be higher than domestic-currency yields before investors choose the foreign-currency alternative; investors need to find it worthwhile to incur the extra transaction costs for a foreign-currency security. Similarly, it might seem that borrowing costs in foreign currency would have to be lower than borrowing costs in domestic currency before borrowers choose the foreign-currency alternative; borrowers face extra costs when borrowing via the foreign-currency swap. In other words, it might seem that there could be deviations from interest parity by up to the extra transaction costs of investing or borrowing in foreign currency before the benefits of the foreign alternative are sufficient to compensate for the added costs. In terms of Figure 8.4, it would appear that transaction costs could allow the situation to be slightly off the interest-parity line; the apparent advantages to foreign-currency investments/borrowing at points just off the line do not trigger foreign borrowing/ investing because the benefits are insufficient to compensate for the costs. Indeed, because the cost of covered interest arbitrage includes the borrowing – investing interest rate spread as well as foreign exchange transaction costs, it might appear that deviations from interest parity could be relatively large before being sufficient to compensate for the transaction costs of covered interest arbitrage.

Despite the preceding, which would suggest that deviations from interest parity could result from transaction costs, it has generally become recognized that transaction costs do not contribute to deviations from interest parity. A major reason for this recognition is the realization that one-way

13 The borrowing-investment spread can be considered as a transaction cost in the same way that we consider the bid-ask spread on currencies a transaction cost, namely, it is the cost of borrowing and then immediately investing the borrowed funds.

interest arbitrage circumvents transaction costs in foreign exchange and securities markets. We can explain the nature of one-way interest arbitrage and how it influences the interest-parity condition by contrasting one-way and **round-trip arbitrage**. In order to do this, we need to be explicit about foreign exchange and borrowing – lending transaction costs. Using the same notation as in Chapter 2 for transaction costs on spot exchange, let us use the following definitions:

$S(\$/ask£)$ and $F_n(\$/ask£)$ are respectively the spot and n-year forward exchange rates when buying pounds with dollars, and $S(\$/bid£)$ and $F_n(\$/bid£)$ are respectively the spot and forward exchange rates when selling pounds for dollars. $r_\$^I$ and $r_£^I$ are the interest rates earned on investments in the two currencies, and $r_\$^B$ and $r_£^B$ are the interest rates on borrowing in the two currencies.

This notation is used in Figure 8.6 to show the difference between one-way and round-trip arbitrage and the implications of this distinction for covered interest parity.

Figure 8.6a illustrates round-trip covered interest arbitrage. As before, the four corners of the diagram show current dollars ($\$_0$), current pounds, ($£_0$), future dollars ($\$_n$), and future pounds ($£_n$). The arrows drawn between the corners of the figure show the interest rates or exchange rates when going between the corners in the directions of the arrows. For example, when going from $\$_0$ to $£_0$ as shown by the downward-pointing arrow in the left-hand panel of Figure 8.6a, the transaction occurs at the spot exchange rate, $S(\$/ask£)$: pounds are being purchased. Similarly, when going from $\$_n$ to $\$_0$ as shown by the upper, horizontal, leftward-pointing arrow in the left-hand panel of Figure 8.6a, this involves borrowing dollars and so occurs at the dollar-borrowing rate, $r_\$^B$.

The left-hand diagram in Figure 8.6a shows round-trip arbitrage involving borrowing in dollars and investing in pounds. To understand the nature of this arbitrage we begin at corner $\$_n$. The top

leftward-pointing arrow from $\$_n$ shows the interest rate on dollar borrowing which gives immediate dollars, $\$_0$, in return for paying dollars back in the future, $\$_n$. The left downward-pointing arrow shows the spot exchange rate at which the borrowed dollars are exchanged into pounds; the pounds must be purchased, so the spot rate is the ask rate for pounds, $S(\$/ask£)$. The bottom rightward-pointing arrow shows the interest rate earned on the pound-denominated investment which converts today's pounds, $£_0$, into future pounds $£_n$. Finally, the right upward-pointing arrow shows the forward exchange rate at which the dollars needed for repaying the dollar loan are purchased with pounds, $F_n(\$/bid£)$. The counterclockwise journey in this left-hand diagram in Figure 8.6a from $\$_n$ and back to $\$_n$ is seen to involve foreign exchange transaction costs – the ask on spot pounds $S(\$/ask£)$ versus bid on forward pounds $F_n(\$/bid£)$, and therefore a bid-ask spread – plus borrowing – investment transaction costs – the borrowing rate on dollars $r_\$^B$ versus the investment rate on pounds, $r_£^I$. That is, round-trip arbitrage is expensive in terms of facing costs in the currency and in the security markets.

The right-hand diagram in Figure 8.6a illustrates the alternative direction of round-trip arbitrage, with borrowing of pounds and investment in dollars. Starting at $£_n$, pounds are borrowed at $r_£^B$ giving the borrower current pounds $£_0$. These are sold spot for dollars at $S(\$/bid£)$ and the dollars invested at $r_\$^I$. The pound-denominated loan is covered by buying forward pounds at the forward ask rate for pounds, $F_n(\$/ask£)$. As with the left-hand figure in Figure 8.6a, we see that the pound borrowing-dollar investment arbitrage also involves a transaction cost spread in the foreign exchange market – spot bid versus forward ask on pounds – and in the securities market – pound borrowing rate versus the dollar investment rate.

If the maximum possible sizes of deviations from covered interest parity due to transaction costs were determined only by round-trip covered interest arbitrage, the deviations could be quite large. This is because for round-trip interest arbitrage to be profitable it is necessary to overcome the

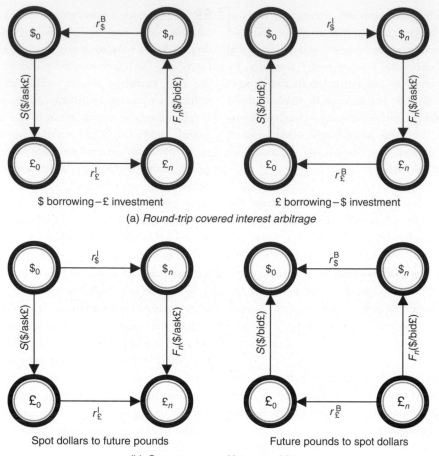

$ borrowing – £ investment   £ borrowing – $ investment

(a) *Round-trip covered interest arbitrage*

Spot dollars to future pounds   Future pounds to spot dollars

(b) *One-way covered interest arbitrage*

Figure 8.6 *One way and round-trip interest arbitrage*

Notes
Round-trip interest arbitrage, illustrated in (a), involves going along all four sides of the diagram at the interest rates
and exchange rates that are shown. The presence of four transaction costs allows for large deviations from interest parity.
One-way interest arbitrage, illustrated in (b), involves comparing two alternative ways of going from one corner to another
corner that is diagonally opposite. Either route involves two transaction costs, but since these are for the same types of
transactions, they do not cause deviations from interest parity.

transaction costs in the foreign exchange markets
and the borrowing – lending spread on interest
rates. Let us attach some numbers to see the size of
deviations that might result. We shall use transactions costs faced by the lowest cost arbitragers, such
as large commercial banks, since it is they who are
likely to act first and preclude others from profiting
from interest arbitrage.

Let us assume a potential interest arbitrager can
borrow for 1 year at $\frac{1}{4}$ percent (25 basis points)
above his or her investment rate, and can borrow

a sufficient amount to reduce the spot and forward
transaction costs both to only $\frac{1}{10}$ of 1 percent. In this
situation, it is necessary that the interest-parity
deviation calculated using interest rates and
exchange rates that exclude transaction costs would
have to be almost $\frac{1}{2}$ of 1 percent for profitable
arbitrage. This is because it is necessary to earn $\frac{1}{4}$ of
one percent to cover the borrowing – investment
spread, and another $\frac{1}{5}$ of 1 percent to cover the two
foreign exchange transaction costs, those for the
spot and forward exchange transactions, both being

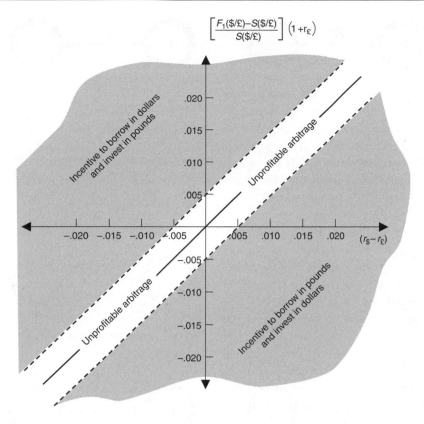

Figure 8.7 *Interest parity in the presence of transaction costs, political risk, or liquidity premiums*

Notes
Interest parity might not hold exactly because of transaction costs, political risk, and liquidity preference. This means interest rates and exchange rates may not plot on the interest-parity line. Rather, they may be somewhere within a band around the line; only outside this band are the covered yield differences enough to overcome the costs and/or political risk of covered interest arbitrage. However, the band is narrow because there are some participants for whom the costs and political risk of arbitrage are unimportant or irrelevant. For example, transaction costs are irrelevant for one-way arbitragers.

$\frac{1}{10}$ of 1 percent. This is illustrated in Figure 8.7. We can interpret the interest rates on the horizontal axis as the midpoints between the borrowing and lending rates, and the exchange rates on the vertical axis as the midpoints between the "bid" and "ask" rates.

We show a band around the interest-parity line within which round-trip interest arbitrage is unprofitable. This band has a width of approximately $\frac{1}{2}$ percent on either side of the interest-parity line, as is seen, for example, along the horizontal axis around the origin. The band reflects the fact that arbitrage must cover the $\frac{1}{2}$ percent lost in transaction costs/spreads. Above and to the left of the band it is profitable to borrow in dollars and

make covered investments in pounds, and to the right of the band it is profitable to do the reverse.[14]

14 If interest rates were for 3 months rather than 1 year, the band would be considerably wider. Even if the borrowing – lending spread remained at $\frac{1}{4}$ of 1 percent and the foreign exchange transaction costs remained at $\frac{1}{10}$ of 1 percent, the band would be more than one full percent on either side of the interest-parity line. The reason is that the costs of buying spot and selling forward are incurred within a 3-month period, and when annualized are effectively 4 times larger. With $\frac{1}{5}$ percent lost in 3 months, it is necessary for the interest arbitrage to generate $\frac{4}{5}$ of a percent to cover foreign-exchange costs, plus $\frac{1}{4}$ of a percent to cover the borrowing–lending spread. If we were dealing with 1-month or shorter arbitrage, the potential deviations from interest parity would be even larger.

Let us next consider the implication of *one-way* arbitrage.

One-way arbitrage can come in various forms. However, we need to consider only the form which involves the lowest transaction cost, because it is this arbitrage that will determine the maximum deviation from interest parity; just as the *arbitrager* with the lowest cost of interest arbitrage drives interest rates and exchange rates to levels closest to the interest-parity line, so it is that the *form* of one-way arbitrage that faces the lowest transaction cost drives us closest to the parity line.

Let us consider first the one-way interest arbitrage illustrated by the left-hand diagram in part b of Figure 8.6. This shows an arbitrager holding dollars ($\$_0$) who wants pounds in the future ($\pounds_n$), perhaps to pay for something purchased from Britain.[15] The arbitrager has two choices to go from current dollars to future pounds. The dollars can be sold for pounds on the spot market and invested in pound-denominated securities until the pounds are needed, or the dollars can be invested in dollar securities and forward pounds can be purchased. The first of these choices is illustrated by the downward-pointing arrow on the left of the diagram from $\$_0$ to $\pounds_0$ and the rightward-pointing arrow along the bottom from $\pounds_0$ to $\pounds_n$. The second choice is illustrated by the upper rightward-pointing arrow from $\$_0$ to $\$_n$ and the downward-pointing arrow on the right from $\$_n$ to $\pounds_n$. We note that both routes take the arbitrager from today's dollars, $\$_0$, to future pounds, $\pounds_n$. The choice is to pick the route providing the future pounds at lower cost.

15 The use of the term "arbitrager" in this context stretches the usual meaning of the term, because we have assumed that dollars are already held, and that there is already a need for pounds in the future. Without engaging in excessive semantics we can note that the essence of what our "arbitrager" is doing is judging which of two ways of going from current dollars to future pounds is the cheaper. This choice of the preferred route is the same type of choice met in deriving cross exchange rates in Chapter 2. The term "arbitrage" comes from "arbitrate," which means "choose." However, a reader who still objects to the term "arbitrager" can substitute his or her own term; the conclusion is the same whatever word we use.

If the choice that is made is to invest in dollar securities and buy pounds forward, each pound purchased will cost $\$F_n(\$/\text{ask}\pounds)$. In order to have this many dollars in n-years requires investing today at $r_\$^I$

$$\$\frac{F_n(\$/\text{ask}\pounds)}{(1+r_\$^I)^n} \qquad (8.21)$$

This is the cost per pound using the dollar investment, forward pound route from $\$_0$ to $\$_n$. If the other choice is made, that is, to buy pounds immediately and invest in pound-denominated securities for n years, the number of pounds that must be purchased immediately for each pound to be obtained in n years is

$$\pounds\frac{1}{(1+r_\pounds^I)^n} \qquad (8.22)$$

The cost of this number of pounds at the spot price of pounds, $S(\$/\text{ask}\pounds)$, is:

$$\$\frac{S(\$/\text{ask}\pounds)}{(1+r_\pounds^I)^n} \qquad (8.23)$$

In the same way that we saw that there are forces pushing interest rates and exchange rates to the interest-parity line, there are forces making the amounts in equations (8.21) and (8.23) equal to each other. For example, if equation (8.23) gave a lower cost per pound than equation (8.21), there would be spot purchases of pounds and funds invested in pound-denominated securities. These actions would increase $S(\$/\text{ask}\pounds)$ and reduce $r_\pounds^I$. At the same time, the lack of forward pound purchases would reduce $F_n(\$/\text{ask}\pounds)$, and the capital outflow from the United States would increase $r_\$^I$. The choice between alternatives would therefore drive them to the same cost, that is,

$$\frac{F_n(\$/\text{ask}\pounds)}{(1+r_\$^I)^n} = \frac{S(\$/\text{ask}\pounds)}{(1+r_\pounds^I)^n} \qquad (8.24)$$

We can rewrite (8.24) as

$$(1+r_\$^I)^n = \frac{F_n(\$/\text{ask}\pounds)}{S(\$/\text{ask}\pounds)}(1+r_\pounds^I)^n \qquad (8.25)$$

If the sizes of transaction costs in the spot and forward foreign exchange markets were the same, then equation (8.25) would plot as a 45-degree line through the origin in the interest-parity diagram, Figure 8.7. This is because we have investment interest rates on both sides of the equation, and we have "ask" exchange rates for both the forward and spot transactions.[16] This means that if spot and forward transaction costs were equal, the choice we have described would drive us all the way to the interest-parity line even though there are transaction costs. The reason this happens is that either method of going from $\$_0$ to £$_n$ requires buying pounds, the only difference being whether they are purchased on the spot or the forward market. Therefore, transaction costs will be paid whatever choice is made. Similarly, investment interest rates are earned if the choice is to buy pounds spot or forward, the only difference being in which currency the interest is earned.

Another form of one-way interest arbitrage is illustrated by the lower right-hand diagram in Figure 8.6b. The choice in this case is between two ways of going from £$_n$ to $\$_0$. (A US exporter who is to receive pounds and needs to borrow dollars would be interested in going from £$_n$ to $\$_0$.) The two ways of going from the £$_n$ to $\$_0$ involve either going from £$_n$ to £$_0$ by borrowing pounds, and then from £$_0$ to $\$_0$ via the spot market, or going from £$_n$ to $\$_n$ via the forward market, and from $\$_n$ to $\$_0$ by borrowing dollars.

If the route that is taken from £$_n$ to $\$_0$ is to borrow pounds and sell them spot for dollars, the number of pounds that can be borrowed today for

each pound to be repaid in n years is

$$£\,\frac{1}{\left(1 + r_£^B\right)^n}$$

This number of pounds, when sold spot for dollars, provides

$$\$\,\frac{S(\$/\text{bid}£)}{\left(1 + r_£^B\right)^n} \qquad (8.26)$$

The alternative route of selling pounds forward and borrowing dollars means receiving in the future for each pound sold

$$\$F_n(\$/\text{bid}£)$$

The number of dollars that can be borrowed today and repaid with these pounds is

$$\$\,\frac{F_n(\$/\text{bid}£)}{\left(1 + r_\$^B\right)^n} \qquad (8.27)$$

The dollar amounts in equations (8.26) and (8.27) show the dollars available today, $\$_0$, for each pound in the future, £$_n$. The choice between the alternative ways of obtaining dollars will drive exchange rates and interest rates to the point that

$$\frac{S(\$/\text{bid}£)}{\left(1 + r_£^B\right)^n} = \frac{F_n(\$/\text{bid}£)}{\left(1 + r_\$^B\right)^n}$$

that is,

$$\left(1 + r_\$^B\right)^n = \frac{F_n(\$/\text{bid}£)}{S(\$/\text{bid}£)}\left(1 + r_£^B\right)^n \qquad (8.28)$$

Again, if forward and spot transaction costs are equal, this is an exact interest-parity line; we have borrowing interest rates on both sides, and both exchange rates are bid rates.

In fact, forward exchange transaction costs are higher than spot costs – recall from Chapter 3 that forward spreads are wider than spot spreads – and so equation (8.25) and equation (8.28) might differ a little from the interest-parity line drawn without transaction costs. However, the departures

---

16 That is, because both exchange rates are "ask" rates, the exchange rates in the numerator and denominator of equation (8.25) are both on the high side of the bid-ask spread. To the extent that transaction costs in the spot and forward markets are equal, they cancel. Similarly, because the interest rates on the two sides of equation (8.25) are investment rates, they are both on the low side of the borrowing-lending spread. The cost-component again cancels.

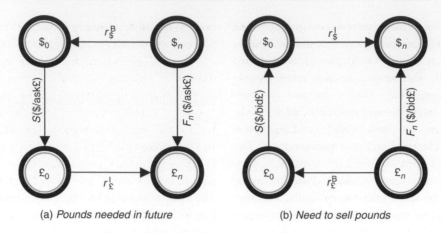

(a) *Pounds needed in future*   (b) *Need to sell pounds*

Figure 8.8 *A more roundabout one-way arbitrage*

Notes
We can reduce the band around the interest-parity line by considering whether to use the forward market or the spot market plus money markets. This choice, however, involves one transaction versus three transactions and is likely to leave larger deviations from interest parity than other, more similar one-way arbitrage choices.

will be much smaller than those obtained from consideration of round-trip interest arbitrage.[17] This is because round-trip interest arbitrage involves the borrowing – investment interest-rate spread and foreign exchange transaction costs of buying spot and selling forward, or of buying forward and selling spot. On the other hand, one-way arbitrage does not involve interest-rate spreads, and foreign exchange transaction costs are faced whatever choice is made.

The one-way arbitrage we have described produces the interest-parity line because we have established situations where the arbitrager has in any case to buy/sell foreign exchange and to invest/borrow. An alternative one-way arbitrage is a choice between buying/selling forward on the one hand, and buying/selling spot and using the money

markets on the other hand.[18] For example an arbitrager could buy pounds forward, or alternatively could borrow dollars, buy pounds spot, and invest the pounds. Either way the arbitrager receives pounds in the future and has to deliver dollars. This is illustrated in Figure 8.8a, where the arbitrager can go from $\$_n$ to $\pounds_n$ via the forward market (the downward-pointing arrow on the right-hand side), or by borrowing dollars (the upper leftward-pointing arrow), buying pounds spot with the borrowed dollars (the left-hand downward-pointing arrow), and investing in pounds (the lower rightward-pointing arrow). This one-way arbitrage does make *foreign exchange* transaction costs irrelevant, or at least less relevant, because it involves ask rates in either case. However, it does not avoid the *borrowing – investing* spread. It does not, therefore, take us as close to the interest-parity line as the type of one-way arbitrage we considered. We reach the same conclusion if we consider the reverse forward exchange, going from $\pounds_n$ to $\$_n$, versus the

17 In fact, even if there are transaction cost differences between spot and forward exchange, when all one-way arbitrages are considered simultaneously with a requirement that there is both supply and demand in every market, interest parity holds exactly. This is shown in Maurice D. Levi, "Non-Reversed Investment and Borrowing, Transaction Costs and Covered Interest Parity," *International Review of Economics and Finance*, 2, 1992, pp. 107–19.

18 This is the more usual one-way arbitrage considered in explaining why transaction costs are not important. For example, see Alan V. Deardorff, "One-Way Arbitrage and its Implications for the Foreign Exchange Markets," *Journal of Political Economy*, April 1975, pp. 351–64.

alternative of borrowing pounds, using these to buy dollars spot, and investing the dollars. This is illustrated in Figure 8.8b; it again gives a line further from the interest-parity line than the one-way arbitrage we described.

An alternative way of concluding that the deviations from interest parity as a result of transaction costs are small is to consider the choice faced by third-country borrowers and investors. For example, if Japanese or German investors and borrowers are looking for the best currency to invest or borrow, they will drive the situation between dollars and pounds to the interest-parity line. This is because the Japanese or Germans pay foreign exchange costs whatever the currency of their investment or borrowing, and compare investment rates in the two currencies, or borrowing rates in the two currencies.[19] For this reason, or because of the presence of one-way arbitrage, we can expect deviations from interest parity to be too small for round-trip arbitrage to ever occur. We conclude that transaction costs are probably not a cause of deviations from interest parity.[20]

Political risk and interest parity

When securities denominated in different *currencies* trade in different *countries*, deviations from interest parity can result from **political risk**. Political risk involves the uncertainty that while funds are invested in a foreign country, they may be frozen, become inconvertible into other currencies, or be confiscated. Even if such extremes do not occur, investors might find themselves facing new or increased taxes in the foreign country. Usually, the investment that involves the least political risk is at home; if funds are invested abroad, to the risk of tax or other changes at home is added the risk of changes in another political jurisdiction. However, it is possible that for investors in some countries, it is politically less risky to send funds abroad. This will be true if investors thereby avoid politically risky possibilities at home. For example, people in some volatile countries have invested in Switzerland and the United States for political safety. In these circumstances, a foreign investment might be made even at a covered interest disadvantage. In general, however, we expect investors to require a premium from a foreign investment versus a domestic investment.

In diagrammatic terms, political risk creates a band like that shown in Figure 8.7; only in the area beyond some covered differential is there an incentive to invest abroad.[21] The political risk band does not have to be of equal width on the two sides of the interest-parity line if one country is viewed as riskier than the other. For example, Canadian yields are generally a little higher than US yields, even after allowance for forward hedging. This can be attributed to US investors viewing Canada as being politically more risky than Canadians view the US, thereby causing a larger political-risk premium on Canadian securities than on US securities.

It is important to remember that political risk relates to the country, not the currency, of investment. For example, there is no political risk involved in the deviations from covered interest-parity in Table 8.1 because the yields are assumed to be on different currency bank deposits in London. That is, there are no political differences between the instruments in Table 8.1, but rather only differences in the currencies of denomination. Indeed, by comparing yield differences when there are no political differences – as on bank deposits (covered) in a given country – with yield differences when there are

19 This assumes that cross exchange rates of pounds for yen or pounds for euros do not have a larger bid-ask spread than direct yen-dollar or euro-dollar exchange rates. When cross-exchange-rate spreads are larger, dollar investments and borrowing will be favored.

20 The arguments we have given for transaction costs to be a minor or irrelevant reason for deviation from interest parity can be supplemented by an argument advanced by Kevin Clinton involving the trading of swaps. See Kevin Clinton, "Transaction Costs and Covered Interest Arbitrage: Theory and Evidence," *Journal of Political Economy*, April 1988, pp. 358–70.

21 Of course, political risk does not create a band via the *borrowing* decision. Borrowers have to pay back their loans whatever happens in the country from which they borrowed.

political differences – as on Treasury bills (covered) in different countries – it is possible to estimate the importance of political risk. The extra spread when political risk is faced versus when it is not faced is a measure of the political risk premium.[22]

Even when covered yields are on instruments which trade in different countries, third-country investors might force interest rates and exchange rates onto the interest-parity line. For example, if Japanese investors view the United States and Britain as equally risky politically from their perspective, then they will drive the interest rates and exchange rates for the United States and Britain onto the interest-parity line. This is true even if investors in the United States and Britain perceive foreign investment as riskier than investment at home. Of course, if conditions are driven onto the interest-parity line, this will encourage US and British investors to keep funds at home, because neither is receiving compensation for the perceived risk of investing in the other country.

Taxes and interest parity

If taxes are the same on domestic and on foreign investment and borrowing, then the existence of taxes will make no difference in our investment and borrowing criteria or the interest-parity line; taxes will cancel out when yield comparisons are made. However, if tax rates depend on the country in which funds are invested or borrowed, the interest-parity condition will be affected. There are two ways in which taxes could conceivably affect the parity condition. One way involves withholding taxes, and the other involves differences between the tax rate on income and that on capital gains. Let us consider these in turn.

Withholding taxes

One might think that a potential cause of higher taxes on foreign earnings than on domestic earnings, and

hence a band around the interest-parity line, is the **foreign resident withholding tax**. A withholding tax is a tax applied to foreigners at the source of their earnings. For example, when a Canadian resident earns $100 in the United States, the payer of that $100 is required to withhold and remit 15 percent of the earnings to the US Internal Revenue Service. Similarly, the earnings of US residents in Canada are subject to a withholding tax. Withholding taxes, however, are unlikely to offer a reason for a band around the covered interest-parity line.

As long as the rate of withholding is less than or equal to the tax rate that would be applied to the earnings at home, domestic **withholding tax credits** that are designed to avoid double taxation of income will offset the tax withheld. For example, suppose that a resident of the United States pays the equivalent of $15 on $100 of interest or dividends earned in Canada, and the total tax payable on the $100 when declared in the United States is $25. The Internal Revenue Service will grant the US resident a $15 credit on taxes paid to the taxing authority in Canada. Only an additional $10 will be payable in the United States. The investor ends up paying a total of $25, which is the same as she would have paid on $100 earned at home. Complete or full withholding tax credit leaves no incentive to choose domestic securities rather than foreign securities. Only if withholding tax credits are less than the amounts withheld will there be a reason to keep money at home.[23] This means that the interest-parity condition is in general not affected, and we have no band around the parity line as a result of withholding taxes.

Capital gains versus income taxes

Taxes can affect the investment and borrowing criteria and the interest-parity condition if investors pay different effective tax rates on foreign exchange

---

22 See Robert Z. Aliber, "The Interest Parity Theorem: A Reinterpretation," *Journal of Political Economy*, November/December 1973, pp. 1451–9.

23 Even when full credit is obtained, interest earnings are lost on the funds withheld in comparison with what might have been earned if taxes had been paid at home at the end of the tax period. This should, however, be a relatively small consideration except when interest rates are very high.

earnings than on interest earnings. This can be the situation for investors who infrequently buy or sell foreign exchange. This is because such investors can obtain capital-account treatment of their foreign exchange gains or losses; gains and losses are normally given capital-account treatment if they are not part of the "normal conduct of business."[24] If the tax rate on capital gains is lower than that on ordinary income, this affects the slope of the interest-parity line. Let us see how, by considering a US investor who pays a lower effective tax rate on capital gains than on interest income.[25]

Let us write the US investor's tax rate on capital gains as τ_K and the US tax rate on income as τ_Y, and let us assume that for this particular investor, $\tau_Y > \tau_K$. Since all interest earnings are considered to be income, after paying taxes and ignoring transaction costs the US investor will receive from each dollar invested in dollar-denominated securities for 1 year

$$1 + (1 - \tau_Y)r_{\$} \qquad (8.29)$$

That is, the investor will lose a fraction τ_Y of the interest earned. If he or she instead invests in pound securities, then before taxes the US dollar receipts will be

$$\frac{F_1(\$/£)}{S(\$/£)}(1 + r_£) = \left[\frac{F_1(\$/£) - S(\$/£)}{S(\$/£)}\right] \\ \times (1 + r_£) + (1 + r_£)$$

or

$$\frac{F_1(\$/£)}{S(\$/£)}(1 + r_£)$$
$$= 1 + r_£ + \left[\frac{F_1(\$/£) - S(\$/£)}{S(\$/£)}\right](1 + r_£)$$

24 Even where the tax rate on realized capital gains is the same as on ordinary income, the *effective* tax rate on capital gains is lower if capital gains can be deferred, or if there are capital losses against which the capital gains can be taken. In many countries the *actual* tax rate on capital gains is lower than that on ordinary income.

25 For the conditions for capital-account treatment of foreign exchange earnings, see Martin Kupferman and Maurice D. Levi, "Taxation and the International Money Market Investment Decision," *Financial Analysts Journal*, July/August 1978, pp. 61–4.

We have expanded the total dollar payback into three parts; the principal; the interest earned on the pounds; and the earnings/losses from exchange rate premiums/discounts on the principal and interest, $(1 + r_£)$. After taxes, if capital gains taxes are paid on foreign exchange earnings, even when hedged, the investor will receive only $(1 - \tau_Y)$ of the interest and $(1 - \tau_K)$ of the gain from the forward premium, that is,

$$1 + (1 - \tau_Y)r_£ + (1 - \tau_K)$$
$$\times \left[\frac{F_1(\$/£) - S(\$/£)}{S(\$/£)}\right](1 + r_£) \qquad (8.30)$$

We have used the income tax rate τ_Y on $r_£$, since all interest, whatever the currency or country of source, is subject to that rate.

We can show the effect of taxes in terms of the graphical presentation of interest parity if we proceed the same way as we did when we included transaction costs. The US investor for whom we have assumed $\tau_Y > \tau_K$ will be indifferent between investing in dollar or pound securities if the amounts in equations (8.29) and (8.30) are equal. This requires that

$$r_{\$} - r_£ = \frac{1 - \tau_k}{1 - \tau_Y}\left[\frac{F_1(\$/£) - S(\$/£)}{S(\$/£)}\right]$$
$$\times (1 + r_£) \qquad (8.31)$$

In comparing equation (8.31) with the equation for the interest-parity line in Figure 8.4, which is

$$r_{\$} - r_£ = \left[\frac{F_1(\$/£) - S(\$/£)}{S(\$/£)}\right](1 + r_£)$$

we see that differential taxes on income versus capital gains/losses adds $(1 - \tau_K)/(1 - \tau_Y)$ to the front of the forward premium/discount term. When the capital gains tax rate is lower than the income tax rate,

$$\frac{1 - \tau_K}{1 - \tau_Y} > 1$$

For example, if $\tau_K = 0.10$ and $\tau_Y = 0.25$, then

$$\frac{1 - \tau_K}{1 - \tau_Y} = 1.20$$

This means that the line of indifference for investors who face lower taxes on foreign exchange earnings than on interest income is flatter than the 45-degree interest-parity line in Figure 8.4; each percent change in $\left[F_1(\$/\pounds) - S(\$/\pounds)\right]/\left[S(\$/\pounds)\right] \times (1 + r_\pounds)$ on the vertical axis in Figure 8.4 is associated with more than a 1 percent change in $r_\$ - r_\pounds$ on the horizontal axis.

While some investors may enjoy a lower tax rate on foreign exchange than on interest earnings, banks and other major financial market players do not; such investors, for whom international investment is part of their normal business, pay the same tax on interest and foreign exchange earnings. For this reason we can expect interest rates and exchange rates to remain on the 45-degree interest-parity line; banks will take positions until the situation is on the line. This implies that those investors who *do* pay lower taxes on foreign exchange earnings than on interest income may find valuable **tax arbitrage** opportunities. For example, suppose interest rates and exchange rates are such that interest parity holds precisely on a before-tax basis with:

$$r_\$ = 8\%$$

$$r_\pounds = 4\%$$

$$\left[\frac{F_1(\$/\pounds) - S(\$/\pounds)}{S(\$/\pounds)}\right](1 + r_\pounds) = 4\%$$

For a US investor for whom $\tau_Y = 0.25$ and $\tau_K = 0.10$, US investments yield $(1 - \tau_Y)r_\$ = 6$ percent after tax, while covered pound investments yield after tax:

$$(1 - \tau_Y)r_\pounds$$

$$+ (1 - \tau_Y)\left[\frac{F_1(\$/\pounds) - S(\$/\pounds)}{S(\$/\pounds)}\right](1 + r_\pounds)$$

$$= 6.6\%$$

The pound investment will be preferred on an after-tax basis even though interest parity holds on a before-tax basis. More generally, if covered interest-parity holds on a before-tax basis, investors with favorable capital gains treatment will prefer investments denominated in currencies trading at a forward premium. It is a natural extension of our argument to show that in the same tax situation, borrowers will prefer to denominate borrowing in currencies at a forward discount.[26]

Liquidity differences and interest parity

The liquidity of an asset can be judged by how quickly and cheaply it can be converted into cash. For example, when a *domestic*-currency denominated asset such as a 90-day security is sold before maturity after only 50 days, domestic security selling transaction costs must be paid that would not have been incurred had the security been held to maturity. If, however, a covered *foreign*-currency 90-day investment is sold after only 50 days, more than security selling costs are faced. This should be explained carefully.

The brokerage costs for selling a foreign-currency denominated security are likely to be similar to those for selling a domestic-currency security. However, transaction costs are faced when investors convert on the spot exchange market, the foreign exchange received from the sale of the foreign-currency security. These costs would have not been faced had the security been held to maturity and the proceeds converted according to the original forward contract. Further, when a foreign-currency denominated security is sold prior to maturity and the funds are converted into domestic currency, there is still the matter of honoring the original forward contract to sell the

---

26 This is because the high interest rates they pay are tax-deductible. For more on taxes and interest parity see Maurice D. Levi, "Taxation and 'Abnormal' International Capital Flows," *Journal of Political Economy*, June 1977, pp. 635–46.

foreign exchange at the maturity of the foreign-currency investment. If cash managers want to avoid the foreign exchange risk that would be faced by leaving the original forward contract in effect, they must cover their position. In our example, if there is a 90-day forward contract and the funds are converted into domestic currency after only 50 days, the investor should buy a new forward exchange contract of 40 days maturity. This purchase of forward foreign exchange will offset the sale of foreign exchange that was part of the original covered investment. At the conclusion of the full 90-day period, the foreign exchange that was originally sold forward will be obtained from that bought forward 40 days previously.

The extra spot and forward exchange transaction costs from the premature sale of a foreign-currency investment require an initial advantage of covered foreign investment to make the initial investment worthwhile. There is also uncertainty at the time of the original investment concerning what the spot rate will be if redemption is early and what the rate will be for offsetting the original forward contract with a reverse contract. The transaction costs and uncertainty make foreign covered investments less liquid than domestic investments. **Liquidity preference** is hence another reason for a band around the covered interest-parity line. The amount of extra required return and hence the potential width of the band due to liquidity preference depend on the likelihood that the funds will be needed early, and on whether these funds can be borrowed by using the original covered investment to secure the loan. Since the required extra return depends on the *likelihood* that the funds will be needed, it is clear that this liquidity consideration is different from the transaction costs consideration discussed earlier, which involved *known* amounts of transaction costs. Liquidity does relate to transaction costs, but these are *expected* costs. Clearly, if it is known that funds will not be required, or if it is known that the foreign investment can be used as the guarantee or security for borrowing funds, no foreign yield premium is required. The more uncertainty there is concerning future needs and

alternative sources of short-term financing, the higher are the premiums that should be required before venturing into foreign-currency securities. This will mean wider bands around the interest-parity line.[27]

As in the case of transaction costs and political risk, the choice by third-country investors of which currency-denominated securities to invest in should be symmetrical as far as liquidity preference is concerned. That is, if there is the same probability of needing to liquidate investments from either currency and the same transaction costs if liquidation occurs, liquidity preference in the presence of third-country investors should not cause deviations from interest parity.

Effect of the reasons for interest disparity on investment and borrowing

Each investor or borrower must evaluate yields and borrowing costs from his or her own perspective. This means using exchange rates that include transaction costs and consideration of applicable tax rates, and then comparing yield or borrowing-cost differences with the difference the investor or borrower believes is necessary to compensate for the risk or illiquidity that is faced. What we have argued suggests that, transaction costs are likely to work towards keeping investing and borrowing in the home currency. Withholding taxes are likely to matter only if withholding rates are higher than domestic tax rates, but differential taxes on interest income versus capital gains could induce investors with favorable capital gains treatment to place funds in currencies at a forward premium. As for political risk, this will create yield and cost differences that are not exploitable for those facing the political risk, although the differences may be exploitable by

27 It might be felt that movements in security values because of changes in market interest rates also affect the liquidity of domestic investment versus foreign investment. Although the reason is not obvious, this view is not, in general, correct, because relative interest-rate movements should be offset by exchange-rate movements, which are all related according to the interest-parity condition.

others.[28] A similar conclusion applies to liquidity preference. That is, to the extent that interest parity does not hold because foreign investments are less liquid, those investors for whom liquidity is not relevant can enjoy higher yields. We can see that it can pay to shop around when investing or borrowing, but it all depends on the specific circumstances of the investor or borrower.

SUMMARY

1 Forward exchange markets allow short-term investors and borrowers to avoid foreign exchange risk and exposure.

2 An investor should be indifferent with respect to investing in domestic or foreign currency when the domestic-currency interest rate equals the foreign-currency rate plus the annualized forward exchange premium or discount on the foreign currency. The investor should invest in domestic currency when the domestic-currency interest rate exceeds the foreign-currency rate plus the forward premium/discount on the foreign currency, and vice versa.

3 A borrower should borrow in foreign currency when the domestic-currency interest rate exceeds the foreign-currency rate plus the forward foreign exchange premium or discount, and borrow in domestic currency when the domestic-currency interest rate is lower than the foreign-currency interest rate plus the forward foreign-exchange premium or discount.

4 Covered interest arbitrage involves borrowing in one currency to invest in another. It is profitable when there are differences between covered borrowing costs and investment yields.

5 The covered interest-parity condition states that there will be no advantage to borrowing or lending in one currency rather than another. Forces set up by interest arbitragers will move the money and foreign exchange markets towards covered interest parity.

6 The uncovered interest-parity condition states that the differences between interest rates equals the market's expected change in the exchange rate.

7 The uncovered interest-parity condition and the PPP condition in terms of expected inflation can be used to derive the equality of real rates of return between countries. This latter relationship is the Fisher-open condition, which has an independent rationale.

8 If round-trip arbitrage were the only force moving exchange rates and interest rates towards interest parity, the deviations could be relatively large. This is because it would be necessary to be compensated in the covered interest differential for foreign exchange transaction costs and borrowing–lending spreads on interest rates.

9 One-way interest arbitrage involves choosing between alternative ways of going from current dollars/pounds to future pounds/dollars. Because the choices involve the same

28 Those that can exploit differences are third-country investors for whom the political risks are similar, and borrowers for whom political risks are irrelevant. Borrowers will tend to borrow in the low-risk countries because covered interest costs there can remain lower than elsewhere.

transaction costs whichever route is taken, one-way arbitrage should drive markets very close to covered interest parity.

10 Third-country investors or borrowers who face the same transaction costs whichever currency of denomination they choose for borrowing or investment should also drive markets very close to covered interest parity.

11 Political risks can also cause deviations from interest parity between countries, and allow a band around the interest-parity line, because investors from each country need compensation for the greater risk of investing in the other country. However, if investors outside the two countries view the countries as equally risky politically, they will drive markets to interest parity.

12 Withholding taxes do not normally affect the interest-parity condition.

13 For those who face differential taxes on income versus capital gains, the relevant interest-parity line has a different slope than the conventional interest-parity line. However, since banks pay the same tax on interest and foreign exchange gains, interest disparity should not result from differential taxes.

14 Covered foreign-currency investments are less liquid than domestic-currency investments because extra exchange transaction costs and uncertainties are met on liquidating covered foreign-currency securities. The liquidity relates to expected rather than actual transaction costs.

15 Each investor or borrower must evaluate opportunities from his or her own perspective of transaction costs, taxes, political risks, and liquidity concerns. There can be advantages from shopping around.

REVIEW QUESTIONS

1 What is the "money market?"

2 How does a forward-covered investment avoid exchange rate risk?

3 According to covered interest parity, if the British pound is at a forward premium vis-à-vis the US dollar, what do we know about pound versus dollar interest rates?

4 What is "covered interest arbitrage?"

5 Does the covered interest-parity condition arise from different perspectives? Name them.

6 If the covered yield on pound-denominated securities were to become temporarily higher than on dollar securities, what would happen to interest rates and the spot and forward exchange rates?

7 What is "uncovered interest-parity?"

8 What is the "Fisher-open condition?"

9 What conditions together imply the Fisher-open condition?

10 What is "round-trip interest arbitrage?"

11 Can transaction costs affect interest parity?

12 Does political risk affect covered yields on different currency-denominated deposits at London banks?

13 Does political risk affect covered yields on US government versus Canadian government bills?

14 What is a "withholding tax credit?"

15 Do low rates of withholding tax affect covered interest parity?

16 What is "liquidity preference," and can it affect covered interest parity if people can borrow without penalty against covered foreign-currency assets?

ASSIGNMENT PROBLEMS

1 Derive the criteria for making covered money-market investment and borrowing decisions when the exchange rates are given in European terms. Derive the equivalent of equation (8.4).

2 You have been given the following information:

$r_\$$	$r_£$	$S(\$/£)$	$F_{1/4}(\$/£)$
5%	6%	1.5000	1.4985

where $r_\$$ = annual interest rate on 3-month US-dollar commercial paper

$r_£$ = annual interest on 3-month British-pound commercial paper

$S(\$/£)$ = number of dollars per pound, spot

$F_{1/4}$ $(\$/£)$ = number of dollars per pound, 3-months forward

On the basis of the precise criteria:

a In which commercial paper would you invest?

b In which currency would you borrow?

c How would you arbitrage?

d What is the profit from interest arbitrage per dollar borrowed?

3 a Use the data in Question 2 and the precise formula on the right-hand side of equation (8.4) to compute the covered yield on investment in pounds. Repeat this using the approximate formula on the right-hand side of equation (8.5).

   b Compare the error between the precise formula and the approximate formula in "a" above with the error in the situation where $r_\$ = 15$ percent, $r_£ = 16$ percent, and $S(\$/£)$ and $F_{1/4}(\$/£)$ are as above.

   c Should we be more careful to avoid the use of the "interest plus premium or minus discount" approximation in equation (8.5) at higher or at lower interest rates?

   d If the interest rates and the forward rate in Question 2 are for 12 months, is the difference between equation (8.4) and equation (8.5) greater than when we are dealing with 3-month rates?

4 Derive the equivalent of Table 8.1 where all covered yields are against pounds rather than dollars. This will require computing appropriate cross spot and forward rates.

5 Draw a figure like Figure 8.4 to show what interest arbitrage will do to the interest-rate differentials and the forward premiums at points A to F in the table below. If all the

adjustment to the interest parity occurs in the forward exchange rate, what will $F_{1/12}(\$/£)$ be after interest parity has been restored?

	A	B	C	D	E	F
$S(\$/£)$	1.6200	1.6200	1.6200	1.6200	1.6200	1.6200
$F_{1/12}(\$/£)$	1.6220	1.6150	1.6220	1.6150	1.6180	1.6120
$r_\$(1\ month)$, %	8.00	8.00	8.00	8.00	8.00	8.00
$r_£(1\ month)$, %	10.00	9.00	8.00	7.00	6.00	5.00

6   Write down the expectations form of PPP, the uncovered interest-parity condition, and the Fisher-open condition. Derive each one from the other two.

7   Assuming that there are a large number of third-country borrowers and investors, do you think that political risk will cause larger deviations from interest parity than are caused by transaction costs?

8   If banks are as happy to advance loans that are secured by domestic-currency money-market investments as they are to advance loans secured by similar foreign-currency covered money-market investments, will firms prefer domestic-currency investments on the grounds of liquidity?

9   How does the importance of liquidity relate to the probability that cash will be needed?

10   Use the framework of Figure 8.7 to show how the band within which one-way arbitrage is unprofitable compares to the band within which round-trip arbitrage is unprofitable.

11   Why might a borrower want to borrow in a currency that is at a forward discount if that borrower faces a higher tax rate on interest income than on capital gains?

12   Why does the Fisher-open condition relate to countries rather than currencies?

13   In general, are transactions costs higher in spot or forward markets? Does this hold any implications for whether interest parity will hold exactly?

14   What role does the rest of the world play in determining whether covered interest parity will hold between any two currency-denominated securities?

15   Suppose that real interest rates are equal for all countries in the world. Does this imply anything for the relationship between covered interest-rate parity and the PPP condition?

BIBLIOGRAPHY

Aliber, Robert, Z. and Clyde P. Stickney, "Accounting Measures of Foreign Exchange Exposure: The Long and Short of It," *The Accounting Review*, January 1975, pp. 44–57.

Bahmani-Oskooee, Mohsen and Satya P. Das, "Transaction Costs and the Interest Parity Theorem," *Journal of Political Economy*, August 1985, pp. 793–9.

Blenman, Lloyd P. and Janet S. Thatcher, "Arbitrage Opportunities in Currency and Credit Markets: New Evidence," *International Journal of Finance*, 3, 1995.

Blenman, Lloyd P. and Janet S. Thatcher, "Arbitrage Heterogeneity, Investor Horizon and Arbitrage Opportunities: An Empirical Investigation," *Financial Review*, 30, 1995.

Blenman, Lloyd P., Louis Henock, and Janet S. Thatcher, "Interest Rate Parity and the Behavior of the Bid-Ask Spread," *Journal of Financial Research*, 22, 1999, pp. 189–206.

Branson, William H., "The Minimum Covered Interest Needed for International Arbitrage Activity," *Journal of Political Economy*, December 1969, pp. 1029–34.

Clinton, Kevin, "Transaction Costs and Covered Interest Arbitrage: Theory and Evidence," *Journal of Political Economy*, April 1988, pp. 358–70.

Deardorff, Alan V., "One-Way Arbitrage and Its Implications for the Foreign Exchange Markets," *Journal of Political Economy*, April 1979, pp. 351–64.

Frenkel, Jacob A. and Richard M. Levich, "Covered Interest Arbitrage: Unexploited Profits?," *Journal of Political Economy*, April 1975, pp. 325–38.

Giddy, Ian H., "An Integrated Theory of Exchange Rate Equilibrium," *Journal of Financial and Quantitative Analysis*, December 1976, pp. 883–92.

Harvard Business School, *Note on Fundamental Parity Conditions*, Case 9–288–016, 1994.

Huang, Roger D., "Expectations of Exchange Rates and Differential Inflation Rates: Further Evidence on Purchasing Power Parity in Efficient Markets," *Journal of Finance*, March 1987, pp. 69–79.

Kubarych, Roger M., *Foreign Exchange Markets in the United States*, Federal Reserve Bank of New York, New York, 1978.

Levi, Maurice D., "Non-Reversed Investment and Borrowing, Transaction Costs, and Covered Interest Parity," *International Review of Economics and Finance*, 1 (2), 1992, pp. 107–19.

——, "Spot versus Forward Speculation and Hedging: A Diagrammatic Exposition," *Journal of International Money and Finance*, April 1984, pp. 105–10.

——, "Taxation and 'Abnormal' International Capital Flows," *Journal of Political Economy*, June 1977, pp. 635–46.

Lewis, Karen K., "Puzzles in International Financial Markets," Working Paper, University of Pennsylvania, July 2000.

Llewellyn, David T., *International Financial Integration: The Limits of Sovereignty*, Macmillan, London, 1980.

Marston, Richard C., "Interest Differentials under Fixed and Flexible Exchange Rates: The Effects of Capital Controls and Exchange Risk," Working Paper, University of Pennsylvania, May 2004.

Officer, Lawrence H. and Thomas D. Willet, "The Covered-Arbitrage Schedule: A Critical Survey of Recent Developments," *Journal of Money, Credit and Banking*, May 1970, pp. 247–57.

Woodward, Robert S., "Some New Evidence on the Profitability of One-Way versus Round-Trip Arbitrage," *Journal of Money, Credit and Banking*, November 1988, pp. 645–52.

Part IV

Managing foreign exchange risk and exposure

Until this point our concern has been with the nature of markets in which currencies and currency derivatives trade. The focus of the remainder of the book is with managerial issues, such as using international financial markets to deal with the special opportunities and risks of international trade and investment. We shall see on numerous occasions on this journey through international managerial finance that an understanding of the financial markets and environment are essential elements of financial decision making. The chapters in Part IV begin our journey with a discussion of the objectives of international financial management and how to achieve these objectives. The focus is on operating issues, from the measurement of foreign exchange risk and exposure, to the methods and potential for success of currency speculation.

The opening chapter of Part IV, Chapter 9, takes us directly to the meaning of foreign exchange exposure. It is shown that exposure is a measure of the sensitivity of changes in domestic currency values of assets and liabilities to unanticipated changes in exchange rates. We show that surprisingly, domestic as well as foreign financial instruments can face foreign exchange exposure, and that under special circumstances, foreign financial instruments may *not* be exposed. The chapter also explains foreign exchange risk, a matter which is often confused with exposure. Exchange-rate risk is shown to relate to the *variability* of domestic currency values of assets and liabilities, whereas exposure is the *amount at risk*. This makes risk

and exposure conceptually and even dimensionally different: the two concepts have different units of measurement.

Chapter 10 provides a brief introduction to international accounting principles and how these impact on exposure as reflected in financial accounts – accounting exposure – versus true, underlying value changes – real exposure. While it is real exposure that should really matter to the owners of a multinational firm, values that show up in accounting statements cannot be ignored when, for example, taxes are based on operating incomes as expressed in a company's "reporting currency."

Chapter 11 is devoted to the effect of exchange rates on sales and operating profitability, so-called "operating exposure." Use is made of the microeconomic theory of the firm which emphasises marginal cost and marginal revenue. It is shown that the amount of operating exposure depends on such factors as elasticity of demand and flexibility of production. The chapter ends with a consideration of situations where exchange rates have different effects on firms in the short-run versus the long-run. This short-run versus long-run distinction for firms is analogous to the short-run versus long-run distinction for the economy as a whole, met in Chapter 6 when we explained the J curve.

With exposure and risk defined and explained in Chapters 9, 10, and 11, in Chapter 12 we shift attention to the management of exposure and risk. We begin by asking whether managers should hedge foreign exchange risk and exposure, or whether they should leave this to shareholders. Alternative means of dealing with risk and exposure are contrasted and compared using the building blocks of payoff profiles. This approach is sometimes called financial engineering.

The opposite to hedging is speculation, which involves purposefully taking exposed positions in foreign exchange. Chapter 13 begins by describing the methods that exist for currency speculation. This leads naturally into a discussion of market efficiency, because as we shall show, speculation cannot be persistently successful if foreign exchange markets are efficient. Chapter 13, and Part IV, end with a discussion of the successes and failures of attempts to forecast exchange rates. This discussion appears alongside the discussions of speculation and market efficiency because, as we shall see, an ability to forecast exchange rates and profit from such forecasts is closely related to market efficiency and the expected returns from speculation.

Chapter 9

Foreign exchange exposure and risk

If you want the fruit you have to go out on a limb.

Ancient saying

THE IMPORTANCE OF UNDERSTANDING RISK AND EXPOSURE AND MEASURING THEM

Even though foreign exchange (forex) risk and exposure have been central issues of international financial management for many years, considerable confusion remains about what exactly they are and how to measure them. For example, it is not uncommon to hear the term "foreign exchange exposure" used interchangeably with the term "foreign exchange risk" when in fact exposure and risk are conceptually and even dimensionally completely different (as we shall explain, foreign exchange risk is related to the *variability* of domestic-currency values of assets or liabilities due to unanticipated changes in exchange rates, whereas foreign exchange exposure is the *amount* that is at risk). This chapter is devoted to clarifying the nature of, and methods of measurement of, risk and exposure, as well as to explaining the factors contributing to them. Several subsequent chapters deal with the management of risk and exposure.

Measurement of foreign exchange exposure and risk is an essential first step in international financial management. Without knowing how large a company's exposure and risk are, it is difficult to know how much effort and cost it is worth incurring to manage them. For example, if exposure represents a tiny fraction of the firm's value, it might be decided to ignore the matter, or at least leave exposure management to the company's shareholders who can decide for themselves whether the exposure on a particular company is diversifiable or otherwise avoidable.[1] Furthermore, a company may find that it is exposed, but not at risk. This is possible in a rigidly fixed exchange rate environment such as Hong Kong or the People's Republic of China through the 1990s and beyond.[2] Only by measuring exposure and risk can a company know how to allocate scarce corporate resources to the management of different sources of uncertainty. Perhaps hedging of key inputs or prices of outputs is more important for earnings stability than hedging foreign exchange-related matters.

---

1 The question of whether a company's managers or the company's shareholders should manage foreign exchange risk is discussed in Chapter 12. We shall see there are some valid reasons why shareholders may prefer that corporate managers hedge the risk on their behalf.

2 As we shall see, while it is possible to be exposed and not be at risk, it is not possible to face foreign exchange risk without being exposed.

THE NATURE OF EXCHANGE-RATE RISK AND EXPOSURE

Definition of foreign exchange exposure

Foreign exchange exposure can be defined in the following way:

> Foreign exchange exposure is the sensitivity of changes in the real domestic-currency value of assets or liabilities to changes in exchange rates.[3]

Several features of this definition are worth noting.

First, we notice that exposure is a measure of the *sensitivity* of domestic-currency values. That is, it is a description of the *extent* or *degree* to which the home-currency value of something is changed by exchange rate changes. This immediately suggests some type of ratio. For example, it suggests exposure takes the form

$$\text{Exposure} = \frac{\Delta V(\$)}{\Delta S(\$/€)} \qquad (9.1)$$

where in this instance we are considering exposure to a manager or shareholder who cares about US dollar values – the presumed domestic currency – to the exchange rate against the euro. If this ratio is zero, there is no exposure to the exchange rate. The bigger is the ratio, whether the ratio is positive or negative, the larger is the exposure to the euro.

The second thing we notice in the definition is that it is concerned with *real domestic-currency values*. By this we mean, for example, that from a US perspective exposure is the sensitivity of changes in real (i.e. inflation-adjusted) US-dollar values of assets or liabilities to changes in exchange rates.

---

3 Exposure was first defined this way by Michael Adler and Bernard Dumas, "Exposure to Currency Risk: Definition and Measurement," *Financial Management*, Summer 1984, pp. 41–50. See also Christine R. Hekman, "Measuring Foreign Exchange Exposure: A Practical Theory and Its Application," *Financial Analysts Journal*, September/October 1983, pp. 59–65; and Lars Oxelheim and Clas G. Wihlborg, *Macroeconomic Uncertainty: International Risks and Opportunities for the Corporation*, Wiley, New York, 1987.

A Euro-zone investor will be concerned with the sensitivity of real euro values. In other words, exposure to an American and a European on the same asset or liability is different.

Third, we notice that exposure exists on assets and liabilities. Assets and liabilities are balance sheet items. There are many ways that the value of assets and liabilities can be affected by exchange rates. The simplest way is through the translation of foreign-currency values into domestic-currency values by multiplication of the relevant exchange rate. For example, a British stock trading for a given amount of pounds in London, changes in dollar value when there is a change in the dollar value of the pound. However, as we shall see, changes in the dollar–pound exchange rate can affect the *pound value* of the British stock. This is because exchange rates affect operating revenues and costs. For example, a decline in the value of the pound could make the British company more competitive and increase its profits. This could raise the stock price.

Alternatively, if the British company depends on imports that become more expensive in pounds when the dollar value of the pound goes down, the company may become less profitable and its share price could decline. The effects on revenues, costs, and profits are the result of **operating exposure** to exchange rates. This is also sometimes called **economic exposure**. Foreign exchange exposure from effects on operations requires separate treatment, and is covered in a later chapter. For the moment we can note that operating exposure has the dimension of a flow, so much per period of time, unlike assets and liabilities which have a stock dimension, so much at a particular point in time. As we shall see when we focus on operating exposure, the flow effects of exchange rates can be converted to present values so that all exposures can be considered to be measured at a point in time.

Fourth, we notice that we have not qualified the list of exposed items by describing them as being *foreign* assets or liabilities. This is because, as we shall see, changes in exchange rates can affect domestic as well as foreign assets and liabilities.

For example, companies that do not export or import, but who compete in their domestic market with imported products, will find themselves gaining when their own currency drops in value because it makes the foreign companies less competitive in their own country's market. Indeed, we shall see that not only is it possible to be exposed without being engaged in any sort of international investment or commerce, it is also possible to *not* be exposed when investing in foreign assets.

It is worth mentioning that exposure, and more importantly risk, relate to *unanticipated* changes in exchange rates. This is because current market prices should reflect changes in exchange rates that are widely anticipated. Consequently, it is only to the extent that exchange rates change by more or less than had been expected that there are likely to be gains or losses on assets or liabilities. We shall consider total changes in exchange rates in what immediately follows, not just the unanticipated change. However, when it comes to measuring exposure and risk, we will explain the importance of distinguishing between changes in exchange rates that are expected and those that are a surprise.

EXAMPLES OF FOREIGN EXCHANGE EXPOSURE

We can gain an understanding of exposure by considering a number of examples, starting with the simplest case, and showing that all exposures are obtained by applying equation (9.1). Let us begin by considering exposure on what are generally referred to as **contractual assets** and **contractual liabilities**. In all cases we take the perspective of an investor or borrower who is concerned with the US dollar value of assets or liabilities. That is, the domestic currency is taken to be the US dollar.

Exposure on contractual assets and liabilities

Contractual assets and liabilities are those with fixed face and market values. Examples of foreign-currency contractual assets are bank deposits and

foreign-currency accounts receivable. Examples of foreign-currency contractual liabilities are loans and accounts payable. Let us begin by considering the exposure on a bank deposit of €1,000.

> Contractual assets and liabilities are those with fixed face and market values, such as bank deposits and accounts receivable, or bank loans and accounts payable.

Exposure on a contractual asset

Table 9.1 shows values of the bank deposit before and after a change in the exchange rate. We assume that the euro appreciates from $1.1000/€ to $1.2000/€. This is a change of $0.1000/€ as shown at the bottom of the first column. The bank account remains at €1,000 before and after the appreciation of the euro, but the dollar value of this contractual asset increases from $1,100 to $1,200. By subtracting the values of the exchange rate and bank deposit (in dollars) before the euro appreciation from the values after the appreciation we have $\Delta V(\$) = \$100$ and $\Delta S(\$/€) = \$0.1000/€$. Using these values in our definition of exposure in equation (9.1) we find:

$$\text{Exposure} = \frac{\Delta V(\$)}{\Delta S(\$/€)} = \frac{\$100}{\$0.1000/€}$$
$$= €1,000$$

where we see that the dollar signs in the numerator and denominator have cancelled. The exposure on a €1,000 bank account is €1,000, as we would expect. Our sensitivity measure in the ratio in equation (9.1) gives us a magnitude in the foreign

Table 9.1 *Exposure on a contractual asset: euro bank deposit*

	Exchange rate	Bank account, €	Bank account, $
Before	$1.1000/€	€1,000	$1,100
After	$1.2000/€	€1,000	$1,200
Change	$0.1000/€	€0	$100

currency, and in this particular case it is equal to the foreign-currency value of the asset. It is also a positive magnitude, telling us that the change in the exchange rate and the dollar value of the asset move in the same direction: when the euro goes up the euro bank account is worth more dollars. In such a case, where the value in domestic-currency value moves in the same direction as the price of the foreign currency, we say there is a **long position** in the foreign currency. That is, if there is a dollar gain when the spot value of the foreign currency increases, and a dollar loss when the value of the foreign currency decreases, we say there is a long position in the foreign currency.

> An investor is long in a foreign currency if she or he gains when the spot value of the foreign currency increases, and loses when it decreases. That is, an investor is long if the foreign exchange value of the foreign currency and the domestic currency value of the investment move in the same direction. In this case, exposure is a positive number.

Exposure on a contractual liability

Let us consider foreign exchange exposure from a dollar perspective on a bank loan of €1,000. The exposure on this contractual liability is illustrated in Table 9.2.

We show the same appreciation of the euro from $1.1000/€ to $1.2000/€ as in Table 9.1. Because in this case we are considering a loan, which is a liability, we prefix this with a minus sign: a loan on itself represents negative worth. The dollar value of

this liability goes from $1,100 to $1,200. When we take the difference between these two amounts by taking the dollar value before the euro appreciation from the dollar value after euro appreciation we obtain

$$\Delta V(\$) = -\$1,200 - (-\$1,100)$$
$$= -\$100$$

The minus sign signifies that more dollars are now owed, a bigger liability. Hence, with $\Delta S(\$/€) = \$0.1000/€$ and $\Delta V(\$) = -\$100$ exposure on this euro loan from equation (9.1) is

$$\text{Exposure} = \frac{\Delta V(\$)}{\Delta S(\$/€)} = \frac{-\$100}{\$0.1000/€}$$
$$= -€1,000$$

As before, exposure has an absolute magnitude of €1,000. However, in this case of a foreign-currency liability, exposure is negative. We say in this case that the euro liability represents a **short position** in the euro. By definition, a short position is where there is a loss in terms of domestic currency if the foreign currency increases in value, or there is a gain if the foreign currency decreases in value. In other words, a short position is where the value of the person's wealth in their own currency and the foreign exchange value of the foreign currency go in opposite directions.

> An investor is short in a foreign currency if she or he loses when the spot value of the foreign currency increases, and gains when it decreases. That is, an investor is short if the value of the foreign currency and the domestic currency value of the investment move in the opposite direction. In this case exposure is a negative number.

So far the conclusions concerning the size of exposure are hardly surprising: exposure is the same as the face value of the contractual assets or liabilities. Let us now consider other assets and liabilities which, to distinguish them from contractual items, we shall call **noncontractual assets and liabilities**.

Table 9.2 *Exposure on a contractual liability: euro bank loan*

	Exchange rate	Bank loan, €	Bank loan, $
Before	$1.1000/€	−€1,000	−$1,100
After	$1.2000/€	−€1,000	−$1,200
Change	$0.1000/€	€0	−$100

These are assets and liabilities that can change in value. Most importantly for foreign exchange exposure and risk, they can change in value due to changes in exchange rates.

Exposure on a noncontractual asset

Shares of foreign exporter or import competer

Table 9.3 considers the foreign exchange exposure facing an investor whose domestic currency is the dollar, and who has bought shares of a Euro-zone company. We assume the company exports to the United States, or else competes with US companies in foreign markets, including the European market. What is this investor's exposure, based on the sensitivity measure in equation (9.1), on each share owned by the investor?

Table 9.3 takes the appreciation of the euro to be the same as in the previous situations. The table also assumes that the share price before the euro appreciation is €10. An appreciation of the euro will harm the profits of a Euro-zone exporter to the United States because it makes the company's products less competitive in the US market. It will also harm the profits of a Euro-zone company that competes in Europe or elsewhere in the world with US companies: the Euro-zone company is less competitive than before when the euro increases in value relative to the dollar.[4] A company that competes in its own market with foreign competitors is called

an import competer. Let us assume that the damage done by the appreciation of the euro versus the dollar in terms of current and future profits puts a dent in the share price of the Euro-zone company. Suppose it declines from €10.00 to €9.50 as in Table 9.3.

The dollar price of the Euro-zone company has increased from $1.1000 × €10 = €11.00 to $1.1200 × €9.5 = $11.40. Hence, $\Delta V(\$) = \$0.40$, and exposure given by equation (9.1) is

$$\text{Exposure} = \frac{\Delta V(\$)}{\Delta S(\$/€)} = \frac{\$0.40}{\$0.1000/€}$$
$$= €4.00$$

The increase in the dollar value of the euro has made the US investor better off, but by less than the value of the investment. The reason is that while the higher spot value of the euro has added to the dollar value of the investment – each euro translates into more dollars – the lower euro share price associated with a stronger euro has eroded some of this. Stated differently, there is negative correlation between the dollar value of the euro and the euro value of the asset. In this particular case this leaves the investor long in the euro: the value of exposure is positive so the investor gains when the foreign-currency gains. However, this may not be so, depending on by how much the euro share price is impacted by the change in the exchange rate.

Table 9.4 shows what may happen if the Euro-zone company's share price falls by more than in Table 9.3. In this case we assume the stronger euro has done more damage to the company's profits, with a consequent decline in share price from €10.00 to €9.00. As we shall see when we discuss

▨ **Table 9.3** *Exposure on a noncontractual asset: Euro-zone exporter*

	Exchange rate	Share value, €	Share value, $
Before	$1.1000/€	€10.00	$11.00
After	$1.2000/€	€9.50	$11.40
Change	$0.1000/€	−€0.50	$0.40

4 This is due to operating exposure. This type of exposure, which can translate into effects on companies' values, is discussed in Chapter 11.

▨ **Table 9.4** *Exposure on a noncontractual asset: Euro-zone exporter*

	Exchange rate	Share value, €	Share value, $
Before	$1.1000/€	€10.00	$11.00
After	$1.2000/€	€9.00	$10.80
Change	$0.1000/€	−€1.00	−$0.20

195 ▨

operating exposure in Chapter 11, a greater effect on the company's profit and share price could be due to more price-sensitivity in the market for the company's products, lower use of tradable inputs which become cheaper after a currency appreciation, and so on. Applying our sensitivity measure of exposure we have the same exchange rate change in the denominator, $\Delta S(\$/€) = \$0.1000/€$, but in the numerator we have $\Delta V(\$) = \$10.80 - \$11.00 = -\$0.20$. Therefore

$$\text{Exposure} = \frac{\Delta V(\$)}{\Delta S(\$/€)} = \frac{-\$0.20}{\$0.1000/€}$$
$$= -€2.00$$

We find that in this case the US investor is short in the euro, specifically by €2 per share: the investor loses from a higher euro, and would gain from a lower euro.

As we can see, the critical issue determining the size and direction of exposure – long versus short – is the extent to which the currency value and asset value are negatively related. Exposure depends on co-variation between the exchange rate and the foreign-currency value.

We have simply assumed numbers as if they are known. In reality, it may be very difficult to know how much an asset price might be dented or boosted by a specific change in the exchange rate. What we need to know is the systematic connection between the spot rate and the asset value, which is what would happen, all else being equal. In reality many things can affect share prices beyond the exchange rate. However, as we shall see later in this chapter, there may be historical data on share prices and exchange rates from which systematic connections may be estimated statistically. There may also be ways of gauging the impact of exchange rates by asking people in the company whose experience can help build a picture of what might happen under specified circumstances. This alternative **scenario approach** is discussed in the following chapter after describing what can influence the extent of the impact of exchange rates on the value of a company.

Shares of foreign import company

Let us consider the reverse situation to that mentioned earlier, specifically, let us analyse a US investor who has bought shares in a Euro-zone company that imports products from the United States for sale in Europe. In this case an appreciation of the euro means a lower euro cost for the company's imported products and associated higher profits. A systematic increase in current and future profits from an appreciation of the euro will favorably affect the company' share price. This is shown in Table 9.5

Table 9.5 assumes the same appreciation of the euro as in the previous situations, so as before, $\Delta S(\$/€) = \$0.1000/€$. Because a stronger euro is good for a Euro-zone company that imports for sale in the European market, we show an increase in the price of the importer's stock, from €11.00 to €12.60, so that, $\Delta V(\$) = \$1.60$. Again applying our definition of exposure we have

$$\text{Exposure} = \frac{\Delta V(\$)}{\Delta S(\$/€)} = \frac{\$1.60}{\$0.1000/€}$$
$$= €16.00$$

We find that an American investor in a European import-oriented company has long exposure of more than the value of the investment. In this case a €10 stock has €16 of long exposure. What has happened is that when the euro goes up the stock price goes up too. Therefore, the US investor gains twice, from the value of the currency and the value of the asset. The asset value and exchange rate are positively correlated.

Having dealt with contractual assets and liabilities and with stocks, let us next turn to bonds. Let us consider first foreign currency-denominated bonds.

Table 9.5 *Exposure on a noncontractual asset: Euro-zone importer*

	Exchange rate	Share value, €	Share value, $
Before	$1.1000/€	€10.00	$11.00
After	$1.2000/€	€10.50	$12.60
Change	$0.1000/€	€0.50	$1.60

Foreign currency-denominated bond

Suppose a US-dollar-based investor buys a euro-denominated bond. Suppose that the European Central Bank (ECB) follows a policy of "leaning against the wind," lowering interest rates when the euro rises and raising interest rates when the euro falls. This is a common policy of central banks which try to smooth variations in the foreign exchange value of their currencies (lowering interest rates when the euro is rising should reduce the currency's appreciation, and raising interest rates when the euro is falling should reduce the depreciation).

Table 9.6 shows exposure on a euro-denominated bond when the ECB leans against the wind. We again assume the euro increases in value by $\Delta S(\$/€) = \$0.1000/€$. The higher value of the euro is assumed to lead to an interest rate reduction by the ECB, causing an increase in the price of the bond from €1,000 to €1,050. This means a change in the dollar price of the bond from $1,100 to $1,260, so that $\Delta V(\$) = \$160$. Applying the measure of exposure:

$$\text{Exposure} = \frac{\Delta V(\$)}{\Delta S(\$/€)} = \frac{\$160}{\$0.1000/€}$$
$$= €1,600$$

The exposure on the bond with initial value of €1,000 is larger than the value of the bond.

Domestic-currency bond

It would seem natural to think that an investor in a domestic bond who buys only domestic products does not face any foreign exchange exposure or risk. This view may be incorrect. In particular, if the investor's country follows a policy of leaning against the wind, the investor will have short exposure in the foreign currency. Let us see how.

Suppose that the dollar decreases in value as before, and as shown in Table 9.7: the higher dollar value of the euro is a depreciation of the dollar. The United States Federal Reserve, to fight against the depreciation of dollar – perhaps to prevent inflation that can result from a lower currency – may raise interest rates. This would make dollar-denominated bonds worth less. Table 9.7 shows the decline in the dollar-denominated bonds from the dollar depreciation and consequent Federal Reserve action. In the table we assume $\Delta V(\$) = -\$50$. It follows that exposure to an American investor in the dollar bond is

$$\text{Exposure} = \frac{\Delta V(\$)}{\Delta S(\$/€)} = \frac{-\$50}{\$0.1000/€}$$
$$= -€500$$

We find that this investor is short €500. This might seem very odd, and is certainly not intuitive. However, the basic fact is that a higher euro is bad for this investor because it makes dollar-bond prices fall. As long as the Fed follows a policy of leaning against the wind, the investor is short in euros and would need to find a long position in the euro, through, for example, buying a euro futures contract or euro asset, to avoid exposure on the euro. It is the systematic application of the Fed's policy of leaning against the wind that is responsible for exposure.

To the extent that increases in a country's interest rates are bad news to its stock market as a whole, investments in the domestic stock market are also exposed to the exchange rate if the central

Table 9.6 *Exposure on a noncontractual asset: euro bond*

	Exchange rate	Bond value, €	Bond value, $
Before	$1.1000/€	€ 1,000	$1,000
After	$1.2000/€	€ 1,050	$1,260
Change	$0.1000/€	€ 50	$160

Table 9.7 *Exposure on a noncontractual asset: dollar bond*

	Exchange rate	Bond value, $
Before	$1.1000/€	$1,000
After	$1.2000/€	$950
Change	$0.1000/€	-$50

bank systematically leans against the wind.[5] As with domestic bonds, when the country's currency declines and the central bank reacts with higher interest rates the stock market declines.

Just as it is possible to be invested in a domestic asset and *face* foreign exchange exposure, it is also possible to invest abroad and *not face* exposure. To see this, let us consider investment in a real asset such as real estate.

Foreign real estate

Table 9.8 shows what can happen on an asset such as real estate if the price of the asset and the exchange rate move in opposite directions as predicted by the dynamic version of Purchasing Power Parity (PPP).[6] We assume that 10 percent inflation in Europe occurs on the investment item. According to the relative or dynamic version of PPP discussed in Chapter 7 and summarized by equation (7.7), if 10 percent inflation also applies to the European economy as a whole and there is zero inflation in the United States,

$$\dot{S}(\$/€) = \frac{\dot{P}_{US} - \dot{P}_E}{1 + \dot{P}_E} = \frac{-0.10}{1.10} = -0.0909$$

We have simply replaced the United Kingdom with Europe and the pound with the euro in equation (7.7). We find that the euro should depreciate by approximately 9.1 percent from the initial value of $S(\$/€) = \$1.10/€$. The new spot rate implied by relative or dynamic PPP is ($\$1.1000/€) \div 1.0909 = \$1.0000/€$ as shown in the table. When we use this exchange rate of $\$1.0000/€$ to convert

Table 9.8 *Exposure on a noncontractual asset: foreign real estate*

	Exchange rate	Asset value, €	Asset value, $
Before	$1.1000/€	€1,000,000	$1,100,000
After	$1.0000/€	€1,100,000	$1,100,000
Change	−$0.1000/€	€100,000	$0

the euro price of the real estate that has increased in euro value by 10 percent we find the dollar value to be unchanged. It follows that with $\Delta V(\$) = 0$, and with $\Delta S(\$/€) = -\$0.1000$, foreign exchange exposure on the European real estate is zero. We can therefore claim that if the relative or dynamic version of PPP holds systematically for a particular overseas asset, there is no foreign exchange exposure on this asset. What happens is that the change in the exchange rate exactly offsets the change in the local-currency value of the asset. Therefore, as stated earlier, it is possible to face foreign exchange exposure on domestic assets, and not face exposure on foreign assets.

EXPOSURE AS A REGRESSION SLOPE

The exposure line

We can further clarify the definition of foreign exchange exposure at the same time as we describe how it can be calculated by considering Figures 9.1a and b. The horizontal axis in both figures shows unexpected changes in exchange rates, $\Delta S^u(\$/€)$, with these being positive to the right of the origin and negative to the left of the origin. Positive values of $\Delta S^u(\$/€)$ are unanticipated appreciations of the euro, and negative values are unanticipated depreciations of the euro. The vertical axis of each figure shows the changes in the values of assets or liabilities in terms of a **reference currency**, which for a US firm is the US dollar. We can interpret $\Delta V(\$)$ as the change in the value of particular individual assets or liabilities, or as the change in the value of a collection of assets or liabilities. As we have said,

---

5 As we have already indicated, some companies within the domestic stock market, such as export-oriented companies, are likely to gain in value from depreciation. We speak here about the stock market in general which tends to fall when interest rates rise because of the higher opportunity cost of holding stocks rather than bonds.

6 To be more precise, we are assuming the law of a single price applies to the asset if we are considering a particular individual investment. We could relate this to PPP if we are talking about a basket of investment items.

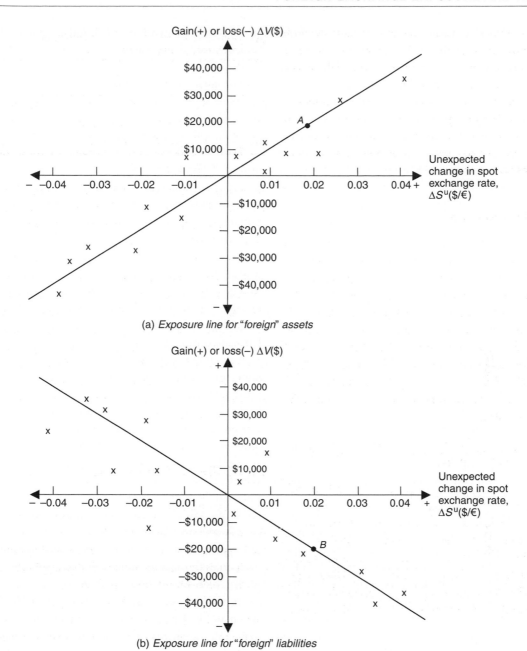

(a) *Exposure line for "foreign" assets*

(b) *Exposure line for "foreign" liabilities*

Figure 9.1 *Exposure as the slope of a regression line*

Note

Each unanticipated change in the exchange rate will be associated with a change in the dollar value of an asset or liability. The unanticipated change in the exchange rate can be plotted against the associated change in dollar value. Because other factors also affect asset and liability values, the same $\Delta S^u(\$/€)$ will not always be associated with the same $\Delta V(\$)$. However, there may be a systematic relationship between $\Delta S^u(\$/€)$ and $\Delta V(\$)$. For example, unanticipated euro appreciations may typically be associated with gains from higher dollar values of euro-denominated assets and losses from higher dollar values of euro-denominated liabilities, the former implying an upward-sloping scatter and the latter a downward-sloping scatter.

$\Delta V(\$)$ should be in real terms, and so it should be adjusted for US inflation.[7]

As we have seen, when there is a change in an exchange rate, there will generally be an accompanying change in the dollar value of assets or liabilities. The change in dollar value depends on whether an asset or liability is contractual or noncontractual. For contractual assets and liabilities the change in dollar value is due only to the change in exchange rate. For noncontractual assets and liabilities the change in dollar value depends on the systematic relationship between the foreign-currency asset or liability value and the exchange rate. If a higher value of the foreign-currency decreases the foreign-currency value, as it does for investments in foreign export- or import-competing companies, the dollar value change is less than the change in the exchange rate: the two effects are offsetting. On the other hand, if a higher foreign currency also makes the foreign asset worth more, as with a foreign import-oriented company, the dollar value changes by more than the exchange rate.

Of course, many factors other than exchange rates can influence dollar market values of assets and liabilities, and so we cannot predict with certainty how values will change with any particular unanticipated change in exchange rates. However, there is often a tendency for values to change in more or less predictable ways. Indeed, as we have seen, there is a particularly strong systematic relationship for contractual assets and liabilities. For example, when the euro unexpectedly jumps from $1.14/€ to $1.16/€, the US dollar value of a €1 million bank deposit changes from $1.14 million to $1.16 million, and this change in dollar value is accurately known. We can then plot a $\Delta V(\$)$ of $20,000 against a $\Delta S^u(\$/€)$ of $0.02/€ in Figure 9.1a. This is shown by point A in the upper right-hand quadrant of the figure. Similarly, an unexpected depreciation of the euro would be associated with

an accurately known lower US dollar value of the bank deposit, giving rise to a point in the lower left-hand quadrant. With the euro value of the bank deposit unchanged by changes in the exchange rate, all points sit exactly on a line called the **exposure line**, which for the bank deposit or any other euro-denominated contractual asset is upward-sloping.

If we consider a euro-denominated bank loan instead of a bank deposit, the effect of unanticipated changes in exchange rates is again accurately known. However, in this case there is a downward-sloping relationship. For example, an unanticipated appreciation in the euro from $1.14/€ to $1.16/€ results in a $20,000 loss on a €1 million bank loan, because this is the extra dollar amount of liability. This gives point B in the lower right-hand quadrant of Figure 9.1b. Similarly, an unanticipated depreciation of the pound gives a point in the upper left-hand quadrant.

It should be emphasized that US dollar values of noncontractual assets and liabilities would not be as predictably affected by changes in exchange as the bank accounts or loans just considered. Rather, a given value of $\Delta S^u(\$/€)$ could be associated with different possible values of $\Delta V(\$)$. Furthermore, as we have seen, domestic assets and liabilities values may also change with changes in exchange rates and therefore may also be exposed to exchange rates. We saw this earlier for domestic bonds and even for the stock market as a whole. As we shall see in Chapter 11, it is also true of individual domestic companies through the impact of exchange rates on prices, sales, production costs, and so on.

As we have said, exposure is measured by the systematic tendency for $\Delta V(\$)$ to change with respect to $\Delta S^u(\$/€)$, where by systematic tendency we mean the way these variables are *on average* related to each other. Of course, because the actual $\Delta V(\$)$ associated with a given $\Delta S^u(\$/€)$ is not always the same, the equation which describes the relationship between these variables must allow for errors. Such an equation is a regression equation, which, for exposure to the dollar–euro exchange rate, takes the form

$$\Delta V_t = \beta \Delta S_t^u(\$/€) + \mu_t \qquad (9.2)$$

7 Inflation itself is unknown in advance and contributes to uncertainty. However, because of the difficulty of dealing with inflation, in much of what follows we ignore the level of inflation as well as uncertainty about inflation.

In equation (9.2) β is the **regression coefficient** describing the systematic relation between $\Delta V(\$)$ and $\Delta S^u(\$/\text{€})$. That is, β shows the tendency for these variables to be related. Indeed, β describes the sensitivity of the systematic relation between unanticipated changes in exchange rates and changes in dollar values of assets and liabilities. The term μ_t is the random error in the relationship, and is called the **regression error**. The role of μ_t is to allow the value of $\Delta V(\$)$ to be less than perfectly predictable for a given $\Delta S^u(\$/\text{€})$.[8] Because β is the slope of the line described by equation (9.2) we can redefine exposure as:[9]

> Foreign exchange exposure is the slope of the regression equation which relates changes in the real domestic-currency value of assets or liabilities to unanticipated changes in exchange rates.

Let us consider how we might estimate β.

Estimating exposure

As we have seen, we can plot the values of $\Delta V(\$)$ and associated $\Delta S^u(\$/\text{€})$ on a graph such as Figure 9.1. Of course, to do this we would have to know how much of the actual changes in exchange rates were unanticipated and also be able to measure the changes in the real dollar values of assets and liabilities. These data problems may be surmountable. In particular, the unanticipated changes in exchange rates may be calculated by obtaining forward exchange rates, which are predictions of future spot exchange rates, and subtracting the

forward rates from the realized spot exchange rates.[10] Similarly, time series of dollar values of assets and liabilities may be available in market stock and bond prices.

If we are unable to calculate *unanticipated* changes in exchange rates and instead use actual changes in exchange rates the effect is to increase the random errors, μ_t. The reason is that there will be some actual changes in exchange rates that are not associated with changes in asset or liability values. Market values reflect what is *expected* to happen to exchange rates. Therefore, what happens to asset or liability values from a given actual change in exchange rate is not always the same: the response of market value depends on the extent that the change in the exchange rate was anticipated. A combination of anticipated and unanticipated changes in exchange rates on the right-hand side of the regression equation will add "noise" to the relationship. This will be apparent in the size of the regression errors.

Interpreting exposure

As we saw in the various examples that motivated our definition of exposure as a sensitivity ratio or as the slope of a regression line, if ΔV is measured in US dollars, as it will be if we are measuring exposure from a US perspective, and if ΔS^u is measured in dollars per euro, then the measurement unit of exposure is the euro. This is because in terms of units of measurement, equation (9.1) involves $\$ = \beta \times (\$/\text{€})$. Rearranging the measurement units we have $\beta = \$ \div (\$/\text{€}) = \text{€}$. We can therefore think of exposure as the amount of foreign currency that is at risk. In the case of contractual assets and liabilities the amount at risk is the face value of the asset or liability. In the case of non-contractual assets and liabilities the amount at risk could be higher or lower than the value of the asset

---

8 If $V(\$)$ is increasing over time from, for example, inflation, we can add a constant to the right-hand side of equation (9.2). For simplicity, we suppress the constant.

9 Those readers with a background in statistics will realize that this means that by definition exposure is $\text{cov}(\Delta V, \Delta S^u)/\text{var}(\Delta S^u)$. This definition makes it clear that long versus short exposure depends on whether ΔV and ΔS^u move in the same direction or in opposite directions. See also Adler and Dumas, op. cit., and Oxelheim and Wihlborg, op. cit.

10 The reason why forward rates can be considered to proxy for expected future spot rates was explained in Chapter 3.

or liability depending on the covariance of exchange rates and local-currency values.

> Foreign exchange exposure is the amount of foreign currency that is at risk. This can be equal to, larger, or smaller than the value of an asset or liability depending on covariance of exchange rates and local-currency values.

What do we do if there are many exchange rates changing at the same time? It is in these situations that the definition of exposure in terms of slope of a line comes to the fore.

Exposure on numerous exchange rates

When many different exchange rates can affect $\Delta V(\$)$, as is the case for a firm that holds assets and liabilities in many countries and currencies or earns incomes in many countries and currencies, we can use an extension of equation (9.2) to estimate exposure. For example if $\Delta V(\$)$ could conceivably be influenced by the exchange rate of the dollar versus the British pound, Japanese yen, Swiss franc, as well as the euro, we can use the **multiple regression equation**

$$\Delta V(\$) = \beta_{\text{€}}\Delta S^{\text{u}}(\$/\text{€}) + \beta_{\text{£}}\Delta S^{\text{u}}(\$/\text{£})$$
$$+ \beta_{\text{¥}}\Delta S^{\text{u}}(\$/\text{¥}) + \beta_{\text{SFr}}\Delta S^{\text{u}}(\$/\text{SFr})$$
$$+ \mu \qquad (9.3)$$

Each slope coefficient or "beta" gives exposure to the associated foreign currency. For example, $\beta_{\text{¥}}$ gives the sensitivity of $\Delta V(\$)$ to unanticipated changes in the US-dollar value of the Japanese yen. We note that as in the case of exposure to a single exchange rate, the coefficients are all measured in units of the foreign currency. For example, if we are measuring exposure to the dollar–yen exchange rate assuming all other ΔS^{u}'s to be zero, then in terms of measurement units in equation (9.3),

$$\$ = \beta_{\text{¥}}(\$/\text{¥})$$

which requires that $\beta_{\text{¥}}$ be a yen amount.

We showed earlier that a central bank policy of "leaning against the wind," which involves raising interest rates to support a declining currency and lowering interest rates to dampen a rising currency, can make domestic bonds and stocks exposed to domestic investors. It also means that from a non-US investor's perspective, US stocks are exposed by more than their value. This follows because the combined effect of a depreciating dollar and a declining dollar value of US stocks from associated higher interest rates is a more substantial decline in the foreign-currency values of US stocks than just the decline in exchange rates.

It is worth repeating that while stock prices in general might decline when the US dollar unexpectedly depreciates, some stocks may benefit from the dollar depreciation. In particular, stocks of US export-oriented firms might increase in value because a cheaper dollar makes these firms more competitive in foreign markets. Indeed, as we have mentioned before, since a dollar depreciation makes imports to the United States more expensive relative to competing American products, US firms which sell exclusively in the US market, but which compete against imports, may also gain from a depreciation of the dollar. If the extra profitability of US export-oriented and import-competing firms shows up in higher stock prices, these particular stocks are long in foreign currency even though the stock market as a whole may be short.

Estimation difficulties

Unfortunately, the calculation of exposure may not be straightforward, even when we have a long interval of time series data on the changes in domestic-currency values for the left-hand side of the regression equation, and unexpected changes in exchange rates for the right-hand side of the equation. One serious problem is that exposure changes over time. For example, a company may have changed its assets and liabilities during the period of fitting the regression equation. Alternatively, the correlations between exchange rates and local asset or liability values may have changed during the time period. Operating exposure may have changed due to numerous conditions affecting revenue and cost, as will be explained in Chapter 11. There is also the problem mentioned earlier concerning possible variation in the extent to which changes in the spot exchange rate had been anticipated. Consequently, we cannot count on collecting the values of ΔV and the relevant ΔS^u's over a period of time and using these to fit an equation like equation (9.3).

An application of exposure measurement

We can illustrate what can be learned from the regression approach for the measurement of foreign exchange exposure, as well as some of the difficulties, by considering estimates of exposure in the Canadian forest products sector calculated by the author.[11] The market segment provides a useful test case, because if there is an industry that should be exposed in a straightforward manner, this is it: roughly 70 percent of the paper and 80 percent of lumber is exported. Overall, almost 85 percent of Canada's exports go to the United States. Therefore we would expect exchange rate exposure, particularly to the US dollar.

Using data on the return from holding the paper and forest products index on the Toronto Stock Exchange as the dependent variable, three potentially relevant exchange rates as regressors, and studying the period January 1979–August 1985, gave the following result:

$$\Delta V(\text{C\$}) = -0.0039 + 0.0001 r_C$$
$$(0.44) \qquad (0.16)$$
$$+ 0.2459 \Delta S(\text{C\$}/\$)$$
$$(0.74)$$
$$- 0.2727 \Delta S(\text{C\$}/\pounds)$$
$$(1.930)$$
$$+ 0.5841 \Delta S(\text{C\$}/\yen)$$
$$(4.23)$$

11 Maurice D. Levi, "Exchange Rates and the Valuation of Firms," in *Exchange Rates and Corporate Performance*, in Yakov Amihud and Richard Levich (eds) Irwin Publishing, Burr Ridge IL, 1994.

As well as three exchange rates, the regression includes r_C, which is the Canadian 3-month treasury bill interest rate. The values in parentheses below coefficients are 't' values: these must exceed approximately 2.0 for statistical significance at the 5 percent level. The R^2 for the equation, which is a measure of the fraction of variation in the dependent explained by the right-hand variables, was 0.11. When $R^2 = 1.0$ the right-hand variables explain all the variation in the dependent variable, and when $R^2 = 0$ none of the variation is explained.

It is notable that despite the importance of the United States as a market for Canadian paper and forest products, the Canadian–US exchange rate is not statistically significant. Also, the effect of the Canadian–British exchange rate is of the wrong sign – a higher pound is associated with lower returns in the sector – although this coefficient is not quite significant at the 5 percent level. The only significant variable that has the sign we would expect is the Canadian dollar–yen exchange rate: a decline in the Canadian dollar versus the yen raises the value of the sector, as we would export for an export industry.

Why would the exchange rate against the US dollar be insignificant while the yen is significant? This could be because Canadian firms hedge their exposure against the US dollar: many Canadian export-oriented firms denominate some of their debt in US dollars. Then, if the US dollar falls in value, they lose on operations but gain on the balance sheet: the US dollar debt then translates into fewer Canadian dollars. If the yen exposure is not hedged, it being more difficult for Canadian firms to borrow yen and more difficult to use other yen hedges, we might find a yen exposure but no US dollar exposure.

We see that exposure to an exchange rate could be zero because the companies had been very capable at hedging exchange rate exposure. It is also possible, however, that the zero coefficient is because the financial markets did not recognize what would happen as a result of the exchange rate changes. That is, either the ignorance of investors or the keen hedging knowledge of corporate financial managers could be responsible for what we observe. Being unable to disentangle these two possibilities limits greatly what we learn.

The fact that the R^2 in the regression is only 0.11 tells us that almost 90 percent of what is happening to returns is the result of factors other than exchange rates and the interest rate. We learn that even if the companies had hedged their exposure they would have reduced the volatility in their returns by only 11 percent – and this includes hedging the interest rate which also appears in the regression equation. R^2 is an important measure to have because it provides an indication of whether exchange rates are important relative to other possible influences on a company's returns. When R^2 is small it may indicate that managerial effort would better be spent trying to reduce other sources of volatility.

Any of the regression difficulties we mentioned earlier could be responsible for the poor explanatory power of the equation. For example, it is possible that we are mixing anticipated and unanticipated changes in exchange rates: sometimes exchange rate changes may have been predicted better than on other occasions. This makes it difficult for the regression procedure to assign a constant value to a regression coefficient. It is also possible that exposure changed over the time period studied. A more careful analysis might be able to disentangle these effects. Indeed, in a study that tried to reduce the problems of regression for estimating exposure, George Allyannis and Jane Ihrig found some significant exposures.[12] Four of the eighteen manufacturing groups they studied were found to be exposed through competitive structure, export share or imported inputs. They found a 1 percent appreciation of the dollar was associated with a 0.13 percent reduction in returns.

DEFINITION OF FOREIGN EXCHANGE RISK

Michael Adler and Bernard Dumas define foreign exchange risk in terms of the variability of unanticipated changes in exchange rates.[13] That is, they define exchange rate risk in terms of the unpredictability of exchange rates as reflected by the standard deviation of Δs^u, that is, SD(Δs^u) where SD stands for standard deviation.

While Adler and Dumas's definition makes it clear that unpredictability is paramount in the measurement of exchange rate risk, this author prefers a different focus on variability. The definition of **exchange rate risk** we shall use is as follows:

> Foreign exchange risk is measured by the standard deviation of domestic-currency values of assets or liabilities attributable to unanticipated changes in exchange rates.

The principal difference between the definition used in this book and that of Adler and Dumas is that the definition used here focuses on the unpredictability of values of assets or liabilities due to uncertainty in exchange rates, not on the uncertainty of exchange rates themselves. This difference in definitions can have important consequences. For example, according to our definition, an asset is not subject to exchange rate risk if its value does not depend on exchange rates, even though exchange rates might be extremely volatile. According to our definition, volatility in exchange rates is responsible for exchange rate risk only if it translates into volatility in real domestic-currency values. This makes exchange rate risk dependent on exposure as well as on SD(Δs^u). Let us see why this is so by reconsidering regression equation (9.2).

Equation (9.2) makes it clear that changes in the values of assets and liabilities, depend both on exchange rates and on other factors, with the effect of the non-exchange rate factors captured by the term μ_t. We can isolate the effect of exchange rates

---

12 See George Allyannis and Jane Ihrig, "Exposure and Markups," *Review of Financial Studies*, 14, 2001, pp. 805–35.

13 Michael Adler and Bernard Dumas, op. cit. We might note that because the probabilities of outcomes are not known, it would be more appropriate to refer to exchange-rate *uncertainty* rather than *risk*. However, because it has become customary to use the term "risk," we also use this term.

from the effect of other factors if we define the variable

$$\Delta \hat{V} = \beta \Delta S^{u}(\$/\pounds) \qquad (9.4)$$

$\Delta \hat{V}$ is the change in domestic-currency value of an asset or liability *that is due to unanticipated changes in the exchange rate*. That is, we have partitioned the total change in value, ΔV, into that due to changes in exchange rates, $\Delta \hat{V}$, and that due to other influences, μ; this follows by relating equation (9.4) to equation (9.2), giving

$$\Delta V \equiv \Delta \hat{V} + \mu \qquad (9.5)$$

With ΔV so partitioned, we can explain how our definition of exchange rate risk relates to exchange rate exposure.

Our definition of exchange rate risk as the standard deviation of the domestic-currency values of assets or liabilities due to unanticipated changes in exchange rates is a definition in terms of $SD(\Delta \hat{V})$, where $\Delta \hat{V}$ is as defined in equation (9.4). Applying standard statistical procedures to equation (9.4), with the average unanticipated change in exchange rate, written as $\overline{\Delta S}^{u}(\$/\pounds)$, being zero, we have[14]

$$SD(\Delta \hat{V}) = \sqrt{\frac{1}{n-1}\sum_{n}\left[\beta\Delta S^{u}(\$/\pounds) - \beta\overline{\Delta S}^{u}(\$/\pounds)\right]^{2}}$$

$$= \beta SD(\Delta S^{u}) \qquad (9.6)$$

Equation (9.6) shows that foreign exchange risk is proportional to foreign exchange exposure. However, exchange rate risk also depends on the volatility of ΔS^{u}, the unanticipated change in exchange rates, which is the risk measure used by Adler and Dumas.

Equation (9.6) makes it clear that exchange rate risk requires both exposure and unpredictability of exchange rates. Having exposure does not mean

having exchange rate risk if exchange rates are perfectly predictable. Similarly, unpredictability of exchange rates does not mean exchange rate risk for items that are not exposed.

EXPOSURE, RISK, AND THE PARITY RELATIONSHIPS

With exchange rate risk and exposure now defined and compared, we can consider how risk and exposure are related to PPP and interest parity. This will allow us to clarify several features of risk and exposure that we have alluded to, but not so far systematically explored.

Exposure, risk, and interest parity

Covered interest parity can be summarized in the dollar–pound context by equation (8.10):

$$(1 + r_{\$})^{n} = \frac{F_{n}(\$/\pounds)}{S(\$/\pounds)}(1 + r_{\pounds})^{n} \qquad (8.10)$$

The right-hand side of equation (8.10) gives the hedged dollar receipts to an investor on a covered n-year British pound interest-bearing security. Clearly, if the pound security is hedged and held to maturity, unanticipated changes in exchange rates can have no effect on the dollar value of the security. That is, the hedged pound security is not exposed and faces no foreign exchange risk. Indeed, this is why the return equals that on US securities. However, the lack of exposure and risk on the pound security is only because the security is combined with a forward contract, and because both the security and forward contract are held to maturity.

When a foreign currency-denominated security is not hedged with a forward contract or may have to be sold before maturity, the security is exposed and subject to exchange rate risk, irrespective of interest parity. Indeed, the presence or absence of interest parity has no bearing on the amount of exchange rate risk or exposure. While uncovered interest parity does suggest that *anticipated* changes in exchange rates are compensated for in interest

---

14 Average unexpected changes of exchange rates are zero if expectations are rational: rational people take all relevant information into account, and *on average* predict correctly.

differentials, there is no compensation for *unanticipated* changes in exchange rates.[15]

Interest parity also has no implication for exchange rate risk, which we have measured by

$$\text{SD}(\Delta \hat{V}) = \beta \text{SD}(\Delta s^{\text{u}}) \qquad (9.6)$$

This is because it has no implications for the exposure, β, or for the variability of unanticipated changes in exchange rates, $\text{SD}(\Delta s^{\text{u}})$.

Exposure, risk, and purchasing power parity

Whereas there are no implications of interest parity for exposure and risk, the situation is quite different for PPP. In the case of PPP there are implications for exposure and risk on real assets such as real estate and equities, the prices of which can systematically vary with exchange rates. There are also implications of PPP for exposure and risk on the operating incomes of firms. It is useful to consider the implications of PPP for real assets – called **fixed assets** by accountants – separately from those for operating incomes.

Purchasing power parity and real-asset exposure

We can see the implications of PPP for risk and exposure on real (or fixed) assets such as real estate from the example of investment in European real estate shown earlier in this chapter. The essential part of the example is summarized by the final column in Table 9.8. This shows an item of European real-estate that is worth $1.1 million when the exchange rate is $1.1000/€, and the same dollar value one period later when the exchange rate is $1.0000/€. In the example, the change in the exchange rate has been assumed to exactly offset the change in local-currency value of the asset. As we pointed out earlier, if this situation systematically occurred the real-estate investment would not be exposed.

The values in Table 9.8 would occur if dynamic or relative PPP holds, *and* if the euro value of the real estate systematically follows the overall European rate of inflation. In such a situation there is zero exposure. There is also no foreign exchange *risk*: foreign exchange risk requires foreign exchange exposure.[16] In reality, two empirical facts force us to reconsider the absence of exposure and risk on real assets such as real estate:

1   PPP does not hold, as we saw in Chapter 7.
2   An individual real-estate investment, or even real estate investment in general, will not usually change in value by the overall rate of inflation.

Considering the first point alone, if PPP fails to hold and there is no tendency for adjustment of prices and/or exchange rates towards PPP levels, then there is exposure. In this case there is no systematic connection between exchange rates and prices of baskets of goods. If, on the other hand, deviations from PPP are random in the sense that relative price levels are sometimes higher and sometimes lower than the exchange rate would suggest, but on average over a period of time exchange rates equal PPP values, exposure is zero, just as if PPP always held. The departures from PPP in this case add to total risk, but to the extent that the deviations from PPP are caused by factors other than changes in exchange rates, they are not part of *foreign exchange* risk.

As for the second point mentioned earlier, if changes in exchange rates do not reflect movements in different countries' prices of real estate, investors can face exposure on real estate even if PPP holds for broad-based baskets of goods – which is the

---

15 As we have seen, there could be a systematic relationship between $\Delta s^{\text{u}}(\$/£)$ and the value of pound-denominated securities if the Bank of England leans against the wind. Then, British security prices will decline as $\Delta s^{\text{u}}(\$/£)$ decreases. However, this has nothing to do with whether covered interest parity holds.

16 Exhibit 9.1 shows that offsets between asset values and exchange rates may depend on the length of investors' horizons.

EXHIBIT 9.1 HEDGING HORIZONS

If currencies depreciate when asset prices denominated in those currencies increase, exposure is less than the value of the foreign assets; the movements in exchange rates and asset prices are offsetting when translating values into a different currency. When there is no connection between asset prices and exchange rates, as with bank deposits, exposure equals the value of foreign assets. Finally, when currencies and asset prices move in the same direction, with appreciation accompanying increasing asset values and vice versa, exposure *exceeds* the value of the foreign assets. As the following explains, the size of exposure appears to depend on the length of the horizon that is studied. Specifically, it appears that an offsetting of exchange rates and asset values resulting in exposure of less than the asset values occurs in the long run, but the reverse occurs in the short run.

Exposure to changes in exchange rates represents a major risk for international investors. During the 1980s, it became common practice for investors to hedge currency risk as fully as possible by methods including the purchase of futures contracts. But for many investors, this simple and seemingly sensible hedging strategy actually may increase exchange-rate risk rather than reducing it, according to NBER Research Associate Kenneth Froot.

In *Currency Hedging Over Long Horizons* (*NBER Working Paper No. 4355*), Froot examines the variability of returns to British residents on U.S. stock and bond investments during the period between 1802 and 1990. Where short-term investments are concerned, currency hedging greatly affects British investors' returns. Over a one-year period, Froot finds, the earnings from unhedged U.S. stock portfolios, expressed in British pounds of constant value, are 13 percent more variable than the earnings from fully hedged portfolios. Unhedged portfolios of U.S. bonds show 56 percent more variance than hedged portfolios for British investors.

But as the time horizon lengthens, the value of hedging drops sharply. After three years, Froot reports, fully hedged U.S. stock portfolios show *greater* variability than unhedged portfolios when their returns are expressed in real pounds. The same is true for bond portfolios at horizons of about seven years.

The length of the investor's time horizon is important where exchange rate hedging is concerned, Froot contends, because while short-term currency fluctuations are random, over the longer term, currencies move toward purchasing-power-parity: the level at which amounts of similar value have similar buying power in each country. That movement creates a "natural" exchange rate hedge for physical assets, such as factories and equipment, and for common stocks. If the value of the currency declines, the local-currency value of such assets will rise over the long term to keep their international value stable.

The value of bonds, however, depends much more heavily on each country's inflation and interest rates, as well as on the real exchange-rate. Convergence toward purchasing-power-parity therefore will have less effect in reducing the variability of foreign bond investors' returns, which is why currency hedging may be more useful.

Multinational corporations' currency hedging strategies, Froot concludes, should be based on the nature of the investment and the duration of the anticipated exposure. If, for example, a company borrows in one currency to build a plant in a country with another currency, then hedging may be unnecessary, as the physical assets will be naturally hedged as exchange rates move toward purchasing-power-parity . . .

Source: "The Value of Exchange-Rate Hedging Depends on Your Horizon," *The NBER Digest*, October 1993, pp. 3–4.

price measure that is relevant for the PPP principle. When dealing with exposure of particular items, it is the law-of-a-single price that determines whether there is exposure. Furthermore, as with deviations from PPP discussed earlier, it is the *systematic* relation between real-estate prices and exchange rates that determines whether or not foreign real-estate investment faces foreign exchange exposure. What is affected by individual asset prices moving differently than overall inflation is the total amount of risk. Added to the risk caused by PPP deviations is relative-price risk. However, if this risk is not due to exchange rate changes, while it adds to total risk, it does not add to exchange rate risk.

Purchasing power parity and operating exposure[17]

There are also implications of PPP for the foreign exchange exposure of operating incomes of firms that export, import, compete with imports, use imports, supply exporters, and so on. This type of exposure is called operating exposure, and the risk is operating risk.[18] In particular, operating exposure is the sensitivity of real operating income to changes in exchange rates. Similarly, operating risk is the volatility of operating income attributable to unanticipated changes in exchange rates. The effects on operations can be considered as effects on the income statement while effects on assets and liabilities can be considered as effects on the balance sheet. The income statement effects are flows and so must be converted to present value amounts – which have a stock dimension – before being added to exposure on assets or liabilities. When combined, the present value of operating effects plus the effects on assets and liabilities gives the total exposure.

We should also note that operating risk and exposure involve effects of exchange rates on the current and future profitability of firms. This is distinct from the effects of exchange rates on the dollar values of foreign-currency accounts receivable and accounts payable. Accounts receivable and payable are fixed, face-value, short-term assets and liabilities, and have risk and exposure like those of foreign-currency bank accounts and loans. We have called such items contractual amounts. On the other hand, operating incomes are not contractual values. Indeed, as we shall see, operating exposure depends on very different factors than those we have met before, such as the elasticity of demand for imports or exports, the fraction of input costs that depend on exchange rates, the flexibility of production to respond to exchange rate-induced changes in demand, and the reference currency for computing incomes.[19]

We can explain the difference between operating risk and exposure on the one hand, and asset and liability exposure on the other hand, as well as show the relevance of PPP for operating risk and exposure, by considering the case of a US exporter selling to Britain. Let us consider under what conditions the profit or operating income of the exporter is systematically affected by exchange rates.

Let us denote the dollar profits of the US exporting firm by π; then from the definition of profits as revenue minus costs we can write

$$\pi = S(\$/\pounds)p_{UK}q - c_{US}q$$

or

$$\pi = [S(\$/\pounds)p_{UK} - c_{US}]q \qquad (9.7)$$

Here p_{UK} is the pound price of the US firm's export good in Britain, and c_{US} is the (constant) per-unit US dollar production cost of the export. The product, $S(\$/\pounds)p_{UK}$, is the export sales price of the company's product in dollars, and so the difference between $S(\$/\pounds)p_{UK}$ and c_{US} is the dollar profit

---

17 This section may be omitted without loss of continuity.
18 Chapter 11 is devoted to the topic of operating exposure.

19 As mentioned, these and other factors influencing operating risk and exposure are explained in Chapter 11. The complexities of operating risk and exposure, as well as the distinction between accounts-receivable exposure versus operating exposure, are covered in Exhibit 9.2, which considers the situation facing American Airlines.

EXHIBIT 9.2   FLYING HIGH: RISK AND EXPOSURE AT AMERICAN AIRLINES

In a study that uses statistical regression for determining foreign exchange risk and exposure facing American Airlines, John Bilson discussed the numerous ways that exchange rates can affect an airline. As the following excerpt explains, the routes through which exchange rates work are many and varied.

Foreign exchange exposure is of increasing importance in the airline industry as the large carriers expand into foreign markets. Net foreign currency cash flows at American Airlines (AMR) have grown from $119 million in 1986 to $393 million in 1990. International revenue has grown from 19.3 percent of the system total in 1986 to an estimated 26.7 percent in 1990. While the bulk of this expansion has been in the European market, service to the Far East is expected to grow rapidly in the near future. It is consequently important to know how the profitability of the airline will be influenced by the inevitable fluctuations in the price of foreign currencies against the dollar.

There are two primary sources of currency exposure. The largest source arises from the timing lag between the sale of a ticket in a foreign currency and the receipt of the revenue in dollars. This delay averages 15 to 45 days in the major markets. After a ticket is sold in a foreign currency, a delay will occur before AMR receives the revenue (denominated in foreign currency) from the sale. If the foreign currency should depreciate between the time the ticket is sold and the time the revenues are repatriated, a loss will be recognized on the transaction. Since AMR has positive excess cash flows in its foreign markets, this analysis suggests that AMR is net long in foreign currencies and that hedge activities should involve short positions in foreign currencies.

The second source of exposure results from the impact of exchange rates on anticipated future cash flows. Since it is impractical to reset ticket prices at short intervals, a depreciation of a foreign currency will reduce the dollar value of future cash flows if the foreign currency price and the load factors are stable. This consideration also suggests that AMR is naturally net long in the foreign currencies where it is operationally involved.

If this approach is correct, an appreciation of foreign currencies should be associated with increased profitability and a rise in the value of AMR stock. However, the effect of the exchange-rate on the profitability of an airline is considerably more complex than its effect on cash flows and contemporaneous load factors. For the American consumer of international air travel services, appreciation in foreign currencies increases the total costs of international travel. While the airline ticket cost, which is denominated in dollars, is typically not affected immediately, all other travel costs should increase in proportion to the change in the exchange rate. It is therefore reasonable to assume that American overseas travel will be adversely affected by the appreciation of foreign currencies. It is true that a depreciation of the dollar should make travel to the United States by foreigners less expensive, but if foreign travelers have a preference for their national airline, U.S. carriers could still be adversely affected. This effect would not be immediately apparent in load factors since international travel typically is planned in advance. However, if the market efficiently forecasts anticipated future revenues, the decline in profitability should be immediately reflected in the stock price.

Movements in exchange rates also reflect underlying economic conditions. The prospect of a recession in the United States will decrease the demand for the U.S. currency and lead to a depreciation of the dollar. Since airline travel is cyclical, anticipated future revenue from both domestic and international travel is likely to decline with prospective recession. While this decline is unlikely to be reflected in current revenues, it should be reflected in the stock price. Finally, the exchange-rate could also have an indirect effect on energy prices. When the dollar depreciates, U.S. energy prices have to rise in order to maintain parity with world prices. If the industry cannot offset the cost increases with higher prices, anticipated future profitability will be adversely affected.

Source: John F.O. Bilson, "Managing Economic Exposure to Foreign Exchange Risk: A Case Study of American Airlines," in Yakov Amihud and Richard M. Levich (eds), Exchange Rates and Corporate Performance, New York University Salomon Center, New York, 1994, pp. 221–46.

("markup") per unit sold. By multiplying this difference by the total quantity of sales, q, we get the US exporter's total profit in dollar terms, or π.

In order to see the conditions under which changes in exchange rates will raise or lower a US exporter's profits, we will write the annual rate of change in exchange rates as $\dot{S}$, and the rate of change of profits as $\dot{\pi}$: as before, a dot over a variable signifies a rate of change. Let us assume that the market selling price of the company's product in the United Kingdom grows at the British general rate of inflation, which we have written as $\dot{P}_{UK}$. Let us also assume that the production cost of the product, which is made in the United States, grows at the general rate of inflation in the United States, $\dot{P}_{US}$. For the given output level q, we can write the US exporter's profit at the end of the year as follows:

$$\pi(1 + \dot{\pi}) = [S(\$/\pounds)p_{UK}(1 + \dot{S})(1 + \dot{P}_{UK})$$
$$- c_{US}(1 + \dot{P}_{US})]q \qquad (9.8)$$

Equation (9.8) is obtained from equation (9.7) simply by replacing π, $S(\$/\pounds)$, and so on, with their values after one year has passed. These year-later values are the values at the beginning multiplied by one plus the annual rates of change.

Subtracting equation (9.7) from equation (9.8) gives

$$\dot{\pi} = \{S(\$/\pounds)p_{UK}[\dot{S}(1 + \dot{P}_{UK}) + \dot{P}_{UK}] - c_{US}\dot{P}_{US}\}q/\pi$$

Profits will grow after, for example, a depreciation or devaluation of the dollar (when $\dot{S}$, which is short for $\dot{S}(\$/\pounds)$, is positive) if $\dot{\pi} > 0$, that is, if

$$S(\$/\pounds)p_{UK}[\dot{S}(1 + \dot{P}_{UK}) + \dot{P}_{UK}] - c_{US}\dot{P}_{US} > 0$$

If the devaluation or depreciation takes place when the profits are zero $[S(\$/\pounds)p_{UK} = c_{US}]$, we can rewrite this as

$$S(\$/\pounds)p_{UK}[\dot{S}(1 + \dot{P}_{UK}) + \dot{P}_{UK} - \dot{P}_{US}] > 0$$

Since $S(\$/\pounds)$ and p_{UK} are positive, a devaluation or depreciation of the dollar will raise a US exporter's profits if $[\dot{S}(1 + \dot{P}_{UK}) + \dot{P}_{UK} - \dot{P}_{US}] > 0$, that is, if

$$\dot{S} > \frac{\dot{P}_{US} - \dot{P}_{UK}}{1 + \dot{P}_{UK}} \qquad (9.9)$$

Similarly, a devaluation or depreciation will reduce profits if

$$\dot{S} < \frac{\dot{P}_{US} - \dot{P}_{UK}}{1 + \dot{P}_{UK}} \qquad (9.10)$$

Comparison of the inequalities (9.9) and (9.10) with the relative form of PPP in equation (7.7) shows that for effects on profits to occur, that is, for there to be operating exposure, it is necessary to have *ex post* violations of PPP. The intuitive explanation of this is that for the US exporter's product to gain in competitiveness in Britain from a dollar depreciation, it is necessary for the product's price to fall vis-à-vis prices of competing British goods. This requires that the depreciation exceed the extent to which US prices are increasing faster than British prices. For example, if US prices are increasing by 8 percent and British prices are increasing by 6 percent, it is necessary for the dollar depreciation to exceed approximately 2 percent for the US exporter's competitiveness to be improved from depreciation.

In deriving equations (9.9) and (9.10) we made an assumption. To repeat, we said: "assume that the market selling price of the company's product in the United Kingdom grows at the British general rate of inflation, (and) that the production cost of the product . . . grows at the general rate of inflation in the United States." Rather than PPP, what matters to an individual firm is its own product price and its own costs. What we have done above is put the conditions in terms of companies collectively.

Consideration of the inequalities (9.9) and (9.10) tells us that if our assumption that an individual company's prices and costs change at overall inflation rates is correct, and if PPP always holds, there is no operating risk or exposure. Similarly, as with assets and liabilities, if PPP is violated but deviations from PPP are as likely to be positive as be negative and on average are zero, there is still no exposure. In terms of Figure 9.1, in this situation we have a scatter of points around the horizontal axis: there is no *systematic* relationship between operating income and exchange rates. Again, as with assets and liabilities, random deviations from PPP add to the total operating risk but do not add to exchange rate risk, which is the variation in operating income due to unanticipated changes in exchange rates. That is, when PPP holds only as a long-run tendency, the firm faces greater risk than when PPP always holds, but this added risk is due to the factors causing the deviations from PPP, not the exchange rate.

In deriving inequalities (9.9) and (9.10) we assumed that the market selling price of the US exporter's product in Britain grows at the overall British rate of inflation and that the cost of production grows at the overall US rate of inflation. If these assumptions are possibly invalid at any moment, but are valid on average, there is still no exposure provided of course that PPP holds, at least on average.[20] However, violation of the assumptions does add a relative price risk to any risk from random deviations from PPP. This conclusion is very similar to that reached for real assets.

It should be remembered that while operating risk and exposure and real-asset risk and exposure relate similarly to PPP, these two types of risk and exposure are completely different in nature. Indeed, gains and losses from operating risk and exposure have a different dimension to those from real-asset exposure and from exposure on any type of asset or liability. Operating gains and losses have the dimension of flows, with profit changes occurring by so much *per month* or *per year*, that is, over a period of time. On the other hand, asset and liability gains or losses have the dimension of stocks, occurring at the moment of the change in exchange rates. Overall exposure is best considered as an amount at a moment in time and so operating exposures which appear on the income statement need to be converted into present values before adding them to balance sheet exposures.

SUMMARY

1 From a US dollar perspective, foreign exchange exposure is the sensitivity of real US-dollar values of assets or liabilities with respect to changes in exchange rates.
2 Exposure is measured in units of foreign currency.
3 Contractual assets or liabilities are those with domestic-currency values that do not depend on exchange rates. Examples are bank deposits and bank loans.

20 By the assumptions being valid "on average" we mean that there is no systematic difference between the rate of change of the product's price and British inflation, and no systematic difference between the rate of change in production costs and US inflation.

4   Exposure on a contractual asset or liability equals the value of the asset or liability.

5   Exposure on a foreign asset or liability can be higher or lower than the
    foreign-currency value of the asset or liability depending on the correlation between
    the local-currency value of the asset or liability and the exchange rate.

6   Exposure is higher than the foreign-currency value of an asset if the local-currency
    asset price and the exchange rate move in the same direction. This can happen with
    investments in foreign import-oriented companies that become more profitable
    when the importer's domestic currency appreciates, and less profitable when the
    importer's currency depreciates.

7   Exposure on a foreign asset is less than the value of the asset if the asset price
    and the exchange rate move in opposite direction. This can happen with investments in
    foreign export-oriented companies that become more profitable when the domestic
    currency falls, and vice versa.

8   Long foreign exchange exposure is when an investor gains when the foreign currency
    rises and loses when the foreign currency declines. Short exposure is when an
    investor loses when the foreign currency rises and gains when the foreign currency
    declines.

9   It is actually possible for an investor in a foreign stock to be short in the foreign currency
    if after an appreciation of the foreign currency the stock price falls by more than the
    foreign-currency increases.

10 An investor in foreign-currency bonds is exposed by more than the value of the
    bonds if the foreign central bank "leans against the wind," raising interest rates when the
    foreign currency falls and lowering interest rates when the foreign currency rises.

11 Domestic currency-denominated bonds can be exposed to exchange rates if the
    home country central bank leans against the wind. If interest rates affect stock prices,
    the domestic stock market as a whole is also exposed.

12 Exposure can be measured by the slope coefficient in a regression equation relating the
    real change in the dollar value of assets or liabilities to changes in exchange rates.

13 There is exposure only if there is a *systematic* relationship between home-currency
    values of assets and liabilities and exchange rates. That is, for exposure to exist,
    dollar values must on average change in a particular way vis-à-vis unanticipated changes
    in exchange rates.

14 Normally there is noise in the relationship between domestic-currency values and
    unanticipated changes in exchange rates. However, the size of foreign exchange exposure
    of, for example, a pound-denominated bond is still the face value of the bond if the
    noise is random and on average equal to zero.

15 When exposures exist against numerous currencies, they can be measured from
    the slope coefficients in a multiple regression.

16 Foreign exchange risk is positively related to both exposure and the standard deviation of
    unanticipated changes in exchange rates.

17 When a foreign currency-denominated security is not hedged with a forward
    exchange contract, it is exposed and subject to exchange rate risk, irrespective of whether
    interest parity holds.

18 If individual asset values do not always change by the overall rate of inflation for
    a country but on average change at the rate of inflation, exposure is still zero if PPP holds

on average. With random departures from PPP there is an added source of risk, but this is part of the total risk, not the foreign exchange risk.

19 The sensitivity of operating income to changes in exchange rates is called operating exposure, and the standard deviation of operating income due to unanticipated changes in exchange rates is called operating risk.

20 If PPP always holds exactly and market prices and production costs always move in line with overall inflation, there is no operating exposure or operating risk. If PPP holds only on average and prices and production costs move on average at the overall rate of inflation, there is still no exchange rate exposure or risk, but there is greater total risk.

REVIEW QUESTIONS

1 What is "foreign exchange exposure?"
2 What is a contractual asset or liability?
3 What is a "reference currency?"
4 What is meant by a "systematic relationship?"
5 What variables go on the axes of an "exposure line?" How do these variables relate to those used for drawing payoff profiles?
6 What are the units of measurement of exposure to a particular exchange rate, for example, euros per US dollar?
7 How does the sign associated with exposure – positive versus negative – relate to whether exposure is "long" or "short?"
8 What is "foreign exchange risk?"
9 Can an asset face exposure larger than the foreign-currency value of the asset?
10 Can a domestic currency-denominated asset face foreign exchange exposure?
11 How does foreign exchange exposure on real assets relate to the PPP condition.
12 How does operating exposure relate to the PPP condition?

ASSIGNMENT PROBLEMS

1 In what sense is the sign – positive versus negative – of the slope coefficient which measures exposure relevant, and in what sense is it irrelevant?
2 How can exposure exceed the face value of a foreign currency-denominated asset or liability?
3 If the Bank of Canada "leans against the wind," which means increasing interest rates when the Canadian dollar depreciates and lowering interest rates when the Canadian dollar appreciates, what would this mean for the exposure of
   a   Canadian residents holding Canadian dollar-denominated bonds?
   b   US residents holding Canadian-dollar bonds?
   Relate your answer to Question 2 above.

4 How does PPP relate to:

a   exposure on real, fixed assets?

b   operating exposure?

5 Would it make sense to add a firm's exposures in different currencies at the spot exchange rate to obtain a measure of the firm's aggregate exposure, and if not, why not?

6 What is the problem in using the standard deviation of exchange rates as a measure of foreign exchange risk?

7 If a company has used its currency of debt denomination and/or forward contracts to make its exposure zero, what would *measured* exposure be from the β of a regression line, if in calculating β, the debt and/or forward contracts were omitted from the regression equation?

8 Would the distinction between real and actual changes in exchange rates be important if inflation and interest rates were everywhere the same and were also small?

9 By studying the stock price of a US-based publicly traded company you have noticed that when the dollar drops against various currencies the company's value on the stock exchange increases. By averaging the link between exchange rates and the company's value you have determined the size of the change in each exchange rate that increases the value of the company by $1 million:

$$\Delta S^u(\text{€}/\$) = 0.1$$
$$\Delta S^u(\text{¥}/\$) = 5$$
$$\Delta S^u(\text{SFr}/\$) = 0.05$$
$$\Delta S^u(\text{C}\$/\$) = 0.04$$

What is the company's exposure to the various currencies?

10 Redo the analysis in this chapter of the effect of exchange rate changes on an exporter by allowing the quantity sold, q, to change with the exchange rate instead of holding it constant. Use calculus to make the problem easier, and note that p_{UK} and q should be at profit-maximization levels in every period (this is a very difficult question).

BIBLIOGRAPHY

Adler, Michael and Bernard Dumas, "Exposure to Currency Risk: Definition and Measurement," *Financial Management*, Summer 1984, pp. 41–50.

Flood, Eugene Jr. and Donald R. Lessard, "On the Measurement of Operating Exposure to Exchange Rates: A Conceptual Approach," *Financial Management*, Spring 1986, pp. 25–37.

Garner C. Kent and Alan C. Shapiro, "A Practical Method of Assessing Foreign Exchange Risk," *Midland Corporate Finance Journal*, Fall 1984, pp. 6–17.

Hekman, Christine R., "Measuring Foreign Exchange Exposure: A Practical Theory and its Application," *Financial Analysts Journal*, September/October 1983, pp. 59–65.

Hodder, James E., "Exposure to Exchange-Rate Movements," *Journal of International Economics*, November, 1982, pp. 375–86.

Jorion, Philippe, "The Exchange Rate Exposure of U.S. Multinationals," unpublished manuscript, Columbia University, February 1986.

Korsvold, Pal E., "Managing Strategic Foreign Exchange Exposure of Real Assets," presented at European Finance Association meetings, Madrid, September 1987.

Lessard, Donald R. and David Sharp, "Measuring the Performance of Operations Subject to Fluctuating Exchange Rates," *Midland Corporate Finance Journal*, Fall 1984, pp. 18–30.

Levi, Maurice D., "Exchange Rates and the Valuation of Firms," in Yakov Amihud and Richard M. Levich, *Exchange Rates and Corporate Performance*, New York University, New York, 1994, pp. 32–48.

—— and Joseph Zechner, "Foreign Exchange Risk and Exposure," in Robert Z. Aliber (ed.), *Handbook of International Financial Management*, Richard Irwin-Dow Jones, New York, 1989.

Nobes, Christopher: *International Guide to Interpreting Company Accounts: Overcoming Disparities in National Accounting Procedures*, Financial Times Management Reports, London, 1994.

Oxelheim, Lars and Clas G. Wihlborg, *Macroeconomic Uncertainty: International Risks and Opportunities for the Corporation*, Wiley, New York, 1987.

Shapiro, Alan C., "Defining Exchange Risk," *The Journal of Business*, January 1977, pp. 37–9.

——, "What Does Purchasing Power Parity Mean?" *Journal of International Money and Finance*, December 1983, pp. 295–318.

Solnik, Bruno, "International Parity Conditions and Exchange Risk," *Journal of Banking and Finance*, August 1978, pp. 281–93.

Stulz, Rene and Rohan Williamson, "Identifying and Quantifying Exposure," Working Paper 96–14, Fisher College of Business, Ohio State University, 1996.

Chapter 10

Accounting exposure versus real exposure[1]

There is no such source of error as the pursuit of absolute truth.

Samuel Butler

The definitions of foreign exchange exposure and risk in Chapter 9 relate to the true *economic* effects of exchange rates, and indeed, exposure and risk as we have defined them are often called **economic exposure** and **economic risk**. While in principle, economic effects should be apparent in companies' accounts, in reality the effects of exchange rates that appear in financial statements rarely if ever correspond with the economic measures. The effect of exchange rates which appears in financial statements is called **accounting exposure**. In this chapter we trace through the ways different accounting principles measure the effects of exchange rates, and how these measures compare to what we refer to as **real changes in exchange rates**, where by "real changes" we mean true economic effects of exchange rates. We begin with an outline of accounting principles that have been or that are currently being used to record international financial transactions.

ACCOUNTING PRINCIPLES

It is necessary to have rules for converting values of foreign assets, liabilities, payments, and receipts

into domestic currency in order to include them in consolidated financial statements in a firm's **domestic reporting currency** (the domestic reporting currency is usually that of the country where the head office is located). Different countries use different conversion rules, and so it is difficult to provide generally valid guidelines in this book. However, by focusing on the accounting principles of one country, the United States, many of the common issues and problems can be identified and addressed.

Acceptable rules for preparing financial statements in the United States are provided by the **Financial Accounting Standards Board (FASB)**. Our focus is on the international dimensions of financial reporting, and not on matters relating to **corporate governance**. This is not meant to diminish the importance of the role that accurate accounting plays in the governance of business. Indeed, as we became so keenly aware in the stunning revelations of accounting irregularities involving Enron and WorldCom, the quality and integrity of financial reporting is critical to properly functioning commerce. However, since this is a book in international finance and since governance issues do not play a particularly important role at the international level, we focus instead on the issue

---

1 This chapter can be omitted without loss of continuity.

of the effect of rules governing the choice of exchange rates for the gains or losses on assets and liabilities appearing in income statements. We also deal with the effect of exchange rates on operating income and expenses.[2]

The income statement, which is also called the profit and loss statement, typically attracts more attention than a firm's balance sheet because taxes are based on income, and as we shall claim, it is usually assumed that shareholders can see through the veil of accounting rules that affect balance sheet values.

It will help the reader's understanding of how US international accounting principles affect gains and losses on assets and liabilities by distinguishing between **translation risk** and **translation exposure** on the one hand, and **transaction risk** and **transaction exposure** on the other. From a US perspective, translation risk is the uncertainty of real US dollar asset or liability values *appearing in financial statements*, where this uncertainty is due to unanticipated changes in exchange rates. Similarly, translation exposure is the sensitivity of values *appearing in financial statements* to changes in exchange rates. On the other hand, transaction risk is the uncertainty of realized US dollar asset or liability values *when the assets or liabilities are liquidated*, due to unanticipated changes in exchange rates. Similarly, transaction exposure is the sensitivity of changes in realized US dollar values of assets or liabilities *when the assets or liabilities are liquidated*, with respect to unanticipated changes in exchange rates (see Exhibit 10.1).[3]

Until 1982, the United States used an accounting standard generally known as Financial Accounting Standard 8, or briefly, **FAS 8**. Under FAS 8 a company was required to show all foreign exchange translation gains or losses (those from converting foreign assets or liabilities into dollar amounts) in the current-period income statement. Different treatment was given to current operating receipts and expenditures and financial assets/liabilities on the one hand, and to fixed (or real) assets on the other hand. This was referred to as a **temporal distinction**, and the rules were as follows.[4]

1   Revenues and expenses from foreign entities (overseas operations) were translated at the average exchange rate prevailing during the period. Financial assets and liabilities were translated at the average exchange rate during the period.

2   Other assets, primarily fixed assets, were translated at historical exchange rates. Historical costs were used in terms of local (foreign) currency.[5]

What FAS 8 therefore required was that if local-currency values were measured at current cost, they were to be translated at current exchange rates, and if they were measured at historical cost, they were to be translated at historical exchange rates.

The fact that FAS 8 required that all translation adjustments appear in the income statement made income appear highly volatile and caused numerous corporate treasurers to take permanently hedged positions. The procedure which has replaced FAS 8 is called **FAS 52**, and this involves two principal changes:

1   The **functional currency** is selected for each subsidiary. This is the primary currency of

---

2   The impact of exchange rates on operations, called operating exposure, is the topic of the next chapter, Chapter 11, while the management of operating exposure is discussed in Chapter 12.

3   The distinction between translation and transaction exposure is discussed in Exhibit 10.1.

4   See *Statement of Financial Accounting Standards, No. 8*, Financial Accounting Standards Board, Stamford, CT, October 1975. The accounting system which replaced the FAS 8 system is described in *Statement of Financial Accounting Standards, No. 52– Foreign Currency Translation*, Financial Accounting Standards Board, Stamford, CT, December 1981.

5   Fixed assets include buildings, equipment, and other items for which prices tend to reflect inflation. While economists refer to fixed assets as "real assets," we use the term preferred by accountants in this chapter to reduce confusion between *real* assets and *real* changes in exchange rates.

EXHIBIT 10.1   TRANSLATING ACCOUNTANTS' AND ECONOMISTS' LANGUAGES

The excerpt below, which is revised slightly to reflect current practices, emphasizes the distinction between translation and transaction exposure according to whether conversion of currencies has occurred. It also makes clear why it is the need to consolidate worldwide income that causes translation exposure.

Transaction exposure

Transaction exposure occurs when one currency must be exchanged for another, and when a change in foreign exchange rates occurs between the time a transaction is executed and the time it is settled. Take the case of ABC Corporation, a U.S.-based multinational with extensive operations in Europe. Suppose ABC's UK subsidiary sells product to a German company. The customer wishes to transact in euros. The sale is made on May 1 on 30-day terms. ABC-UK receives euros on June 1 and converts to British pounds. If the £/€ exchange rate changes in May, ABC-UK receives more or fewer pounds than anticipated at the time of the transaction. The risk here thus involves uncertainty about a specific identifiable cash flow; it is referred to as "transaction" exposure because it involves an actual gain or loss due to conversion of one currency into another.

Translation exposure

Translation exposure arises in multinational firms from the requirement that U.S. companies (and those foreign firms following U.S. accounting practices) produce consolidated financial statements. Subsidiaries of multinational companies operating in different countries typically transact in local currencies. Local currency is also normally the unit of account for accounting, performance measurement, and taxation at the local level; and thus the operating financial statements of subsidiaries are generally denominated in local currencies.

Periodically (often quarterly but at least annually), however, these subsidiary statements must be summed into consolidated statements for the entire multinational enterprise and denominated in the home currency. In ABC's case, this means consolidating statements denominated in a wide variety of currencies around the globe and expressing them in U.S. dollar equivalents. To provide a measure of ABC's worldwide performance in the home currency, operating results and asset values denominated in foreign currencies must be *translated* into dollar equivalents.

Although there is a restatement of values into a different currency, there is no actual *conversion* of one currency into another.

Source: John P. Pringle, "Managing Foreign Exchange Exposure," *Journal of Applied Corporate Finance*, Winter 1991, pp. 73–82. Minor revisions made to reflect current practices.

---

the subsidiary. For example, a British subsidiary of a US parent firm will declare that the pound is its functional currency. Any foreign-currency income of the subsidiary (e.g. euros or Swiss francs earned by the British subsidiary) is translated into the functional currency according to the FAS 8 rules. After this, all amounts are translated from the functional currency into dollars at the current exchange rate.

2   Translation gains and losses are disclosed and accumulated in a separate account showing shareholders' equity. Only when foreign assets or liabilities are liquidated do they become transaction gains or losses and appear in the income statement (see Exhibit 10.2).[6]

6 See Exhibit 10.2 for more on the rules and rationale for the exchange rates used to compute gains or losses on assets and liabilities, and on where these gains or losses should appear.

EXHIBIT 10.2   FROM HISTORICAL TO CURRENT RATES: THE RATIONALE FOR A CHANGE IN APPROACH

US international accounting rules went through a major revision in 1982. The following excerpt, revised to reflect current practices, explains these revisions, their rationale, and the reasons it was decided to separate foreign exchange translation gains or losses from income.

What exchange rate should be used in making the translation?

This issue has been the center of a longstanding controversy among accountants and financial officers. Should it be the *current* exchange rate at the time the translation is done? Or should it be the *historical* rate at the time the asset or liability went on the books? It can make a big difference, especially in the case of long-lived items such as fixed assets.

Financial Accounting Standard #8, promulgated in the U.S. in 1975, mandated the so-called *temporal* method, which uses the rate at the time the asset or liability was booked. This meant different rates for different items.

FAS #8 was widely criticized and gave way to FAS #52 in 1982, which mandates the *current rate* method. Under the current rate method, all assets and liabilities are translated at the current exchange rate at the time of the translation; equity accounts are translated at historical rates; and income statement items are converted at a weighted average rate for the period.*

Translation *exposure* thus arises because changes in exchange rates change the dollar equivalents of foreign currencies. A profit of EUR (euro) 10 million in ABC-France would translate into USD (U.S. dollar) 11,764,706 at an exchange rate of EUR 0.85 per USD. But if the dollar strengthens to EUR

0.95 per USD, the same EUR 10 million falls to USD 10,526,316. An asset worth EUR 25 million translates into USD 29.41 million at an exchange rate of EUR 0.85 per USD, but into only USD 26.32 million at 0.95. In short, the USD representation of the asset's value depends on the exchange rate.

And so it should. The shareholders of the parent company ABC Corporation are ultimately interested in results expressed in dollar terms. And, for this reason, ABC Corporation's profits and market value are vulnerable to shifts in the EUR/USD exchange rate. There is no impact on the subsidiary's financial statements in EUR terms; the impact is only in the dollar equivalents. Note also that in this case there is no conversion of euros into actual dollars; we have merely expressed or translated EUR into U.S. dollar equivalents.

Note

* FAS #52 was promulgated in 1982 and made mandatory for US companies in 1983. It required the selection of a "functional currency" for foreign subsidiaries, defined as the currency of the "primary economic environment." If the US dollar were selected as the functional currency, the translation rules were identical to those of FAS #8. If the local currency were chosen, FAS #52 permitted two important changes: (1) it mandated the current rate method in place of the temporal method, thus permitting the use of the current forex (foreign exchange) rate for translating fixed assets: and (2) it allowed firms to separate transactions and translation exposures, and to charge translation gains and losses to a special equity account rather than running them through the profit and loss (P & L) statement, as had been required under FAS #8. Transaction gains and losses continued to go through the P & L as before.

Source: John J. Pringle, "Managing Foreign Exchange Exposure," *Journal of Applied Corporate Finance,* Winter 1991, pp. 73–82. Adapted to reflect current practices.

The rule on using current exchange rates on all items is relaxed when there is extremely high inflation in the country whose currency is being translated. Extremely high inflation means a cumulative amount of over 100 percent during the proceeding 3 years. If this condition is met, the temporal distinction used in FAS 8 still applies. This means that in circumstances of extreme inflation, current exchange rates are used for current-cost items such as financial assets and liabilities, and historical rates are used for historical-cost items. This means that different exchange rates are used within the same account for converting different items from the same foreign country/currency, something that some believe could add more confusion than clarity.

The best way to illustrate the effects of these accounting procedures is to take examples. However, before we consider these examples it is useful to define the concept of real changes in exchange rates. This is because our examples show not only the implications of US accounting principles for translation and transaction gains and losses but also the extent to which the accounts accurately reflect what has really happened to exchange rates.

REAL CHANGES IN EXCHANGE RATES

Definition of the real change in exchange rates

We can define a real change in exchange rates in this way:

A real change in exchange rates is a change that produces a difference between the rates of return on domestic versus foreign assets/liabilities or in the operating profitability of firms.

As we proceed, we shall see that in order for real changes in exchange rates to occur there must be *ex post* departures from interest parity or PPP. We have already seen that PPP departures are necessary for there to be exchange-rate *exposure*.[7] However, this is as far as the analogy goes. The real change in exchange rates is a measure of how much *a particular change in exchange rates* has affected domestic versus foreign returns or profitability. On the other hand, exchange-rate exposure is a measure of the sensitivity of asset or liability values or operating incomes to

exchange-rate values that could occur. Therefore, while the sources of exchange-rate exposure and of real changes in exchange rates are similar, they are measures of very different phenomena.[8]

Financial assets and liabilities and real changes in exchange rates

Suppose that Aviva Corporation, which we introduced in Chapter 8, has invested in British bonds. Let us assume that these are long-term bonds. Clearly, a depreciation of the British pound will decrease the dollar value of these financial securities when they are translated (i.e. converted) into dollars at the new exchange rate. But would we want to consider Aviva as being worse off by holding pound-denominated bonds rather than dollar-denominated bonds if the interest rates on the two bonds are different? Alternatively, under what circumstances would an appreciation of the pound make Aviva better off?

A depreciation of a currency that is fully compensated for in terms of higher interest rates on financial assets should not be considered a real depreciation from the point of view of these assets. For example, if the pound fell in value against the dollar by 10 percent but British interest rates were 10 percent higher than those in the United States, the firm would be no worse off from British than from US investments.[9] According to our definition of a real change in exchange rates, that is, a change which affects the rate of return on foreign versus domestic assets, we might therefore define the real change for financial assets held for a year as follows:

$$\text{Real change in } (\$/\pounds) = \left[\frac{S_1(\$/\pounds) - S(\$/\pounds)}{S(\$/\pounds)} \right] - (r_\$ - r_\pounds)$$

8 Indeed, the units of measurement are different. We measure real changes in exchange rates in percent, whereas exchange-rate exposure has the dimension of units of a particular currency.

9 For simplicity we talk here of countries rather than currencies. The currency difference is the important difference.

7 In Chapter 9 we showed that exposure on real assets and on operating incomes depend on departures from PPP.

$S_1(\$/£)$ is the actual spot rate at year end, and $r_\$$ and $r_£$ refer to interest earnings during that year. The definition consists of the actual proportional increase in the value of the pound – assuming $S_1(\$/£) > S(\$/£)$ – adjusted for the extent to which higher dollar versus pound interest rates have compensated for this percentage increase in the pound.

Because translation losses or gains are made on the interest earned on pound bonds as well as on the principal, a more precise definition is:

Real change in $(\$/£)$

$$= \frac{S_1(\$/£) - S(\$/£)}{S(\$/£)}(1 + r_£) - (r_\$ - r_£)$$

$$(10.1)$$

The real change of $\$/£$ shown in equation (10.1) is equal to the *ex post* deviation from unhedged interest-parity, which can be seen as follows.

Each dollar a US investor invests in Britain will buy $1/S(\$/£)$ of British pounds, which will pay back after 1 year

$$£\frac{1}{S(\$/£)}(1 + r_£)$$

If the British investment is not hedged by selling the pounds forward, the pounds will be sold and converted into dollars at the following year's spot rate, $S_1(\$/£)$, giving

$$\$\frac{S_1(\$/£)}{S(\$/£)}(1 + r_£)$$

The return from the unhedged British security is therefore this amount minus the original dollar invested, that is

$$\frac{S_1(\$/£)}{S(\$/£)}(1 + r_£) - 1$$

The difference between this return and the US dollar return is

$$\frac{S_1(\$/£)}{S(\$/£)}(1 + r_£) - (1 + r_\$)$$

By subtracting and adding $(1 + r_£)$ this can be written as

$$\frac{S_1(\$/£) - S(\$/£)}{S(\$/£)}(1 + r_£) + (1 + r_£)$$
$$- (1 + r_\$)$$

or

$$\frac{S_1(\$/£) - S(\$/£)}{S(\$/£)}(1 + r_£)$$
$$- (r_\$ - r_£)$$

$$(10.2)$$

Comparison of equation (10.2) with equation (10.1) shows that a real change in the exchange rate for financial securities occurs when there is an *ex post* departure from uncovered interest parity.

Financial assets and liabilities and financial accounts: learning by example

In order to describe how US international accounting principles show translation gains or losses on financial assets and liabilities, and to compare the situation shown by the accounting treatment with the definition of the real change in exchange rates, suppose that in the previous year Aviva placed $1 million in a US dollar long-term bond yielding 12 percent ($r_\$ = 0.12$), and $1 million in a pound long-term bond yielding 20 percent ($r_£ = 0.20$). Suppose that last year the spot rate was $S(\$/£) = 2.0$ and that during the year the pound depreciates to $S_1(\$/£) = 1.8$.

The actual pound depreciation is 10 percent. However, higher pound versus dollar interest rates make up for some of this. The real depreciation of the pound given by equation (10.1) is

$$\text{Real change in } (\$/£) = \frac{1.8 - 2.0}{2.0}(1.20)$$
$$- (0.12 - 0.20)$$
$$= -0.04$$

The negative value means a real depreciation of the pound of 4 percent, which is a real appreciation of the dollar. The 10 percent decline in the value of the

Table 10.1 *Earnings on domestic versus foreign financial assets*

Realized spot rate	Interest earnings	Declared income, FAS 52	Shareholder equity, FAS 52	Overall income	Real gain/loss on pound bond
$S_1(\$/£)$ = 1.8000	+$180,000	+$180,000	−$100,000	+$80,000	−$40,000
$S_1(\$/£)$ = 1.8667	+$186,667	+$186,667	−$66,667	+$120,000	$0
$S_1(\$/£)$ = 1.9000	+$190,000	+$190,000	−$50,000	+$140,000	+$20,000

pound is not fully compensated by the higher pound interest rate.

In terms of the financial accounts, after placing $1 million in the dollar bond for 1 year, there will be $120,000 in interest appearing in the income statement, and if interest rates and hence dollar bond prices do not change, there is no change in the value of financial assets. Therefore, total earnings on the dollar bond are $120,000. How does this compare to the pound bond?

Placing $1 million in a pound bond at the initial exchange rate $S(\$/£) = 2.0$ means investing £500,000. At $r_£ = 0.20$, this will earn £100,000. At the exchange rate of $1.8/£ at the end of the year, the £100,000 will be translated into $180,000 of income. This is shown as interest earnings in the top row of Table 10.1.

The £500,000 pound bond is worth only $900,000 at the rate of $1.8/£. Since the initial value was $1 million, there is a translation loss of $100,000. Under FAS 8 this would have appeared in the income account, but with the FAS 52 accounting procedure it will appear separately as shown in the third column of Table 10.1. We see that under the FAS 52 system, there is a declared income of $180,000 if the translation loss is not realized, that is, if the bond is not sold, and a $100,000 loss in the shareholder-equity account. Combining the shareholder-equity account with the declared income, we have an overall income on the pound bond of $180,000 − $100,000 = $80,000. Compared with the $120,000 that would have been earned on the dollar bond, this involves a relative loss of $40,000, which is 4 percent of the

original investment. The real depreciation or devaluation of 4 percent found from the FAS 52 procedure agrees with what we found in the definition, equation (10.1). But we note that we must include shareholder-equity effects if we are to make the correct judgment of the real change in the exchange rate from the accounting statements based on FAS 52.

If the exchange rate after a year of investment had moved to $S_1(\$/£) = 1.8667$, then the real change in the exchange rate would have been zero, since the definition, equation (10.1), tells us that

$$\frac{1.8667 - 2.0}{2.0}(1.20) - (0.12 - 0.20) = 0.0$$

This result occurs because the end-of-year exchange rate of $1.8667/£ is the rate that produces *ex post* unhedged interest-parity.[10]

In terms of the entries in the financial accounts, $1 million invested in the pound bond at $S(\$/£) = 2.0$ is £500,000, which as before earns £100,000. At $S_1(\$/£) = 1.8667$, the £100,000 of interest is worth $186,667. The translation loss on the financial asset at the realized exchange rate is $66,667 [= ($1.8667/£ × £ 500,000) − $1,000,000]. Using FAS 52, this gives total earnings

---

10 With $r_£ = 0.20$, $r_s = 0.12$, and $S(\$/£) = 2.0$ we can rearrange the unhedged interest-parity condition

$$S_1(\$/£) = S(\$/£)\frac{1 + r_s}{1 + r_£}$$

to find $S_1(\$/£) = 1.8667$.

of $120,000 (= $186,667 − $66,667) if we are careful to aggregate the interest earnings from the income account and the foreign exchange loss given in the separate shareholder-equity account. We obtain the same recorded earnings on both bonds, $120,000. This corresponds with the conclusion from equation (10.1) of no real change in the exchange rate.

If the pound falls in actual value by only 5 percent from $S(\$/£) = 2.0$ to $S_1(\$/£) = 1.9$, then the £100,000 in earnings from the pound bond will be worth $1.9/£ × £100,000 = $190,000, and the translation loss will be $50,000 [($1.9 × 500,000) − $1,000,000]. The total recorded earnings are therefore $140,000 ($190,000 − $50,000) if we are careful to include all earnings. This is $20,000 more than the earnings from the dollar bond, or a 2 percent extra return. Even though the pound has fallen in value, the compensation in the relatively higher British interest rate is a real gain from the British bond of 2 percent. This will be found as the real percentage change in the exchange rate from the definition, equation (10.1), but we again note that in order for the accounts to give the correct result, they must be integrated so that equity effects are added to income earned.

Judging the borrowing decision, which means judging financial liabilities, is the reverse of judging the investment decision, and we must reverse the interpretation of equation (10.1). When borrowing is unhedged, real borrowing costs are the same on foreign and domestic currency if the depreciation in the value of the foreign currency is compensated for by higher interest payments. There is an *ex post* real gain from borrowing foreign instead of domestic currency if the realized depreciation of the foreign currency is more than the extra interest rate that is paid on the foreign-currency borrowing. There is a real loss from borrowing foreign rather than domestic currency if the realized depreciation of the foreign currency is less than the extra interest paid. These effects can be found in financial statements using FAS 52, provided we integrate the shareholder-equity account with the income statement.

Fixed assets and real changes in exchange rates

If fixed-asset prices have risen at the rate $\dot{P}_{US}$ and the real rate of return (in the form of, e.g. rental income or dividends on the assets) has been, ρ_{US}, then the overall rate of return on each dollar of fixed assets held at home is [11]

$$\rho_{US} + \dot{P}_{US} \qquad (10.3)$$

Each dollar placed in British fixed assets that rose with inflation at $\dot{P}_{UK}$ with a rent or dividend rate of ρ_{UK} will produce, when translated at the new realized exchange rate $S_1(\$/£)$, dollar receipts of

$$\$ \frac{S_1(\$/£)}{S(\$/£)} (1 + \rho_{UK} + \dot{P}_{UK}) \qquad (10.4)$$

This is because the original dollar will purchase £$[1/S(\$/£)]$ of British fixed assets, on which there is a rental or dividend of ρ_{UK} and inflation of $\dot{P}_{UK}$, and which is translated back into dollars at $S_1(\$/£)$. The rate of return on the dollar invested in the British fixed asset is therefore

$$\frac{S_1(\$/£)}{S(\$/£)} (1 + \rho_{UK} + \dot{P}_{UK}) - 1 \qquad (10.5)$$

According to our definition of the real change in the exchange rate as the change causing a difference between the overall return on domestic versus foreign investments, from (10.5) minus (10.3)

11 We use the subscripts US and UK rather than $ and £ because fixed assets are specific to a *country*, not a *currency*. For simplicity we refer to US and British inflation even though we are dealing with asset prices, not with overall price levels. We do this because "fixed assets" is a big category, making it inappropriate to refer to the law of one price. Thinking in terms of inflation allows us to reach conclusions in terms of PPP which can be related to other parts of the book.

we have:

Real change in $(\$/£)$

$$= \left[\frac{S_1(\$/£)}{S(\$/£)} (1 + \rho_{UK} + \dot{P}_{UK}) - 1 \right]$$
$$- (\rho_{US} + \dot{P}_{US})$$

(10.6)

By adding and subtracting $\dot{P}_{UK}$ this can be written as

Real change in $(\$/£) = \frac{S_1(\$/£)}{S(\$/£)} (1 + \dot{P}_{UK})$
$$- (1 + \dot{P}_{UK}) + \dot{P}_{UK}$$
$$+ \frac{S_1(\$/£)}{S(\$/£)} \rho_{UK}$$
$$- \rho_{US} - \dot{P}_{US}$$

which by combining terms gives

Real change in $(\$/£)$

$$= \frac{S_1(\$/£) - S(\$/£)}{S(\$/£)} (1 + \dot{P}_{UK})$$
$$- (\dot{P}_{US} - \dot{P}_{UK})$$
$$- \left[\rho_{US} - \frac{S_1(\$/£)}{S(\$/£)} \rho_{UK} \right]$$

(10.7)

Examination of equation (10.7) shows that if rental or dividend yields in the United States and Britain are equal when we include the translation gain/loss in the British yield, that is, if $\rho_{US} = [S_1 (\$/£)/S(\$/£)]\rho_{UK}$, then equation (10.7) becomes

Real change in $(\$/£)$
$$= \dot{S}(1 + \dot{P}_{UK}) - (\dot{P}_{US} - \dot{P}_{UK})$$ (10.8)

where $S = [S_1(\$/£) - S(\$/£)]/S(\$/£)$ is the proportional change in the exchange rate. A comparison of equation (10.8) with the relative form of PPP in equation (7.7) shows that real changes in exchange rates on fixed assets require *ex post* deviations from PPP.[12] We recall that this conclusion also applies to real changes in exchange rates for the

operating profitability of firms; as we saw in our discussion of operating exposure in Chapter 9, a change in profitability requires *ex post* departures from PPP.

Fixed assets and financial accounts: learning by example

When we examine the financial accounts in order to judge the performance of domestic versus foreign fixed investments we face even more problems than with financial assets and liabilities. With financial assets and liabilities we can obtain the correct judgment as long as we are sure to include both the income and the separate shareholder-equity effects within total earnings. With fixed assets, this is not sufficient. Indeed, by including shareholder-equity effects as they are measured with the FAS 52 accounting procedure, we might distort the picture even more than by leaving these effects out of the calculations. These points are by no means obvious, so we will show them by taking an example.

Suppose that at the beginning of the previous year, $1 million was invested in US fixed assets that provided a 5 percent real rate of return and $1 million was invested in British fixed assets that provided a 5.5556 percent real rate of return. Suppose that during the previous year, inflation in the United States was 10 percent and inflation in Britain was 16 percent, with fixed-asset prices and general prices moving at the same rates. Suppose that at the beginning of the previous year the exchange rate was $2.0/£ and that by the end of the year it was $1.8/£. We have

$$\rho_{US} = 0.0500 \quad \rho_{UK} = 0.05556 \quad \dot{P}_{US} = 0.10$$
$$\dot{P}_{UK} = 0.16 \quad S(\$/£) = 2.0 \quad \text{and}$$
$$S_1(\$/£) = 1.8$$

What we want to know from the example is what we will find in a company's accounts.

The actual pound depreciation or devaluation is 10 percent. However, the higher inflation in asset values in Britain has made up for some of this. The real pound depreciation (dollar appreciation)

---

12 Alternatively, if we think of a specific type of fixed asset so that $\dot{P}_{US}$ and $\dot{P}_{UK}$ refer to specific prices, we can conclude that real changes in exchange rates require deviations from the law of one price rather than PPP.

Table 10.2 *Earnings on foreign fixed assets*

Realized spot rate	Rental or profit income	Translation gain		Income plus *declared* translation gain		Income plus *actual* translation gain	
		FAS 52	Correct method	FAS 52	Correct method	FAS 52	Correct method
$S_1(\$/£)$ = 1.8000	+$50,000	−$100,000	+$44,000	+$50,000	+$94,000	−$50,000	+$94,000

against which to judge the measured accounting effects is calculated with equation (10.7), which gives

Real change in $(\$/£)$

$$= \frac{1.8 - 2.0}{2.0}(1.16)$$
$$- (-0.06)$$
$$- \left(0.05 - \frac{1.8}{2.0}0.05556\right)$$
$$= -0.056, \text{ or } -5.6\%$$

Since the change is negative, we call it a real pound depreciation. It is smaller than the actual depreciation because the change in the exchange rate has been partially compensated by higher rates of return in Britain and higher inflation in the market value of British fixed assets. But what will the financial accounts show?

In terms of the financial accounts, the $1 million in the US fixed assets earned a return of $\rho_{US} \times \$1,000,000 = \$50,000$. In addition, the 10 percent inflation in the United States raised the dollar value of the fixed assets by $100,000, which is a "gain" to the company even if it does not show in accounts until it is realized. Therefore, the total earned on the US fixed asset is $150,000. How does this compare to the British asset?

The $1 million sent to Britain at $S(\$/£) = 2.0$ had an initial value of £500,000. At $\rho_{UK} = 0.05556$, the £500,000 earned $\rho_{UK} \times £500,000 = £27,778$. When translated into US dollars at the current exchange rate $S_1(\$/£)$ as current earnings, this £27,778 becomes $1.8/£ × £27,778 = $50,000 which appears in the income statement. The $50,000 is shown as the first item in Table 10.2. Translation

gains and losses – those resulting from converting foreign asset values into units of domestic currency – require more careful treatment than income on the investments.

With FAS 52, the values of fixed assets are translated at current exchange rates, but historical costs are used for the value of the assets in the local currency. The current exchange rate is $S_1(\$/£) = 1.8$, and the historical cost is £500,000, and so the value is recorded as $900,000. There is a translation loss of $100,000 from the original $1 million value of the British fixed asset. This is excluded from current income and goes only into the separate shareholder-equity account, and so the declared income is only the $50,000 of earnings.[13] However, if exchange rates do not return to the previous levels before the British fixed asset is sold, the $100,000 will appear as income when it becomes a transaction loss, showing a loss of −$50,000 ($50,000 − $100,000).

The economically correct method for handling foreign fixed assets uses the current exchange rate and the current market value of assets. This is different from both the current FAS 52 procedure and the older FAS 8 procedure. We note that by the year end, the initial £500,000 invested in the British fixed asset has increased with 16 percent inflation to £580,000. At the current exchange rate of $S_1(\$/£) = 1.8$, this translates into $1,044,000 on the income statement, and so there is a translation

---

13 Our treatment is valid for countries which do not suffer from extreme inflation and for which the straightforward forms of FAS 52 rules apply. Countries with extreme inflation (over 100 percent cumulative inflation in 3 years) continue to use the temporal distinction of FAS 8.

gain of $44,000 ($1,044,000 − $1,000,000). If this is included as income, the total earnings from Britain are $50,000 + $44,000 = $94,000, compared with the total return from US fixed assets of $150,000. The relative loss from the change in exchange rates is −$56,000 ($94,000 − $150,000), which is 5.6 percent of the original investment, the same as the real percentage change in exchange rate computed with equation (10.7). This correct result is in contrast with the outcome of FAS 52. When the shareholder-equity effect is included in FAS 52 and the total return from the British fixed asset is compared with the return from the US asset, we have a relative loss on the British asset of −$200,000 (−$50,000 − $150,000), implying a real change in exchange rate of −20 percent, far larger than the −5.6 percent obtained from equation (10.7). We do not obtain the correct picture from the FAS 52 procedure.

The relevance of translation exposure

FAS 8 rules were frequently criticized because by bringing translation gains and losses into income statements, corporate taxes were affected. While many were willing to accept *transaction* gains and losses as part of income – as they were under FAS 8

rules and continue to be under FAS 52 – *translation* gains or losses were another matter. In order to prevent volatile income from FAS 8 translation rules it was common for firms to hedge their accounting exposure. Some economists believed this hedging to be unnecessary because, on average, gains and losses from fluctuating exchange rates average out to zero. Therefore, provided that corporate tax rates are not progressive, the long-run situation should not be affected by what appeared in income statements from year to year. These economists also believed that actual and potential shareholders would be able to see through the veil of accounting rules to the true economic effects. Therefore, they believed that if a firm decided to hedge it should hedge against exposure as measured by β in equation (9.1), rather than hedge accounting exposure. However, as we shall see in Chapter 12, there are arguments that suggest that firms should not bother to hedge their exposure *whatever way it is measured*. Rather, a case can be made that if certain conditions are not present, hedging decisions should be left to the shareholders who can reduce exposure and risk by diversifying their portfolios, and who can hedge from their own personal perspectives.

SUMMARY

1 Accounting exposure concerns the effect that exchange rates have on values appearing in financial statements.

2 Translation risk and exposure have to do with how asset and liability values appear when converted into a firm's domestic reporting currency for inclusion in financial accounts. Transaction risk and exposure have to do with the effect of exchange rates on asset or liability values when they are liquidated.

3 The real change in exchange rates is the change that produces a difference between the rate of return on domestic versus foreign assets/liabilities, or in the profitability of firms.

4 There are no real changes in exchange rates on financial assets and liabilities if unhedged interest-parity always holds *ex post*.

5 There are no real changes in exchange rates for fixed (real) assets if PPP (or more precisely the law of one price) always holds *ex post*.

6   FAS 52 procedure values assets using historical costs and current exchange rates, but puts translation gains or losses in a separate shareholder equity account.

7   FAS 52 produces correct measures of real changes in exchange rates for financial assets if shareholder equity effects are included as part of income.

8   FAS 52 produces incorrect measures of real changes in exchange rates for fixed assets. Correct values on fixed assets require using current exchange rates and current market values.

REVIEW QUESTIONS

1   What is "accounting exposure?"

2   What are "translation risk" and "translation exposure?"

3   What are "transaction risk" and "transaction exposure?"

4   What is the nature of the "temporal distinction" under FAS 52 when inflation is high?

5   What is meant by a "real change in exchange rates?"

6   What is the relationship between *ex post* departures from uncovered interest parity and real changes in exchange rates for financial assets?

7   What items in the financial statements must be combined in order for accounting exposure on financial assets to reflect the real change in exchange rates?

8   What is the relationship between *ex post* departures from PPP and real changes in exchange rates for fixed assets?

9   How well do financial statements reflect real changes in exchange rates on fixed assets?

10 If the choice could be made between current exchange rates and current costs, and historical exchange rates and historical costs, what would you select in order to accurately reflect real changes in exchange rates in financial statements?

ASSIGNMENT PROBLEMS

1   Suppose you had invested $500,000 for 6 months in the United States and in Europe and interest rates and exchange rates are as follows:

$r_\$$	$r_{€}$	$S(\$/€)$	$S_{1/2}(\$/€)$
5%	8%	1.1000	1.0800

$S(\$/€)$ is the exchange rate when the investment was made, and $S_{1/2}(\$/€)$ is the actual rate 6 months later. Was foreign investment a good idea?

2   Using the information in Question 1, what values will appear in the income account and the shareholder-equity account with the FAS 52 accounting procedure?

3   Suppose you had invested $1 million in US fixed assets and in Italian fixed assets under
    the following conditions:

ρ_{US}	ρ_{IT}	$\dot{P}_{US}$	$\dot{P}_{IT}$	$S(\$/€)$	$S_1(\$/€)$
2%	4%	5%	4%	1.1500	1.1200

Assume that fixed-asset prices in local currency have kept pace with prices in general.

a   Which investment yielded higher returns over the year?

b   What will appear in the income statement and the shareholder equity
    account under the FAS 52 procedure?

c   What should appear as income?

d   Why does your answer to "b" (where income and shareholder equity are
    aggregated) disagree with your answer to "c"?

4   Redo the analysis in the text of a real change in exchange rates for financial liabilities
    instead of assets. Describe how a declining value of a currency of denomination of
    liabilities retires debt.

5   If capital moves around the world so that *expected* rates of return on fixed assets are
    the same, are overseas investors exposed to exchange rates?

6   Why do the FAS 52 rules for translating assets in very high inflation countries –
    accumulated inflation exceeding 100 percent in the previous 3 years – use
    a "temporal distinction?" (the temporal distinction involves translating current-cost
    items at current exchange rates and historical-cost items at historical exchange rates).

7   To what extent do you think that the difficulty of verifying declared current costs of
    fixed assets has limited the use of current cost – current exchange rate reporting
    in financial statements?

8   FAS 8 rules, which caused exchange rate effects to show directly in financial statements,
    caused managers to cover foreign exchange exposure very actively. Do you agree
    with the decision to hedge accounting exposure?

BIBLIOGRAPHY

Adler, Michael and Bernard Dumas, "Should Exposure Management Depend on Translation Accounting
    Methods?" *Economoney*, June 1981, pp. 132–8.

Carsberg, Bryan, "FAS #52 – Measuring the Performance of Foreign Operations," *Midland Corporate Finance
    Journal*, Summer 1983, pp. 48–55.

Evans, Thomas G. and Thimothy S. Doupnik, *Determining the Functional Currency under Statement 52*, Financial
    Accounting Standards Board, Stamford, CT, 1986.

Garlicki, T. Dessa, Frank J. Fabozzi, and Robert Fonfeder, "The Impact of Earnings under FAS 52 on Equity
    Returns," *Financial Management*, Autumn 1987, pp. 36–44.

Houston, Carol O., "Translation Exposure Hedging Post SFAS No. 52," *Journal of International Financial
    Management and Accounting*, Summer/Autumn 1990, pp. 145–70.

Miller, Martin A., *Comprehensive GAAP Guide*, Harcourt Brace Jovanovich, New York, 1989.

Pringle, John J., "Managing Foreign Exchange Exposure," *Journal of Applied Corporate Finance*, Winter 1991, pp. 73–82.

—— and Robert A. Connolly, "The Nature and Causes of Foreign Currency Exposure," *Journal of Applied Corporate Finance*, Fall 1993, pp. 61–72.

Rosenfeld, Paul, "Accounting for Foreign Operations," *Journal of Accountancy*, August 1987, pp. 103–12.

Shapiro, Alan, C., *Statement of Financial Accounting Standards No. 52 – Foreign Currency Translation*, Financial Accounting Standards Board, Stamford, CT, December 1981.

Wyman, Harold E., "Analysis of Gains and Losses from Foreign Monetary Items: An Application of Purchasing Power Parity Concepts," *The Accounting Review*, July 1976, pp. 545–58.

Chapter 11

Operating exposure

International companies now know that what happens to the currencies in which they tot up the costs, revenues and assets affects their results as much as their success in making and selling products.

The Economist, April 4, 1987

This chapter explains the implications of exchange rates for the revenues, costs, and profits of companies directly or indirectly involved in international commerce, and is hence concerned with **operating exposure**. For example, it describes the effects of exchange rates on an exporter's product price and sales (which affect cash inflows) as well as on production costs (which affect cash outflows). It explains how the elasticity of demand for a company's products, the types of inputs used, and other market factors influence the extent to which profits are affected by exchange rates. We discover, for example, how the effect of changes in exchange rates depends on such things as the use of internationally traded inputs that may cost more after devaluation, the flexibility of production to meet changes in demand due to changes in exchange rates, the time span considered, and the degree of competition faced in the markets where goods are sold.

We reach the important conclusion in this chapter that even if a company has hedged its foreign-currency receivables and payables and has no foreign assets or liabilities, there is still an important element of foreign exchange exposure. This is the operating exposure which occurs because current and, more importantly, future profits from operations depend on exchange rates. The techniques used for

hedging assets and liabilities are not designed to eliminate operating exposure. Indeed, because operating exposure is so difficult to eliminate, it has been called **residual foreign exchange exposure**.

OPERATIONS AFFECTED BY EXCHANGE RATES

Before beginning, we should point out that some firms face operating exposure without ever dealing in foreign exchange. For example, restaurants in US resorts that are visited by foreign tourists gain or lose customers according to the exchange rate. US restaurants also gain or lose domestic customers with changes in exchange rates that affect the vacation destinations of American travelers: exchange rates influence whether American tourists travel abroad or vacation at home. This exposure happens despite the fact that the US restaurants are generally paid in US dollars and pay for food, labor, rent, and interest in US dollars. Similarly, industries which compete with imported goods face operating exposure. For example, US firms that supply beef to US supermarkets and that never see foreign exchange can find stiffer competition from foreign beef suppliers when the US dollar gains against other suppliers' currencies, lowering prices of the non-US product. Any company that uses inputs that are internationally tradable, whether imported or not, will find costs changing with exchange rates. For example, a US company using oil from Texas will find the price of oil increasing with a decline in the foreign exchange value of the dollar.[1] Companies can even be affected by exchange rates of countries with which they have no trading relationship. For example, a German car manufacturer can be hurt by a decline in the Japanese yen even if the company does not export to Japan and German consumers do not buy from Japan. This can happen if the German manufacturer sells cars in the United States, and if American car buyers see German and Japanese cars as alternatives.

Since the links in the economic chain of interdependence are many, industries that provide supplies to US resort hotels, US beef producers, or other industries more directly involved in international trade will find themselves affected by changes in exchange rates. That is, there can be indirect effects of exchange rates via derived demand from others who are directly affected. Even banks with no international asset or liability positions can be affected by exchange rates in their loan portfolios. If they have made loans to companies whose fortunes depend on exchange rates, their own fortunes also depend on exchange rates through the ability of borrowers to repay loans. Governments whose tax base includes corporate income are exposed to the extent that profitability depends on exchange rates.[2] It should therefore be apparent that operating exposure requires an extremely broad perspective. It should also be apparent that operating exposure is difficult to avoid with the exposure-reducing techniques we have met so far: forwards, futures and so on are geared to current, known payments or receipts rather than to future operating consequences of exchange rates. Let us begin by examining what influences the extent of operating exposure. We start with exporters. What we say about exporters also applies to import competers because both gain when their own country's currency declines, making foreign competitors' goods more expensive (an import competer is a domestic company that faces competition from foreign firms in the domestic market).

THE EXPORTER

Competitive markets in the short run

The most straightforward situation of operating exposure involves an export-oriented company facing perfectly elastic demand, meaning that it can sell as much as it wishes without affecting the market price. To put this in context, let us suppose that before a devaluation of the US dollar, Aviva Corporation was able to sell in Britain all the jeans that it wished to produce at a pound price of $p_1^{\pounds}$ a pair. The pound superscript denotes that the price is expressed in terms of pounds, the currency the British buyer pays. After devaluation, Aviva Corporation will still be able to sell all the jeans it wishes at this same price. This is because in a competitive market, there are many other firms – at home, in Britain, and around the world – that are prepared to supply similar jeans. There is no reason for the non-US suppliers, including the British, to change their pound prices just because the United States has experienced a depreciation/devaluation.[3]

---

1 It is sometimes erroneously thought that because oil prices are usually quoted in dollars, the dollar price does not depend on exchange rates. A weaker dollar means more dollars are required to buy internationally tradable products because market prices are determined in the global marketplace.

2 This could provide a motive for a country to issue some foreign-currency debt. Then if the country's currency appreciates and this reduces the tax base from lower international competitiveness, the country has an offsetting gain in its balance sheet through a reduction in the domestic-currency value of its foreign currency-denominated debt.

3 Henceforth, by "devaluation" we mean either devaluation, which occurs with fixed exchange rates, or depreciation, which occurs with flexible exchange rates. Similarly, "revaluation" refers either to revaluation, which happens with fixed rates, or appreciation, which happens with flexible rates.

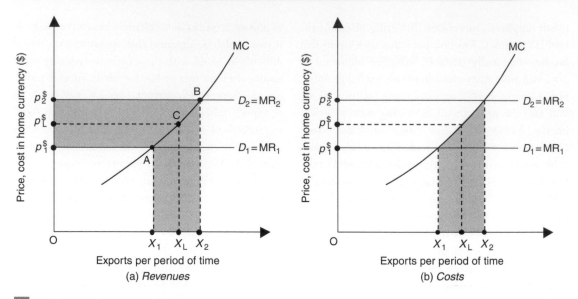

Figure 11.1 *Exporter and devaluation in a competitive market*

Notes

A depreciation or devaluation raises the price an exporter can charge in terms of his or her own currency. In the perfectly competitive situation the price rises by the percentage of devaluation/depreciation. This raises profit-maximizing output, sales revenues, and the total cost of production. In the long run, new firms and the expansion of older firms reduce prices, output, and profits towards original levels. If the country's exporters are a small part of the overall market, some benefits will remain.

If the pound price is unchanged by devaluation this means that Aviva can charge a higher US dollar price: there are more dollars to the pound after dollar devaluation.

We can go further in this competitive situation and say precisely how much higher the new dollar price, $p_2^\$$, will be relative to the dollar price before the devaluation, $p_1^\$$. To determine this, note that before the devaluation the dollar price of jeans sold in Britain for $p_1^£$ is

$$p_1^\$ = S(\$/£)p_1^£ \tag{11.1}$$

This equation merely defines the relationship between the price charged in Britain in pounds and the equivalent price in dollars. After dollar devaluation to an exchange rate of $S'(\$/£)$, and with the pound price unchanged at $p_1^£$, the dollar-equivalent price is:

$$p_2^\$ = S'(\$/£)p_1^£ \tag{11.2}$$

Taking the ratio of equation (11.2) to equation (11.1), we have

$$\frac{p_2^\$}{p_1^\$} = \frac{S'(\$/£)}{S(\$/£)}$$

This tells us that after a devaluation of the dollar to $S'(\$/£)$, the US dollar-equivalent price of jeans in Britain will rise by the same percent as the dollar devaluation. This is the direct result of the pound price of the jeans being unchanged.[4]

The pre-devaluation and post-devaluation prices, $p_1^\$$ and $p_2^\$ = [S'(\$/£)/S(\$/£)]p_1^\$$, are shown in Figure 11.1, where the price axes are drawn in home-currency (\$) units. In this figure we assume that none of the inputs used by Aviva are internationally tradable so that their prices are unaffected by the exchange rate. As a result, the marginal cost (MC) curve does not shift. Note that it is the international *tradability* of inputs, not whether

---

4 For simplicity, we assume inflation is zero in both countries.

inputs are *imported* that determines whether devaluation increases input costs. After a devaluation, domestically produced inputs which could be sold abroad increase in price because the opportunity cost of selling them at home is higher. Of course, by definition, imported inputs are tradable and therefore cost more after devaluation. However, so do domestically produced goods that could be sold overseas. For the time being we assume no internationally tradable inputs.

While the MC curve itself does not shift, the MC per unit does increase as output increases. Because the firm is in a perfectly competitive market, the demand curve is a horizontal line at the market price, and the horizontal demand curve is also the marginal revenue (MR) curve: more goods can be sold without reducing the price.

In Figure 11.1, before the devaluation, our firm, Aviva Corporation, would have produced and sold X_1 units per period by seeking its optimum output where marginal revenue MR_1 equals marginal cost, MC. This is the point of maximum profit. If output is less than X_1, $MR > MC$, and profit is increased by producing more and adding more revenue than costs. At an output greater than X_1, we have $MC > MR$, and profit is increased by producing less and thereby reducing costs by more than revenue.

With the price and hence MR of jeans in dollar terms rising to $p_2^\$ = [S'(\$/\pounds)/S(\$/\pounds)]p_1^\$$ after the devaluation, and the MC remaining unchanged, Aviva will want to raise its production to X_2 per period. This is the new profit-maximizing output, where $MR_2 = MC$. We find that a higher price in dollars and a higher level of sales have resulted from the devaluation.

Figure 11.1a shows how total revenue in units of domestic currency increases as a result of the higher price and the greater quantity sold. Total revenue increases by the shaded area as shown in Figure 11.1a. We conclude that there is an unambiguous increase in total revenue measured in terms of home currency after a devaluation. A simple reversal of interpretation in the diagram to determine the effects of a *revaluation* would similarly show that there would be an unambiguous decrease in total

revenue for an exporter when measured in terms of the home currency: the dollar price and number of units sold would both be reduced.

In the short run, if no US inflation results from the dollar devaluation, and if per-unit costs of inputs are unaffected by devaluation because they are not tradable, the total production cost will rise by only the cost of producing the additional quantity that is sold. Since MC is the cost of producing each additional item, the area under the MC curve between X_1 and X_2 will be the additional cost incurred in providing the extra goods. Hence, the total manufacturing cost will increase by the shaded area as shown in Figure 11.1b. We can see that with total revenue rising by the shaded area seen in Figure 11.1a and total cost rising by the shaded area in Figure 11.1b, profit, which rises by the difference between total revenue and total cost, will rise by the area $p_1^\$ AB p_2^\$$ in Figure 11.1a. We find that after a devaluation, the increase in export revenues exceeds the increase in costs, so that profits rise.

What are the factors affecting the amount by which profits will increase? We note that with $p_2^\$$ exceeding $p_1^\$$ by the percentage of the devaluation, the increase in profits in terms of dollars – assuming that output remains at X_1 – will be equal to the percentage of the devaluation multiplied by the original total dollar revenue. For example, with a 10 percent devaluation, $p_2^\$$ exceeds $p_1^\$$ by 10 percent, and so if initial revenues were \$1,000, nominal profits will rise by \$100, assuming the quantity sold does not increase. However, in general we might expect output to increase because of upward slope in the MC curve. Then there is an increase in the profit-maximizing output, and profits will rise by an even bigger percentage than the percentage of devaluation. This is clear from Figure 11.1a by comparing the size of the extra profit, shown by area $p_1^\$ AB p_2^\$$, with the original revenue given by the unshaded rectangle, $Op_1^\$ AX_1$.

We notice also from Figure 11.1 that the flatter is the MC curve, the greater is the increase in profit resulting from a devaluation. That is, production flexibility increases the profit gained from a devaluation. This is what one would expect, namely, that firms that are able to increase production benefit more after devaluation than firms that are producing at capacity. The reader is urged to draw Figure 11.1a with MC curves of different slopes and show that changes in profits are larger with a flatter curve. In redrawing Figure 11.1, allow all MC curves to pass through point A.

When asked what effect devaluation will have on a company's profit, many managers say things such as: "every one-percent decline in the value of our currency increases our company's profit by one-million dollars." When asked how they come up with that amount, a common explanation is "total revenue is one-hundred million dollars, so a one-percent increase in amount of domestic currency received for each unit of foreign exchange is one million dollars." What we can see from Figure 11.1 is that this view of the impact of devaluation on an exporter's profit is correct in a perfectly competitive market if the company is producing at capacity – resulting in a vertical MC curve – and if unit costs at any given output do not increase. For costs not to increase, inputs must not be internationally tradable. As we have stated, tradable input prices are determined in the world market and cost more in terms of a devalued currency. When the firm is not producing at capacity and does use tradable inputs it is necessary to consider the cost side of operations as well as revenues to determine the consequences of devaluation of revaluation.

Long-run effects: tradable inputs

Since the accurate forecasting of cash flows is an important job for the financial manager, we should not limit our discussion to the immediate effects of devaluation on flows of revenue and production costs. When we are dealing with a firm in an industry with free entry of new firms and where existing firms can expand output, it is important to appreciate that increases in profit that accompany devaluation may be temporary.[5] The additional

profit that might be available after a real devaluation (i.e. one that does not just make up for differences in inflation between countries) will serve as an incentive for new firms to get involved and existing firms to expand. This will reduce the product price via an increase in market supply. This can bring the rate of profit back to its pre-devaluation level. Therefore, it is possible that only in the interim will higher-than-normal profits be made. Let us show this conclusion graphically.

The immediate higher profits after devaluation will induce firms in purely domestic endeavors to move into the export sector until the "last" firm to enter can reap a profit equal to the best it could achieve in some alternative endeavor. Competition from new firms might move the price that the original firms such as Aviva receive for their product back towards $p_1^\$$. As a result, we would move back towards the pre-devaluation situation of price $p_1^\$$ and output X_1 with original revenues and costs. Extra profits will last only as long as it takes for old firms to expand and new firms to get involved. This will depend largely on the nature of the industry.

It is important to note that if the devaluing country produces only a small fraction of the world's output of a particular good, then the free entry of firms *within* the country may have little effect when cutting into the extra profit from devaluation. This is true because many new firms might enter the industry within the devaluing country without significantly affecting the world price. What is required for profits to persist is that the country with the devalued currency remains a small part of the world market. We can think of the devaluation as favoring only producers within the country. Other world producers do not enjoy the "subsidy" enjoyed by the firms in the devaluing country.[6] If the devaluing country does remain a small part of the world market, prices might move

---

5 The characteristics of perfectly elastic demand and free entry are elements of a perfectly competitive industry. However, as we shall see, free entry *within* the devaluing country may still leave profit, so the situation is a little different from the usual perfectly competitive case.

6 A devaluation can be thought of as a subsidy to exporters offset by a tax on importers. The fact that only firms in the devaluing country receive the "subsidy" is why we can have free entry into the industry globally as we do in perfect competition, and yet still have long-term abnormal profit after devaluation.

back very little from $p_2^\$$, perhaps only to $p_L^\$$ in Figure 11.1. Output would be X_L. Profits would remain abnormally high and be given by area $p_L^\$ CAp_1^\$$. Furthermore, industry-level profits are higher from the profits of newly entering firms as well as the original firms.

There is another route that is possible through rising costs that can also limit the period of obtaining extra profit after a real devaluation and hence limit the post-devaluation celebrations of an exporter. This involves the eventual reduction in the *real* devaluation via the inflation that the *actual* devaluation itself sets up. This will work in all market settings, not only in competitive markets, and so we will consider the effect separately. The effect will come about even if none of the inputs used by the firm under consideration are tradable, in which case there is no immediate increase in the firm's costs. Cost increases may nevertheless take place eventually.

Tradable consumer goods prices tend to rise after a depreciation or devaluation. To the extent that tradable products figure in the cost-of-living

index, a devaluation increases the cost of living and thereby reduces the buying power of wages. If efforts to maintain real or price-adjusted wages result in nominal wage increases to compensate for the higher cost of living, then the firm's production costs will rise. That is, the firm's production costs can increase because of indirect effects of devaluation-induced price increases on wages, even if there are no direct effects on input prices. Figure 11.2 describes the effect of higher wages caused by the devaluation.

In Figure 11.2a, we show the MC of production rising from MC to MC_L and average cost rising from AC to AC_L. Every unit is shown to cost more to produce as nominal wages rise. We can think of MC and AC moving up by the US inflation rate that is induced by the devaluation. If a devaluation increases the dollar price of the product from $p_1^\$$ to $p_2^\$$, and devaluation-induced inflation increases costs to MC_L and AC_L, output goes from X_1 to X_L and total revenue increase from $Op_1^\$ SX_1$ to $Op_2^\$ TX_L$. Total cost is AC multiplied by the output, which before the devaluation was $Op_1^\$ VX_1$. After the

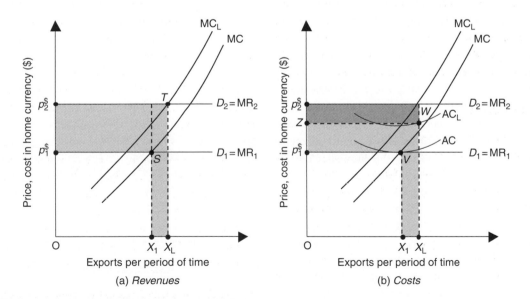

Figure 11.2 *Exporter and devaluation in a competitive market: effect of cost increases*

Notes
A devaluation raises the costs of tradable inputs and may eventually raise all costs. This means a reduction in the extent of the real devaluation. Profit-maximizing output and profits return toward original levels. However, as long as some real devaluation remains, there are extra sales and profits for exporters from devaluation.

devaluation, at the output X_L, the total cost is area $OZWX_L$. This cost exceeds the pre-devaluation cost by the lightly shaded area in Figure 11.2b. Since revenues increase by the shaded area in Figure 11.2a, or the entire shaded area in Figure 11.2b, and costs rise by the lightly shaded area in Figure 11.2b, profits rise by the difference, shown by the darkly shaded rectangle in Figure 11.2b.[7]

In the long run, the dampening effect on profits from the competition-induced price reduction shown in Figure 11.1a must be added to the profit reduction from higher costs. Both effects contribute to a smaller profit increase from devaluation in the long-run than occurs in the short run.

The effect of having internationally tradable inputs is, diagrammatically, precisely the same as the effect of wage pressure from devaluation-induced inflation that we have just discussed. Consequently, Figure 11.2 also describes the effect of having tradable inputs. Devaluation makes tradable inputs more expensive. As a result, MC and AC both shift upward to the extent that tradable inputs figure in production. We know that this vertical shift will be less than the shift in the selling price when at least some inputs are non-tradable. As before, the shift is given in Figure 11.2 by the MC_L and AC_L curves, and the output increase is smaller than it would be without tradable inputs. Output increases to X_L, where MC_L cuts D_2. Profits rise by the darkly shaded area in Figure 11.2b.

The difference between the effect of tradable inputs and of wage increases from devaluation-induced inflation is only in the immediateness of effect, with input prices probably rising much more quickly than with the link through wages. We should remember, however, that tradable input and wage effects can work together in the long run. From this point on, we shall consider only the

short run. We shall see that this can become complicated enough.

Imperfect competition

There are a large number of imperfect-market settings, but in general an imperfectly competitive firm can still sell some of its product if it raises the price. This is the case when only imperfect substitutes are available, and occurs frequently, since products of different firms generally have different characteristics.

To examine a firm like Aviva in an imperfect-market setting, we allow for some inelasticity in demand; that is we draw a conventional downward-sloping demand curve. When, as before, the home currency is on the vertical axis, what is the effect on the demand curve of a devaluation? We shall see that the demand curve and associated MR curve will move vertically upward, just as in a competitive market. Indeed, the argument will differ little from the one we used in the discussion of perfectly elastic demand.

Let us consider any particular sales volume on demand curve D_1 in Figure 11.3, for example, X_1. Note that when the demand curve is at the

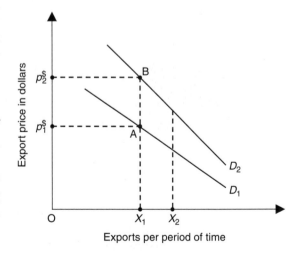

Figure 11.3 Devaluation and the demand curve

Notes
For each sales level, the price that can be charged after the devaluation with sales unchanged rises by the percentage of the devaluation. This means that the demand curve shifts vertically upwards by the percentage of the devaluation.

---

7 To simplify the argument, we have drawn area $Op_1^\$ SX_1$ so that it is equal to area $Op_1^\$ VX_1$. This means that before the devaluation, total revenue equals total cost, and profits are zero. Any profit after the devaluation is a result of the devaluation itself. We have also simplified the argument by ignoring the long-run envelope of AC curves.

pre-devaluation level, D_1, a volume X_1 can be sold at the exporter's currency (dollar) price $p_1^\$$. After the devaluation, the same quantity – that is, X_1 – will be sold abroad if the foreign-currency price is still the same as other suppliers. Sales depend on the price buyer's faces, and if Aviva keeps its pound price in line with the prices charged by other suppliers to the British market it will remain competitive. This is because the British do not look at the price tag of a pair of US-made jeans on sale in Britain in terms of the US dollar. Rather, they consider the number of pounds that must be paid for the jeans, just as a US car buyer considers the dollar price of an imported car. But at the devalued exchange rate of the dollar the unchanged pound price means a higher dollar price. Indeed, the dollar price is higher by the percent of dollar devaluation. In other words, if the dollar price changes by the amount of devaluation from $p_1^\$$ to $p_2^\$$ in Figure 11.3, then sales will remain unchanged at X_1. That is, before the devaluation at price $p_1^\$$ Aviva will sell X_1 abroad and hence be at point A. After the devaluation, Aviva

will sell the same amount, X_1, abroad if the dollar price is $p_2^\$ = [S'(\$/\pounds)/S(\$/\pounds)]p_1^\$$. This gives point B. We find that the percent vertical shift of the demand curve is equal to the percent of devaluation.

We can now take another sales volume, say X_2, and follow precisely the same argument. Each and every point on the new demand curve, D_2, will be vertically above the old demand curve, D_1, in proportion to the devaluation.

We should think in terms of vertical movements of the demand curve, rather than think of "rightward shifts" of the demand curve along the lines that "more is sold for the same dollar price after devaluation." Although this is true, it does not tell us how much the demand curve shifts, whereas we know the vertical shift is in the same proportion as the change in the exchange rate. Of course, we notice that since the vertical shift is always in the same *proportion* as the change in exchange rate, the *absolute* shift is less at lower prices on the demand curve. This is shown in Figure 11.3, with demand curve D_2 closer to D_1 at lower prices.

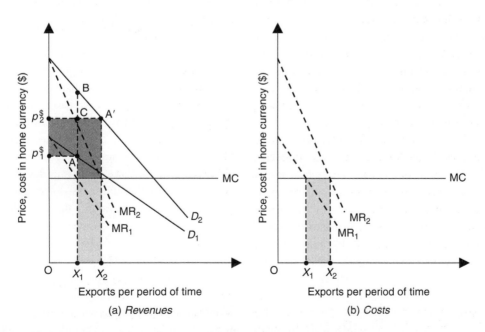

Figure 11.4 Exporter and devaluation in an imperfectly competitive market

Notes
In an imperfectly competitive market the home-currency price of exports will increase by a smaller percentage than the devaluation. Sales revenue will increase by a smaller fraction than in the case of perfect competition.

Figure 11.4a shows the vertical shift in the demand curve (D_1 to D_2) from a US dollar devaluation, along with the corresponding shift in the MR curve. We have assumed that costs do not depend on output in Figure 11.4b by drawing a flat MC. It would complicate matters only a little to allow for increasing costs with increasing output by drawing an upward-sloping MC curve and associated AC curve. Rising costs would reduce the positive effects of devaluation on profits, but they would not eliminate these effects. We have also assumed no tradable inputs.

We see from Figure 11.4 that before the devaluation, the firm will produce X_1 per period, which is where $MC = MR_1$, and it will be able to sell this output at the price $p_1^\$$. After the devaluation, the firm will produce X_2 per period and sell this at the price $p_2^\$$. The increase in revenue from $Op_1^\$ A X_1$ to $Op_2^\$ A' X_2$ is represented by the total shaded area in Figure 11.4a. An important point to realize is that with a downward-sloping curve, the price increase from $p_1^\$$ to $p_2^\$$ is less than the vertical shift in the demand curve ($AC < AB$). We discover that export prices when stated in the exporter's own currency rise by *less than* the percentage of devaluation. This is different from the case of perfect competition, where the product price rises by an amount *equal* to the devaluation.

With output rising from X_1 to X_2, and with each unit costing the manufacturer the amount given by the height of the MC curve, total cost increases by the lightly shaded area in Figure 11.4b (shown also in Figure 11.4a). Profits increase by the difference between the change in total revenue, given by the total shaded area in Figure 11.4a, and the change in total cost, given by the lightly shaded area. The change in profits is therefore represented by the darkly shaded area in Figure 11.4a, which is the difference between the total shaded area and the lightly shaded area.

In general, the extent to which prices rise, output increases, and profits are affected depends on the slope (elasticity) of the demand curve and the slope of the MC curve, which we have made horizontal so that profits can be easily computed. The reader might note that if the firm is up against a rigid constraint in raising output, then MC can be

vertical, and a devaluation will leave output and sales unchanged, with domestic-currency prices rising by the full percentage of devaluation — just as in the case of perfect competition. Supporting this implication of a production capacity constraint is the observation that, for example, auto exporters have typically raised their home-currency prices in proportion to any devaluation; that is, they have usually left foreign prices unchanged. This has been attributed to their inability to raise output in the short run. Why lower your foreign-currency selling price if you cannot satisfy any extra demand that this might create? Similarly, when facing a revaluation of their currency, they have lowered their own-currency price in proportion to the revaluation to leave the foreign-currency price unchanged. The slopes of the demand and cost curves are seen to be vital parameters for effective financial planning in an exporting firm. The demand sensitivity of the firm should be estimated, and the degree of capacity utilization should be measured to determine the response to changes in exchange rates.

Analysis in foreign-currency units

So far we have measured the vertical axes in our diagrams in units of the domestic currency, which we have taken as the US dollar. By drawing our diagrams in terms of what we have taken to be the home currency, we have been able to examine the effects of exchange-rate changes when these effects are measured in the same units. Our revenue, cost, and profit changes that result from devaluations or revaluations are therefore US dollar amounts; in general, they are the amounts that are relevant for US firms. Some firms that are operating within a country, however, will be concerned with revenues, costs, and profits in some particular foreign-currency unit. For example, a British firm with a manufacturing operation in the United States may not be directly concerned with whether devaluation of the US dollar raises its US-dollar earnings. Since the dollar is less valuable after devaluation, the higher US-dollar earnings might bring fewer pounds than before the devaluation, or so it might seem.

Similarly, a US firm with a subsidiary in, for example, Canada, may not be thrilled if a depreciation of the Canadian dollar raises the Canadian-dollar earnings of its subsidiary. These higher earnings might, it might seem, be worth less in US dollars. However, as we shall show, these possibilities need not concern parent firms.

Interest in the effects of a devaluation or revaluation, when measured in foreign-currency units, may not be limited to firms with subsidiaries abroad. Any firm that denominates borrowing in a foreign currency – even if it enjoys only one location – will care about the effect of exchange-rate changes on its operating revenues, measured in units of the currency of its debt. For example, a US firm that has borrowed in British pounds will care about its trading revenues as measured in pounds after an exchange-rate change: the firm has payables in British pounds. Similarly, Canadian firms that borrow in US dollars care about their US-dollar

revenues, since they must service US-dollar debts. For these reasons, we should consider the effects of exchange-rate changes on revenues, costs, and profits when measured in units of foreign currency. We will limit our discussion to an imperfectly competitive market; the simple case with a flat demand curve and an upward-sloping MC curve is similar and is left as an exercise for the reader.

As we said, the price that is relevant to a purchaser of a product is the price he or she has to pay in terms of his or her own currency. When the price of Aviva jeans in Britain remains unchanged in terms of British pounds but changes in terms of US dollars, there is no reason for sales volumes in Britain to change. It follows that when there is, for example, a devaluation of the US dollar, there is no reason for the demand curve for Aviva's jeans to shift if it is drawn against the pound price. At the same pound price as before, the same monthly volume of jeans will be sold. Therefore, the demand curve in

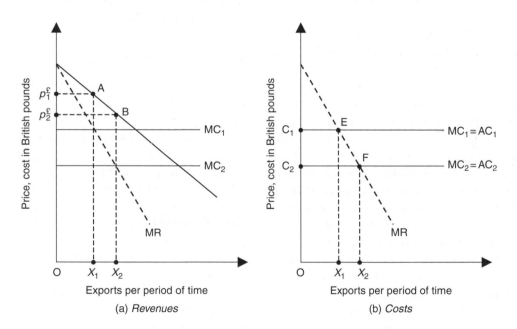

Figure 11.5 *Exporter and devaluation in an imperfectly competitive market: foreign-currency units*

Notes
The relevant price for demanders is the price denominated in their own, that is, the buyers' currency. When we measure the vertical axis in the buyers' currency, the positions of the demand and MR curves are unaffected by changes in exchange rates: buyers move along the curves. If there are no tradable inputs so production costs are unchanged in the producers' currency, a devaluation of that currency will lower costs denominated in the buyers' currency by the percent of devaluation. The export price will decline in the buyers' currency after a devaluation, and the quantity of exports will increase.

Figure 11.5, and hence also the MR curve, are the same before and after the devaluation.

The effect of changes in exchange rates on the cost curves is different from the effect on the demand curve. When our diagrams are drawn in units of foreign currency and there is an exchange-rate change, the cost curves will move vertically in proportion to the exchange rate. Why is this so?

If it costs, say, $MC_1^\$$ to produce an extra pair of Aviva's jeans and no inputs are tradable, then after a devaluation the production cost should still be $MC_1^\$$ if the devaluation has not induced general inflation. However, before the devaluation, with an exchange rate of $S(\$/£)$, the cost in units of foreign exchange was

$$MC_1^£ = \frac{1}{S(\$/£)} MC_1^\$$$

After the devaluation to $S'(\$/£)$, with the dollar cost the same, the foreign exchange cost becomes

$$MC_2^£ = \frac{1}{S'(\$/£)} MC_1^\$$$

By simply taking ratios, we get

$$\frac{MC_2^£}{MC_1^£} = \frac{S(\$/£)}{S'(\$/£)}$$

That is, the MCs, in terms of British pounds, change in proportion to the exchange rate. Since a devaluation of the dollar means that $S'(\$/£) > S(\$/£)$, the MC, in terms of British pounds, falls as the dollar is devalued. In Figure 11.5, this is shown with MC curve moving downward from MC_1 to MC_2. Since we have drawn Figure 11.5 with a constant MC, we know that $MC = AC$, and so the AC curve moves downward with the devaluation of the dollar when the vertical axis is in British pounds.

With profit maximization requiring that $MC = MR$, we see from Figure 11.5 that a devaluation of the US dollar increases Aviva's profit-maximizing output from X_I to X_2, With the demand curve remaining at D, the pound price falls from $p_1^£$ to $p_2^£$. We see that even with the demand curve unaffected by a devaluation, the devaluation lowers the foreign exchange price of exports and raises the

quantity sold.[8] With lower prices and higher sales – movements in opposite directions – what has happened to total revenue in terms of the British pound?

The answer clearly depends on whether sales have risen by a larger or smaller proportion than the reduction in the pound price. If the increase in quantity sold is greater than the price reduction, total revenue will be higher. Such a situation requires that the elasticity of demand exceed unity, that is, demand is elastic, which we know to be the case by making a straightforward observation. Since MC is positive, and the firm produces where $MR = MC$, MR must also be positive. With MR positive, an extra unit of sales, even though it requires a reduction in price, must increase total revenue. We know, therefore, that pound total revenue must rise, with area $Op_2^£BX_2$ necessarily greater than area $Op_1^£AX_1$.

Figure 11.5b gives the required curves for considering the effect of a devaluation on total cost. Since total cost is given by AC multiplied by output, whether total cost has increased depends on the slope of MR. Total cost has changed from area OC_1EX_1 to area OC_2FX_2 in Figure 11.5b. Has total cost increased, and if so, by how much? Well, continuing at this point without the help of mathematics is difficult. Mathematics helps us show that for profitable firms, total cost in terms of pounds increases after the dollar is devalued, but by a smaller amount than the increase in total revenue. In terms of pounds, profit is therefore increased.

THE IMPORTER

It is generally presumed that importers lose from devaluation and gain from revaluation of their own currency. This presumption is correct, with the exact magnitude of effect of exchange rates depending on such factors as the degree of competition and which currency we use for our analysis. The amount of

---

8 By referring back to the equivalent home-currency diagram, Figure 11.4, the reader will see that while the pound price *falls*, devaluation *raises* the export price in terms of dollars (from $p_1^\$$ to $p_2^\$$).

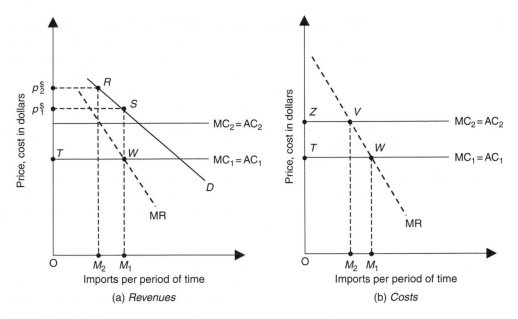

Figure 11.6 *The importer and a devaluation*

Notes
If the price that an importer pays is unchanged in terms of the foreign supplier's currency after the importer's currency is devalued, the cost curves will move up by the percentage of devaluation when measured against the importer's currency. The demand curve is not affected if it is drawn against the demander's currency. Only the amount demanded – a move along the curve – is affected, not the position of the curve. A devaluation will raise import prices and lower sales. The importer's profit declines.

change in cash flows is important information for the financial manager of an importing firm, whether the firm is importing finished goods for sale at home or some of the inputs used in producing its local output. If the goods are finished goods for sale, determining the effects of changes in real exchange rates requires that the financial manager knows the elasticity of demand for the product. The financial manager must also decide on the relevant currency for measurement. To illustrate these points we will begin by measuring in dollar amounts.

Analysis in home-currency (dollar) units

Let us again consider Aviva Corporation and assume that it has decided to import finished jeans that are manufactured in Britain for sale in the United States. The most straightforward case is one in which Aviva can import whatever quantity of jeans it wishes at the same pound cost per pair. This would be the case if Aviva is a small part of the market for the jeans and is therefore a price taker. In fact, however, an

assumption of constant costs is not necessary and only aids in computing total costs and profits. Being able to buy jeans at a constant cost means that before devaluation we have the horizontal cost curve $MC_1 = AC_1$ shown in Figure 11.6a and b. We can think of the constant per unit dollar cost as being the constant pound cost that is faced whatever the exchange rate, translated into dollars.

Assume that Aviva faces market demand conditions that are less than perfectly elastic in selling the imported British jeans in the US market. This requires that there not be many other *sellers* of the same brand of jeans. This could very easily be the case in practice if, for example, Aviva is licensed as the sole importer of these jeans in the United States.[9] This situation is very common. Many of the

9 If the import were freely available to any importer or potential importer, any one firm would face a flat demand curve for the good at the going price. This perfect competition would put the demand curve at the level of the cost curve, and so no profit would be made above the normal return on the capital and effort involved.

products produced in foreign countries are sold in each market by licensed firms or sales subsidiaries with exclusive marketing rights.

The demand curve is shown along with the associated MR and cost curves in Figure 11.6. Before the devaluation, Aviva Corporation will import and sell M_1, pairs of jeans per period, which is the profit-maximizing quantity where $MR = MC_1$. The jeans will be sold at the price $p_1^\$$ per pair, giving total revenue in dollars of area $Op_1^\$ SM_1$ in Figure 11.6a. The cost of the jeans, $MC_1 = AC_1$ per unit, gives a total cost of $OTWM_1$ dollars in Figure 11.6b. The initial profit is the difference between total revenue and total cost, which is area $Tp_1^\$ SW$ Figure 11.6a.

After a devaluation of the dollar to $S'(\$/\pounds)$, there is no reason for the British-pound production cost to be affected. With the British-pound cost unchanged, the new dollar cost must increase in proportion to the exchange value of the British pound against the dollar. The cost curves in Figure 11.6a and b shift vertically upward by the percentage of the dollar devaluation, from MC_1 and AC_1 to MC_2 and AC_2. The importer will reduce the amount imported and sold to M_2 per period, where $MR = MC_2$, and will sell this new amount, with the demand curve D, at the price $p_2^\$$. We see that the effect of a dollar devaluation is to reduce the quantity imported and sold and raise the product price.

The effect on revenues, costs, and profits of the importer is less obvious from Figure 11.6 than the effect on quantities and prices. Revenues have changed from $Op_1^\$ SM_1$ dollars to $Op_2^\$ RM_2$ dollars. However, we know from the straightforward observation made for the exporter that as a result of dollar devaluation, revenues have fallen for the importer. All profit-maximizing firms sell at a point where the demand curve for their product is elastic. This is because they choose to be where $MR = MC$, and since MC must be positive, MR is positive – that is, revenues are increased by additional sales, even though higher sales require lower prices. With the importer on an elastic part of his or her demand curve, the percentage reduction in the quantity sold

must exceed the percentage increase in price – that is, total revenue is reduced by devaluation.

To determine the effect of devaluation on profits, we must determine the effect on total cost and compare this with the effect on total revenue. This is not easily done with the diagrammatic analysis of Figure 11.6. However, with the aid of mathematics it can be shown that devaluation also reduces the total costs of the imports; that is, area $OZVM_2$ is less than area $OTWM_1$. It can also be shown that provided we begin with positive profits, the reduction in total cost is smaller than the reduction in total revenue, and so the dollar profits of the importer fall from devaluation. The effects of devaluation in terms of British pounds are more easily obtained from a diagrammatic analysis than are the effects in terms of dollars. Let us consider this.

Analysis in foreign-currency (pound) units

The effects of a dollar devaluation in terms of British pounds are shown in Figure 11.7. With the cost of the jeans to Aviva Corporation at $MC^\pounds$ and the demand curve at D_1, Aviva will import and sell M_1 pairs of jeans per period at the price $p_1^\pounds$ per pair. The volume and the price were obtained by choosing the profit-maximizing position, where $MC^\pounds = MR_1$.

Now, if the British-pound cost of the import does not change from a dollar devaluation, then $MC^\pounds = AC^\pounds$ will remain in its original position. The quantity of items our importer can sell, however, will depend on the dollar price charged. At any level of sales – for example, M_1 – the same quantity will be sold after the devaluation only if the dollar price remains unchanged (buyers consider the dollar price). An unchanged dollar price means a lower British pound price (lower by the percentage of the devaluation). Therefore, in terms of British pounds, the demand curve of the American buyers of Aviva's imported jeans must shift vertically downward by the percentage of the dollar devaluation. This is shown as a move from D_1 to D_2, with the associated MR curves moving from MR_1 to MR_2 in Figure 11.7.

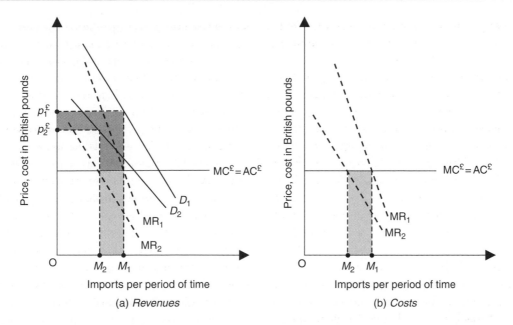

Figure 11.7 *Importer and devaluation in foreign-currency units*

Notes

A devaluation shifts the demand curve downward by the percent of devaluation when the curve is drawn against the producer's, not the consumer's, currency. If the producer's cost is unaffected by a devaluation, total revenue, total cost, and profit are all reduced by a devaluation.

Figure 11.7 tells us that a devaluation will reduce the profit-maximizing amount of imports from M_1 to M_2 (not surprisingly the same reduction as in Figure 11.6) and result in a lower British pound price for the jeans (which, nevertheless, is a higher dollar price, as is seen in Figure 11.6). With both the quantity and the pound price falling, the British pound total revenue must fall by the entire shaded area in Figure 11.7a.

With the British pound per unit cost of the jeans unaffected by devaluation, but with a smaller amount imported, the total cost is reduced by the shaded area in Figure 11.7b. Profits fall by the difference between the reduction in British pound total revenue and in total cost. This decline in profits is shown by the darkly shaded area in Figure 11.7a. We conclude that an importer's pound profits are reduced from a devaluation of the importer's currency. This should be no surprise because we saw previously that dollar profits are reduced, and with fewer pounds per dollar after the devaluation, pound profits must be reduced *a fortiori*.

Tradable inputs

Suppose that instead of importing finished jeans, Aviva is importing the denim cloth or perhaps cut denim that is ready for final manufacture in the United States. When a firm imports unfinished goods or other inputs for production, a devaluation of the domestic currency will raise production costs at each level of output.[10]

Let us consider the general case where MCs and average costs increase with output. The effect of a dollar devaluation will be to shift the upward-sloping cost curves upward, as shown in Figure 11.8. The amount by which the curves shift depends on the importance of imported inputs in the total production cost, and on whether alternative sources of inputs can be substituted. As Figure 11.8 shows, the effect of the dollar devaluation is to raise the product price and reduce the quantity manufactured and sold.

10 The same consequence follows from the use of any internationally tradable input, whether the input is imported or domestically produced.

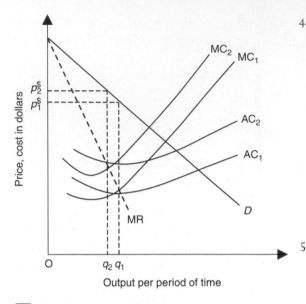

Figure 11.8 *Importer of inputs and devaluation*

Notes
When inputs are imported, a devaluation will raise production costs. Higher production costs will lower the output of goods domestically and raise prices.

SUMMARY OF EFFECTS OF EXCHANGE RATES ON EXPORTERS AND IMPORTERS

Before we add to our discussion the complications of forward hedging and the invoicing of exports or imports in different currencies, we shall summarize what we have learned:

1   Even with no foreign assets or liabilities or foreign-currency payables or receivables, changes in exchange rates will affect operations. This is called operating or residual exposure which can be difficult to avoid.

2   Devaluations raise export prices in home-currency terms and at the same time raise export sales volumes. Therefore, total revenue in terms of home-currency is increased by devaluation. The reverse occurs from revaluation.

3   Devaluations raise an exporter's profits. The gains are reduced by using internationally tradable inputs and may be in any case removed in the long run by free entry of new firms or by general inflation brought about by devaluation.

4   Foreign-owned companies or companies with foreign-currency debts care about receipts and payments in units of foreign currency. Devaluation lowers prices in foreign-currency units (while raising prices in units of the devalued currency) and raises an exporter's sales. Total revenues increase because the percentage sales volume increase exceeds the price reduction. This follows because firms sell where demand is elastic. Production costs also increase, but it can be shown that if profits are being made, an exporter's total revenues will rise more than total costs, and so profits will increase.

5   Import prices rise in units of the devalued currency and fall in units of the foreign currency. The quantity of imports falls from devaluation. The importer's total sales revenue falls in terms of the devalued currency because price increases are smaller than quantity reductions. The total cost of imports also falls, but if profits are being made, not by as much as total revenue. The profits of importers therefore decline from devaluation. This is true whether we measure profits in terms of the local currency or in terms of foreign currency.

EFFECT OF CURRENCY OF INVOICING AND FORWARD HEDGING

In our discussion of operating exposure we have so far allowed the quantity sold and the price the exporter receives or the importer pays to vary immediately as the exchange rate changes. However, these variations in quantity and price do not always occur immediately. Often, quantities and prices are fixed for a period into the future in sales or purchase contracts. This temporarily postpones the effects of operating exposure, causes a translation/transaction exposure to be faced in addition to the operating exposure, and results in conclusions that are potentially different from those reached earlier. For example, exporters can lose from devaluations and importers can gain – the reverse of the normal effects.

The effect of changes in exchange rates depends on whether sales and inputs are covered by existing contracts, and on which currency is used in the contracts. We will consider the following two cases for exporters:

1 A fixed volume of exports has been promised for future delivery at prices fixed in dollars (or in pounds, which have been sold on the forward market), but inputs are subject to inflation or are at pound-contracted prices. This situation involves what is in effect a translation or transaction exposure on payables and the removal of this exposure on export revenues.

2 A fixed volume of exports has been promised for delivery at prices stated in British pounds, and the pounds have *not* been sold on the forward market. This situation involves a translation or transaction exposure on receivables.

We should note that what we shall be discussing involves the pre-contracting of prices and/or quantities. So far in this chapter we have taken price determination, production, and settlement as being contemporaneous. Without there being any delays in payments or receipts there is no transaction or translation exposure on payables or receivables, even though exchange rates do change profitability through operating exposure. When we have pre-contracting of prices and quantities, we have translation or transaction exposure and postponed operating exposure. Since this situation occurs frequently, we will sketch the potential consequences.

The exporter with exposed inputs

Dollar accounting

Assume that Aviva Corporation has fixed the US dollar receipts from exports of a fixed number of pairs of jeans at an agreed price. As we shall explain in Chapter 12, dollar receipts can be fixed either by invoicing the jeans in dollars or by invoicing in the foreign buyer's currency and selling the foreign currency forward for a known, fixed number of

dollars. With dollar receipts per pair of jeans and the quantity supplied fixed, total dollar revenues are fixed.

While total dollar revenues will not change from devaluation, total costs could increase. This increase could stem from general inflation induced by rising tradable-goods prices, or it could occur because some inputs are internationally tradable or are imported and priced in pounds. (As we shall see in Chapter 12, it is possible to fix dollar costs of pound-priced inputs by buying the required pounds forward. It is more difficult to hedge against inflation.) Let us take input prices to be fixed in pounds which are not bought forward. This means facing a payables exposure on pounds, and the situation shown in Figure 11.9.

The total revenue from sales is represented by area $Op_1^{\$}SX_1$. However, costs could increase to $OHJX_1$. If Aviva's profits were minimal before the devaluation, the devaluation will result in losses equal to the area $p_1^{\$}HJS$. We can see that a US exporter might lose from devaluation of the dollar.[11] Of course, the loss is temporary and exists only while sales revenues are fixed and while more is paid for inputs.

If production costs as well as revenues from sales are fixed by buying forward foreign exchange for imported inputs and arranging a period of fixed dollar wages, then, of course, both costs and revenues will be unaffected by exchange rates while the various agreements are in effect. The exporting firm can therefore avoid temporary losses from devaluation if foreign exchange is sold forward or invoicing is in dollars by trying also to fix dollar input costs, including wages, for the same period.

We should note that the temporary decline in profits from devaluation as a result of paying more for inputs is analogous to the temporary worsening of the balance of payments, which in Chapter 6 was called the J-curve effect. The balance of payments

11 Aviva would prefer to reduce output and sales to the level where MC_L cuts $p_1^{\$}$. Losses would be reduced if this were done, but with an agreement to deliver X_1, it might not be possible.

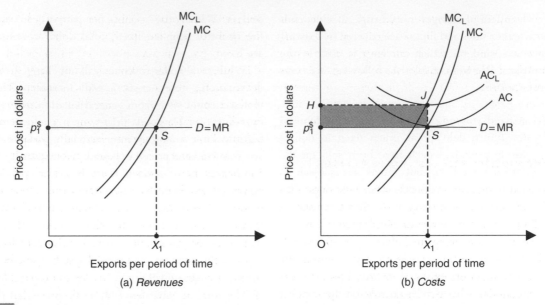

(a) *Revenues* (b) *Costs*

Figure 11.9 *Exporter with payables exposure: dollar accounting*

Notes
If a fixed number of goods are sold at a fixed dollar price, revenues will be unchanged after devaluations. We can think of operating exposure on sales revenues as being postponed. If, however, a devaluation raises input costs, total costs will rise. This is because of transaction exposure if the prices of imported inputs are denominated in foreign currency. The higher input costs could reduce profits, and so exporters can temporarily lose from a devaluation.

can temporarily worsen because the value of imports may increase in dollars, and this may offset extra revenues from exports. Our analysis in this chapter shows for an individual firm the J curve that is usually shown for the economy. The J curve for the firm or the economy is shown in Figure 11.10. The figure shows that if a devaluation takes place at time t_o profits could temporarily fall or the balance of payments could temporarily worsen, but eventually the operational effects of the devaluation will begin to improve both profits and the balance of payments.

Pound accounting

With the price of jeans fixed in dollars from selling export proceeds forward or from dollar invoicing, a US dollar devaluation means that these contracted dollars represent fewer pounds. Therefore, total revenue in pounds declines. A given amount of production costs, which are in dollars, will also represent fewer pounds, but if devaluation causes inflation or if some inputs are tradable and become

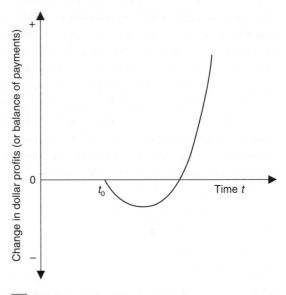

Figure 11.10 *The J curve*

Notes
When prices of inputs increase, a devaluation can lower an exporter's profits just as it can worsen the balance of payments of nations. However, the negative effects are temporary, and eventually the beneficial effects of a devaluation for an exporter's profit will begin to dominate.

more expensive, total revenue will fall more than total cost. Thus profit will decline or losses will increase. We find that exporters might lose not only in dollar terms but also in terms of pounds. This is no surprise, since lower profits in dollars are certainly lower profits in pounds after a dollar devaluation, because there are fewer pounds for each dollar.

The exporter with receivables exposure

We have considered the case where the exporter's dollar receipts are temporarily fixed, either by selling foreign-currency-invoiced receivables forward or by invoicing in dollars. This temporarily eliminates operating exposure on revenues but leaves transaction exposure on payables. We can now consider what will happen when export prices are pre-contracted in the foreign currency, but the foreign currency is not sold forward. This postpones the operating exposure and causes a transaction exposure on receivables.

It is relatively easy to compute the effect of Aviva's having pre-contracted to supply jeans to Britain at a fixed pound-per-pair price when the pounds have not been sold forward. A dollar devaluation would make these pounds more valuable by the percentage of devaluation – a gain on pound receivables – but postpone the effect of operating exposure. Production costs might also rise because of tradable inputs or wage pressure from devaluation-induced inflation, but this effect is likely to be smaller than the effect on revenues, and so dollar profits will rise. This gain on receivables in pounds for jeans that have already been sold will be followed by gains on jeans not yet sold, resulting from the operating exposure described earlier.

The importer

If Aviva is operating as an importer and agrees to purchase a given quantity of jeans at a dollar invoice price, or at a pound price when the pounds are bought forward, there is no immediate effect of a dollar devaluation in dollar terms. Aviva's costs are in dollars and are unaffected by exchange rates, as

are Aviva's revenues. Only after the period during which dollar prices are fixed will a devaluation have the operating-exposure effect described earlier in this chapter. A revaluation of the dollar will also leave costs, revenues, and profits unaffected in dollar terms. We have a case where there is no translation or transaction exposure and where the effects of operating exposure have been postponed.

If Aviva agrees to purchase a given quantity of imports at pound prices, there is a fixed payable in pounds and hence payables transaction exposure. A dollar devaluation, which means a pound revaluation, will increase the dollar value of this payable. For given total revenue in dollars from sales of the contracted imported quantity, we have a reduction in dollar profits via losses on payables. The losses on payables will be followed by the importer's losses from operating exposure; recall that devaluations lower operating incomes of importers. Therefore, there are immediate and longer term negative consequences.

A reminder: importance of lags

If sales, delivery, and payment could all occur simultaneously, there would be no need to worry about the contract currency or the presence of forward agreements. There would be no receivables or payables in trade, and the only effects of changes in exchange rates would be those from the operating exposure described earlier in this chapter. The currency used for sales invoicing and forward market covering are important only when price agreements and actual payments are separated in time. This, however, frequently happens to be the case. We then have the combined effects of translation/transaction exposure and operating exposure.

An example: Aviva's different exposures

Suppose that Aviva has contracted to sell 100 pairs of jeans per year to Britain at $24/pair and to buy 200 yards of denim from Britain in this same period for £2/yard. Suppose that 2 yards of denim are required per pair and that the labor cost for each pair is $8.

Suppose that at the time of contracting the exchange rate is $S(\$/£) = 1.5$ and that the dollar is then devalued or depreciates to $S(\$/£) = 2.0$. Suppose also that the elasticity of demand for Aviva jeans in Britain is -2, which is elastic as is the case at a profit-maximizing output, and that after the current sales contract expires Aviva raises the price of jeans to $25 per pair.[12]

1 What are the gains/losses from the dollar devaluation on the jeans sold and on the denim bought at pre-contracted prices? (i.e. what are the gains/losses from transaction exposure on Aviva's payables and receivables?)
2 What are the gains/losses from the extra competitiveness of Aviva's jeans, that is, from operating exposure?

Assume that Aviva can buy all the denim it wishes at £2/yard – it is a price taker – and that wages do not increase as a result of the devaluation.

Effect of transaction exposure

Before the devaluation:

Expected total revenue/year
$$= 100 \text{ pairs} \times \$24/\text{pair} = \$2,400$$

Expected total cost/year
$$= 100 \text{ pairs} \times 2\text{yd}/\text{pair} \times £2/\text{yd} \times \$1.5/£$$
$$+100 \text{ pairs} \times \$8/\text{pair} = \$1,400$$

Expected profit $= \$2,400 - \$1,400$
$$= \$1,000/\text{year}$$

After the devaluation:

Total revenue $= 100 \text{ pairs} \times \$24/\text{pair}$
$$= \$2,400$$

Total cost $= 100 \text{ pairs} \times 2\text{yd}/\text{pair} \times £2/\text{yd}$
$$\times \$2/£ + 100 \text{ pairs} \times \$8/\text{pair} = \$1,600$$

Expected profit $= \$2,400 - \$1,600$
$$= \$800/\text{year}$$

We find that the exporter's profit on contracted quantities and prices of jeans supplied and denim purchased is *reduced* by $200 per year because of the transaction exposure.

Effect of operating exposure

Before the devaluation:

Expected profit $= \$1,000/\text{year}$
(as we just showed)

After the contract expires: When the dollar price of jeans rises from $24 per pair to $25 per pair, the pound price falls from $24 ÷ \$1.5/£ = £16$ to $25 ÷ \$2/£ = £12.5$. This is a 21.875 percent price reduction. With a demand elasticity of -2, it will result in sales increasing by 43.75 percent to 143 pairs per year. It follows that after the contract expires

Expected revenue $= 143 \text{ pairs} \times \$25/\text{pair}$
$$= \$3,575$$

Expected cost $= 143 \text{ pairs} \times 2\text{yd}/\text{pair}$
$$\times £2/\text{yard} \times \$2.0/£$$
$$+ 143 \text{ pairs} \times \$8/\text{pair}$$
$$= \$2,288$$

Expected profit $= \$3,575 - \$2,288$
$$= \$1,287/\text{year}$$

We find that the exporter's profit is increased by $287 ($1,287 - $1,000) per year from the devaluation because of operating exposure.

In this specific example the firm is likely to feel happy about the devaluation because in the long run it will come out ahead. It should be clear, however, that temporary setbacks from transaction exposure on payables can occur.

---

12 Firms do not generally know the elasticity of demand for their products. An alternative practical approach taken by a European chemicals subsidiary of a US-based multinational is described in Exhibit 11.1.

EXHIBIT 11.1   A PRACTICAL SOLUTION TO ESTIMATING OPERATING EXPOSURE

Rather than knowing elasticities of demand, firms have an idea of the extent to which the quantity demanded is sensitive to price changes. The following excerpt explains how one firm gains an idea of the price sensitivity of demand for its products, and takes steps based on what it finds.

> One company that manages economic exposure explicitly is the European chemicals subsidiary of a U.S.-based multinational. As an executive of the company commented, 'Although a lot of people talk about economic exposure, we wanted to actually measure it and do something about it.'
>
> This company's system begins with a projection of cash flows for each of eight major geographical regions for one year ahead. The next step is to determine the sensitivity of the revenues of each product group and each major element of cost to forex (foreign exchange) movements. Because it is based in the U.S., the company is most concerned about movements against the dollar.
>
> To measure this sensitivity, an analysis is made by taking a representative sample of products from each product group and interviewing the product marketing manager in each case. Questions concern the general characteristics of the market, who the competitors were, how pricing was determined, and what factors had the largest impact. Based on these interviews, a rating is assigned to each product group signifying the

extent to which the product price is sensitive to movements in the U.S. dollar....

> The product rating in a sense is a measure of the company's ability to pass on changes in exchange rates to customers. If a product is completely dollar-sensitive, forex changes can be passed on immediately; if completely insensitive, changes cannot be passed on....
>
> A similar analysis is done for costs. Each major cost component is given a rating using the same scale used for revenues. Feedstocks, for example, which consist of petroleum derivatives, are viewed as completely dollar-sensitive. Electric power was entirely local, while fuel and gas was entirely dollar-sensitive. Locally-sourced inputs such as labor and services were judged to be completely dollar-sensitive....
>
> Projected cash flows are then transformed into "economic" cash flows by multiplying them by the product ratings.... This procedure is repeated for revenues and costs for each of the company's European subsidiaries and then aggregated to obtain an estimate of total exposed and non-exposed cash flows for the company overall for the year ahead. The results provide the company with a measure of its effective exposure in each currency relative to the U.S. dollar.

Source: John J. Pringle, "Managing Foreign Exchange Exposure," *Journal of Applied Corporate Finance*, Winter 1991, pp. 73–82.

MEASURING EXPOSURE: AN ALTERNATIVE APPROACH

The regression equation approach described in Chapter 9 for estimating exposure from time series data on exchange rates and a company's market value provides a measure of overall exposure. That is, it gives the combined exposure from effects of exchange rates on assets and liabilities and on operations. The effect on operations showing up in

the share price from which the market value is calculated should be the present value of future effects on profitability of operations. However, sometimes, times series data on a share price is not available. The company could be relatively new, or be privately held. Furthermore, management may be interested in operating exposure alone, excluding exposure on the balance sheet that would be part of overall exposure. What does a company need to do to find its operating exposure? There are two possibilities.

First, if there is a long history of profits (as opposed to share price), a regression can be run to see the sensitivity of profits with respect to past changes in exchange rates. These are flow effects because they are effects on income which is a flow. It is necessary to take the present value of the effect on income to compute exposure. This would have to be done at an appropriate risk-adjusted discount rate. But what does a company do when it has no history of profits from which to compute exposure? Perhaps the company is new, or perhaps the nature of its business changed. Maybe the company is now exporting, importing, or being forced to compete in the home market with imported substitutes. The past profits data, even if they exist, are not useful for calculating foreign exchange exposure. Even in such a situation, however, it may be possible to glean a reasonable sense of a company's exposure from interviewing knowledgeable company personnel.

To gain a sense of operating exposure, the interviewing might begin with talking to those in charge of sales and/or marketing. The head sales manager might be asked: "How badly would sales be affected if our currency were to appreciate 5 percent?" "How about a rise of 10 percent?" "What if our currency were to increase 15 percent?" Then the same person(s) could be asked how much sales would increase from a 5, 10, and 15 percent depreciation. Factored into the predictions about sales revenues would be judgment of the extent to which changes in exchange rates could be passed on to buyers through the prices that customers pay. As we have seen in this chapter, depending on the elasticity of demand for a company's product, the profit-maximizing price will reflect different proportions of the change in exchange rates (under perfect competition price rises in proportion to devaluation. With some inelasticity in demand, the price effect is smaller). Depreciation of currency is like a subsidy, at the same time reducing the price the buyer pays and increasing what the producer receives.

An appreciation of currency is like a tax, raising the price the buyer pays and reducing the amount the producer receives.

After asking relevant personnel about the impact of possible exchange rate changes on sales volumes and the prices buyers will pay – and hence on total revenue – attention can be turned to those with knowledge of the impact of exchange rates on costs, specifically company personnel involved with input acquisitions and/or production. The question is again what would happen from various amounts of currency appreciation and currency depreciation. Guidance of those responding is required here because they may need to be told that costs of all internationally tradable inputs, not just those inputs that are imported, are likely to increase with a depreciation of the buyer's currency, and vice versa for a revaluation. As we have explained, this is because, *ceteris paribus*, buyers have to compete for their own country's tradable inputs (depreciation of the producer's currency increases the amount foreign producers can pay for inputs in terms of the depreciated currency).

As we have seen in this chapter, in addition to impacts on sales volumes, product prices and input costs, the implications of changes in exchange rates for profits also depend on the ability of a company to change its output level without substantially affecting its unit production costs. Specifically, it depends on whether marginal and average costs are relatively constant as output is varied, or whether instead unit costs increase with output, at least in the short run. This can be determined from production managers.

The ability to substitute between domestic and foreign inputs is also a factor affecting how costs change with changing exchange rates. The greater the extent to which domestic input substitutes are available, the less production costs are likely to rise when the producer's currency depreciates. This may be determined from procurement personnel.

After dealing with implications of changes in exchange rates for sales revenue and costs, it is necessary to put these in present value terms by discounting at an appropriate rate. The exposure on operations can then be added to any balance-sheet exposure that may exist if the interest is in total exposure. As explained in Chapter 9, the size of balance-sheet exposure depends on the investments and debt of the company. For example, if a company has any contractual foreign-currency debt it is short the amount of the debt and this can be combined with the exposure on operations in present value form. A company may also hold exposed assets. It should be remembered that the exposure is the sensitivity of the value of assets and liabilities.

It depends on whether the exchange rate and the asset of liability price move in the same direction or the opposite direction.

The procedure we have described for determining exposure by combining the operating and balance-sheet effects of exchange rates is a complicated one, and not something that would be done frequently. It is, however, important that a company checks periodically how big its exposure is relative to the size of the company before deciding what if anything should be done about it.[13]

SUMMARY

1   An exporting firm in a competitive market will experience an increase in sales revenues and production costs after a real devaluation/depreciation of its currency. Total revenue will rise by more than total cost, and so profits will increase.

2   The higher profit for a competitive firm from devaluation will encourage existing firms to expand output and new firms to enter the industry, lowering the product price. This may limit the period of extra profit for any particular pre-existing firm.

3   Higher input costs associated with devaluation also limit profit improvements. Increases in input costs can result from the effect of devaluation on wages via a general inflationary impact or from the use of internationally tradable inputs.

4   The home-currency price of an exporter's product will rise by the percentage of the devaluation when the product is sold in a perfectly competitive market.

5   An exporting firm in an imperfectly competitive market will experience an increase in total revenue and total cost after devaluation when amounts are measured in the firm's home currency. Total revenue will rise by more than total cost, and so profit will increase. The higher profits can persist if they are not offset by higher input costs. Revenues, costs, and profits that are measured in terms of foreign exchange will also increase from devaluation, although by a lesser amount.

6   In an imperfectly competitive market the price of the goods sold by an exporter will, after a devaluation of the home currency, rise in terms of the home currency but fall in terms of the amount of foreign exchange. This happens because the home-currency price rises by a smaller percentage than the devaluation.

13 As we shall see in Chapter 12, what a company should do about exposure also depends on the ability of the company's shareholders to hedge exposure themselves, perhaps by holding a portfolio of assets for which the exposures cancel. For example, a shareholder could hold importing and exporting firms shares, or exporters' shares from different countries, so when some lose from a currency change, others in the portfolio gain.

7 Devaluation raises the prices of imports in terms of the devalued currency and reduces the quantity that is imported and sold. Total revenue and total cost in terms of dollars will fall, and so will the importer's profit. A revaluation lowers input prices and raises an importer's dollar total revenue, total cost, and profit.

8 Devaluation lowers the prices of imports when these prices are measured in the foreign currency.

9 Dollar devaluation lowers an importer's total revenue, total cost, and profit in terms of the foreign currency. Revaluation will raise them.

10 When an arrangement exists to export a stated quantity at a price fixed in home currency (or in foreign exchange that is sold forward), devaluation can temporarily hurt an exporter's profit. This is true in both dollar and foreign-currency units.

11 If prices in an export sales agreement are stated as foreign-currency amounts and these are not sold forward, devaluation will raise dollar revenues, costs, and profits of a US exporter via both transaction and operating exposure.

12 An importer buying an agreed-upon quantity at an agreed-upon price in dollars (or with required foreign exchange bought forward) will experience no change in dollar revenues, costs, or profits after devaluation. An importer buying an agreed-upon quantity at prices invoiced in foreign exchange will temporarily experience unchanged dollar revenues, increased costs, and reduced profits.

REVIEW QUESTIONS

1 What is meant by "operating exposure?"

2 What is a "tradable input?"

3 Are all imported inputs "tradable?"

4 In what way does an exporter's operating exposure depend on the elasticity of demand facing the exporter?

5 How does an exporter's operating exposure depend on the flexibility of production?

6 How does free entry in an industry affect operating exposure in the short run versus the long run?

7 How does the importance of tradable versus non-tradable inputs affect an exporter's exposure?

8 How is exposure of a perfectly competitive exporter affected by the exporter's country being and remaining only a tiny part of the world supply of the product the exporter sells?

9 Does the demand curve for an imperfectly competitive firm's product shift after devaluation if the demand curve is drawn again the currency of the buyer, and if so how does it shift?

10 Does the exporter's demand curve shift after devaluation when the curve is drawn against the exporter's home currency, and if not, what does happen?

11 Why might an exporter care about the effect of a change in an exchange rate on the exporter's revenue, cost and profit measured in terms of the currency of the *buyer* of the exporter's product?

12 How does the effect of a revaluation on an importer's domestic-currency price depend on the elasticity of demand for the product that is imported?

13 How does change in domestic-currency price of an import compare to the size of devaluation?

14 What happens to the quantity imported after a devaluation of the importer's currency?

15 What happens to an importer's total revenue after a devaluation of the importer's currency?

ASSIGNMENT PROBLEMS

1   Rank the following export industries according to the amount of increase in sales volume you would expect to result from a fall in the value of the US dollar.
    a   Wheat farming
    b   Automobile production
    c   Foreign travel to the United States
    d   Computer hardware
    Use diagrams in your answers.

2   Rank the industries in question 1 according to the effects of a devaluation/depreciation on profits. You may assume that there are different amounts of tradable inputs, different elasticities of demand, and so on.

3   Do you think that the United States is a sufficiently large importer of products in general so that the effect of a dollar depreciation would be eliminated by pressure on nominal wages from tradable-goods price increases? How about Canada, Fiji, or Iceland?

4   Assume that the elasticity of demand for Aviva's jeans is −2. Assume that production costs are constant and that there is a 10 percent dollar depreciation.
    a   By how much will the quantity sold increase?
    b   By how much will dollar revenues increase?
    c   By how much will foreign exchange revenues increase?
    d   By how much will costs increase?
    e   By how much will profits increase?

5   As in question 4, assume that Aviva's jeans face an elasticity of demand of −2 with constant costs, and assume also approximately half the total cost is accounted for by denim cloth, which is imported. To an approximation, what will this mean for your answers in question 4?

6   Redraw Figure 11.2 to show the *short-run effect* of a dollar *revaluation* on the profits of a US exporter that sells in a competitive market.

7   Redraw Figure 11.2 to show the *long-run effect* of a dollar *revaluation* on the profits of a perfectly competitive US exporter.

8   Redraw Figure 11.4 to show the effect of a *revaluation* of the dollar on a US exporter selling in an imperfectly competitive market.

9　Redraw Figure 11.2 to show the effect of devaluation-induced cost increases when amounts are measured in foreign currency.

10　Why does devaluation simultaneously raise export prices as measured in home currency and lower them as measured in foreign currency?

11　Redraw Figure 11.6 and Figure 11.7 to show the effect of a *revaluation* on revenues, costs, and profits.

12　Reconcile a rising domestic-currency price and a falling foreign-currency price for an imported good after a devaluation of the domestic currency. Why does this mean that the domestic-currency price rises by less than the percentage of devaluation?

13　What would the availability of very close substitutes for an import mean for the elasticity of demand of the firm that competes with imports? Who will bear the burden of devaluation in this case?

14　The "maquiladoras" are manufacturing facilities located on the Mexican side of the US-Mexican border, including factories owned by US firms assembling goods for sale in the United States. What factors influence the size of operating exposure of these maquiladoras for their US owners?

15　Due to the North American Free Trade Agreement, NAFTA, the operations of many firms are more integrated across the continent with, for example, manufacturers sourcing parts from United States, Canadian and Mexican factories. How might such integration influence operating exposure of a firm that integrates production, but which also sells its products throughout North America?

BIBLIOGRAPHY

Bodnar, Gordon M. and William M. Gentry, "Exchange Rate Exposure and Industry Characteristics: Evidence from Canada, Japan and the U.S.A.," *Journal of International Money and Finance*, February 1993, pp. 29–45.

Bodnar, Gordon M., Bernard Dumas, and Richard C. Marston, "Pass-through and Exposure," *Journal of Finance*, February 2002, pp. 199–231.

Ceglowski, Janet, "Dollar Depreciation and U.S. Industry Performance," *Journal of International Money and Finance*, June 1989, pp. 233–51.

Dufey, Gunter, "Corporate Finance and Exchange Rate Changes," *Financial Management*, Summer 1977, pp. 23–33.

Flood, Eugene Jr., "The Effect of Exchange Rate Changes on the Competitive Firm's Pricing and Output," unpublished, Massachusetts Institute of Technology, December 1981.

Hekman, Christine R., "Measuring Foreign Exchange Exposure: A Practical Theory and its Applications," *Financial Analysts Journal*, September/October 1983, pp. 59–65.

Hung, Wansing, Yoonbai Kim, and Kerichi Ohno, "Pricing Exports: A Cross-Country Study," *Journal of International Money and Finance*, February 1993, pp. 3–28.

Kalter, Elliot R.J., "The Effect of Exchange Rate Changes upon International Price Discrimination," International Finance Discussion Paper 122, Board of Governors of the Federal Reserve, Washington, DC.

Marston, Richard, "Pricing to Market in Japanese Manufacturing," National Bureau of Economic Research, Working Paper 2905, 1989.

——, "The Effects of Industry Structure on Economic Exposure," Working Paper, University of Pennsylvania, 1998.

Shapiro, Alan C., "Exchange Rate Changes, Inflation and the Value of the Multinational Corporation," *Journal of Finance*, May 1975, pp. 485–502.

Sundaram, Anant K. and Veena Mishra, "Exchange Rate Pass Through and Economic Exposure: A Review," Dartmouth College, Working Paper, October 1989.

Chapter 12

Hedging risk and exposure

A good hedge keeps dogs off the yard.

Chicago Fed Letter, November 1989

With the various forms of foreign exchange risk and exposure defined in Chapters 10 and 11 we can turn our attention to how they can be managed. However, before we proceed we must answer the question of whether corporate managers – the agents of the company – should hedge exposure, or whether this should be left to shareholders – the principals. The choice between corporate – (or managerial-) level and shareholder-level exposure is important because the preferred exposure of shareholders may differ from that of company managers. Indeed, shareholders may want to undo hedging done by managers, thereby incurring hedging transaction costs twice. After dealing with the question of who should hedge, we consider a variety of means of hedging, employing the technique of **financial engineering** to contrast and compare the consequences of different hedging vehicles.

WHETHER TO HEDGE: MANAGERIAL HEDGING VERSUS SHAREHOLDER HEDGING

It is usually argued that the objective of management should be to maximize the utility of the company's shareholders. However, even though hedging reduces or even eliminates exchange-rate risk, and lower risk is valued by shareholders, it does not pay for a firm to hedge exchange-rate risk if shareholders can reduce this risk themselves for the same or lower cost; shareholders will not value risk reduction they can achieve as or more effectively themselves. This is particularly relevant because shareholders may be residents of different countries and buy different baskets of goods and therefore have different risk perspectives.[1] However, several arguments have been advanced which suggest that managers rather than shareholders should hedge foreign exchange exposure. These arguments include:

1   *Progressive corporate tax rates*   A stable before-tax corporate income results in a higher average after-tax income than a volatile income of the same average value if corporate tax rate are progressive. This is because with progressive tax rates more taxes are paid in high-income periods than are saved in low-income periods.[2]

1 If PPP holds, the residence of shareholders should not matter provided tastes are similar; with PPP the same bundle of goods should cost the same in different countries. However, the buying of different baskets of goods by different shareholders can cause different real exposures for different shareholders.

2 This and some of the other reasons given here for why managers rather than shareholders should hedge can be found in Rene Stulz and Clifford W. Smith, "The Determinants of Firms" Hedging Policies, *Journal of Financial and Quantitative Analysis*, December 1985, pp. 391–405, and Alan C. Shapiro, "Currency Risk and Relative Price Risk," *Journal of Financial and Quantitative Analysis*, December 1984, pp. 365–73.

2   *Economies of scale in hedging* It may be difficult for shareholders to determine the amount of exposure in each currency that exists at any particular moment. Furthermore, even if the overall exposure is known, the share of total exposure facing an individual shareholder may be so small that forward or swap hedging by the shareholder is impractical. This occurs because of economies of scale in foreign exchange and derivatives markets.[3]

3   *Product marketing* Marketing of a company's product may be adversely affected by an unstable corporate income if buyers want assurance that the company will stay in business to maintain and service its product or supply parts. This motive for hedging is particularly important in such industries as computer software and telecommunications. Software producers, for example anti-virus providers, are expected to update their product continuously, and if their income was so volatile that their continuation in business was in doubt, sales would be adversely impacted.

4   *Attracting personnel* Corporate employees may be frightened away by volatile corporate earnings which might suggest less job security. Alternatively, those that accept employment might demand higher salaries to compensate for the employment uncertainty.

5   *Expected costs of bankruptcy* Bankruptcy costs, which refer to the expected costs of reorganization in the event of bankruptcy, constitute a higher reduction in corporate value when earnings are more volatile. Furthermore, suppliers of capital will demand higher returns to cover expected bankruptcy costs.

6   *Debt repayment clauses* Loan repayments can sometimes be triggered when earnings fall below a stated low level. The company must then incur costs of refinancing.

7   *Information on performance and profit centers* Managers of multi-division companies need to know the profit centers within the company in order to properly allocate marketing and capital expansion budgets. Leaving hedging to shareholders reduces the quality of internal information available to managers, because incomes of different divisions of the company can be a mixture of foreign exchange gains and losses and of operating income.[4]

8   *Instrument availability* There are hedging techniques involving selecting the currency of invoicing and buying inputs in markets or currencies of exports that are available to the firm but not to its shareholders.[5]

Let us assume that for one or more of these reasons it is the firm that should hedge. Before evaluating the techniques that are available for this purpose, let us give the problem a context by considering the hedging decision of importers and exporters dealing first with the source of their foreign exchange risk and exposure.

---

3   This impracticality is manifest in the large bid-ask spreads on small swap and forward transactions: a shareholder whose share of exposure is $1,000 might face a percent bid-ask spread that is 50 times that of the company whose exposure is, say, over $1 million, if the shareholder can find forward cover at all. We should note, however, that shareholders have ways of hedging other than using forward contracts and swaps. For example, they can hold a portfolio of shares in import- and export-oriented companies. If shareholders can select an alternative to the swap or forward markets, higher spreads are not a reason for firms rather than their shareholders to hedge.

4   Of course, firms can calculate the profitability of different divisions "as if" they had hedged. However, this requires maintaining a lot of data on foreign-currency inflows and outflows as well as on forward exchange rates.

5   Some of the reasons for corporate-level hedging given here, as well as further reasons, are mentioned in Exhibit 12.1, which discusses how the pharmaceutical giant, Merck & Co. Inc., views hedging.

EXHIBIT 12.1   TO HEDGE OR NOT TO HEDGE: MERCK'S MOTIVES

The pharmaceutical giant, Merck & Co. Inc., does business in over 100 countries through approximately 70 subsidiaries. Because the company has 40 percent of total assets overseas and also has an important non-US marketing presence, Merck's management has carefully considered whether it should hedge its foreign exchange exposure. The following excerpt from an article by the Treasurer and an Assistant Treasurer at Merck reinforces some of the reasons for hedging stated in the text. The article also adds some other reasons which are relevant in a technologically driven industry, such as the need for a steady income when committing to long-term R&D.

> Over the long term, foreign exchange rate movements have been – and are likely to continue to be – a problem of volatility in year-to-year earnings rather than one of irreversible losses.... The question of whether or not to hedge exchange risk thus becomes a question of the company's own risk profile with respect to interim volatility in earnings and cash flows.

The desirability of reducing earnings volatility due to exchange can be examined from both external and internal perspectives.

External concerns

These center on the perspective of capital markets, and accordingly involve matters such as share price, investor clientele effects, and maintenance of dividend policy. Although exchange fluctuations clearly can have material effects on reported accounting earnings, it is not clear that exchange-related fluctuations in earnings have significant effects on stock price. Our own analysis... suggests only a modest correlation in recent years between exchange gains and losses and share price movements, a slight relationship in the strong dollar period – the scenario of greatest concern to us...

With respect to investor clientele, exchange would seem to have mixed effects. To the extent that some investors – especially overseas investors – see Merck's stock as an opportunity for speculating on a weak dollar, hedging would be contrary to investors' interests. But, for investors seeking a "pure play" on the stocks of ethical drug companies, significant exchange risk could be undesirable. Thus, given this potential conflict of motives among investors, and recognizing our inability to ascertain the preferences of all of Merck's investor clienteles (potential as well as current), we concluded that it would be inappropriate to give too much weight to any specific type of investor.

On the issue of dividend policy, we came to a somewhat different conclusion. Maintaining Merck's dividend, while probably not the most important determinant of our share price, is nevertheless viewed by management as an important means of expressing our confidence in the company's prospective earnings growth. It is our way of reassuring investors that we expect our large investment in future research (funded primarily by retained earnings) to provide requisite returns. And, although both Merck and the industry in general were able to maintain dividend rates during the strong dollar period, we were concerned about the company's ability to maintain a policy of dividend *growth* during a future dollar strengthening. Because Merck's (and other pharmaceutical companies') dividend growth rates did indeed decline during the strong dollar 1981–1985 period, the effect of future dollar strengthening on company cash flows could well constrain future dividend growth. So, in considering whether to hedge our income against future exchange movements, we chose to give some weight to the desirability of maintaining growth in the dividend.

In general, then, we concluded that although our exchange hedging policy should consider capital market perspectives (especially dividend policy), it should not be dictated by them. The direct effect of exchange fluctuations on shareholder value, if any, is unclear; and it thus seemed a better course to concentrate on the objective of maximizing long-term cash flows and to focus on the potential effect of exchange rate movements on our ability to meet our internal objectives. Such actions, needless to say, are ultimately intended to maximize returns for our stockholders.

Internal concerns

From the perspective of management, the key factors that would support hedging against exchange volatility are the following two: (1) the large proportion of the company's overseas earnings and cash flows; and (2) the potential effect of cash flow volatility on our ability to execute our strategic plan – particularly, to make the investments in R & D that furnish the basis for future growth. The pharmaceutical industry has a very long planning horizon, one which reflects the complexity of the research involved as well as the lengthy process of product registration. It often takes more than 10 years between the discovery of a product and its market launch. In the current competitive environment, success in the industry requires a continuous, long-term commitment to a *steadily increasing* level of research funding.

Given the cost of research and the subsequent challenges of achieving positive returns, companies such as Merck require foreign sales in addition to U.S. sales to generate a level of income that supports continued research and business operations. The U.S. market alone is not large enough to support the level of our research effort. Because foreign sales are subject to exchange volatility, the dollar equivalent of worldwide sales can be very unstable. Uncertainty can make it very difficult to justify high levels of U.S.-based research when the firm cannot effectively estimate the pay-offs from its research. Our experience, and that of the industry in general, has been that the cash flow and earnings uncertainty caused by exchange rate volatility leads to a reduction of growth in research spending.

Such volatility can also result in periodic reductions of corporate spending necessary to expand markets and maintain supportive capital expenditures. In the early 1980s, for example, capital expenditures by Merck and other leading U.S. pharmaceutical companies experienced a reduction in rate of growth similar to that in R & D.

Our conclusion, then, was that we should take action to reduce the potential impact of exchange volatility on future cash flows. Reduction of such volatility removes an important element of uncertainty confronting the strategic management of the company.

Source: Judy C. Lewent and A. John Kearney, "Identifying, Measuring, and Hedging Currency Risk at Merck," *Journal of Applied Corporate Finance*, Winter 1990, pp. 19–28. Emphasis in original.

HEDGING OF RECEIVABLES AND PAYABLES

The source of risk and exposure for importers and exporters

Importing and exporting firms can face significant exposure because of settlement delays when their trade is denominated in a foreign currency. An importer, for example, does not normally receive a product immediately after ordering it. Often, the ordered product has not yet been produced, and this takes time. Even after production is completed, the goods must be shipped, and this also takes time. After delivery, it is customary for the vending firm to grant the importer a period of trade credit. As a result of all these delays the importer may not be required to pay for many months after the order has been placed. Yet the price and amount purchased are generally agreed on at the time of ordering. As we explained in Chapter 11, if an importer agrees on a price that is stated in the vendor's currency, the importer faces exposure on the account payable if steps are not taken to hedge it. Alternatively, if the price that is agreed upon is stated in the importer's currency, the exporter faces exposure on the account receivable if nothing is done to hedge it.[6] The exposure is due both to the delay between agreeing on the price and settling the transaction, and to the settlement price being in terms of a foreign currency. However, the exposure can be hedged in various ways. Let us begin by considering hedging via the forward market.

Hedging via the forward market

Suppose that Aviva Corporation has placed an order with a British denim-cloth manufacturer for £1 million of fabric to be delivered in 2 months. Suppose also that the terms of agreement allow for 1-month trade credit after delivery, so that the sterling payment is due in 3 months.

One alternative open to Aviva is to buy £1 million forward for delivery on the settlement date. This will eliminate all uncertainty about the dollar cost of the denim. However, before Aviva can decide if forward hedging is a good idea, it must consider the cost. This can then be compared with the benefit of making the dollar cost certain. Let us therefore consider the cost and benefit of forward hedging.[7]

THE COST OF FORWARD HEDGING

If a firm hedges forward, there will be a gain or loss vis-à-vis not hedging and exchanging currency on the spot market. However, this gain or loss is known only *ex post*, that is, after the spot rate becomes eventually known. The relevant cost in deciding whether to hedge is not this *ex post* cost, but rather the *expected* or *ex ante* cost. The expected cost of forward hedging is equal to the known cost of foreign currency if it is bought forward, minus the expected cost of the foreign currency if the buyer waits and the currency is bought spot. That is, in the context of our example, the expected cost of buying pounds 3 months forward versus waiting and buying the pounds at the time of payment is

$$\text{Expected cost of hedging £ payables}$$
$$= F_{1/4}(\$/\text{ask£}) - S^*_{1/4}(\$/\text{ask£})$$

where $S^*_{1/4}$ ($\$/\text{ask£}$) is the expected future spot cost of buying pounds in 3 months' time. Note that both exchange rates are dollar prices that must be paid to the bank to purchase pounds.[8] As we showed in Chapter 3, *if speculators are risk-neutral and there are no transaction costs*, speculators will buy pounds forward when

$$F_{1/4}(\$/£) < S^*_{1/4}(\$/£) \qquad (12.1)$$

This is because there is an expected gain from selling the pounds in the future at a higher spot price than will be paid when taking delivery of the pounds under the forward contract. Similarly, if

$$F_{1/4}(\$/£) > S^*_{1/4}(\$/£) \qquad (12.2)$$

risk-neutral speculators will sell pounds forward and expect to gain by buying pounds spot when it is time to deliver the pounds on the forward contract. With speculation occurring whenever inequality (12.1) or (12.2) holds, and with this speculation forcing the forward rate towards the expected future spot rate, risk-neutral speculation and zero-transaction costs ensure that

$$F_{1/4}(\$/£) = S^*_{1/4}(\$/£) \qquad (12.3)$$

---

6 Both buyer and seller can be exposed if the import or export price is stated in any currency other than that of the importer or exporter. The frequent practice of stating prices in a major international currency such as the US dollar or euro means the importer and exporter can both face exposure if neither is an American firm.

7 Exhibit 12.2 describes the choice between hedging and non-hedging alternatives.

8 If we were instead to consider the expected cost of hedging pound receivables, the expected cost of hedging would be $F_{1/4}(\$/\text{bid£}) - S^*_{1/4}(\$/\text{bid£})$.

EXHIBIT 12.2 DIFFERENT CORPORATE CHOICES OVER HEDGING

Firms facing foreign exchange exposure should decide at the highest managerial level what their corporate policy is on the matter, and convey this policy first and foremost to those in charge of treasury operations. Since sales, investment, borrowing and procurement can all affect a company's exposure to foreign exchange risk, the decision that top-level management makes on what the company is to do with exposure should have wide distribution. Furthermore, the chosen policy should be periodically reviewed. In the review, a comparison of what would have happened with different foreign exchange protocols would provide useful input to the decision of whether or not to change the company policy.

The first matter that should enter the policy decision is how large is the company's exposure relative to the size of the company. This will in turn affect the contribution of exchange-rate variations to the overall volatility of company earnings or to the market value of the company. If it is determined that exchange rates are a minor matter compared to other influences on the company's performance, the policy could easily be to leave matters alone. Alternatively, it might be decided that only transactions greater than a pre-selected size need to be hedged. Of course, since it is the company's overall exposure that counts, long and short exposures would need to be considered at the same time.

If it is decided to do nothing the company should expect to gain sometimes and to lose at other times from changes in exchange rates. On average over a long period of time the gains and losses should average out to zero. For example, in the time between contracting to make a payment for inputs and making the payment the foreign currency may go up or down, and in a rational market each direction should have equal probability. Some people think the zero average hides a lot of what might be going on. Indeed, economists have been criticized for having one foot in the freezer and one foot in the oven and saying that on average things are just about right! This is why the determination of company policy should depend on

how much variation in performance might possibly occur. It is only if the company feels it can live with the ups and downs that it should leave forex risk management alone.

Since there will be losses if the policy is to not hedge, one factor that is relevant is whether the company has good enough credit to carry itself over until things improve, or whether it has sufficient capitalization to handle anything that is likely to hit it. Another consideration is the length of the cycles over which exchange rates tend to travel. If the swings are long, then there could be lengthy periods of forex losses to deal with, and a policy of hedging makes more sense. If exchange rates just bob up and down, the company might decide to ride it out. Casual observation of exchange rate cycles of major currencies seems to show quite long waves which should result in sober thought among those who must decide on the corporate policy.

Foreign exchange risk on receivables and payables matters because of delays between agreeing on sales or purchases and receiving or making payment. Therefore, at least as far as these simple types of exposures are concerned, the amount of delay between contracting and payment needs to be included in what the protocol is to be. The longer the delays, the more exchange rates might change and consequently the bigger the impacts might be.

Unfortunately, not all exposures are as simple as those on accounts receivable and payable. In the case of exposure on assets and liabilities a critical element is the correlation between exchange rates and asset/liability prices. These correlations have to be calculated, a matter made most difficult by the fact that the correlations change over time. Even worse is the exposure on operations. Operating exposure depends on the price sensitivity of a company's product market. Some companies have an ability to pass on any price increases that might be prompted by changes in exchange rates. The ability to do this is sometimes referred to as "pass through." Others companies are price takers. Production costs vary with exchange rates, even when inputs are not imported from overseas. This is because tradable inputs from a company's home market can be influenced by ups and downs of currencies. Fortunately, the uncertainty in what the exposure and risks are can often be reduced by careful analysis, although some uncertainly is almost certain to remain even when the matter is carefully studied.

Foreign exchange risk not only depends on exposure, but also on the volatility of exchange rates. Consequently, when a company is dealing in an environment where exchange rates are fixed and seem likely to remain fixed, there is little need to pay a great deal of attention to the matter. There have been times when a company could count on

a currency moving in at most a very narrow band, at least in the period between agreeing on a sale or purchase and the payments being made. The Hong Kong dollar has not changed in value against the US dollar for nearly two decades. With their huge foreign exchange reserves and restrictions on who can buy and sell their currency, the People's Republic of China has been able to enjoy long periods of exchange-rate stability. This has enabled Chinese companies to do business without great fear of exchange-rate losses.

Clearly, different companies are in different positions as far as exchange rate exposure and risk are concerned. The challenge is to find what that position is and what if anything to do about it.

---

as was shown in Chapter 3. That is, with risk-neutral speculation and zero-transaction costs the expected cost of hedging is zero.[9]

It is clear that for there to be an expected cost of hedging, one or both of the assumptions made in arriving at equation (12.3) must be invalid. These assumptions were:

1 Speculators are risk-neutral.
2 There are no transaction costs.

As it turns out, only the transaction-cost assumption is relevant for the existence of an expected cost of forward hedging. Let us see why.

Risk premiums on forward contracts

If speculators are risk-averse, they may not buy forward when the inequality (12.1) holds or sell forward when (12.2) holds. This is because

with risk aversion, speculators will require an expected return for taking risk. This expected return is equal to the difference between $F_{1/4}(\$/\pounds)$ and $S^*_{1/4}(\$/\pounds)$. That is, risk aversion may result in a **risk premium** in the forward exchange rate; the risk premium is equal to the expected cost of hedging, assuming zero-transaction costs.

Of course, there is no reason *a priori* why the need for a risk premium would result in inequality (12.2) holding rather than (12.1). The situation that prevails depends on how the forward market is imbalanced without any speculation occurring. For example, if forward purchases and sales of pounds from the combined hedging activities of importers, exporters, borrowers, investors, and interest arbitragers result in a net excess demand for forward pounds, then speculators will have to be drawn in to be sellers of forward pounds; otherwise, the forward exchange market will not be in equilibrium with supply equal to demand. In this case speculators will need an expected return from selling pounds forward, causing inequality (12.2) to be an equilibrium situation; with speculators selling pounds forward for more than the expected future spot value of the pound, speculators collect

---

9 This has given rise to the view that forward hedging is a "free lunch." See Andre F. Perold and Evan C. Shulman, "The Free Lunch in Currency Hedging: Implications for Policy and Performance Standards," *Financial Analysts Journal*, May/June 1988, pp. 45–50.

a forward risk premium.[10] Similarly, if there is an excess supply of forward pounds without the action of speculators, they will have to be induced to demand pounds forward to balance the market. In this case there will be a forward discount on the pound – forward premium on the dollar – to induce speculators to buy pounds forward. The forward discount, that is, a forward price of pounds below the expected future spot price, provides speculators with an expected return, in the form of a risk premium, from buying pounds forward. However, the presence of such a risk premium is irrelevant for the hedging decision, for the following reason.

If there is an expected cost of hedging when buying pounds forward because $F_{1/4}(\$/\pounds) > S_{1/4}^*(\$/\pounds)$, the risk premium earned by the speculators who sell pounds forward must be just appropriate for the risk they take; otherwise, more speculators would enter the market to sell pounds forward. If the hedgers who *buy* pounds forward have the same risk concerns as the speculators who *sell* them pounds forward, the hedgers receive a benefit that equals the expected cost. That is, the risk premium is paid by hedgers when buying pounds forward because this reduces risk to the hedger, just as it adds to the risk of the speculator. This means that if a company's shareholders are typical in their attitude towards the pound, the risk premium paid to buy (or sell) pounds forward comes with an offsetting benefit: there is a risk premium which just compensates for the risk aversion. As a result of the offsetting of the expected cost of hedging and the benefit of risk reduction, the presence of the forward risk premium is irrelevant in deciding whether to hedge forward.[11]

10 The nature of the forward-market equilibrium, with speculators earning a premium for taking up imbalances in the forward market from the activities of hedgers, is described in Maurice D. Levi, "Spot versus Forward Speculation and Hedging: A Diagrammatic Exposition," *Journal of International Money and Finance*, April 1984, pp. 105–09.

11 In reality, speculators and hedgers are not similar in their attitude to risk, and so both can gain by taking opposite positions in the forward market.

Transaction costs in forward versus spot exchange markets

Whereas the presence of a risk premium is irrelevant to the forward-hedging decision, this is not the case for transaction costs, because transaction costs constitute an expected cost of hedging. This cost arises because the bid-ask spreads on forward exchange are larger than those on spot exchange. It might be argued that the bid-ask spread is larger on forward than on spot transactions because forward trading is riskier than spot trading, thereby basing the risk-premium and transaction-cost arguments both on the same source, namely, risk. However, in principle we might distinguish two types of risk. One risk is that faced by speculators who maintain open positions over intervals of time before the contracts mature, the open positions being needed to balance the aggregate supply of, and demand for, forward exchange (the mirror image of the imbalance of forward contracts being absorbed by speculators consists of the net holdings of forward contracts by hedgers). The other type of risk is that of banks quoting forward buy and sell rates in the open-bid market, each bank knowing it cannot ensure balance of buy and sell orders at every moment in time. The former risk will cause what we have called a risk premium, while the latter risk will cause a larger bid-ask spread on forward than on spot transactions. Of course, both risks are related to uncertainty in exchange rates, and they differ only in the period of time over which the risk is faced.

The preceding discussion means that even if *in the absence of transaction costs* it were the case that

$$F_{1/4}(\$/\pounds) = S_{1/4}^*(\$/\pounds) \qquad (12.3)$$

(i.e. there is no risk premium), it would still be the case *with transaction costs* that

$$F_{1/4}(\$/\text{ask}\pounds) > S_{1/4}^*(\$/\text{ask}\pounds)$$

That is, transaction costs make the forward price for buying pounds higher than the expected future spot

263

price of pounds. At the same time, we would expect transaction costs to result in

$$F_{1/4}(\$/bid£) < S^*_{1/4}(\$/bid£)$$

That is, the number of dollars received from selling pounds forward will be less than the expected number of dollars to be received from pounds by waiting and selling the pounds spot. While the larger spread on forward than on spot transactions does mean an expected cost of forward hedging, this expected cost is small. This is because the expected transaction cost of buying pounds forward versus waiting and buying them spot is only the *difference* between the two transaction costs; a transaction cost is paid to buy the pounds whether they are bought forward, or bought spot when needed. Similarly, the expected cost of selling pounds forward rather than waiting and selling them spot is only the difference between the two transaction costs.

To quantify the cost, consider the choice between buying *and* also selling forward on the one hand, and buying *and* also selling spot on the other hand. Then the extra expected cost of forwards is:

$$[F_{1/4}(\$/ask£) - F_{1/4}(\$/bid£)]$$
$$- [S^*_{1/4}(\$/ask£) - S^*_{1/4}(\$/bid£)]$$

This is the expected cost of buying *and* selling forward versus buying *and* selling spot: it is positive because the forward bid-ask spread is larger than the spot bid-ask spread. Therefore, to calculate the cost of just buying forward versus buying spot, or of just selling forward versus selling spot, we take half of the amount above. That is, the expected cost of using the forward versus the spot market when just buying or when just selling foreign currency is:

$$\tfrac{1}{2}[F_{1/4}(\$/ask£) - F_{1/4}(\$/bid£)]$$
$$- [S^*_{1/4}(\$/ask£) - S^*_{1/4}(\$/bid£)]$$

That is, the expected cost of forward hedging is one half of the difference between the forward spread and the spot spread. The longer the maturity forward, the greater will be the expected cost.

It is relatively easy to find this expected cost of hedging because it is possible to ask a bank what its spot and forward buy and sell rates are every now and again. Spreads do not change much over time, and therefore finding the expected cost of hedging does not require calling the bank very often. However, the spread will depend on the size of transaction as well as the distance into the future of the forward quote. A conversation with the bank on normal spreads that relate to different amounts of currency and a range of maturities should give a company a good sense of the expected cost of hedging.[12]

The second reason why the expected cost of hedging is small is because banks that buy and sell forward can readily hedge their positions. That is, the bid-ask spread on forward exchange is not due to the risk of changes in exchange rates over the maturity of the forward contract. Rather, it is due to the risk of changes in exchange rates *while covering a position the bank has taken* by having to quote in the open-bid market. This risk is higher in forward than in spot markets because forward markets are thinner.[13] However, the market for short maturity contracts is almost as deep as the spot market, and so the spreads on forward contracts used for hedging importers' and exporters' receivables and payables – which are typically three months or less – are only slightly higher than those on spot transactions. This makes the size of the spread difference between spot and forward exchange a small amount.

THE BENEFIT OF FORWARD HEDGING

What we have found is that the possibility of a risk premium on forward contracts is irrelevant because the expected cost of hedging is matched by a benefit, and that transaction costs constitute only a small

---

12 The forward spread is likely to be higher in very turbulent times because banks take on more risk due to the nature of the open-bid quotations in the interbank market. However, while the expected cost of hedging is high in turbulent times, so is the benefit from hedging.

13 This was mentioned in Chapter 3.

Table 12.1 *Dollar payments on £1-million accounts payable using different hedging techniques*

Technique	Dollar payment, millions				
	Rate[a] = 1.3	1.4	1.5	1.6	1.7 $/£
Unhedged	1.3	1.4	1.5	1.6	1.7
Forward £ purchase @ 1.5£	1.5	1.5	1.5	1.5	1.5
Futures £ purchase @ 1.5£	1.5±	1.5±	1.5±	1.5±	1.5±
$1.50/£ call option @ $0.06/£	1.36	1.46	1.56	1.56	1.56
$1.40/£ call option @ $0.12£	1.42	1.52	1.52	1.52	1.52
$1.60/£ call option @ $0.02/£	1.32	1.42	1.52	1.62	1.62

Note
a Realized future spot exchange rates.

cost of hedging via forward exchange. That is, there is an expected cost of buying or selling forward rather than waiting and buying or selling spot, but it is a relatively small cost. But what about the *benefit* of buying or selling forward? As we have explained earlier in this chapter, there are several benefits of forward hedging which are enjoyed if management hedges foreign exchange exposure. For example, forward hedging reduces taxes if tax rates are progressive, reduces expected bankruptcy costs, reduces refinancing costs, has marketing and hiring benefits, and can improve information on profit centers and subsidiary performance. These benefits accrue because hedging reduces the volatility of receipts, payments, and profits. Let us show how forward hedging reduces volatility within the context of our example of Aviva having agreed to pay £1 million due in 3 months.

If Aviva does not hedge its £1 million account payable in 3 months, the dollar cost of the pounds will depend on the realized spot exchange rate at the time of settlement. The possible payments resulting from remaining unhedged are shown in the top line of Table 12.1. If instead of being unhedged Aviva decides to buy forward at $1.50/£, the cost of the pounds is $1.5 million, regardless of what happens to the spot rate by the time of settlement. This is shown on the second line of Table 12.1. Comparing the certain payment of $1.5 million via the forward contract with the uncertain payment if Aviva waits and buys pounds spot, we see that *ex post* it is sometimes better to hedge and sometimes better

not to hedge. However, since by considering the various possibilities or "states" we find the gains from hedging balance the losses from hedging, the average or expected cost of the pounds is the same with forward and spot purchase of pounds.[14] Let us make this our base case against which to compare alternative ways of hedging. Let us consider next hedging via the currency futures market.

Hedging via the futures market

If Aviva decides to hedge its pound payables exposure in the futures market and buys £1 million of futures contracts, it is necessary to post a margin. If subsequent to buying the futures contracts the price of these contracts declines, it may be necessary to add to the margin account.[15] Alternatively, if the futures price increases, the margin account is credited by the amount gained. This addition or subtraction to the margin account is done on a daily basis and is called marking to market, as we said in Chapter 4. What marking to market means is that if, for example, the pound increases in value more than had been anticipated in the original pricing of the futures contract, at the maturity of the contract

14 The average of $1.3 million, $1.4 million, $1.5 million, $1.6 million, and $1.7 million, with equal probabilities of all outcomes, equals $1.5 million. Of course, this outcome is the result of assuming a zero expected hedging cost in determining the forward rate.
15 As mentioned in Chapter 4, it is necessary to supplement the margin only if it falls below the maintenance level.

265

the margin account will include the value of the unanticipated increase in the value of the pounds represented by the futures contracts, as well as the original margin.

The gain or loss from buying pound futures contracts rather than waiting to buy spot pounds is the amount added to or taken from the margin. A gain made on a futures contract can be put towards buying the pounds on the spot market. As we saw in Chapter 4, the net result of paying a higher-than-anticipated spot rate for the pounds, and the gain made on the futures contracts when the spot rate ends up higher than was anticipated, is to end up paying approximately the same for the pounds as if a forward contract had been purchased. For example, if, in the pricing of the futures contracts for £1 million, the expected future spot exchange rate had implicitly been $1.5/£, and it turns out at the maturity date of the futures contracts that the actual spot rate is $1.7/£, then if Aviva buys futures it will find it has gained about $200,000 in its margin account. Aviva will, of course, have to pay $1.7 million for the £1 million pounds it needs, rather than $1.5 million that would have been paid with a forward contract. However, after the compensating gain in the margin account, Aviva will be paying only approximately $1.5 million, the same as if the pounds had been purchased on the forward market. On the other hand, if the expected future spot rate had been $1.5/£, but the actual spot rate ended up at $1.3/£, Aviva would find it had contributed $200,000 to its margin account. Aviva would then buy the required £1 million for $1.3 million at the going spot rate, making the total cost of pounds $1.5 million. We find that whatever happens to the spot rate, Aviva pays approximately $1.5 million for its £1 million. A difference between using the forward and futures markets is that in the forward market all the payment is made at the end, whereas with the futures market some of the payment or compensation received occurs before the pounds are eventually bought at the spot rate.

As we explained in Chapter 4, because interest rates vary over time, it is possible that the amount in the margin account at the maturity of the futures contract, or the amount paid into the account and lost, does not bring the eventual price of the £1 million to exactly $1.5 million. For example, if interest rates are low when the margin account has a large amount in it and high when the margin account goes below the maintenance level, it could be that slightly more than $1.5 million is paid for the pounds. Alternatively, varying interest rates could make the eventual cost of the pounds slightly less than $1.5 million. This is the marking-to-market risk of futures contracts discussed in Chapter 4. Because of this risk, in Table 12.1 we write the cost of the £1 million when using the futures market as $1.5 ± million.

Hedging via the options market

If Aviva buys call options on pounds at a strike price of $1.50/£, the options will be exercised if the spot rate for the pound ends up above $1.50/£. The options to buy pounds will not be exercised if the spot rate for the pound is below $1.50/£, because it will be cheaper to buy the pounds at the spot rate; the option has no exercise value at maturity. Table 12.1 shows the result of buying £1 million of $1.50/£ strike-price call options if the option premium, that is, the option price, is $0.06/£. At this option premium the cost of the option for £1 million is £1 million × $0.06/£ = $60,000. Let us examine the entries in Table 12.1 for the $1.50/£ call option to see how the entries are obtained.

If the realized spot rate at the time of payment is $1.30/£, then the $1.50/£ strike-price call option will not be exercised, and the pounds will be bought spot for $1.3 million. However, $60,000 has been paid for the option, so we can think of the pounds as having a total cost of $1.36 million, as shown in Table 12.1.[16] Similarly, if the spot rate ends up at $1.40/£, the total cost of the

16 Our description is directly applicable to options on spot exchange, such as those trading on the Philadelphia Stock Exchange. For simplicity we exclude the opportunity cost of forgone interest on the payment for the option contract.

pounds including the option premium is $1.46 million. If the spot rate is the same as the strike rate, both $1.50/£, then Aviva will be as well off to exercise as to buy spot, and in either case the total cost of pounds is $1.56 million. If the spot rate ends up at $1.60/£ or $1.70/£, Aviva will exercise and pay the call rate of $1.50/£, which with the option premium included, brings the total cost of the pounds to $1.56 million.

It is clear from examining Table 12.1 that the benefit of buying a call option on the pound when there is a pound payable is that it puts a ceiling on the amount that is paid for the pounds but allows the option buyer to benefit if the exchange rate ends up below the strike rate. It can similarly be demon-strated that if a firm has a receivable in pounds, by buying a put option it can ensure that a minimum number of dollars is received for the pounds, and yet can still benefit if the dollar value of the pound ends up higher than the strike rate.

Let us suppose that instead of buying a call option at a strike price of $1.50/£, Aviva buys one at a strike price of $1.40/£, which, if the spot rate at the time of buying the option is above $1.40/£, is an in-the-money option. Table 12.1 shows the effect of buying this option if it costs $0.12/£.

Aviva will not exercise the $1.40/£ call option if the eventually realized spot rate is $1.30/£. Instead, it will buy the pounds spot for $1.3 million. Adding the $0.12/£ × £1 million = $120,000 price of the option gives a total cost for the £1 million of $1.42 million. At a realized spot rate of $1.40/£ Aviva will be indifferent between exercising the option and buying spot. Either way the pounds will cost $1.52 million, including the cost of the option. At any spot rate above $1.40/£, the $1.40/£ call option will be exercised, and whatever the spot rate happens to be, the cost of the pounds is $1.40 million. When we include the amount paid for the option, this brings the cost to $1.52 million.

If Aviva chooses a $1.60/£ call option – which, if the spot rate of the pound at the time it is purchased is below this value, is an out-of-the-money option – and if the option premium is $0.02/£, then the effect is as shown on the bottom line of Table 12.1.

These values are obtained in a similar fashion to those for the other options, recognizing that the option is exercised only when the spot rate ends up above $1.60/£.

A comparison of the effects of the different-strike-price options and of using options versus forwards and futures can be made by looking along each row in Table 12.1. We can see that with the exposure of a payable in pounds, the out-of-the-money option (that with a strike price of $1.60/£) turns out to have been the best option hedge if the pound ends up at a low value, but the in-the-money option (that with a strike price of $1.40/£) is best if the pound ends up at a high value. The at-the-money option is somewhere in between. All options are better than forwards and futures if the pound ends up very low, but options are worse if the pound ends up high. If the pound ends up at its expected value, $1.50/£, having used forwards or futures is *ex post* a little cheaper than having used options: the payment for the option time value is avoided.

Hedging via borrowing and lending: swaps

In the discussion of interest parity in Chapter 8 we pointed out that it is possible to use borrowing, investing, and the spot exchange market to achieve the same result as would be obtained by using the forward market. For example, Aviva can hedge its import of £1 million of denim fabric with payment due in 3 months by borrowing dollars immediately, buying pounds spot with the borrowed dollars, and investing the pounds for 3 months in a pound-denominated security. If this is done, then in 3 months Aviva has to pay a known number of dollars – the repayment of its dollar loan – and receives a known number of pounds. This is the same as with a forward contract. Let us consider the cost of hedging via borrowing and lending so that we can compare it with the cost of the forward market. We will use the notation introduced in Chapter 8 and will be careful to distinguish between borrowing and lending interest rates on the one hand, and between bid- and ask-exchange rates on the other.

For every £1 Aviva wants in n years' time, where $n = \frac{1}{4}$ in our particular example, the company must purchase

$$\pounds \frac{1}{(1 + r_\pounds^I)^n} \qquad (12.4)$$

on the spot market. Here $r_\pounds^I$ is the interest rate the pounds will earn – the pound investment rate – in the chosen pound-denominated security. For example, if $r_\pounds^I = 0.12$, then if Aviva buys £970,874 immediately and invests it at 12 percent, it will receive £1 million in 3 months. The dollar cost of the spot pounds in equation (12.4) is

$$\$S(\$/\text{ask}\pounds)\frac{1}{(1 + r_\pounds^I)^n} \qquad (12.5)$$

where $S(\$/\text{ask}\pounds)$ is the cost of buying pounds spot from the bank. If the number of dollars in equation (12.5) has to be borrowed, then in n years Aviva will have to pay for each pound

$$\$S(\$/\text{ask}\pounds)\frac{(1 + r_\$^B)^n}{(1 + r_\pounds^I)^n} \qquad (12.6)$$

where $r_\$^B$ is Aviva's US dollar borrowing rate.[17]

We should recall that this hedging technique involves:

1 borrowing, if necessary, in home currency;
2 buying the foreign exchange on the spot market;
3 investing the foreign exchange;
4 repaying the domestic-currency debt.

Clearly, if the value in equation (12.6) is the same as the forward exchange rate for buying the pounds n years ahead, $F_n(\$/\text{ask}\pounds)$, then Aviva will be indifferent to the choices of buying forward and going through this borrowing-investment hedging

procedure. Indifference between these two hedging methods therefore requires that

$$S(\$/\text{ask}\pounds)\frac{(1 + r_\$^B)^n}{(1 + r_\pounds^I)^n} = F_n(\$/\text{ask}\pounds) \qquad (12.7)$$

or

$$(1 + r_\$^B)^n = \frac{F_n(\$/\text{ask}\pounds)}{S(\$/\text{ask}\pounds)}(1 + r_\pounds^I)^n \qquad (12.8)$$

Equation (12.8) is one of the forms of the interest-parity condition. We find that when interest parity holds, an importer should not care whether he or she hedges by buying forward or by borrowing domestic currency and investing in the needed foreign currency. However, we note that since equation (12.7) involves a borrowing-investment spread – $r_\$^B$ versus $r_\pounds^I$ – interest parity may not hold exactly in this form. Specifically, because, *ceteris paribus*, $r_\$^B$ is high relative to $r_\$^I$ as a result of borrowing interest rates exceeding investment interest rates, we expect the forward cost $F_n(\$/\text{ask}\pounds)$ to be smaller than $S(\$/\text{ask}\pounds)(1 + r_\$^B)^n/(1 + r_\pounds^I)^n$. This would favor the use of forwards versus a swap.

Borrowing and investing can also be used by an exporter to hedge foreign exchange exposure. The exporter does the reverse of the importer. For example, if Aviva is to receive foreign currency for its jeans, it can sell it forward. Alternatively, it can

1 borrow in the foreign currency that is to be received;
2 sell the borrowed foreign currency spot for dollars;
3 invest or otherwise employ the dollars at home;
4 repay the foreign-currency debt with its export earnings when they are received.

Since the foreign-currency debt will offset the foreign exchange proceeds on its exports, Aviva will not have foreign exchange exposure or risk. The amount borrowed should be such that the amount needed to repay the debt is equal to the export

---

17 If Aviva does not have to borrow because it has the dollars, we use Aviva's opportunity cost of dollars used to buy pounds now, $r_\$^I$, in place of $r_\$^B$.

revenues that are to be received. If, for example, payment is due in n years, Aviva should borrow

$$\pounds \frac{1}{\left(1 + r_{\pounds}^{B}\right)^{n}}$$

for each pound it is due to receive; this will leave Aviva owing £1 in n years.[18] This number of pounds will be exchanged for

$$\$ S(\$/\text{bid}\pounds) \frac{1}{\left(1 + r_{\pounds}^{B}\right)^{n}}$$

of dollars, where we use the bid rate on pounds because the borrowed pounds are sold when they are received. When invested in US dollar securities this will provide

$$\$ S(\$/\text{bid}\pounds) \frac{\left(1 + r_{\$}^{I}\right)^{n}}{\left(1 + r_{\pounds}^{B}\right)^{n}} \quad (12.9)$$

at the time that payment for the jeans is received. The alternative is to sell the foreign pound receipts on the forward market at $F_{n}(\$/\text{bid}\pounds)$. Clearly, an exporter will be indifferent between selling the foreign-currency proceeds forward, and borrowing the foreign-currency and investing in domestic currency when

$$S(\$/\text{bid}\pounds) \frac{\left(1 + r_{\$}^{I}\right)^{n}}{\left(1 + r_{\pounds}^{B}\right)^{n}} = F_{n}(\$/\text{bid}\pounds) \quad (12.10)$$

or

$$\left(1 + r_{\$}^{I}\right)^{n} = \frac{F_{n}(\$/\text{bid}\pounds)}{S(\$/\text{bid}\pounds)} \left(1 + r_{\pounds}^{B}\right)^{n} \quad (12.11)$$

Equation (12.11) is another form of interest parity. Again, we conclude that if interest parity holds in this form, exporters receiving pounds are indifferent between selling them forward and using a swap. However, as before we note that, *ceteris paribus*, with $r_{\$}^{B}$ high relative to $r_{\$}^{I}$ from the borrowing-investment

spread, the left-hand side of equation (12.10) is likely to be low vis-à-vis the right-hand side of equation (12.10), that is, $F_{n}(\$/\text{bid}\pounds)$.[19] Thus, more dollars are received from selling the pounds forward than by using the swap arrangement.

Hedging via currency of invoicing

While it is usually a simple matter to arrange hedging via forwards, futures, options, or swaps, we should not overlook an obvious way for importers or exporters to avoid exposure, namely, by invoicing trade in their own currency.[20] For example, if Aviva can negotiate the price of its imported denim cloth in terms of US dollars, it need not face any foreign exchange risk or exposure on its imports. Indeed, in general, when business convention or the power that a firm holds in negotiating its purchases and sales results in agreement on prices in terms of the home currency, the firm that trades abroad will face no more receivables and payables exposure than the firm with strictly domestic interests. However, even when trade can be denominated in the importer's or exporter's local currency, only part of the risk and exposure is resolved. For example, an American exporter who charges for his or her products in US dollars will still find the level of sales dependent on the exchange rate, and hence faces operating exposure and risk. This is because the quantity of exports depends on the price the foreign buyer must pay, and this is determined by the rate of exchange between the dollar and the buyer's currency. Therefore, even when all

19 For more on how borrowing-investment spreads and currency transaction costs affect costs of alternative hedging techniques, see Maurice D. Levi, "International Financing: Currency of Issue and Management of Foreign Exposure," *World Congress Proceedings*, 14th World Congress of Accountants, Washington, DC, October 1992, pp. 13A.1–12.

20 The fact that this method has been overlooked became clear from a survey of firms conducted by Business International. See "Altering the Currency of Billing: A Neglected Technique for Exposure Management," *Money Report*, Business International, January 2, 1981, pp. 1–2.

18 You can think of this as the present value of the amount owing.

trade is in local currency, some foreign exchange exposure – operating exposure – will remain.

Of course, only one side of an international deal can be hedged by stating the price in the importer's or exporter's currency. If the importer has his or her way, the exporter will face the exchange risk and exposure, and vice versa.

When there is international bidding for a contract, it may be wise for the company calling for bids to allow the bidders to state prices in their own currencies. For example, if Aviva invites bids to supply it with denim cloth, Aviva may be better off allowing the bids to come in stated in pounds, euros, and so on, rather than insisting on dollar bids. The reason is that the bidders cannot easily hedge because they do not know if their bids will succeed (they can use options, but options contracts from options exchanges are contingent on future spot exchange rates rather than the success of bids for orders, and so are not ideally suited for the purpose). When all the foreign-currency-priced bids are in, Aviva can convert them into dollars at the going forward exchange rates, choose the cheapest bid, and then buy the appropriate foreign currency at the time it announces the successful bidder. This is a case of asymmetric information, where the buyer can hedge and the seller cannot, and where the seller may therefore add a risk premium to the bid. When the *seller* is inviting bids, as when equipment or a company is up for sale, the seller knows more than the buyer, and so bidding should be in the buyer's currency. The seller can convert the foreign-currency bids into their own currency, choose the highest bid, and then sell the foreign currency forward at the same time as they inform the successful bidder.

When hedging is difficult because tendering companies insist on being quoted in their own currency, the shorter is the cycle between quoting prices and contracts being signed, the smaller is the bidder's risk. The tendering company might bear this in mind, knowing that a short cycle between receiving quotes and announcing winners could translate into lower prices: the bidding company may translate lower risk into lower quotes.

So far we have considered situations in which all of the exposure is faced by the importer or the exporter. However, another way of hedging, at least partially, is to mix the currencies of trade.

Hedging via mixed-currency invoicing

If the British mill were to invoice its denim at £1 million, Aviva would face the exchange exposure. If instead Aviva agreed to pay the equivalent in dollars, for example, $1.5 million, then it would be the British mill that accepted the exposure. In between these two extreme positions is the possibility of setting the price at, for example, £500,000 plus $750,000. That is, payment could be stated partly in each of the two currencies. If this were done and the exchange rate between dollars and pounds varied, Aviva's exposure would involve only half of the funds payable – those that are payable in pounds. Similarly, the British mill would face exposure on only the dollar component of its receivables.

The mixing of currencies in denominating sales contracts can go further than a simple sharing between the units of currency of the importer and exporter. It is possible, for example, to express a commercial agreement in terms of a composite currency unit – a unit that is formed from many different currencies. A prominent composite unit is the Special Drawing Right, or SDR. This unit is constructed by taking a weighted average of five of the major world currencies. Another officially maintained currency unit is the European Currency Unit (ECU), which consists of an average of the exchange rates of all the European Union countries, not just those in the Euro-zone: the ECU includes, for example, the British pound and Swedish crown. Besides the official SDR and ECU units, there are private currency baskets, or cocktails, which are also designed to have a relatively steady value. They are formed by various weighted averages of a number of different currencies.

The composite currency units will reduce risk and exposure because they offer some diversification benefits. However, they cannot eliminate risk and exposure as can a forward contract, and they themselves can be difficult to hedge forward. It is perhaps because of this that cocktails and baskets are not as common in denominating trade, where forward, futures, options, and swaps are frequently available, as they are in denominating long-term debt, where these other hedging techniques are not as readily available.

A large fraction of the world's trade is, by convention and for convenience, conducted in US dollars. This is an advantage for American importers and exporters in that it helps them avoid exchange-rate exposure on receivables and payables.[21] However, when the US dollar is used in an agreement between two non-American parties, *both* parties experience exposure. This situation occurs often. For example, a Japanese firm may purchase Canadian raw materials at a price denominated in US dollars. Often both parties can hedge, for example, by engaging in forward exchange contracts. The Japanese importer can buy and the Canadian exporter can sell the US dollars forward against their own currencies. In the case of some of the smaller countries where foreign business is often expressed in dollar terms, there may not be regular forward, futures, options, or swap markets in the country's currency. However, the denomination of trade in US dollars might still be seen as a way of reducing exposure and risk if the firms have off-setting business in the dollar, or view the dollar as less volatile in value than the currency of either party involved in the trade.

Hedging according to predictive accuracy of cash flows

While we have spoken as if foreign-currency receivables or payables are known with certainty, this may not be the case. It may well be that a company knows with great accuracy what is to be received or paid in the next 30 days, because settlement practices may be to pay invoices within

30 days. However, the amount to be received or paid more than 30 days in the future may not be quite so well known. These amounts will depend on sales and purchases yet to be made. Some sales and purchases might be relatively certain, being the result of ongoing discussions: they may be awaiting settlement of a few technical details or even sitting on a manager's desk waiting for a final signature. In such a case, a company may hedge all the amount to be paid or received. Other sales or purchases may be less certain. Perhaps negotiations are ongoing, with the final decision still in some doubt. In such a situation, it may be prudent to nevertheless hedge, but perhaps not 100 percent of what is paid or received if the deal is completed. Perhaps the hedge could be 50 percent or 75 percent depending on the likelihood that the payable or receivable will occur. A company could consider establishing a hedging protocol. This might be to hedge all already contracted amounts, 90 percent of highly likely amounts, 75 percent of probable amounts, 50 percent of reasonable expected amounts, and so on. It should be pointed out, however, that this just applies to receivables and payables, and really hedging should be based on the effects of exchange rates on the value of a company as explained in Chapter 9 – if indeed hedging is deemed by management to be in the interest of shareholders.

Hedging via selection of supplying country: sourcing

A firm that can invoice its inputs in the same currency as it sells its goods can offset foreign-currency payables against receivables. This type of hedging practice is called **sourcing**. For example, Aviva Corporation might buy its denim cloth in the currencies in which it sells its jeans. If about one half of the wholesale value of jeans is the value of the material, then on each pair of jeans the firm has only about one half of the foreign exchange exposure of the jeans themselves. Aviva could buy the denim in the various currencies in rough proportion to the volume of sales in those currencies. Sourcing can also involve the use of local labor. For example,

---

21 As we have repeatedly said, US firms face operating exposure irrespective of the currency of invoicing.

large multinational accounting, marketing, and consulting firms use staff in local offices. These employees are paid in the currency of the projects and hence reduce foreign exchange exposure.

The risk-reducing technique of buying inputs in the currencies in which outputs are sold has a clear disadvantage: Aviva should buy its denim where the material is cheapest, and it should not pay more for its cloth just to avoid foreign exchange exposure. However, after an input source has been chosen at the best price, there will be some automatic hedging occurring in that currency. For example, if Aviva settles on buying its denim in Britain because the cloth is cheapest there, the total value of the jeans that it sells in that market should be netted against its denim purchases.

Now that we have explained the different techniques that are available for hedging exposure, we can consider their different consequences. This can be done most easily by examining payoff profiles, which, as we saw in Chapters 3 and 4, show graphically the rewards and/or costs of selecting different methods of hedging.

FINANCIAL ENGINEERING: PAYOFF PROFILES OF DIFFERENT HEDGING TECHNIQUES

Forward profile

As before, let us assume the expected future spot rate is $1.50/£. Then the difference between the realized spot rate and this expected rate is the unanticipated change in the exchange rate, which we have previously written as ΔS^u.

When the expected spot rate for 3 months ahead is $1.50/£, and the spot rate indeed turns out to be $1.50/£, if Aviva has bought pounds forward at $1.50/£, the forward contract has a value of zero. Let us write this as $\Delta V = 0$, where we can think of ΔV as the gain or loss by having purchased the forward contract. If instead of $1.50/£, the realized spot rate happens to be $1.70/£ so that $\Delta S^u = \$0.2/£$, Aviva's forward contract to buy £1 million at $1.50/£ is worth $\$0.2/£ \times £1$ million $= \$0.2$ million. Then we can write ΔV as $0.2 million. Alternatively, if for example, the realized spot rate is $1.30/£ so that $\Delta S^u = -\$0.2/£$, then Aviva's $1.50/£ contract has a negative value of $-\$0.2/£ \times £1$ million $= -\$0.2$ million, because forward contracts, unlike options, must be honored. These and other values of ΔV are shown against the unanticipated changes in spot rates that bring them about in the first column of Table 12.2.

The values of ΔV and ΔS^u for the £1-million forward contract at $1.50/£ are plotted against each other in the left-hand panel of Figure 12.1a. We find an upward-sloping line because the forward contract has positive value when the pound experiences unanticipated appreciation ($\Delta S^u > 0$) and negative value when the pound experiences unanticipated depreciation ($\Delta S^u < 0$).

The middle panel of Figure 12.1a shows the underlying exposure for the £1-million account payable. The exposure is represented by a line

Table 12.2 Payoffs from different hedging techniques

$\Delta S^u(\$/£)$	Forward contract	Futures contract	At-the-money option	In-the-money option	Out-of-the-money option
−0.2	−0.2	−0.2±	−0.06	−0.12	−0.02
−0.1	−0.1	−0.1±	−0.06	−0.12	−0.02
0	0.0	−0.0±	−0.06	−0.02	−0.02
0.1	0.1	−0.1±	0.04	0.08	−0.02
0.2	0.2	−0.2±	0.14	0.18	0.08

ΔV, millions of $

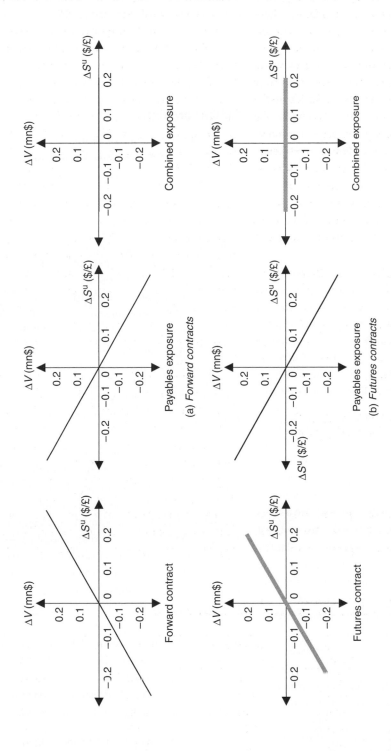

Figure 12.1 *Payoff profiles, payables exposure, and resulting exposure with forward and futures contracts*

Notes
When there is exposure on foreign-currency payables, as in the middle figures of (a) and (b), the exposure can be hedged by buying the foreign-currency forward or by buying a futures contract. The payoff profiles on the forward and futures contracts are shown in the left-hand figures of a and b. When the exposure profiles are combined, as in the right-hand figures of a and b, we can visualize the effects of hedging. The forward contract removes all exposure and risk, while the futures contract leaves marking-to-market risk.

with negative slope, showing a loss if the pound unexpectedly appreciates and a gain if the pound unexpectedly depreciates.

The right-hand panel of Figure 12.1a shows the effect of hedging pound payables with a forward purchase of the needed pounds. The figure is obtained by adding the two ΔV's from the left-hand and middle panels at each ΔS^u. We find that the combination of a forward purchase of pounds and the underlying payables exposure produces a line with a zero slope. That is, the forward contract eliminates exposure on the account payable. Figure 12.1 is an example of how to use payoff profiles to see the effect of different hedging techniques. The approach of adding profiles is called financial engineering.

Futures profiles

Table 12.2 shows the gains or losses on futures contracts to purchase £1 million at different unanticipated changes in the exchange rate. We see, for example, that if the future spot rate had been expected to be $1.50/£, but the realized rate turns out to be $1.30/£, that is, $\Delta S^u(\$/£) = -0.2$, then by buying £1 million via pound futures Aviva will find that it has lost approximately $0.2 million. This $0.2 million will have been moved through Aviva's margin account. We note that the expected loss on futures contracts is the same as the loss from buying pounds forward. However, in the case of futures we add $\pm$ to the amount lost because the actual ΔV is unknown due to volatility of interest rates. Other values of ΔS^u also give rise to the same expected ΔV's on futures contracts as on forward contracts, but the actual ΔV's are uncertain for futures contracts, due to marking-to-market risk.

The values *of* ΔV and ΔS^u for the purchase of £1 million of futures contracts are plotted against each other in the left-hand panel of Figure 12.1b. We show a broadened line because of marking-to-market risk. The middle panel of the figure shows the underlying exposure on the $1-million account payable. When the two panels

are combined by adding the ΔV's at each ΔS^u we obtain the right-hand panel. We see that the resulting combined exposure line has zero slope, thereby signifying elimination of exchange rate exposure.

Options profiles

The middle column of Table 12.2 shows the values of an option to buy £1 million at a strike price of $1.50/£ for different realized spot exchange rates.[22] As before, we assume the option premium is $0.06/£, so that the option costs Aviva $60,000. Table 12.2 shows that if the realized spot rate is $1.30/£, $1.40/£, or $1.50/£, the option is not exercised, and so by buying the option Aviva loses $0.06 million. At a realized spot rate of $1.60/£ the option is worth $0.10 million, which, after subtracting the $0.06 million cost of the option, is a gain of $0.04 million. Similarly, at a spot rate of $1.70/£ the option is worth $0.20 million, or $0.14 million after considering its cost. These values of ΔV are plotted against the associated ΔS^u's, assuming the expected spot exchange rate is $1.50/£, in the left-hand panel of Figure 12.2a.

The middle panel of Figure 12.2a again shows the underlying exposure of £1-million of payables, and the right-hand panel shows the effect of combining the option and the underlying exposure. As before, this involves adding the ΔV's at each ΔS^u. We find that hedging with the pound call option allows Aviva to gain when the pound ends up somewhat cheaper than expected, because unlike the forward or futures contracts, the option does not have to be exercised if this occurs. However, this benefit comes at the expense of being worse off than by buying pounds forward when the pound ends up above or at its expected value. This is the same conclusion that we reached earlier, but the payoff profile gives us a straightforward way of seeing

22 This is an at-the-money option if the spot rate at the time the option is purchased is $1.50/£.

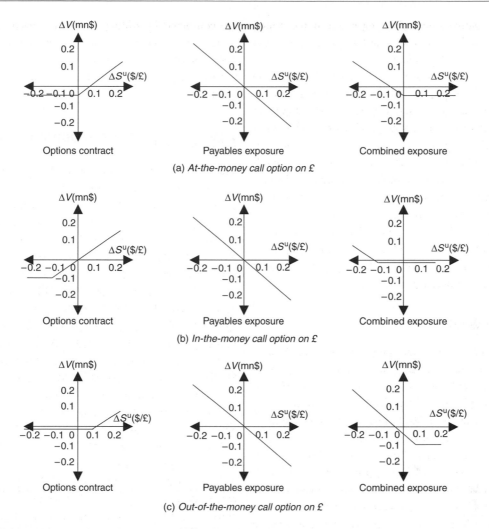

Figure 12.2 *Payoff profiles from option hedges*

Notes
The center figures in (a)–(c) show the exposure line for a foreign-currency payable. The left-hand figures in (a)–(c) show the payoff profiles for call options on the foreign currency. In a the option is at-the-money, in (b) the option is in-the-money, and In c the option Is out-of-the-money. By combining the profiles for the underlying exposure and the different options the hedges can be visually compared.

this, and of comparing the outcomes from different hedging techniques.[23]

23 For other examples of payoff profiles for hedging strategies see "Why Do We Need Financial Engineering?" *Euromoney*, September 1988, pp. 190–9. Another excellent introduction to the ways different instruments can be "clipped together" to form different payoff profiles is Charles W.Smithson, "A LEGO Approach to Financial Engineering: An Introduction to Forwards, Futures, Swaps, and Options," *Midland Corporate Finance Journal*, Winter 1987, pp. 16–28.

The effects of using in-the-money and out-of-the-money call options to hedge an underlying short pound exposure – the need to pay $1 million pounds – are described in Figure 12.2b and 12.2c. These graphs are based on the values in Table 12.2, which were obtained in the same fashion as the values for the at-the-money option. We see from the payoff profiles that both options allow the hedger to benefit if the pound is lower than was expected.

However, the gain is less for the in-the-money option, because this is more expensive. On the other hand, if the pound unexpectedly appreciates, the in-the-money option is exercised at a lower price of the pound and so there is a benefit that offsets the higher price of the option. The choice between options with different strike prices depends on whether the hedger wants to insure only against very bad outcomes for a cheap option premium (by using an out-of-the money option) or against anything other than very good outcomes (by using an in-the-money option).

The payoff profile for swaps is exactly the same as for forward contracts, because, as with forward contracts, payment or receipt of dollars occurs in the future at the time the pounds are received or must be paid. For example, the borrowing of dollars combined with the spot purchase and investment of pounds produces an upward-sloping payoff profile like that in the left-hand panel of Figure 12.1a, which when combined with the underlying exposure on pound payables leaves Aviva with zero exposure.

Hedging via denominating trade in domestic currency eliminates the underlying exposure, giving a flat exposure profile. Mixed-currency invoicing and buying inputs in the currency of exports reduce the slope of the exposure line but leave some exposure and hence some risk. For example, putting half of a contract value in each of the two countries' currencies will halve the exposure and risk.

HAVING A COMPANY HEDGING POLICY

Foreign exchange gains or losses in one division of a company can spill over to other divisions. For example, with capital being constrained, a large foreign exchange loss by one part of a company could starve other parts of needed capital for promising ventures. Since the cost of foreign exchange losses are borne by the entire enterprise, the company policy on foreign exchange hedging should be clear to all. The protocol might stipulate the maximum size of exposure that can go unhedged. It might also stipulate the hedging procedure to be used. As we shall see in Chapter 14, this is all best coordinated centrally so as to avoid hedging overlaps to save costs. However, before turning to the issue of international cash management, let us consider the opposite activity to hedging, namely speculation.

SUMMARY

1   There are several reasons why hedging should be performed by the firm rather than by its shareholders. These include progressive corporate income tax, scale economies in hedging transactions, marketing and employment benefits, lower expected bankruptcy costs, and better internal information.

2   An importer or exporter faces exposure and risk because of delay between agreeing on a foreign-currency price and settling the transaction.

3   The expected cost of hedging is the difference between the forward exchange rate for buying/selling and the expected future spot rate for buying/selling.

4   The expected cost of hedging can be estimated as one half of the difference between the forward spread and the spot spread. This magnitude can be determined by consulting a bank on what its bid and ask rates would be for spot and forward transactions, with this amount being unlikely to change much over time, but being dependent on the amount of the transaction and the maturity.

5   The decision to use forward hedging does not depend on there being a forward-risk premium. The premium represents a cost and a benefit.

6   The bid-ask spread on short-maturity forward transactions does not substantially exceed that on spot transactions, so that the expected cost of forward hedging is small. Because there are several benefits of forward hedging, it generally pays to use the forward market.

7   Futures-market hedging achieves essentially the same result as forward hedging. However, with futures the foreign exchange is bought or sold at the spot rate at maturity, and the balance of receipts from selling a foreign currency or cost of buying a foreign currency is reflected in the margin account. Because interest rates vary, the exact receipt or payment with currency futures is uncertain.

8   Foreign-currency accounts payable can be hedged by buying a call option on the foreign currency, and accounts receivable can be hedged by buying a put option on the foreign currency. Options set a limit on the worst that can happen from unfavorable exchange-rate movements without preventing enjoyment of gains from favorable exchange-rate movements.

9   An importer can hedge with a swap by borrowing in the home currency, buying the foreign-currency spot, and investing in the foreign currency. Exporters can hedge with a swap by borrowing in the foreign currency, buying the home-currency spot, and investing in the home currency: the loan is repaid from the export proceeds.

10   Foreign exchange exposure can be eliminated by invoicing in domestic currency. Exposure can be reduced by invoicing in a mixture of currencies or by buying inputs in the currency of exports.

11   Payoff profiles provide a graphical comparison of the consequence of using different hedging techniques.

REVIEW QUESTIONS

1   How is the manager-versus-shareholder hedging choice influenced by progressivity of the corporate income tax rate?

2   How is the manager-versus-shareholder hedging choice influenced by economies of scale when buying or selling forward exchange?

3   Are there informational gains to managers if they hedge foreign exchange exposure? How might the information be obtained without hedging?

4   What types of products might sell better when firms hedge foreign exchange exposure?

5   Why might expected bankruptcy costs be higher for firms that do not hedge than for those that do?

6   How does the expected cost of hedging forward relate to spot versus forward exchange-rate spreads?

7   Would a typical hedger be willing to pay a risk premium in order to hedge by buying foreign currency forward?

8   How does the risk of hedging via futures compare to that of hedging via forward exchange?

9   What type of swap would an American importer of Japanese-yen-invoiced products use?

10   Can importers and exporters both hedge by selecting the currency of invoicing, and are there any compromise invoicing currency strategies?

11   What is a composite currency unit?

12   Name two composite currency units.

13   What is meant by "sourcing?" Should this be used as a method of hedging foreign exchange exposure?

14   Why do you think financial engineering has been referred to as a "LEGO© approach" to decision making?

ASSIGNMENT PROBLEMS

1   In what sense are the forward-risk premium and the bid-ask spread on forward contracts both related to risk? Does the fact that the bid-ask spread is always positive and yet the forward risk premium can be positive or negative suggest that the nature of the two risks is different?

2   Suppose that you were importing small electric transformers, that delivery from all suppliers would take approximately 6 months, and that you faced the situation shown in the table below:

	United States	Canada	Great Britain	Switzerland	Germany
Local cost	$20,000	Can$22,000	£10,000	SFr 22,000	€18,000
$S(\$/j)$	1	0.84	2.00	0.80	1.20
$S^*_{1/2}(\$/j)$	1	0.82	2.05	0.79	1.22
$F_{1/2}(\$/j)$	1	0.83	2.02	0.81	1.24

a   Where would you buy if you decided on forward hedging?

b   Where would you buy if you decided on being unhedged?

c   If you knew that your own expected future spot rates were also the market's expected spot rates, could you deduce from the table if there is a forward-risk premium?

3   Why might managers' motivations to hedge against foreign exchange exposure differ from those of company shareholders?

4   It has been said that expected bankruptcy costs can help explain the use of equity versus debt in corporate financial structure, even when interest but not dividends are tax-deductible. Can bankruptcy costs also explain hedging practices that on average reduce expected earnings?

5   If a currency can be sold forward for more than the currency's expected future value because of a risk premium on the currency, do the sellers of that currency enjoy a "free lunch?"

6   Why is the cost of forward hedging half of the difference between the forward and spot bid-ask spreads?

7   Assume that you are importing German transformers and that you face the following:

$r^B_\$$	6%
$r^I_{€}$	4%
$S(\$/ask€)$	1.2000
$F_{1/2}(\$/ask€)$	1.2400

a   How would you hedge? Would you buy euro forward or would you borrow dollars, buy euro spot, and invest in euro for 6 months?

b   Would it make any difference in your choice of hedging technique if you already had dollars that were earning 5 percent?

8   Suppose that as the money manager of a US firm you faced the following situation:

$r_\$^B$	9.0%
$r_\$^I$	8.0%
$r_{C\$}^B$	10.5%
$r_{C\$}^I$	9.5%
$S(C\$/ask\$)$	1.2400
$S(C\$/bid\$)$	1.2350
$F_1(C\$/ask\$)$	1.2600
$F_1(C\$/bid\$)$	1.2550

Here, $r_\$^B$ and $r_\$^I$ are the 1-year interest rates at which you can, respectively, borrow and invest in the United States, and $r_{C\$}^B$ and $r_{C\$}^I$ are the 1-year borrowing and investing interest rates in Canada.

a   If you had funds to invest for 1 year, in which country would you invest?

b   If you wished to borrow for 1 year, from which country would you borrow?

c   What might induce you to borrow and invest in the same country?

d   If you needed Canadian dollars to pay for Canadian goods in 1 year and were not holding US dollars, would you buy forward or use a swap?

e   If you needed Canadian dollars to pay for Canadian goods in 1 year and already had some US dollars, would you buy forward or use a swap?

BIBLIOGRAPHY

Euromoney, "Why Do We Need Financial Engineering?" *Euromoney*, September 1988, pp. 190–99.

Khoury, Sarkis J. and K. Hung Chan, "Hedging Foreign Exchange Risk: Selecting the Optimal Tool," *Midland Corporate Finance Journal*, Winter 1988, pp. 40–52.

Levi, Maurice D., "Spot versus Forward Speculation and Hedging: A Diagrammatic Exposition," *Journal of International Money and Finance*, April 1984, pp. 105–09.

Perold, Andre F. and Evan C. Shulman, "The Free Lunch in Currency Hedging: Implications for Investment Policy and Performance Standards," *Financial Analysts Journal*, May/June 1988, pp. 45–50.

Smithson, Charles W., "A LEGO Approach to Financial Engineering: An Introduction to Forwards, Futures, Swaps, and Options," *Midland Corporate Finance Journal*, Winter 1987, pp. 16–28.

Stulz Rene and Clifford W. Smith, "The Determinants of Firms' Hedging Policies," *Journal of Financial and Quantitative Analysis*, December 1985, pp. 391–405.

Chapter 13

Exchange-rate forecasting and speculation

The proportion of (monthly or quarterly) exchange rate changes that current models can explain is essentially zero.

Richard Meese

The topics discussed in this chapter, namely, exchange-rate forecasting and speculation, are both closely related to the issue of the efficiency of foreign exchange markets. For example, if speculators can profit from forecasting exchange rates markets cannot be efficient. By efficiency we mean here the effective use of all relevant information by people buying and selling foreign exchange. Because of the closeness of connections between the issues, this chapter deals first with foreign exchange speculation, then with market efficiency, and finally with forecasting. After explaining the vehicles of foreign exchange speculation, the evidence on market efficiency is examined. The chapter then turns to the record on exchange-rate forecasting, including a comparison of chartist versus fundamental forecasting techniques. The record of chartists versus fundamentalists is linked back to market efficiency, specifically to the ability to earn from speculation using simple trading rules.

It should be mentioned at the outset that opinions differ widely on the topics discussed in this chapter, and by no means do all finance researchers agree that abnormal speculative returns and market inefficiencies have been detected. Nevertheless, despite a traditional predisposition against finding abnormal returns to speculation, market inefficiencies,

and chartist-forecasting success, when it comes to foreign exchange markets, traditional notions face a challenge. For example, central banks and international organizations have at times been major players in the foreign exchange market, whereas in most financial markets such as stock markets, there are generally no massive players. Some believe speculators may be able to profit from judging the actions of official organizations.

SPECULATION

When many think of foreign exchange speculators, they have an image of fabulously rich people in large limousines, wearing vested suits and making handsome profits with little regard for the ordinary citizen. The graphic phrase "the gnomes of Zurich" was coined by a former British Chancellor of the Exchequer when his country faced what he perceived as an outright attack on its currency by those ever-hungry and apparently heartless manipulators. In spite of the images we might have, it can be argued, as we do later in this book, that speculators may play a useful role by stabilizing exchange rates. However, our initial purpose here is not to discuss the possible merits or evils of speculation, but rather to simply describe the different ways to speculate. As we shall see, these are the same as the different ways to hedge, but when actions are taken *without* the offset of an underlying exposure such as a foreign-currency account receivable or payable.

Speculating via the forward market

Speculating without transaction costs

If we write a speculator's expected spot exchange rate in n years as $S_n^*(\$/\pounds)$, then, as we indicated in Chapters 3 and 8, if the speculator is risk neutral and we ignore transaction costs, she or he will want to buy pounds n years forward if[1]

$$F_n(\$/\pounds) < S_n^*(\$/\pounds)$$

On the other hand, the risk-neutral speculator, ignoring transaction costs, will want to sell pounds n years forward if

$$F_n(\$/\pounds) > S_n^*(\$/\pounds)$$

However, if the speculator is averse to risk, he or she will not buy or sell forward unless the expected return is sufficient for the systematic risk that is taken. This risk depends on the correlation of the exchange rate with the values of other assets and liabilities. To the extent that exchange-rate risk is not diversifiable, there may be a risk premium in the forward rate. This can cause the forward rate to differ from the market's expected future spot rate.

Speculating with transaction costs

When there are transaction costs in the spot and the forward foreign exchange market, a risk neutral speculator will buy pounds n years forward when

$$F_n(\$/ask\pounds) < S_n^*(\$/bid\pounds) \tag{13.1}$$

---

1 We should distinguish the *individual speculator's* expected future spot rate from the *market's* expected future spot rate. In this current discussion expected future spot rates are those of the individual speculator.

That is, the speculator will buy pounds forward if the *buying* price of the forward pounds is less than her or his expected future spot *selling* price of pounds. For example, if the speculator can buy pounds 1 year forward for $F_1(\$/ask\pounds) = 1.5500$, and the speculator thinks that in 1 year the spot rate at which the pounds can be sold will be $S_1^*(\$/bid\pounds) = \$1.5580/\pounds$, then the speculator will buy pounds forward in the hope of selling them at a profit. The expected profit is $[S_1^*(\$/bid\pounds) - F_1(\$/ask\pounds)] = \$0.0080/\pounds$ purchased, or $8,000 per £1,000,000. We see that in order to profit, the expected movement of the exchange rate has to be sufficient to cover the transaction costs on the forward and spot transactions. Similarly, the risk-neutral speculator will sell pounds n years forward if

$$F_n(\$/bid\pounds) > S_n^*(\$/ask\pounds) \tag{13.2}$$

For example, if the speculator can sell pounds 1 year forward for $F_1(\$/bid\pounds) = 1.5500$, and the speculator thinks the spot rate for buying pounds in 1 year will be $S_1^*(\$/ask\pounds) = \$1.5420$, then the speculator will sell pounds forward in the hope of being able to buy the pounds spot when making delivery on the forward contract. The expected profit is $[F_1(\$/bid\pounds) - S_1^*(\$/ask\pounds)] = \$0.0080/\pounds$ sold forward, or $8,000 per £1,000,000. The remarks about risk premiums that were made in the context of zero transaction costs also apply when transaction costs exist.

Speculating via the futures market

The decision criteria for speculation in the futures market are, not surprisingly, essentially the same as those for the forward market: the risk-neutral speculator buys pound futures if he or she believes the future spot price for selling pounds will exceed the current futures buying rate, that is, if inequality (13.1) holds where the "F" refers to the futures price. The risk-neutral speculator sells pound futures when the reverse is the case, that is, if inequality (13.2) holds. However, there are two small differences between the decision to buy or sell futures, and the decision to buy or sell forward, namely

1   Because of marking-to-market risk on futures, if speculators are risk averse they might want a larger gap between the ask (bid) futures price and the expected future bid (ask) spot price to compensate for the extra risk. That is, there is risk from unanticipated changes both in the spot exchange rate, as there is on forwards, and in the interest rate, which adds marking-to-market risk to futures.

2   Futures contracts are rarely held to their maturity, and the speculator may therefore be comparing today's futures price with an expected futures exchange rate for a date prior to the futures contract's maturity.

Speculating via the options market

A speculator buys an option if the expected payoff exceeds the cost of the option by enough to compensate for the risk of the option, and for the opportunity cost of money paid for the option. Of course, the value of an option varies with the underlying asset price which can move the option into or out of the money at different times during its maturity and by different amounts.[2] Furthermore, each of the different possible extents of being in or out of the money occurs with a different probability. This means that to calculate the expected payoff the different possible outcomes must be weighted by the probabilities of these outcomes.

Clearly, a speculator will buy an option if he or she values the option at more than its market price. This may occur if the speculator believes that the option will be in-the-money with a higher probability than the market in general believes. For example, a speculator may buy a call option on the pound with a strike price of $1.60/£ if he or she believes the probability of the pound moving above

$1.60/£ is higher than the probability attached to this eventuality by the market in general. Similarly, a speculator may buy a put option at $1.40/£ if he or she believes the probability of the pound moving below this "strike" rate is higher than the probability attached to this eventuality by the market.

A speculator who is prepared to accept the possibility of large losses can also sell, or write, currency options. As we saw in Chapter 4, if the speculator writes a call option on the pound, she or he gives the buyer the right to buy the pound at the strike price, and if the speculator writes a put option, she or he gives the buyer the right to sell the pound at the strike price. Option writing provides an expected return on the risk taken. That is, the expected payout is less than the premium received for the option. Option writing is a risky speculative strategy unless, as usually is the case, the speculator creates offsetting exposure via other options, forwards, or futures, or by holding the currency against which a call option is written.

Speculating via borrowing and lending: swaps

We saw in Chapters 8 and 12 that by borrowing dollars, buying pounds spot, and investing in pound-denominated securities, it is possible to achieve essentially the same objective as buying pounds forward. That is, at maturity, dollars are paid on the loan and pounds are received from the investment.

For each pound a speculator wants to have in n years, he or she must invest in pounds today

$$£ \frac{1}{\left(1 + r_£^I\right)^n}$$

where $r_£^I$ is the per annum pound-denominated security investment return. The dollar cost of buying this number of pounds on the spot market, the number that will provide £1 in n years, is

$$\$ \frac{S(\$/ask£)}{\left(1 + r_£^I\right)^n}$$

---

2 The pricing of European options based on put-call parity was discussed in Appendix A in Chapter 4.

If the speculator borrows the dollars to do this at $r_\$^B$, the number of dollars that must be repaid on the loan is

$$\frac{\$ S(\$/\text{ask}£) \cdot (1 + r_\$^B)^n}{(1 + r_£^I)^n} \qquad (13.3)$$

In summary, the amount in expression (13.3) is the dollar amount to be paid in n years in order for the speculator to receive £1 in n years. The timing of the dollar payment and pound receipt is the same as with a forward purchase of pounds.

A risk-neutral speculator would use the swap to speculate in favor of the pound if

$$S(\$/\text{ask}£) \cdot \frac{(1 + r_\$^B)^n}{(1 + r_£^I)^n} < S_n^*(\$/\text{bid}£) \qquad (13.4)$$

where $S_n^*(\$/\text{bid}£)$ is the number of dollars the speculator expects to be able to sell one pounds for in n years time. That is, the speculator will borrow in the US, buy pounds spot, and invest in pound-denominated securities if he or she thinks the pounds to be received can be sold spot in n years for more dollars than must be repaid on the dollar loan used to buy the pounds.[3]

Speculating via not hedging trade

While it might not seem like speculation, when a firm has a foreign currency receivable or payable and does *not* hedge this by one of the procedures we have described, that firm is speculating: by not hedging an exposure the firm accepts the exposure, just as it does when there is no underlying exposure and the firm uses one of the techniques for speculating that we have described. For example, a US importer who receives an invoice in pounds and does nothing to hedge the exposure is speculating against the pound. the importer is short pounds.

This should seem obvious after what we have said in Chapter 9, because it should be clear that speculation is synonymous with having an exposure line with nonzero slope. Yet despite the obvious fact that not hedging foreign-currency receivables or payables means speculating, it is remarkable how many firms, when asked if they use the forward, futures, options or swap markets to hedge their trade, say, "Oh no! We don't speculate!" As we have seen, in fact they are unwittingly speculating by *not* using these markets to hedge exposure. It is also not uncommon to hear an export company, for example, say that they *sometimes* hedge, selling foreign currency forward only when they think the foreign currency will depreciate. They are, of course, speculating.

Speculating on exchange-rate volatility

It is possible to speculate, not on whether an exchange rate will unexpectedly increase or decrease, but rather on the possibility that the exchange rate will change by an unexpectedly large amount in one direction or the other. That is, it is possible to speculate on the exchange rate being volatile, not on the exchange rate moving in a particular direction. One way to speculate on volatility is to simultaneously buy a call option and a put option at the same strike price, or perhaps buy a call with a higher price than the put.[4] Then, if the value of the foreign currency increases substantially, the call can be exercised for a profit, while the loss on the put is limited to the price paid for it. Likewise, if the value of the foreign currency decreases substantially, the put can be exercised. Such a speculative strategy is called a **straddle**.

MARKET EFFICIENCY

Foreign exchange speculation is worthwhile only if foreign exchange markets are inefficient. This is because in an inefficient market, by definition, there are abnormal returns from using information when

---

3 The criterion for speculating *against* the pound by borrowing pounds, buying dollars spot, and investing in dollar-denominated securities is left as an exercise for the reader.

4 The more the call strike price exceeds the put strike price, the cheaper is the strategy.

taking positions in foreign exchange.[5] An abnormal return is equal to the actual return minus the return that would be expected, given the level of risk, if all available information concerning the asset had been utilized in the market's determination of the asset's price. Since it is necessary to specify the expected return when evaluating whether markets are efficient, tests of market efficiency are really joint tests of the model used to generate the expected returns, and of market efficiency.

Efficiency can take on different meanings according to what we include in the set of information that is assumed to be available to decision makers, and that is therefore reflected in an asset's market price. If information only on historical prices or returns on the particular asset is included in the set of information, we are considering **weak-form efficiency.** That is, with weak-form efficiency, the current asset price reflects everything relevant in past prices of the asset. (So-called "technical trading" is based on past patterns of prices and returns, so any profitability of such a strategy would indicate markets are not weak-form efficient.) With all publicly known information included in the information set, we are considering **semi-strong efficiency**, and with all information, including that available to insiders, we are considering **strong-form efficiency**. Because of central-bank involvement in foreign exchange markets, exchange rates could well prove to be influenced by an important "insider," and its information. (A possibility that markets could be strong-form efficient, with prices thereby reflecting even insider information, can be based on the view that if market participants know which traders are insiders, they may deduce what insiders know from what they do. For example, if insiders are buying an asset, it might suggest they have knowledge of good news that is not yet public.)

An important aspect of efficiency in the international context concerns the foreign exchange market's ability to form forecasts of spot exchange rates. As we have seen earlier in this chapter and in Chapters 3 and 8, if speculators are risk neutral and we ignore transaction costs, speculators buy and sell forward until

$$F_n(\$/\pounds) = S_n^*(\$/\pounds)$$

that is, until the forward rate equals the market's expected future spot rate. Two questions arise in this context:

1   Do forward rates tend, on average, to equal the market's expected future spot rates, or are they systematically different?
2   Is all relevant information used by the market in determining the forward rate as a predictor of future spot rates, or are there observable factors which would be helpful in making predictions which the market overlooks?

The first of these questions relates to possible bias in forward exchange rates, and the second relates to market efficiency.

It is possible to construct a joint test of possible bias in the forward rate and of market efficiency by running a regression on data for forward exchange rates and the eventually realized spot exchange rates. Specifically, for any value of n we choose, it is possible to estimate the equation:[6]

$$S_n(\$/\pounds) = \beta_0 + \beta_1 F_n(\$/\pounds) + \beta_2 Z + \mu \qquad (13.5)$$

In equation (13.5), $S_n(\$/\pounds)$ is the realized spot rate for the maturity date of the forward contract, $F_n(\$/\pounds)$ is the forward rate for the matching maturity date, Z represents any information that may be relevant for exchange rates, and μ is the regression error. Values of the forward rate, $F_n(\$/\pounds)$, the realized spot rate, $S_n(\$/\pounds)$, and Z exist for each

---

5 On the concept of market efficiency see Stephen F. LeRoy, "Efficient Capital Markets and Martingales," *Journal of Economic Literature*, December 1989, pp. 1583–621.

6 We show the regression equation in the context of the dollar–pound exchange rate, but it is naturally extendable to other exchange rates.

point in time during the period over which the regression equation is estimated. In principle, monthly, weekly, or even daily data could be used for the exchange rates, and different n values can be considered. For example, we could study weekly or monthly data for n of 1 month, 3 months and so on. The variable (or variables) that Z represents depends on the form of market efficiency for which we are testing. If Z consists only of past values of the dollar–pound exchange rate – spot or forward – available to the market when forming expectations, the test is of weak-form efficiency; if Z consists of all publicly available information the test is of semi-strong efficiency; and if Z also includes information available only to central bankers and other insiders, the test is of strong-form efficiency.

The principal interest in equation (13.5) is with the estimated values of β_0, β_1, and β_2. The value of β_0 is the constant (or intercept) term. β_1 and β_2 represent the partial impacts of $F_n(\$/£)$ and Z respectively on the spot rate, that is, the impacts of each variable where the other variable is assumed constant.

Let us first consider β_2, the coefficient on potentially relevant information for the future spot rate other than that already impounded in the forward rate. If relevant information were not incorporated in the forward rate by the market, the market would be inefficient. In this case, the estimate of β_2 would be significantly different from zero. Equation (13.5) can be estimated using a variety of alternative variables representing Z. If it is not possible to find any variables Z for which the null hypothesis that $\beta_2 = 0$ is rejected, then we can conclude that the market is efficient: an absence of statistically significant variables means that no relevant matters were ignored by the market in forming its expectation of future spot rates as incorporated in forward rates.[7] That is, whether or

not we can reject the null hypothesis that $\beta_2 = 0$ is a test of efficiency.

If it could be argued under the null hypothesis that $\beta_2 = 0$, it is possible to estimate equation (13.5) *without* including Z. This is because if β_2 is indeed zero, then omission of Z should have no effect on the outcome of the regression in terms of other coefficient estimates, the extent to which forward rates predict future spot rates, and so on. Judging whether Z can be omitted requires studying the behavior of the actual regression errors, that is, those based on the actual coefficient estimates for β_0 and β_1. The behavior of the errors through time – called **serial correlation**, or **autocorrelation** – suggests whether relevant variables were omitted. If relevant variables were left out when estimating equation (13.5) excluding Z that is, when estimating

$$S_n(\$/£) = \beta_0 + \beta_1 F_n(\$/£) + \mu$$

then measured regression errors are likely to exhibit patterns over time. The patterns arise because omitted relevant variables usually move through time with patterns; if the omitted variables are purely random, their omission does not create non random behavior of errors. For example, forward rates may underestimate spot rates again and again for a period of time if we ignore a relevant variable. There are statistical summaries which indicate whether significant serial correlation of errors is present. One such measure is the **Durbin–Watson statistic, D–W**. Values of D–W close to 2 mean the null hypothesis of zero serial correlation cannot be rejected.

Before considering the evidence on whether $\beta_2 = 0$, let us see how β_0 and β_1 are related to the possible presence of bias in forward exchange rates. The joint null hypothesis concerning the presence of forward-rate bias is whether $\beta_0 = 0$ and $\beta_1 = 1$. This is because in this situation, from equation (13.5) and continuing to assume that $\beta_2 = 0$

$$S_n(\$/£) = F_n(\$/£) + \mu \tag{13.6}$$

If the regression errors, μ, average zero, then equation (13.6) says that on average, forward rates correctly predict realized spot rates. On the other

---

7 If a 95 percent confidence interval is used for determining whether a coefficient is significantly different from zero, then by design, one in 20 variables chosen will be significant just by chance. It is necessary to check whether variables help prediction outside the sample period and to do other diagnostic tests of whether statistically significant variables really do matter.

hand if, for example, $\beta_0 = \alpha \neq 0$, then even if $\beta_1 = 1$ and $\beta_2 = 0$

$$S_n(\$/£) = \alpha + F_n(\$/£)$$

This means the forward rate is a biased predictor of the future realized spot rate. For example, if $\alpha > 0$ then on average the forward price of the pound, $F_n(\$/£)$, is less than the realized spot value of the pound. Therefore, buying the pound forward, which means selling dollars forward, earns a speculator a positive return on average. This suggests a risk premium being earned by the purchaser of forward pounds, a premium earned for going long on pounds. On the other hand, if $\alpha < 0$ there is a premium for going short on pounds – or long on the dollar.

The empirical evidence suggests there is a risk premium in the forward rate, and that it does vary over time.[8] However, it appears that the risk premium is very small. For example, Jeffrey Frankel has considered the change in risk premium that would occur if there were an increase in the supply of dollar assets of 1 percent of global assets. Theory suggests that in order to induce people to hold the extra dollar assets the market would have to provide a bigger forward premium on dollars: people need to be rewarded more to hold extra dollars. Frankel estimates that such a 1-percent increase in dollar-assets would change the risk premium by 2.4 basis points, that is, by less than 1/40th of 1 percent.[9] Moreover, the evidence for there being a significant risk premium at all was thrown into question by further research by Jeffrey Frankel and his coresearcher Kenneth Froot.[10] Indeed, even some of those who originally identified a risk premium subsequently obtained evidence that casts doubt on the model used to find it.[11]

Results of one particular joint test of the hypotheses that $\beta_0 = 0$; $\beta_1 = 1$, which implies a zero risk premium in forward rates, and of $\beta_2 = 0$, which implies market efficiency, are shown in Table 13.1. The table gives the results from estimating equation (13.5) under the null hypothesis that $\beta_2 = 0$. Results are shown for the dollar–pound rate as well as for the dollar–mark and dollar–yen rates. The estimates cover the period 1978–87 and are reported in a comprehensive and insightful survey of foreign exchange market efficiency by Douglas

---

8 A by no means exhaustive list of papers reaching this conclusion includes Richard T. Baillie, Robert E. Lippens, and Patrick C. McMahon, "Testing Rational Expectations and Efficiency in the Foreign Exchange Market," *Econometrica*, May 1983, pp. 553–63; Eugene F. Fama, "Forward and Spot Exchange Rates," *Journal of Monetary Economics*, November 1984, pp. 320–38; Lars P. Hansen and Robert J. Hodrick, "Forward Exchange Rates as Optimal Predictors of Future Spot Rates: An Economic Analysis," *Journal of Political Economy*, October 1980, pp. 829–53; David A. Hsieh, "Tests of Rational Expectations and No Risk Premium in Forward Exchange Markets," *Journal of International Economics*, August 1984, pp. 173–84; Rodney L. Jacobs, "The Effect of Errors in the Variables on Tests for a Risk Premium in Forward Exchange Rates," *Journal of Finance*, June 1982, pp. 667–77; Robert A. Korajczck, "The Pricing of Forward Contracts for Foreign Exchange," *Journal of Political Economy*, April 1985, pp. 346–68; and Christian C.P. Wolff, "Forward Foreign Exchange Rates, Expected Spot Rates and Premia: A Signal-Extraction Approach," *Journal of Finance*, June 1987, pp. 395–406.

9 See Jeffrey A. Frankel, "In Search of the Exchange Risk Premium: A Six-Currency Test Assuming Mean-Variance Optimization," *Journal of International Money and Finance*, December 1982, pp. 255–74.

10 Jeffrey A. Frankel and Kenneth A. Froot, "Using Survey Data to Test Some Standard Propositions Regarding Exchange Rate Expectations," *American Economic Review*, March 1987, pp. 133–53.

11 Robert J. Hodrick and Sanjay Srivastava, "An Investigation of Risk and Return in Forward Foreign Exchange," *Journal of International Money and Finance*, April 1984, pp. 5–29. Other research that does not support the notion of a risk premium includes Bradford Cornell, "Spot Rates, Forward Rates and Exchange Market Efficiency," *Journal of Financial Economics*, August 1977, pp. 55–65; David L. Kaserman, "The Forward Exchange Rate: Its Determination and Behavior as a Predictor of the Future Spot Rate," *Proceedings of the American Statistical Association*, 1973, pp. 417–22; David Longworth, "Testing the Efficiency of the Canadian–U.S. Exchange Market under the Assumption of No Risk Premium," *Journal of Finance*, March 1982, pp.43–9; and Alan C. Stockman, "Risk, Information and Forward Exchange Rates," in Jacob A. Frenkel and Harry G. Johnson (eds), *The Economics of Exchange Rates: Selected Studies*, Addison-Wesley, Boston, MA, 1978, pp. 159–78.

Table 13.1 *Test of unbiasedness of forward rates as predictors of future spot rates, monthly data 1978–87*

Rate	Coefficients/Statistics $S(i/\$) = \beta_0 + \beta_1 F_{1/12}(i/\$) + \mu$, $i =$ DM, ¥, £			
	β_0	β_1	R^2	D–W
(DM/$)	0.013	0.988	0.962	1.71
	(0.867)	(0.667)		
(¥/$)	0.028	0.995	0.926	1.59
	(0.197)	(0.192)		
(£/$)	−0.002	0.993	0.974	1.57
	(−0.222)	(0.467)		

Note
t-statistics in parentheses below coefficients, based on $\beta_0 = 0$; $\beta_1 = 1$.
Source: Douglas K. Pearce, "Information, Expectations, and Foreign Exchange Market Efficiency," in Thomas Grennes (ed.), *International Financial Markets and Agricultural Trade*, Westview Press, Boulder, CO, 1989, pp. 214–60.

Pearce.[12] The values in parentheses below the coefficient estimates for β_0 and β_1 are *t*-statistics, which allow us to see whether the point estimates are statistically significantly different from zero, for β_0, and from 1.0, for β_1, as implied by the null hypothesis that there is no bias in forward rates; if the estimate of $\beta_0 = 0$, and $\beta_1 = 1$, the forward rate predicts the realized spot rate correctly on average. Estimated *t*-statistics less than approximately 2.0 indicate insignificance. We see from the numbers in parentheses below the coefficient estimates that β_0 is insignificantly different from 0 and β_1 is insignificantly different from 1.0. In addition, the Durbin–Watson statistic is close to 2.0, indicating that relevant variables were not overlooked in forming expectations. Unfortunately, however, we can have only limited confidence in these results because the test statistics are based on the assumption that the process generating the data is **stationary,** which means that the underlying model, including any forward risk premium, is the same over the time period that is studied. Analysis of the data suggests that the process is not stationary.[13]

There is an alternative means of testing for efficiency of foreign exchange markets. This second method also tests whether forecasts of future spot exchange rates are **rational**; by "rational" forecasts we mean forecasts that are on average correct and which do not reveal persistent errors.[14] This test replaces the forward rate, $F_n(\$/£)$, in equation (13.5) with the expected future spot rate as given in surveys of opinions of important market participants. That is, we estimate not equation (13.5), but instead

$$S_n(\$/£) = \gamma_0 + \gamma_1 S_n^*(\$/£) + \gamma_2 Z + \mu \qquad (13.7)$$

where S_n^* is the average forecasted future spot rate of those who are surveyed. In this case we can still judge market efficiency by whether γ_2 is significantly different from zero for any variable(s) Z. Furthermore, we can interpret a γ_0 that is insignificantly different from zero and a γ_1 that is insignificantly different from 1.0 as implying rational forecasts, because under these joint conditions the market's forecasts are on average correct. Furthermore, if forecasts are rational, then prediction errors in

12 Douglas K. Pearce, "Information, Expectations, and Foreign Exchange Market Efficiency," in Thomas Grennes (ed.), *International Financial Markets and Agricultural Trade*, Westview Press, Boulder, CO, 1989, pp. 214–60.
13 See Richard A. Meese and Kenneth J. Singleton, "On Unit Roots and the Empirical Modelling of Exchange Rates," *Journal of Finance*, September 1982, pp. 1029–35.

14 The concept of rationality was also used in the context of the expectations form of PPP in Chapter 7, where we argued that rational people are as likely to overestimate as to underestimate and do not make persistent mistakes.

287

forecasts should not be related between successive time periods.[15]

The evidence from the estimation of equation (13.7) is not supportive of market efficiency. Specifically, other variables *do* appear to help forecast future spot rates; in the regression, γ_2 is sometimes significantly different from zero. This is the conclusion of, for example, Peter Liu and G.S. Maddala, and of Stefano Cavaglia, Willem Verschoor and Christian Wolff.[16] However, on the matter of rationality of expectations, the same researchers reach different conclusions. Rationality is supported by Liu and Maddala, but rejected by Cavaglia, Verschoor, and Wolff who find consistent biases in experts' forecasts.[17]

EXCHANGE-RATE FORECASTING

Forecasting models' successes and failures

A further, indirect way of testing foreign exchange market efficiency and whether speculation offers positive excess expected returns is to examine the forecasting performance of exchange-rate models. If markets are efficient so that exchange rates reflect all available information, it should not be possible to make abnormal returns from speculation by following any forecasting model's predictions; exchange rates should reflect the model's predictions, with the market behaving "as if" it knew the forecasts implied by the model.

In a frequently cited paper, Richard Meese and Kenneth Rogoff compared the forecasting performance of a number of exchange-rate models.[18] The models generally predicted well during the period of time over which they were estimated. That is, when using the estimated equations and the known values of the explanatory variables, these models predicted exchange rates that were generally close to actual exchange rates. However, when predicting *outside* the period used to fit the models to the data, the models did a poorer job than a naive forecast that future spot rates equal current spot rates.[19] This is despite the fact that the out-of-sample forecasts — those made outside the estimation period — were made using actual, realized values of explanatory variables. (In practice, forecasting would be based on forecast values of explanatory variables, adding to the forecast error.)

A comparison of the forecasting performances of the major macroeconomic models developed since the 1970s has been made by Mark Taylor and Robert Flood.[20] Models considered included several based on theories discussed later in this book, including the monetary theory of exchange rates, the sticky-price overshooting model, the portfolio-balance model, and the asset approach. The authors used data for 21 industrialized countries for which exchange rates were flexible. Their results confirm those of Meese and Ragoff for forecasts of up to 1 year, namely that macroeconomic fundamentals provide a poor prediction of movements in exchange rates. However, as we might expect,

15 As we said earlier, this can be judged by the Durbin–Watson statistic, given assumptions about the stationarity of the process generating the data.

16 See Peter C. Liu and G.S. Maddala, "Rationality of Survey Data and Tests for Market Efficiency in the Foreign Exchange Markets," *Journal of International Money and Finance*, August 1992, pp. 366–81, and Stefano Cavaglia, Willem F.C. Verschoor, and Christian C.P. Wolff, "Further Evidence on Exchange Rate Expectations," *Journal of International Money and Finance*, February 1993, pp. 78–98. See also Frankel and Froot, op. cit.

17 Cavaglia, Verschoor, and Wolff, op. cit.

18 Richard A. Meese and Kenneth Rogoff, "Empirical Exchange Rate Models of the Seventies: Do They Fit Out of Sample?," *Journal of International Economics*, February 1983, pp. 3–24.

19 Support for this conclusion with fixed coefficients, but of improvements in forecasts when coefficients are allowed to change, can be found in Garry J. Schinasi and P.A.V.B. Swamy, "The Out-of-Sample Forecasting Performance of Exchange Rate Models when Coefficients are Allowed to Change," *Journal of International Money and Finance*, September 1989, pp. 375–90.

20 Mark Taylor and Robert P. Flood, "Exchange Rate Economics: What's Wrong with the Conventional Macro Approach?," conference paper in *Microstructure of Foreign Exchange Markets*, sponsored by National Bureau of Economic Research, the Centre for Economic Policy Research (London), and the Bank of Italy, July 1994.

Table 13.2 Correlation coefficients between the yen–dollar spot rate and various possible spot-rate predictors, 1974–87

	Variable				
	$S(¥/\$)$	$(r_\$ - r_¥)$	P_{US}/P_{JP}	M_{US}/M_{JP}	Y_{US}/Y_{JP}
$S(¥/\$)$	1.00				
$(r_\$ - r_¥)$	−0.50	1.00			
P_{US}/P_{JP}	−0.59	0.63	1.00		
M_{US}/M_{JP}	−0.46	−0.08	0.72	1.00	
Y_{US}/Y_{JP}	0.30	−0.26	−0.88	−0.57	1.00

Source: Richard Meese, "Currency Fluctuations in the Post-Bretton Woods Era," *Journal of Economic Perspectives,* Winter 1990, p. 120.

Table 13.3 Correlation coefficients between the Deutschemark–dollar spot rate and various possible spot-rate predictors, 1974–87

	Variable				
	$S(DM/\$)$	$(r_\$ - r_{DM})$	P_{US}/P_{GY}	M_{US}/M_{GY}	Y_{US}/Y_{GY}
$S(DM/\$)$	1.00				
$(r_\$ - r_{DM})$	−0.20	1.00			
P_{US}/P_{GY}	−0.04	0.42	1.00		
M_{US}/M_{GY}	0.37	−0.25	0.50	1.00	
Y_{US}/Y_{GY}	0.04	0.51	0.80	0.45	1.00

Source: Richard Meese, "Currency Fluctuations in the Post-Bretton Woods Era," *Journal of Economic Perspectives,* Winter 1990, p. 120.

Taylor and Flood do find that macroeconomic fundamentals have considerably more explanatory power over longer forecasting horizons.

Forward rates offer freely available estimates of the market's expectation of future spot rates since they are available by calling a bank or checking a financial newspaper. Therefore, the test of efficiency we normally make is whether a model's predictions outperform the forward exchange rate, not whether the model's predictions outperform naive forecasts of future spot rates as being equal to current spot rates. Surprisingly, however, it has been shown that the current spot rate is often a better predictor of the future spot rate than is the forward rate. Therefore, if the models do worse than predicting future spot rates from current spot rates, they do *a fortiori* worse than predicting future spot rates from current forward rates.[21]

21 See Thomas C. Chiang, "Empirical Analysis of the Predictors of Future Spot Rates," *The Journal of Financial Research,* Summer 1986, pp. 153–62.

The lack of success of forecasting models is reflected in the low correlations between the variables which would normally be associated with exchange rates. Indeed, many of the correlations are opposite to what one would normally expect. The low and sometimes surprising correlations are indicated in Tables 13.2 and 13.3. Table 13.2 shows the correlations between the level of the Japanese yen–US dollar exchange rate, $S(¥/\$)$, and several variables which would be expected to be related to the exchange rate.[22] These variables include the US–Japanese interest rate differential, $(r_\$ - r_¥)$, US versus Japanese prices, P_{US}/P_{JP}, US versus Japanese narrowly-defined money supplies, (M_{US}/M_{JP}), and US versus Japanese industrial production,

22 The correlations are provided by Richard Meese, "Currency Fluctuations in the Post-Bretton Woods Era," *Journal of Economic Perspectives,* Winter 1990, pp. 117–34. All data are in logarithms, except interest rates, and cover the period January 1974–July 1987.

(Y_{US}/Y_{JP}). Table 13.3 shows the correlations for the equivalent variables for the US versus Germany.

The first feature of these tables that is noticeable is the low level of some of the correlations. As Meese himself concludes, the correlations "suggest that it may be challenging to explain exchange-rate fluctuations . . . with macroeconomic fundamentals."[23] The second thing we notice is that some of the correlations have the opposite sign to what we would expect. For example, relatively rapid US money-supply growth causes the dollar to appreciate vis-à-vis the Deutschemark, the opposite to the prediction of the so-called Monetary Theory of Exchange Rates which suggests a declining currency value from relatively rapid expansion of the money supply; the positive correlation in Table 13.3 suggests that as M_{US}/M_{GY} goes up, $S(DM/\$)$ also goes up, which means a dollar appreciation from rapid money-supply growth.[24] The negative correlations between the interest differentials and exchange rates are even more curious: relatively higher US interest rates are associated with a dollar depreciation in both tables.

News and exchange rates

When events occur that are relevant for exchange rates, but which were widely expected to occur, these events should have no impact on exchange rates. Therefore, in regressions of measures of expected events on exchange rates, regression coefficients should be zero; when the explanatory variables on the right-hand side of the equation change as expected, the exchange rate on the left-hand side should not change. The situation is different for unexpected events, which are frequently referred to as "surprises." Examples of surprises are interest rate changes that were not anticipated, money

supply growth that differed from expectations, and so on. These surprise events are the ones that should affect exchange rates. The low correlations and statistical insignificance of macroeconomic variables that have been found could be due to using the actual values of the variables instead of only the surprise components: in general, a large part of actual values, especially in the *levels* of variables, should be expected.

Basing his approach on the preceding argument, Jacob Frenkel examined how exchange rates respond to surprises in the interest rate differential.[25] Specifically, he estimated the regression, stated in dollar–pound form but estimated also for the Deutschemark and French franc.

$$
\begin{aligned}
S_n(\$/\pounds) = {} & \beta_0 + \beta_1 F_n(\$/\pounds) \\
& + \beta_2[(r_\$ - r_\pounds) - (r_\$ - r_\pounds)^*] \\
& + \mu
\end{aligned}
\tag{13.8}
$$

where $(r_\$ - r_\pounds)$ is the actual interest differential on dollar- and pound-denominated securities, and $(r_\$ - r_\pounds)^*$ is the expected interest rate differential. The surprise is therefore $[(r_\$ - r_\pounds) - (r_\$ - r_\pounds)^*]$. Interest rate expectations are implied in the **term structure** of interest rates, based on the principle that long-term interest rates involve forecasts of future short-term interest rates. Expected interest rate differentials are also based on forward exchange premiums/discounts. Frenkel finds a statistically significant β_2, suggesting that "news" in the form of unexpected interest differentials does relate to exchange rates. However, non-stationarity of the

---

23 Meese, ibid., p. 120.

24 However, we should be careful interpreting simple correlations when the explanatory variables are correlated. For example, exchange-rate money correlations could reflect effects of money working indirectly on exchange rates through interest rates and other variables.

25 Jacob A. Frenkel, "Flexible Exchange Rates, Prices, and the Role of 'News': Lessons from the 1970s," *Journal of Political Economy*, August 1981, pp. 665–705. See also the summaries of Frenkel's study in Douglas K. Pearce, "Information, Expectations, and Foreign Exchange Market Efficiency," in Thomas Grennes (ed.), *International Financial Markets and Agricultural Trade*, Westview Press, Boulder, Co, 1989, p. 241, and Mack Ott and Paul T.W.M. Veugelers, "Forward Exchange Rates in Efficient Markets: The Effects of News and Changes in Monetary Policy Regimes," *Review*, Federal Reserve Bank of St. Louis, June/July 1986, pp. 5–15.

spot rate limits confidence in the findings. Following Frenkel, Sebastian Edwards includes news on money supply and national income as well as on interest rates, and finds, as expected, that unexpectedly rapid money growth leads to depreciation.[26] On the other hand, using vector auto regression – a technique which bases expectations on the best fitted relationship found from a long list of potential factors – Christian Wolff finds no effect of news.[27]

The role of surprises has also been investigated using **event study** methodology in which specific news events are related to subsequent changes in exchange rates. This allows implications to be drawn about the possibility of predicting exchange rates – we can see if exchange rates respond to certain variables – as well as on market efficiency. (In an efficient market, prices respond immediately, not with a lag.) Craig Hakkio and Douglas Pearce find that during 1979–82, when the US Federal Reserve was trying to achieve target growth rates of the money supply, following an announcement that money-supply growth was higher than expected, the dollar appreciated.[28] This appreciation was completed within 20 minutes of the release of the money-supply statistics. This is consistent with an efficient market, and with the market's view that excessive money growth will be curbed in the future, forcing interest rates and hence the dollar higher. (The curbing of money growth in the future is necessary to keep the longer term money growth within the target range. The slower money growth makes money relatively scarce, and thereby raises interest rates. Higher interest rates increase the demand for the currency and hence its price.) The dollar did not respond to *expected* changes in the money supply, just as we would predict. While some effect of surprises in money growth persisted after the money-supply targeting period ended in 1982 – perhaps because the market believed the Fed had not entirely given up money targeting – the effect did eventually disappear. This is consistent with the view that after the market had concluded that the Fed had finished targeting the money supply, surprises in money had no implication for future money supply, and hence no implication for interest rates or exchange rates. Similar studies of the effects of announcements of trade-balance statistics on exchange rates show similar results; trade-balance surprises have effects which depend on how markets expect governments to respond.[29]

Rather than separating variables into expected and unexpected components, Martin Evans and James Lothian have separated variables into **transitory** (temporary) and **permanent** components.[30] Normally, it would be expected that transitory shocks would play a small role in variations in exchange rates. However, contrary to expectations, Evans and Lothian have shown a significant role for transitory shocks.

26 Sebastian Edwards, "Exchange Rates and News: A Multi-Currency Approach," *Journal of International Money and Finance*, December 1982, pp. 211–24.

27 Christian C.P. Wolff, "Exchange Rates, Innovations and Forecasting," *Journal of International Money and Finance*, March 1988, pp 49–61.

28 Targeting the money-supply involves attempting to keep the money-supply growth rate within a specific range. For the details see Craig S. Hakkio and Douglas K. Pearce, "The Reaction of Exchange Rates to Economic News," *Economic Inquiry*, October 1985, pp. 621–36. See also G.A. Hardouvelis, "Economic News, Exchange Rates and Interest Rates," *Journal of International Money and Finance*, March 1988, pp. 23–5.

29 See Ken Hogan, Michael Melvin, and Dan J. Roberts, "Trade Balance News and Exchange Rates: Is There a Policy Signal," *Journal of International Money and Finance*, supplement, March 1991, pp. S90–S99; Raj Aggarwal and David C. Schirm, "Balance of Trade Announcements and Asset Prices: Influence on Equity Prices, Exchange Rates and Interest Rates," *Journal of International Money and Finance*, February 1992, pp. 80–95; and Keivan Deravi, Philip Gregorowicz, and Charles E. Hegji, "Balance of Trade Announcements and Movements In Exchange Rates," *Southern Economic Journal*, October 1988, pp. 279–87.

30 Martin D. Evans and James R. Lothian, "The Response of Exchange Rates to Permanent and Transitory Shocks Under Floating Exchange Rates," *Journal of International Money and Finance*, December 1993, pp. 563–86.

291

Changing regimes

As we explained when describing the effects of money-supply surprises on exchange rates during the period of money targeting, the nature of government economic policy plays an important role. In particular, we showed that if the Fed is attempting to keep the money-supply growth rate within a stated target range, surprise increases in the money supply should cause a dollar appreciation: the Fed would respond to excessive money growth by restricting the growth of money in the future, thereby increasing interest rates, and in turn, the dollar. On the other hand, if instead of targeting the money supply the Fed were to target interest rates, which means trying to keep interest rates at a given level, then a surprise increase in the money supply would have a different effect. Specifically, a surprisingly large money-supply growth would imply future inflation. This would tend to push up interest rates, a tendency that the Fed might try to offset by increasing the money supply even further. The resulting inflation could eventually cause a dollar depreciation.[31]

In reality, market participants do not hold a given view of the policy **regime** that is in effect. Rather, there is a **probability distribution** about the market's view of the policy regime behind government action. The probability distribution could take the form of some investors believing that it is one policy that the government is following, while other investors think it is a different policy. Alternatively, the probability distribution could take the form of *all* investors attaching common probabilities to possible different regimes being behind government actions. Whatever the nature of the probability distribution we have in mind, beliefs about the underlying policy regime that is in effect change slowly, and this has important implications for market efficiency. Let us explain this in terms of the **peso problem**, which is one of the earliest

contexts in which the issue of perceived regime changes was raised.[32]

When the Mexican peso was under heavy selling pressure in 1982, beliefs in the willingness of the authorities to maintain the exchange rate started to shift. More and more market participants began to think the Mexican government would let the peso drop, and/or each participant began to reduce their estimate of the probability the authorities would continue to prop up the peso. This shifting of beliefs took place gradually over a period of time. However, empirical tests of market efficiency assume that a *given* regime is in effect. Estimating models which assume a given regime is in effect when in fact beliefs are shifting gradually over time produces sequentially related prediction errors. For example, while the government manages to hold the exchange rate, the prediction of a possible depreciation means the market underestimates the value of the peso time and again. The sequentially related errors could be interpreted as a market inefficiency: in an efficient market people do not make sequentially related (repeated) errors. However, instead of market inefficiency, the errors could represent shifting regime beliefs. Unless researchers can model the evolution of beliefs about the underlying policy regime, it is not possible to disentangle the alternate hypotheses of market inefficiency versus regime shifting and reach a definitive conclusion.[33] In other words, researchers may conclude that foreign exchange markets ignore relevant information

---

31 See Martin Eichenbaum and Charles Evans, "Some Empirical Evidence on the Effects of Monetary Policy Shocks on Exchange Rates," *National Bureau of Economic Research*, Working Paper 4271, 1993.

32 See William S. Krasker, "The Peso Problem in Testing the Efficiency of the Forward Market," *Journal of Monetary Economics*, April 1980, pp. 269–76.

33 On regime switching see Richard G. Harris and Douglas D. Purvis, "Incomplete Information and the Equilibrium Determination of the Forward Exchange Rate," *Journal of International Money and Finance*, December 1982, pp. 241–53; René Stultz, "An Equilibrium Model of Exchange Rate Determination and Asset Pricing with Nontraded Goods and Imperfect Information," *Journal of Political Economy*, October 1987, pp. 1024–40; and Karen K. Lewis, "The Persistence of the 'Peso Problem' when Policy is Noisy," *Journal of International Money and Finance*, March 1988, pp. 5–21.

Table 13.4 *The performance of econometric-oriented services*

Currency	Forward rate	Berkeley Consulting Group	DRI	Forex Research	Predex	Service 5	Service 6	Arithmetic average (services only)
Share of forecasts for which the exchange rate moved in the indicated direction in the subsequent 3-month period								
Canadian dollar	62	83	53[a]	n.a.	30	31	n.a.	49
French franc	37	63	43[a]	30	73	27	25[a]	44
Deutschemark	67	57	77[a]	60	73	45	63	63
Yen	54	50	67[a]	67	47	37	n.a.	54
Swiss franc	80	n.a.	n.a.	n.a.	47	n.a.	10	29
Sterling	50	60	63[a]	60	43	37	29[a]	49
Arithmetic average	58	63	61	54	52	35	32	50
Share of forecasts in which the predicted rate was closer to the spot rate than was the comparable forward rate								
Canadian dollar	60	27[a]	n.a.		13	37	n.a.	34
French franc	57	33[a]	48		40	38	57[a]	46
Deutschemark	24	63[a]	57		41	33	53	45
Yen	37	60[a]	62		30	20	n.a.	42
Swiss franc	n.a.	n.a.	n.a.		30	n.a.	10	20
Sterling	70	33[a]	47		47	40	48[a]	48
Arithmetic average	50	43	54		34	34	42	43

Note
a Based on part period data.
Source: Stephen Goodman, "No Better than the Toss of a Coin," *Euromoney*, December 1978, pp. 75–85.

because they consistently over- or under-estimate future exchange rates, when in fact the model the researcher is using is the cause of the persistent errors: the prediction model being used is the same in all periods, when in reality it should allow for a gradual change in beliefs over time.

The record of forecasting services

Closely related to the question of market efficiency is the success of exchange-rate forecasting services. Do they give their users a better idea of where exchange rates are going than can be obtained by looking at other generally available sources of information such as the forward rate? The answer appears to be that forecasting services have different levels of success, but in general do a poor job. Let us consider the evidence.

Stephen Goodman performed a number of statistical tests on a large group of forecasting

services.[34] He classified the services according to the techniques they employ. He separated those that use econometric (i.e. statistical) techniques from those that use subjective evaluations and those that use technical decision rules. The econometric approach involves estimation of the relation between exchange rates and interest rates, inflation differentials, and other explanatory variables. The models mentioned earlier would fit in this category. The technical rules are generally based on relating future to past exchange rates. The subjective approach is what you would think it is – forecasting by personal opinion. Goodman compared predictions made by the forecasting services with what eventually occurred. He examined the accuracy of predictions made between January and June in 1978.

Table 13.4 summarizes the results for the econometric forecasts in predicting trends and in

34 See Stephen H. Goodman, "No Better than the Toss of a Coin," *Euromoney*, December 1978, pp. 75–85.

predicting actual spot exchange rates ("point estimates"). The first column in the top half of the table on predicting trends shows how often the forward rate was on the correct side of the current spot rate. Because speculators move the forward rate towards the expected future spot rate, the forward rate provides a benchmark against which to judge whether the forecasting services provide information in addition to what is readily available without charge: the forward rate can be seen in the newspaper or obtained from a bank. We see that except in the case of the French franc, the forward rate is in the correct direction more than 50 percent of the time. On the other hand, the remainder of the top half of Table 13.4 shows that forecasters are

sometimes correct about trends less than 50 percent of the time. This suggests that the predictive accuracy of forecasting services is weak. The bottom half of Table 13.4 compares the point estimate predictions of the forecasting services with the forward-rate "predictions." The table shows that predicted levels of spot rates are frequently further away from the realized rates than forecasts based simply on forward rates.

Tables 13.5 and 13.6 show the results of an additional test that Goodman performed. In order to compare forecasting success, Goodman computed the rates of return from following the advice of the different services. The rates of return from following the advice of the econometric-based

Table 13.5 *Speculative return on capital from following the advice of econometric services (in percentages)*

Currency		Buy and Hold	Berkeley Consulting Group	DRI	Forex Research	Predex	Service 5	Service 6	Arithmetic average (Services only)
Canadian dollar	Buy	(15.12)	2.52	(2.88)	n.a.	(4.96)	(0.60)	n.a.	(1.48)
	Sell		6.88	5.16[a]	n.a.	(2.08)	3.52	n.a.	3.37
	Total	(15.12)	4.40	1.64[a]	n.a.	(3.60)	0.28	n.a.	0.68
French franc	Buy	3.20	7.32	5.76[a]	2.40	7.20	3.24	10.08[a]	6.00
	Sell		2.28	(0.64)[a]	(3.16)	3.68	(2.68)	13.80[a]	(2.39)
	Total	3.20	4.20	1.40[a]	0.02	5.92	0.08	2.60[a]	2.37
Deutschemark	Buy	6.80	5.72	13.00[a]	6.52	7.56	16.08	10.84	9.95
	Sell		(13.92)	(1.96)[a]	(7.00)	(4.40)	(4.04)	(4.88)	(6.03)
	Total	6.80	(1.56)	5.80[a]	(1.60)	4.68	0.64	0.36	1.39
Yen	Buy	12.52	7.36	15.56[a]	12.92	21.08	4.80	n.a.	12.34
	Sell		(16.40)	(13.68)[a]	(8.92)	(9.56)	(15.76)	n.a.	(12.86)
	Total	12.52	(5.32)	3.88	6.16	(2.40)	(7.96)	n.a.	(1.13)
Swiss franc	Buy	9.64	n.a.	n.a.	n.a.	18.80	n.a.	n.a.	18.80
	Sell		n.a.	n.a.	n.a.	(6.12)	n.a.	n.a.	(6.12)
	Total	9.64	n.a.	n.a.	n.a.	0.52	n.a.	n.a.	0.52
Sterling	Buy	0.12	14.04	4.56	8.40	2.76	2.16	6.20[a]	6.35
	Sell		10.48	(12.40)[a]	4.68	2.44	1.12	(9.32)[a]	(0.50)
	Total	0.12	12.04	(2.24)[a]	6.04	2.60	1.52	(2.52)[a]	2.91
Arithmetic average		2.86	2.75	2.10	2.66	1.29	(1.09)	0.15	1.12

Notes
a Based on part period data. Parentheses indicate a negative. The total is the return on all transactions, both buy and sell; it is equal to the weighted average of the return on buys and on sells, where the weights are the share of transactions which are buys and sells respectively. Totals for arithmetic average column represent horizontal sums; arithmetic average for arithmetic average column represents vertical sum of totals.

Source: Stephen Goodman, "No Better than the Toss of a Coin," *Euromoney*, December 1978, pp. 75–85.

Table 13.6 *Speculative return on capital from following the advice of technical services (in percentages)*

Currency		International forecasting	Shearson Hayden, Stone	Waldner	Arithmetic average
Canadian dollar	Buy	0.99	4.61	2.50	2.70
	Sell	4.60	5.19	6.22	5.34
	Total	5.59	9.80	8.72	8.04
Number of transactions/year		5	17	11	11
French franc	Buy	(2.42)	n.a.	3.82	0.70
	Sell	(3.66)	n.a.	0.53	(1.57)
	Total	(6.08)	n.a.	4.35	(0.87)
Number of transactions/year		5	n.a.	15	10
Deutschemark	Buy	10.49	8.78	7.53	8.93
	Sell	2.46	3.02	1.19	2.22
	Total	12.95	11.80	8.72	11.16
Number of transactions/year		5	25	13	14
Yen	Buy	12.42	10.95	11.78	11.72
	Sell	(1.73)	(1.63)	(1.52)	(1.63)
	Total	10.69	9.32	10.26	10.09
Number of transactions/year		5	21	12	13
Swiss franc	Buy	9.52	12.99	2.76	8.42
	Sell	2.07	3.11	(10.28)	(1.70)
	Total	11.60	16.10	(7.52)	6.73
Number of transactions/year		5	22	14	14
Sterling	Buy	6.70	2.62	9.24	6.19
	Sell	5.55	2.64	9.93	6.04
	Total	12.25	5.26	19.17	12.23
Number of transactions/year		4	24	12	13
Arithmetic average	Total	7.83	10.46	7.28	7.90
Number of transactions/year		5	22	13	13

Notes
Parentheses indicate a negative. Total is the return on all transactions, both buy and sell. Totals for arithmetic average column represent horizontal sums. Arithmetic average column represents vertical sum of totals.

Source: Stephen Goodman, "No Better than the Toss of a Coin," *Euromoney*, December 1978, pp. 75–85.

services are given in Table 13.5. The performance of the advisory services can be compared with the strategy of just buying currencies and holding them, a practice which because the US dollar dropped against most currencies during the period, offered gains on every currency other than the Canadian dollar. The econometric forecasters had a poor record. However, the technically oriented services, whose performances are summarized in Table 13.6, did a good job. Before adjustments for transaction costs or risk, the total returns from buying and selling according to their advice show an average yield of almost 8 percent. This means that if the advice of these services had been followed with the maintenance of a 5 percent margin, the return on the margin after adjusting for transaction costs would have been 145 percent. However, there would also have been periods of losses, and a follower of the advice might not have survived to enjoy the profit available to those currency speculators who did survive. Stated differently, we do not know whether the return of 145 percent is sufficient for the risk that is involved.

Richard Levich has also examined the performance of the advisory services, but his conclusions are rather different from the conclusions of Stephen Goodman.[35] While Levich also found the subjective and technical forecasts to be more accurate than econometric forecasts in the short run, he found the opposite for forecasts of a year (a period not checked by Goodman). Levich did find some gain from following the advice of the advisory services. Further evidence of success of professional forecasters over 1-year and 3-month horizons is described in Exhibit 13.1, while Exhibit 13.2 describes the success of a renowned forecaster, George Soros. Unfortunately, as explained earlier, it is difficult to decide whether the return from following the forecasters is sufficient to compensate for the risk of taking positions based on these forecasts.

Success of different forecasting methods

A manifestation of the risk of following the advice of exchange-rate forecasters is that there is a large dispersion of opinion among them. This is directly evident from examination of the expressed opinions of forecasters, and indirectly from the immense volume of transactions that occur in foreign exchange markets. If all participants agreed on how exchange rates would evolve, transactions would occur only for commercial and investment reasons. There would be no transaction due to buyers believing a currency is worth more than what the sellers believe if buyers and sellers hold the same opinion. Furthermore, transactions would largely involve non-financial firms – notably importers, exporters, borrowers and investors – trading with financial firms, notably banks. However, analysis of foreign exchange transactions data collected biannually by the Federal Reserve Bank of New York shows that over 95 percent of foreign exchange changes hands between banks and other financial firms. That is, less than 5 percent of transactions involve non-financial firms. In other words, banks and other financial establishments are trading between themselves, presumably because buyers of a currency believe it to be worth more than the sellers believe.[36]

Jeffrey Frankel and Kenneth Froot have examined data for the British pound, German mark, Japanese yen, and Swiss franc and found that trading volume and dispersion of expectations were positively related in these four currencies.[37] They have also shown that the volatility of exchange rates is related to trading volume.

The connection between volatility of exchange rates and dispersion of expectations of forecasters can be related to one of the explanations of exchange overshooting discussed later in this book. This explanation involves a choice between following the advice of technical forecasters, those

---

35 Richard Levich, "Analyzing the Accuracy of Foreign Exchange Advisory Services: Theory and Evidence," in Richard Levich and Clas Wihlberg (eds), *Exchange Risk and Exposure: Current Developments in International Financial Management*, D.C. Heath, Lexington, MA, 1980. See also Richard J. Sweeney, "Beating the Foreign Exchange Market," *Journal of Finance*, March 1986, pp. 163–82.

36 If the value of a currency is judged in portfolio terms, diversification value would be behind trading as well as the expected change in the exchange rate. Therefore, it is possible that both buyer and seller agree on the expected change in exchange rate, but differ in terms of the value from diversification.

37 Jeffrey A. Frankel and Kenneth A. Froot, "Chartists, Fundamentalists, and Trading in the Foreign Exchange Market," *American Economic Review*, Papers and Proceedings, May 1990, pp. 181–5.

EXHIBIT 13.1   THE SUCCESS OF PROFESSIONAL FORECASTERS

It has been said that an economist is a person with one foot in the freezer and the other in the oven who believes that on average things are just about OK. The cynicism behind this comment reflects the view that averages can hide wide dispersions. Therefore, even if forecasters were able on average to predict exchange rates better than freely available forward rates, we might still wonder how this average was formed. Were all forecasters successful, or were they widely different and successful only on average? Similarly, were some forecasters right year after year and others wrong year after year, or were the successful forecasters themselves difficult to predict? The summary below, which describes the research of Jeffrey Frankel and Menzie Chinn, tells us only of the success of forecasters, on average. We must still ask whether the risk, which would be present if it were different forecasters who were successful at different times or if forecasters were widely different and correct only on average, is excessive for the returns earned.

Banks, multinationals, and anyone else who participates in international currency markets could use more accurate forecasts of foreign exchange rates. Yet predictions in this area have been notoriously bad. It often has been found that investors would do better to ignore current forecasts. Instead, they could view the exchange rate as an unpredictable random walk, just as likely to rise as to fall. Now a new study by NBER Research

Associate Jeffrey Frankel and Menzie Chinn finds that professional forecasts, under certain conditions, can help to predict changes in exchange rates. Frankel and Chinn examine the monthly predictions from an average of about 45 forecasters regarding the currencies of 25 developed and developing countries between February 1988 and February 1991. The data come from *Currency Forecasters' Digest*. Frankel and Chinn also examine monthly predictions for these currencies based on the value of their exchange rates in forward markets, where participants promise to exchange currencies in the future at a specified price.

In "Are Exchange Rate Expectations Biased? Tests for a Cross Section of 25 Currencies," Frankel and Chinn report that the prediction based on forward markets is wrong more often than not. Both the three-month-ahead predictions and the 12-month-ahead predictions of exchange rate shifts have the wrong sign more than half the time. The average of the professional forecasters when they look either three or 12 months ahead across the 25 currencies, on the other hand, is right more than half the time.

Source: "Forecasting Foreign Exchange Rates," *The NBER Digest*, National Bureau of Economic Research, November 1991.

---

basing views on past exchange rates; and following the advice of fundamentalist forecasters, those basing views on economic fundamentals. The explanation of overshooting assumes a positive association between the success of forecasters and the numbers of market participants who follow the forecasters.[38] If the chartists who follow trends

38 See Jeffrey A. Frankel and Kenneth A. Froot, "The Dollar as an Irrational Speculative Bubble: A Tale of Fundamentalists and Chartists," *National Bureau of Economic Research*, Working Paper 959, January 1988.

happen to be more correct than the fundamentalists, the chartists will gain followers thereby reinforcing the trend. For example, when a currency is rising, the chartists who base beliefs on extrapolating the past will be correct, people will buy according to the chartists' recommendations, and therefore the chartists' forecasts will prove to be correct. This "positive feedback" can, according to the theory, cause exchange rates to move well beyond their values based on economic fundamentals. Eventually, however, the rates will be so inappropriate

EXHIBIT 13.2 GOOD LUCK OR GOOD JUDGEMENT?

In 1992, with the British pound being pummeled by speculators, one individual was particularly closely associated with the huge losses incurred by the Bank of England as it tried to keep the pound within the European Exchange Rate Mechanism (ERM) band. His name is George Soros, and his story is told briefly in the following paragraphs.

While Norman Lamont was dithering last autumn, unable to make up his mind whether to take the U.K. out of the European exchange rate mechanism, the Hungarian-born financier, George Soros, was clear that the pound was overvalued and needed to free itself from its constricting currency strait jacket. What is more, he was ready to gamble $10 billion backing his judgment.

Mr. Soros was the one who read the economic runes correctly. With his now renowned sense of timing, he committed his Quantum Fund, based in the Netherlands Antilles, to selling sterling short up to this value (and, in fact, more). The Chancellor countered that he would spend up to $15bn defending his currency. But Mr. Soros's sales of sterling provided the momentum that put the pound into an uncontrollable spin. On Black Wednesday, 16 September 1992, Mr. Lamont was ignominiously forced to backtrack and bring sterling out of the ERM. Over the previous few days, the U.K. had lost around $10bn trying to shore up its currency, while Mr. Soros made a cool $1bn for the Quantum Fund out of his punt.

Today Mr. Lamont is out of his job, while the iconoclastic Mr. Soros is riding on the crest of a wave. One up for the hidden hand of the market? Or simply another dubious achievement for international speculators?

His gamble on sterling certainly put Mr. Soros on the world media map. Previously he was known to the general public only as the reclusive millionaire who in 1990 sacked his butler and his wife after a row involving the use of a £500 bottle of Château Lafite as cooking wine in a goulash. After Black Wednesday he became as a Thames Television documentary dubbed him, The Man Who Broke the Pound . . .

Mr. Soros was born in Budapest in 1930. His father was a Hungarian Jewish lawyer who survived internment as a prisoner of war in Siberia between 1917 and 1921. Similarly George Soros, then known as Dzjehdzhe Shorosh, survived the Nazi occupation of Hungary during the Second World War. In 1947 he escaped the communist regime, coming first to Berne and then to London. Still only a teenager, he worked as a farm hand, house painter and railway porter before winning a place to study economics at the London School of Economics in 1949. There he met his intellectual mentor, the Austrian philosopher Karl Popper, whose theories on scientific method and whose book, *The Open Society and its Enemies*, deeply influenced the young fugitive from communism . . .

Mr. Soros's break came in 1963 when he was hired by Arnhold and S. Bleichroader to advise American institutions on their European investments. He persuaded his employers to start up two offshore funds – the First Eagle Fund in 1967 and the Double Eagle Fund in 1969. By 1973, he wanted more of the action himself. With his then partner James Rogers, he took many of the Double Eagle investors and started up the Soros Fund (later the Quantum Fund) in Curaçao. By the end of the decade the fund was chalking up annual returns of over 100% and George Soros was up among the seriously rich.

Source: Andrew Lycett, "Soros: Midas or Machiavelli?" *Accountancy*, July 1993, pp. 36–40.

Table 13.7 *Connection between past changes in exchange rates and median forecasts of future rates: different forecast horizons*

Source of data on forecasts				
MMS International[a]		The Economist[b]		
1-week	4-week	3-month	6-month	12-month
0.13^c	0.08	-0.08^c	-0.17^c	-0.33^c
(4.32)	(1.60)	(−2.98)	(−4.98)	(−5.59)

Notes
t-statistics given in parentheses below coefficients.
a Period, October 1984–January 1988.
b Period, June 1981–August 1988.
c Significant at 99 percent confidence level.

Source: Jeffrey A. Frankel and Kennett A. Froot, "Chartists, Fundamentalists, and Trading in the Foreign Exchange Market," *American Economic Review*, Papers and Proceedings, May 1990, p. 184.

Table 13.8 *Forecasting methods of Euromoney respondents*

Year	Number using chartist methods	Number using fundamentals	Number using both methods
1978	3	19	0
1981	1	11	0
1983	8	1	1
1984	9	0	2
1985	15	5	3
1986	20	8	4
1987	16	6	5
1988	18	7	6

Source: Jeffrey A. Frankel, "Chartists, Fundamentalists, and Trading in the Foreign Exchange Market," National Bureau of Economic Research, *NBER Reporter*, February 1991.

that the chartists' projections will prove wrong, followers of forecasters will switch to the fundamentalists' advice, reinforcing the opinion of the fundamentalists, causing more to follow the fundamentalists' advice, and so on.

Survey data from a variety of sources indicate a large and growing influence of chartist-forecasting techniques, especially for short horizons. For example, Table 13.7 shows the result of analysis of forecasts gathered by *MMS International* and *The Economist* for overlapping time periods.[39] The table shows the extent that a 1 percent increase in the value of the US dollar in a 1-week period causes forecasters, as measured by the median (middle) forecast, to anticipate a further dollar appreciation. We see that for 1 week horizons a 1 percent dollar appreciation is associated with a median belief in a further 0.13 percent dollar appreciation. This drops to 0.08 percent at the 4-week horizon. However, the longer horizon forecasts using survey data from *The Economist* reveal reversions, with forecasters believing that past-week changes in exchange rates will eventually be reversed. Indeed, the median forecast is for a third of past-week changes to be reversed within 1 year.

The overshooting role of chartists is indirectly supported by the forecasting techniques used by the

services surveyed by *Euromoney*.[40] Table 13.8 shows the shift from economic fundamentals to chartist techniques in the period 1978–88. The data also reveal, however, an increasingly large number of forecasting services using both methods. These conclusions are supported by a questionnaire survey conducted on behalf of the Bank of England in 1988.[41] The questionnaire, which solicited the views of chief foreign exchange dealers based in London, revealed that more than 90 percent considered technical – that is, chartist – factors in making forecasts over one or more time horizons, with the dependence on technical views being more pronounced over shorter horizons. As with the evidence from *MMS International* versus *The Economist*, more attention is paid to fundamental analysis the longer the forecasting horizon.

The reliance on technical forecasts has been reinforced by the success of technical trading rules. These include rules based on past exchange rates

39 Jeffrey A. Frankel and Kenneth A. Froot, op. cit.

40 See Jeffrey A. Frankel, "Chartists, Fundamentalists, and Trading in the Foreign Exchange Market," National Bureau of Economic Research, Annual Research Conference, 1991.

41 See Mark P. Taylor and Helen Allen, "The Use of Technical Analysis in the Foreign Exchange Market," *Journal of International Money and Finance*, June 1992, pp. 304–14.

such as "buy if the 1-week moving average moves above the 12-week moving average, and sell when the opposite occurs." A popular form of technical trading rule involves the use of a so-called **filter**. A filter rule might be to buy whenever a currency moves more than a given percentage above its lowest recent value, and to sell when it moves a given percentage above its highest recent value.[42]

The success of a variety of relatively simple rules has been reported by several researchers looking at different parts of the foreign exchange market. For example, Michael Dooley and Jeffrey Shafer, and also Dennis Logue, Richard Sweeney, and Thomas Willett, found profits from trading in the spot market.[43] These profits persisted even after allowance for transaction costs, although it is not clear whether they are sufficient for the risk involved. Trading rules have also been found profitable in the forward market and the futures market. However, there is an indication that trading based on simple rules is becoming less profitable.[44] This is what one would expect because as the rules become known, they are followed by more speculators, and profits are then competed away. Therefore, perhaps the inefficiencies found in the various studies discussed above are a matter of history, a mere artifact of foreign exchange market participants learning about the instruments in which they are trading. Alternatively, perhaps the inefficiencies are the result of predictability of central-bank intervention policies of the past, with central banks shifting to less predictable or to less activist behavior.

SUMMARY

1　In the absence of transaction costs, a risk-neutral forward speculator buys a foreign currency forward if the forward price of the currency is below the expected future spot price. A risk-neutral speculator sells forward if the forward price of the foreign currency exceeds the expected future spot price.

2　With transaction costs, a risk-neutral speculator buys if the forward ask price of the foreign currency is less than the expected future spot bid price, and sells if the forward bid price exceeds the expected future spot ask price.

3　Futures speculation is similar to forward speculation except that the futures contract can be sold back to the exchange prior to maturity allowing gains and losses to be taken. There is also marking-to-market risk on currency futures.

4　A speculator buys a call on a foreign currency if the probability-weighted sum of possible payouts based on the speculator's opinion exceeds the price of the option by enough to compensate for the opportunity cost and risk involved.

42　On forward market trading rules see Paul Boothe, "Estimating the Structure and Efficiency of the Canadian Foreign Exchange Market," unpublished PhD dissertation, University of British Columbia, 1981, and on futures market rules see Richard M. Levich and Lee R. Thomas III, "The Significance of Technical Trading-Rule Profits in the Foreign Exchange Market: A Bootstrap Approach," *Journal of International Money and Finance*, October 1993, pp. 451–74.

43　See Michael Dooley and Jeffrey Shafer, "Analysis of Short-Run Exchange Rate Behavior: March 1973 to November 1981," in David Bigman and Teizo Taya (eds), *Exchange Rates and Trade Instability*, Ballenger, Cambridge, MA, 1983, pp. 43–9; Dennis Logue, Richard Sweeney, and Thomas Willett, "Speculative Behavior of Foreign Exchange Rates During the Current Float," *Journal of Business Research*, 6, 1979, pp. 159–74; and Stephan Schulmeister, "Currency Speculation and Dollar Fluctuations," *Quarterly Review*, Banca Nationale del Lavoro, December 1988, pp. 343–65.

44　See Levich and Thomas, op. cit.

5 Investment in favor of a foreign currency can be achieved by borrowing domestic currency, buying the foreign currency spot, and purchasing an investment instrument denominated in the foreign currency. This is a swap and is equivalent to buying the foreign currency forward.

6 It is possible to speculate against a foreign currency by borrowing that currency, converting it spot into domestic currency, and investing in the domestic currency.

7 Not hedging an exposure that can be avoided is speculation.

8 Speculation offers abnormal returns if markets are inefficient. In an efficient foreign exchange market, relevant information is reflected in exchange rates. Weak-form efficiency occurs when relevant information on past exchange rates is reflected in current rates; semi-strong efficiency when all publicly available information is reflected; and strong-form efficiency when *all* information, public and private, is reflected.

9 A difference between the forward rate and the expected future spot rate is called forward bias. A joint test of forward bias and of foreign exchange market efficiency is to regress forward rates and other relevant information on realized spot exchange rates. The absence of forward bias is implied by a zero constant and a forward-rate coefficient of unity. Efficiency is implied by zero coefficients on any other included variables.

10 Efficiency can also be tested by examining the sequential errors in forward forecasts of realized spot exchange rates. Omitted information is likely to cause sequentially related (persistent) prediction errors.

11 Forward bias is the risk premium that forward market participants require to compensate them for taking positions in particular currencies. Others are willing to pay this compensation to avoid risk.

12 Exchange-rate forecasting models have not generally predicted well outside the estimation period. This is the case even when realized values of variables believed to influence exchange rates are used in the formation of predictions.

13 Correlations between exchange rates and variables believed to affect exchange rates are generally low and sometimes have the opposite signs to those we would expect.

14 While widely expected events should not cause exchange rates to change, surprise events should affect exchange rates. Evidence on the effect of surprises is mixed.

15 Slowly changing opinions among market participants about the underlying policy regime governing exchange rates can generate data that appears to support market efficiency, when in fact it is caused by shifting beliefs about the relevant regime. It is important that any model used to judge market efficiency be based on the regime beliefs that market participants hold.

16 Exchange-rate forecasting services have a generally poor record of outdoing the forward rate when predicting future spot exchange rates. This is what market efficiency would imply. However, some forecasts based on chartist techniques which project according to past exchange rates, have allowed speculators to make profits. More emphasis seems to have been given to chartist forecasting techniques based on their success. This could cause exchange-rate volatility in the form of overshooting exchange rates.

REVIEW QUESTIONS

1 In what ways are speculation, market efficiency, and forecasting closely related matters?
2 Taking into account transaction costs, what does a speculator compare when deciding whether to go long in a particular foreign currency via a forward exchange contract?
3 Taking into account transaction costs, what does a speculator compare when deciding whether to go short in a particular foreign currency via a forward contract?
4 Are futures more or less liquid than forwards for a currency speculator?
5 What is the main advantage of options versus forwards or futures as an instrument of currency speculation?
6 What is required to go long in the euros vis-à-vis the US dollar via a swap?
7 How would you short the euro via a swap?
8 Why is doing nothing when importing or exporting tantamount to speculation on exchange rates?
9 What is meant by weak-form, semi-strong form, and strong-form market efficiency?
10 Are there any "insiders" in the foreign exchange markets?
11 What type of regression equation could you use to simultaneously test the efficiency of the foreign exchange market and the existence of forward bias?
12 Is it possible to test for the omission of important factors in the pricing of foreign currencies without any measures of these factors?
13 What is meant by "rational" forecasts?
14 Why might you compare the performance of a spot exchange-rate forecasting model with the ability of forward exchange rates to predict eventually realized spot rates?
15 Is the correlation coefficient between the ratio of US to Japanese prices and the exchange rate of the Japanese yen per dollar, likely to be positive or negative?
16 Why might anticipated changes in variables appear statistically insignificant when related to exchange rates?
17 What is an "event study" and how could it be applied to learning about what influences exchange rates?
18 What problem is presented by "changing regimes" in a study of market efficiency?
19 What type of information is used in "technical" forecasting?
20 What might you deduce about what has happened to different peoples' opinions on exchange rates from an increase in the volume of foreign exchange transactions?

ASSIGNMENT PROBLEMS

1 Why might a speculator prefer speculating on the futures market to speculating with forward exchange contracts?
2 What is the advantage of speculating with options?
3 If foreign exchange markets were very efficient, what would this imply about the profits from foreign exchange cash management?

4   Why might foreign exchange markets be efficient even if it is possible to make a positive return from using forecasting techniques?

5   Why does forward bias depend on risk aversion?

6   How might you speculate on the exchange rate being *less* volatile than the market as a whole believes?

7   Why can we test for market efficiency without including any variables which might influence exchange rates in our test?

8   How might low correlations of individual variables with exchange rates hide a strong relationship of many variables when included together?

9   What different interpretations can be given to the shifting of the probability distribution of beliefs about a policy regime?

10 Do huge profits by an individual speculator such as George Soros necessarily imply markets are inefficient?

BIBLIOGRAPHY

Baillie, Richard and Patrick C. McMahon, *The Foreign Exchange Market: Theory and Econometric Evidence*, Cambridge University Press, New York, 1989.

Boothe, Paul and David Longworth, "Foreign Exchange Market Efficiency Tests," *Journal of International Money and Finance*, June 1986, pp. 135–52.

Chen, T.J. and K.C. John Wei, "Risk Premiums in Foreign Exchange Markets: Theory and Evidence," *Advances in Financial Planning and Forecasting*, 4, 1990, pp. 23–42.

Chiang, Thomas C., "Empirical Analysis of the Predictors of Future Spot Rates," *The Journal of Financial Research*, Summer 1986, pp. 153–62.

Chinn, Menzie and Jeffrey Frankel, "Patterns in Exchange Rate Forecasts for Twenty-five Currencies," *Journal of Money, Credit and Banking*, November 1994, pp. 759–70.

Dunis, Christian and Michael Feeny (eds), *Exchange Rate Forecasting*, Woodhead-Faulkner, New York, 1989.

Everett, Robert M., Abraham M. George, and Aryeh Blumberg, "Appraising Currency Strengths and Weaknesses: An Operational Model for Calculating Parity Exchange Rates," *Journal of International Business Studies*, Fall 1980, pp. 80–91.

Frankel, Jeffrey A. and Kenneth A. Froot, "Using Survey Data to Test Some Standard Propositions Regarding Exchange Rate Expectations," *American Economic Review*, March 1987, pp. 133–53.

Froot, Kenneth A. and Richard H. Thaler, "Anomalies: Foreign Exchange," *Journal of Economic Perspectives*, Summer 1990, pp. 179–92.

Goodman, Stephen H., "No Better than the Toss of a Coin," *Euromoney*, December 1978, pp. 75–85.

Hodrick, Robert J., *The Empirical Evidence on the Efficiency of Forward and Futures Foreign Exchange Markets*, Harwood Academic Publishers, New York, 1988.

——and Sanjay Srivastava, "An Investigation of Risk and Return in Forward Foreign Exchange," *Journal of International Money and Finance*, April 1984, pp. 5–29.

Koedjik, Kees G. and Mack Ott, "Risk Aversion, Efficient Markets and the Forward Exchange Rate," *Review*, Federal Reserve Bank of St. Louis, December 1987, pp. 5–8.

Kohers, Theodor, "Testing the Rate of Forecasting Consistency of Major Foreign Currency Futures," *International Trade Journal*, Summer 1987, pp. 359–70.

Krugman, Paul and Maurice Obstfeld, *International Economics: Theory and Policy*, Harper-Collins, New York, 1994.

Kwok, Chuck C.Y. and LeRoy D. Brooks, "Examining Event Study Methodologies in Foreign Exchange Markets," *Journal of International Business Studies*, 21, 2, second quarter 1990, pp. 189–224.

Levich, Richard M., "On the Efficiency of Markets for Foreign Exchange," in Rudiger Dornbusch and Jacob A. Frenkel (eds), *International Economic Policy: Theory and Evidence*, Johns Hopkins University Press, Baltimore, MD, 1979.

——"Analyzing the Accuracy of Foreign Exchange Advisory Services: Theory and Evidence," in Richard Levich and Clas Wihlberg (eds), *Exchange Risk and Exposure: Current Developments in International Financial Management*, D.C. Heath, Lexington, MA, 1980.

——and Lee R. Thomas III, "The Significance of Technical Trading-Rule Profits in the Foreign Exchange Market: A Bootstrap Approach," *Journal of International Money and Finance*, October 1993, pp. 451–74.

Lewis, Karen K., "Can Learning Affect Exchange Rate Behavior? The Case of the Dollar in the Early 1980s," *Journal of Monetary Economics*, 23, 1989, pp. 79–100.

Mark, Nelson C., "Exchange Rates and Fundamentals: Evidence on Long-Horizon Predictability," *American Economic Review*, March 1995, pp. 201–18.

Meese, Richard A. and Kenneth Rogoff, "Empirical Exchange Rate Models of the Seventies: Do They Fit Out of Sample?" *Journal of International Economics*, February 1983, pp. 3–24.

——, "Currency Fluctuations in the Post-Bretton Woods Era," *The Journal of Economic Perspectives*, Winter 1990, pp. 117–34.

Pearce, Douglas K., "Information, Expectations, and Foreign Exchange Market Efficiency," in Thomas Grennes (ed.), *International Financial Markets and Agricultural Trade*, Westview, Boulder, CO, 1989, pp. 214–60.

Sarno, Lucio and Mark P. Taylor, *The Economics of Exchange Rates*, Cambridge University Press, New York, 2003.

Sweeney, Richard J., "Beating the Foreign Exchange Market," *Journal of Finance*, March 1986, pp. 163–82.

Taylor, Dean, "Official Intervention in the Foreign Exchange Market, or Bet against the Central Bank," *Journal of Political Economy*, April 1982, pp. 356–68.

Part V

International investment and financing

If there is any individual factor which commands principal responsibility for the astonishingly rapid globalization of the world economy, that factor is surely international investment in its various forms. For example, the global flow of foreign direct investment, FDI, which involves managerial control overseas through the extent of ownership, grew from under $180 billion in 1991 to approximately $1.5 trillion in 2000, an eight-fold increase in a decade. The growth in multinational organizations which has resulted from this direct investment is partly responsible for the fact that by 2001, over 28 percent of the global GDP was produced by 200 companies. It is the factors behind and the consequences of these startling statistics that are the focus of Part V of this book.

The first three chapters of Part V consider the three categories of international capital flows appearing in the balance-of-payments accounts, namely, short-term investments (Chapter 14), portfolio investments (Chapter 15), and direct investments (Chapter 16). These categories are identified by balance-of-payments statisticians and presented separately in this book because they represent different degrees of liquidity, with short-term investments being the most liquid and direct investments the least liquid.

Chapter 14, which deals with short-term investments, begins with a discussion of the criterion for making short-term covered investments when there are costs of transacting in the foreign exchange markets. Since short-term investments are an important aspect of cash management, the chapter looks also at short-term borrowing decisions and a number of other aspects of the management of working capital in a multinational context.

Chapter 15, which deals with portfolio investment, considers international aspects of stock and bond investment decisions, paying particularly close attention to the benefits of international portfolio diversification. It is shown that international diversification offers significant advantages over domestic diversification, despite uncertainty about exchange rates. A section is included on the international capital asset pricing model. This model is used to compare the implications of internationally segmented versus integrated capital markets. Chapter 15 ends with a discussion of bond investments, again with a focus on diversification issues.

Chapter 16 considers a capital-budgeting framework that management can employ when deciding whether or not to make FDIs. We shall see that a number of problems are faced in evaluating foreign investments that are not present when evaluating domestic investments. These extra problems include the presence of exchange-rate and country risks, the need to consider taxes abroad as well as at home, the issue of which country's cost of capital to use as a discount rate, the problem posed by restrictions on repatriating income, and the frequent need to account for subsidized financing. The means for dealing with these difficulties are clarified by an extensive example.

Chapter 16 includes an appendix in which various topics in taxation are covered, some of which are relevant for the capital-budgeting procedure used for evaluating FDIs. The appendix offers a general overview of taxation in the international context, covering such topics as value-added tax – which is assuming increasing international importance – tax-reducing organizational structures, and withholding tax.

It is through FDI that some companies have grown into the giant multi-national corporations (MNCs) whose names have entered every major language – Sony, IBM, Shell, Ford, Nestlé, Mitsubishi, Citibank, and so on. Chapter 17 examines various reasons for the growth in relative importance of MNCs, as well as the reasons for international business associations that have resulted in transnational alliances. The chapter also considers some special problems faced by multinational corporations and transnational alliances, including the need to set transfer prices of goods and services moving between divisions and the need to measure and monitor country risk. The difficulties in obtaining and using transfer prices are described, as are some methods of measuring country risk. Clarification is given of the differences between country risk and two narrower concepts, political risk and sovereign risk. Methods for reducing or eliminating country risk are described. Chapter 17 concludes with an account of the problems and benefits that have accompanied the growth of multinational corporations and transnational alliances. This involves a discussion of the power of these giant organizations to frustrate the economic policies of host governments, and of the transfer of technology and jobs that results from FDI.

The final chapter of Part V, Chapter 18, deals with project financing. The issues addressed include the country of equity issue, foreign bonds versus Eurobonds, bank loans, government lending, and matters that relate to financial structure. Overall, we shall see in Part V that there are important matters which are unique to the international arena, whether the issue concerns the uses or the sources of funds. We shall also see that substantial progress has been made in understanding many of the thornier multinational matters.

Chapter 14

Cash management

Where credit is due, give credit. When credit is due, give cash.

Evan Esar

THE OBJECTIVES OF CASH MANAGEMENT

Inflows and outflows of funds are generally uncertain, especially for large multinational corporations with sales and production activities throughout the world. It is therefore important for companies to maintain liquidity. The amount of liquidity and the form it should take constitute the topic of working-cash (or working-capital) management. Liquidity can take a number of forms, including coin and currency, bank deposits, overdraft facilities, and short-term readily marketable securities. These involve different degrees of opportunity cost in terms of forgone earnings available on less liquid investments. However, there are such highly liquid short-term securities in sophisticated money markets that virtually no funds have to remain completely idle. In some locations there are investments with maturities that extend no further than "overnight," and there are overdraft facilities which allow firms to hold minimal cash balances. This makes part of the cash management problem similar to the problem of where to borrow and invest.

The objectives of effective working-capital management in an international environment are

1   to allocate short-term investments and cash-balance holdings between currencies and countries to maximize overall corporate returns;

2   to borrow in different money markets to achieve the minimum cost.

These objectives are to be pursued under the conditions of maintaining required liquidity and minimizing any risks that might be incurred.

The problem of having numerous currency and country choices for investing and borrowing, which is the extra dimension of international finance, is also faced by firms which deal only in local markets. For example, a firm that produces and sells only within the United States will still have an incentive to earn the highest yield, or borrow at the lowest cost, even if that means venturing to foreign money markets. There *are* additional problems faced by firms that have a multinational orientation of production and sales. These include the questions of local versus head-office management of working capital, and how to minimize foreign exchange transaction costs, political risks, and taxes. We address these questions in this chapter along with matters faced by all firms concerned with investment returns and borrowing costs. We will also describe some actual international cash management systems that have been devised.

Let us begin our discussion of cash management by considering whether a company should invest or borrow in domestic versus foreign currency, where any foreign exchange exposure and risk is hedged by using forward exchange contracts. While this choice was discussed in Chapter 8, in that chapter we focused on arbitrage and interest parity, rather than hedged investment and borrowing choices with transaction costs. After discussing the investment and borrowing criteria we turn to whether a company with receipts and payments in different countries and currencies should manage working capital locally or centrally. We shall see that there are a number of advantages to centralization of cash management, and only a few disadvantages.

INVESTMENT AND BORROWING CHOICES WITH TRANSACTION COSTS

Investment criterion with transaction costs

An investment in pound-denominated securities by a holder of US dollars requires first a purchase of spot pounds. The pounds must be bought at the pound offer or ask rate, $S(\$/\text{ask}£)$, so that \$1 will buy

$$£\frac{1}{S(\$/\text{ask}£)}$$

This initial investment will grow in n years at the investment return of $r_£^I$

$$£\frac{1}{S(\$/\text{ask}£)}\left(1 + r_£^I\right)^n$$

This can be sold forward at the buying or bid rate on pounds, $F_n(\$/\text{bid}£)$, giving a US investor, after n years,

$$\$\frac{F_n(\$/\text{bid}£)}{S(\$/\text{ask}£)}\left(1 + r_£^I\right)^n$$

The amount received from \$1 invested instead in US dollar-denominated securities for n years at an annual rate $r_\$^I$ is $\$(1 + r_\$^I)^n$. Therefore, the rule for a holder of US dollars is to invest in pound securities when

$$\frac{F_n(\$/\text{bid}£)}{S(\$/\text{ask}£)}\left(1 + r_£^I\right)^n > \left(1 + r_\$^I\right)^n \quad (14.1)$$

and to invest in dollar securities when the reverse inequality holds.

If we had ignored foreign exchange transaction costs, then instead of the condition (14.1) we would have written the criterion for investing in pound securities as

$$\frac{F_n(\$/£)}{S(\$/£)}\left(1 + r_£^I\right)^n > \left(1 + r_\$^I\right)^n \quad (14.2)$$

In comparing the conditions (14.1) and (14.2) we can see that because transaction costs ensure that $F_n(\$/\text{bid}£) < F_n(\$/£)$ and $S(\$/\text{ask}£) > S(\$/£)$, where $F_n(\$/£)$ and $S(\$/£)$ are the middle exchange rates (i.e. the rates half way between the bid and ask rates), the condition for advantageous hedged investment in pound securities by a dollar-holding investor is made less likely by the presence of transaction costs on foreign exchange. That is, the left-hand side of (14.1), which includes transaction costs, is smaller than the left-hand side of (14.2), which excludes transaction costs. However, because both interest rates are investment rates, transaction costs on securities represented by a borrowing–lending spread have no bearing on the decision, and do not discourage foreign versus domestic-currency investment.

For example, suppose we have

$S(\$/\text{bid}£)$	$S(\$/\text{ask}£)$	$F_{1/2}(\$/\text{bid}£)$	$F_{1/2}(\$/\text{ask}£)$	$r_\$^I$	$r_£^I$
1.5800	1.5850	1.5600	1.5670	7%	10%

where $r_\$^I$ and $r_£^I$ are respectively the dollar and pound interest rates on 6-month securities, expressed on a full year, or per annum, basis. Then, receipts from the dollar investment at the end of the 6 months on each dollar originally invested are

$$\$\left(1 + r_\$^I\right)^n = \$(1.07)^{1/2} = \$1.03441$$

If the investor does not bother to calculate the receipts from the pound security using the correct side of the spot and forward quotations, but instead uses the midpoint values half way between "bids" and "asks," that is, $S(\$/£) = 1.5825$ and

$F_{1/2}(\$/\pounds) = 1.5635$, then receipts from the hedged pound security are

$$\$\frac{F_{1/2}(\$/\pounds)}{S(\$/\pounds)}(1+r_\pounds^I)^{1/2} = \$\frac{1.5635}{1.5825}(1.10)^{1/2}$$
$$= \$1.03622$$

This amount exceeds the $1.03441 from the dollar-denominated security, making the pound security the preferred choice. However, if the correct exchange rates are used, reflecting the fact that hedged investment in pound-denominated securities require *buying* pounds spot at the ask price and *selling* pounds forward at the bid price, then the proceeds from the pound security are calculated as

$$\$\frac{F_{1/2}(\$/\mathrm{bid}\pounds)}{S(\$/\mathrm{ask}\pounds)}(1+r_\pounds^I)^{1/2} = \$\frac{1.5600}{1.5850}(1.10)^{1/2}$$
$$= \$1.03227$$

The dollar-denominated security with receipts of $1.03441/\$ invested is seen to be better than the pound-denominated security for a dollar-holding investor. That is, the correct choice is the dollar security, a choice that would not be made without using the exchange rates which reflect the transaction costs of buying and selling pounds. The example confirms that inclusion of transaction costs on foreign exchange tends to favor the choice of domestic-currency investments.

Borrowing criterion with transaction costs

When a borrower considers using a swap to raise US dollars by borrowing pounds, the borrowed pounds must be sold at the pound selling rate, $S(\$/\mathrm{bid}\pounds)$. For each $1 the dollar borrower wants he or she must therefore borrow

$$\pounds\frac{1}{S(\$/\mathrm{bid}\pounds)}$$

The repayment on this number of borrowed pounds after n years at $r_\pounds^B$ per annum is

$$\pounds\frac{1}{S(\$/\mathrm{bid}\pounds)}(1+r_\pounds^B)^n$$

This number of pounds can be bought forward at the buying rate for pounds, $F_n(\$/\mathrm{ask}\pounds)$, so that the number of dollars paid in n years for borrowing $1 today is

$$\$\frac{F_n(\$/\mathrm{ask}\pounds)}{S(\$/\mathrm{bid}\pounds)}(1+r_\pounds^B)^n$$

Alternatively, if $1 is borrowed for n years in US dollars at $r_\$^B$ per annum, the repayment in n years is

$$\$(1+r_\$^B)^n$$

The borrowing criterion that allows for foreign exchange transaction costs is that a borrower should obtain dollars by borrowing hedged British pounds (i.e. via a swap) whenever

$$\frac{F_n(\$/\mathrm{ask}\pounds)}{S(\$/\mathrm{bid}\pounds)}(1+r_\pounds^B)^n < (1+r_\$^B)^n \qquad (14.3)$$

Because $F_n(\$/\mathrm{ask}\pounds) > F_n(\$/\pounds)$ and $S(\$/\mathrm{bid}\pounds) < S(\$/\pounds)$, the condition (14.3) is more unlikely than the condition without transaction costs on foreign exchange, which is simply

$$\frac{F_n(\$/\pounds)}{S(\$/\pounds)}(1+r_\pounds^B)^n < (1+r_\$^B)^n \qquad (14.4)$$

where $S(\$/\pounds)$ and $F_n(\$/\pounds)$ are mid-points between "bid" and "risk" exchange rates. For example, suppose a borrower who needs US dollars for 6 months faces the following.

$S(\$/\mathrm{bid}\pounds)$	$S(\$/\mathrm{ask}\pounds)$	$F_{1/2}(\$/\mathrm{bid}\pounds)$	$F_{1/2}(\$/\mathrm{ask}\pounds)$	$r_\$^B$	$r_\pounds^B$
1.5800	1.5850	1.5500	1.5570	8%	12%

where $r_\$^B$ and $r_\pounds^B$ are respectively the per annum 6-month borrowing rates in dollars and pounds. The dollar repayment after 6 months from dollar borrowing is

$$\$(1+r_\$^B)^{1/2} = \$(1.08)^{1/2} = \$1.03923$$

If the borrower did not bother to calculate the cost of a "swap out" of pounds using the correct bid or ask exchange rates but instead used mid-point rates, the repayment per dollar borrowed would be computed from the left-hand side of equation (14.4) as

$$\$\frac{F_n(\$/£)}{S(\$/£)}\left(1 + r_£^B\right)^n = \$\frac{1.5535}{1.5825}\left(1.12\right)^{1/2}$$
$$= \$1.03891$$

The borrower would choose the pound-denominated loan because it requires a smaller repayment. However, if the borrower selected the proper bid and ask rates as in the left-hand side of equation (14.3), the repayment on the swap would be

$$\$\frac{F_n(\$/\text{ask }£)}{S(\$/\text{bid }£)}\left(1 + r_£^B\right)^n = \$\frac{1.5570}{1.5800}\left(1.12\right)^{1/2}$$
$$= \$1.04289$$

This is larger than the repayment from borrowing dollars. We find that the incentive to venture into foreign-currency denominated borrowing is reduced by the consideration of foreign exchange transaction costs, just as is the incentive to invest in foreign currency.

Unlike the situation with investment, where borrowing–lending spreads are irrelevant, in the case of borrowing, foreign-currency borrowing may be discouraged by borrowing–lending spreads. This is because *when foreign funds are raised abroad,* lenders may charge foreign borrowers more than they charge domestic borrowers because they consider loans to foreigners to be riskier. For example, the mark-up over the prime interest rate for dollars facing a US borrower in the United States might be smaller than the markup over prime for the same US borrower when raising pounds in Britain. This may be due to greater difficulty collecting on loans to foreigners, or to the difficulty of transferring credible information on credit-worthiness of borrowers between countries. However, if the pounds can be raised in the United States, there should be no difference between dollar–pound investment spreads and borrowing spreads.

Firms invest and borrow cash because sometimes they have net cash inflows and at other times they have net cash outflows. While the investing and borrowing criteria that we have given provide a way of choosing between alternatives, they do not provide guidance on some of the complexities of multinational cash management. For example, how should a company respond when one subsidiary has surplus amounts of a currency, while another subsidiary which operates independently needs to borrow the same currency? Should a company hedge all its foreign-currency investments and/or borrowing when it deals in numerous different foreign currencies and thereby enjoys some natural diversification? Good cash management in these and other situations requires some centralization of financial management and perhaps also central holding of the funds themselves. As we shall see later, centralization has several advantages but also some disadvantages when the holdings of funds, as well as management decisions concerning the funds, are centralized.

INTERNATIONAL DIMENSIONS OF CASH MANAGEMENT

Advantages of centralized cash management

Netting

It is extremely common for multinational firms to have divisions in different countries, each having accounts receivable and accounts payable, as well as other sources of cash inflows and outflows, denominated in a number of currencies. If the divisions are left to manage their own working capital, it can happen, for example, that one division is hedging a long pound position while at the same time another division is hedging a short pound position of the same maturity. This situation can be avoided by **netting**, which involves the calculation of the overall position in each currency. This calculation requires some central coordination of cash management.

The benefit that is enjoyed from the ability to net cash inflows and outflows through centralized cash management comes in the form of reduced transaction costs. The amount that is saved depends on the extent that different divisions deal in the same currencies and have opposite positions in these currencies.[1] The benefit also depends on the length of the period over which it is feasible to engage in netting. This in turn depends on the ability to practice **leading and lagging.**

Leading and lagging involve the movement of cash inflows and outflows forward and backward in time so as to permit netting and achieve other goals?[2] For example, if Aviva has to pay £1 million for denim on June 10 and has received an order for £1 million of jeans from Britain, it might attempt to arrange payment for about the same date and thereby avoid exposure. If the payment for the jeans would normally have been after June 10 and the receivable is brought forward, this is called leading of the export. If the payment would have been before June 10 and is delayed, this is called lagging of the export. In a similar way it is possible to lead and lag payments for imports.

When dealing at arm's length, the opportunities for netting via leading and lagging are limited by the preferences of the other party. However, when transactions are between divisions of the same multinational corporation, the scope for leading and lagging (for the purpose of netting and achieving other benefits such as deferring taxes by delaying receipts) is considerable. Recognizing this, governments generally regulate the length of credit and acceleration of settlement by putting limits on leading and lagging. The regulations vary greatly from country to country, and are subject to change, often with very little warning. If cash managers are to employ leading and lagging successfully and not find themselves in trouble with tax authorities, they must keep current with what is allowed.[3]

Currency diversification

When cash management is centralized it is possible not only to net inflows and outflows in each separate currency, but also to consider whether the company's foreign exchange risk is sufficiently reduced via natural diversification that the company need not hedge all the individual positions. The diversification of exchange-rate risk results from the fact that exchange rates do not all move in harmony. Consequently, a portfolio of inflows and outflows in different currencies will have a smaller variance of value than the sum of variances of the values of the individual currencies.[4] We can explain the nature of the diversification benefit by considering a straightforward example.

Suppose that in its foreign operations, Aviva buys its cloth in Britain and sells its finished garments in both Britain and Germany in the following amounts:

	Germany (€)	Britain (£)
Denim purchase	0	2,000,000
Jeans sales	1,500,000	1,000,000

The timing of payments for British denim and the timing of sales of jeans are the same. (Alternatively, we could think of the revenue from the export of jeans as receipts from foreign investments, and the

1 Clearly, if all divisions are long in a foreign currency, or all divisions are short in the foreign currency, the transaction-cost advantage of centralized cash management exists only if there are economies of scale in transacting. Of course, there *are* in fact such economies of scale.

2 Leading and lagging are practised to defer income and thereby delay paying taxes and to create unhedged positions in order to speculate; cash managers may delay paying out currencies they expect to appreciate and accelerate paying out currencies they expect to depreciate. Leading and lagging are therefore used to hedge, speculate, and reduce taxes.

3 The regulations governing leading and lagging are described each year by Business International in its *Money Report*. The large multinational accounting firms also publish the current regulations.

4 For an account of the size of diversification benefits see Mark R. Eaker and Dwight Grant, "Cross-Hedging Foreign Currency Risk," Working Paper, University of North Carolina, August 1985.

payment for imports of cloth as repayment of a debt.)

One route open to Aviva is to sell forward the €1.5 million it is to receive and, after netting its pound position, buy forward £1 million. Aviva would then be hedged against changes in both exchange rates versus the dollar. An alternative, however, is to consider how the British pound and the euro move vis-à-vis the dollar and hence between themselves. Let us suppose for the purpose of revealing the possibilities, that when the euro appreciates vis-à-vis the dollar, generally the pound does so as well. In other words, let us suppose that the euro and pound are highly positively correlated. Such a correlation will occur if the source of exchange-rate movements stems from economic developments in the United States. For example, good news concerning the US currency such as a reduced current account deficit would likely increase the value of the dollar against both the euro and the pound.

With net pound payables of £1 million, euro receivables of €1.5 million, and spot exchange rates of, for example, $S(\$/\text{€}) = 1.2$ and $S(\$/\text{£}) = 1.8$, the payables and receivables cancel out: the payable to Britain is £1 million $\times$ \$1.8/£ = \$1.8 million at the current rate, and the receivable from Germany is €1.5 million $\times$ \$1.2/€ = \$1.8 million. The risk is that exchange rates can change before payments are made and receipts are received. However, if the pound and the euro move together and the US dollar depreciates against both of the currencies by, for example, 10 percent to $S(\$/\text{€}) = 1.32$ and $S(\$/\text{£}) = 1.98$, then payments to Britain will be £1 million $\times$ \$1.98/£ = \$1,980,000, and receipts from Germany will be €1.5 million $\times$ \$1.32/€ = \$1,980,000, which is still the same. The amount that is lost through extra dollar payments to Britain will be offset by extra dollar revenue from Germany. We find in this case that Aviva is quite naturally unexposed if it can be sure that the currencies will always move together vis-à-vis the dollar.

In our example, we have, of course, selected very special circumstances and values for convenience.

In general, however, there is safety in large numbers. If there are receivables in many different currencies, then when some go up in value, others will come down. There will be some canceling of gains and losses. Similarly, if there are many payables, they can also cancel. Moreover, as in our example, receivables and payables can offset each other if currency values move together. There are many possibilities that are not obvious, but it should be remembered that although some canceling of gains and losses might occur, some risk will remain. A firm should use forward contracts or some other form of hedging if it wishes to avoid all foreign exchange risk and exposure. However, a firm with a large variety of small volumes of payables and receivables (i.e. small volumes in many different currencies) might consider that all the transaction costs involved in the alternative forms of hedging are not worthwhile in view of the natural hedging from diversification. The determination of whether the diversification has sufficiently reduced the risk can only be made properly when cash management is centralized.

Pooling

Pooling occurs when cash is held as well as managed in a central location. The main advantage of pooling is that higher returns can be enjoyed due to economies of scale in returns offered on investment vehicles such as bank deposits.[5] At the same time, cash needs can be met wherever they occur out of the centralized pool without having to keep precautionary balances in each country. Uncertainties and delays in moving funds to where they are needed require that some balances be maintained everywhere, but with pooling, a given probability of having sufficient cash to meet liquidity needs can be achieved with smaller cash holdings than if holdings are decentralized. The reason

5 See Antoine Gautier, Frieda Granot, and Maurice D. Levi, "Alternative Foreign Exchange Management Protocols: An Application of Sensitivity Analysis," *Journal of Multinational Financial Management*, February 2002, pp. 1–20.

pooling works is that cash surpluses and deficiencies in different locations do not move in a perfectly parallel fashion. As a result, the variance of total cash flows is smaller than the sum of the variances of flows for individual countries. For example, when there are large cash-balance outflows in Britain, it is not likely that there will also be unusually large outflows in Australia, Japan, Sweden, Kuwait, and so on. If a firm is to have sufficient amounts in each country, it must maintain a large cash reserve in each. However, if the total cash needs are pooled in, for example, the United States, then when the need in Britain is unusually high, it can be met from the central pool because there will not normally be unusually high drains in other countries at the same time.

Security availability and efficiency of collections

All of the advantages of centralized cash management that we have mentioned so far, which are all particular aspects of economies of scale, would accrue wherever centralization occurs. However, if the centralization occurs in a major international financial center such as London or New York, there are additional advantages in terms of a broader range of securities that are available and an ability to function in an efficient financial system.

It is useful for a firm to denominate as many payments and receipts as its counterparties will allow in units of a major currency and to have bills payable in a financial center. Contracts for payment due to the firm should stipulate not only the payment date and the currency in which payment is to be made, but also the branch or office at which the payment is due. Penalties for late payment can help ensure that payments are made on time. The speed of collection of payments can be increased by using post-office box numbers wherever they are available. Similarly, if a firm banks with a large-scale multinational bank, it can usually arrange for head-office accounts to be quickly credited using an electronic funds transfer system, even if payment is made at a foreign branch of the bank.

Disadvantages of centralized cash management

Unfortunately, it is rarely possible to hold all cash in a major international financial center. This is because there may be unpredictable delays in moving funds from the financial center to other countries. If an important payment is due, especially if it is to a foreign government for taxes or to a local supplier of a crucial input, excess cash balances should be held where they are needed, even if these mean opportunity costs in terms of higher interest earnings available elsewhere. When the cash needs in local currencies are known well ahead of time, arrangements can be made in advance for receiving the needed currency, but substantial allowances for potential delay should be made. When one is used to dealing in North America, Europe, and other developed areas, it is too easy to believe that banking is efficient everywhere, but the delays that can be faced in banks in some countries can be exceedingly long, uncertain, and costly.

In principle it is possible to centralize the *management* of working capital even if some funds do have to be held locally. However, complete centralization of management is difficult because local representation is often necessary for dealing with local clients and banks. Even if a multinational bank is used for accepting receipts and making payments, problems can arise that can only be dealt with on the spot. Therefore, the question a firm must answer is the degree of centralization of cash management and of cash holding that is appropriate, and in particular, which activities and currencies should be decentralized.[6]

If interest parity always held exactly, the cash management problem would be simplified in that it would then not matter in which currency or country a firm borrowed or invested. However, as we explained in Chapter 8, there are factors which do allow limited departures from interest parity to occur, at least from the perspective of any one borrower or lender. Let us consider what each of

6 Exhibit 14.1 explains how General Electric arrived at its decision about currency management centralization.

313

EXHIBIT 14.1 DECENTRALIZING CURRENCY MANAGEMENT AT GENERAL ELECTRIC

Having considered the pros and cons of centralization of currency management, the US-based global giant General Electric decided to download responsibility. Their reasons are given below.

General Electric (GE) is a global company, with 13 key business operations all over the world, dealing in dozens of currencies. International activities include export sales, international sourcing, manufacturing and sales affiliates abroad, and joint ventures, and other business associations. For some years now, GE managers have been challenged to "think globally" in all aspects of their business, and this mindset permeates our organization.

Management of currency risk goes hand-in-hand with the globalization of today's business environment. GE's philosophy of foreign exchange exposure management is consistent with what we refer to as "Work-Out" — GE shorthand for empowerment of those closest to the action, and the consequent elimination of layers of staff review and bureaucracy. Thus, at GE, foreign exchange is not a staff responsibility, but an integral part of managing a global business. It is one of a number of external factors that a business must manage. Businesses are empowered to do it themselves, not only by the company's philosophy, but by the reality of the situation. They are closest to the strategic and tactical decisions which are most relevant to FX (foreign exchange) exposure management. They must decide such things as how and where to source materials and components; where to locate manufacturing facilities, and how to manage their working capital. Treasury's job is to work with the businesses as they go through their analysis and come up with a comprehensive currency management plan, but the business itself is responsible for implementation and results...

Our major objectives for foreign exchange management are earnings and cash flow. Ultimately, we must deliver earnings in dollars to our shareholders. As such, the businesses are responsible for dollar net income, and therefore for management of their income-related currency exposures. The objective is to neutralize exposure, not to take views on the markets. Hedging is encouraged, as a short-term tactical solution, to stabilize near-term net income. It is not seen as a substitute for a long-term, strategic mindset. Nor is it seen as a profit center, either within the business or in treasury.

Source: Marcia B. Whitaker, "Strategic Management of Foreign Exchange Exposure in an International Firm," in Yakov Amihud and Richard M. Levich (eds), *Exchange Rates and Corporate Performance*, New York University Salomon Center, New York, 1994, pp. 247–51.

the factors discussed earlier – transaction costs, political risk, liquidity preference, and taxes – implies for working-capital management. We shall see that each factor has slightly different implications.

Transaction costs, political risk, liquidity preference, taxes, and cash management

Transaction costs are a reason for keeping funds in the *currency* that is received if the funds might be needed later in the same currency. For example, if a firm receives 2 million won in payment for sales from its subsidiary in South Korea and needs approximately this quantity of won to meet a payment in a month or two, the funds should be left in Korean won if expected yields are not sufficiently higher in other currencies to cover two sets of transaction costs — out of won and back into won.

Political risk is a reason to keep funds in the company's home *country* rather than in the country in whose currency the funds are denominated. This is because the home jurisdiction is generally safer for investors than foreign jurisdictions.[7] The reduction in political risk that results from moving funds home must, of course, be balanced against the extra costs this entails. Between most developed countries, the transaction costs of temporarily moving funds home are likely to exceed the benefit from reduced political risk, and so cash balances are maintained offshore. However, the political situation in some third-world countries might be considered sufficiently volatile that only minimal working balances should be maintained in those countries.

Liquidity considerations argue in favor of keeping funds in the currency in which they are *most likely* to be needed in the future. This might not be the currency in which the funds arrive or the company's home currency. The liquidity factor is hence different from transaction costs, which suggest that funds should be kept in the currency in which they arrive, and it is also different from political risk, which suggests that funds should be kept at home. We use the words "most likely" because it is the uncertainty of cash flows that is responsible for the need to maintain liquidity. If inflows and outflows were *perfectly* predictable, a firm could arrange the maturities, currencies and locations of securities so that securities would mature at the precise time, place, and in the needed currency. Complete certainty would do away with the precautionary motive for holding money balances. However, even with uncertainty in the timing and amounts of cash inflows and outflows, extremely liquid money-market investments and overdraft facilities at banks have allowed firms to keep most of their funds in interest-bearing instruments.

Withholding taxes are a reason to avoid countries in which withholding tax rates exceed the investor's domestic tax rate, because in such a case it will not in general be possible to receive full withholding tax credit. Lower taxes on foreign exchange gains than on interest income are a reason to invest in countries whose currencies are at a

forward premium if the premium is treated as a capital gain and capital gains face favorable tax rates. However, for firms that are heavily involved in dealing in many countries, foreign exchange gains and interest earnings are likely to face the same tax rates. There is therefore little need to favor any particular market. The factors affecting the location of working capital are summarized in Table 14.1.

Examples of cash management systems

It will be illustrative to end our discussion of cash management by considering the cash management systems of two US multinational corporations. Both of these corporations have undergone name changes and reorganizations as part of mergers and acquisitions, but what they set up illustrates how netting can be done, and how centralized cash management through a **currency center** can be effected.

Navistar International

Navistar was formed in a reorganization of International Harvester, the farm and transportation equipment manufacturer. The company established a netting system that worked as follows.[8]

Table 14.1 Factors affecting working-capital management

Factor	Implication
Absence of forward markets	Keep funds in the currency received if an anticipated future need exists
Transaction costs	Keep funds in the currency received
Political risk	Move funds to the domestic market
Liquidity requirements	Keep funds in the currency most likely to be needed in the future
Taxes	Avoid high withholding taxes and keep funds in appreciating currencies

7 This is not always the case. There are countries where investors would rather hold their funds in an offshore jurisdiction such as the United States or Switzerland than at home.

8 See "Multilateral Netting System Cuts Costs, Provides Flexibility for International Harvester," *Money Report*, Business International, December 20, 1979.

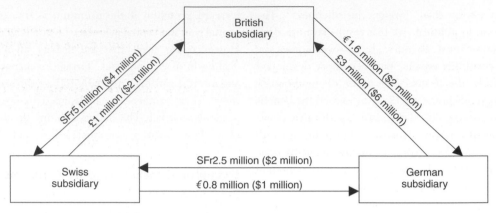

(a) *Receivables and payables reported to currency center before the 15th of the month*

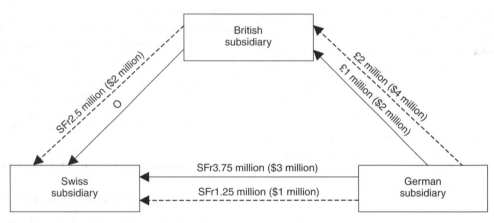

(b) *Net payables/receivables (broken lines) and actual cash flows (solid lines) made on the 25th of the month*

Figure 14.1 *Example of Navistar International's foreign exchange netting system*

Notes
It is assumed that on the 15th of the month $S(€/\$) = 0.8$, $S(£/\$) = 0.5$, and $S(SFr/\$) = 1.25$. Information on receivables and payables is provided for the Swiss currency center on or before the 15th of the month. The currency center converts the amounts of foreign exchange into dollars at the going exchange rate (as shown in Figure 14.1(a)) and evaluates the net amounts owed between subsidiaries (as shown by the broken lines in Figure 14.1(b)). Rather than having the German subsidiary pay the British subsidiary the equivalent of $4 million while the British subsidiary in turn pays the Swiss subsidiary $2 million, the German subsidiary will be instructed to add $2 million onto what it pays the Swiss subsidiary and to reduce what it pays the British subsidiary by this amount. The British and Swiss subsidiaries will receive no instructions to pay anybody. The total number of transactions will be reduced from six to only two. Transaction costs will be faced on only $5 million worth of transactions.

The netting system was based at a currency clearing center, located in a finance company in Switzerland. Prior to clearing foreign exchange, the Swiss finance company had been responsible for transactions involving foreign currencies. The netting scheme worked on a monthly cycle, as illustrated in Figure 14.1. By the 15th day of each month, all participating subsidiaries sent information to the currency clearing center on payables and receivables existing at that time in local currencies. The clearing center converted all amounts into dollars at the current spot exchange rate, and sent information to those subsidiaries with net payables on how much they owed and to whom.

These paying subsidiaries were responsible for informing the net receivers of funds and for obtaining and delivering the foreign exchange. Settlement was on the 25th of the month or the closest business day, and the funds were purchased two days in advance so that they were received on the designated day. Any difference between the exchange rate used by the Swiss center on the 15th and the rate prevailing for settlement on the 25th gave rise to foreign exchange gains or losses that were attributed to the subsidiary.

The original clearing system was for intra-company use and did not include outside firms. After a decade with this system, the company introduced a scheme for foreign exchange settlements for payments to outsiders. There were two different dates, the 10th and the 25th or the nearest business day, on which all foreign exchange was purchased by and transferred from the Swiss center. The payment needs were sent electronically to the center from the subsidiary more than 2 days before the settlement date, and the center netted the amounts of each currency so as to make the minimum number of foreign exchange transactions. The subsidiary which owed the foreign exchange settled with the clearing center by the appropriate settlement date. According to the company, netting cut the total number of transactions with outsiders in half, saving the company transaction costs.

More flexibility was given to the cash management system by the use of interdivisional leading and lagging. If, for example, a subsidiary was a net payer, it could delay or lag payment for up to two months while compensating the net receiver at prevailing interest rates. Net receivers of funds could at their discretion make funds available to other subsidiaries at interest. In this way the need to resort to outside borrowing was reduced; the Swiss clearing center served to bring different company subsidiaries together. The netting with leading and lagging allowed the company to eliminate intra-company floats and reduce by over 80 percent the amount of money that would otherwise have been transferred.

Compaq (HP)

When it was known as Digital Equipment, Compaq, which is now part of Hewlett Packard, centralized its cash management in two currency centers.[9] The cash positions of European subsidiaries were monitored and managed from the European headquarters in Geneva. Cash management for other subsidiaries was handled by the company's principal headquarters in Acton, Massachusetts. The subsidiaries and appropriate headquarters communicated electronically, and the movement of cash was facilitated by the use of a limited number of US banks with offices in many countries. The cash management system worked as shown in Figure 14.2.

Foreign exchange positions were established and adjusted on a weekly basis. Every Thursday, all subsidiaries sent a report to the currency center at their headquarters. In their statements they gave projected cash inflows and outflows in each foreign currency for the following week. They also gave their bank-account positions. Foreign sales subsidiaries were generally net receivers of foreign exchange. On the following Monday the subsidiary borrowed its anticipated net cash inflow via an overdraft facility and transferred the funds to the corporate headquarters' account at the same bank from which it drew the overdraft funds. For example, if the British sales subsidiary expected net receipts of £10 million and had no bank balance, it would call its banks for the best exchange rate. If the most favorable rate for buying dollars was $S(\$/£) = 2.0$, it would transfer $20 million to the Geneva currency center by borrowing £10 million and converting it into dollars. The selected bank – the one which offered the best rate

9 An excellent account of Compaq's centralized cash management system can be found in "How Digital Equipment's Weekly Cash Cycle Mobilizes Idle Funds," *Money Report*, Business International, January 30, 1981. A similar system that uses a currency center in London was operated by RCA. The company adapted a system available from Citibank for large clients which kept track of currency needs and netting. For a full account, see "Standard Netting System Remodeled to Suit RCA's Own Needs," *Money Report*, Business International, July 13, 1979.

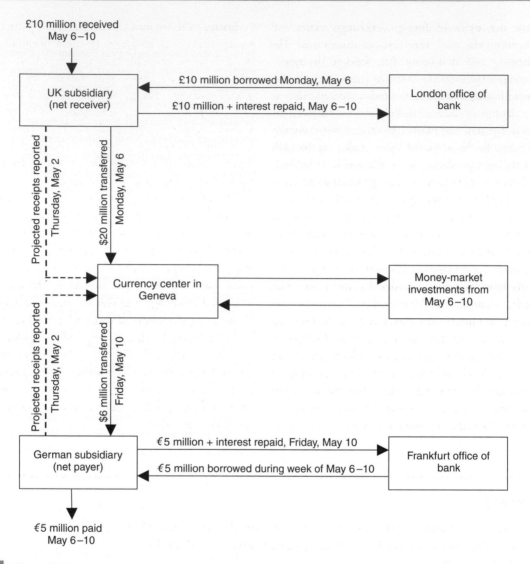

Figure 14.2 *Digital Equipment's weekly cash cycle*

Notes
We assume that the UK subsidiary is a net receiver of pounds and that the German subsidiary is a net payer of euros. Both subsidiaries send their cash-flow projections to the currency center on Thursday, May 2. On the following Monday the UK subsidiary borrows its expected cash receipts and then transfers the dollar equivalent to Geneva. (It is assumed that $S(\$/£) = 2.0$.) The debt is repaid in the currency of borrowing during the week of May 6–10. The German subsidiary borrows euros during the week of May 6–10 as its payments fall due. On Friday, May 10, the Geneva currency center transfer the dollar equivalent to the subsidiary. (It is assumed that $S(\$/€) = 1.2$.) This is used to repay the overdraft on the day. During the week the currency center has $20 million to invest in the money market.

on dollars – debited the British subsidiary's account in London by £10 million and, on the same day, credited the Geneva headquarter's account with $20 million. The British subsidiary would repay the £10 million debt incurred due to the overdraft as the receipts came in.

In order to ensure that it was able to make the same-day transfers and obtain the overdrafts, Compaq maintained close ties with a limited number of multinational US banks. The subsidiaries obtained funds only via overdrafts; they did not use other means of borrowing funds. Subsidiaries that were net users of foreign exchange instead of net receivers used the reverse procedure. The subsidiary reported its need for cash to the appropriate headquarters on Thursday, and beginning on the following Monday, it used overdraft lines as payments were met. On the following Friday the subsidiary received funds from the parent company to pay off the overdraft and make up for any unanticipated disbursements that had been made.

There were occasions when a subsidiary received more funds than it anticipated, with this resulting in transfers to headquarters more than once a week. Alternatively, sometimes a subsidiary faced small unprojected disbursements or late receipts. It then used backup overdrafts. If a subsidiary faced unusually large payments it called its parent for extra funds. Compaq used post-office lock boxes in Canada and the United States in order to speed up the handling of receivables, and in Europe, it instructed customers to pay its bank directly rather than the local subsidiary itself. All investing or borrowing in currencies other than the US dollar was hedged on the forward market to reduce foreign exchange exposure and risk.

Because the amount of cash handled by the two headquarters was so large, it could generally be invested more favorably than if each separate subsidiary placed it. Funds were invested in various money markets. The parent had the total amount of funds from its many subsidiaries to invest for a week. A subsidiary would, however, repay the overdraft *during* the week. It follows that the interest costs on overdrafts were not as large as the interest earnings of the headquarters.

The major advantage of Compaq's system was that there was no foreign exchange exposure for the subsidiary. This is because the payable on the overdraft was in the local currency, as was the receivable against which the funds were borrowed. Local currency was paid out as it arrived. An additional advantage was that the currency centers handled large amounts of cash and could therefore get lower spreads when buying and selling foreign exchange. They could also take a broader perspective of investment and borrowing opportunities as well as enjoy the advantages of netting, currency diversification, pooling, and financial efficiency that we discussed earlier.

SUMMARY

1 The choice between domestic-currency and foreign-currency investment or borrowing should be based on spot and forward exchange-rate quotations which reflect transaction costs.

2 The need to buy/sell spot and then sell/buy forward for hedged foreign-currency investment/borrowing tends to favor the domestic-currency alternative.

3 Centralized cash management allows netting of long and short positions in each currency, where the positions are those of different divisions of a multinational company. The scope for netting is enhanced by leading and lagging cash inflows and outflows.

4 Centralized cash management provides an ability to consider how exposure to numerous exchange rates provides natural diversification.

5 Centralization permits a broad view of investment and borrowing opportunities.

6 Centralized cash management reduces the precautionary cash needs via pooling; funds can be moved from the central location to where they are needed.

7 Complete centralization is limited by the need to maintain local personnel to deal with unpredictable delays that can occur when moving funds between countries, and for dealing with local banks and clients.

8   The different reasons why interest parity may not hold have different implications for the management of working capital. In particular, transaction costs induce keeping funds in the currency in which cash arrives, political risk induces keeping funds at home, liquidity considerations induce holding currencies that are most likely to be needed, and taxes induce avoiding countries with very high withholding rates and holding appreciating currencies if facing favorable capital gains tax treatment on foreign exchange gains.

REVIEW QUESTIONS

1   What are the objectives of international cash management?
2   Why do transaction costs on spot and forward exchange reduce the incentive to invest in foreign-currency securities?
3   Why do transaction costs on spot and forward exchange reduce the incentive to borrow in a foreign-currency?
4   What is meant by "netting?"
5   What is meant by "leading" and "lagging?"
6   What are the advantages of centralized cash management?
7   How can "pooling" provide benefits for international cash management?
8   How does liquidity preference affect international cash management decisions?

ASSIGNMENT PROBLEMS

1   Assume that you face the following money-market and exchange-rate quotations:

$r_\$$	$r_{C\$}$	$S(C\$/ask\$)$	$S(C\$/bid\$)$	$F_{1/2}(C\$/ask\$)$	$F_{1/2}(C\$/bid\$)$
4.20%	6.80%	1.3850	1.3830	1.4000	1.3960

a   If $r_\$$ and $r_{C\$}$ are respectively the per annum 6-month US dollar and Canadian dollar borrowing rates facing a US firm that wishes to remain hedged, should that firm borrow in US or Canadian dollars?

b   If $r_\$$ and $r_{C\$}$ are respectively the per annum interest rates available on 6-month US and Canadian treasury bills, in which country should a US firm place its funds?

2   Suppose that as the money manager of a US firm you face the following situation:

$r_\$^B$	9.0%
$r_\$^I$	8.0%
$r_{C\$}^B$	10.5%
$r_{C\$}^I$	9.5%
$S(C\$/ask\$)$	1.2400
$S(C\$/bid\$)$	1.2350
$F_1(C\$/ask\$)$	1.2600
$F_1(C\$/bid\$)$	1.2550

Here $r_\$^B$ and $r_\$^I$ r are the 1-year interest rates at which you can respectively borrow and invest in US dollars, and $r_{C\$}^B$ and $r_{C\$}^I$ are the 1-year borrowing and investing interest rates in Canadian dollars.

   a   If you had funds to invest for 1 year, in which currency would you invest?

   b   If you wished to borrow for 1 year, in which currency would you borrow?

3   Suppose that you face the situation in Question 2, except that the effective tax rate on interest income is 50 percent, and the effective tax rate on capital gains is 30 percent. In which currency-denominated securities would you wish to invest?

4   What is the connection between the size of the gain from netting and the nature of long and short positions of the different divisions of a multinational firm?

5   Which of the gains from centralization of cash management are related to foreign exchange transaction costs?

6   What are the differences and similarities between the gain from centralization of cash management via pooling, and the gain via diversification of different currencies?

7   Will allowance for co-movement between currencies allow a firm to eliminate foreign exchange risk or foreign exchange exposure?

8   Why might we be suspicious that any apparent covered interest arbitrage opportunity must be due to not considering transaction costs, political risk, taxes, or liquidity?

9   Why do multinational firms tend to use multinational banks, rather than local banks in their local markets?

10   Why do many governments restrict the maximum length of time over which firms can practise leading and lagging of accounts receivable and payable?

BIBLIOGRAPHY

Business International, *Automated Global Financial Management*, Financial Executives Research Foundation, Morristown, NJ, 1988.

Essayyad, Mussa and Paul C. Jordan, "An Adjusted-EOQ Model for International Cash Management," *Journal of Multinational Financial Management*, 1 and 2, 1993, pp. 47–62.

Shapiro, Alan C. "Payments Netting in International Cash Management," *Journal of International Business Studies*, Fall 1978, pp. 51–8.

Srinivasan, Venkat and Yong H. Kim, "Payments Netting in International Cash Management: A Network Optimization Approach," *Journal of International Business Studies*, Summer 1986, pp. 1–20.

——, Susan E. Moeller, and Yong H. Kim, "International Cash Management: State of the Art and Research Directions," *Advances in Financial Planning and Forecasting*, Vol. 4, Part B, 1990, pp. 161–94.

Chapter 15

Portfolio investment

Economic forecasting houses . . . have successfully predicted fourteen of the last five recessions.

David Fehr

As we explained in Chapter 1, the world as a whole benefits from international investment via a better allocation of financial capital, and a smoother wealth or consumptive stream from lending and borrowing. Individual investors gain in these same ways from engaging in international investment and thereby achieving a more **efficient portfolio**. Stated in the vernacular of finance, diversified international investment offers investors higher expected returns and/or reduced risks vis-à-vis exclusively domestic investment. This chapter focuses on the sources and sizes of these gains from venturing overseas for portfolio investment, which is investment in equities and bonds where the investor's holding is too small to provide any effective control. (Direct investment, defined in Chapter 5 as investment where the investor achieves some control – via 10 percent or more ownership – is discussed separately in Chapters 16 and 17.)

THE BENEFITS OF INTERNATIONAL PORTFOLIO INVESTMENT

Spreading risk: correlations between national asset markets

Because of risk aversion, investors demand higher expected return for taking on investments with greater risk. It is a well-established proposition in portfolio theory that whenever there is imperfect correlation between different assets' returns, risk is reduced by maintaining only a portion of wealth in any individual asset. More generally, by selecting a portfolio according to expected returns, variances of returns, and correlations between returns, an investor can achieve minimum risk for a given expected portfolio return, or maximum expected return for a given risk. Furthermore, *ceteris paribus*, the lower are the correlations between returns on different assets, the greater are the benefits of portfolio diversification.

Within an economy there is some degree of independence of asset returns, and this provides some diversification opportunities for investors who do not venture abroad. However, there is a tendency for the various segments of an economy to feel jointly the influence of overall domestic activity, and for asset returns to respond jointly to prospects for domestic activity, and uncertainties about these prospects. This limits the independence of individual security returns, and therefore also limits the gains to be made from diversification within only one country.

Because of different industrial structures in different countries, and because different economies do not trace out exactly the same business cycles, there are reasons for smaller correlations of

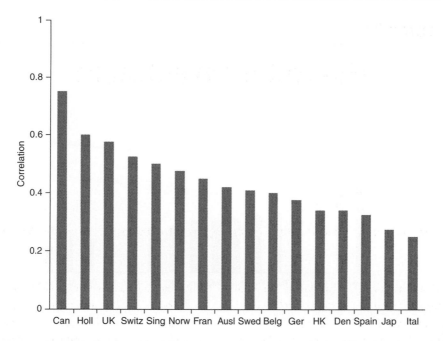

Figure 15.1 *Correlations between US and other countries' stock markets, US dollars, 1980–90*

Notes
The US stock market is not very highly correlated with stock markets in other countries: correlation coefficients average about 0.5. These relatively low correlations mean a potential gain from holding an internationally diversified portfolio of stocks.

Source: Patrick Odier and Bruno Solnik, "Lessons for International Asset Allocation." Copyright 1993, CFA Institute. Reproduced and republished from *Financial Analysts Journal* with permission from CFA Institute. All rights reserved.

expected returns between investments in different countries than between investments within any one country. This means that foreign investments offer diversification benefits that cannot be enjoyed by investing only at home and means, for example, that a US investor might include British stocks in a portfolio even if they offer lower expected returns than US stocks: the benefit of risk reduction might more than compensate for lower expected returns.

Figure 15.1 graphically illustrates the degree of independence of foreign versus US stock markets during the period 1980–90 as reported by Patrick Odier and Bruno Solnik.[1] The coefficients in the

figure are based on US dollar values of stock markets, and have an average of about 0.5. This means a squared-correlation, called R^2, of 0.25. The R^2 statistic is an indicator of the extent to which two variables – in this case two countries' stock markets – respond jointly to common factors. Figure 15.1 suggests that different countries' stock markets have substantial idiosyncrasies of returns; with $R^2 = 0.25$, 75 percent of returns are due to factors specific to individual countries. In principle, the low correlations that are found could be the consequence of different economic and political events in different countries, or of different countries' stock-market indexes being formed from dissimilar mixes of industries. We shall show in the following paragraphs that the latter explanation is not supported by the empirical evidence.

Figures 15.2 and 15.3 show, respectively, the correlation coefficients between the Japanese and

1 Patrick Odier and Bruno Solnik, "Lessons for International Asset Allocation," *Financial Analysts Journal*, March/April 1993, pp. 63–77. This excellent survey of international portfolio investment provides much useful data in addition to that cited in this chapter.

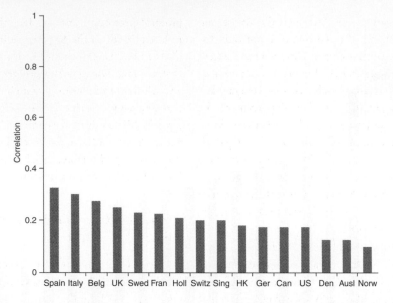

Figure 15.2 *Correlations between Japanese and other countries' stock markets, Japanese yen, 1980–90*

Notes
Japan's stock market follows a path which appears to be quite independent of the stock markets of other countries, with correlation coefficients averaging about 0.2. This situation suggests substantial potential benefits for Japanese investors holding an internationally diversified stock portfolio.

Source: Patrick Odier and Bruno Solnik, "Lessons for International Asset Allocation." Copyright 1993, CFA Institute. Reproduced and republished from *Financial Analysts Journal* with permission from CFA Institute. All rights reserved.

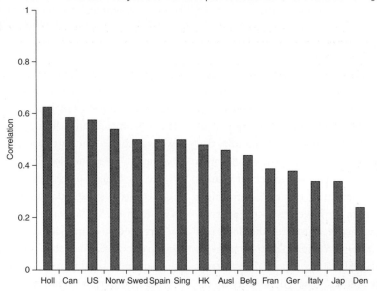

Figure 15.3 *Correlations between British and other countries' stock markets, British pounds, 1980–90*

Notes
The British stock market is correlated with stock markets of other countries to about the same extent as is the US stock market, with correlation coefficients averaging about or slightly below 0.5. As is the case for investors from the United States, Japan, and other countries, British investors stand to benefit for international diversification.

Source: Patrick Odier and Bruno Solnik, "Lessons for International Asset Allocation." Copyright 1993, CFA Institute. Reproduced and republished from *Financial Analysts Journal* with permission from CFA Institute. All rights reserved.

non-Japanese markets, and between the British and non-British markets. We see that it is not only the United States which has a major idiosyncratic element in its stock market. Indeed, for Japan in particular, the very low correlation coefficients – averaging less than 0.2 – suggest that less than 4 percent of the factors behind the Japanese stock market are affecting other stock markets. (The R^2 for Japan is approximately $0.2 \times 0.2 = 0.04$, or only 4 percent.)

Correlations between a slightly different group of stock markets, but for a more up-to-date period than reflected in Figures 15.1, 15.2, and 15.3, are shown in Table 15.1. (Figures 15.1, 15.2, and 15.3 provide correlations for 1980–90, while Table 15.1, which was constructed for this book, provides correlation for the period 1994–2002). Despite the different time periods and consideration of a slightly different set of countries, the picture that emerges from the table is similar to that given by the figures. For example, the US market correlation is relatively high with Canada: Canadian and US stock markets move together closely which is not surprising, given their

physical proximity and the fact that US–Canadian bi-lateral trade is the largest trading relationship in the world. The US market is less closely related to that of Japan which is at a greater physical distance and which has a different industrial structure. France and Germany, which are close neighbors in Europe, have highly connected markets. The Indian stock market moves differently from all the other markets considered in the table, all of which are at a higher level of economic development.

Country-specific volatility versus industrial structure

As we have mentioned, two possible explanations for the generally low correlations between different countries' stock markets are

1   that the countries' economies evolve differently over time with different business cycles;
2   that the countries have different industries in their stock-market indexes.

Table 15.1 *Monthly US dollar returns and risks for national stock markets, 1994–2002*[a]

	Correlation coefficient											Monthly mean return (%)	Risk (Standard deviation) (%)
	Aus	Can	Fr	Ger	Ind	Ital	Jap	Holl	Sing	Swed	UK		
Australia												0.18	4.38
Canada	0.66											0.36	5.50
France	0.46	0.59										0.37	6.19
Germany	0.50	0.62	0.85									0.39	6.83
India	0.43	0.41	0.21	0.21								−0.67	7.82
Italy	0.37	0.47	0.70	0.68	0.31							0.63	7.05
Japan	0.57	0.44	0.37	0.32	0.25	0.28						−0.62	6.55
Holland	0.54	0.60	0.87	0.88	0.27	0.67	0.37					0.64	6.07
Singapore	0.63	0.53	0.40	0.41	0.36	0.28	0.41	0.44				−0.23	9.29
Sweden	0.59	0.71	0.80	0.83	0.38	0.68	0.39	0.76	0.45			0.31	7.06
UK	0.55	0.64	0.75	0.74	0.13	0.50	0.34	0.76	0.49	0.70		0.29	4.26
USA	0.57	0.76	0.67	0.74	0.25	0.49	0.43	0.72	0.54	0.71	0.82	0.64	4.71

Note
a India 1997–2002, Sweden 1996–2002.

Source: International Monetary Fund, *International Financial Statistics*, December 2003. *Yahoo* finance website www.yahoo.com

Table 15.2 *Correlations between US dollar monthly returns in automobile manufacturing, 1986–91*

	GM	Ford	Chrysler	Fiat	Volks	Peugot	Honda	Nissan
GM	1.0000							
Ford	0.8020	1.0000						
Chrysler	0.6829	0.6150	1.0000					
Fiat	0.4909	0.3541	0.3393	1.0000				
Volkswagon	0.4016	0.3350	0.2604	0.6177	1.0000			
Peugot	0.4517	0.4105	0.2994	0.5166	0.6347	1.0000		
Honda	0.2321	0.2195	0.1635	0.4162	0.1755	0.2503	1.0000	
Nissan	0.2980	0.2505	0.3722	0.3908	0.1974	0.2837	0.5957	1.0000

Source: Tania Zouikin, "Is International Investing Losing Its Lustre?" *Canadian Investment Review*, Winter 1992, p. 18.

Table 15.3 *Correlations between US dollar monthly returns in the consumer electronics industry, 1986–91*

	GE	Zenith	Phillips	Siemens	Matsushita	Sony
GE	1.0000					
Zenith	0.4816	1.0000				
Phillips	0.4295	0.3931	1.0000			
Siemens	0.4938	0.5389	0.5389	1.0000		
Matsushita	0.2562	0.1915	0.1885	0.1657	1.0000	
Sony	0.2035	0.1389	0.1108	0.2062	0.8286	1.0000

Source: Tania Zouikin, "Is International Investing Losing Its Lustre?" *Canadian Investment Review*, Winter 1992, p. 18.

In the latter case, the low correlations between overall stock market indexes could occur despite firms in a given industry, but in different countries, having highly correlated stock values; high correlations *within* industries might be swamped by low correlations *between* industries. Evidence suggesting that the low correlations are not due to different industrial compositions of different countries' market indexes is shown in Tables 15.2 and 15.3.[2] The tables show correlation coefficients between monthly returns measured in US dollars of major firms in given industries, but from different countries. We see from Table 15.2 that correlations between automobile manufacturers in different countries are low. For example, Honda and GM have a correlation coefficient of only 0.23. Table 15.3 shows a similar pattern in the consumer electronics industry. With firms in given industries but different countries offering such different return experiences, international portfolio diversification offers significant potential.

The size of the gain from international diversification

Gain from stock diversification

An indication of the size of the gain from including foreign stocks in a portfolio has been provided by the

2 Steven Heston and K. Geert Rouwenhorst have examined industrial structure versus country-specific sources of low correlations between country indexes. By considering 12 European countries during the period 1978–92, Heston and Rouwenhorst concluded that industrial structure plays very little role. Rather, low correlations between country indexes are almost exclusively due to country-specific factors. See Steven L. Heston and K. Geert Rouwenhorst, "Does Industrial Structure Explain the Benefits of International Diversification," *Journal of Financial Economics*, August 1994, pp. 3–27.

research of Bruno Solnik.[3] Solnik computed the risk of randomly selected portfolios of n securities for different values of n in terms of the volatility of these portfolios. For example, a large number of portfolios of two randomly selected companies were formed, and their return and volatility calculated. Then, portfolios of three randomly selected companies were formed, with average returns and volatilities calculated, and so on. As expected, it was found that volatility declines as more stocks are included. Moreover, Solnik discovered that an international portfolio of stocks has about half as much risk as a portfolio of the same size containing only US stocks. This result is shown in Figure 15.4. We see that the risk of US portfolios of over 20 stocks is approximately 25 percent of the risk of a typical security, whereas the risk of a well-diversified international

portfolio is only about 12 percent of that of a typical security. When Solnik considered other countries which have far smaller stock markets, he found that the gains from international diversification were, not surprisingly, much larger than for the United States. In smaller countries there is less opportunity to diversify within the country than in larger countries. For example, in the United States it is possible to invest in most of the world's industries, something you could not do in a small country such as Denmark or Egypt. Furthermore, in large countries such as the United States and Britain, there are often numerous multinational corporations trading on their stock markets. As we shall see, this means that investors holding only "domestic" stocks are actually achieving international diversification indirectly because of the extensive overseas activities of their own countries' companies. However, the evidence indicates that there are opportunities for further diversification by venturing into foreign stock markets even for the United States.

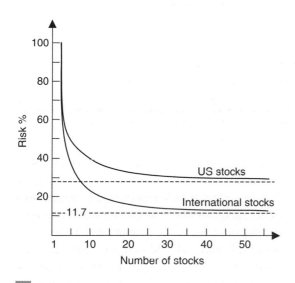

Figure 15.4 *The size of the gain from international diversification*

Notes
For any given number of stocks, an internationally diversified portfolio typically has less than half the risk of a domestically diversified portfolio.

Source: Bruno H. Solnik, "Why Not Diversify Internationally Rather than Domestically?" Copyright 1974, CFA Institute. Reproduced and republished from *Financial Analysts Journal* with permission from CFA Institute. All rights reserved.

3 Bruno H. Solnik, "Why Not Diversify Internationally Rather than Domestically?" *Financial Analysts Journal,* July–August 1974, pp. 48–54.

Risk from exchange rates

While there are gains from international diversification because of the independence between foreign and domestic stock returns, there is a possibility of added risk from unanticipated changes in exchange rates when foreign stocks are held. Therefore, it is important to consider whether the gains from imperfect correlations between stock returns when measured in terms of local currency more than compensate for the risk introduced by exchange rates. As we saw in Chapter 9 when dealing with the measurement of foreign exchange risk and exposure, the extent to which holding foreign stocks increases risk from unanticipated changes in exchange rates depends on both the volatility of exchange rates and on the way exchange rates and stock prices are related. The added risk from exchange rates also depends on whether stocks from only one foreign country, or from a number of different foreign countries, are added to a portfolio of domestic stocks.

The potential for exchange rates to add risk can be judged by comparing the volatility of stock values

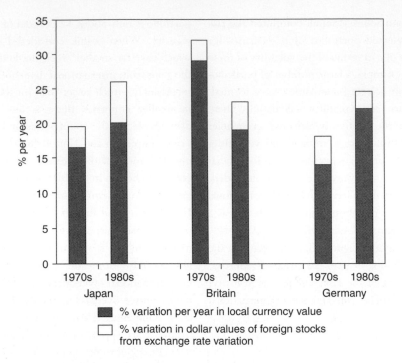

Figure 15.5 *Local-market versus exchange-rate components of volatility of US dollar values of non-US stocks, 1970s and 1980s*

Notes
Most of the variation in the US dollar value of non-US stocks is the result of volatility in the local-currency value of the stocks, rather than in exchange rates. Typically, exchange rates contribute 10–15% of the US dollar valuation of foreign stock markets.

Source: Patrick Odier and Bruno Solnik, "Lessons for International Asset Allocation." Copyright 1993, CFA Institute. Reproduced and republished from *Financial Analysts Journal* with permission from CFA Institute. All rights reserved.

measured in local currencies to the volatility of stock values measured in US dollars; US dollar values involve converting foreign currency values into dollars at the spot exchange rate, with variations in the spot rate possibly providing volatility depending on the covariation between exchange rates and stock prices. The difference between these two volatilities – local-currency value versus US dollar value – is an indication of the volatility contributed to the US dollar value by variations in exchange rates.[4] Figure 15.5 graphically

illustrates the volatility from the currency and local stock-market value components for Japanese, British, and German stocks. While exchange rates contribute risk, the exchange-rate element is seen to be the distinctly smaller of the two risk-contributing factors.

Evidence on exchange-rate risk from investing in one foreign country and in a group of foreign countries has also been provided by Cheol Eun and Bruce Resnick.[5] Eun and Resnick decompose the volatility of returns on foreign stocks into the volatility of stock returns in terms of local currency, the

4 Exchange rates contribute to volatility both via the variance of exchange rates, and via the covariance of exchange rates with local-currency values of stocks. The measure we use combines these two sources of volatility from exchange rates. So, implicitly, do the results of Solnik in Figure 15.4; Solnik's portfolio returns and risks involve the use of US dollar values.

5 Cheol S. Eun and Bruce G. Resnick, "Exchange Rate Uncertainty, Forward Contracts and International Portfolio Selection," *Journal of Finance*, March 1988, pp. 197–215.

volatility of exchange rates, and the comovement of stock prices in local currency and changes in exchange rates. That is, they separate the two sources of volatility from exchange rates, namely volatility of exchange rates themselves, and the volatility from covariance of exchange rates with local-currency stock prices. Specifically, they write the expected dollar rate of return to a US holder of, for example, British stocks as

$$\text{Expected dollar return on British stocks} = \dot{S}^* + r^*_{\text{UK}} \tag{15.1}$$

Here, r^*_{UK} is the expected stock return in terms of pounds, which consists of the expected dividend return plus the expected change in market value in pounds. $\dot{S}^*$ is the expected rate of change of the dollar value of the pound. This allows Eun and Resnick to write the variance of the dollar return on British stocks as

$$\text{Var(\$return on British stocks)} = \text{var}(\dot{S}) + \text{var}(r_{\text{UK}}) + 2\text{cov}(\dot{S}, r_{\text{UK}}) \tag{15.2}$$

This expression shows that the variance of the US dollar rate of return on British stocks can be decomposed into the variance of the dollar–pound exchange rate, the variance of the return on British stocks valued in pounds, and the covariance between the exchange rate and the pound rate of return on British stocks.

Table 15.4 shows the percentage composition of the US dollar return from holding the stock-market indexes of six foreign countries, when each market is held on its own. The first column gives $\text{var}(\dot{S})$ as a percentage of the variance of the dollar return from each foreign market, the second column gives $\text{var}(r)$ as a percentage of the variance of the dollar return, and the final column gives two times the covariance between the exchange rate and associated local return as a percent of the dollar return. We see that on its own the volatility in the exchange rate can contribute anything from less than 5 percent to over 50 percent of the volatility of dollar returns. We can also see that the covariance between exchange rates and local-currency returns contributes to the variance of US dollar returns. That is, movements in exchange rates are reinforced by movements in local stock markets. For example, on average, when the pound is declining, so is the British stock-market index. This means that exchange rates add to the volatility both directly in being volatile themselves, and indirectly by being positively related to local stock-market returns.

The situation for a portfolio of stocks from different countries is essentially the same as that for stocks from an individual country. According to the same study referred to in Table 15.4 by Cheol Eun and Bruce Resnick, approximately one-third of the variance of US dollar returns from holding an equally-weighted portfolio of the stock markets of seven countries, the United States and the six countries in Table 15.4, is directly due to the

Table 15.4 *Composition of US dollar weekly returns on individual foreign stock markets, 1980–85*

Country	Percentage of variance in US dollar returns from		
	Exchange rate	Local return	2 × Covariance
Canada	4.26	84.91	10.83
France	29.66	61.79	8.55
Germany	38.92	41.51	19.57
Japan	31.85	47.65	20.50
Switzerland	55.17	30.01	14.81
UK	32.35	51.23	16.52

Source: Cheol S. Eun and Bruce G. Resnick, "Exchange Rate Uncertainty, Forward Contracts, and International Portfolio Selection," *Journal of Finance*, March 1988, pp. 197–215.

exchange rate. In addition, about one quarter of the variance of this equally-weighted international portfolio is due to the covariance between exchange rates and local market returns: this is twice the covariance as described by equation (15.2). This leaves just over 40 percent of the variance of dollar returns as being due to the stock portfolio itself. We see the exchange rate contributes a substantial fraction of the volatility of dollar returns via the direct effect of the exchange-rate volatility, and via the indirect effect of positive covariance between exchange rates and local market returns. It would not appear that diversification among currencies has a substantial effect in reducing the *proportion* of risk attributable to changes in exchange rates.

With volatility directly or indirectly resulting from unanticipated changes in exchange rates, it is important to confirm whether this completely nullifies the benefits from international diversification attributable to the presence of some independence between stock-market returns in different countries. The answer is no. One reason is that it is possible to diversify internationally without adding exchange-rate exposure – by hedging in the forward market, by borrowing in the foreign currencies, or by using futures or currency options. The hedges would have to be based on the exposure in each currency, as given by regression coefficients according to Chapter 9.[6] A second reason international portfolio diversification is beneficial despite exchange-rate variability is that, even without hedging, the variance of the dollar return on an internationally diversified portfolio of stocks remains lower than the variance of the expected dollar return

from investing in the domestic stock market. This has been shown by Bruno Solnik, who compared the variance of returns on portfolios of US stocks with the variance of returns on internationally diversified portfolios, both when not hedging exchange-rate exposure and when hedging on the forward market.[7] Different-sized portfolios of US stocks and internationally diversified stocks were compared, with the results shown in Figure 15.6. This figure reveals that even though there is exchange-rate risk – given by the gap between the hedged and unhedged curves – it is still better to diversify internationally than to hold only US stocks. It is clear that the gain

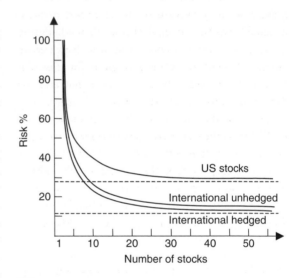

Figure 15.6 *The advantages of international diversification with and without exchange risk*

Notes
There are further gains from risk reduction through international diversification if forward markets are used to hedge exchange-rate risk.

Source: Bruno H. solnik, "Why Not Diversify Internationally Rather than Domestically?" Copyright 1974, CFA Institute. Reproduced and republished from *Financial Analysts Journal*, with permission from CFA Institute. All rights reserved.

---

6 It was explained in Chapter 9 that the exposure on a foreign stock depends on how the stock price covaries with the exchange rate, and, consequently, the exposure is not simply the market value of the stock. The appropriate hedge would have to take this into account. We should note that while exposure at a given moment in time can be eliminated by appropriate hedging, it is not feasible to eliminate exposure indefinitely. This is because the market value of foreign stocks varies, so that the hedge will not always be the correct amount, unless, of course, the hedge is changed continuously.

7 Solnik, op. cit. Solnik's hedges on the international portfolios are not the optimal hedges as given by regression coefficients, but rather are equal to the values of the foreign stocks at the time of investment. Consequently, Solnik's results, if anything, understate the benefits of hedged international diversification.

from having independence of returns due to holding securities of different countries in a portfolio more than offsets any exchange-rate risk that this implies, even when not hedging. And of course, when hedged, the benefits from international portfolio diversification are even greater.

Many researchers other than Eun and Resnick, and Solnik, have studied the gains from international diversification, and while all agree on the existence of gains, they differ substantially in the estimated size of these gains.[8] One major reason the estimates of gains are different is that some of the studies use past returns over different sample periods to form efficient, internationally diversified portfolios, rather than using the distribution of future returns as is called for by the theory.[9] The problem introduced by using past returns and covariances for forming efficient diversified portfolios is that if, for example, the past return in Belgium was very high during the estimation period, Belgian stocks will be heavily weighted in the internationally diversified portfolio.[10] This is the case even though it may have been just by chance that Belgian stocks did so well. It is then little surprise that the internationally diversified portfolio with its abnormally high proportion of high-return Belgian stocks outperforms the domestic portfolio when applied to past data. The

problem is that there is an upward bias in the estimated benefits of international diversification due to basing international portfolios on past returns rather than the distribution of future returns. This bias can be verified by taking the internationally diversified portfolio that is formed using past-return data during a given interval of time and seeing how it performs out of sample, that is, over other intervals. The results of this type of test suggest that the benefits of international diversification have indeed been overestimated in many studies.[11]

In an attempt to partially overcome the problem of using past returns to construct portfolios for judging the gain from international diversification, Philippe Jorion used statistical procedures which "shrink" past returns in different countries toward the mean return for all countries' markets combined.[12] This means, for example, that if the observed past return for Belgium happened to have been very high, a realistic investor is assumed to expect a future return in Belgium that is less than the past return, and somewhere between the past return for Belgium and the past average return for all countries combined. The results from Jorion's study show that the gains from international diversification in earlier studies have been greatly overstated. His conclusions are supported by the fact that the portfolios he constructed outperform portfolios based on unadjusted past returns when their returns are compared with out-of-sample data. Nevertheless, Jorion shows there is still some gain from international portfolio diversification.

INTERNATIONAL CAPITAL ASSET PRICING

The central international financial question concerning the pricing of assets, and hence their expected rates of return, is whether they are determined in an **integrated**, international capital market or in local, **segmented** markets. If assets

8 Earlier, frequently referenced research showing the size of gains from international diversification includes Donald Lessard, "World, Country, and Industry Relationships in Equity Returns: Implications for Risk Reduction through International Diversification," *Financial Analysts Journal*, January/February 1976, pp. 2–8, and Haim Levy and Marshall Sarnat, "International Diversification of Investment Portfolios," *American Economic Review*, September 1970, pp. 668-75.

9 An **efficient portfolio** is one which is constructed to have maximum expected return for a given volatility, or minimum volatility for a given expected return. The studies by Solnik and by Eun and Resnick are not based on efficient portfolios and consequently are not subject to the problems we are about to describe.

10 Belgian stocks will receive high weighting if their return is high relative to the risk they contribute to the international portfolio. The risk depends on the covariance between Belgian and other returns.

11 See Philippe Jorion, "International Diversification with Estimation Risk," *Journal of Business*, July 1985, pp. 259–78.

12 See Jorion, op. cit.

are priced in an internationally integrated capital market, expected yields on assets will be in accordance with the risks of the assets when they are held in an efficient, internationally diversified portfolio, such as the world-market portfolio. This means that while in such a situation it is better to diversify internationally than not to, the expected yields on assets will merely compensate for their systematic risk when this is measured with respect to the internationally diversified world portfolio. That is, with internationally integrated capital markets the expected returns on foreign stocks will be appropriate for the risk of these stocks in an internationally diversified portfolio. There will be no "free lunches" from foreign stocks due to higher expected returns for their risk. On the other hand, if assets are priced in segmented capital markets, their returns will be in accordance with the systematic risk of their domestic market. This means that if an investor happens to have an ability to circumvent whatever it is that causes markets to be segmented, this investor will be able to enjoy special benefits from international diversification. It is consequently important for us to consider whether assets are priced in internationally integrated or in segmented capital markets. However, before doing this it is useful to review the theory of asset pricing in a domestic context, because if we do not understand the issues in the simpler domestic context, we cannot understand the international dimensions of asset pricing.

The domestic capital asset pricing model, CAPM

The domestic variant of the **capital asset pricing model (CAPM)**, familiar from the so-called "beta analysis" used in security selection, can be written as follows[13]

$$r_j^* = r_f + \beta(r_m^* - r_f) \tag{15.3}$$

13 See William Sharpe, "Capital Asset Pricing: A Theory of Market Equilibrium under Conditions of Risk," *Journal of Finance*, September 1964, pp. 424–47. The model is explained in many finance textbooks and is only stated here.

where

$$\beta = \frac{\text{cov}(r_j, r_m)}{\text{var}(r_m)} \tag{15.4}$$

and where

r_j^* = equilibrium or required expected return on security or portfolio j,

r_f = risk-free rate of interest,

r_m^* = expected return on the market portfolio m,

$\text{cov}(r_j, r_m)$ = covariance between security or portfolio j and the market m,

$\text{var}(r_m)$ = variance of the market portfolio.

The essential point of the CAPM is that a security or portfolio offers an equilibrium expected return, r_j^*, equal to the risk-free interest rate plus a risk premium. The risk premium, $\beta(r_m^* - r_f)$ is linearly related to the risk that the asset or portfolio contributes to the market as a whole, cov $(r_j, r_m)/$ var(r_m). This is the risk which cannot be diversified away, the **systematic risk**. If a security compensated for more than systematic risk, it would be a bargain, and investors would buy it and combine it with other securities. The buying of the security would raise its current market price and thereby lower its expected return until the security was no longer a bargain, even within a diversified portfolio.

The international capital asset pricing model, ICAPM

With the domestic variant of the CAPM explained, we can clarify the conclusion stated earlier about internationally integrated versus segmented markets. If assets are priced in internationally integrated capital markets, expected yields are given by

$$r_j^* = r_f + \beta^w(r_w^* - r_f) \tag{15.5}$$

where

$$\beta^w = \frac{\mathrm{cov}(r_j, r_w)}{\mathrm{var}(r_w)} \qquad (15.6)$$

and where $r_w^* = $ "world market" expected return. Unfortunately, it is difficult in practice to apply the **international CAPM**, or **ICAPM**, because this requires being able to define a world risk-free interest rate, making assumptions about preferences of investors from different countries who face different real returns according to the basket of goods they purchase, and dealing with other thorny problems.[14]

If the international CAPM as summarized in equations (15.5) and (15.6) is valid, then investors do not receive abnormal returns from investing in foreign assets; returns appropriately compensate for the systematic risk of assets in an internationally diversified portfolio.[15] On the other hand, if assets are priced in segmented capital markets, then if an investor or firm could overcome the cause of the market segmentation, perhaps by getting around capital flow regulations, such an investor could enjoy abnormal returns. (Later we shall explain that US multinational corporations appear to be in this situation, investing where ordinary US investors cannot.)

Segmentation versus integration of capital markets: a graphical view

The implications of integrated versus segmented capital markets can be viewed graphically in terms

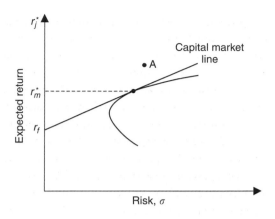

Figure 15.7 *The relationship between expected return and total risk*

Notes
If assets are priced in segmented markets, it may be possible for an investor to enjoy a combination of expected return and risk above the capital market line for a *particular country* if the investor can overcome the causes of segmentation and diversify internationally. If assets are priced in internationally integrated capital markets, then by not diversifying internationally an investor will be accepting higher risk and/or lower return than is necessary.

of the risk-return framework that is used frequently in the domestic context to describe diversification benefits. Figure 15.7 shows expected returns on the vertical axis, and total risk, given by the standard error, σ, of expected returns, on the horizontal axis. The upward-sloping part of the curve, or **envelope**, gives the best combinations of expected returns and risk that can be achieved with different portfolios; combinations of risk and return along the envelope above the minimum value of σ are those of efficient portfolios. As before, r_f is the risk-free interest rate, and r_m^* is the expected return on the market portfolio. Again as before, the interpretation of r_f and r_m^* depends on whether we are considering integrated or segmented capital markets. We note that r_m^* is the tangency point on a straight line drawn between the risk-free rate and the envelope of efficient portfolios' risks and returns. This line is the **capital market line**, which gives the expected returns and risks of combinations of the risk-free asset and the market portfolio. It is a well-known proposition in finance that an investor cannot do better than select such a

14 Notable attempts to determine the conditions required for the international CAPM, and the implications if these conditions are satisfied, include those of Bruno Solnik, "An Equilibrium Model of the International Capital Market," *Journal of Economics Theory*, August 1974, pp. 500–24, and Michael Adler and Bernard Dumas, "International Portfolio Choice and Corporation Finance: A Synthesis," *Journal of Finance*, June 1983, pp. 925–84. For a summary of empirical applications and new test results see Bruno Solnik, "The World Price of Foreign Exchange Risk," Working Paper, H.E.C. School of Management, Paris, July 1993.

15 Indeed, by not investing internationally, investors face more risk than is necessary.

combination and therefore be somewhere on the capital market line.

If capital markets are internationally integrated, then we can interpret r_f in Figure 15.7 as the risk-free rate, and r_m^* as the expected world-market return, r_w^*.[16] That is, with integrated capital markets the international CAPM is an extension of the domestic CAPM where we reinterpret r_m^* as the expected world-market return, r_w^*. Indeed, if the capital market is integrated, by not holding the world-market portfolio the investor will be below the capital market line in Figure 15.7; the investor could reduce risk and increase expected return by holding the world portfolio. On the other hand, if capital markets are segmented so that we can interpret r_m^* as the expected return in the domestic market, then by overcoming the obstacles to foreign investment an investor might be able to create a risk-return portfolio that is above the domestic capital market line. For example, the investor might be able to reach a point such as A and enjoy gains from international diversification, since these are not priced by the market due to the segmentation.

The potential gain from integration of capital markets

The extent to which integration of world financial markets could empirically make a difference to the opportunities facing investors in terms of the risk-return profile is indicated in Figure 15.8. The figure shows a constructed efficiency frontier, with risk and return in US dollars, from combining the stock-market indexes of different countries.[17] We see, for example, that an internationally efficient allocation of assets with a risk of 16.2 percent per annum, same as the US market, provides a return almost 8 percent

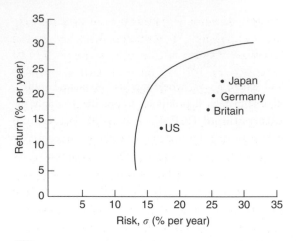

Figure 15.8 *Efficiency frontier of global stocks, US dollar, 1980–90*

Notes
The efficiency frontier shows the highest return for a given risk and/or the lowest risk for a given return by optimally combining the stock market of different countries. The returns and risks of the individual countries' markets are seen to be below the efficiency frontier. This indicates the size of potential gains from international diversification if capital markets are integrated. For example, an internationally efficient allocation with the same risk as the US market offers approximately 8 percent more return per annum than the US market.

Source: Patrick Odier and Bruno Solnik, "Lessons for International Asset Allocation." Copyright 1993, CFA Institute. Reproduced and republished from *Financial Analysts Journal*, with permission from CFA Institute. All rights reserved.

higher than the US market return, that is, 21 percent versus 13.3 percent per annum. The potential gains for the riskier but higher return stock markets of Britain, Germany, and Japan are also indicated. The performance of the internationally diversified portfolio could be further enhanced by periodically revising the asset allocation – the figure uses fixed allocations – and by hedging the risk from exchange rates, but even without such refinements the diversification benefits are substantial. But are capital markets integrated so as to offer investors such benefits, or are they segmented?

The evidence on market segmentation: is there a home-equity bias?

The most immediately obvious evidence that markets are segmented in the form of a bias

---

16 As we have mentioned, in practice, defining r_f and r_w^* is far from easy. The risk-free rate r_f requires forming a portfolio of different treasury bills plus forward exchange contracts to remove exchange-rate risk, and the expected world-market return r_w^* and world β require complex calculations and numerous assumptions.

17 See Odier and Solnik, op. cit.

towards domestic investments is in data showing the composition of portfolios held by typical investors. Despite the relatively rapid *rate* of expansion of US and other countries' overseas portfolio investment in recent years, the *level* of foreign investment is still low. For example, according to values reported by Ian Cooper and Evi Kaplanis, US investors held 98 percent in domestic equity versus the 36.4 percent proportion of world equity market capitalization represented by the US equity market.[18] For the United Kingdom, investors held 78.5 percent domestic equity versus the UK's 10.3 percent of the world-market capitalization. The average for five continental European countries was 85 percent domestic investments versus their 1.9 percent share of world equity market capitalization. The situation for the US is confirmed by Karen Lewis who shows that US holdings of foreign equities are suboptimal, being below that for the minimum-variance portfolio for any set of preferences.[19] The bias towards domestic equity is even more extreme than these numbers suggest if we entertain the argument of Marianne Baxter and Urban Jermann.[20] They suggest that given the exposure investors have on their human capital which makes them long on their home country which is the source of their working income, investors might want to actually go short on domestic equities by borrowing against them. Whether or not we go this far, there is clearly an **equity home bias puzzle** as it has become known. Investors around the globe are not fully availing themselves of international diversification opportunities: they hold fewer foreign securities than would be representative of the world portfolio.[21]

Possible reasons for home-equity bias

Segmentation of capital markets with disproportionate investments in the investors' home markets can occur for a variety of different reasons.[22] The most obvious cause of segmentation is the presence of legal barriers to foreign investment. These barriers can take the form of outright restrictions on investing abroad, or can involve higher rates of tax on income from foreign than domestic investment.[23] Transaction costs may also be higher on foreign equities, although according to Frank Warnock, turnover rates on foreign equities are comparable to domestic turnover rates, thereby not supporting the transaction-cost based argument.[24] Furthermore, even if the majority of investors are

18 See Ian Cooper and Evi Kaplanis, "Home Bias in Equity Portfolios, Inflation Hedging and International Market Equilibrium," *Review of Financial Studies*, Spring 1994, pp. 45–60.

19 Karen K. Lewis, "Trying to Explain Home Bias in Equities and Consumption," *Journal of Economic Literature*, June 1999, pp. 571–608. For an alternative view see Exhibit 15.1.

20 Marianne Baxter and Urban J. Jermann, "The International Diversification Puzzle is Worse than You Think," *American Economic Review*, March 1997, pp. 170–80.

21 For discussion of the extent of international diversification and possible explanations of why a home-country bias occurs, see Raman Uppal, "The Economic Determinants of the Home Country Bias in Investors' Portfolios: A Survey," *Journal of International Financial Management and Accounting*, 4, 1992, pp. 171–89, and "A General Equilibrium Model of International Portfolio Choice," *Journal of Finance*, June 1993, pp. 529–53. For the extent of turnover in foreign stocks, which has been very rapid, see Linda L. Tesar and Ingrid M. Werners, "Home Bias and High Turnover," *Journal of International Money and Finance*, August 1995, pp. 467–92.

22 For a discussion of the possibility that the bias has been overstated due to model misspecification see Debra A. Glassman and Leigh A. Riddick, "Why Empirical International Portfolio Models Fail: Evidence that Model Misspecification Creates Home Asset Bias," *Journal of International Money and Finance*, April 1996, pp. 275–312.

23 See René Stultz, "On the Effects of Barriers to International Investment," *Journal of Finance*, September 1981, pp. 923–34.

24 Higher transaction costs would imply low turnover that does not appear to occur. See Frank E. Warnock, "Home Bias and High Turnover Reconsidered," *Journal of International Money and Finance*, November 2002, pp. 795–805.

EXHIBIT 15.1   HOME BIAS AND CORPORATE GOVERNANCE

Normally, the vast majority of shares that have been issued by American corporations trade freely in financial markets, with no individual shareholder holding more than a tiny fraction of the stock. This limits the amount of control that individual shareholders or coordinated groups of shareholders can exert on the companies' management. The situation is not the same in many other countries. Controlling interests in some countries, where families or individuals hold large amounts of voting stock, can exceed 50 percent. According to the paper summarized below, this can explain up to half the apparent home-equity bias.

The fact that domestic companies represent 90 percent of the holdings in an average U.S. investor's stock portfolio – even though U.S. stocks represent only 49 percent of the world market – has prompted a range of theories, but no generally accepted explanation of this so-called "home bias." Some analysts have blamed market barriers. Others view U.S. investors as lacking sufficient information on foreign equities. And then there are those who see in this imbalance overly optimistic expectations about the performance of homegrown assets. But in "Corporate Governance and the Home Equity Bias" . . . Lee Pinkowitz, Rene Stultz, and Rohan Williamson assert that at least some of the oft-noted tilt is not a bias at all but simply a reflection of the fact that a sizable number of shares worldwide are not for sale to the average investor. They find that comparisons of U.S. portfolios to the world market for equities have failed to consider that the "controlling shareholders" who dominate many a foreign corporation do not make their substantial holdings available for normal trading.

Take this into account, the authors argue, and as much as half of the home bias disappears. A more accurate assessment of globally available shares,

they say, would show about 67 percent of a properly balanced U.S. portfolio would be invested in U.S. companies.

"We show that the home bias is intricately linked to corporate governance," the authors write. "When companies are controlled by large investors, portfolio investors are limited in the fraction of a firm they can hold." For example, in examining 51 countries they find that, on average, 32 percent of the shares are not available for trading. The United States has the lowest percentage of controlling shareholders, with only 7.9 percent of domestic stocks "closely held" followed by the United Kingdom at 9.9 percent. But the authors note that, except for Ireland, Sri Lanka, the United States, and the United Kingdom, " no country has a . . . controlling ownership of less than 20 percent," and in 23 countries, controlling ownership exceeds 50 percent.

Pinkowitz, Stulz, and Williamson observe that controlling shareholders are not interested in selling off their stock at the mere market price. The authors point to previous studies demonstrating that "the benefits of control are substantial in most countries," placing the value of such holding above those of ordinary shares and thus not practical for the typical foreign investor.

Therefore, the authors believe efforts to make foreign stocks more attractive to domestic investors need to move beyond the current focus on market barriers. They conclude that considerably more attention must be given to how corporate governance repels investors who might otherwise replace some of their domestic stocks with foreign equities.

Source: "Why Don't Americans Hold More Foreign Stocks?" a summary of Lee Pinkowitz, Rene Stultz, and Rohan Williamson Working Paper 8680, National Bureau of Economic Research, Cambridge, MA, in *The NBER Digest,* May 2002.

subject to legal barriers and higher transaction costs, assets could still in principle be priced according to integrated markets. This is because some investors, such as giant multinational firms with operations in numerous countries, might be able to circumvent the legal barriers and avoid costs.

A slightly less obvious form of market segmentation occurs as a result of so-called **indirect barriers**.[25] Indirect barriers include the difficulty of finding and interpreting information about foreign securities and reluctance to deal with foreigners. As is true for legal barriers, those who can overcome the indirect barriers through, for example, access to better information or freedom from xenophobia, might be able to enjoy abnormal returns by diversifying internationally. That is, those who can overcome the barriers might achieve a risk-return combination such as that at A in Figure 15.7.

When we interpret market segmentation in the more general terms of having different expected returns or risks according to where an investor lives, it becomes clear that as well as arising from legal and indirect barriers, segmentation can arise because prices of what investors consume relative to the returns they earn change differently in different countries.[26] In such a case the buying power of returns would depend on where investors live. It turns out, however, that this cause of segmentation requires that PPP does not hold. This is because, for example, if PPP holds and investors in one country, say Canada, happen to earn a lower nominal return than investors elsewhere because of an appreciation of the Canadian dollar, then the lower nominal return to Canadians is compensated for by lower inflation in Canada; an appreciation of the

Canadian dollar is associated with lower prices in Canada.[27] It follows that if PPP holds, securities should be priced according to equation (15.5), in which the market return is the global-market return, provided of course there are no legal or indirect causes of segmentation.

When PPP does not hold, there is exchange-rate risk, and markets are segmented with different real rates of return for investors according to where they live; the changes in exchange rates will not be exactly offset by changes in prices. The effect of having exchange-rate risk for the asset pricing relationship in equation (15.5) is to make the international CAPM more complex than a mere reinterpretation of the domestic CAPM.[28]

Evidence on whether securities are priced in an integrated or a segmented capital market has been provided by Philippe Jorion and Eduardo Schwartz.[29] They begin by noting that integration means expected returns depend only on international factors, and in particular on the systematic risk of securities vis-à-vis the world-market portfolio. That is, if markets are completely integrated, the r_j^*'s of different securities should depend only on their β's calculated vis-à-vis the return on the world market. On the other hand, if markets are completely segmented, expected returns will depend on only domestic factors, and in particular the β's vis-à-vis the domestic market return. By isolating the international and domestic β's Jorion and Schwartz were able to show that domestic

---

25 Philippe Jorion and Eduardo Schwartz, "Integration vs. Segmentation in the Canadian Stock Market," *Journal of Finance*, July 1986, pp. 603–16.

26 For an excellent account of this interpretation of segmentation see Michael Adler and Bernard Dumas, "International Portfolio Choice and Corporation Finance: A Synthesis," *Journal of Finance*, June 1983, pp. 925–84.

27 The appreciation of the Canadian dollar means that to Canadians, there is a depreciation of the US dollar, the pound, the yen, and so on. This would reduce the return on foreign securities to Canadians but would also reduce the prices of products that Canadians buy.

28 For accounts of the international CAPM in the presence of exchange-rate risk due to deviations from PPP see Piet Sercu, "A Generalization of the International Asset Pricing Model," *Revue Française de Finance*, June 1980, pp. 91–135, and René Stultz, "A Model of International Asset Pricing," *Journa of Financial Economics*, December 1981, pp. 383–406. See also the excellent survey in Adler and Dumas (1983), op. cit.

29 Jorion and Schwartz, op. cit.

factors are relevant for expected returns on Canadian securities, suggesting some degree of market segmentation.[30]

Jorion and Schwartz also separated out inter-listed Canadian stocks – those trading simultaneously on both US and Canadian stock exchanges – and found the same result, namely, that Canadian returns are related to systematic risk vis-à-vis the Canadian market. This suggests that the segmentation is not attributable to reporting of information on Canadian stocks, because Canadian companies with shares trading on US exchanges must report the same types of information as that reported by US companies.

Limited further support for segmentation based on an examination of inter-listed stocks has been provided by Gordon Alexander, Cheol Eun, and S. Janakiramanan.[31] They begin by stating that if markets are segmented, the listing of a security abroad should reduce the security's expected rate of return. This should come about as a result of a jump in the stock price at the time the market learns of the additional listing. They find evidence consistent with a lower expected return after overseas listing for their sample of non-Canadian firms. However, they do not detect the implied jumps in stock prices and find insignificant effects for Canadian firms.

An alternative, although even more indirect, way of testing whether markets are integrated or segmented is to see whether securities of companies that can overcome segmentation have returns more related to systematic risk vis-à-vis the international

than vis-à-vis the domestic market. For example, if US multinational corporations can invest in countries where private US citizens cannot, then the returns on US multinationals' securities should be more closely related to their β's vis-à-vis the international market than vis-à-vis the US market, whereas returns on non-multinational US securities should not. Indeed, the extent to which the US multinationals' securities are priced according to international or domestic risk should depend on their international orientation, judged, for example, by the fraction of sales made overseas. One test of this was performed by Tamir Agmon and Donald Lessard, who found some weak indication that multinationals can achieve something investors cannot achieve themselves.[32] However, it has been pointed out that the US market index itself contains companies which earn a substantial fraction of their earnings overseas – consider, for example, Coca Cola, McDonalds, Microsoft, General Electric and General Motors – so that the β's of securities vis-à-vis the US market are not really measuring systematic risks vis-à-vis the domestic market. That is, the r_m^* for the US market includes a substantial amount of the effect of international returns, so that studies comparing the use of r_m^* for an international index and a US index understate the role of internationalization of investment by US multinationals. When US stock indexes are constructed in a way that removes the international returns in them, the results show a more significant benefit from the ability of multinational corporations to invest

30 It has been argued that if investors in the different countries care about different measures of inflation, so that PPP cannot hold, then the pricing of domestic factors does not necessarily mean that markets are segmented. See Mustafa N. Gultekin, N. Bulent Gultekin, and Alessandro Fenati, "Capital Controls and International Capital Markets Segmentation: The Evidence from the Japanese and American Stock Markets," Paper presented to European Finance Association Meetings, Madrid, 1987.

31 Gordon J. Alexander, Cheol S. Eun, and S. Janakiramanan, "International Listings and Stock Returns; Some Empirical Evidence," *Journal of Financial and Quantitative Analysis*, June 1988, pp. 135–51.

32 Tamir Agmon and Donald R. Lessard, "Investor Recognition of Corporate International Diversification," *Journal of Finance*, September 1977, pp. 1049–56. The results of Agmon and Lessard disagree with those of Bertrand Jacquillat and Bruno Solnik, "Multinationals are Poor Tools for Diversification," *Journal of Portfolio Management*, Winter 1978, pp. 8–12; H.L. Brewer, "Investor Benefits from Corporate International Diversification," *Journal of Financial and Quantitative Analysis*, March 1981, pp. 113–26; and A.J. Senschak and W.L. Beedles, "Is Indirect International Diversification Desirable?" *Journal of Portfolio Management*, Winter 1980, pp. 49–57.

overseas.[33] This suggests that markets are segmented for the ordinary US investor. Exhibit 15.2 suggests this segmentation has increased.

While the preceding arguments try to explain segmentation taking the form of home-equity bias in terms of rational financial arguments, it has been suggested that what we observe could be the results of investor-behavior characteristics. For example, Kenneth French and James Poterba have suggested investors may be relatively more optimistic about domestic versus foreign prospects.[34] They calculate the extent to which expected returns on domestic investments would have to exceed those on foreign investments to produce the observed degree of home-equity bias. They show, for example, that US investors would have to expect about 2.4 percent more from US equities than Japanese investors expect, and about 1 percent more than British investors. Optimism about domestic prospects supporting the behavioral line of argument has been noted in survey data by Norman Strong and Xinzhong Xu who investigated the monthly Fund Manager Survey conducted by Merrill Lynch.[35] Investment managers from the United States, the United Kingdom, Europe and Japan all showed a significant relative optimism towards their own domestic market.

BONDS AND INTERNATIONAL PORTFOLIO DIVERSIFICATION

When considering international investment in bonds, issues arise that are similar to those we have already discussed concerning stocks, including the extent to which foreign bonds, unhedged, introduce exchange-rate risk, and the extent to which bonds further allow investors to improve the risk-return opportunity set. As for the issue of the currency risk associated with bonds, the evidence indicates that the contribution of exchange rates to the riskiness of bonds is much larger than it is for stocks.[36] Some difference in this regard would be expected from the PPP principle. Specifically, if expected income streams and hence stock prices kept pace with inflation, then higher inflation in a country would increase stock prices at the same time as it caused depreciation of the country's currency: the inflation increases prices, including those of real assets such as stocks, but at the same time causes depreciation. In such a situation the effect of inflation in the local-currency stock price is offset by the depreciation when the stock price is measured in terms of US dollars. Stated differently, the local-currency stock price and the currency value are negatively correlated, at least to the extent PPP holds. This reduces volatility measured in US dollars. Of course, factors other than PPP are at work affecting the correlation, so any reduction in stock-price volatility in dollars is against the background of these other factors.

In the case of bonds, the opposite could be occurring to the situation for stocks. Currency depreciation could lead to government action to increase interest rates in an attempt to prop up the currency, a practice called "leaning against the wind." Higher interest rates reduce bond prices in local currency, so that depreciation of the currency is associated with a decline in the local currency value of the bond. In this case, unlike the case with stocks discussed previously, the asset value and exchange-rate movement are reinforcing, making variations in US bond values higher; the correlation between the local-currency asset value and the exchange rate is positive, thereby adding to volatility.

33 See John S. Hughes, Dennis E. Logue, and Richard J. Sweeney, "Corporate International Diversification and Market Assigned Measures of Risk and Diversification," *Journal of Financial and Quantitative Analysis*, November 1975, pp. 627–37.

34 Kenneth R. French and James M. Poterba, "Investor Diversification and International Equity Markets," *American Economic Review*, May 1991, pp. 222–6.

35 Norman Strong and Xinzhong Xu, "Understanding the Equity Home Bias: Evidence from Survey Data," *The Review of Economics and Statistics*, May 2003, pp. 307–12.

36 See Patrick Odier and Bruno Solnik, op. cit.

EXHIBIT 15.2 EVOLUTION OF CAPITAL MARKET INTEGRATION

There is a presumption that international financial markets are more open and freer today than they have ever been before. Indeed, we think of hot money flowing according to the slightest differential between countries' interest rates, with no loyalty other than to the rate of return. In other words, it is commonly believed that financial markets are more integrated than at any time in history. This belief is based on the view that legal barriers to investment have all but disappeared, and that information travels around the globe at the speed of light. Therefore, it may comes as a surprise to many that evidence indicates capital markets may be less integrated than they were in the late nineteenth century.

How well-integrated have the world's capital markets been in the modern industrial era? In recent decades economic historians have agreed that capital markets were well-integrated in the late 19th century, that they disintegrated somewhat in the period between the two world wars, and that they have been reintegrating speedily since then. Some economists have sought to measure capital-market integration by examining the correlation between domestic saving and investment rates among the developed countries, on the theory that domestic saving would seek out the highest returns in world capital markets independent of local investment demand. A key unexpected finding of this research was that capital markets were not well integrated in the 1960s and 1970s.

Now, in an NBER study, Alan Taylor revisits the question and presents a more nuanced picture of the evolution of capital markets. He finds that the conventional wisdom seems to be broadly correct, and he develops and extends the more recent analyses which have found that the re-integration of capital markets since World War II has been slow. He concludes, among other things, that capital markets today – despite all the journalistic and anecdotal evidence of "globalization" – are still less integrated than they were 100 years ago.

In "International Capital Mobility in History: The Saving-Investment Relationship," Taylor assembles and reviews data for a group of 12 countries (Argentina, Australia, Canada, Denmark, France, Germany, Italy, Japan, Norway, Sweden, the United Kingdom, and the United States) over the period from 1850 to 1992. While data are missing for some countries for some years, this is both a larger sample and a longer time span than had been utilized previously. Taylor finds that the average size of capital flows in the pre-World War I era was often as high as 4 to 5 percent of national income. Flows diminished during the 1920s, however, and international capital flows were less than 1.5 percent of national income in the late 1930s. But the all-time low was in the 1950s and 1960s – around 1 percent of national income – and while flows increased in the late 1970s and 1980s, they still didn't approach the levels of a century ago.

Taylor also extends the analysis of the correlations between domestic saving and domestic investment to analyze the entire 1850–1992 period for the 12-country group. The results broadly support the conventional view of the late 19th and early 20th centuries, and confirm the earlier research suggesting that capital mobility was low in the post-World-War II era.

Source: A summary of Alan Taylor's "Capital Markets Today are Less Integrated Today than 100 years Ago," in *The NBER Digest*, Working Paper 5743, National Bureau of Economic Research, Cambridge, MA, June 1997.

The empirical importance of international portfolio diversification of bonds is addressed in Figure 15.9.[37] The figure shows two efficiency frontiers, one for an optimally internationally diversified portfolio of stocks only, and the other for stocks plus bonds. The frontier when bonds are included in the portfolio shows reduced risk for given returns. This reduction in risk does not,

37 See Odier and Solnik, op. cit.

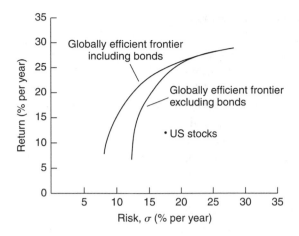

Figure 15.9 *Contribution of bonds to the globally efficient frontier, US dollars, 1980–90*

Notes
Including bonds as well as stocks in an internationally diversified portfolio provides an opportunity to reduce risk for a given return vis-à-vis a stock-only portfolio. The benefit from holding bonds comes despite the relatively high exchange-rate risk on bonds.

Source: Patrick Odier and Bruno Solnik, "Lessons for International Asset Allocation." Copyright 1993, CFA Institute. Reproduced and republished from *Financial Analysts Journal* with permission from CFA Institute. All rights reserved.

of course, occur at high rates of return because to achieve such returns it is necessary to hold only stocks. At lower expected returns the advantage of including bonds is substantial with, for example, a volatility reduction from 12 to 8 percent at a 10 percent rate of return. The position of the combined stock and bond efficiency frontier in Figure 15.9 makes the gains from international portfolio diversification very evident.

SETTLEMENTS OF INTERNATIONAL PORTFOLIO INVESTMENTS

When an investor acquires a stock or bond in an overseas market the settlement and exchange of assets occur in more than one regulatory environment. The mechanics of such multi-country exchange and settlement is handled by **global custodians**. Custodians provide the services of holding securities and making payments. For further fees, they also handle foreign exchange transactions, collect dividends, handle proxies, forward relevant corporate information to asset owners, and arrange to reclaim withholding taxes.[38] While some countries such as the US and Canada have so integrated their settlement procedures that the border does not represent much of a barrier, in situations where language and regulatory differences exist settlement can be complex. For example, changes in exchange rates as well as asset prices make the timing of transactions related to settlement extremely important. In essence, by overcoming the complexities custodians help to integrate markets. However, they have clearly not yet made markets a seamless whole, or we would not observe so much evidence supporting market segmentation.

SUMMARY

1   If different countries' economic performances are not perfectly synchronized, or if there are other differences between nations such as in the types of industries they have, there are benefits from international diversification of portfolios beyond those from diversification within a single country. Therefore, investments in foreign

38 For an account of the growing role of global custodians see "Global Custody: Speeding the Paperchase," special supplement to *Euromoney*, March 1989; Keith Martin, "The Changing Role of the Global Custodian," *Benefits and Pensions Monitor*, May/June 1994, pp. 12–15; and Jodi G. Scarlata, "Institutional Developments in the Globalization of Securities and Futures Markets," *Review*, Federal Reserve Bank of St. Louis, January/February 1992, pp. 17–30. For an alternative procedure for dealing with overseas portfolio investments, see the discussion of American Depository Receipts in Chapter 18.

countries might be made even if they offered lower expected returns than some domestic investments; the diversification benefits might more than compensate for lower expected returns.

2   The evidence shows considerable independence between different countries' stock returns, suggesting large gains from international diversification. Portfolios that are internationally diversified do indeed prove to have lower volatility than portfolios of domestic stocks of the same size.

3   Stocks of companies in different countries but in the same industry are not highly correlated. This indicates that stock-market indexes have low correlations because of idiosyncratic economic circumstances, not because the indexes of different countries' markets have different industrial compositions.

4   Even if internationally diversified portfolios are not hedged against exchange-rate risk, they show lower volatility than domestically diversified portfolios. This is despite the fact that exchange rates are an important component of overall volatility of foreign stocks both directly, and indirectly via their covariance with local market returns.

5   Many early studies of the gains from international diversification overstated the gains because they constructed portfolios on the basis of past actual returns rather than expected future returns.

6   If assets are priced in internationally integrated capital markets, their returns are appropriate for their risk when combined with the world-market portfolio. Then, by not diversifying internationally, an investor is accepting more risk than is necessary for a given expected return, or lower expected return than is necessary for a given risk.

7   If capital markets are segmented, those who can overcome the cause of segmentation and invest abroad can enjoy abnormal returns for the risk taken. This is because assets are then priced only to compensate for the risk in internationally *un*diversified portfolios.

8   Evidence indicates that there is some segmentation of capital markets.

9   Multinational corporations' shares appear to be priced according to their systematic risk vis-à-vis an internationally diversified portfolio. Investors appear to value the ability of multinationals to invest abroad, overcoming the barriers which the investors themselves face on overseas investments.

10   Home-equity bias may be due to people in different countries facing different consumption prices, or because domestic investors are more optimistic about their own country's prospects than are foreign investors.

11   Exchanges rates add substantially more to the volatility of foreign bonds than they do to the volatility of foreign stocks. This could be explained by PPP applying to stocks, and to the policy of "leaning against the wind" on bonds, whereby central banks increase interest rates, thereby lowering bond prices, when their currencies are depreciating.

12   Despite the exchange-rate risk on bonds, the inclusion of bonds in an internationally diversified portfolio lowers risk and raises return vis-à-vis a stock-only diversified portfolio.

13   Global custodians help handle the exchange and settlement of foreign securities. In this way they help to integrate capital markets.

REVIEW QUESTIONS

1   What types of investments are included in "international *portfolio* investment?"
2   Why are the correlation coefficients between different countries' stock markets and stocks relevant for the potential benefit from international portfolio diversification?
3   How could different compositions of stock-market indexes reduce the correlation between returns on different countries' markets?
4   What are the different components of volatility from investment in stocks of an individual foreign country?
5   What do we mean by "integrated capital markets?"
6   What assumptions must be made to apply the international capital asset pricing model to an explanation of the pricing of securities?
7   How would *you* characterize the gains from international portfolio diversification?
8   What is meant by "home-equity bias?"
9   How can the level of information cause international capital market segmentation?
10 How would *you* interpret the conclusion that returns are more closely related to systematic risk in the domestic market than to systematic risk in the international market?
11 How might multinational firms offer a vehicle for overcoming segmented capital markets?
12 What does a global custodian do?

ASSIGNMENT PROBLEMS

1   Why are the benefits from international diversification overstated if efficient portfolios are constructed on the basis of past investment returns?
2   Why are there gains from international diversification without hedging exchange-rate risk even though exchange rates contribute a substantial *proportion* of overall risk?
3   Could we judge whether markets are segmented or integrated by examining rules governing the international flow of capital?
4   Why does the calculation of the risk-free rate for the ICAPM involve the use of forward contracts? Could we use any one country's risk-free rate if covered interest-parity holds?
5   What possible reasons exist for the segmentation of capital markets?
6   Why might an investor who is able to diversify globally benefit if, for most other investors, capital markets are segmented?
7   How might we calculate the importance of currency risk to the total risk on
    a   an individual foreign stock?
    b   a portfolio of foreign stocks?
8   Could multinationals provide a vehicle for overcoming market segmentation?
9   How is the expected equilibrium return on bonds likely to vary with the covariance between the local-currency market value of bonds and the exchange rate?
10 What impact might global custodians have on capital markets if they do their job cheaply and effectively?

BIBLIOGRAPHY

Adler, Michael and Bernard Dumas, "Optimal International Acquisitions," *Journal of Finance*, March 1975, pp. 1–19.

——, "International Portfolio Choice and Corporation Finance: A Synthesis," *Journal of Finance*, June 1983, pp. 925–84.

Baxter, Marianne and Urban Jermann, "The International Diversification Puzzle is Worse than You Think," *American Economic Review*, March 1997, pp. 170–80.

Cohen, Kalman, Walter Ness, Robert Schwartz, David Whitcomb, and Hitoshi Okuda, "The Determinants of Common Stock Returns Volatility: An International Comparison," *Journal of Finance*, May 1976, pp. 733–40.

Cooper, Ian and Evi Kaplanis, "Home Bias in Equity Portfolios, Inflation Hedging, and International Capital Market Equilibrium," *Review of Financial Studies*, Spring 1994, pp. 45–60.

Dimson, Elroy, Paul Marsh, and Mike Staunton, *Triumph of the Optimists: 101 Years of Global Investment Returns*, Princeton University Press, Princeton, NJ, 2002.

Eun, Cheol S. and Bruce G. Resnick, "Exchange Rate Uncertainty, Forward Contracts, and International Portfolio Selection," *Journal of Finance*, March 1988, pp. 197–215.

Frankel, Jeffery A., "The Diversifiability of Exchange Risk," *Journal of International Economics*, August 1979, pp. 379–93.

French, Kenneth R. and James M. Poterba, "Investor Diversification and International Equity Markets," *American Economic Review*, May 1991, pp. 222–6.

Grauer, Frederick L., Robert H. Litzenberger, and Richard E. Stehle, "Sharing Rules and Equilibrium in an International Capital Market under Uncertainty," *Journal of Financial Economics*, June 1976, pp. 223–56.

Hughes, John S., Dennis E. Logue, and Richard J. Sweeney, "Corporate International Diversification and Market Assigned Measures of Risk and Diversification," *Journal of Financial and Quantitative Analysis*, November 1975, pp. 627–37.

Jorion, Philippe, "International Diversification with Estimation Risk," *Journal of Business*, July 1985, pp. 259–78.

—— and Eduardo Schwartz, "Integration vs. Segmentation in the Canadian Stock Market," *Journal of Finance*, July 1986, pp. 603–14.

Lessard, Donald R., "World, Country, and Industry Relationships in Equity Returns: Implications for Risk Reduction through International Diversification," *Financial Analysts Journal*, January–February 1976, pp. 2–8.

Levy, Haim and Marshall Sarnat, "International Diversification of Investment Portfolios," *American Economic Review*, September 1970, pp. 668–75.

Lewis, Karen K., "Trying to Explain Home Bias in Equities and Consumption," *Journal of Economic Literature*, June 1999, pp. 571–608.

Odier, Patrick and Bruno Solnik, "Lessons for International Asset Allocation," *Financial Analysts Journal*, March/April 1993, pp. 63–77.

Serçu, Piet, "A Generalization of the International Asset Pricing Model," *Revue Française de Finance*, June 1980, pp. 91–135.

Solnik, Bruno H., "Why Not Diversify Internationally Rather than Domestically?" *Financial Analysts Journal*, July–August 1974, pp. 48–54.

——, "An Equilibrium Model of International Capital Market," *Journal of Economic Theory*, August 1974, pp. 500–24.

——, "International Arbitrage Pricing Theory," *Journal of Finance*, May 1983, pp. 449–57.

Stultz, René, "A Model of International Asset Pricing," *Journal of Financial Economics*, December 1981, pp. 383–406.

Uppal, Raman, "A General Equilibrium Model of Portfolio Choice," *The Journal of Finance*, June 1993, pp. 529–53.

——, "The Economic Determinants of the Home Country Bias in Investors' Portfolios," *Journal of International Financial Management and Accounting*, Autumn 1993, pp. 171–89.

Chapter 16

Capital budgeting for foreign investments

All the world's a stage.

William Shakespeare
As You Like It

SELECTING PROJECTS

The massive multinational corporations (MNCs), whose names are household words around the globe and which have power that is the envy and fear of many governments, grew large by making foreign direct investment (FDI). A criterion used for making these investments will be presented in this chapter as we develop the principle of **capital budgeting** that can be used in evaluating foreign projects.

A typical FDI is the building of a plant to manufacture a company's products for sale in overseas markets. The choice of building a plant is one of several alternative ways of selling the company's products in a foreign country. Other options include exporting from domestic facilities, licensing a producer in the foreign market to manufacture the good, and producing the good in a facility outside the intended market which the firm already operates. As Exhibit 16.1 explains, the choice is complex and has to be made in a world in which conditions are continually changing. Nevertheless, as is explained in Exhibit 16.2, increasing competition from globalized trade is forcing companies to seriously consider FDI.

Project evaluations, generally referred to as capital budgeting, are discussed in a domestic context in almost all introductory corporate finance courses. However, in the international arena, capital budgeting involves complex problems that are not shared in a domestic context. These include, for example, the dependence of cash flows on **capital structure** – the amount of debt versus equity used in company financing – because of cheap loans from foreign governments. This makes the cost of capital to the corporation different from the opportunity cost of capital of shareholders, where the latter is the correct discount rate. There are also exchange-rate risks, country risks, multiple tiers of taxation, and sometimes restrictions on repatriating income. We will show the conditions under which some of the more complex problems in the evaluation of overseas direct investments can be reduced to manageable size.

There are several approaches to capital budgeting for traditional domestic investments, including **net present value (NPV)**, **adjusted present value (APV)**, **internal rate of return**, and **payback period**. We shall use the APV technique, which has been characterized as a "divide and

EXHIBIT 16.1 INVESTMENT STRATEGIES: A DYNAMIC MATTER

In a matter of than less than a decade, General Electric's rationale for a joint venture to manufacture appliances in Mexico changed several times. As the following excerpt explains, in GE's case the company was fortunate that new developments gave further support for the original choice.

> Our major appliance (white goods) business had a mainly domestic focus for many years. In the mid-1980s, GE Appliances decided to enter the North American gas range business through a Mexican joint venture with a local partner. They built a plant in Mexico to serve both the export market and eventually, what they foresaw (correctly, as it turns out) as a growing Mexican market for modern domestic appliances. Their initial foreign exchange concern was a 1982-style devaluation and *de facto* confiscation of dollar-denominated financial assets. The solution had two principal elements: one was an offshore sales company, to minimize locally-held dollar assets to the extent possible, the other was careful management of working capital and cash flow exposure to maintain a balanced position. These are classic strategies in devaluation-prone currencies where hedging instruments are either unavailable or prohibitively expensive.

> The strategy worked well throughout the 1980s, but within the last two years, the environment has changed. First of all, the local Mexican market for major appliances (including refrigeration and home laundry products, which the joint venture also supplies) has expanded, and GE Appliances is well-positioned to take advantage of the increased local demand. The result, of course, is that we now have more peso assets on the books. Also, financing these assets by borrowing in local currency – a classic hedging technique – remains stubbornly expensive. The business did a lot of homework on the Mexican economic situation and on forecasting cash flows and income statements by currency. Their assessment of the former and their analysis of cash flows and expected returns in the business led them to a greater degree of comfort with an increased level of Mexican asset exposure. The strategy is working well, and Appliances is very enthusiastic about the second stage, as it were, of their Mexican investment.

Less than two years after this item was written, Mexico experienced a serious financial crisis. Between December 1994 and March 1995 the peso lost almost half its foreign exchange value. A strategy of having Mexican asset exposure meant resulting translation or transaction losses; peso assets, such as peso accounts receivable, became worth half their previous value when converted into dollars. However, to the extent that Mexican facilities produced for the US market, the peso devaluation meant increased profitability; see Chapter 11. *A priori*, the net result of the asset versus operating exposures is difficult to discern. Nevertheless, the scale of the 1994–95 peso crisis helps reinforce the importance of maintaining close scrutiny of foreign direct investments.

Source: Marcia B. Whitaker, "Strategic Management of Foreign Exchange Exposure in an International Firm," in Yakov Amihud and Richard M. Levich (eds), *Exchange Rates and Corporate Performance*, New York University Salomon Center, 1994, pp. 247–55.

conquer" approach because it tackles each difficulty as it occurs. The APV approach involves accounting separately for the complexities found in foreign investments as a result of such factors as subsidized loans and restrictions on repatriating income. Before we show how the difficulties can be handled, we shall enumerate the difficulties themselves. Our explanations will show why the APV approach has been proposed for the evaluation of overseas projects, rather than the traditional NPV approach which is generally the preferred choice in evaluating domestic projects.

EXHIBIT 16.2   COMPETITIVE PRESSURE TO PURSUE FDI

Companies in many industries can no longer survive as exclusively domestic operations. Competition from foreign-based firms which have made FDIs and which enjoy economies of large-scale production is forcing previously inward-looking companies to consider investing abroad. In other words, some companies are considering FDI because *other* companies have made FDIs. The need to pursue FDIs to remain competitive is discussed in the following excerpt. Other developments which are adding to the global level of direct investment and the coordination of the resulting multinational activities are also mentioned.

> Multinational corporations (MNCs) today not only participate in most major national markets, but are also increasingly coordinating their activities across these markets to gain advantages of scale, scope, and learning on a global basis. The emergence of global competition represents a major threat, as well as an opportunity, to those European and American companies that gained competitive advantage under an older mode of multinational competition. Labeled "multidomestic" competition by Michael Porter, this now passing phase in the development of international business was characterized by large MNCs with overseas operations that operated for the most part independently of one another. What centralization existed in this stage of the evolution of the MNC was typically restricted to areas such

as R&D and finance. With global competition, a much larger proportion of corporate activities is coordinated globally, including aspects of manufacturing, marketing, and virtually all R&D.

> The emergence of global competition reflects the merging of previously segmented national markets caused by a variety of forces, including reductions in trade barriers, a convergence of tastes, and significant advances in product and process technologies. New global strategies also take advantage of changes in information technology and increased organizational sophistication to improve coordination among geographically dispersed operations...

> National financial markets have become increasingly linked into a single global market, as a result of both deregulation and an increase in the market power, global reach, and financial skills of both corporate and institutional users of financial services. At the same time, a significant deepening of financial technology has taken place not only in terms of the information, trading, and document-processing systems, but also in the refinement of analytical techniques that have given rise to new financial instruments, more precise pricing of assets, and new economic risk management approaches.

Source: Donald R. Lessard, "Global Competition and Corporate Finance in the 1990s," *Journal of Applied Corporate Finance*, Winter 1991, pp. 59–72.

DIFFICULTIES IN EVALUATING FOREIGN PROJECTS[1]

Introductory finance textbooks tend to advise the use of the NPV technique for capital budgeting

decisions. The NPV is defined as follows

$$\text{NPV} = -K_0 + \sum_{t=1}^{T} \frac{CF_t^*(1 - \tau)}{(1 + \bar{r})^t} \qquad (16.1)$$

where

K_0 = project cost
CF_t^* = expected before-tax cash flow in year t
τ = tax rate
$\bar{r}$ = weighted average cost of capital
T = life of the project

---

1 Our account of the adjusted-present-value technique draws on a paper by Donald Lessard: "Evaluating International Projects: An Adjusted Present Value Approach," in Donald R. Lessard (ed.), *International Financial Management: Theory and Application*, Warren, Gorham and Lamont, Boston, MA, 2nd edn, 1985.

The **weighted average cost of capital**, $\bar{r}$, is in turn defined as follows

$$\bar{r} = \frac{E}{E+D}r^e + \frac{D}{E+D}r(1-\tau)$$

where

$r^e =$ equilibrium cost of equity reflecting only the systematic risk

$r =$ before-tax cost of debt

$E =$ total market value of equity

$D =$ total market value of debt

$\tau =$ tax rate

We see that the cost of equity and the cost of debt are weighted by the relative importance of equity and debt as sources of capital, and that an additional adjustment is made to the cost of debt due to the fact that interest payments are generally a deductible expense when determining corporate taxes. The adjustment of $(1 - \tau)$ gives the effective cost of debt after the fraction τ of interest payments has been saved from taxes. While not universally accepted, this NPV approach has enjoyed a prominent place in finance textbooks.[2]

There are two categories of reasons why it is difficult to apply the traditional NPV technique to overseas projects and why an alternative framework such as the adjusted-present-value technique is preferred by many managers. The first category of reasons involves the difficulties which cause cash flows – the numerators in the NPV calculation – to be seen from two different perspectives: that of the investor's home country and that of the country in which the project is located. The correct perspective is that of the investor's home country, which we assume to be the same for all company shareholders.[3]

The second category of reasons involves the degree of risk of foreign projects and the appropriate discount rate – the denominator of the NPV calculation. We shall begin by looking at why cash flows differ between the investor's perspective and the perspective of the foreign country in which the project is located.

CASH FLOWS: HOME VERSUS FOREIGN PERSPECTIVES

Blocked funds

If funds that have been blocked or otherwise restricted can be utilized in a foreign investment, the effective project cost to the investor may be below the local project construction cost. From the investor's perspective there is a gain from activated funds equal to the difference between the face value of those funds liberated by pursuing the project, and the present value of the funds if the next best thing is done with them. This gain should be deducted from the capital cost of the project to find the effective cost from the investor's perspective. For example, if the next best thing that can be done is to leave blocked funds idle abroad, the full value of the activated funds should be deducted from the project cost. Alternatively, if half of the blocked funds can be returned to the investor after the investor pays taxes, or if the blocked funds earn half of a fair market interest rate, then half of the value of the blocked funds should be subtracted from the capital cost of the project.

Effects on sales of other divisions

From the perspective of the foreign manager of an overseas project, the total cash flows generated by the investment would appear to be relevant. However, factories are frequently built in countries in which sales have previously taken place with goods produced in other facilities owned and operated by the same parent company. When the MNC exports to the country of the new project

2 For the traditional textbook account of the NPV approach with the weighted average cost of capital, see James C. Van Horne, *Financial Management and Policy*, 12th edn, Prentice-Hall, Englewood Cliffs, NJ, 2002. For an account of the alternative APV approach using an adjusted cost of capital, see Richard Brealey and Stewart Myers, *Principles of Corporate Finance*, 6th edn, McGraw Hill, New York, 2001.

3 Michael Adler has tackled the challenging problem of having company shareholders from different countries. See Michael Adler, "The Cost of Capital and Valuation of a Two-Country Firm," *Journal of Finance*, March 1974, pp. 119–32.

from the home country or some other preexisting facility, only the increment in the MNC's corporate income due to the investment is relevant. This means deducting from the new project's cash flow, the income lost from other projects due to the new project. It should be noted that it may not be necessary to deduct *all* losses of cash flows from other facilities because sales in the foreign market will sometimes decline or be lost in the absence of the new project, and this is why the investment is being made. For example, the foreign investment may be to preempt another company entering the foreign market. What we must do is net out whatever income would have otherwise been earned by the MNC without the new project.

Remittance restrictions

When there are restrictions on the **repatriation** of newly generated income earned on a foreign project – the amount that can be remitted to the parent investor's country – only those cash flows that are remittable to the parent company are relevant from the MNC's perspective. This is true whether or not the income is actually remitted. When remittances are legally limited by the foreign government, sometimes the restrictions can be circumvented to an extent by using charges for parent company overhead and so on. If we include only the income which is remittable via legal and open channels, we will obtain a conservative estimate of the project's value. If this is positive, we need not add any more. If it is negative, we can add income that is remittable via illegal transfers, for example. The ability to perform this two-step procedure is a major advantage of the APV approach. As we shall see, a two-step procedure can also be applied to taxes.

Different levels of taxation

International taxation is an extremely complex subject that is best treated separately, as it is in Appendix A. However, for the purpose of evaluating overseas direct investment, what matters is the total taxes paid, and not which government collects them, the form of taxes collected, the expenditures allowed against taxes, and so on. The essential point is that for a US-based multinational, when the US corporate tax rate is above the foreign rate, the effective tax rate will be the US rate if full credit is given for foreign taxes paid. For example, if the foreign project is located in Singapore and the local tax rate for foreign-based corporations is 22 percent while the US corporate tax rate is 40 percent, then after the credit for foreign taxes paid is applied, only 18 percent will be payable in the United States. If, however, the project is located in Japan and faces a tax rate of 42 percent, full credit will not be available, and the effective tax rate will be 42 percent. This means that when we deal with foreign projects from the investor's point of view, we should use a tax rate, τ, which is the higher of the home-country and foreign rates.

Taking τ as the higher of the tax rates at home and abroad is a conservative approach. In reality, taxes are often reduced to a level below τ through the judicious choice of transfer prices, through royalty payments, and so on. These techniques can be used to move income from high-tax countries to low-tax countries and thereby reduce overall corporate taxes. In addition, the payment of taxes can be deferred by leaving remittable income abroad, and so if cash flows are measured as all remittable income whether or not remitted, some adjustment is required since the actual amount of taxes paid will be less than the cash-flow term suggests. The adjustment can be made to the cost of capital or included as an extra term in an APV calculation.[4]

---

4 A method for valuing foreign investment that is based on net present value and the weighted average cost of capital that takes care of taxes has been developed by Alan C. Shapiro, "Financial Structure and the Cost of Capital in the Multinational Corporation," *Journal of Financial and Quantitative Analysis*, November 1978, pp. 211–26. In general, the NPV and APV approaches will be equivalent if they take care of all complexities. This has been shown by Lawrence D. Boothe, "Capital Budgeting Frameworks for the Multinational Corporation," *Journal of International Business Studies*, Fall 1982, pp. 113–23.

DISCOUNT RATES: CORPORATE VERSUS SHAREHOLDER PERSPECTIVES

While governments sometimes offer special financial terms and other kinds of help for certain domestic projects, it is very common for foreign investors to receive some sort of assistance. This may come in the form of low-cost land, reduced interest rates on debt, and so on. Low-cost land can be reflected in project costs, but **concessionary financing** is more problematic in the NPV approach. However, with the APV technique we can add an extra term to the calculation to reflect the value of the debt subsidy. As we shall see, the advantage of the APV approach is due to the fact that special concessionary loans are available to the corporation but not to the shareholders of the corporation. Concessionary financing also makes the appropriate cost of capital for foreign investment projects differ from that for domestic projects, which is what happens in segmented capital markets.[5]

THE ADJUSTED-PRESENT-VALUE TECHNIQUE

The APV for a foreign project can be written as follows:

$$APV = -S_0 K_0 + S_0 AF_0$$
$$+ \sum_{t=1}^{T} \frac{(S_t^* CF_t^* - LS_t^*)(1 - \tau)}{(1 + DR_e)^t}$$
$$+ \sum_{t=1}^{T} \frac{DA_t \tau}{(1 + DR_a)^t} + \sum_{t=1}^{T} \frac{r_g BC_0 \tau}{(1 + DR_b)^t}$$
$$+ S_0 \left[CL_0 - \sum_{t=1}^{T} \frac{LR_t}{(1 + DR_c)^t} \right]$$
$$+ \sum_{t=1}^{T} \frac{TD_t^*}{(1 + DR_d)^t}$$
$$+ \sum_{t=1}^{T} \frac{RF_t^*}{(1 + DR_f)^t} \qquad (16.2)$$

5 Indeed, blocked funds, remittance restrictions, and different levels of taxation are also *causes* of market segmentation.

where

S_0 = spot exchange rate, period zero

S_t^* = expected spot rate, period t

K_0 = capital cost of project in foreign-currency units

AF_0 = restricted foreign funds activated by project

CF_t^* = expected remittable cash flow in foreign currency units

LS_t^* = profit from lost sales, in dollars

τ = the higher of US and foreign corporate tax rates

T = life of the project

DA_t = depreciation allowances in dollar units

BC_0 = contribution of project to borrowing capacity in dollars

CL_0 = face value of concessionary loan in foreign currency

LR_t = loan repayments on concessionary loan in foreign currency

TD_t^* = expected tax savings from deferrals, inter-subsidiary transfer pricing

RF_t^* = expected illegal repatriation of income

DR_e = discount rate for cash flows, assuming all-equity financing

DR_a = discount rate for depreciation allowances

DR_b = discount rate for tax saving on interest deduction from contribution to borrowing capacity

DR_c = discount rate for saving via concessionary interest rate

DR_d = discount rate for tax saving via inter-subsidiary transfers

DR_f = discount rate for illegally repatriated project flows

r_g = market borrowing rate at home

We can describe each of the terms in the APV equation and show how these terms take care of the difficulties in evaluating foreign investment project s.

$-S_0 K_0$ The cost of the project, K_0 is assumed to be denominated in foreign currency and incurred in year 0 only. It is converted into dollars at S_0.

$S_0 AF_0$ We reduce the project cost by the value, converted into dollars, of the blocked funds activated by the project. AF_0 is the face value of the blocked funds minus their value in the next best use.

$\sum_{t=1}^{T} (S_t^* CF_t^* - LS_t^*)(1 - \tau)/(1 + DR_e)^t$ The term CF_t^* represents the expected legally remittable project net cash flows on sales from the new project in year t, beginning after a year.[6] This is measured in foreign currency and converted into dollars at the expected exchange rate, S_t^* From this is subtracted the lost income that was made on sales from other facilities which are replaced by the new facility, LS_t^*. If the lost income is measured in US dollars, as it will be if due to the new foreign plant sales are lost to the US parent company, we do not multiply by the exchange rate. However, if the lost income is measured in units of foreign currency, S_t^* applies to LS_t^*. Other funds remitted via inter-subsidiary transfer pricing and other illegal means are included in a later term. The cash flows are adjusted for the effective tax rate, τ, which as mentioned earlier is the higher of the domestic and foreign corporate tax rates. Any reduction from this level that results from managing to move income from high-tax countries to low-tax countries through internal transfers can be added later. We assume here that the same tax rate applies to lost income on replaced sales as well as to income from the new investment. If the lost income would have faced a different tax rate, LS_t^* must be considered separately from CF_t^*. The discount rate is the all-equity cost of capital that reflects all systematic risk, including unavoidable country risk and exchange-rate risk.[7] We use the all-equity cost of capital because the benefit of any tax savings from the use of debt financing is included in a separate term, discussed later.

$\sum_{t=1}^{T} DA_t \tau/(1 + DR_d)^t$ Depreciation is an allowable expense when determining corporate taxes, whether the source of income is from abroad or from home. The benefit of the depreciation allowance is the amounts of allowance times the corporate tax rates against which the allowance is applied. We have assumed DA_t is a dollar amount and therefore have not included S_t^*. This will be appropriate if the higher of the foreign and domestic tax rates is the domestic rate; in this case depreciation allowances are deducted against US taxes. If the higher tax rate is the rate in the foreign country, DA_t will probably be in foreign-currency units, and we need to convert at S_t.

$\sum_{t=1}^{T} r_g BC_0 \tau/(1 + DR_b)^t$ When debt is used to finance a project at home or abroad, the interest payments are tax-deductible, providing a **tax shield**. Whether or not the project in question fully utilizes the potential borrowing made possible by the project, the tax savings on the amount that *could be* borrowed should be included as a benefit.[8] We use the *potential* to borrow because if, for example, a firm does not use the entire borrowing potential provided by a particular new project, the firm can use more borrowing elsewhere in its operations and enjoy the tax shield from this borrowing. On the other hand, if a firm borrows in excess of the capacity provided by a particular project, it will be able to borrow less for other projects, losing the tax savings from debt financing on these projects.

The annual benefit that is included in the APV equals the tax saving due to the interest payments associated with the borrowing capacity. The interest rate is the market borrowing rate at home. For example, if the project has a value of $1 million and the firm likes to maintain 50 percent of its value in debt, the project will raise borrowing capacity by $BC_0 = \$500,000$, and the interest payment on

---

6 As before in the book, asterisks stand for expected values. Quantities without asterisks are assumed to be known at the time of the investment decision.

7 We are not yet ready to give a full account of country risk, which includes political risk. This will be covered in the next chapter.

8 **Borrowing capacity** is the amount of borrowing made possible by investing in a project. This is not a limit imposed on the investor from outside, but rather results from a firm's decision on how much debt it wishes to carry.

Table 16.1 *Value of a £1-million concessionary loan*

Year	Loan outstanding(£)	Principal repayment(£)	Interest payment(£)	Total payment(£)	Present value of payment(£)
1	1,000,000	100,000	100,000	200,000	173,913
2	900,000	100,000	90,000	190,000	143,667
3	800,000	100,000	80,000	180,000	118,353
4	700,000	100,000	70,000	170,000	97,198
5	600,000	100,000	60,000	160,000	79,548
6	500,000	100,000	50,000	150,000	68,849
7	400,000	100,000	40,000	140,000	52,631
8	300,000	100,000	30,000	130,000	42,497
9	200,000	100,000	20,000	120,000	31,111
10	100,000	100,000	10,000	110,000	27,190
					834,957

this amount, that is, $r_g BC_0$ should be included each year. The tax saved from the interest cost deduction is this amount times the effective tax rate, that is, $r_g BC_0 \tau$. As we have said, this is the amount used in the APV calculation even if the amount borrowed is larger or smaller than $500,000. For example, if only $200,000 is borrowed on the $1 million project, an additional $300,000 can be borrowed elsewhere in the corporation, with consequent tax savings from the interest payments on this $300,000. If $800,000 is borrowed, the project will reduce the capacity to borrow for other activities by $300,000, and thereby lower the tax savings on this amount of debt.

$$S_0\left[CL_0 - \sum_{t=1}^{I} LR_t/(1 + DR_c)^t\right]$$ The current value of the benefit of a concessionary loan is the difference between the face value of the loan, CL_0, and the present value of the repayments on the loan discounted at the rate of interest that would have been faced in the absence of the concessionary financing. The loan is assumed to be in the foreign currency and must be converted into dollars. Since it is a present or current amount it is converted at the current exchange rate. For example, if a 10-year loan with a 10 percent interest rate and ten equal principal repayments is made available when the market rate would have been 15 percent, the

present value of the repayment on a £1 million loan is £834,957. This is shown in Table 16.1. The value of the subsidy from the loan concession is hence £1,000,000 − £834,957 = £165,043. This amount has a dollar value of $330,086 if, for example, $S_0 = 2.0$.[9]

$$\sum_{t=1}^{T} TD_t^*/(1 + DR_d)^t$$ By using the higher of the domestic and foreign tax rates for τ we have taken a conservative approach. In practice, a multinational is likely to be able to move income from high-tax locations to low-tax locations, and may also be able to defer the payment of taxes, thereby reducing the effective tax rate to a level below τ. Corporate income can be moved by adjusting **transfer prices**, head-office overhead, and so on, and the payment of taxes can be deferred by reinvesting in the foreign country rather than remitting any income.[10] The APV technique allows us to include an estimate of tax savings as a separate term

9 A general account of the valuation of subsidized financing can be found in Richard Brealey and Stewart Myers, *Principles of Corporate Finance*, 6th edn, McGraw-Hill, New York, 2001.

10 Transfer prices are those charged for goods and services moving between divisions of a company. They are discussed more fully in Chapter 17.

in the calculation. We can evaluate APV without TD_t and see if it is positive. If it is, we need not do anything else: the project is worthwhile. If it is not, we can see how much of a tax saving will be required to make APV positive and determine whether such a saving can reasonably be expected. That is, the APV procedure allows us to take a two-step approach when necessary.

$\sum_{t=1}^{T} RF_t^* / (1 + DR_f)^t$ The cash flow we use for CF_t^* is a conservative estimate. CF_t^* includes only the flows which are remittable when transfer prices, royalties, and so on reflect their legitimate, market values. However, a multinational might try to manipulate transfer prices or royalty payments to repatriate more income (as well as to reduce taxes as explained immediately above). Any extra remittable income from additional (and perhaps illegal) channels may be included after the APV from the legal cash flows has been computed, if APV is negative. This two-step procedure can be applied simultaneously to extra remittable income and tax savings, both of which involve transfer price tinkering.

SELECTING THE APPROPRIATE DISCOUNT RATES

All-equity rates that reflect systematic risk

So far we have said little about the discount rates. The first important matter involving the choice of discount rates is that since the tax shield from debt is evaluated in a separate term in the APV formula, cash flows should be discounted at an *all-equity* discount rate. Recall that the separate term in APV is the one that reflects the project's borrowing capacity. This is different from the NPV approach where the tax saving from debt appears in the weighted average cost of capital calculation. With the tax shield accounted for separately in APV, the opportunity cost of capital to the shareholder is the expected return on alternative applications of their equity. The relevant alternatives are those of equivalent risk.

As we noted in Chapter 15, only the systematic component of total risk matters. To some extent the additional risks of doing business abroad are mitigated by the extent to which cash flows from foreign projects are imperfectly correlated and therefore reduce the variance of corporate income. If there is risk reduction from having some independence of cash flows from different countries, and the diversification of flows from different countries is not directly available to shareholders, the diversification offered by the MNC should be reflected in discount rates as well as in the market value of the stock.[11]

The risks faced with foreign investments that are not explicitly faced with domestic investments are first foreign exchange risk, that is, *currency* risk, and second, *country* risk. These are the two "C" words that distinguish international finance from ordinary finance. The two risks provide further reason, in addition to those already mentioned, why the NPV technique is difficult to apply to FDI projects. Both country risk and exchange-rate risk can, for example, make the optimal capital structure change over time. One possibility is that relatively more debt is used early on when there is concessionary finance. Debt denominated in the currency of income might also reduce foreign exchange risk. It is difficult to incorporate **dynamic capital structure** within the weighted average cost of capital used in the NPV technique. However, in the APV technique, where we use the all-equity cost of capital, (DR_e), the effect of capital structure on, for example, interest tax shields, is treated in a separate term.

Country risk can be diversified by holding a portfolio of investments of many different countries. Similarly, currency risk can be diversified by holding investments denominated in many different currencies. It is also possible to use debt denomination in the currency of income, forward

---

11 As we mentioned in Chapter 15, an ability of a multinational corporation to do what its shareholders cannot requires capital market segmentation from the shareholders' perspective, that the corporation can circumvent.

contracts, options, and other hedges. This means that the risk premium in the discount rate, which reflects only the systematic risk, may not be very large.[12] It follows from our discussion of the ICAPM in Chapter 15 that knowing the systematic risk requires that we have a covariance for the project's value with the relevant market portfolio. It is extremely difficult to obtain such a project covariance because, while a company's market value may be known, there is no market value of the *project*, and no past data to use to estimate the covariance with *proposed* projects. Moreover, the relevant risk premium for the APV approach must be for an all-equity investment. This adds even more difficulty when any existing risk premium reflects the company's debt. But these are only some of the problems in selecting appropriate discount rates. We have already mentioned the problem of the shareholder perspective, which is difficult when different shareholders are from different countries and capital markets are segmented. Yet another problem is inflation and the connected question of the currency in which cash flows are measured.

Inflation and discount rate choice

A question that arises in all capital budgeting applications, whether the investment project being evaluated is foreign or domestic, concerns the choice of the "nominal" versus the "real"

discount rate. (As mentioned in Chapter 8, the real interest rate is the nominal rate minus expected inflation.) The answer is that the choice does not matter provided we are consistent. That is, we reach the same conclusion if we discount nominal cash flows (those not adjusted for inflation) by the nominal discount rate, or real (inflation adjusted) cash flows by the real discount rate. However, if cash flows are easier to forecast in today's prices so that the forecasts are of real cash flows, as a practical matter it is easier to use the real flows and discount at the real rate. (Companies may find it easier to forecast quantities of goods they may sell than to forecast values of goods sold which depend on future prices. Therefore, it is often easier to deal with real cash flows than try to build inflationary expectations into cash flows and then use the nominal discount rate, a far more roundabout procedure.)

A related question to that of nominal versus real discount rates concerns the currency of expected cash flows. Should we use foreign-currency flows and discount these at the foreign-currency discount rate, or convert foreign-currency cash flows into domestic currency, and then discount at the domestic-currency discount rate? Again, the answer is that it does not matter which method we use provided everything is done consistently. That is, if cash flows are measured in foreign currency we use the foreign-currency discount rate, and if cash flows are measured in domestic currency we use the domestic-currency discount rate. Similarly, if we use real cash flows, in terms of either currency, we should use the real discount rate, in the same currency. These conclusions are not obvious, and are explained in Appendix B. The appendix also shows that despite the theoretical equivalence of methods, when foreign-currency cash flows are predetermined, or contractual, we do not have a choice between real and nominal discount rates and between current and future expected exchange rates. Examples of contractual cash flows are revenues from exports sold at fixed prices and depreciation allowances based on historical costs. The contractual amounts are fixed in nominal

12 Instead of including the country risk in the discount rate, we can incorporate it within the cash-flow term. This procedure, which can also be followed with other types of risk, involves putting cash flows into their "certainty equivalents." A method of dealing with risk that avoids the need to find certainty equivalents or risk premiums is to deduct from cash flows the cost of country risk insurance or a foreign exchange risk management program. This is the recommendation of Arthur I. Stonehill and Leonard Nathanson in "Capital Budgeting and the Multinational Corporation," *California Management Review*, Summer 1968, pp. 39–54. The ability of shareholders to diversify foreign exchange risk has been examined by Jeffery A. Frankel, "The Diversifiability of Exchange Risk," *Journal of International Economics*, August 1979, pp. 379–93.

terms and should therefore be converted into dollars at the expected future exchange rate and then discounted at the nominal dollar discount rate. Contractual flows do not lend themselves to simplification through the use of today's cash flows of foreign exchange at today's exchange rates. It is for this reason that in the cash flow term in equation (16.2) we convert foreign-currency cash flows into US dollars, and then discount at the nominal US dollar discount rate. However, as we shall show below, the discount rates for other terms in equation (16.2) take different forms.

Discount rates for different items

Now that the methods for handling inflation with the discount rate have been stated, we are ready to describe the nature of the different discount rates in the APV formula.

DR_e This should be nominal for contractual cash flows resulting from sales made at fixed future prices. Since the cash flows are converted into dollars at S_t^* the discount rate should be the nominal rate for the United States. DR_e should also be the all-equity rate, reflecting the project's systematic risk, including the risk from exchange rates. When the cash flows are noncontractual, we can use a real discount rate, today's actual exchange rate, and initial-period expected cash flows at today's prices. This is explained in Appendix B.

DR_a Since in many countries depreciation is based on historical costs, the depreciation allowance, DA_t, will be contractual, and DR_a should therefore be the nominal discount rate. Since we have written DA_t directly in dollar terms, we should use the US rate. The only risk premium should be for the chance that the depreciation allowances will go unused. If the investor feels very confident that the project will yield positive net cash flows, this risk is small, and then DR_a should be the riskless nominal rate of the United States. This is true even if the depreciation allowance, DA_t, is measured in

foreign-currency units, provided we convert them into US dollars.

DR_b If the project's contribution to borrowing capacity is measured in nominal US dollar terms – and it is very likely that it will be – we should discount at the US nominal rate. The risk is that the tax shield cannot be used, and if this is considered small, we can use the riskless rate.

DR_c The value of a concessionary loan depends on the interest rate that would otherwise be paid. If the loan repayments will be nominal foreign exchange amounts, we should use the nominal foreign-currency interest rate that would have been paid in the absence of the financing concession.

DR_d and DR_f Tax savings, additional repatriated income via transfer prices, and the deferment of tax payments via reinvestment in low-tax countries could be estimated at either today's prices or future prices. If the estimates of TD_t^* and RF_t^* are at today's prices and are therefore real, we must use a real rate, and if they are at future (inflated) prices, we must use a nominal rate. If the estimates are in US dollars, as they probably will be, we must use a US rate. Since the risk is that of not being able to find techniques for making these tax savings and additional remittances, the appropriate discount rate requires a risk premium. Donald Lessard advises the use of the same rate used for cash flows, DR_e.[13]

With the nature of the terms in the APV formula carefully defined and the factors influencing the discount rates also explained, we are ready to consider an example of capital budgeting. We consider whether Aviva Corporation should build a jeans manufacturing factory in Turkey.

AN EXAMPLE

Suppose that as a result of possible admission of Turkey into the European Union, and concern that competition from new producers in the Turkish market will erode sales and profits of its plants

13 See Donald R. Lessard, op. cit.

currently supplying Turkey, Aviva is considering opening a jeans production facility in Turkey. The construction costs of the plant have been estimated at TL2 trillion (or TL2,000 billion), where TL represents the Turkish lira. At the current exchange rate of approximately 1 million Turkish liras to the US dollar, the construction cost is equivalent to about $2 million. Suppose the factory is expected to add about $1 million to Aviva's borrowing capacity, this being about half the value of the facility and consistent with the company's chosen policy of financing its overall operations with roughly equal amounts of debt and equity. Because of partial retention of earnings from Aviva's previously established sales subsidiary in Turkey, the proposed factory can be partially financed with TL600 billion held in the country, which, if it had been remitted, would have faced taxes of TL400 billion in Turkey. Of this amount, a tax credit for the equivalent of only TL280 billion would have been received in the United States.

The current exchange rate between the Turkish lira and the US dollar is TL1,000,000/$, and so $S_0 = 0.000001$ where $S = S(TL/\$)$. The spot rate is expected to move at the rate given by the relative inflation rates according to PPP. Turkish inflation is expected to proceed at 25 percent, while US inflation is expected to be 10 percent.

Jeans sales, which will begin when the plant is completed after a year, are expected to average 50,000 pairs per year. At the beginning of the year of construction, the jeans have a unit price of TL20,000,000 (TL20 million) per pair, and this is expected to rise at the general rate of inflation. The average production cost based on material prices at the time of construction is TL15,000,000 per pair, and this cost is also expected to keep in line with general Turkish inflation.

The Turkish market has previously been supplied by Aviva's main plant in the United States, and recent sales to the Turkish market were 10,000 pairs per year. The most recent profit on US-manufactured jeans has been $5 per pair, and future profit is expected to keep pace with general US

inflation. However, it is expected that in the absence of a Turkish factory, Aviva would lose 9.1 percent per annum of its Turkish sales to new, local entrants. This is one of the reasons why Aviva is considering opening the Turkish plant.

The factory is expected to require little in the way of renovation for 10 years. The market value of the plant in 10 years is extremely difficult to estimate, and Aviva is confident only in the belief that it will have some substantial value.

Aviva has by great art and ingenuity managed to arrive at an all-equity cost of capital that reflects the project's systematic risk (including country risk that is not covered by insurance, the deviation of exchange rates from predicted levels, and so on) of 20 percent. This allows for the fact that some of the risk can be diversified by the shareholders and/or avoided by insurance, forward cover, and so on.

In return for locating the factory in an area of heavy unemployment, Aviva will receive from the Turkish government TL600 billion of the TL1400 billion it needs in addition to the previously blocked funds, at the subsidized rate of 10 percent. The principal is to be repaid in equal installments over 10 years. If Aviva had been required to borrow competitively in Turkey, it would have faced a 35 percent borrowing cost, as opposed to its 15 percent borrowing cost in the United States. This is a little above the US riskless rate of 12 percent. The remaining TL800 billion that is needed for construction will be provided as equity by Aviva USA. Income on the project is subject to a 25 percent tax in Turkey and a 46 percent tax in the United States, and Turkish taxes are fully deductible against US taxes.

The US Internal Revenue Service (IRS) will allow Aviva to write off one-tenth of the dollar equivalent of the historical construction cost each year over 10 years. By using carefully arranged transfer prices and royalties, Aviva thinks it can reduce taxes by deferrals by $5,000 in the initial year of operation, and it expects this to hold steady in real terms, but it does not expect to be able to remit more income than the amount declared.

357

In summary and in terms of the notation used in defining APV in equation (16.2), Aviva faces the following situation.

$K_0 =$ TL2,000,000 million

$BC_0 =$ $1,000,000

$AF_0 =$ TL600,000 million

$\qquad - ($TL600,000 $-$ TL400,000$)$ million

$\qquad =$ TL400,000 million

$S_0 =$ 0.000001

$S_t^* =$ $0.000001(1 - 0.12)^t$

$CF_t^* =$ TL50,000$(20,000,000 - 15,000,000)$

$\qquad \times (1 + 0.25)^t + ($scrap value when $t = 10)$

$LS_t^* =$ $10,000(5)(1 + 0.1)^t(1 - 0.091)^t$

$\qquad =$ $50,000

$CL_0 =$ TL600,000 million

$LR_t =$ (see Table 16.2)

$DA_t =$ $200,000

$TD_t =$ $5,000(1 + 0.1)^{t-1}$ for $t > 0$

$RF_t =$ 0

$\tau =$ 0.46

$DR_e = DR_d = DR_f = 0.20$

$DR_a = DR_b = 0.12$

$DR_c =$ 0.35

$r_g =$ 0.15

We will solve the problem by using all nominal values for cash flows and all nominal discount rates.

Many of the values attached to the terms of the APV formula are self-evident. For example, the construction cost is TL2,000,000 million and the borrowing capacity that the plant contributes is $1,000,000. The value of activated funds, AF_0, is their face value minus their value in their next best use. If the next best use is to bring them home and face taxes, the next best value is TL600,000 million $-$ TL400,000 million. We exclude the tax credit in the United States on repatriated funds because it is smaller than the taxes paid

in Turkey; thus the effective tax rate is the Turkish rate. (If the credit cannot be applied against other income, it has no value.) This means that if the blocked funds had been brought back, TL200,000 million would have been received after taxes. We subtract this from the TL600,000 million that can be used in the project to find TL400,000 million for AF_0.

The expected exchange rates are obtained from the definition $S_t = S_0(1 + \dot{S}^*)^t$. We obtain $\dot{S}^*$ from the PPP condition; that is,

$$\dot{S}^* = \dot{S}^* = \frac{\dot{P}_{US}^* - \dot{P}_{TK}^*}{1 + \dot{P}_{TK}^*} = \frac{0.10 - 0.25}{1.25}$$

$$= -0.12$$

The expected cash flow, CF_t^*, is obtained by multiplying the expected sales of 50,000 pairs of jeans per annum by the expected profit per pair. The profit per pair during the plant construction year, when prices and costs are known, would be TL20,000,000 $-$ TL15,000,000 if production could begin immediately, but by the initial year of operation the profit per pair is expected to rise to (TL20,000,000 $-$ TL15,000,000)(1 + 0.25). The profit is expected to continue to rise at 25 percent per annum, with an expected cash flow by year t of

$$(\text{TL20,000,000} - \text{TL15,000,000})(1 + 0.25)^t$$

from each of the 50,000 pairs. The value of this is shown in Table 16.2. The present value of the cash flow at Aviva's chosen cost of capital of $DR_e = 0.20$ is also shown.

The scrap value of the project is uncertain. As a result, we can take a two-step approach to see whether the project is profitable without estimating a scrap value, since if it is profitable without including the scrap value, it is a fortiori profitable with some scrap value.

Sales from the US plant that will be lost due to the project, LS_t^*, have most recently been producing a profit for Aviva USA of $5 \times 10,000 = $50,000 per year. With the profit per unit expected to grow at the US inflation rate of 10 percent and the

Table 16.2 *Adjusted-present-value elements for Turkish jeans factory*

Year	S_t^* ($\times 0.000001$)	CF_t^* (million)	$S_t^* CF_t^*$	$S_t^* CF_t^* - LS_t^*$	$(1-\tau)\dfrac{S_t^* CF_t^* - LS_t^*}{(1+DR_e)^t}$	$\dfrac{DA_t \tau}{(1+DR_a)^t}$
1	$0.8800/TL	TL312,500	$275,000	$225,000	$101,250	$82,143
2	0.7744	390,625	302,500	252,500	94,688	73,342
3	0.6815	488,281	332,764	282,764	88,364	65,484
4	0.5997	610,351	366,028	316,028	82,299	62,203
5	0.5277	762,939	402,603	352,603	76,520	48,468
6	0.4644	953,674	442,886	392,886	71,051	46,610
7	0.4087	1,192,092	487,208	437,208	65,889	41,616
8	0.3596	1,490,116	535,846	485,846	61,016	37,157
9	0.3165	1,862,645	589,527	539,527	56,465	33,176
10	0.2785	2,328,306	648,433	598,433	52,191	29,622
					749,733	519,821

Year	$r_g BC_0 \tau$	$\dfrac{r_g BC_0 \tau}{(1+DR_b)}$	TD_t^*	$\dfrac{TD_t^*}{(1+DR_d)^t}$	Loan balance TL million	Loan interest TL million	LR_t TL million	$\dfrac{LR_t}{(1+DR_c)^t}$ TL million
1	$69,000	$61,607	$5,000	$4,167	600,000	60,000	120,000	88,889
2	69,000	55,007	5,500	3,819	540,000	54,000	114,000	62,551
3	69,000	49,113	6,050	3,501	480,000	48,000	108,000	43,896
4	69,000	43,851	6,655	3,209	420,000	42,000	102,000	30,709
5	69,000	39,153	7,321	2,942	360,000	36,000	96,000	21,409
6	69,000	34,957	8,053	2,697	300,000	30,000	90,000	14,868
7	69,000	31,212	8,858	2,472	240,000	24,000	84,000	10,279
8	69,000	27,868	9,744	2,266	180,000	18,000	78,000	7,070
9	69,000	24,882	10,718	2,077	120,000	12,000	72,000	4,834
10	69,000	22,216	11,790	1,904	60,000	6,000	66,000	3,283
		389,866		29,054				287,788

number of units expected to decline by 9.1 percent, expected profits from replaced sales remain at their current level of $50,000 per year; the product of 1.10 and $(1 - 0.091)$ equals unity.

The amount of the concessionary loan is $CL_0 = TL600,000$ million. The repayments of principal are TL60,000 million each year, with interest computed on the unpaid balance at 10 percent per annum. LR_t in Table 16.2 shows the annual loan repayments discounted at the market rate in Turkey of $DR_c = 0.35$. The table also gives the values of the discounted net-of-tax depreciation allowances of

$200,000 per year. This is 10 percent of the historical cost in dollars, $S_0 K_0$. We use the dollar cost because the depreciation is effectively against US corporate taxes. These are at the rate $\tau = 0.46$. We have discounted depreciation allowances at the riskless dollar rate, $DR_a = 0.12$. Use of the riskless rate presumes there will be sufficient income to be able to use the depreciation allowances.

The debt or borrowing capacity of the project is such that Aviva can borrow $1,000,000 (which is half the dollar cost of construction) to obtain tax shields somewhere within its operations. The

359

interest rate Aviva would pay if it took the tax shields by borrowing more at home is $r_g = 0.15$. This will save taxes on $0.15 \times \$1,000,000$ at the tax rate $\tau = 0.46$. We have discounted the saving from the tax shield at the riskless dollar rate, $DR_b = 0.12$. As with the depreciation allowance, this presumes enough income to enjoy the tax shield.

The extra tax benefits, TD_t^*, of $5,000 are assumed to keep pace with US inflation. We have discounted $TD_t^* = \$5,000$ at Aviva's cost of equity of 20 percent.

We can form an opinion concerning the feasibility of the jeans factory if we use the values of the terms as we have stated them, including the totals from Table 16.2, in the APV formula, equation (16.2).

$$
\begin{aligned}
APV = &- (0.000001 \times 2,000,000 \text{ million}) \\
&+ (0.000001 \times 4,000,000 \text{ million}) \\
&+ 749,733 + 519,821 + 389,866 \\
&+ 0.000001 \times (600,000 \text{ million} \\
&- 287,788 \text{ million}) + 29,054 + 0 \\
= &\ \$400,686
\end{aligned}
$$

We discover that the APV is positive. This means that the project is worthwhile. Furthermore, the APV does not yet include any estimate for the market value of the factory and land at the end of 10 years. If Aviva feels that while it cannot estimate this value, it should exceed half the original cost in real terms, it can take an even more confident position. Half the original project cost is $1 million, and since this is a real value, it should be discounted at the real interest rate relevant for dollars. Using Aviva's risky rate, this is DR_e minus the US expected inflation rate of 10 percent; that is, $DR_e = 0.20 - 0.10 = 0.10$. At this rate the present value of $1 million in 10 years is $385,543, which makes the APV clearly positive. The $385,543 would be subject to a capital-gain tax if it were to be realized because the entire project has been depreciated, but even after taxes the project would clearly seem to be worthwhile.

ACTUAL PRACTICE OF CAPITAL BUDGETING

The adjusted-present-value approach using the correct discount rate to reflect the contractual or non-contractual nature of cash flows and the systematic risk of the investment project requires management to take a very scientific view. We can expect that constraints on the knowledge of managers and the time available to make decisions will result in approaches that are often more pragmatic – perhaps a simple "rule-of-thumb" – than the approach we presented. According to a survey of multinational corporations this appears to be the case. The survey was made of 10 US multinationals by Business International to see how they analyze acquisitions.[14] It showed that only 7 of the 10 corporations used any sort of discounting method at all.

Only one of the respondents in the Business International survey said that it looked at synergy effects, that is, the effects the acquisition would have on other subsidiaries measured by our LS_t^* term. Five of the 10 firms used the same hurdle discount rate for all acquisitions, whatever the country. Projected exchange rates were used by five of the respondents, while two used the projected rate if they considered a currency to be unstable and the current rate if they considered it to be stable. The remainder used current rates to convert all currency flows, but it was not clear from the survey whether these flows were measured in current price terms. At least one company assumed that exchange-rate movements would be reflected in relative interest rates and therefore used the US interest rate on cash flows converted into dollars at the current exchange rate.

A survey of the foreign-investment evaluation practices of 225 US manufacturing MNCs conducted by Marie Wicks Kelly and George Philippatos

---

14 See "BIMR Survey Reveals How U.S. Multinationals Analyze Foreign Acquisitions," *Money Report*, Business International, November 28, 1980. See also "Stress on Currency Fluctuations as MNCs Analyze Foreign Acquisitions," *Money Report*, Business International, November 5, 1980.

produced results revealing practices somewhat more in line with theory than those found in the much smaller Business International survey.[15] For example, the majority of companies used cash flow calculations and costs of capital which, while not exactly the kind explained in this chapter, are approximately in line with appropriate procedures.

SUMMARY

1   The net-present-value, NPV, technique is difficult to use in the case of foreign investment projects. The adjusted-present-value, APV, technique is frequently recommended instead.

2   Foreign investment projects should be evaluated from the parent company's perspective. Factors which must be considered include blocked funds (which reduce effective project costs to investors), reduced sales from other corporate divisions, restrictions on remitting earnings, extra taxes on repatriated income, and concessionary loans. These factors can be included in the adjusted present value. The APV approach can also include the benefit of concessionary finance, effects on the borrowing capacity of the company, and so on.

3   The APV technique allows a two-step evaluation. The first step involves a conservative estimate that includes only benefits of the project that are legitimate and for which there are reasonable estimates. The second step, including other benefits which may not be legitimate or well measured, is needed only if the first step gives a negative estimate.

4   Each item in the APV calculation must be discounted at an appropriate discount rate. With the benefits of the debt shield included in a separate term, the discount rates are all-equity rates for a similar amount of risk.

5   Discount rates should reflect only the systematic risk of the item being discounted. Doing business abroad can help reduce overall corporate risk when incomes are more independent between countries than between operations within a particular country, and this can mean lower discount rates for foreign projects.

6   Discount rates can, however, be higher on foreign investment projects than domestic projects because of country risk and currency risk. These risks can be diversified by shareholders if they invest in a number of countries/currencies, and this reduces required risk premiums.

7   We must be consistent in foreign-project evaluations. We can use domestic or foreign currency as long as we use the corresponding discount rates, and we can use real values of cash flows if we use real interest rates, or nominal cash flows if we use nominal interest rates.

8   When we are dealing with noncontractual flows, we can choose the method of handling inflation that we prefer. However, with contractual flows, which are nominal amounts, we must use nominal discount rates. The choice of approach with noncontractual flows exists because inflation in cash flows will be offset by movements in exchange rates.

15 Marie E. Wicks Kelly and George C. Philippatos, "Comparative Analysis of the Foreign Investment Evaluation Practices by U.S.-Based Manufacturing Multinational Companies," *Journal of International Business Studies*, Winter 1982, pp. 19–42.

REVIEW QUESTIONS

1 It what ways can the view of a foreign investment project differ according to whether it is viewed from the perspective of the investor, or from the perspective of a project manager in the country where investment occurs?

2 Which of the two perspectives in Question 1 is the correct perspective for judging foreign direct investments?

3 What does concessionary lending imply for the cost of capital of a corporation enjoying the favorable terms, versus the opportunity cost of capital to shareholders?

4 If blocked, or not fully repatriable, funds can be liberated by a new foreign project, how can the value of these funds to the investor be factored into a project's APV?

5 What is meant by "borrowing capacity" or "debt capacity," and how is the tax shield from this incorporated into a project's APV?

6 How do the levels of corporate tax rates influence whether an investor's home-country rate or the rate in the country of investment is used for calculating after-tax cash flows?

7 What amount of risk, total or only systematic, should be included in the all-equity discount rate used in the APV calculation?

8 What is the nature of the discount rate that is used for cash flows in the APV approach?

9 If cash flows are converted into the investor's domestic currency, and are adjusted for inflation so they are real, what discount rate should be used?

10 What is a "contractual" cash flow?

11 In what way is the handling of contractual foreign-currency cash flows different from the handling of noncontractual foreign-currency cash flows?

12 What discount rate should be used for calculating the current value of interest payments on a concessionary loan, where the payments are in terms of the foreign currency?

ASSIGNMENT PROBLEMS

1 Will withholding taxes that are at rates below domestic corporate tax rates affect direct investment when full withholding tax credit is available? How will withholding tax rates affect the distribution of total tax revenues between countries?

2 A US automobile manufacturer, National Motors, is considering building a new plant in Britain to produce its sports car, the Sting. The estimated construction cost of the plant is £50,000,000, and construction should be completed in a year. The plant will raise borrowing capacity by about $40,000,000. National Motors can reinvest £20,000,000 already held in Britain. If these funds were repatriated to the United States, they would face an effective tax rate of 46 percent. Inflation in Britain is expected to be at 15 percent; in the United States, at 10 percent. The current exchange rate is $S(\$/£) = 2.00$, and it is believed that PPP will hold on average over the relevant time frame.

National Motors expects to sell the Sting with only minor modifications for 5 years, and after this period the plant will require remodeling. The value of the plant for future use is expected to be £40,000,000 in nominal terms after 5 years. The Sting will have an initial sticker price of about £8,000, and it is expected that 10,000 will be sold each year. Production costs are estimated at £6,000. These values are expected to move in line with the general price level in Britain.

National Motors also builds a two-seater car in Germany called the Racer and expects 4,000 Racers to be replaced by the Sting. Since Racers are in short supply, 2,000 of the 4,000 Racers can be sold in Japan at the same profit as in Germany. The expected before-tax profit on the Racer during the initial year of producing the Sting is €2,500 per car, with $S(€/£) = 2.00$. This is expected to keep in line with German inflation, and PPP is expected to prevail over the relevant time frame between Britain and Germany.

Because National Motors will be building the Sting in Merseyside, an area of heavy unemployment, the British government has offered the company a loan of £20,000,000 at a 10 percent interest rate. The principal is to be repaid in five equal annual installments, with the first installment due at the beginning of the initial year of production. The competitive market rate in Britain is 20 percent, while in the United States, National Motors faces a borrowing rate of 12 percent and the riskless rate is 10 percent. The balance of the capital will be provided as equity. The tax rate in Britain is 50 percent, which is higher than the 46 percent rate in the United States. British tax law allows car plants to be depreciated over 5 years.

The British and US tax authorities are careful that appropriate transfer prices are used so that no taxes can by saved by using inter-company pricing techniques. National Motors believes a 20 percent discount rate is appropriate for the project.

Should the Sting be built?

3   Which items in the previous question are contractual and which are noncontractual? Could you discount the cash flows with a real rate of interest?

4   Compare the treatments of tax shields from debt in using the NPV and APV approaches to foreign investments.

5   How would you allow for lost income due to displaced sales from a subsidiary located in another foreign country, rather than from domestic, parent operations? Consider both exchange rate and tax problems.

6   How would you include depreciation allowances in the calculation of adjusted present value when the effective corporate income tax is that of the foreign country in which an investment is located? Consider both the exchange-rate issue, and the appropriate discount rate.

BIBLIOGRAPHY

Adler, Michael, "The Cost of Capital and Valuation of a Two-Country Firm," *Journal of Finance,* March 1974, pp. 119–32.

Booth, Lawrence D., "Capital Budgeting Frameworks for the Multinational Corporation," *Journal of International Business Studies,* Fall 1982, pp. 113–23.

Dinwiddy, Caroline and Francis Teal, "Project Appraisal Procedures and the Evaluation of Foreign Exchange," *Economics,* February 1986, pp. 97–107.

Dotan, Amihud and Arie Ovadia, "A Capital-Budgeting Decision – The Case of a Multinational Corporation Operating in High-Inflation Countries," *Journal of Business Research,* October 1986, pp. 403–10.

Eaker, Mark R., "Investment/Financing Decisions for Multinational Corporations," in Dennis E. Logue (ed.), *Handbook of Modern Finance,* Warren, Gorham and Lamont, Boston, MA, 1984, pp. 42-1–42-29.

Hodder, James E., "Evaluation of Manufacturing Investments: A Comparison of U.S. and Japanese Practices," *Financial Management,* Spring 1986, pp. 17–24.

Lessard, Donald R., "Evaluating International Projects: An Adjusted Present Value Approach," in Donald Lessard (ed.), *International Financial Management: Theory and Application,* 2nd edn, John Wiley & Sons, New York, 1985.

Shapiro, Alan C., "Capital Budgeting for the Multinational Corporation," *Financial Management,* Spring 1978, pp. 7–16.

Stonehill, Arthur I. and Leonard Nathanson, "Capital Budgeting and the Multinational Corporation," *California Management Review,* Summer 1968, pp. 39–54.

APPENDIX A

A survey of international taxation

International taxation is a complex subject, and we can do little more here than explain variations in the types of taxes encountered and the methods that can be used to help reduce them. We will view taxation questions in the most general terms, recognizing that even generalities about tax are subject to unpredictable change.

THE DIFFERENT FORMS OF TAXES

Corporate taxes

Income taxes are the chief source of revenue for the US government, and the corporate income tax is an important although declining component of the total of income taxes. Income taxes are **direct taxes**, and the United States is dependent on direct taxes for a greater proportion of its total revenue than most other countries. Members of the European Union collect direct taxes, but these are augmented by a **value-added tax**, or **VAT**, which is an **indirect tax**.[16] Sales taxes in US states have crept up over the years. Many poorer countries have a tax on imports as their primary revenue source. Other taxes that are found are based on wealth, inheritance, sales, turnover, employees, and so on.

Table 16A.1 shows that standard corporate tax rates are on average around 30 percent, although they vary substantially between countries. Variations in allowable deductions in determining income subject to tax vary from country to country, and can make effective rates differ even more than the standard rates imply. However, to the extent that high-tax rate countries have more generous allowances for deductions, the effective rate variations can be diminished. Outside the industrialized countries some nations charge no corporate tax at all. Countries with zero rates

---

16 By definition, direct taxes cannot be shifted and are borne directly by those on whom they are levied. In contrast, indirect taxes can be shifted in part or in full to somebody who is not directly taxed. For example, corporate and personal income taxes are paid by those on whom they are levied. On the other hand, sales taxes and import duties charged to firms are at least in part paid by consumers. The consumer therefore pays indirectly.

Table 16A.1 *Corporate income tax rates, 2003 (Percentages)*

Australia	30
Canada	37
Denmark	30
Finland	29
France	34
Germany	40
Hong Kong	17
Ireland	13
Italy	38
Japan	42
Netherlands	35
New Zealand	33
Singapore	22
Sweden	28
United Kingdom	30
United States	40

Note
Rates are principal corporate levels, rounded to the nearest percent.

Source: KPMG's Corporate Tax Rate Survey – January 2003.

include the Bahamas and Bermuda. The absence of corporation taxes is designed to encourage multinationals to locate offices for sheltering income and thereby gain rental and employment income as well as registration and other fees.

The United States considers that it has jurisdiction over all the income of its citizens and residents wherever it is earned. However, credit is given for taxes paid elsewhere as long as the credit does not cause taxes to fall below what would have been paid had the income been earned in the United States.[17] While citizens and residents of the United States are taxed on their full income wherever it is earned, nonresidents are taxed only on their income in the United States. This is the practice in other countries. The resident versus nonresident status of a corporation is determined by where it is incorporated, with some departures from this principle as explained in the following paragraphs.

Some countries that appear to have low national corporate tax rates have more normal rates when local corporate taxes are added. For example, while Switzerland has federal corporate rates below 10 percent, the local authorities, called cantons, have tax rates of between 10 and 30 percent. Different provincial rates in Canada can make rates vary more than 5 percent. Further variation and complication are introduced by the fact that some national tax authorities give full credit for local taxes, while others do not. In addition, as mentioned earlier, there is considerable variation between countries according to what expenditures are deductible in determining taxable income. Capital cost allowances on expenses such as computers and research and development also vary from country to country, with some countries using rapid write-offs as a stimulus to investment.

---

17 Since the Tax Reform Act of 1986, US-based multinationals have been subject to a minimum corporate tax rate. For the nature of this minimum tax and its consequences, see Andrew Lyon and Gerald Silverstein, "The Alternative Minimum Tax and the Behavior of Multinational Corporations," *National Bureau of Economic Research,* Paper No. 4783, 1994.

Value-added tax (VAT)

A value-added tax is similar to a sales tax, but each seller can deduct the taxes paid at previous stages of production and distribution. If, for example, the VAT rate is 25 percent and a company cuts trees and sells $100 worth of wood to a furniture manufacturer, the tax is $25, since there are no previous stages of production. If the wood is made into furniture that is sold for $240, the furniture manufacturer must pay $60 (25 percent of $240) minus the already collected VAT. Since the wood producer paid $25, the VAT of the furniture manufacturer is $35. Since the eventual effect is the collection of 25 percent of the final selling price, the VAT is like a sales tax that is collected on the value added to a product at each stage of production, distribution, and sale, rather than only at the final retail stage.[18]

Because each payer receives credit for taxes paid at previous stages of production, there is an incentive to collect complete tax records from suppliers. This reduces tax evasion but can give rise to complaints about burdensome, costly paperwork. The value-added tax has partially replaced income taxes on individuals in the European Union. It has been promoted because it is a tax on spending and not on income. Taxes on income are a disincentive to work and invest, while taxes on spending can be considered a disincentive to spend, that is, an incentive to save. Another advantage of VAT to countries promoting exports is that the rules of the World Trade Organization allow rebates of VAT to exporters, while a potential drawback is that VAT can artificially distort patterns of output when applied at differential rates to different products.

Import duties

Before income tax and value-added tax became primary sources of government revenue, import duties or tariffs (two terms for the same thing) were major sources of fiscal receipts.[19] Since goods entering a country are shipped to specific ports where policing can be intensive, import duties are a good source of revenue when income or sales records are poor. This partly explains why some underdeveloped countries depend heavily on tariffs. Also, tariffs can explain why an automobile or refrigerator can cost five times more in some countries than in others. Because tariffs can be levied more heavily on luxuries than on necessities, they do not have to be regressive.[20]

Tariffs explain why some firms move production facilities abroad. For example, if automobiles made in the United States and sold in Europe face a tariff and this can be avoided if the vehicles are produced in Europe, a European plant may be opened. Tariffs are used to protect jobs that are believed to be threatened by cheap foreign imports. For example, if sales of imported footwear or automobiles increase while domestically produced goods face sluggish sales, there may be lobbying to impose tariffs or quantitative restrictions (quotas) on imports. Tariffs tend to distort the pattern of international trade because countries may produce goods and services for which they do not have a comparative advantage, but on which they can make profits behind protective trade barriers. Duties have been imposed by the US government in the form of countervailing tariffs when it was believed that foreign competitors were dumping (selling at lower prices abroad than at home) or receiving "unfair" export help from their governments.

Withholding taxes

Withholding taxes are collected from foreign individuals or corporations on income they have received from sources within a country. For example, if a US resident earns dividends in Canada, taxes are withheld by the Canadian

---

18 For more on VAT, see *Value Added Tax*, Price Waterhouse, New York, November 1979.

19 Tariffs are also called excise taxes. They can be based on value *(ad valorem)* or on the weight of imports.

20 With a regressive tax, the poor pay a larger *fraction* of their income or spending than do the rich. A tax can be regressive even if the rich pay a larger *absolute amount*.

corporation and paid to the Canada Revenue Agency. Credit is generally received on taxes withheld, and so the level of the withholding tax rate primarily affects the amount of taxes received by the respective tax authorities. For example, if the US resident has 15 percent withheld in Canada and is in a 25-percent tax bracket in the United States, the US tax payable will be reduced to 10 percent of the income after credit for the 15 percent is given. Higher withholding rates therefore generally mean that more is collected by the foreign authorities where the income is being earned.

There are some circumstances in which the level of withholding does matter. Clearly, if the rate of withholding exceeds the effective tax rate at home, full credit may not be obtained. This can happen even if the tax *rate* at home is higher than the withholding rate if the definition of income or eligible deductions differs between the countries. For example, if little depreciation is deductible in the foreign country but generous allowances exist at home, the taxable income may differ, and more taxes may be paid abroad than are payable at home even if the foreign rate is lower. In the United States there is an overall limitation on credit for taxes withheld that equals taxes payable in the United States, but when tax returns for a number of countries are combined in a consolidated tax return, full credit may be obtained even when on an individual-country basis there would have been unused withholding tax credit.[21]

Branch versus subsidiary taxes

An important element in corporate tax planning is deciding whether to operate abroad with a **branch** or a **subsidiary**. A branch is a foreign operation that is incorporated at home, while a subsidiary is incorporated in the foreign country.

If a foreign activity is not expected to be profitable for a number of years, there may be an advantage to starting out with a branch so that negative earnings abroad can be used to offset profits at home in a consolidated tax return. US tax laws and the tax laws of a number of other countries allow branch income to be consolidated.[22] If a company expects positive foreign income and this income is not to be repatriated, there may be an advantage to operate as a subsidiary. Foreign branches pay taxes on income as it is earned, while subsidiaries do not pay US taxes until the income is repatriated. Whether this is sufficient reason to form an overseas subsidiary depends on relative tax rates and on whether the company wishes to repatriate earnings.[23]

ORGANIZATIONAL STRUCTURES FOR REDUCING TAXES

The foreign-sales corporation (FSC)

The **foreign-sales corporation (FSC)** is a device for encouraging US export sales by giving a tax break on the generated profits. The possibility of establishing a foreign-sales corporation was part of the Tax Reform Act of 1984 Prior to this Act, the US Internal Revenue Service (IRS) offered tax breaks to exporters via the operation of **domestic international-sales corporations (DISCs)**. While some DISCs still exist, the FSC has effectively replaced the DISC as the preferred tax-saving vehicle of exporters.

---

21 When high levels of withholding are combined with low levels, the unused credit on the low levels of withholding is utilized by the high levels of withholding within the combined tax return. Even if the combined return does not provide full credit, in the United States unused credit can be carried back 2 years or forward 5 years.

22 Companies can opt for a country-specific or global basis of filing, with the choice being binding for an indefinite time.

23 Withholding tax credits and the taxation of subsidiary income only when it is repatriated have both contributed to FDI of US firms, according to Alan Auerbach and Kevin Hassett in "Taxation and Foreign Direct Investment in the United States: A Reconsideration of the Evidence," National Bureau of Economic Research, Paper No. 3895, 1992.

The main advantage offered by an FSC is that the goods or services "bought" by the FSC for subsequent sale do not have to be priced at **arm's length**, that is, at proper market value. Rather the FSC can use an artificial or **administered price** to increase its own profit and consequently reduce the profit and tax of the firm producing the US goods or services for export. For example, if Aviva were to establish an FSC, Aviva itself could "sell" its jeans to its FSC for a below-market price. Aviva's FSC could then sell the jeans abroad. Only a portion of Aviva's FSC's income is then subject to tax, and Aviva's own taxable income is reduced. That is, there is a shifting of income by using the artificially low prices, from Aviva to its FSC. The tax paid by the FSC is less than the tax saving of Aviva.

There are, however, some limitations on the administrative prices and the portion of an FSC's income which escapes tax, as well as in the structure of an FSC. Some of the more important of the limitations and requirements are as follows.

1   An FSC must have its office in a possession of the United States or in a country with a tax information exchange program with the IRS.[24] This is to ensure the FSC is an "offshore" corporation.
2   Tax and accounting information must nevertheless be available at a location in the United States.
3   At least one director must not be a US resident. This is also to ensure the FSC is "foreign."
4   An FSC may not coexist with a DISC that is controlled by the same corporation(s). An FSC may serve more than one corporation, but must have fewer than 25 shareholders.
5   Qualifying income is generated from the sale of US "property," which essentially means goods or services produced or grown in the United States, including leasing, rental property, and management services unrelated to the FSC.
6   The prices "paid" by the FSC to the producer can be set so that the FSC's income is the largest of the following three amounts:
    a   1.83 percent of the FSC's revenue.
    b   23 percent of the combined taxable income of the FSC and related suppliers associated with the export transactions.
    c   The FSC's income that would occur using arm's-length pricing. (The effect of this is that the worst that could happen is that the FSC's income would be as if the goods were priced at arm's length. However, in general the FSC can enjoy higher profits than this. These profits are taxed more favorably than if the profits had been made by the US producer.)
7   Only part of the FSC's income is taxed. If pricing is at arm's length, all the FSC's income is called foreign-trade income, and 30 percent of this is exempt from tax. If one of the two alternative administrative pricing rules is used, foreign-trade income involves adding the FSC's operating expenses to the taxable income – excluding the cost of goods sold – and 15/23, or approximately 62.22 percent, of this is exempt. This can be very advantageous if expenses are low.
8   Domestic corporate shareholders of the FSC receive a 100 percent deduction on dividends received when disbursements occur, except for the taxable component of income under arm's-length pricing.[25]

80–20 subsidiaries

If 80 percent or more of a corporation's income is earned abroad, dividends and interest paid by the corporation are considered foreign-source income by the US IRS. An 80–20 subsidiary is formed to raise capital for the parent,

---

24 The US possessions are Guam, American Samoa, the US Virgin Islands, and the Mariana Islands.
25 The alternative minimum tax provisions of the 1986 Tax Reform Act changed the incentives and structure of taxes from establishing an FSC. It should be noted that very frequent and often complicated changes of tax regulations make any summary of taxation, especially international taxation, difficult to keep current. The summary in this appendix is simply to describe how international taxation has been structured.

since it is considered foreign by the IRS and therefore does not need to deduct withholding taxes. Payments made to 80–20 corporations may well be taxed by foreign governments, but when the income is consolidated, credit will be obtained for taxes already paid. If an 80–20 corporation is incorporated in the Netherlands Antilles or in another country with a treaty with the United States permitting no withholding taxes, then when interest is paid by the US parent to the 80–20 subsidiary, the parent can also avoid having taxes withheld. This means that a company can avoid withholding taxes completely by having an 80–20 corporation in a treaty country. However, after the passage of the Deficit Reduction Act of 1984, which removed the need for US corporations to withhold tax on incomes paid to foreigners, the need for 80–20 subsidiaries was reduced.

Internal pricing

A corporation can save taxes if it is able to shift profits from high-tax countries to low-tax countries by, for example, charging a relatively high price for internally transferred items when they move from a low-tax country to a high-tax country. This raises income in the low-tax country and lowers it in the high-tax country. However, the potential for US corporations to do this is reduced by an important section of the US Internal Revenue Code. Section 482 allows the Treasury to reallocate income and/or expenses to prevent evasion of taxes within commonly owned entities. The IRS requires internal prices to be as if they had been determined competitively. Of course, this does not apply to FSCs.

Tax havens

Some countries charge extremely low corporate taxes to encourage corporations to locate within their jurisdiction, bring jobs, and so on.[26] The jurisdictions are called **tax havens**.[27] These countries include the Bahamas, Bermuda, Cayman Islands, and Grenada, and they are all endowed with delightful climates. The ability of US corporations to take full advantage of tax havens is limited by Section 882 of the US Tax Code. This says that foreign corporations doing business in the United States are taxed at US rates. There is therefore no advantage to locating the corporate headquarters in the tax haven for doing business at home.

APPENDIX B

Inflation and the choice of discount rates

We will concentrate on the expected-cash-flow term of equation (16.2), but our conclusions are valid for any term in the APV formula. The cash-flow term is

$$\sum_{t=1}^{T} \frac{S_t^* CF_t^* (1 - \tau)}{(1 + DR_e)^t}$$

26 "Tax rate competition" has led to political disputes when one nation is seen as using "beggar-thy-neighbor policy" to enjoy economic expansion at other countries' expense. For example, the low corporate tax rates of Ireland have caused partners in the European Union to accuse Ireland of profiting at the expense of other EU members. This is a version of the so-called "Laffer Curve" in which more tax revenue is raised at lower tax rates. In this case it is not by extra work and investment by fellow citizens. Rather, it involves drawing activity from other countries.

27 A student of the author inadvertently called these "tax heavens," an apt term for those who manage to end up there.

The numerator of this expression consists of the expected cash flow in the foreign currency, CF_t^*, converted into US dollars at the expected spot exchange rate, S_t^*. This is put on an after-tax basis by multiplying by $(1 - \tau)$. What we show in this appendix is that as an alternative to using the nominal foreign-currency cash flow converted into dollars, and then using the nominal dollar discount rate, we can use a simpler alternative: we can use the real initial-period dollar cash flow and discount this at the real dollar discount rate. However, we shall also show that this does not work for contractual cash flows.

The exact form of the link between nominal and real interest rates, known as the **Fisher equation**, can be written as

$$(1 + \rho_{US})^t = \frac{(1 + DR_e)^t}{(1 + \dot{P}_{US}^*)^t}$$

or

$$(1 + DR_e)^t = (1 + \rho_{US})^t (1 + \dot{P}_{US}^*)^t \tag{16B.1}$$

Here, ρ_{US} is the real US discount rate, DR_e is the nominal US discount rate, and $\dot{P}_{US}^*$ is the expected US inflation rate. What the Fisher equation does is define the real discount rate as the nominal rate deflated by the expected inflation rate. We have selected the all-equity US dollar *nominal* discount rate, DR_e, because that is the one of particular concern. Consequently, ρ_{US} is the all-equity *real* US dollar discount rate.

If we think that exchange rates will be changing at a steady forecast rate of $\dot{S}_t^*$ we can write

$$S_t^* = S_0(1 + \dot{S}_t^*) \qquad t = 1, 2, \ldots, T$$

If, in addition, we believe that cash flows in the foreign currency will grow at the foreign rate of inflation, we can write

$$CF_t^* = CF_1^*(1 + \dot{P}_{UK}^*)^t \qquad t = 1, 2, \ldots, T$$

where $\dot{P}_{UK}^*$ is the annual rate of inflation and CF_1^* is the initial cash flow, which we assume is unknown. Using this, our definition of S_t^* and the Fisher equation in equation (16B.l), we have

$$\sum_{t=1}^{T} \frac{S_t^* CF_t^*(1 - \tau)}{(1 + DR_e)^t} = S_0 \frac{CF_1^*}{1 + \dot{P}_{UK}^*} \sum_{t=1}^{T} \frac{(1 + \dot{S}^*)^t (1 + \dot{P}_{UK}^*)^t (1 - \tau)}{(1 + \rho_{US})^t (1 + \dot{P}_{US}^*)^t} \tag{16B.2}$$

The magnitudes S_0 and $CF_1^*/(1 + \dot{P}_{UK}^*)$ have been placed in front of the summation because they do not depend on t.[28] We can reduce equation (16B.2) to a straightforward expression if we invoke the purchasing-power-parity (PPP) condition.

We have been writing the precise form of PPP as

$$\dot{P}_{US} = \dot{P}_{UK} + \dot{S}(1 + \dot{P}_{UK})$$

---

28 We remove $CF_1^*/(1 + \dot{P}_{UK}^*)$ rather than just CF_1^* because we wish to have all expressions in the summation raised to the power t. The interpretation of $CF_1^*/(1 + \dot{P}_{UK}^*)$ is that it is the value of the initial foreign cash flow at today's prices.

If the best forecast we can make is that PPP will hold – even though we know that in retrospect we could well be wrong – we can write PPP in the expectations form.

$$\dot{P}^*_{US} = \dot{P}^*_{UK} + \dot{S}^*(1 + \dot{P}^*_{UK})$$

By adding unity to both sides, we get

$$1 + \dot{P}^*_{US} = (1 + \dot{P}^*_{UK}) + \dot{S}^*(1 + \dot{P}^*_{UK}) = (1 + \dot{P}^*_{UK})(1 + \dot{S}^*)$$

or

$$\frac{(1 + \dot{S}^*)(1 + \dot{P}^*_{UK})}{(1 + \dot{P}^*_{US})} = 1$$

By using this in equation (16B.2), we can write the APV cash-flow term in equation (16B.2) in the straightforward form

$$\sum_{t=1}^{T} \frac{S^*_t CF^*_t(1 - \tau)}{(1 + DR_e)^t} = S_0 \frac{CF^*_t(1 - \tau)}{1 + \dot{P}^*_{UK}} \sum_{t=1}^{T} \frac{1}{(1 + \rho_{US})^t} \qquad (16B.3)$$

In the special case of a perpetual expected cash flow so that $T = \infty$, equation (16B.3) becomes

$$\sum_{t=1}^{T} \frac{S^*_t CF^*_t(1 - \tau)}{(1 + DR_e)^t} = S_0 \frac{CF^*_1(1 - \tau)}{\rho_{US}(1 + \dot{P}^*_{UK})} \qquad (16B.4)$$

All we need to know to evaluate (16B.3) or (16B.4) is the initial exchange rate S_0, the initial cash flow at today's prices, $CF^*_1/(1 + \dot{P}^*_{UK})$ the tax rate, τ; and the real discount rate that reflects the systematic risk, ρ_{US}. There is no need to forecast future exchange rates and foreign-currency cash flows. In reaching this conclusion, we assumed only that cash flows can be expected to grow at the overall rate of inflation, that PPP can be expected to hold – that is, hold on average – and that the Fisher equation does hold. Any noncontractual term can be handled in this straightforward way which avoids the need to forecast inflation and exchange rates at which to convert the foreign-currency amounts. Our conclusion is based on the view that inflation and changes in exchange rates are offsetting – requiring PPP – and that local inflation in cash flows and inflation premiums in discount rates are also offsetting, requiring the Fisher equation.

While it is reasonable to *expect* PPP and the Fisher equation to hold, when events are *realized,* it is very unlikely that they will have held. However, the departures from the conditions are as likely to be positive as negative. This is part of the risk of business. The risk is that realized changes in exchange rates might not reflect inflation differentials, and the interest rate might poorly reflect the level of inflation. This risk should be reflected in DR_e or ρ_{US} which should contain appropriate premiums.

When we are dealing with contractual values, we cannot use the real interest rate with uninflated cash flows. This is because the foreign-currency streams are nominal amounts that must be converted at the exchange rate at the time of payment/receipt and discounted at the nominal rate. What we have if the cash flows are contractual is

$$\sum_{t=1}^{T} \frac{S^*_t CF^*_t(1 - \tau)}{(1 + DR_e)^t} = \sum_{t=1}^{T} \frac{S_0(1 + \dot{S}^*)^t CF^*_t(1 - \tau)}{(1 + DR_e)^t}$$

We cannot expand CF_t^* in order to cancel terms, since all values are fixed contractually. We are left to discount at the nominal rate of interest, DR_e. We discount the nominal CF_t^* converted into the investor's currency at the forecast exchange rate.

When the profiles of cash flows or incremental effects such as tax shields vary in real terms and do not grow at the inflation rate (perhaps they initially increase in real terms and later decline), we cannot use PPP and the Fisher equation to reduce the complexity of the problem, even for noncontractual cash flows. We must instead use the APV formula – equation (16.2) – with forecasted nominal cash flows and the nominal discount rate.

Chapter 17

The growth and concerns about multinationals

"If everybody minded their own business," the Duchess said in a hoarse growl, "the world would go round a deal faster than it does."

Lewis Carroll
Alice's Adventures in Wonderland

Regardless of where you live, chances are you have come across the names of numerous multinational corporations (MNCs) such as those listed in Table 17.1. These mammoth organizations, which measure sales by the tens of billions of dollars and employment by the tens or even hundreds of thousands, have evaluated expected cash flows and risks and decided that foreign direct investment (FDI) is worthwhile. But what makes expected cash flows and risks what they are? Furthermore, can anything he done to influence them? For example, can **transfer prices** of goods and services moving within an MNC be used to reduce taxes or otherwise increase net cash flows from a given project? Can **financial structure** – the mix between debt and equity for financing activities – be used to reduce political risk? Indeed, can an MNC correctly measure the cash flows and political risks of foreign investments? Furthermore, do the matters relating to MNCs apply also to members of transnational alliances – firms in different countries working in cooperation – or are transnational alliances a means of avoiding problems faced by MNCs? These questions, which are central to the emergence and management of MNCs and transnational alliances, are addressed in this chapter. In addition, we look at

the problems and benefits that have accompanied the growth of multinational and transnational forms of corporate organization.

THE GROWTH OF MNCs

The growth of the MNC has been a result of FDIs which have taken place in the past. In the extensive example in Chapter 16, Aviva's overseas direct investment was a result of the movement of indigenous firms into its market. Such strategic overseas investment is especially important in dynamic and changing markets, such as publishing and fashion clothing, where overseas subsidiaries must keep in line with local needs or where shipping time is vital. In addition to strategic reasons for direct investment, numerous other reasons have been put forward, and while these are not all strictly financial, they deserve mention in this book.

Reasons for the growth of MNCs

Availability of raw materials

If there are mills producing denim cloth in other countries, the quality is good, and the price is attractive why should a firm like Aviva Corporation

Table 17.1 *The 50 largest nonfinancial MNCs, ranked by total assets, 2000*

Rank	Corporation	Home country	Industry	Total assets (billion $)	Total sales (billion $)	Total employment in thousands
1	GE	United States	Electrical equipments	437	129	313
2	GM	United States	Motor vehicles	303	184	386
3	Ford Motor	United States	Motor vehicles	283	170	350
4	Vodafone Communications	United Kingdom	Telecommunications	222	11	29
5	Verizon Communications	United States	Telecommunications	164	63	552
6	Toyota Motor	Japan	Motor vehicles	154	125	709
7	Exxon/Mobil	United States	Petroleum	149	206	97
8	Vivendi Universal	France	Diversified	141	39	327
9	Deutsche Post	Germany	Transport and storage	139	30	278
10	Royal Dutch/Shell	United Kingdom	Petroleum	122	149	95
11	SBC Communications	Unites States	Telecommunications	98	51	89
12	Fiat	Italy	Motor vehicles	95	53	223
13	Hitachi	Japan	Electrical equipments	92	75	337
14	IBM	United States	Electrical equipments	88	88	316
15	Telefonica	Spain	Telecommunications	87	26	148
16	Total Fina Elf	France	Petroleum	81	105	123
17	Wal-Mart Stores	United States	Retail	78	191	1,300
18	Chevron Texaco	United States	Petroleum	77	117	69
19	BP	United Kingdom	Petroleum	75	148	107
20	Volkswagen	Germany	Motor vehicles	75	79	324
21	Matsushita Electric Industrial	Japan	Electrical equipments	72	68	290
22	Sony	Japan	Electrical equipments	68	63	181
23	Mitsui & Company	Japan	Wholesale trade	64	128	39
24	RWE	Germany	Electricity, Gas	60	44	125
25	Hutchison Whampoa	Hong Kong	Diversified	56	7	49
26	Unilever	United Kingdom	Diversified	52	44	295
27	Nissan Motors	Japan	Motor vehicles	51	48	133
28	Daimler/Chrysler	Germany	Motor vehicles	48	83	24
29	Repsol YPF	Spain	Petroleum	48	42	37
30	Honda Motors	Japan	Motor vehicles	46	57	112
31	Peugeot	France	Motor vehicles	46	42	172
32	BMW	Germany	Motor vehicles	45	34	93
33	Eni	Italy	Petroleum	45	44	69
34	Suez	France	Electricity	43	32	173
35	Texas Utility Company	United States	Electricity	43	22	16
36	Roche	Switzerland	Pharmaceuticals	42	17	64
37	Motorola	United States	Telecommunications	42	37	147

Table 17.1 Continued

Rank	Corporation	Home country	Industry	Total assets (billion $)	Total sales (billion $)	Total employment in thousands
38	E. On	Germany	Electricity	41	83	39
39	Itochu	Japan	Wholesale trade	41	97	867
40	Merck & Co.	United States	Pharmaceuticals	40	40	49
41	News Corporation	Australia	Media	39	14	33
42	Nestle	Switzerland	Food products	39	49	224
43	Alcatel	France	Machinery	39	29	598
44	Sumitomo	Japan	Wholesale trade	39	80	30
45	Aventis	France	Pharmaceuticals	38	20	102
46	Diageo	United Kingdom	Food and beverages	37	18	72
47	BASF	Germany	Chemicals	36	33	103
48	Philips Electronics	Netherlands	Electrical equipments	35	34	219
49	DOW Chemicals	United States	Chemicals	35	29	53
50	Procter & Gamble	United States	Diversified	34	39	48

Source: *World Investment Report 2002*: *Transnational Corporations and Export Competitiveness*, United Nations Conference on Trade and Development, New York and Geneva 2002.

buy the denim material abroad, ship it to the United States, manufacture the jeans, and then ship the finished garments overseas again? Clearly, if the ability exists to manufacture the jeans in the foreign market, the firm can eliminate two-way shipping costs – for denim in one direction and jeans in the other – by directly investing in a manufacturing plant abroad.[1]

Many firms, most particularly mining companies, have little choice but to locate at the site of their raw materials. If copper or iron ore is being smelted, it often does not make sense to ship the ore when a smelter can be built near the mine site. The product of the smelter – the copper or iron bars which weigh less than the original ore – can be shipped out to the market. However, even in this rather straightforward situation we still have to ask why it would be a foreign firm rather than an indigenous firm that owned the smelter. With an indigenous firm there would be no FDI. Thus, to explain FDI, we must explain why a multinational corporate organization

can do things better or cheaper than local firms. As we shall see in the following paragraphs, there are numerous advantages enjoyed by MNCs versus local, single country companies.

Integrating operations

When there are advantages to vertical integration in terms of assured delivery between various stages of production and the different stages can be performed better in different locations (as with the smelting of ores and the use of the product of the ore), there is good reason to invest abroad. This reason for direct investment has been advanced by Charles Kindleberger, who along with Richard Caves did some of the earlier work on FDI.[2]

---

1 A model of overseas direct investment that considers transportation costs as well as issues involving stages of production and economies of scale has been developed by Jimmy Weinblatt and Robert E. Lipsey, "A Model of Firms' Decisions to Export or Produce Abroad," *National Bureau of Economic Research*, Working Paper 511, July 1980.

2 We refer to Charles P. Kindleberger, *American Business Abroad*, Yale University Press, New Haven, CT, 1969. See also Richard E. Caves, "International Corporations: The Industrial Economics of Foreign Investment," *Economica*, February 1971, pp. 1–27. A number of papers on direct investment are contained in John H. Dunning (ed.), *International Investment*, Penguin Books, Harmondsworth, UK, 1972. For factors affecting the initial decision, the reader may consult J. David Richardson, "On Going Abroad: The Firm's Initial Foreign Investment Decision," *Quarterly Review of Economics and Business*, Winter 1971, pp. 7–22.

The advantage of ownership of the various stages of the supply chain is based on the lower inventory levels that are required when there is good communication of information between the different stages of production: inventory arrival can then move closer to just-in-time levels. The advantage of common ownership to achieve this is perhaps less important than it used to be because of electronic data interchange that can link separately owned companies when the flow of information between stages of the supply chain is mutually beneficial.

Nontransferable knowledge

It is often possible for firms to sell their knowledge in the form of patent rights, and to license a foreign producer. This relieves a firm of the need to make FDI. However, sometimes a firm that has a production process or product patent can make a larger profit by doing the foreign production itself. This is because there are some kinds of knowledge which cannot be sold and which are the result of years of experience. Aviva, for example, might be able to sell patterns and designs, and it can license the use of its name, but it cannot sell a foreign firm its experience in producing, and more importantly, marketing the product. This points to another reason why a firm might wish to do its own foreign production.

Protecting reputations

Products develop good or bad names, and these are carried across international boundaries. For example, people everywhere know the names of certain brands of jeans, fast food, soft drinks, and commercial banks. It would not serve the good name of a multinational company to have a foreign licensee do a shoddy job providing the good or service. Whether we are talking about restaurant chains where people could become sick, accounting firms which might use unlawful or ethically questionable practices, or pharmaceutical

companies that can make mistakes, it is important for multinationals to maintain high and homogeneous standards to protect their reputations. A bad experience in one location can easily spill over to sales and profits in other locations. This is the nature of **negative externalities** which are internalized if foreign production is kept within the company rather than being licensed out to a separate corporate entity. We find that there is good reason for FDI rather than alternative ways of expanding into overseas markets such as granting foreign licences.

Exploiting reputations

FDI may occur to exploit rather than protect a reputation. This motivation is probably of particular importance in FDI by banks, and it takes the form of opening branches and establishing or buying subsidiaries. One of the reasons why banking has become an industry with mammoth multinationals is that an international reputation can attract deposits; many associate the size of a bank with its safety. For example, a name like Barclays, Chase, or Citibank in a small, less-developed nation is likely to attract deposits away from local banks. Reputation is also important in accounting, as Exhibit 17.1 explains. This is why many large industrial nations such as the United States and Britain have argued in global trade negotiations for a liberalization of restrictions on services, including accounting and banking. It is also the reason why the majority of less-developed nations have resisted this liberalization.

Protecting secrecy

Direct investment may be preferred to the granting of a license for a foreign company to produce a product if secrecy is important. This point has been raised by Erich Spitaler, who argues that a firm can be motivated to choose direct investment over licensing by a feeling that, while a licensee may take precautions to protect patent

EXHIBIT 17.1   COUNTING ON A GOOD NAME

The economics of information suggests that reputation has value when a supplier's reputation is a signal of good quality. Reputation is important when quality is difficult to observe directly, and thus this issue is particularly relevant with services.

One service for which reputation has become increasingly important, especially since the Enron and Worldcom revelations and accusations, is accounting. While there are other reasons for accounting having become multinational, including benefits to multi-national corporations of maintaining confidentiality when dealing with the same accounting firm worldwide, the company's name has played a central role in the success of many of today's international accounting firms. This is all the more incredible in light of the fact that accounting rules vary a great deal from country to country, a matter that would tend to favor local firms with detailed knowledge of the local procedures.

Reputation matters because it is very difficult for those employing accounting services to distinguish a good accountant from a bad one. It is too late if discovery of an accountant's "type" is determined only after the fact. Yes, there have been revelations involving at least one major multinational accoun-tancy firm which found itself in court for questionable practices. Furthermore, there are other advantages to multinationalization in the industry, such as econo-mies of scale in information technology and econo-mies of scope with providing consultancy services: an economy of scope is where there are advantages to different production activities being provided side-by-side. However, the bottom line – something that accountants pay a lot of attention to – is that the power of an accountancy firm is in its name. Brand is as important in the sale of international services as it is for familiar manufactures.

---

rights, it may be less conscientious than the original owner of the patent.[3]

The product life-cycle hypothesis

It has been argued, most notably by Raymond Vernon, that opportunities for further corporate expansion at home eventually dry up.[4] To maintain the growth of profits, the corporation must venture abroad to where markets are not as well penetrated and where there is perhaps less competition. This makes direct investment the natural consequence of being in business for a long enough time and having exhausted possibilities of expansion at home. There is an inevitability in this view that has concerned

those who believe that American firms are further along in their life-cycle development than the firms of other nations and are therefore dominant in foreign expansion.[5] However, even when US firms do expand into foreign markets, their activities are often scrutinized by the host governments. More-over, the spread of US multinationals has been matched by the inroads of foreign firms into the United States. Particularly noticeable have been auto and auto-parts producers such as Toyota, Honda, Nissan, and Michelin. Foreign firms have an even longer history as leaders in the US food and drug industry (Nestle, Hoffmann-La Roche); in oil and gas (Shell, British Petroleum – as BP – and so on); in insurance, banking, and real-estate development; and in other areas.

3 See Erich Spitaler, "A Survey of Recent Quantitative Studies of Long-Term Capital Movements," *IMF Staff Papers*, March 1971, pp. 189–217.

4 Raymond Vernon, "International Investment and International Trade in the Product Life-Cycle," *Quarterly Journal of Economics*, May 1966, pp. 190–207.

5 Inevitable US domination of key businesses in Europe and the world was a popular view in parts of Europe in the 1960s and 1970s. Particularly influential was J.J. Servain-Schreiber's *The American Challenge*, Hamish Hamilton, London, 1968.

Capital availability

Robert Aliber has suggested that access to capital markets can be a reason why firms themselves move abroad.[6] The smaller one-country licensee does not have the same access to cheaper funds as the larger firm, and so larger firms are able to operate within foreign markets with a lower discount rate. However, Edward Graham and Paul Krugman have questioned this argument on two grounds.[7] First, even if large multinational firms have a lower cost of capital than small, indigenous firms, the form of overseas investment does not have to be direct investment. Rather, it can take the form of portfolio investment. Second, the majority of FDI has been two-way, with, for example, US firms investing in Japan while Japanese firms invest in the United States. This pattern is not an implication of the differential-cost-of-capital argument which implies one-way investment flows.

Strategic FDI

As we indicated in Chapter 16, companies enter foreign markets to preserve market share when this is being threatened by the potential entry of indigenous firms or multinationals from other countries. This strategic motivation for FDI has always existed, but it may have contributed to the multinationalization of business as a result of improved access to capital markets. This is different from the argument concerning the differential cost of capital, given previously. In the case of increased strategic FDI, it is globalization of financial markets that has reduced entry barriers due to large fixed costs. Access to the necessary capital means a wider set of companies with an ability to expand into any given market. This increases the incentive to move and enjoy any potential first-mover advantage.

Organizational factors

Richard Cyert and James March emphasize reasons given by organization theory, a theme that is extended to FDI by E. Eugene Carter.[8] The organization-theory view of FDI emphasizes broad management objectives in terms of the way management attempts to shift risk by operating in many markets, achieve growth in sales, and so on, as opposed to concentrating on the traditional economic goal of profit maximization.

Avoiding tariffs and quotas

Another reason for producing abroad instead of producing at home and shipping the product concerns the import tariffs that might have to be paid.[9] If import duties are in place, a firm might produce inside the foreign market in order to avoid them. We must remember, however, that tariffs protect the firm engaged in production in the foreign market, whether it be a foreign firm or an indigenous firm. Tariffs cannot, therefore, explain why foreign firms move abroad rather than use the licensing route, and yet the movement of firms is the essence of direct investment. Nor, along similar lines, can tax write-offs, subsidized or even free land offerings, and so on, explain direct investment, since foreign firms are not usually helped more than domestic ones. We must rely on our other listed reasons for direct investment and the overriding desire to make a larger profit, even if that means moving abroad rather than expanding into alternative domestic endeavors.

6 Robert Aliber, "A Theory of Direct Foreign Investment," in Charles P. Kindleberger (ed.), *The International Corporation: A Symposium*, MIT Press, Cambridge, MA, 1970.

7 Graham, Edward M. and Paul R. Krugman, *Foreign Direct Investment in the United States*, Institute for International Economics, Washington, DC, 1991.

8 Richard M. Cyert and James G. March give an account of organization theory in The *Behavioral Theory of the Firm*, Prentice-Hall, Englewood Cliffs, NJ, 1963. E. Eugene Carter extends the theory to direct investment in "The Behavioral Theory of the Firm and Top Level Corporation Decisions," *Administrative Science Quarterly*, December 1971, pp. 413–28.

9 A geometrical explanation of the effect of tariffs on direct investment has been developed by Richard E. Caves in *Multinational Enterprise and Economic Analysis*, Cambridge University Press, Cambridge, UK 1982, pp. 36–40.

There have been cases where the threat of imposition of tariffs, or quantitative restrictions on imports in the form of quotas, have prompted direct investment overseas. For example, a number of foreign automobile and truck producers opened plants, or considered opening plants, in the United States to avoid restrictions on selling foreign-made cars. The restrictions were designed to protect jobs in the US industry. Nissan Motors built a plant in Tennessee, and Honda built a plant in Ohio. For a period of time Volkswagen assembled automobiles and light trucks in the United States and Canada. Other companies having made direct investments included Renault and Daimler-Benz.[10]

Avoiding regulations

As is explained in Chapter 19 in our discussion of the multinationalization of banking, FDI has been made by banks to avoid regulation. This has also been a motivation for foreign investment by manufacturing firms. For example, a case might be made that some firms have moved to escape standards set by the US Environmental Protection Agency, the Occupational Safety and Health Administration, and other agencies. Some foreign countries with lower environmental and safety standards offer a haven to firms using dirty or dangerous processes. The items produced, such as chemicals and prescription drugs, may even be offered for sale back in the parent companies' home countries.

Production flexibility

A manifestation of departures from purchasing power parity (PPP) is that there are periods when production costs in one country are particularly low because of a real depreciation of its currency. Multinational firms may be able to relocate production to exploit the opportunities that real depreciations offer. This requires, of course, that

trade unions or governments do not make the shifting of production too difficult. Small manufactured goods such as computer components and TVs lend themselves to such shuffling of production, whereas automobile production, with its international unions and expensive setup costs, does not.[11]

Symbiotic relationships

Some firms follow clients who make FDIs. For example, large US accounting firms which have knowledge of parent companies' special needs and practices have opened offices in countries where their clients have opened subsidiaries. These US accounting firms have an advantage over local firms because of their knowledge of the parent and because the client may prefer to engage only one firm in order to reduce the number of people with access to sensitive information; see Exhibit 17.1. The same factor may apply to consulting, legal, and securities firms, which often follow their home-country clients' direct investments by opening offices in the same foreign locations. Similarly, it has been shown that manufacturing firms may be drawn to where other manufacturing firms from the same country are located. By being in the same region they can work together and benefit from their knowledge of each other. The benefits from being in the same region as other companies are called **agglomeration economies**.[12]

---

10 Offsetting the incentive to produce within a country to avoid import tariffs is the preference that buyers of a product may have for imports. For example, it may be that a German car from Germany will be valued more than if the car is manufactured in the United States.

11 See Victoria S. Farrell, Dean A. DeRosa, and T. Ashby McCown, "Effects of Exchange Rate Variability on International Trade and Other Economic Variables: A Review of the Literature," *Staff Studies*, no. 130, Board of Governors of the Federal Reserve System, January 1984; Bruce Kogut, "Designing Global Strategies: Comparative and Competitive Value-Added Chains," *Sloan Management Review*, Summer 1985, pp. 15–28; John H. Dunning, "Multinational Enterprises and Industrial Restructuring in the UK," *Lloyds Bank Review*, October 1985, pp. 1–19; and David de Meza and Frederick van der Ploeg, "Production Flexibility as a Motive for Multinationality," *Journal of Industrial Economics*, March 1987, pp. 343–55.

12 See Keith Head, John Ries, and Deborah Swenson, "Agglomeration Benefits and Location Choice: Evidence from Manufacturing Investments in the United States," *Journal of International Economics*, 1995, pp. 223–47.

EXHIBIT 17.2 MULTINATIONALS: CREATURES OF MARKET IMPERFECTIONS

The numerous reasons given in the text for the growth in the relative importance of multinational corporations are all aspects of market imperfections. For example, they are based on transportation costs, tariff barriers, quotas, different regulations in different countries, protection of industrial or commercial secrets, and costly information, all of which represent "frictions" to the free international flow of goods and services.

Some frictions are natural barriers, such as transportation costs which force companies to operate in multiple locations or else face the costs of shipping to every market from a single, central location. This is especially true for products such as gasoline which is expensive to move and difficult to handle. Another natural friction is perishability which forces companies to be close to the final consumer when dealing with food, newspapers, and so on which have to be "fresh." Other frictions are man-made. For example, tariff barriers which force companies to produce where they sell or else face import duties are the result of human interventions in what would otherwise be freer trade. Quotas are another means of encouraging companies to operate where they sell, and which are the result of government action, usually at the urging of local interest groups who wish to reduce competition.

Exchange rates represent a friction in that they introduce an added cost and uncertainty when doing business across currency areas. Foreign exchange markets are human creations, although humans can hardly be blamed for the fact that most countries – those in the Euro zone being an exception – like to have their own currencies. There is an issue of sovereignty that works against throwing your lot in with other countries for a one-size-fits-all exchange rate and monetary policy.

When we see what the causes are of multinationalization of business we can begin to figure out what the future might hold. Some natural barriers are being reduced, as for example from the reduction in transportation costs and faster, cheaper telecommunications. Even human barriers are coming down with free-trade agreements and actions such as the 2004 decision by the World Trade Organization members to eventually abolish subsidies and other distortions to trade in agricultural commodities. The same forces that enabled multinationals to grow to their importance at the turn of the twenty-first century could be the very same influences that eventually lead to their demise.

Source: Based in part on *Multinationals*, a supplement in *The Economist*, March 27, 1993, p. 9.

Indirect diversification

We should not leave our discussion of factors contributing to the growth of MNCs without mentioning the potential for the MNC to indirectly provide portfolio diversification for shareholders.[13] This service will, of course, be valued only if shareholders are unable to diversify themselves. This requires the existence of segmented capital markets that only the MNC can overcome. This argument was mentioned in Chapter 15 in the context of international asset pricing. It is also mentioned in Exhibit 17.2, which argues that all the causes of growth of MNCs, including that relating to diversification, depend on market imperfections.

Empirical evidence on the growth of MNCs

It should be apparent from glancing down the list of factors that can be responsible for the growth

13 A formal theory of FDI based on indirect provision of portfolio diversification has been developed by Vihang R. Errunza and Lemma W. Senbet, "The Effects of International Operations on the Market Value of the Firm: Theory and Evidence," *Journal of Finance*, May 1981, pp. 401–17.

of MNCs that the relative importance of different factors will depend on the nature of the MNC's business. Partly as a result of this, the empirical evidence we have on MNCs tends to be limited to some stylized facts about the nature of the industries in which most direct investment occurs.

In an investigation of the characteristics of approximately 1,000 US publicly owned companies investing abroad, Irving Kravis and Robert Lipsey found a number of characteristics of investing firms vis-à-vis firms not investing abroad.[14] The characteristics were separated into those that could be attributed to the industry of the investor and those distinguishing investing firms from other firms within their industry.

Investing firms spent relatively heavily on research and development (R&D); this was attributable both to the investors' industries and to the firms investing abroad within each industry. That is, the industries with heavy investments abroad spent more on R&D than other industries, and the firms that invested abroad spent more on R&D than the average spending of firms in their industries. (This characteristic of FDI is consistent with the secrecy-protection explanation given earlier: high R&D investors have more intellectual capital to protect, thereby discouraging production overseas through licensees. It is also consistent with the size of market being a determinant of R&D investments which are often large and risky.) Investors were also more capital intensive than noninvestors, this being mostly attributable to the industries investing overseas. (This is consistent with the capital-availability argument; capital-intensive investors presumably need to raise a relatively large amount of financial capital.) Other characteristics of investors were that they were large relative to both other industries and other firms within their industries (which is consistent with the life-cycle hypothesis), and that investing

firms were more profitable.[15] Profitability is a factor affecting investment when there are imperfections or frictions in capital markets, with internally generated funds being lower cost than external capital.

Kravis and Lipsey also noted that there appeared to be an order of countries when investing overseas. If an investor had made one foreign investment, it would most likely be in Canada. With two investments, an investor would be in Canada and in Mexico or the United Kingdom. After this, investments were found in Germany, France, and possibly Australia.

Evaluation of direct-investment statistics also suggests, as we would expect from the procedures used to evaluate foreign projects, that more investment occurs in those countries that have offered investors higher returns.[16] There also appears to be a connection between domestic economic activity and foreign investment, with good economic conditions at home discouraging investment abroad. Such a situation, that suggests that at times profitable overseas investments are avoided when there are profitable domestic investments, indicates that there is **capital rationing**. When capital is rationed not all positive NPV or APV projects are pursued. Rationing happens when a company appropriates a capital budget that is fixed irrespective of what the investment possibilities are.

SPECIAL ISSUES FACING MNCs: TRANSFER PRICING

While any firm with multiple divisions must price goods and services transferred between its divisions if it is to be able to judge its profit centers correctly,

---

14 Irving B. Kravis and Robert E. Lipsey, "The Location of Overseas Production and Production for Export of US Multinational Firms," *Journal of International Economics*, May 1982, pp. 201–23.

15 These conclusions are also supported by Irving B. Kravis, Robert E. Lipsey, and Linda O'Connor, "Characteristics of US Manufacturing Companies Investing Abroad and Their Choice of Production Locations," *National Bureau of Economic Research*, Working Paper 1104, April 1983.

16 See *International Letter*, Federal Reserve Bank of Chicago, no. 537, October 19, 1984.

there are few, if any, political or tax implications of transfer pricing in the domestic context. The situation is very different for the MNC.

The measurement of transfer prices

If correct measures of prices of goods or services moving between corporate divisions are not available, management will have difficulty making APV calculations for new projects, and will even face difficulties judging past projects and performances of corporate divisions: performance is important for monitoring where profits are being made and for allocation of bonuses. But how are managers to calculate correct transfer prices?

The prices managers must determine are those of intermediate products moving through the value chain of vertically integrated firms. The most obvious source for these prices is the market. However, market prices do not always exist for intermediate products. Furthermore, even when there are market prices for the goods and services transferred between divisions within a firm, using these prices may result in incorrect decisions. Let us consider why.[17]

The theoretically correct transfer price is equal to the marginal cost.[18] This is because the price paid then correctly reflects the cost of producing another unit.[19] If a good or service transferred between corporate divisions is available in the marketplace, where it trades in a textbook-type "perfectly competitive" market, the market price will equal the marginal cost, and this market price can then be used as the transfer price. However, goods and services moving between divisions are frequently available only in monopolistic or monopolistically competitive markets. In this case, market prices will typically exceed marginal costs. This means that by setting transfer prices equal to market prices a buying division will be paying above marginal cost for inputs. This will induce the use of too few inputs to achieve the profit-maximizing output from the firm's overall perspective. The firm's output of its final product will also be less than the profit-maximizing level. In addition, with transfer prices equal to market prices, and these being higher than the firm's marginal costs of the transferred goods and services, input combinations will be inappropriately intensive in products bought from outside the firm. That is, if, instead of setting transfer prices of intermediate products equal to market prices, the firm sets them equal to its marginal costs of production, buying divisions would correctly use more of the firm's own intermediate products as inputs.

While setting transfer prices equal to marginal costs will maximize the firm's overall profits, it will make it difficult to attribute the company's profit to the correct divisions; marginal costs are typically lower than market prices, so that divisions supplying intermediate products will show losses. This will make bonus allocations and expansion budgets difficult to determine properly. One way around this is to use marginal costs as the transfer prices that are paid, but to calculate divisional profitability at market prices. This requires, of course, that market prices of intermediate products are available, and that marginal costs are known. In reality, neither requirement is likely to be satisfied.

Strategic considerations in transfer pricing

Repatriation of profits by a multinational firm from its overseas operations can be a politically sensitive problem. It is important that host governments do not consider the profit rate too high, or else the multinational is likely to face accusations of price gouging and lose favor with foreign host

17 The background economic analysis behind the points made here was first provided by Jack Hirschleifer, "On the Economics of Transfer Pricing," *Journal of Business*, July 1956, pp. 172–84, and "Economics of the Divisionalized Firm," *Journal of Business*, April 1957, pp. 96–108.

18 This assumes constant returns to scale. See Hirschleifer, op. cit.

19 The rationale is the same as for selecting the quantity of any input that maximizes profits: profits are reduced by using less or by using more than the quantity of input at which the marginal revenue product of the input equals the input's marginal cost.

governments. In order to give an appearance of repatriating a lower profit without reducing the actual profit brought home, the multinational may use transfer prices. It may set high transfer prices on what is supplied to a foreign division by the head office or by divisions in environments that are politically less sensitive. For example, it can extract high payments for parts supplied by other divisions or for general overheads such as R&D and marketing expenses. Alternatively, the multinational can lower the transfer prices of products which the foreign division sells to the parent company or to other divisions. These methods of reducing foreign profits while repatriating income are particularly advantageous when foreign reinvestment opportunities are limited. Unfortunately for the multinational, the misstatement of transfer prices is illegal with fines and even more serious punishments.

Manipulating transfer pricing to reduce overall corporate taxes can be particularly advantageous. The multinational has an incentive to shuffle its income to keep profits low in high-tax countries and relatively high in low-tax countries. There are complications if within a country there are different tax rates on retained versus repatriated income. The gains from profit shuffling via transfer prices are limited by the legal powers of the Internal Revenue Service (IRS), and of taxing authorities in some other countries, which can reallocate income and impose fines if it is determined that transfer prices have distorted profits.[20]

20 For a detailed account of the tax implications of transfer pricing see Donald R. Lessard, "Transfer Prices, Taxes, and Financial Markets: Implications of International Financial Transfers within the Multinational Corporation," *International Business and Finance*, 1979, pp. 101–35, and J. William Petty and Ernest W. Walker, "Optimal Transfer Pricing for the Multinational Firm," *Financial Management*, Winter 1972, pp. 74–87. We might note that if MNCs are in a position to reduce taxes in ways unavailable to local firms, this provides an additional reason for the growth of MNCs. See David Harris, Randall Morck, Joel Slemrod, and Bernard Yeung, "Income Shifting in US Multinational Corporations," National Bureau of Economic Research, Summer Institute's International Taxation Workshop, 1991.

A multinational firm is likely to be in a better position to avoid foreign exchange losses than a firm with only local operations. There have been times, especially under fixed exchange rates in the period before 1973, when the devaluation of certain currencies and the revaluation of others were imminent. Because of extensive involvement by central banks, the interest-rate differential between countries did not always reflect the anticipated changes in exchange rates, and so compensation was not offered for expected exchange-rate movements. There were incentives for all corporations to reduce their holdings of the currencies which faced devaluation. However, an attempt to move from these currencies was viewed as unpatriotic when undertaken by domestic firms and as unfair profiteering when undertaken by multinationals. As a result, considerable constraints were placed on moving funds in overt ways, but multinationals were in a better position than their domestic counterparts to move funds disguised as transfer payments.

Transfer prices can be used to reduce import tariffs and to avoid quotas. When tariffs on imports are based on values of transactions, the value of goods moving between divisions can be artificially reduced by keeping down the transfer prices. This puts a multinational firm at an advantage over domestic firms. Similarly, when quotas are based on values of trade, the multinational can keep down prices to maintain the volume. Again, the multinational has an advantage over domestic counterparts, but import authorities frequently adopt their own "value for duty" on goods entering trade to help prevent tax revenues from being lost through the manipulation of transfer prices.

Large variations in profits may be a concern to shareholders. In order to keep local shareholders happy, fluctuations in local foreign profits can be reduced via transfer prices. By raising the prices of goods and services supplied by foreign operations or lowering prices on sales to foreign operations, unusually high profits can be brought down so that subsequent falls in profits are reduced. Of course, shareholders are normally assumed to be concerned only with systematic risk and not with total risk, so the premise that profit volatility is of concern to shareholders is not universally accepted.

To the extent that transfer prices apply to financial transactions such as credits granted between corporate divisions, the scope for meeting the many strategic objectives we have described, such as reducing host-government criticism over profits and reducing taxes, are substantially enhanced. Indeed, when we add discretion over timing of repayment of credits, the MNC may be at a substantial advantage over non-multinational competitors.[21]

Practical considerations in transfer pricing

Transfer prices can be used to "window-dress" the profits of certain divisions of a multinational so as to reduce borrowing costs. The gains from having seemingly large profits by paying a subsidiary high transfer prices for its products must, of course, be balanced against the potential scorn of foreign host governments, higher taxes or tariffs that might result, and so on.

For the long-term prosperity of a multinational, it is important that interdivisional profitability be measured accurately. The record of profitability of different divisions is valuable in allocating overall spending on capital projects and in sharing other corporate resources. In order to discover the correct profitability, the firm should be sure that interdivisional transfer prices are the prices that would have been paid had the transactions been with independent companies, so-called **arm's-length prices**. This can be particularly difficult in the international allocation of such items as research and consulting services or headquarters' overheads; there is rarely a market price for research or other services of corporate headquarters. Profit allocation will usually be according to the distribution of corporate sales, with the sales valued at the "correct" exchange rate. The internal management

advantages of preventing distortions in transfer prices must be balanced against the potential gains from using distorted transfer prices to reduce tariffs, taxes, political risks, and exchange losses. This balance requires the attention of the upper tiers of management.

SPECIAL ISSUES FACING MNCs: COUNTRY RISK

As we mentioned in our account of capital budgeting in Chapter 16, when making FDIs it is necessary to allow for risk due to the investment being in a foreign country. In this section we consider both the measurement and the management of this so-called **country risk**, which, as with transfer pricing, takes on special importance in the multinational corporation.

The term "country risk" is often used interchangeably with the terms **political risk** and **sovereign risk**. However, country risk is really a broader concept than either of the other two, including them as special cases. Country risk involves the possibility of losses due to country-specific economic, political, and social events, and therefore all political risk is country risk, but not all country risk is political risk.[22] Sovereign risk involves the possibility of losses on claims to foreign governments or government agencies, whereas political risk involves the additional possibility of losses on private claims including direct investments. Sovereign risk exists on bank loans and bonds and is therefore not of special concern to MNCs – unless they are banks. Since our concern here is with the risk faced on FDI, we are concerned with country risk and are not particularly interested in the subcomponent of country risk which consists of sovereign risk. Nevertheless, much of what we say about country-risk measurement applies to sovereign risk.

21 See Lessard, op. cit. We recall that to some extent, timing discretion on credits is reduced by leading and lagging restrictions discussed in the appendix A to Chapter 16.

22 For example, see US Comptroller of the Currency, news release, November 8, 1978.

The measurement of country risk

Among the country risks that are faced on an overseas direct investment are those related to the local economy, those due to the possibility of **confiscation** (which refers to a government takeover without any compensation), and those due to the possibility of **expropriation** (which refers to a government takeover with compensation, which at times can be fairly calculated[23]). As well as the political risks of confiscation and expropriation, there are political/social risks of wars, revolutions, and insurrections. While these are not the result of action by foreign governments specifically directed at the firm, they can damage or destroy an investment. In addition, there are risks of currency inconvertibility and restrictions on the repatriation of income beyond those already reflected in the cash-flow term of the APV calculation in Chapter 16. The treatment of these risks requires that we make adjustments in the APV calculation and/or allowances for late compensation payments for expropriated capital. The required adjustments can be made to the discount rates by adding a risk premium, or to expected cash flows by putting them into their certainty equivalent.[24]

We know that when we view the adjustment for risk in terms of the inclusion of a premium in the discount rate, only systematic risk needs to be considered. Since it is possible by investing in a large number of countries to diversify unsystematic risk, the remaining systematic component of economic and political/social risk may be relatively small. Risk diversification requires only a degree of economic and political/social independence between countries. Diversification is made even more effective if the economic and political/social misfortunes from events in some countries provide benefits in other countries. For example, risk on diversified copper investments are small if war or revolution in African countries that produce copper raise the market value of South American producers of copper.

Before a company can consider how much of its country risk is systematic, it must be able to determine the risk in each country. Only later can it determine by how much its country risk is reduced by the individual country risks being imperfectly or even negatively correlated. But how can it determine each country's risk? The most obvious method is to obtain country-risk evaluations that have been prepared by specialists. But this merely begs the question how the specialists evaluate country risk. Let us consider a few of the risk-evaluation techniques that have been employed.

One of the best known country-risk evaluations is that prepared by *Euromoney*, a monthly magazine that periodically produces a ranking of country risks. *Euromoney*'s evaluation procedure is summarized in Figure 17.1.[25]

Euromoney consults a cross section of specialists. These specialists are asked to give their opinions on each country with regard to one or more of the factors used in their calculations. There are three broad categories of factors considered. These are analytical indicators (50 percent), credit indicators (30 percent), and market indicators (20 percent). Each of these broad categories is further subdivided into more specific components as shown in Figure 17.1.

The analytical indicators consist of economic and political-risk evaluations. The economic evaluation is based on actual and projected growth in GNP. The political-risk evaluation is provided by a panel of experts consisting of risk analysts, insurance brokers, and bank credit officers. The credit indicator includes measures of the ability of the country to service debt based on debt service versus exports, the size of the current-account deficit or surplus versus GNP, and external debt versus

23 Clearly, when investors can count on timely and fair compensation at market value, there is no added risk due to expropriation.

24 We have already indicated that the two methods are conceptually equivalent.

25 Figure 17.1 is based on a description of the *Eurocurrency* method in "Country Risk: Methodology," *Euromoney*, September 1994, p. 380.

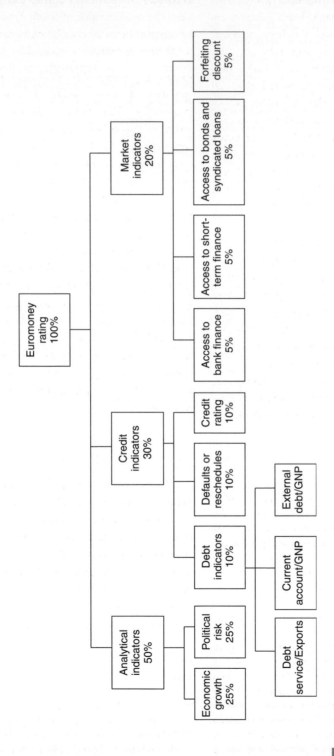

Figure 17.1 Euromoney's country-risk rating scheme

Notes

Euromoney allocates 50 percent of the weight in its country risk evaluation index to analytical indicators, with this 50 percent being divided equally between economic and political factors. The remaining 50 percent of Euromoney's risk evaluation is based on the credit experience and position of a country, and on risk premia set in financial markets.

GNP.[26] Market indicators are based on assessments of a country's access to bank loans, short-term credits, syndicated loans, and the bond market, as well as on the premiums occurring on non-recourse loans made to exporters.[27] Large premiums are a sign of market-perceived risk. Of course, the market also considers the other factors used in *Euromoney*'s ranking, and so there is double-counting; the factors considered by *Euromoney* appear directly in the computation of the ranking, and also indirectly via the premiums on loans. *Euromoney*'s country-risk rankings of the safest and riskiest 20 countries in 2003 are shown in Table 17.2.

Measures of country risk do not distinguish the different risks facing different *industries*; they measure only the risk of *countries*. Yet a number of studies show that some industries, especially those involving natural resources or utilities, face higher risks than other industries.[28] Indeed, country risk may even differ between firms in the same industry. This potential for different country risks can to some extent be influenced by firms themselves, because there are a number of things firms can do to affect the odds of some political-risk events occurring.

Methods of reducing country risk

Keeping control of crucial elements of corporate operations

Some companies making FDIs take steps to prevent operations from being able to run without their cooperation. This can be achieved if the investor maintains control of a crucial element of operations. For example, food and soft drink manufacturers keep secret their special ingredients. Auto companies can produce vital parts, such as engines, in some other country and can refuse to supply these parts if their operations are seized.[29] The multinational oil companies have used refining capacity coupled with alternative sources of oil to reduce the probability that their oil wells will be expropriated. Similarly, many companies have kept key technical operations with their own technicians, who can be recalled in the event of expropriation or confiscation. This has not always been an effective deterrent, as more mercenary technicians can often be found if the salary is sufficient. Moreover, given sufficient time, local people can pick up the important skills.

Programmed stages of planned divestment

An alternative technique for reducing the probability of expropriation is for the owner of an FDI to promise to turn over ownership and control to local people at a specified time in the future. This is sometimes required by the host government. For example, the **Cartagena Agreement** of 1969 requires the foreign owners of enterprises in the Andean countries of South America to lower their ownership, over time, to below 50 percent.

---

26 While the ratio of debt-service payments to export earnings provides an indication of the foreign exchange earnings that may be available for debt service, it does not reflect the diversity of goods and services that earn foreign exchange. Presumably, a country with a single export is a poorer risk than a country with diversified export earnings, even if the two countries have the same ratio.

27 Nonrecourse loans to exporters are discussed in Chapter 20 under the heading "Forfaiting: A Form of Medium-Term Finance."

28 See J. Frederick Truitt, "Expropriation of Foreign Investment: Summary of the Post World War II Experience of American and British Investors in Less Developed Countries," *Journal of International Business Studies*, Fall 1970, pp. 21–34; Robert Hawkins, Norman Mintz, and Michael Provissiero, "Government Takeovers of US Foreign Affiliates," *Journal of International Business Studies*, Spring 1976, pp. 3–16; and John Calverly, *Country Risk Analysis*, Butterworths, London, 1985.

29 According to Roy E. Pederson, who cited the case of IBM, the risk can be reduced by keeping all research and development at home. See Roy E. Pedersen, "Political Risk: Corporate Considerations," *Risk Management*, April 1979, pp. 23–32.

Table 17.2 Euromoney's country-risk ranking, 2003

Top twenty		Bottom twenty	
Country	Rating/100	Country	Rating/100
Luxembourg	99.44	Tajikistan	24.19
Switzerland	97.36	Mauritania	23.98
United States	95.60	Libya	23.38
Norway	95.49	Eritrea	23.14
Denmark	94.31	Burundi	21.90
Netherlands	93.48	Rwanda	21.87
Sweden	93.34	Guinea-Bissau	21.74
Austria	92.80	Sierra Leone	20.93
United Kingdom	92.57	Myanmar	20.75
Finland	92.13	Sao Tome & Principe	20.58
Ireland	92.10	New Caledonia	20.51
Germany	91.92	Micronesia (Fed. States)	18.70
Canada	91.79	Marshall Islands	17.41
France	91.40	Dem. Rep. of the Congo (Zaire)	15.92
Belgium	90.90	Liberia	15.36
Australia	90.36	Cuba	13.44
Iceland	89.51	Somalia	12.01
Spain	88.46	Iraq	6.39
Japan	88.30	Korea North	6.33
Italy	87.27	Afghanistan	3.07

Source: Euromoney, March 2003.

Joint ventures

Instead of promising shared ownership in the future, an alternative technique for reducing the risk of expropriation is to share ownership with foreign private or official partners from the very beginning. Such shared ownerships, known as **joint ventures**, have been tried by US, Canadian, European, and Japanese firms with partners in Africa, Central and South America, and Asia. China has almost exclusively relied on joint ventures in hosting FDI in their country, and as of 2003 became the largest recipient of FDI in the world, moving ahead of the United States which had previously held that record. Joint ventures as a means of reducing expropriation risks rely on the reluctance of local partners, if private, to accept the interference of their own government. When the partner is the government itself, the disincentive to expropriate is the concern over the loss of future investments. Joint ventures with multiple participants from different countries reduce the risk of expropriation, even if there is no local participation, if the government wishes to avoid being isolated simultaneously by numerous foreign powers.

Even if joint ventures with government-controlled enterprises work well while that government remains in power, they can backfire if the government is overthrown by the opposition in a polarized political climate. Extreme changes in governments have been witnessed so many times that the risks of siding with a government that falls are well known. In addition, even when the local partner is a private corporation, if expropriation means more ownership or control for the partner, there is likely to be muted local opposition at best.

It is these reasons which may explain the observation that the risk of joint ventures has been greater than that of ventures with total US ownership. A study of US affiliates in the 1960–76 period showed that joint ventures with host governments were expropriated 10 times more often than fully US-owned ventures and that joint ventures with private firms were expropriated 8 times more often.[30]

Local debt

The risk of expropriation as well as the losses from expropriation can be reduced by borrowing within the countries where investment occurs. If the borrowing is denominated in the local currency, there will often also be a reduction of foreign exchange risk. These obvious gains from engaging in local debt are limited by the opportunities. Those countries where expropriation is most likely tend to be the countries with the least developed capital markets and host governments unwilling to make loans. The opportunities for reducing risk by having local people hold equity in the firm are also limited by the frequent shortage of middle class shareholders in the high-risk countries and by the absence of a viable market in which to sell shares.

Despite the techniques for reducing risk, some danger will remain. Fortunately, something can be done to reduce or eliminate the harmful consequences of political developments by purchasing investment insurance.

The purchase of investment insurance

Many countries will insure their companies that invest overseas against losses from political events such as currency inconvertibility, expropriation, war, and revolution. In the United States this insurance is offered by the Overseas Private Investment Corporation (OPIC). This corporation has been in operation since 1971, having replaced programs in effect since the Economic Co-operation Act of 1948.[31] OPIC will insure US private investments in developing nations, where there tends to be more risk. Over 60 percent of US non-oil-related FDIs in underdeveloped countries are covered by OPIC.

In addition to investment insurance, OPIC offers project financing. This involves assistance in finding sources of funds, including OPIC's own sources, and assistance in finding worthwhile projects. Reimbursement for losses on loans is also offered. There is no coverage for losses due to changes in exchange rates, but there is also no need for such coverage because of the private means that are available, such as the forward and futures markets. OPIC charges a fee for complete coverage that is between 1 and 2 percent per annum of the amount covered on the insurance policy. Insurance must generally be approved by host governments and is available only on new projects. Since 1980, OPIC has joined with private insurance companies in the Overseas Investment Insurance Group. This has been done to move the insurance into the private sector of the economy. OPIC is financially self sustaining.

In Canada, foreign-investment insurance is provided by Export Development Canada (EDC). EDC will insure against losses due to war, insurrection, confiscation, expropriation, and events which prevent the repatriating of capital or the transfer of earnings. This role of the EDC is similar to the role of OPIC. EDC also offers insurance against non-payment for Canadian exports, a function performed by the Export–Import Bank in the United States. The insurance coverage offered in the United Kingdom is very similar to the coverage offered by OPIC and the Canadian EDC, and similar programs exist in most other trading nations.

---

30 These observations may be biased. It could be that joint ventures are used disproportionately in situations where expropriation is likely. For the record on what has happened, see David Bradley, "Managing Against Expropriation," *Harvard Business Review*, July–August 1977, pp. 75–83. For a survey of work on political risks, see Stephen Kobrin, "Political Risks: A Review and Reconsideration," *Journal of International Business Studies*, Spring/Summer 1979, pp. 67–80.

31 See www.opic.gov for a description of the work of OPIC.

If the compensation provided by project insurers is received immediately and covers the full value of the project, the availability of insurance means that the only required adjustment for country risk is a deduction for insurance premiums from cash flows. We can deduct available premiums even if insurance is not actually purchased, since the firm will then be self-insuring and should deduct an appropriate cost for this.

Some of the country risk that MNCs face and that forces them to insure or take other steps is a result of their visibility. This is largely due to their immense size and the difficulty of regulating them. However, there are other factors that have made MNCs the target of criticism and concern. Let us turn our discussion of the growth and special problems of MNCs to these criticisms and concerns, and explain why so much attention has been attracted by MNCs. We shall see that while some of the common concerns over the power and practices of MNCs may be well-founded, there are many benefits that MNCs have brought host countries through the transfer of technology and jobs that can be attributed to their direct investments.

PROBLEMS AND BENEFITS FROM THE GROWTH OF MNCs

As we have mentioned, much of the concern about MNCs stems from their size, which can be formidable. Indeed, the profits of some of the larger corporations can exceed the operating budgets of the governments in smaller countries. It is the power that such scale can give that has led to the greatest concern. Can the MNCs push around their host governments to the advantage of the shareholders and the disadvantage of the citizens of the country of operation? This has led several countries and even the United Nations to investigate the influence of MNCs. The issues considered include the following.

Blunting local economic policy

It can be difficult to manage economies in which multinationals have extensive investments, such as the economies of Canada and Australia. Since MNCs often have ready access to external sources of finance, they can blunt local monetary policy.[32] When the host government wishes to constrain economic activity, multinationals may nevertheless expand through foreign borrowing. Similarly, efforts at economic expansion may be frustrated if multinationals move funds abroad in search of yield advantages elsewhere. You do not have to be a multinational to frustrate plans for economic expansion — integrated financial markets will always produce this effect — but MNCs are likely to participate in any opportunities to gain profits. Furthermore, as we have seen, multinationals can also shift profits to reduce their total tax burden; they can try to manipulate transfer prices to move profits to countries with lower tax rates. This can make the MNC a slippery animal for the tax collector, even though, on the other side of the ledger, by buying local goods they contribute to tax revenue.

Destabilizing exchange rates

It has been argued that multinationals can make foreign exchange markets volatile. For example, it has been claimed that when the US dollar is moving rapidly against the world's major currencies, the Canadian dollar swings even further. In particular, it has been argued that a declining value of the US dollar against, for example, the euro or sterling, has been associated with an average larger decline of the Canadian dollar against these currencies. Although the existence of this phenomenon has not been formally verified, MNCs have been blamed for such an effect. It has been claimed that when US parent companies are expecting an increase in the value of the euro, sterling, and so on, they buy these foreign currencies and instruct their Canadian subsidiaries

32 While MNCs may reduce the effectiveness of monetary policy, they may also increase the effectiveness of changes in exchange rates on the balance of trade. In particular, they may speed up the increase in exports from countries experiencing depreciations by quickly moving their production to those countries to take advantage of the lower production costs.

to do the same. With a thinner market in the Dominion currency, the effect of this activity could be greater movement in the Canadian dollar than the US dollar.

Defying foreign policy objectives

Concern has been expressed, especially within the United States, that US-based multinationals can defy foreign policy objectives of the US government through their foreign branches and subsidiaries. This concern has been heightened by the focus on terrorism, especially in the aftermath of the events of September 11, 2001. For example, a US MNC might break a blockade and avoid sanctions by operating through overseas subsidiaries. This has caused even greater concern within some host countries. Why should companies operating within their boundaries have to follow orders of the US government or any other foreign government?

Multinational corporations present a potential for conflict between national governments. There is even potential for conflict within international/multinational trade unions. For example, in 1980 and 1981 Chrysler Corporation was given loan guarantees to help it continue in operation. The US government insisted on wage and salary rollbacks as a condition. Chrysler workers in Canada did not appreciate the instruction from the US Congress to accept a reduced wage.

Creating and exploiting monopoly power

It is not uncommon to hear the view that because MNCs are so large they have reduced competition. However, the truth may be the opposite. In some industries such as automobiles, computers, steel, and shipbuilding where a single country might support one or only a few firms in the industry, competition is increased by the presence of foreign MNCs. That is, the MNCs themselves compete in international markets, and without them monopoly powers in some sectors might be even greater.

Accusations have been made, most notably with regard to the oil industry, that multinationals can

use monopoly power to withhold output to effect price increases for their products. Because the multinationals have such extensive operations, much of the data on which the governments must rely are often data collected and reported by the MNCs themselves. There is no guarantee that the data are accurate, and there is no easy way to enforce controls and punish culprits. This became one of the leading political issues of the new millennium.

Keeping top jobs at home

Multinationals tend to concentrate and specialize their "good" and "bad" activities within certain locations. This can mean doing R&D within the home country. Highly trained university and technical-school graduates who find their employment and promotion opportunities diminished would prefer locally owned and managed enterprises in their country to foreign MNCs. This has been a controversial problem in countries that consider themselves "branch plant" economies. Canadian and Australian scientists and engineers have been particularly outspoken.[33]

While MNCs have improved prospects for some better-paid workers in their home countries, it has been argued that they have "exported" lower-wage jobs, especially in manufacturing. The evidence does not appear to support this claim. Indeed, Exhibit 17.3 argues that the opposite may be true. FDI is frequently motivated by strategic considerations, and it can help investing firms retain

---

33 The data support the claim that multinationals keep a disproportionate share of R & D activity at home. For example, according to the US Department of Commerce, in 1977 only 10 percent of US-based multinationals' R&D was spent by foreign affiliates, and these foreign affiliates employed only 13 percent of the MNCs' scientists and engineers. See US Department of Commerce, Bureau of Economic Analysis, news release, June 2, 1981. See also Irving Kravis and Robert Lipsey, "The Effect of Multinational Firms' Foreign Operations on Their Domestic Employment," *National Bureau of Economic Research*, Working Paper 2760, March 1989.

EXHIBIT 17.3   DO US MULTINATIONALS EXPORT JOBS?

Given that everybody knows American workers earn far more than their counterparts in newly industrialized and developing countries, it has not been difficult to convince people that US multinationals have exported Americans' jobs. But do firms make their FDIs to gain access to "cheap labor," or is there more to it than that?

The idea that FDI by US multinationals has exported jobs has arisen largely from some highly publicized cases, such as the movement of Smith-Corona's typewriter assembly from Connecticut to Mexico and the serious, protracted labor unrest over International Harvester's decision to relocate production. However, the data do not support popular opinion. First, statistics show that 85 percent of manufacturing output by overseas operations of US MNCs is in other relatively high-wage countries such as Canada and Britain. Second, exports from US subsidiaries abroad to the United States are only 12 percent of the subsidiaries' production. The rest is sold abroad. Indeed, the need to supply overseas subsidiaries with partly-processed inputs and capital equipment and to carry out R&D has been claimed to *create* jobs in the United States. One study convincingly supporting this conclusion, by Robert Lipsey, found that for US multinationals, the higher the share of overseas operations in the firm's total

production, the larger the share of employment at home. The same study suggests that *without* the FDI, the US market share would have been taken by other countries' multinationals. In other words, US foreign investment has a strategic element and has helped the United States retain its share of markets, even though the importance of goods supplied from the United States itself has declined; foreign subsidiaries have helped US firms retain markets, and, thereby, R&D and factor-supply-related jobs at home.

Clearly, there is more to production-location decisions than wages. Overall unit labor costs can be low even when wages are high if workers have high productivity. As long as US workers are more productive, jobs will not be exported. Of course, this requires investment in education as well as in physical capital. Therefore, if there is a danger of losing jobs, it comes from educational and investment levels in the United States versus those levels abroad, not from globally successful US multinationals.

Source: Based on Robert Lipsey, "Outward Direct Investment and the US Economy," *National Bureau of Economic Research*, Paper Number 4691, 1994, and M. Blomström and Ari Kokko, "Home Country Effects of Foreign Direct Investment: Evidence from Sweden," *National Bureau of Economic Research*, Paper Number 4639, 1994.

---

markets threatened by new entrants. In this way jobs at home – those supplying partly processed inputs and R&D – are protected.

Also on the positive side, MNCs have transferred technology and capital to less-developed countries (LDCs), and in this way helped accelerate their economic development.[34] US- and Japanese-based MNCs have been particularly active building production facilities in LDCs.[35] For example, US multinationals' influence in Latin America has been

particularly strong.[36] The Japanese MNCs' influence has also risen, particularly in Asian LDCs.[37]

Homogenization of culture

There is little doubt that MNCs spread a common culture. Chain hamburger outlets become the same on Main Street in Iowa and on the Champs-Elysées in Paris. Soft drink bottles with a familiar shape can

---

34 However, many have argued that the transferred technology is often inappropriate.

35 To the extent MNCs provide training, they may also add to the stock of human capital in LDCs.

36 Magnus Blomstrom, Irving Kravis, and Robert Lipsey, "Multinational Firms and Manufactured Exports from Developing Countries," *National Bureau of Economic Research*, Working Paper 2493, June 1988.

37 See Blomstrom, Kravis, and Lipsey, ibid.

wash up on any beach with no way of telling from which country they came. Hotel rooms are alike everywhere. The same corporate names and product names appear in every major Western language. Even architecture shows a common influence – the "international style." Many have decried this development, complaining that it is robbing the world of a good deal of its variety and local interest. Yet the local people demand the products of the MNCs. This is all part of the unending love–hate relationship between concerned people everywhere and the MNC.

TRANSNATIONAL ALLIANCES

MNCs own and control their overseas operations. An alternative to ownership which still allows companies to enjoy some of the benefits of multi-nationalization is the formation of **transnational alliances**. These alliances involve associations of firms in different countries working together to overcome the limitations of working alone. One motivation to form a transnational alliance is cooperation over research where costs and risks may be too high for any one firm, or where different firms may possess different abilities. Such alliances are popular in biotechnology and computers: Quadra Logic of Canada with American Cyanamide in genetic engineering, for example, and IBM with Siemens of Germany in memory-chip development. Cooperation may be between producers and mar-keters: Chrysler marketed the Colt produced by Mitsubishi; GM marketed the Geo produced in Korea. Other cooperations have involved design, product assembly, component production, and distribution.

The extent and complexity of transnational alliances can be found by writing the names of the global members of any industry in matrix form on a sheet of paper. Lines can then be drawn to represent contacts, whether these are joint ventures, licensing arrangements, production agreements, or research connections. Doing this for computer firms or automobile manufacturers shows an intimate cob-web of tangled connections. Pharmaceutical, aero-space, telecommunications, and defense industry alliances also reveal a highly complex web.

Transnational alliances appear to be formed most frequently for three reasons:

1   to gain access to foreign markets
2   to exploit complementary technologies and
3   to reduce the time taken for innovation.[38]

The alliances are usually for specific purposes, although once formed, they may be used for further purposes. Typically, ownership connections are limited, unlike the consortia so popular in Japan, called **keiretsu**, and in South Korea, called **chaebols**. Keiretsu and chaebols involve owner-ship cross-holdings not usually present with trans-national alliances. Transnational alliances are a compromise between a firm doing everything itself, and dealing with a complete stranger.[39] As such, they are somewhere between independent national operations and multinational corporations.

SUMMARY

1   MNCs have grown by making FDIs.
2   Among the reasons MNCs have made direct investments are to gain access to raw materials, to integrate operations for increased efficiency, to avoid regulations, to

38 See *Multinational*, a supplement in *The Economist*, March 27, 1993, pp. 14–17.
39 Ibid.

protect industrial secrets and patents, to expand when domestic opportunities are exhausted, avoid tariffs and quotas, to increase production flexibility and thereby profit from fluctuations in real exchange rates, to preempt others entering a market, to follow client MNCs, and to increase diversification.

3   MNCs are generally larger and more R&D-intensive than firms in general. These differences are characteristic both of the industries in which MNCs are found, and of the MNCs versus other firms within the same industries.

4   MNCs face two measurement problems to a greater degree than other firms, namely measuring transfer prices and country risks.

5   For maximum overall corporate profits and correct buy-versus-make decisions, transfer prices should be set equal to marginal costs. This means that the use of market prices as transfer prices is appropriate only if the market for intermediate products is perfectly competitive.

6   If intermediate-product markets are not perfectly competitive, prices will exceed marginal costs, and so, by using market prices of intermediate products, less than the optimal final output will be produced, and suboptimal use will be made of the MNCs own intermediate products.

7   Even if market prices equal marginal costs, so that transfer prices can be set equal to market prices, if divisional profits are calculated using these transfer prices, then supplying divisions may appear to be unprofitable even when they add to overall corporate profitability.

8   Transfer prices can be used to reduce political risk, taxes, foreign exchange losses, the impact of tariffs and quotas, and shareholder frustration resulting from fluctuating profits. Offsetting the gains from distorting transfer prices is the loss from losing information on divisional profitability.

9   Country risk is a broader concept than either political risk or sovereign risk. Country risk includes economic and social risk, as well as risk faced on private-sector investments.

10   There are a number of published rankings of country risks and political risks which can help in evaluations of direct investments.

11   Political risk can be reduced by keeping control of essential operations, by having a program of planned divestment, or by the use of local debt. Joint ventures can also reduce political risk, but they can backfire with changes in polarized host governments.

12   Losses from political events can be reduced or eliminated by buying investment insurance. In the United States, this is available from the Overseas Private Investment Corporation (OPIC).

13   MNCs have brought numerous problems. They can make it difficult to manage an economy; they may be able to defy the political directions of their own or foreign governments; they can concentrate skilled jobs at home and more menial jobs abroad. MNCs may also be able to manipulate prices and spread a common culture.

14   Transnational alliances are associations of firms from different countries working in cooperation. They are particularly common in the computer, biotechnology, pharmaceutical, defense, and automobile industries where they give access to foreign markets and/or permit the sharing of technology.

REVIEW QUESTIONS

1 Why might a producer want to own resources located in another country, rather than buy them in the open market?
2 What are the limitations of licences as an alternative to FDI?
3 Why are some accounting firms multinationals?
4 What role do market imperfections play in FDI?
5 What is a transfer price?
6 Can a company set any transfer prices that it wishes?
7 What is meant by "country risk," and how does this risk differ from political risk?
8 How does country risk differ from sovereign risk?
9 How does expropriation differ from confiscation?
10 Why does local debt or equity help reduce country risk?
11 Is country risk the same for all industries and firms?
12 What is a transnational alliance?

ASSIGNMENT PROBLEMS

1 What examples can you list of foreign multinationals operating in the United States?
2 Which of the reasons for the growth of MNCs do you think are the primary reasons for the development of multinationals in the following industries?
   a Pharmaceutical development and manufacturing
   b Automobile manufacturing
   c Metal refining
   d Hotel operation
   e Commercial banking
   f Energy development
   g Fast food
   h Fashion clothing.
3 Which explanation(s) of the growth of MNCs is/are supported by the evidence that MNCs are relatively capital intensive?
4 What are the pros and cons of setting transfer prices equal to marginal costs?
5 Under what circumstances are market prices appropriate to use as transfer prices?
6 How can conflicts exist when a firm sets transfer prices for maximizing overall profits? Could these conflicts arise from differential tax rates, import tariffs, imminent changes in exchange rates, and political risks?
7 Why are risk premiums on bonds a useful way of ranking risks for direct investments, but not very useful for making bond purchasing decisions?
8 Why might country risk depend on the diversity of exports as well as on the value of exports versus debt-service payments?

9   In what ways might country risk be influenced by a country's political and economic associations and its geography?

10 Do you think the standard of living overseas has been raised by the direct investments of multinationals? Does this provide a reason for offering MNCs concessionary loans?

BIBLIOGRAPHY

Aliber, Robert Z., *The Multinational Paradigm*, MIT Press, Cambridge, MA, 1993.

Bird, Graham, "New Approaches to Country Risk," *Lloyds Bank Review*, October 1986, pp. 1–16.

Calverley, John, *Country Risk Analysis*, Butterworths, London, 1985.

Calvet, A. Louis, "A Synthesis of Foreign Direct Investment Theories and Theories of the Multinational Firm," *Journal of International Business Studies*, Spring/Summer 1981, pp. 43–59.

Casson, Mark, *The Firm and the Market: Studies on the Multinational Enterprise and the Scope of the Firm*, MIT Press, Cambridge, MA, 1987.

Davidson, William H., "Location of Foreign Direct Investment Activity: Country Characteristics and Experience Effects," *Journal of International Business Studies*, Fall, 1980, pp. 9–22.

Dunning, John H. (ed.), *International Investment*, Penguin, Harmondsworth, UK, 1972.

——, *Economic Analysis and the Multinational Enterprise*, Praeger, New York, 1975. *The Economist: Multinationals*, a supplement, March 27, 1993.

Goldberg, Michael, Robert Heinkel, and Maurice D. Levi, "Foreign Direct Investment: The Human Dimension," *Journal of International Money and Finance*, forthcoming, 2005.

Granick, David, "National Differences in the Use of Internal Transfer Prices," *California Management Review*, Summer 1975, pp. 28–40.

Kobrin, Stephen J., "The Environmental Determinants of Foreign Direct Investment: An Ex Post Empirical Analysis," *Journal of International Business Studies*, Fall 1976, pp. 29–42.

Magee, Stephen P., "Information and the Multinational Corporation: An Appropriability Theory of Direct Foreign Investment," in Jagdish N. Bhagwati (ed.), *The New International Economic Order*, MIT Press, Cambridge, MA, 1977.

Melvin, Michael and Don Schlagenhauf, "A Country Risk Index: Econometric Formulation and an Application to Mexico," *Economic Inquiry*, October 1985, pp. 601–19.

Ragazzio, Giorgio, "Theories of the Determinants of Direct Foreign Investment," *IMF Staff Papers*, July 1973, pp. 471–98.

Reich, Robert B., *The Work of Nations*, Knopf, New York, 1991.

Rummel, R. J. and David A. Heenan, "How Multinationals Analyze Political Risk," *Harvard Business Review*, January/February 1978, pp. 67–76.

Vernon, Raymond, *Storm Over the Multinationals: The Real Issues*, Harvard University Press, Cambridge, MA, 1977.

Wei, Shang-Jin, "How Taxing is Corruption on International Investors?" *Review of Economics and Statistics*, February 2000, pp. 1–11.

Chapter 18

International dimensions of long-term financing

Let us all be happy and live within our means, even if we have to borrow the money to do it with.

Artemus Ward

The integration and associated globalization of capital markets has opened up a vast array of new sources and forms of financing. Today's corporate treasurers of large multinational as well as domestic corporations can often access foreign capital markets as easily as they can access those at home. This chapter considers these broadened opportunities by explaining the central international financial issues involved in each of the major methods of raising financial capital, some of which are unique to the international sphere. We consider the international aspects of raising capital via stocks, bonds, parallel loans between corporations, credit swaps between banks and corporations, and loans from host governments and development banks. We shall see the importance of exchange-rate risk, taxes, country risk, and issuance costs for the form of financing chosen. The chapter concludes with a discussion of the appropriate relative amounts of each type of financing, that is, the appropriate **financial structure**.

EQUITY FINANCING

The principal international financial question concerning equity financing is in which country stocks should be issued. A second question concerns the legal vehicle that should be used for raising equity capital; should this be done by the parent company or by a subsidiary, and if by a subsidiary, where should it be registered?

The country in which shares should be issued

Clearly, shares should be issued in the country in which the best price can be received, net of issuing costs. If for the time being we assume the costs of issue to be the same everywhere, the country in which the best price can be received for the shares is the country in which the cost of equity in terms of the required expected rate of return for investors is lowest. There is no concern about risk from the equity *issuer's* perspective, other than to the extent that through equity buyer's concern for systematic risk, the riskiness of shares issued affects the required expected rate of return and hence the price received for the shares; the required expected rate of return of shareholders is, of course, the expected rate of return paid by the firm.

It should be clear from our discussion of equity investment in Chapter 15 that if international capital markets are integrated, the expected cost of equity financing will be the same in every country.

That is, the expected return on the company's shares will be the same everywhere.[1]

If capital markets are segmented, the expected returns on the same security *could* be different in different markets. A company might then be able to receive more for its shares in some markets than others. Of course, when a company's shares are listed simultaneously in different countries, the share price measured in a common currency will have to be the same everywhere up to the transaction costs of arbitrage. Otherwise, the shares will be bought in the cheaper market and sold in the more expensive market until the price difference has been eliminated. However, the cause of the capital-market segmentation may prevent arbitrage. Furthermore, a company may not be considering simultaneous issue in different countries, but rather, a single country in which to float an issue.

Ceteris paribus, when capital markets are segmented, the higher the savings rates relative to investment rates in a particular country, the lower is the cost of capital in that country. This means, for example, that a country such as Japan, which has a high savings rate, should have a lower cost of financial capital than the United States, which has a low savings rate, provided that investment opportunities are similar. Of course, if markets are integrated, we shall not see these different costs of capital, because those countries which would have had low costs of capital in segmented markets would have outflows of capital until the rates of return are the same as elsewhere: the outflows reduce the supply of funds, thereby forcing up rates of return. Similarly, those countries which would have had high costs of capital with segmentation would have inflows of capital until their rates of return are the same as elsewhere: the inflows add to the supply of funds and

bring down the cost.[2] This was seen graphically in Appendix B in Chapter 1.

Euroequities

Sometimes, as a result of capital-market segmentation, it can be advantageous for a company to issue shares in one or more foreign markets at the same time as it issues shares at home. The reason is that each individual market can absorb only a limited amount of the new share issue. In other words, there is a downward-sloping demand curve for the shares in any one country, so selling more requires a lower share price which in turn implies a higher expected return. Share issues involving sales of new shares outside the home country are called **Euroequity issues**. In the 1980s, the number of Euroequity issues grew rapidly and has continued to grow as globalization of financial markets has proceeded. For example, in May 1988, Occidental Petroleum floated $212 million of Euroequities, this being 18 percent of the company's total share issue. In May 1987, US Air floated $90 million of Euroequities, 20 percent of its total issue, and in September 1986 Home Shopping Network sold $56.1 million of shares in the Euromarket, 50 percent of its share offering. *Euromoney Magazine* documents these and further issues on a regular basis.

What is the source of market segmentation that has prompted so many companies to raise equity capital by sales in foreign equity markets, rather than issue all the shares at home and allow foreign shareholders to buy their shares in that market? In other words, what is limiting the ability or willingness of foreign investors to buy shares in the company's home market instead of in the Eurodollar market? As Exhibit 18.2 explains, one possible explanation is the preference of many non-American investors for the anonymity enjoyed

---

1 The expected return must, of course, be in terms of a given currency. For example, the expected average annual US-dollar rate of return on shares trading in, for example, Britain includes the expected appreciation/ depreciation of the pound as well as the expected change in the pound price of the shares and the expected dividend yield.

2 Claims have been made that costs of capital in the United States and Japan have not moved together from international financial flows, with Japanese firms facing lower financing costs. However, as Exhibit 18.1 explains, borrowing cost differences may be smaller than many people believe.

EXHIBIT 18.1 OVERSTATING DIFFERENCES: US–JAPANESE BORROWING COSTS MORE SIMILAR THAN IT SEEMS

Theory suggests that borrowing costs, or more generally, the costs of capital, should be equal in different markets after allowance for exchange rates. Indeed, Chapter 8 was devoted to showing this, in the form of the interest-parity principle. Nevertheless, many people have claimed that vital differences in costs of capital exist, especially between Japan and the United States, with Japanese capital costs well below those faced by Americans. Were this to be so, it would give an advantage to Japanese firms, especially in capital-intensive industries. However, as the item below argues, the appearance of a lower cost of capital in Japan than the United States, specifically for bank borrowing, may be due to an incomplete understanding of institutional arrangements in these two countries.

Few subjects in international economics have touched as many political nerves in recent years as the comparison of relative financing costs in different countries. The apparent financing advantage enjoyed by Japanese firms over their U.S. competitors in past decades – short-term real bank loan rates 1 percent to 2.8 percent lower, according to some research – even has been cited as evidence of "unfair trade" that should be redressed by changes in U.S. policy. But a new NBER (National Bureau of Economic Research) study by Richard Marston shows that bank financing costs in Japan were underestimated systematically, and those in the United States overestimated, in the past. In any event, Marston finds, most of the reported gap in financing costs between the two countries can be traced to features of national markets that have largely disappeared.

In "Determinants of Short-Term Real Interest Differentials Between Japan and the United States" (NBER Working Paper No. 4167), Marston focuses on bank loan financing, which continues to be the most important source of external finance for Japanese firms. He finds that interest rates in Japan were governed by market conventions and regulations that often obscured the true cost of funds. Prior to 1989, the most widely reported lending rate was called the "standard rate." This was defined as the rate on loans of "especially high credit standing" and was tied through informal guidelines to the Bank of Japan's discount rate. The cost of borrowing at this rate was understated because Japanese banks typically required that borrowers maintain compensating balances on deposit, raising the effective cost of the loan. For most of the 1970s, the only short-term rate free to reflect monetary conditions was the "gensaki" rate, paid on repurchase agreements. Between 1973 and 1991, the standard rate averaged 5.96 percent while the gensaki rate averaged 6.99 percent: more than one percentage point higher.

Measuring the true cost of bank loans in the United States is also difficult. The meaning of the widely quoted "prime rate" (the rate at which banks traditionally lent to their most creditworthy customers) has changed fundamentally as borrowers gained greater access to direct financing from the 1970s onward. Marston finds that, from 1973 to 1991, the average gap between the prime rate and the rate at which creditworthy firms could borrow on the commercial paper market was 1.57 percent.

Source: "Japan and U.S. Real Interest Rates Converge," *The NBER Digest,* February 1993.

with **bearer shares**. (US shares sold in Euromarkets are bearer shares, which means that they do not carry the name of the owner. US shares sold in US markets are all registered in the owners' names, with the registration changed when the shares are exchanged.)

Investor protection and disclosure requirements

Just as US firms have found it beneficial to sell shares abroad, non-US firms have found it beneficial to sell shares in US stock markets. What is the cause of

EXHIBIT 18.2   GOING ABROAD: THE APPEAL OF EUROEQUITIES

If capital markets are integrated it does not matter in which country a company issues shares; people will buy them wherever they live. The fact that US companies have sold some of their shares overseas is evidence that markets are not fully integrated, posing the important question of why this is so. In a survey of the Chief Financial Officers (CFOs) of large firms issuing Euroequities during 1985–88, Wayne Marr, John Trimble, and Raj Varma found an answer. As the excerpt below indicates, they found that the preference for bearer shares by non-US investors and the requirement of the US Securities Exchange Commission (SEC) that US-based shares be registered in the owners' names has encouraged some large US companies to sell shares in the Euromarket.

> On more than 200 occasions since 1985, American corporations have raised capital with a new kind of equity offering made available simultaneously to U.S. and foreign investors. Such "Euroequity" issues have also been considerably larger, on average, than traditional domestic offerings during the same period. It's true that U.S. companies have long had the option of listing their stock on foreign exchanges, and thus expanding the potential market for their securities. But, for all except a handful of the American firms, such listings have not proved a cost effective method of raising new equity.
>
> What is behind the rise and rapid growth of these overseas equity sales? In an informal survey of the CFOs of U.S. issuers, we found the most common reason for choosing Euroequity was "to take advantage of our good name in overseas markets." But what does this mean? The financing advantages of having a "good name in overseas markets" may be various and thus difficult to quantify. But presumably chief among them is that European investors are willing to pay a higher price for the company's shares – or, alternatively, their added demand enables the issuer to sell a greater quantity of its shares than otherwise without being forced to drop the price.

For financial economists, however, such an alleged financing bargain is puzzling. The existence of a price differential large enough to influence the financing decisions of U.S. corporations appears to run counter to the conventional economic wisdom that international capital markets are becoming progressively more "integrated." And such integration in turn implies that the free flow of capital across international boundaries should erase all but minor and momentary differences in capital costs. How, therefore, does one explain the sudden popularity of Euroequity? And are there genuine equity cost savings for corporate issuers?

[T]he findings of our recently completed study of 32 Euroequity issues by non-financial firms between 1985 and 1988 [reveal] market-based evidence of significant savings by issuers ... [A]n explanation for these savings – one that centers on recent changes in U.S. tax laws and Treasury Department regulations – [is] that Euroequities allow overseas investors to hold *bearer* shares in U.S. corporations. Thanks to new registration procedures cleared by the SEC, such bearer shares can often be made as liquid as the registered shares traded in U.S. capital markets.

Source: Wayne Marr, John L. Trimble, and Raj Varma, "Innovation in Global Financing: The Case of Euroequity Offerings," *Journal of Applied Corporate Finance*, Spring 1992, pp. 50–4.

segmentation that prevents or discourages Americans from buying shares of non-US firms in foreign stock markets? One possible explanation is US reporting requirements that, in accordance with the Securities Exchange Act of 1934, require all companies listing on US exchanges to disclose information conforming to US Generally Accepted Accounting Principles (GAAP). If investors value the security provided by the disclosure requirements, then more shares may be sold by issuing shares in the United States. In other words, it is probably because US reporting rules are more stringent than those of some foreign stock exchanges that so many foreign firms have found it necessary to list in the United States to tap the huge US equity market; American and other nationals would otherwise be more wary about buying the stocks.

The relevance of disclosure requirements and associated shareholder protection has been studied in a series of papers by Rafael La Porta and his co-researchers.[3] By examining the financial market development and investor protection levels in a sample consisting of 49 countries, it was shown that the presence of legally enforceable rules protecting shareholders and the quality of enforcement are important determinants of external finance. Specifically, countries with weaker rules and poorer enforcement were found to have smaller and narrower financial markets: poor investor protection, by limiting funds coming to financial markets, forces firms to use their own income to finance further expansion. The conclusions concerning external finance were true for debt as well as equity. The study also showed that common law countries, such as the United States and United Kingdom, have stronger investor protection and more developed, broader capital markets, especially when compared to countries operating on the Napoleonic Code. Indeed, the relevance of investor protection is sufficiently strong that it has been associated with variations across countries in their rates of economic growth: better investor protection is associated with faster economic growth.[4] On the

other hand, it has also been argued that, at least in principle, when investors are better protected they may feel the need to save less, and this could work against economic growth since less savings means less available to borrow.[5] The empirical evidence, however, supports the positive association of faster growth with better investor protection.

American Depository Receipts (ADRs)

While some non-US firms have listed on US stock exchanges – mostly the New York Stock Exchange and NASDAQ – the shares of many more foreign firms trade indirectly as **American Depository Receipts (ADRs)**. The idea of trading ADRs originated with the Morgan Guarantee Bank, but numerous other US banks, including Citibank, Chase Manhattan, and the Bank of New York, have become involved. What happens is that the bank holds the foreign shares, receives dividends, reports, and so on, but issues claims against the shares it holds.[6] These claims – the ADRs – then generally trade in the relatively unregulated over-the-counter market. This has the advantage for foreign firms of reducing listing fees and the information that they must report.

Issue costs

When we mentioned that the highest price a firm could obtain for its shares, net of issuance costs, is in the market with the lowest required rate of return, we assumed that the costs of issue are the same everywhere. The correct rule for where to issue shares is that they should be sold where the price *net of issue costs* is the highest.

In fact, issue costs do vary from country to country and can be an important consideration. The costs of underwriting can be several percent of

3 See Rafael La Porta, Florencio Lopez-De-Silanes, Andrei Shleifer, and Robert W. Vishny, "Legal Determinants of External Finance," *Journal of Finance*, July 1997, pp. 1131–50.

4 See, for example, Ross Levine and Sara Zervos, "Stock Markets, Banks, and Economic Growth," *American Economic Review*, June 1998, pp. 537–58, and, Asli Demirgue-Kunt and Vojislav Maksimovic, "Law, Finance, and Economic Growth," *The Journal of Finance*, December 1998, pp. 2107–37. See also the survey by Ross Levine, "Financial Development and Economic Growth· Views and Agenda," *Journal of Economic Literature*, June 1997, pp. 688–726, and Raghuram Rajan and Luigi Zingales, "Financial Dependence and Growth," *American Economic Review*, June 1998, pp. 559–86.

5 See Michael B. Devereux and Gregor W. Smith, "International Risk Sharing and Economic Growth," *International Economic Review*, August 1994, pp. 535–50.

6 In the terminology of Chapter 15, the bank acts as the global custodian.

401

the value of funds raised and can vary significantly between different countries' markets. Generally, the lowest costs are faced in large equity markets such as those of the United States. This may explain why a substantial number of foreign companies have sold shares on the New York Stock Exchange and NASDAQ. Indeed, the competitiveness of the US financial markets has increased since 1991 when the Federal Reserve Board allowed a subsidiary of JP Morgan to underwrite an initial public offering (IPO) – the first commercial bank underwritten IPO since the passing of the Glass–Steagall Act of 1933. By 1997 the commercial bank share of the IPO market had grown to almost 30 percent. Then, in 1999 the Gramm–Leach–Bliley Act effectively removed the distinction between commercial banking and investment banking – where the latter was the traditional equity underwriting institution – meaning even more competition and presumably even lower costs by US equity issuing institutions.[7]

The vehicle of share issue

A firm that has decided to issue shares abroad must decide whether to issue them directly, or to do so indirectly via a subsidiary located abroad. There is frequently a motive to use a specially established financing subsidiary to avoid the need to withhold tax on payments made to foreigners. For example, many US firms established subsidiaries in the Netherlands Antilles and other tax havens to avoid having to withhold 30 percent of dividend or interest income paid to foreigners. As was explained in Appendix A of Chapter 16, the US financing subsidiaries took advantage of a ruling of the US Internal Revenue Service that if 80 percent or more of a corporation's income is earned abroad, then dividends and interest paid by the corporation are considered foreign and not subject to the need to withhold. To the extent that foreign creditors or shareholders of

US companies are unable to receive full credit for taxes withheld, they may be willing to pay more for securities issued by US subsidiaries than for the securities of the parent company in the United States.

BOND FINANCING

The same two issues arise with bond financing as with equity financing, namely, (1) the country of issue and (2) the vehicle of issue. The conclusions concerning these matters with bonds are also very similar to those we have described above in connection to equities. In particular, companies tend to issue in markets with relatively full disclosure rules and strong investor protection because these are the markets which attract investors. Companies also choose markets with relatively low issue costs of debt, just as they do when issuing equity.[8] However, an extra international issue does arise with bond financing, namely the *currency* of issue.

The currency of issue is not the same as the country of issue, although the two may coincide. For example, if a US company sells a pound-denominated bond in Britain, the currency of issue is that of the country of issue. However, if a US company sells a US-dollar-denominated bond in Britain, the currency of issue is not that of the country of issue. In the former of these situations the bond is called a **foreign bond**; in the latter it is called a **Eurobond**. Let us provide a more general description of foreign bonds and Eurobonds.

Foreign bonds versus Eurobonds

A foreign bond is a bond sold in a foreign country in the currency of the country of issue. The borrower is

---

7 See Paige Fields, Donald Fraser, and Rahul Bhargava, "A Comparison of Underwriting Costs of Initial Public Offerings of Investment and Commercial Banks," *Journal of Financial Research*, December 2003, pp. 517–34.

8 See Darius P. Miller and John J. Puthenpurackal, "The Costs, Wealth Effects, and Determinants of International Capital Raising: Evidence from Public Yankee Bonds," Working Paper 445, Kelley School of Business, Indiana University, October 2001. A Yankee bond, which is a US-dollar-denominated bond issued in the United States by a foreign bank or corporation, is a form of a "foreign bond" which is described in the section Foreign bonds versus Eurobonds.

foreign to the country of issue, hence the name. For example, a Canadian firm or a Canadian provincial government might sell a bond in New York denominated in US dollars. Similarly, a Brazilian company might sell a euro-denominated bond in Germany. These are examples of foreign bonds, also referred to as **Yankee bonds**. A Eurobond, on the other hand, is a bond that is denominated in a currency that is not that of the country in which it is issued. For example, a US-dollar-denominated bond sold outside of the United States – in Europe or elsewhere – is a Eurobond, a **Euro*dollar* bond**. Similarly, a sterling-denominated bond sold outside of the United Kingdom is a Eurobond, a **Euro*sterling* bond**.

Foreign bonds are usually underwritten and sold by brokers who are located in the country in which the bonds are issued. Eurobonds, on the other hand, are sold by international syndicates of brokers because they are generally sold simultaneously in a number of countries. The syndicates will normally have a lead manager which underwrites the largest proportion of the issue, and a number of smaller members, although some syndicates have co-lead managers. The lead managers include Merrill Lynch, Goldman Sachs, Union Bank of Switzerland (UBS), Morgan Stanley, Deutsche Bank, JP Morgan, and others. Eurobond issues tend to be very large, and their existence is an indication in itself that capital markets are segmented. This is because if there was no capital market segmentation, big bond issues could take place in a single market with foreign bond buyers purchasing what they want in that market. The need to sell parts in different countries' markets suggests that in any individual market there is a downward-sloping demand curve for any particular issue.

Selecting the currency of issue

Whether a firm issues a foreign bond, a Eurobond, or an ordinary domestic bond it must decide on the bond's currency of denomination. Of course, with foreign bonds the currency of denomination is that of the country of issue, so deciding on the currency of denomination is the same as deciding on the country of issue; with Eurobonds the currency and the country or countries of issue must both be decided.

Suppose that Aviva is neutral to exchange-rate risk and is choosing between denominating a bond in pounds or in dollars.[9] For simplicity, let us assume all payments are made at maturity.[10] Writing $r_\$$ for the annual interest cost of a dollar-denominated bond, Aviva's eventual payment on an n year bond per dollar raised is

$$\$(1 + r_\$)^n$$

Each $1 raised by selling a pound-denominated bond means raising $£1/S(\$/£)$. Assuming again that all payments are made at maturity, Aviva's payment in terms of pounds per dollar raised on an n year bond is

$$£\frac{1}{S(\$/£)}(1 + r_£)^n$$

where $r_£$ is the annual interest cost on a pound-denominated bond. The expected dollar cost of this payment is

$$\$\frac{S_n^*(\$/£)}{S(\$/£)}(1 + r_£)^n$$

where $S_n^*(\$/£)$ is the expected exchange rate at the end of year n.[11] Aviva will prefer issuing the pound-denominated bond if the eventual expected cost is less, that is, if

$$\frac{S_n^*(\$/£)}{S(\$/£)}(1 + r_£)^n < (1 + r_\$)^n \qquad (18.1)$$

9 Later we drop the assumption of risk neutrality and show how having pound receivables can make pound borrowing *preferred* on grounds of foreign exchange exposure and risk reduction.

10 If we drop this assumption and allow for periodic coupons, the algebra is more complex but the conclusion is the same.

11 We use the expected future spot rate rather than the forward rate because forward cover may not be available for the maturity of a long-term bond. Of course, so far we have assumed Aviva is neutral to any exchange-rate risk involving the bond.

Writing

$$S_n^*(\$/\pounds) \equiv S(\$/\pounds)[1 + \dot{S}^*(\$/\pounds)]^n$$

where $\dot{S}^*(\$/\pounds)$ is the expected average annual rate of change of the spot exchange rate, inequality (18.1) becomes

$$[1 + \dot{S}^*(\$/\pounds)]^n(1 + r_\pounds)^n < (1 + r_\$)^n$$

Taking the nth root of both sides,

$$[1 + \dot{S}^*(\$/\pounds)](1 + r_\pounds) < (1 + r_\$)$$

Expanding the left-hand side, canceling the ones, and ignoring the cross-product term $\dot{S}^*(\$/\pounds) \cdot r_\pounds$, gives[12]

$$r_\pounds + \dot{S}^*(\$/\pounds) < r_\$ \qquad (18.2)$$

That is, if inequality (18.2) holds and the company is risk neutral, Aviva should denominate its bond in the pound rather than the dollar. (If Aviva sells a pound bond in Britain, the bond is a foreign bond, and if it sells the pound bond in some country other than Britain, it is a Eurosterling bond.) Alternatively, if interest rates and expected exchange rates are such that

$$r_\pounds + \dot{S}^*(\$/\pounds) > r_\$ \qquad (18.3)$$

Aviva should sell a US-dollar-denominated bond, whether this be sold in the United States, making it an ordinary domestic bond, or outside the United States, making it a Eurodollar bond.

For example, suppose as before that Aviva is risk neutral and the borrowing costs and Aviva's expected change in the exchange rate are as follows.

$r_\$$	$r_\pounds$	$\dot{S}^*(\$/\pounds)$
10%	14%	-5%

That is, Aviva sees a higher borrowing cost for the firm on pound-denominated bonds, but also expects

a decline in the foreign exchange value of the pound against the dollar of 5 percent per annum over the life of the bond. It would be advantageous to denominate in terms of pounds, assuming Aviva is not averse to risk involving exchange rates, because in the example

$$r_\$ > r_\pounds + \dot{S}^*(\$/\pounds)$$

Ex post, the actual exchange rate will often change by a considerable amount over the life of a bond, creating a potential for sizable gains or losses. In other words, actual changes can deviate markedly from the changes which had been expected by the firm. History is full of examples of currencies which have changed in value against the dollar by substantial amounts. Even some of the major currencies have moved considerably in value over a number of years. Relatively small annual changes in exchange rates build up into very large changes over the life of long-term bonds.

To show how great the mistake can be, we can examine the results of a survey by William R. Folks, Jr, and Josef Follpracht. These results are shown in Table 18.1. Folks and Follpracht examined the cost of a number of foreign-currency denominated bonds issued by US-based multinational firms over the period July 1969–December 1972. The table allows us to compare the coupon rates with the eventual effective annual costs computed as of March 1976 or at the bonds' maturities. We can see that the appreciation of the German mark, Swiss franc, Dutch guilder, and Luxembourg franc made the borrowing costs of bonds considerably higher than the rates given by the coupons. We cannot tell whether the costs were high compared with the dollar rates that were available when the bonds were originally sold, but there is reason to believe that they were. The only foreign-currency bond which turned out to offer a lower cost than the coupon rate as of the end of the study was the pound-sterling bond issued by Amoco. The fall in value of the pound reduced the effective dollar repayment cost by over 2.7 percent per annum. The conclusion of any study like this depends on where

12 As we have noted before, the cross-product term is typically very small: it is a percent of a percent.

Table 18.1 Costs of foreign-currency bonds

Currency	Issue	Coupon rate %/year	Before-tax cost of borrowing, %/year
Deutschemark	Studebaker-Worthington	$7\frac{1}{4}$	14.69
	International Standard Electric	7	12.31
	TRW	$7\frac{1}{2}$	12.38
	Tenneco	$7\frac{1}{2}$	12.33
	Tenneco	$7\frac{3}{4}$	12.77
	Kraftco	$7\frac{1}{2}$	12.27
	Continental Oil	8	15.83
	Transocean Gulf	$7\frac{1}{2}$	12.50
	Firestone	$7\frac{3}{4}$	11.83
	Philip Morris	$6\frac{3}{4}$	9.87
	Goodyear	$7\frac{1}{4}$	10.44
	Teledyne	$7\frac{1}{4}$	10.44
Swiss franc	Burroughs	$6\frac{1}{4}$	12.31
	Standard Oil (California)	$6\frac{1}{4}$	12.42
	Goodyear	7	13.69
	American Brands	$6\frac{1}{2}$	13.08
	Texaco	$6\frac{3}{4}$	13.37
	Cities Services	$7\frac{1}{4}$	19.27
Dutch guilder	General Electric	$8\frac{1}{4}$	20.08
	GTE	$8\frac{1}{4}$	19.44
	IBM	8	16.46
	Cities Service	8	17.65
	International Harvester	8	17.65
	Philip Morris	$7\frac{1}{2}$	12.67
	Sperry Rand	$6\frac{1}{2}$	10.44
	Holiday Inns	$6\frac{1}{2}$	10.62
	Teledyne	$6\frac{1}{4}$	10.27
	Standard Brands	$6\frac{1}{2}$	10.85
	Textron Atlantic	$6\frac{3}{4}$	11.21
Pound Sterling	Amoco	8	5.29
Luxembourg franc	International Standard Electric	$6\frac{1}{2}$	7.85

Source: William R. Folks, Jr, and Josef Follpracht, "The Currency of Denomination Decision for Offshore Long-Term Debt: The American Experience," Working Paper, Center for International Business Studies, University of South Carolina, 1976.

the examination ends, but it does show that what may appear to be a cheap debt may end up being expensive.

Because of the potential for large unanticipated costs when borrowing by issuing bonds in currencies that rapidly appreciate, some nontrivial advantage may be required before any added exposure by foreign-currency borrowing is considered worthwhile. In such a case, our criteria (18.2) and (18.3) need some modification. For example, if management determines that any added foreign exchange exposure and risk will be worth taking only with an expected 2 percent saving, we must revise condition (18.2) to the following.

$$r_\$ > r_£ + \dot{S}^*(\$/£) + 0.02 \qquad (18.4)$$

Only when (18.4) holds will the expected borrowing cost be sufficiently lower in pounds to warrant borrowing in that currency. For example, if $r_\$$ is 10 percent, $r_£$ is 14 percent, and $\dot{S}^*(\$/£)$ is −5 percent (a 5-percent-per-annum expected depreciation of the pound), then the exposure and risk of borrowing in pounds will not be warranted, for although the criterion (18.2) is met, the revised criterion (18.4) is not.

When foreign-currency bonds do add to exposure and risk, the required risk premiums will have to be established by management. During times of greater economic uncertainty and potential volatility in foreign exchange markets, higher premiums should generally be required to compensate for the greater risk. Borrowing in a foreign currency involves risk because the actual rate of change of the exchange rate, $\dot{S}(\$/£)$ in the dollar–pound case, will in general differ from the *ex ante* expectation, $\dot{S}^*(\$/£)$. If $\dot{S}(\$/£) > \dot{S}^*(\$/£)$ this will make the *ex post* borrowing cost greater than the *ex ante* cost.

For example, if as before we have $r_\$ = 10$ percent, $r_£ = 14$ percent, and $\dot{S}^*(\$/£) = -5$ percent, then by using the straightforward *ex ante* criteria in inequalities (18.2) and (18.3), we know that the US borrower facing these particular conditions should borrow in pounds. Suppose that this is done and that *ex post* we discover that $\dot{S}(\$/£) = -2$ percent. The actual cost of borrowing pounds will be

$$r_£ + \dot{S}(\$/£) = 0.14 - 0.02$$
$$= 0.12, \text{ or } 12\% \text{ per annum}$$

Having borrowed in pounds will in retrospect turn out to have been a bad idea vis-à-vis the 10 percent dollar interest rate.

In general, if it turns out that, $\dot{S}(\$/£)$ the actual per annum change in the exchange rate, has been such that

$$r_£ + \dot{S}(\$/£) > r_\$$$

then we know that borrowing in pounds was a mistake. We see that it is necessary to compare the actual, not the expected, per annum change in the exchange rate with the interest differential. A management-determined risk premium such as the 0.02 premium we used in writing the revised criterion in inequality (18.4) will help to ensure that correct decisions are made. The larger the required premiums, the more often the decision will in retrospect appear correct, but larger premiums also mean missing many opportunities, and they will never guarantee *ex post* correct decisions.

Borrowing with foreign-source income

There may be *less* foreign exchange exposure and risk involved in foreign-currency borrowing than in domestic-currency borrowing when the borrower is receiving income in foreign exchange and is facing a long exposure in the foreign currency. That is, foreign-currency receivables can require a *negative* premium when borrowing in foreign exchange because exposure is reduced. We have already pointed out in Chapters 9 and 12 that firms receiving foreign income can hedge by borrowing foreign funds in the money market. The point is even more valid with long-term borrowing and is extremely important for firms which have sizable foreign operations. When a steady and predictable long-term income is received in foreign currency, it makes sense from a hedging perspective to denominate some long-term payments in that same currency. The amount of debt that should be denominated in each foreign currency will depend on the size of income in that currency, and also on the extent that the firm's income is exposed. As we showed in Chapter 11, the exposure depends on the elasticity of demand, the flexibility of production, the proportion of inputs that are tradable, and so on. That is, it is not simply a matter of borrowing enough in a foreign currency so that debt payments match income in the currency, although that would be the case when the foreign-currency income is contractual.

An example of a situation where the sale of bonds denominated in foreign exchange will reduce foreign exchange exposure and risk involves a Canadian firm that sells Canadian resources in world markets at contracted amounts in US dollars.[13] If lumber or coal is sold by the Canadian firm to, for example, the US or Japanese market at prices stated in US dollars, then the firm faces a long exposure in US dollars, and it makes good sense for the firm to borrow in New York, Europe, or Canada in US dollars. Then the repayments on the debt can come out of the firm's US dollar revenues. Alternatively, losses on the dollars earned after a US dollar depreciation are matched by a gain in the form of reduced debt when this is translated into Canadian dollars. Similarly, if an Australian manufacturer is selling to Japan in yen, it makes sense to borrow with yen-denominated bonds, or if a Venezuelan oil exporter is selling to Chile in dollars, it makes good sense to borrow by selling US-dollar-denominated bonds in the Eurobond market or in the United States.

Tax considerations

Bond buyers who pay a lower tax rate on capital gains than on interest income prefer a dollar of capital gain from foreign-currency appreciation to a dollar of interest income. This means that if, for example, the dollar-bond interest rate was equal to the yen-bond rate plus an expected appreciation of the yen, the yen bond would be preferred by lenders because it provides expected capital gain from an appreciation of the yen. *Ceteris paribus*, bond buyers who pay a lower tax rate on capital gains than on interest income prefer bonds denominated in strong currencies – those that the market expects to appreciate. Such bonds provide a higher after-tax return. On the other hand, bond issuers who can deduct the full cost of their bonds as an expense of doing business will be

indifferent between interest rates and expected changes in exchange rate. This will lead to borrowing in strong currencies. Let us explain this by an example. The example assumes a particular tax situation to illustrate one possibility. Other assumptions will produce different outcomes.

Suppose that

$$r_\$ = 12\% \qquad r_\yen = 5\% \qquad \dot{S}^*(\$/\yen) = 6\%$$
$$\tau_K = 0.2 \qquad \tau_Y = 0.4$$

where $\dot{S}^*(\$/\yen)$ is the expected appreciation of the Japanese yen by both bond issuers and buyers, $r_\yen$ is the interest rate on yen bonds, τ_K is the tax rate on foreign exchange gains of bond buyers, and τ_Y is the tax rate on ordinary income, including interest income, of both bond buyers and bond issuers. The after-tax expected returns from US dollar and yen bonds to bond *buyers* are

$$\text{Dollar bond: } (1 - \tau_Y)r_\$ = (1 - 0.4) \times 0.12$$
$$= 7.2\%$$
$$\text{Yen bond: } (1 - \tau_Y)r_\yen + (1 - \tau_K)\dot{S}^*(\$/\pounds)$$
$$= (1 - 0.4) \times 0.05 + (1 - 0.2) \times 0.06$$
$$= 7.8\%$$

The buyers therefore prefer yen bonds to dollar bonds; they yield more after tax. However, to *borrowers* who can deduct the full cost of bond financing – interest plus exchange-rate movements – against income, the after-tax costs are

$$\text{Dollar bond: } (1 - \tau_Y)r_\$ = (1 - 0.4) \times 0.12$$
$$= 7.2\%$$
$$\text{Yen bond: } (1 - \tau_Y)r_\yen + (1 - \tau_Y)\dot{S}^*(\$/\pounds)$$
$$= (1 - 0.4) \times 0.05 + (1 - 0.4) \times 0.06$$
$$= 6.6\%$$

Bond issuers therefore also prefer yen bonds. We see that tax factors can explain the popularity of strong-currency-denominated bonds – those widely expected to appreciate – among bond buyers and bond sellers.

---

13 Most natural-resource exports – oil, coal, gas, minerals, and lumber – are sold at US dollar prices. This reduces the foreign exchange problem for US-based firms that sell or buy natural resources when compared to foreign firms.

Other bond-financing considerations

Issue cost

As is the case with equities, bond flotation costs are lower in some financial markets than in others. Because flotation costs are nontrivial, the differences in costs between financial markets can influence the country in which bonds are floated.[14] Firms should approach a number of bond underwriters situated in different countries before determining where to issue bonds. With markets in most of the European financial centers, as well as in Asia and North America, and with considerable variation in the flotation costs within and between these financial centers, the benefits of shopping around can be substantial.

Issue size

Another factor bond issuers should consider when issuing bonds is the size of the issue relative to the sizes of issues handled in different markets. The New York and London capital markets can handle very large individual bond issues. In many of the other capital markets of the world, a $200 million bond issue would be considered large, and a $500 million bond issue would be huge. In New York or London, such issues are not uncommon. Indeed, the volume of funds handled by some of the bigger institutions such as the pension funds and insurance companies is such that these institutions can often buy an entire bond issue that is privately placed with them. Private placements offer one the means of reducing issue costs of an intermediary, although of course, an intermediary will be required to bring the borrowing and lending partners together. The bond-issue size that the New York and London markets can handle and the lower costs of issuing bonds under private placement make New York and London attractive markets for large American and foreign borrowers, even when the interest cost is a little higher than elsewhere.[15]

Multicurrency bonds

Types of multicurrency bonds

Not all Eurobonds are denominated in a single currency. Rather, some Eurobonds are **multicurrency bonds**. Some multicurrency bonds give the lender the right to request repayment in one or two or more currencies. The amounts of repayment are often set equal in value at the exchange rates in effect when the bond is issued. If, during the life of the bond, exchange rates change, the lender will demand payments in the currency that has appreciated the most or depreciated the least. This reduces the risk to the lender in that it can help him or her avoid a depreciating currency. It does, however, add to the borrower's risk.

A variant of the multicurrency Eurobond using pre-established fixed exchange rates is the **unit-of-account bond**, such as the European Currency Unit (ECU) bond. The ECU is a weighted "basket" of the fifteen European currencies that existed before twelve of the countries adopted the euro, with interest in the ECU having been greatly diminished by the new common currency. The idea of denominating bonds in a "cocktail" of currencies is to reduce the risk from individual exchange-rate changes; the currency unit is a portfolio of currencies and enjoys

---

14 Rodney Mills and Henry Terrell have shown that front-end fees on Eurobonds on an interest-equivalent basis account for an average of approximately 20 percent of 1 year's annual return, and vary between 9 percent and 43 percent. See Rodney H. Mills and Henry S. Terrell, "The Determination of Front-End Fees on Syndicated Eurocurrency Credits," International Finance Discussion Paper Number 250, Board of Governors of the Federal Reserve System, Washington, DC, undated.

15 The importance of transaction costs and the size of borrowing in encouraging Canadian borrowers to look at the U.S. capital market is examined by Karl A. Stroetmann in "The Theory of Long-Term International Capital Flows and Canadian Corporate Debt Issues in the United States," unpublished PhD dissertation, University of British Columbia, 1974.

EXHIBIT 18.3 SPECIAL DRAWING RIGHTS (SDRs)

The International Monetary Fund describes the valuation and role of SDRs as follows.

> The value of the SDR was initially defined as equivalent to 0.888671 grams of fine gold-which, at the time, was also equivalent to one U.S. dollar. After the collapse of the Bretton Woods system in 1973, however, the SDR was redefined as a basket of currencies, today consisting of the euro, Japanese yen, pound sterling, and U.S. dollar. The U.S. dollar-value of the SDR is posted daily on the IMF's website. It is calculated as the sum of specific amounts of the four currencies valued in U.S. dollars, on the basis of exchange rates quoted at noon each day in the London market.

> The basket composition is reviewed every five years to ensure that it reflects the relative importance of currencies in the world's trading and financial systems. In the most recent regular review that took place in October 2000, the method of selecting the currencies and their weights was revised in light of the introduction of the euro as the common currency for a number of European countries, and the growing role of international financial markets. These changes became effective on January 1, 2001.

Source: International Monetary Fund, Washington, DC. Item is available at http://www.imf.org/external/np/exr/facts/sdr.htm

---

diversification advantages. Another unit-of-account that is still in use today is Special Drawing Rights (SDRs). The SDR is based on the value of the US dollar, the euro, Japanese yen, and British pound – the four most widely traded currencies. It is described in Exhibit 18.3.

Currency cocktails can offer significant savings. For example, in January 1981 the rate on a 5-year SDR-denominated bond offered by Nordic Investment Bank was approximately 11.5 percent, while at the same time the rate on a straight 10-year US dollar bond offered by Du Pont of Canada was 13.69 percent, and the rate on a 7-year bond offered by GM's offshore finance subsidiary, General Motors Acceptance Corporation (or GMAC) Overseas Finance N.V., was 12.87 percent. While the rates are not strictly comparable, the lower rate on the SDR bond shows that investors value the diversification of individual currency exchange-rate risk provided by currency cocktails. They will be particularly desirable during unstable times.[16]

16 For more on SDR bonds, see "Slimmed Down SDR Makes Comeback: Techniques Include Opening Up Market for Negotiable SDR CDs," *Money Report*, Business International, January 16, 1981.

The rationale for multicurrency bonds

Bond buyers can form their own multicurrency bond portfolios by combining different bonds, each of which is denominated in a single currency. Because this is possible, it is worth asking why some firms have found it advantageous to issue multicurrency bonds. The answer must be that there are limitations faced by some bond buyers in forming their own portfolios. One possible limitation is that the total wealth they have to allocate to bonds is too small to achieve significant diversification, which in turn depends on there being economies of scale when buying bonds; if the costs do not increase as smaller amounts of bonds are bought, the bond buyers can form diversified portfolios of separate bonds as cheaply as buying multicurrency bonds. This size-of-wealth limitation may be a major consideration with bonds, which are frequently sold only in very large minimum denominations.

An example of multicurrency denomination of a lease contract rather than a bond involved the Australian carrier Qantas Airlines. In 1980 Qantas arranged to lease two Boeing 747s from an owner who was willing to accept multicurrency payment. The lease required payment in German marks, Dutch guilders, Australian dollars, and pounds sterling – all currencies that the airline received in its business. With this arrangement, Qantas could match the multicurrency nature of its income with the payments on the lease. If Qantas had bought rather than leased the planes, it could have matched the currencies of incomes and payments by financing the planes with a currency-cocktail Eurobond requiring repayment in the various currencies of income.

The vehicle of bond issue

Whether the bond that is issued is a Eurobond, foreign bond, or domestic bond, and whether it is denominated in a single currency or in several currencies, a decision must be made either to issue the bond directly as a liability of the parent company, or to issue it indirectly through a financing subsidiary or some other subsidiary. Companies issue bonds via an overseas subsidiary if they do not want the bonds to be an obligation of the parent company. This has the additional advantage of reducing country risk if some of the subsidiary's bonds are held locally (see Chapter 17). However, because the parent is almost invariably viewed as less risky than subsidiaries, the reduction in the parent's liability and also in country risk must be traded off against the fact that the interest rates that must be paid are generally higher when having a subsidiary issue bonds.

BANK FINANCING, DIRECT LOANS, AND THE LIKE

So far we have examined international aspects of equity and bond financing. We have stated that gains on selling equity in one market rather than another or simultaneously in several markets – Euroequities – depend on the segmentation versus integration of markets. We have also stated that bonds may be sold in a foreign-currency denomination in the country using that currency (foreign bonds) or in countries not using the denomination currency (Eurobonds). The ability to select the currency of issue can lower

borrowing costs but can also introduce foreign exchange exposure and risk because forward markets are not always available for hedging on bonds with long maturities. However, a firm might actually reduce foreign exchange exposure and risk by borrowing in a foreign currency if it has an income in that currency.

A large part of the financing of foreign subsidiaries of MNCs involves neither bonds nor equity. According to a survey of foreign direct investors by the US Department of Commerce, approximately half of the financing of US-based MNCs was generated inside the corporation.[17] The results of the survey are summarized in Table 18.2. If anything, the true percentage of internally generated funds is probably larger than the percentage shown because, according to a different survey by Sidney Robbins and Robert Stobaugh, lending and borrowing by different subsidiaries net out in the Commerce Department's financial survey.[18] Robbins and Stobaugh estimated that the total for outstanding loans was $14 billion. This amount is much larger than the amount quoted for loans outstanding to the parent companies in the Commerce Department's survey. We can note from Table 18.2 that subsidiaries raise little equity. The debt incurred by subsidiaries is almost 20 times the equity they themselves raise.

When a subsidiary borrows from its parent, because this is a transfer within the MNC, there is no increase in the expected cost of bankruptcy which is usually considered to be a factor limiting the debt/equity ratio of a firm. (Firms prefer debt to equity because interest on debt is tax deductible, but too much debt means a higher chance of

17 US Department of Commerce, Office of Foreign Direct Investments, *Foreign Affiliate Financial Survey*, 1966–69, July 1971. This study has not been revised, because the office that prepared it was eliminated; but the proportion of funds generated within the corporation has probably not changed greatly.

18 Sidney M. Robbins and Robert B. Stobaugh, "Financing Foreign Affiliates," *Financial Management*, Winter 1973, pp. 56–65.

Table 18.2 *Sources of funds for subsidiaries*

	Billions of dollars		Percentage	
From within the multinational enterprise		6.1		60
Internally generated by affiliate	4.7		46	
Depreciation	2.9		29	
Retained earnings	1.7		17	
From parent	1.4		14	
Equity	1.0		9	
Loans	0.5		5	
From outside the multinational enterprise		4.0		40
Loans	3.9		39	
Equity	0.2		2	
Total		10.1		100

Source: US Department of Commerce, Office of Foreign Direct Investments, *Foreign Affiliate Financial Survey, 1966–1969,* July 1971, p. 34.

bankruptcy.) A subsidiary is able to deduct its interest payments from income when computing corporate tax, while the parent treats the interest as income. This has an advantage if the subsidiary's tax rate is higher than that of the parent. However, the incentive to use all intra-MNC debt to finance a subsidiary is limited by the need to rationalize the interest rate charged to the subsidiary. According to Bhagwan Chowdhry and Vikram Nanda, subsidiaries use some external debt to justify the interest rate charged on internal debt.[19]

According to the survey by Robbins and Stobaugh mentioned above, most MNCs prefer to use intra-company credit rather than discretionary loans. This is because credit requires less documentation than does a discretionary loan and because there are potential gains from avoidance of withholding tax on credit advances, whereas withholding by the foreign government is likely on interdivisional loans.

Some of the earliest work in financing subsidiaries, done by Edith Penrose, revealed a varying financial structure as MNCs' subsidiaries grew larger.[20] Penrose argued that after receiving initial help from the parent company, subsidiaries move onto an independent growth path using funds from retained earnings and local borrowing. James Hines has suggested that the motivation to provide initial help from the parent is limited by the rational expectation that rather than repatriate future income and pay taxes, multinationals will prefer to reinvest subsidiary income in further expansion.[21] This view is consistent with that of Penrose: subsidiary self-financing expands with time. Hines argues that the incentive to minimize initial help in order to preserve future investment opportunities for a subsidiary is highest when foreign corporate income tax rates are low vis-à-vis parent rates.

Some of the debt raised outside companies takes on a character which is peculiarly international. For example, only in the international arena do we find the so-called "back-to-back" or parallel loans.

19 Bhagwan Chowdhry and Vikram Nanda, "Financing of Multinational Subsidiaries: Parent Debt vs. External Debt," *Journal of Corporate Finance,* August 1994, pp. 259–81.

20 Edith T. Penrose, "Foreign Investment and the Growth of the Firm," *Economic Journal,* June 1956, pp. 220–35. Reprinted in John H. Dunning (ed.), *International Investment,* Penguin Books, Harmondsworth, UK, 1972.

21 James R. Hines, Jr, "Credit and Deferral as International Investment Incentives," *National Bureau of Economic Research,* Working Paper w4574, May 1994.

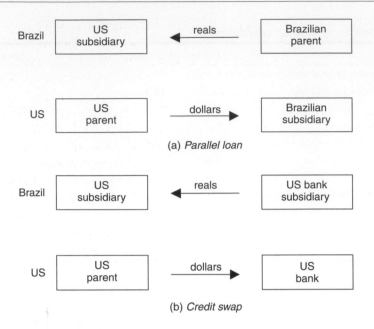

Figure 18.1 *Parallel loans and credit swaps*

Notes
A parallel loan involves two companies, whereas a credit swap involves one company and a bank. In both cases the companies and/or banks are located in two countries. Both types of financing avoid money flows between the countries. Parallel loans are more difficult to arrange than credit swaps because the parties must find each other. In the case of a credit swap, the parent or its subsidiary contacts a bank.

Parallel loans

A **parallel loan** involves an exchange of funds between firms in different countries, with the exchange reversed at a later date. For example, Figure 18.1a shows a situation in which a US company's subsidiary in Brazil needs Brazilian reals while a Brazilian company's subsidiary in the United States needs dollars. The Brazilian firm can lend reals to the US-owned subsidiary in Brazil while it borrows an approximately equivalent amount of dollars from the US parent in the United States.[22] After an agreed-upon term, the funds can be repaid. There is no exchange-rate risk or exposure for either firm, because each is borrowing and repaying in the same currency. Each side can pay interest within the country where funds are lent according to the relevant going market rates.

The advantages of parallel loans over bank loans are that they can circumvent foreign exchange controls and that they help avoid banks' spreads on borrowing versus lending and on foreign exchange transactions. The problem with parallel loans is locating the two sides of the deals. As in other barter-type deals, the needs of the parties must be harmonious before a satisfactory contract can be achieved. While the banks might well know of financing needs which are harmonious, they have little incentive to initiate a deal which avoids their spreads. Consequently, a large portion of parallel loans are arranged by brokerage houses rather than banks.

22 The loan agreement could just as well involve subsidiaries of the Brazilian and US firms in a different country. For example, the US firm might lend the Brazilian firm dollars in New York, while a German subsidiary of the Brazilian firm lends euros to a German subsidiary of the US firm.

Credit swaps

A **credit swap** involves the exchange of currencies between a bank and a firm rather than between two firms. It is an alternative method of obtaining debt capital for a foreign subsidiary without sending funds abroad. In a credit swap the parent makes funds available to a bank at home. For example, a US firm may place US dollars in an account in New York. The US bank then instructs one of its foreign subsidiaries to lend foreign currency to a subsidiary of the parent that made the deposit. For example, an office of the US bank in Rio de Janeiro might lend reals to a subsidiary of the US firm operating in Brazil: see Figure 18.1b. As with parallel loans, a major advantage of credit swaps is that they allow firms (and banks) to circumvent foreign exchange controls. In addition, they allow the parent and subsidiary to avoid foreign exchange exposure: the parent deposits and receives US dollars in our example, while the subsidiary borrows and receives Brazilian reals.

GOVERNMENT AND DEVELOPMENT-BANK LENDING

It is not at all uncommon for financing to be provided by governments or development banks. Because government and development-bank financing is generally at favorable terms, many corporations consider these official sources of capital before considering the issue of stock, the sale of bonds, loans from commercial banks, or parallel loans from other corporations.

Host governments of foreign investments provide financing when they believe projects will generate jobs, earn foreign exchange, or provide training for their workers. There are numerous examples of loans being provided to MNCs by the governments of, for example, Australia, Britain, Canada, and Spain, to attract manufacturing firms to make investments in their countries. Sometimes the state or provincial governments also offer financing, perhaps even competing with each other within a country to have plants built in their jurisdiction. Several US states have provided cheap financing and other concessions to induce Japanese and other foreign firms to establish operations. Canadian provincial and Australian state governments have

also used special financing arrangements to attract investors.

Even though the governments of poorer countries do not usually have the means to offer concessionary financing to investors, there are a number of development banks which specialize in providing financing for investment in infrastructure, for irrigation, and for similar projects. While this financing is usually provided to the host government rather than to corporations involved in the construction of the projects, the corporations are indirectly being financed by the development-bank loans to the host governments.

A leading provider of financial assistance is the International Bank for Reconstruction and Development (IBRD), commonly known as the **World Bank**. The World Bank, which was established in 1944, is not a bank in the sense of accepting deposits and providing payment services on behalf of countries. Rather, it is a lending institution that borrows from governments by selling them its bonds, and then uses the proceeds for development in undeveloped (or developing) nations. World Bank or IBRD loans have a maturity of up to 20 years. Interest rates are determined by the (relative low) cost of funds to the bank.

Many developing countries do not meet the conditions for World Bank loans, so in 1960 an affiliated organization, the **International Development Agency (IDA)**, was established to help even poorer countries. Credits, as the loans are called, have terms of up to 50 years and carry no interest charges. A second affiliate of the World Bank is the **International Finance Corporation (IFC)**. The IFC provides loans for private investments and takes equity positions along with private-sector partners.

OTHER FACTORS AFFECTING THE FINANCING OF SUBSIDIARIES

We have presented a number of international financial considerations affecting bond and equity decisions and decisions involving bank loans, parallel loans, and credit swaps. There are, however, a number of other factors which can affect the financing decision. Frequently these are based on the politically sensitive nature of a large amount of FDI. Sometimes, however, they are based on concern for exchange-rate risk or on restrictions imposed by host governments. We shall quickly mention some of the more notable factors.

The freezing or seizing of assets by inhospitable governments should not be a worry to those who borrow abroad. Instead, it should be a concern to the investors whose assets are lost. It might therefore be thought that while political risks are important in the investment decision, they are relatively inconsequential in the borrowing decision. However, some firms may borrow abroad in the countries of investment *because* they fear confiscation or expropriation. If assets are seized, these firms can refuse to repay local debts and thereby reduce their losses. Furthermore, the probability of confiscation or expropriation may be reduced by having foreign private bondholders or shareholders. Unfortunately, as we have noted, it may be difficult to raise equity or even debt from local private sources.

Generally, the more financing is denominated in local currency of income, the lower the danger from changing exchange rates. This supports the use of debt. Reinforcing the tendency toward using debt is the greater political sensitivity with regard to repatriating income on equity than with regard to receiving interest on debts. However, offsetting the factors leading to more debt is the fact that if equity is kept small, profits can look unreasonably high on the equity invested in foreign operations. The profit rate on equity can be used in claims of exploitation by foreign governments.

Certain governments require that a minimum equity/debt ratio be maintained, while some banks also set standards to maintain the quality of debt. According to Sidney Robbins and Robert Stobaugh, US firms have generally kept their equity well above that required by local regulations.[23] However, this does not mean that local regulations are not binding. Firms may keep their equity higher than necessary as a cushion against any future need to borrow.

When earnings are retained abroad, US corporations can postpone the payment of US corporate income taxes and foreign withholding taxes on income from subsidiaries. According to Walter Ness, the saving from the deferral of tax payments lowers the cost of equity capital for multinational corporations and induces the corporations to have a lower debt/equity ratio in financing foreign subsidiaries.[24] However, according to Ian Giddy and Alan Shapiro, the alternatives for repatriating income via pricing of inter-subsidiary trades, royalties, and interdivisional fees override any advantage from deferred tax payments encouraging the use of equity capital.[25]

FINANCIAL STRUCTURE

Subsidiary or parent determination of financial structure

If the success or failure of an overseas subsidiary has little or no effect on the ability of the parent or other subsidiaries to raise capital, decisions on financial structure can be left to subsidiaries.[26] A subsidiary can then weigh the various economic and political pros and cons of different sources of funds and adopt a financial structure that is appropriate for its own local circumstances. However, if

23 Robbins and Stobaugh, op. cit.

24 Walter L. Ness, Jr, "U.S. Corporate Income Taxation and the Dividend Remittance Policy of Multinational Corporations," *Journal of International Business Studies*, Spring 1975, pp. 67–77.

25 Alan C. Shapiro, "Financial Structure and the Cost of Capital in Multinational Corporations," Journal of Financial and Quantitative Analysis, June 1979, pp. 211–26; Ian H. Giddy, "The Cost of Capital in the Multinational Firm," unpublished paper, Columbia University, 1976.

26 By financial structure we mean the composition of a firm's sources of capital. That is, financial structure involves the amount of equity, versus bond debt, versus bank debt, versus credit swaps, and so on.

there are spillovers from the failure of a subsidiary which reduce the financing opportunities of the parent or its other subsidiaries, decisions on subsidiary financial structure should be made by the parent. Full consideration should be given to the implications of a default by one subsidiary for global operations. Because spillovers will exist if the parent is legally or morally bound to support subsidiaries, we should consider the evidence on corporate responsibility for subsidiary debt.

Survey evidence shows clearly that even when not bound by legal guarantees on subsidiary-incurred debt, parent firms rarely if ever admit they will allow a subsidiary to default. For example, in a survey by Robert Stobaugh, all 20 of the large MNCs in the sample, and all but one of the smaller MNCs, said they would not allow a subsidiary to default whatever the circumstances.[27] Similar responses were received in later surveys conducted by Business International.[28] This evidence suggests that multinationals realize that a default in a subsidiary will affect operations elsewhere. There is no other obvious explanation for the almost universal willingness to support subsidiaries.

With a parent company having a *de facto* obligation to honor debt incurred by its subsidiaries, the parent must monitor its subsidiaries' debt/equity ratios as well as the corporation's overall debt/equity ratio. This does not, however, mean that a parent should keep its subsidiaries' debt/equity ratios equal to its own overall preferred debt/equity ratio. For example, subsidiaries facing high country risk and no ability to raise local equity capital might be allowed to take on relatively high debt loads. Similarly, subsidiaries in countries with relatively high tax savings from deducting interest but not dividend payments should be allowed to

take on relatively large amounts of debt to exploit the tax shield that debt provides. All the time, however, a parent company should make compensating adjustments to the capital structure of itself and its other subsidiaries so that the company's global debt/equity ratio is maintained at the level it deems appropriate. (Recall from Chapter 16 that borrowing capacity is a firm-level choice variable, and incurring higher or lower levels in one project/country requires compensation in debt levels elsewhere in the company's operations.)

Capital structure in different countries

Financial structure varies from country to country. This is seen in Table 18.3. Possible reasons for the

Table 18.3 Mean and standard deviation of debt to asset ratios, sorted by type of legal system: group mean in parentheses.

	Mean	Standard deviation
German Civil Law (0.61)		
Austria	0.65	0.34
Germany	0.41	0.36
Japan	0.62	0.28
Korea	0.80	0.17
French Civil Law (0.56)		
France	0.56	0.34
Netherlands	0.49	0.29
Italy	0.65	0.35
Spain	0.57	0.26
Scandinavian Civil Law (0.49)		
Denmark	0.57	0.32
Finland	0.55	0.26
Norway	0.47	0.27
Sweden	0.43	0.29
English Common Law (0.42)		
Australia	0.54	0.33
Canada	0.39	0.27
United Kingdom	0.56	0.34
United States	0.39	0.26
Overall (0.46)		

Source: Joon Y. Song and George C. Philippatos, "Revisiting Variations in International Capital Structure: Empirical Evidence from 16 OECD Countries," Conference of the Eastern Finance Association, Mystic, CT, 2004.

27 Robert B. Stobaugh, "Financing Foreign Subsidiaries of U.S.-Controlled Multinational Enterprises," *Journal of International Business Studies*, Summer 1970, pp. 43–64.

28 See "Policies of MNC's in Debt/Equity Mix," *Money Report*, Business International, 1979, and "Determining Overseas Debt/Equity Ratios," *Money Report*, Business International, 1986.

variations can be found in explanations of capital structure commonly advanced in a domestic context. These explanations hinge on the tax deductibility of interest payments but not dividends, and on bankruptcy and agency costs.

Countries in which interest payments are deductible against corporate taxes will, *ceteris paribus*, have relatively high debt/equity ratios. However, if interest rates are particularly high *because* borrowers can deduct interest and lenders must pay tax on interest, this will militate against the advantage of debt.[29]

The risk and expected cost of bankruptcy increase with the amount of debt.[30] If expected costs of bankruptcy are lower in some countries than others, debt/equity ratios will, *ceteris paribus*, be higher in the countries with low expected bankruptcy costs. In countries where banks are both providers of debt and holders of companies' equity, the probability of bankruptcy is relatively low because the banks are likely to help in times of trouble. It follows that in countries such as Japan and Germany, where banks hold considerable amounts of equity, debt/equity ratios are higher than in countries such as the United States and Canada, where banks provide debt but little or no equity. Indeed, Table 18.3 shows Canada and the United States as having low debt ratios.

Lenders know that once they have made loans to firms, the managers of the firms will be more concerned with taking care of their own and their shareholders' well being than with protecting the lenders' interests. This is one of the agency costs of debt, and because lenders are aware of this cost, they demand corresponding high interest rates on their loans. These high interest rates reduce typical debt/equity ratios. The greater is the agency cost of debt, the lower is the typical debt/equity ratio. Agency costs are reduced when banks hold directorships in firms, because they can then very directly represent their interests as creditors when attending board meetings. The high degree of horizontal integration in Japan, where banks and manufacturers are frequently subdivisions of the same giant MNC, has greatly reduced agency costs, and this, combined with reduced expected bankruptcy costs, probably explains Japan's high debt-to-equity ratio.

Even though there does seem to be differences between countries in financial structure, with these having been attributed to tax deductibility as well as the country's legal system and other factors, it has been suggested that these differences are small compared to the variations across industries with countries, and idiosyncratic variations across firms within industries.[31] An indication of this is evident from Table 18.3 which shows the standard deviations of debt ratios in OECD countries as well as their means. Recalling that 95 percent of a normal distribution is between approximately two standard deviations either side of the mean, the distribution of debt ratios in every country is extremely broad. In many cases, the 95-percent interval includes zero and extends beyond twice the mean. This is immediately suggestive that within each country, industry and firm-specific effects are more important than country effects.[32]

---

29 An account of the effect of differential tax shields that considers the role of both corporate and individual income tax rates has been provided by Moon H. Lee and Josef Zechner, "Debt, Taxes, and International Equilibrium," *Journal of International Money and Finance*, December 1984, pp. 343–55. Lee and Zechner point out that in order to have an advantage in debt, corporate tax rates relative to individual tax rates must be higher in one country than in other countries. This is because high individual tax rates on interest earnings push up interest rates and thereby reduce the attractiveness of debt. For debt to be attractive the corporate deductibility needs to be high relative to the extent interest rates are pushed higher by individual tax rates.

30 The expected cost of bankruptcy depends on the probability that bankruptcy will occur as well as on legal and other costs if it does occur.

31 See the paper by Joon Y. Song and George C. Philippatos, "Revisiting Variations in International Capital Structure: Empirical Evidence from Sixteen OECD Countries," Conference of the Eastern Finance Association, Mystic, CT, 2004.

32 See Joon Y. Song and George C. Philippatos, op. cit. for this line of argument.

SUMMARY

1   If capital markets are internationally integrated, the cost of capital should be the same wherever the capital is raised.

2   If capital markets are segmented, it pays to raise equity in the country in which the firm can sell its shares for the highest price. It may also pay to consider selling equity simultaneously in several countries; such shares are called Euroequities.

3   Low issuance costs may make some markets better than others for selling shares. Generally, the costs of selling shares are lowest in big financial markets such as New York.

4   Firms must decide on the best vehicle for issuing equity and raising other forms of capital. In particular they must determine whether capital should be raised by the parent company or a financing subsidiary.

5   A foreign bond is a bond sold in a foreign country and in the currency of that country. A Eurobond is a bond in a currency other than that of the country in which it is sold.

6   Firms must decide on the currency of issue of bonds. All foreign-pay bonds are by definition in a foreign currency for the firm, and many Eurobonds are also in a foreign currency for the firm.

7   Large gains or losses are possible from denominating bonds in currencies that are not part of a firm's income. For this reason a risk premium may be demanded before speculating by issuing foreign-currency-denominated bonds.

8   When a firm has foreign-currency income, foreign-currency borrowing reduces exchange-rate exposure. Therefore, a firm may be prepared to pay higher interest on a foreign-currency-denominated bond than on a bond denominated in domestic currency.

9   When bond buyers face lower tax rates on foreign exchange gains than on interest income, it may pay to issue strong-currency bonds. These will have relatively low interest rates because they offer bond buyers part of their return as capital gain.

10   Bond issuers should consider costs and sizes of bond issues when determining the country of issue.

11   Bonds denominated in two or more different currencies, called multicurrency or currency-cocktail bonds, will appeal to lenders if there are costs associated with forming portfolios of bonds denominated in single currencies.

12   A substantial proportion of financing of overseas subsidiaries is provided from within multinational corporations.

13   Parallel loans are made between firms. They are particularly useful when there are foreign exchange controls.

14   Credit swaps are made between banks and firms. They are also a way of avoiding foreign exchange controls.

15   Political risk can be reduced by borrowing in countries in which investment occurs; this tends to increase debt/equity ratios of subsidiaries.

16   Because parent companies tend to honor subsidiaries' debts whether legally obligated to do so or not, a parent company should monitor subsidiaries' debt/equity ratios as well as its own global debt/equity ratio. Nevertheless, parent companies should allow variations in debt/equity ratios between subsidiaries to take advantage of local situations.

17 If a country has a high debt/equity ratio, this can be because of high tax shields on debt, or low bankruptcy or agency costs.

18 The links between banks and corporations in Japan, Germany, and some other countries may explain the high debt/equity ratios in these countries. However, it does appear in general from the within-country variations in financial structure that industry- and firm-specific influences on financial structure are more important than country effects.

REVIEW QUESTIONS

1 What do integrated capital markets imply for the decision of where to raise capital?
2 What is a Euroequity?
3 What is an American Depository Receipt?
4 What is a foreign bond?
5 What is a Eurobond?
6 Under what condition will a risk-neutral borrower borrow pounds?
7 Why might some borrowers pay *more* to borrow foreign rather than domestic currency?
8 Why are strong-currency bonds preferred by lenders facing lower tax rates on capital gains than on interest income?
9 What is the advantage of a multicurrency bond to lenders?
10 What is a parallel loan?
11 What is a credit swap?
12 How does country risk affect parent versus subsidiary borrowing?
13 How does liability for debt affect parent versus subsidiary borrowing?
14 How might the extent of equity ownership by banks in different countries affect financial structure differences between countries?

ASSIGNMENT PROBLEMS

1 Why might a firm want to issue shares simultaneously in a number of financial centers?
2 How can the availability of savings and the opportunities for investment influence the cost of capital in different countries?
3 Is a US dollar bond sold by a British firm in the United States a foreign bond or a Eurobond? How about a pound bond sold by a British firm in the United States?
4 Why do Canadian firms borrow so heavily in US dollars?
5 When lenders are more optimistic about the future value of a currency than borrowers, what do you think this implies about the likelihood of debt denomination in that currency?
6 How is the tax shield on debt mitigated by a high tax rate on interest earnings, thereby making debt/equity ratios in different countries depend on individual income versus corporate tax rates?

7 With $r_\$ = 12.50$ percent, $r_£ = 14.00$ percent, $S(\$/£) = 2.25$, and $S^*_{10}(\$/£) = 1.50$, in which currency would you borrow? What is the expected gain on each $1 million borrowed from making the correct choice?

8 If $r_\$ = 12.50$ percent, $r_£ = 14.00$ percent, and $S(\$/£) = 2.25$, what must the actual exchange rate after 10 years, $S_{10}(\$/£)$, be in order to make borrowing in pounds a good idea?

9 Why does having an income in foreign currency reduce required borrowing risk premiums? What type of risk – translation/transaction risk or operating risk – is reduced?

10 What determines whether you would issue a Eurosterling bond or a sterling bond (i.e. a foreign bond) in Britain?

BIBLIOGRAPHY

Brown, Robert L., "Some Simple Conditions for Determining Swap Feasibility," unpublished, Monash University, Australia, 1986.

Chowdhry, Bhagwan, and Vikram Nanda, "Financing of Multinational Subsidiaries: Parent Debt vs. External Debt," *Journal of Corporate Finance*, August 1994, pp. 259–81.

Edwards, Franklin R., "Listing of Foreign Securities on U.S. Exchanges," *Journal of Applied Corporate Finance*, Winter 1993, pp. 28–36.

Hodder, James E., "Hedging International Exposure: Capital Structure under Flexible Exchange Rates and Expropriation Risk," unpublished, Stanford University, Stanford, CA, 1982.

—— and Lemma W. Senbet, "International Capital Structure Equilibrium," unpublished, Stanford University, Stanford, CA, 1988.

Lee, Moon H. and Josef Zechner, "Debt, Taxes, and International Equilibrium," *Journal of International Money and Finance*, December 1984, pp. 343–55.

Lessard, Donald R. and Alan C. Shapiro, "Guidelines for Global Financing Choices," *Midland Corporate Finance Journal*, Winter 1983, pp. 68–80.

Marr, Wayne, John L. Trimble, and Raj Varma: "Innovation in Global Financing: The Case of Euroequity Offerings," *Journal of Applied Corporate Finance*, Spring 1992, pp. 50–4.

Nauman-Etienne, Rudiger, "A Framework for Financial Decisions in Multinational Corporations – A Summary of Recent Research," *Journal of Financial and Quantitative Analysis*, November 1974, pp. 859–75.

Ness, Walter L., Jr, "A Linear Approach to Financing the Multinational Corporation," *Financial Management*, Winter 1972, pp. 88–100.

Remmers, Lee, "A Note on Foreign Borrowing Costs," *Journal of International Business Studies*, Fall 1980, pp. 123–34.

Shapiro, Alan C., "Financial Structure and the Cost of Capital in the Multinational Corporation," *Journal of Financial and Quantitative Analysis*, June 1978, pp. 211–26.

——, "The Impact of Taxation on the Currency-of-Denomination Decision for Long-Term Foreign Borrowing and Lending," *Journal of International Business Studies*, Spring 1984, pp. 15–25.

Stonehill, Arthur, Theo Beekhuisen, Richard Wright, Lee Remmers, Norman Toy, Antonio Pares, Douglas Egan, and Thomas Bates, "Financial Goals and Debt Ratio Determinants: A Survey of Practice in Five Countries," *Financial Management*, Autumn 1975, pp. 27–41.

Toy, Norman, Arthur Stonehill, Lee Remmers, Richard Wright, and Theo Beekhuisen, "A Comparative International Study of Growth, Profitability, and Risk as Determinants of Corporate Debt Ratios in the Manufacturing Sector," *Journal of Financial and Quantitative Analysis*, November 1974, pp. 875–86.

Wihlborg, Clas, "Economics of Exposure Management of Foreign Subsidiaries of Multinational Corporations," *Journal of International Business Studies*, Winter 1980, pp. 9–18.

Part VI

Institutional structure of international trade and finance

The theory and practice of international finance described in the preceding chapters are built on an institutional framework which is shaped and defined by important private and government institutions. This part of the book describes these institutions and the functions they serve.

The first of the two chapters in Part VI deals with multinational banking. While banks are frequently ignored when considering multinational corporations – for example, Table 17.1, which is a standard table of MNCs, lists only *nonfinancial corporations* – banking is the epitome of an industry that is multinational in nature. When we focus on, for example, the countries in which operations occur and where foreign direct investments have been made, banks are more widespread than firms from just about any other industry, and their effects are as pervasive as their territorial coverage.

An important activity of banks is the acceptance of deposits, and here the multinational dimension is both fascinating and controversial. Chapter 19 begins by looking at "offshore deposits," often simply but inaccurately called "Eurodollars," and explains what they are, where they come from, and what they imply for regulatory agencies. After describing alternative views of the creation and relevance of offshore deposits, the chapter deals with the organization of international banking. We then explain why banking

has become multinational, and conclude with a discussion of anxieties that have been expressed about the fragility of international banking due to "derivatives" trading and a discussion of the "deregulation wars" that have radically changed the activities in which banks are engaged.

Chapter 20 looks at the structure, instruments, and institutions of international trade. No course in international finance is complete without an explanation of the nature and role of letters of credit, bills of exchange, payments drafts, bills of lading, waybills, and other such documents. The chapter explains how methods of payment and trade credit have evolved to meet the special needs of international trade. Several forms of export financing are explained, including short-term credits involving delayed payment dates on bills of exchange, and medium-term credits involving forfaiting. We also discuss a form of trade called countertrade and why it is used.

Chapter 20 ends with a description of the institutions that monitor and regulate international trade, such as the World Trade Organization (WTO), which replaced the General Agreement on Tariffs and Trade (GATT) in January 1995. Since a substantial portion of international trade is between partners of free-trade pacts such as the members of the European Union and the NAFTA, a brief overview of free-trade arrangements is given.

Chapter 19

Multinational banking

Think global, act local.

Theodore Levitt

Currencies have leaped beyond their traditional boundaries, so that today it is possible to write checks in US dollars against bank accounts in Tokyo, or to write checks in Japanese yen against bank accounts in New York. Indeed, bank accounts in different currencies exist side by side in just about every financial center, so that in, for example, London, we find bank accounts in dollars, yen, euros, Swiss francs, and every other major currency. Similarly, it has become possible to arrange loans in US dollars in Hong Kong or in euros in Sydney. The growth rate of these so-called "offshore currency" deposits and loans has been nothing short of startling, and is part of the increased globalization of financial markets, in general, and of the banking industry, in particular.

Spearheading the growth of offshore currencies and loans was the appearance of Eurodollars in the 1950s. Despite several decades of study of the causes and consequences of the emergence of Eurodollars, there are few topics in international finance that have attracted as much controversy and disagreement. The most important parts of this disagreement center on the extent banks can create Eurodollars and the danger Eurodollar creation involves. We shall attempt to give a balanced view of these issues and shall also explain the many aspects of Eurodollars, and more generally of offshore currencies, on which there is

consensus. Then we shall describe the nature of the banks which deal in the offshore currency market. However, before we begin, we should define what we mean by "Eurodollars" and "offshore currencies."

THE EURODOLLAR AND OFFSHORE CURRENCY MARKETS

What are Eurodollars and offshore currencies?

Here is a short, accurate definition:

A Eurodollar deposit is a US-dollar-denominated bank deposit outside the United States.

Hence, a dollar-denominated bank deposit in Barclays Bank in London or in Citibank in Singapore is a Eurodollar deposit, while a dollar deposit in Barclays or Citibank in New York is not.[1] Offshore currency deposits are a generalization of Eurodollars and include other externally held currencies. For example, a Eurosterling deposit is a pound-denominated bank deposit held outside Britain, and

---

1 The Singapore market is also referred to as part of the Asiadollar market that includes Hong Kong, Tokyo, and other centers.

a Euroyen deposit is a Japanese-yen deposit held outside Japan.

The existence of the offshore currency market means that in making hedged or covered investment and borrowing decisions such as those described in Chapter 8 or Chapter 14, there is no need to go to the different currency centers to arrange deals. For example, an American investor could compare covered 3-month yields on dollars, sterling, euros, yen, and various other currencies in London and arrange for investment or borrowing in the currency of his or her choice in that single market. Moreover, as we shall see later in this chapter, the multinational nature of banks means that this American, dealing in London in foreign currencies, might well be trading with an American bank. The larger US, British, Japanese, French, German, and Swiss banks, along with many others, maintain sizable operations in the larger money-market offshore currency centers. As we explained in Chapter 8, the ease of comparing yields on different currency-denominated deposits with banks and their deposits side-by-side in many centers has resulted in covered yields being very similar: see Table 8.1.

Why did Eurodollar deposits develop?

In order to explain why Eurodollars developed and why later other offshore currency deposits became popular, we must explain why holders of US dollars preferred to keep them in banks located outside the United States rather than in the United States. We must also explain why borrowers of US dollars arranged their loans with banks located outside the United States rather than with banks in the United States.

The original establishment of Eurodollar accounts is usually credited to the former Soviet Union, although in reality its role was probably rather small.[2] During the 1950s, the Soviet Union found itself selling gold and some other products in order to earn US dollars. These dollars were to be

used to purchase grain and other western products, many of which came from the United States. What were the Moscow Narodny bank and its fellow financial institutions to do with dollars between the time they were received and the time they would be needed? Of course, banks in New York were willing to take them on deposit. This, however, was generally unacceptable to the Soviets because of the risk that the dollars might be frozen if the cold war became hotter. Also, placing dollars in New York banks would have meant that the Soviet government was "making loans" to capitalist banks, which would channel the funds to other capitalist enterprises. So instead of using New York banks as the place of deposit for their dollars, the Soviets made their dollars available to banks in Britain and France. In turn, the British and French banks took the Soviet dollars and lent them out at interest. This partly involved making loans in the United States by buying US treasury bills, private commercial and financial paper, and so on.[3] With the interest earned on these investments, the dollar-accepting banks in Europe were able to pay interest on the Soviet deposits.

As intriguing as the covert Soviet role in the creation of Eurodollars may sound, in reality the development and expansion of the offshore currency market had its roots in more overt events. We can classify these events as affecting the supply of deposits moving to the Eurodollar market or affecting the demand for loans from Eurodollar banks.

The supply of Eurodollar deposits

The role of bank regulation

During the 1960s and 1970s, US banks and other deposit-taking institutions were subject to limitations on the maximum interest rates they could offer on deposits. The most notable of these

---

2 See especially Gunter Dufey and Ian Giddy, *The International Money Market*, Prentice-Hall, Englewood Cliffs, NJ, 1978.

3 The truth, therefore, is that the Soviet government was, via British and French banks, making loans to the US government, defense manufacturers, and so on.

limitations came from the US Federal Reserve Board's Regulation Q. Banks in London and other global financial centers were not subject to such interest limitations, and so were able to pay more on US dollar deposits than US-based banks could. With higher interest rates offered on dollars deposited in London and other financial centers than in the United States, there was an obvious incentive to deposit dollars outside the United States. This was particularly true for large deposits such as those of US multinational corporations. Several US banks opened overseas offices to receive these funds. Most US interest-rate restrictions were removed after the mid-1970s, but to the extent that limitations were effective before that time, they contributed to the flow of US dollars abroad. The dollars placed abroad to avoid US interest ceilings on deposits were reinvested, often back in the United States.

The supply or availability of Eurodollar deposits also grew from the advantage for US banks in moving operations overseas to avoid Federal Reserve Regulation M. This regulation required the keeping of reserves against deposits. Until 1969, this regulation did not apply to deposits of overseas branches of US banks (and since 1978 this regulation has not applied to such deposits). Since reserves mean idle funds, the cost of operations overseas was reduced vis-à-vis the cost of operations in the United States. This encouraged US banks to move some of their depositors' accounts, including the accounts of many Americans, to the relatively unregulated overseas market, principally to London and other large European financial centers. Also, the absence of reserve requirements and other troublesome Federal Reserve regulations, such as the need to pay for deposit insurance on deposits held in the United States, has allowed US banks operating overseas to offer higher interest rates on dollar deposits.[4]

4 Banks operating in tax havens such as the Cayman Islands and the Netherlands Antilles had an additional advantage of paying low corporate income taxes. This allowed them to cover operating costs with a lower spread between deposit and lending rates.

The role of convenience

Since the late 1960s, growth in Eurodollars has come from sources other than Federal Reserve and US government regulations. For example, Eurodollars are more convenient for some depositors than dollars that are in the United States. Europeans and other non-Americans have uneven cash flows in US dollars. On some occasions, they have dollar inflows, and on others, they have dollar outflows. They could, of course, sell the dollars for their home currency when their inflows are large and repurchase dollars with the home currency when outflows are large. However, this involves transaction costs. Alternatively, these non-Americans could leave their dollars in banks in the United States. However, this means dealing with bankers who are thousands of miles away and possibly unfamiliar with the customers' problems. It is easier to keep the dollars in a bank with offices close by which can respond quickly to the customers' needs. Therefore, the offshore currency market has expanded at a rapid rate. The convenience of Eurodollars is, of course, augmented by the higher yields available on them due to the absence of reserve requirements and deposit insurance mentioned earlier.

The demand for Eurodollar loans

Borrowing regulations

Eurodollars could have developed without a local desire to borrow the funds left on deposit, but the banks would have been required to recycle their Eurodollar holdings back into the US money market. However, as a result of limitations in the 1960s and 1970s on obtaining loans within the United States that did not apply overseas, a demand for borrowing US funds outside the United States was created. This encouraged the growth of Eurodollars on the asset side of the overseas banks' balance sheets. The controls and restrictions on borrowing funds in the United States for reinvestment abroad began with a voluntary restraint program in 1965.

This was followed by mandatory controls in 1968. These controls forced many borrowers to seek sources of loans in the Eurodollar market, and the loans were often arranged with US banks.

Another regulation affecting foreign demand for Eurodollar loans was the US interest equalization tax, introduced in 1963 and in effect until 1974. This was a tax on US residents' earnings on foreign securities. To encourage US residents to lend to foreign borrowers, the foreigners were forced to offer higher yields in order to cover this tax. By channeling funds via Eurodollars, the interest equalization tax was avoided, and this allowed lower interest rates to be offered by the Eurobanks.

With deposits going abroad to escape Regulation Q, banks going abroad to escape Regulation M and US Federal Reserve requirements such as deposit insurance, and with borrowing going abroad to escape the interest equalization tax and credit and direct investment controls, the Eurodollar market expanded very rapidly. Furthermore, despite the removal of most of the regulations, taxes, and controls in the 1970s the Eurodollar market continued to grow.

Convenience again

Considerations of convenience affected the demand for Eurodollars as well as the supply of Eurodollars. Taking Eurodollar loans is often more convenient than taking loans in the United States. The same is true for other currency loans; it is sometimes more convenient to arrange for them locally instead of in a currency's home market. Local bankers know the creditworthiness and talents of local borrowers in a way that is rarely possible for distant bankers. Consequently, instead of taking dollar loans in New York, sterling loans in London, and so on, borrowers take loans in the different currencies in their local market.

The role of narrow spreads

In the final analysis, the most important factor affecting the supply of and demand for Eurodollars is the desire of dollar depositors to receive the highest yield and the desire of dollar borrowers to pay the lowest cost. Because of the absence of reserve requirements, deposit-insurance requirements, and other costly regulations, the Eurobanks can offer higher yields on dollar deposits than can US banks. At the same time, the Eurobanks can charge lower borrowing costs. The lower interest rates on loans are made possible by the absence of severe regulations and by the sheer size and number of informal contacts among the Eurobanks. These factors are important advantages in making large loans. Higher rates to depositors and lower costs to borrowers mean operating on narrower spreads. Nevertheless, the Eurobanks are left with profits despite the lower spreads because of their lower costs. While the growth of the Eurodollar market is best attributed to the ability of the Eurobanks to operate on a narrow spread, this has not always been the accepted explanation.

The role of US deficits

During the early period of development of the Eurodollar market, the market's growth was often attributed to US trade deficits. A trade deficit does mean that dollars are being received and accumulated by non-Americans. This does not, however, have much to do with the expansion of Eurodollar deposits. The dollars being held by non-Americans could be placed in banks within the United States or invested in US financial securities. Eurodollar deposits will grow only if the dollars are kept in overseas banks. Similarly, the Eurodollar market will not disappear if the United States runs trade surpluses. We need the reasons given above, such as convenience and liberal offshore banking regulations, for the Eurodollar market to exist. As long as banks located outside the United States offer greater convenience and/or operate on smaller spreads than banks operating within the United States, they will continue to prosper.

Markets for other Eurocurrencies

The same factors that are behind the emergence and growth of the Eurodollar market are behind the emergence and growth of the markets in other Eurocurrencies. For example, Japanese-yen deposits and loans are found in London and New York because British and American businesses have found it more convenient to make yen deposits and arrange yen loans locally than in Japan, and because banks in London and New York can avoid restrictions faced by banks in Tokyo. Similarly, the market for euro-denominated securities in London is vast. The restrictions that are avoided by operating overseas vary from country to country and have generally become less important in recent years with the global trend towards the deregulation of banking. The role of convenience has increased as a result of the growth in importance of international trade versus domestic trade. As more international trade comes to be denominated in the Japanese and European currencies, we can expect more deposits and loans to be denominated in these currencies in offshore currency market.

Determination of offshore currency interest rates

Offshore currency interest rates cannot differ much from rates offered on similar deposits in the home country. If this were not so there would be arbitrage, with borrowing in the low interest-rate location and lending in the high interest-rate location. As a result of the potential for arbitrage the rate offered to Eurodollar depositors is only slightly higher than in the United States, and the rate charged to borrowers is only slightly lower. Each country's market interest rates influence the offshore currency interest rates and vice versa. The total supply of each currency in the global market, together with the total demand, determines the rate of interest. As a practical matter, however, each individual bank bases its rates on the rates it observes in the market in which it competes.

The interest rates charged to borrowers of Eurocurrencies are based on **London Interbank Offer Rates (LIBOR)** in the particular currencies. LIBOR rates are those offered in interbank

transactions (i.e. when banks borrow from each other) and are the base rates for non-bank customers. LIBOR rates are calculated as the averages of the lending rates in the respective currencies of leading London banks. Non-bank borrowers are charged on a "LIBOR-plus" basis, with the interest premium based on the creditworthiness of the borrower. For example, a corporation might be offered a loan at LIBOR plus 2 percent. With borrowing maturities of over 6 months, a floating interest rate is generally charged. Every 6 months or so, the loan is rolled over, and the interest rate is based on the current LIBOR rate. This reduces the risk to both the borrower and the lender (the bank) in that neither will be left with a long-term contract that does not reflect current interest costs. For example, if interest rates rise after the credit is extended, the lender will lose the opportunity to earn more interest for only 6 months. If interest rates fall after a loan is arranged, the borrower will lose the opportunity to borrow more cheaply for only 6 months. With the lower interest-rate risk, credit terms frequently reach 10 years.

Different types of offshore currency instruments

Offshore currency deposits are primarily conventional term deposits, which are bank deposits with a fixed term, such as 30 days or 90 days. The interest rate is fixed for the term of the deposit, and this keeps the maturity of deposits short.

Not as important as any of the individual offshore currency denominations, but nevertheless of some importance, are the offshore currency deposits denominated in Special Drawing Rights (SDRs). As mentioned in Chapter 18 and explained in Exhibit 18.3, SDRs were originally introduced as central-bank reserve assets by the International Monetary Fund. SDR term deposits were first offered by Chemical Bank in London. Like the bulk of other offshore deposits, SDR-denominated deposits are mostly nonnegotiable term deposits.

427

A relatively small proportion of the liabilities of offshore banks are not term deposits, but instead take the form of **certificates of deposit (CDs)**. Unlike offshore currencies in the form of term deposits, the CDs are negotiable instruments that can be traded in a secondary market. This makes the CDs more liquid than term deposits, which have a penalty on early withdrawal. In the case of US dollars approximately 20 percent of offshore bank liabilities are CDs, the balance being conventional term deposits. Since 1981, some London-based banks have offered SDR-denominated CDs as well as conventional deposits. The banks that first offered the SDR-denominated CDs were Barclays Bank International, Chemical Bank, Hong Kong and Shanghai Bank (HSBC), Midland Bank (now part of HSBC), National Westminster Bank, and Standard Chartered Bank.[5]

An expansion of offshore currency operations within the United States has been made possible by rules allowing the establishment of **international banking facilities (IBFs)**. The IBFs are, in effect, a different set of accounts within an existing bank; they date back to 1981. The facilities can accept foreign-currency deposits and are exempt from both US reserve requirements and insurance premiums on deposits as long as the deposits are used exclusively for making loans to foreigners. Two days' notice for withdrawals is required. These facilities compete with other countries' offshore currency banks and have brought some of the offshore business back to the United States.

Offshore banks generally remain well hedged. They accept deposits in many different currencies, and they also have assets in these same currencies. When they balance the two sides of their accounts with equal volumes and maturities of assets and liabilities in each currency of denomination, they are perfectly hedged and therefore unaffected by changes in exchange rates. Sometimes it is difficult to balance the maturities of assets and liabilities, and

until 1981 this situation involved banks in risk. However, since 1981 banks have been able to avoid risk from unbalanced maturities in US dollars by using the Eurodollar futures market at the International Monetary Market operated by the Chicago Mercantile Exchange. Since the early 1980s banks and other financial institutions have also been able to use the Eurodollar futures markets of the Chicago Board of Trade, the New York Futures Exchange, the London International Financial Futures Exchange, and the Singapore Exchange. It is worthwhile to explain the risk from unbalanced maturities and the way this can be avoided with Eurodollar futures.

Suppose that a bank accepts a 3-month Eurodollar deposit of $1 million on March 1 at 4 percent and at the same time makes a Eurodollar loan for 6 months at 5 percent. In June, when the 3-month deposit matures, the Eurobank must refinance the 6-month loan for the remaining 3 months. If by June the deposit rate on 3 month Eurodollars has risen above 4 percent, the spread on the remaining period of the loan will be reduced. To avoid this risk, on March 1, when making the 6-month loan, the bank could sell a 3-month Eurodollar future for June. (On the International Monetary Market in Chicago, contracts are traded in $1 million denominations for March, June, September, and December.) If by June the Eurodollar rates have gone up, the bank will find that it has made money on the sale of its Eurodollar future. This follows because, as in the bond market, purchases of interest-rate futures (long positions) provide a profit when interest rates fall, and sales (short positions) provide a profit when interest rates rise. The profit made by the bank in selling the Eurodollar future will offset the extra cost of refinancing the 6-month Eurodollar loan for the remaining 3 months.

Offshore banks perform "intermediation" when they convert offshore currency deposits into, for example, commercial or government loans. This term is used because the banks are intermediaries between the depositors and the borrowers. If the two sides of the offshore bankers' accounts are equally liquid — that is, if the IOUs they

---

5 See "Slimmed-Down SDR Makes Comeback; Techniques Include Opening Up Market for Negotiable SDR CDs," *Money Report*, Business International, January 16, 1981.

purchase are as marketable as their offshore currency deposits – then according to the view of some researchers, the banks have not created any extra liquidity or "money."[6] However, it could happen that the original foreign currency that was deposited in a bank is redeposited in other banks before finding its way back to the home country. In this way we can have a total of offshore currency deposits that is a multiple of the original deposit. Before demonstrating how we can have an offshore currency multiplier we should state that this remains a topic of considerable controversy, and there is even some dispute over whether Eurodollar multipliers can be defined at all.[7]

Redepositing and multiple offshore currency expansion

Let us construct a situation in which a multiple expansion of offshore deposits does occur. Assume that a British exporter, Britfirm A, receives a $100 check from an American purchaser of its products and that this check is drawn against a US bank. This is an original receipt of dollars in Europe. Assume that Britfirm A does not need the dollars immediately but that it will need them in 90 days. The $100 is held in Britfirm A's account in a British bank as a dollar term deposit, that is, a Eurodollar. The British bank will, after accepting the check from Britfirm A, send the check to the US bank with which it deals. The British bank will be credited with $100.

The $100 deposit in the British bank probably will not be removed during the term of the deposit, since removing it would involve a substantial interest penalty for Britfirm A. The British bank will therefore look for an investment vehicle that approximately matches the term of Britfirm A's deposit. Suppose that the British bank decides to maintain a cash reserve of 2 percent with an American bank and discovers a British firm, Britfirm B, which wishes to borrow the remaining $98 for 90 days to settle a payment with an Italian supplier, Italfirm A. The British bank will give to Britfirm B a check for $98 drawn against the British bank's account at the US bank and payable to Italfirm A. We have the situation in the top part of Table 19.1. (If the dollars are loaned to a US borrower, as they could well be, the effects end here with the British bank merely intermediating, that is, serving as go-between for the depositor and the borrower.)

On receiving the check from Britfirm B, Italfirm A will deposit it in its account at an Italian bank, which will in turn send it for collection to the United States. If the Italian bank deals with the same US bank as the British bank, all that will happen in the United States is that $98 will be removed from the British bank's account and credited to the Italian bank's account. The British bank's account with the US bank will be reduced to $2. The British bank's account will have the entries shown in Table 19.1; it will show the $100 Eurodollar deposit offset by a $2 reserve and a $98 IOU. (If the British and Italian banks maintain reserves at different US banks, the outcome will be the same after US interbank clearing.) We see that the clearing of Eurodollars takes place in New York, with the banks in the United States merely showing different names of depositors after Eurodollars have been transferred. Originally, they showed the owner of the dollars who paid Britfirm A. Afterwards, the US banks showed the British bank and then the Italian

6 This is the view in Jurg Niehans and John Hewson, "The Euro-Dollar Market and Monetary Theory," *Journal of Money, Credit and Banking*, February 1976, pp. 1–27.

7 The controversy began after the publication of Milton Friedman's article "The Euro-Dollar Market: Some First Principles," (*Morgan Guarantee Survey*, October 1969, pp. 4–14, reprinted with clarifications in *Review*, Federal Reserve Bank of St. Louis, July 1971, pp. 16–24). Friedman treated the Eurodollar multiplier as a conventional domestic banking multiplier, and this prompted a criticism from Fred H. Klopstock ("Money Creation in the Euro-Dollar Market: A Note on Professor Friedman's Views," *Monthly Review*, Federal Reserve Bank of New York, January 1970, pp. 12–15). The controversy expanded with the publication of Niehans and Hewson's paper (see note 6). Gunter Dufey and Ian H. Giddy have introduced a variety of multipliers (*The International Money Market*, Prentice-Hall, Englewood Cliffs, NJ, 1978). We will use the conventional multiplier and treat the question in the conventional way.

Table 19.1 *Change in balance sheets from $100 of primary deposits*

Bank	Assets		Liabilities	
British	Deposit in US bank	+ $2.00	Term deposit of	
	Loan to Britfirm B	+ $98.00	Britfirm A	+ $100.00
		+ $100.00		+ $100.00
Italian	Deposit in US bank	+ $1.96	Term deposit of	
	Loan to Italfirm B	+ $96.04	Italfirm A	+ $98.00
		+ $98.00		+ $98.00
Dutch	Deposit in US bank	+ $1.92	Term deposit of	
	Loan to Dutchfirm B	+ $94.12	Dutchfirm A	+ $96.04
		+ $96.04		+ $96.04
Canadian	Deposit in US bank	+ $1.88	Term deposit of	
	Loan to Canafirm B	+ $92.24	Canafirm A	+ $94.12
		+ $94.12		+ $94.12

bank as the depositor. Since only the names change, nothing happens inside the United States to increase or decrease the number of loans.

After Italfirm A deposits the check in the Italian bank, the Italian bank will have a $98 deposit at the US bank to offset its Eurodollar liability to Italfirm A. Like its British counterpart, it will not leave the funds idle. Let us suppose that it maintains 2 percent, or $1.96, in the US bank, and lends the balance of $96.04 to Italfirm B. The loan will be effected by the Italian bank's drawing a check for $96.04 against its US bank account on behalf of Italfirm B. We assume that this check is made payable to Dutchfirm A.

If Dutchfirm A deposits the check in a Dutch Eurodollar term account, the Italian bank will be left with $1.96 in reserves in the US bank. The Dutch bank will be credited with $96.04. We now assume that the Dutch bank keeps 2 percent of the $96.04 deposit, that is, $1.92, as a cash reserve, and lends the balance of $94.12 to Dutchfirm B by drawing a check on Dutchfirm B's behalf to Canafirm A. After Canafirm A deposits the check, the Dutch bank will have $1.92 in reserves, and the Canadian bank with which the check is deposited will have $94.12. If the Canadian bank lends Canafirm B 98 percent of this, or $92.24, and Canafirm B pays an American company that banks

in the United States, then the process of Eurodollar creation will end. The Canadian bank will have its account in its US bank reduced by $92.24 and will be left with 2 percent, or $1.88, against its Eurodollar deposit of $94.12. The books are balanced, and every bank is in its desired position of having a 2-percent reserve backing its Eurodollar deposit, with the remaining 98 percent out as loans. By the time the Eurodollar creation comes to an end, there is a total of $100.00 + $98 + $96.04 + $94.12, or $388.16, in Eurodollars. The original deposit of $100 has grown 3.8816 times, and this might be called the Eurodollar multiplier vis-à-vis the original $100 base. However, the $388.16 in Eurodollars vis-à-vis *the reserves still remaining in Eurobanks* – that is, $2 + $1.96 + $1.92 + $1.88, or $7.76, gives a **deposit ratio** of 50. That is, $388.16 is 50 times the remaining dollar reserves of $7.76. This is what we would expect with a reserve ratio of 0.02, since each $1 of reserves supports $50 of deposits.

The interesting magnitude is not the deposit ratio but rather the multiplier, which is the expansion on the base of the original deposit. Only if there are no leakages back to the United States will the multiplier be as large as the deposit ratio. If funds deposited in the Euromarket are loaned back in the United States at the outset, the leakage is immediate and the Eurobank is merely intermediating.

The rate of leakage depends on how extensively US dollars are used for settling payments between parties outside the United States. The more any currency is used between offshore parties, the larger the multiplier is likely to be.

When dollar loans offered by commercial banks outside the United States are made to central banks, a leakage back to the United States is almost certain to occur. Central banks tend to hold their dollars in US banks or place them in US treasury bills. This will drain any extra dollar reserves back into the US banking system. However, when many central banks kept dollars at the Bank for International Settlements (BIS) in Basle, Switzerland, in the 1960s, the leakage back to the United States did not occur. The BIS frequently reinvested in the Eurodollar market and thus contributed to the expansion of Eurodollars.

Estimates of the value of the Eurodollar multiplier vary. As we have seen, the value of the multiplier depends on the definition and on the speed with which funds return to the United States. Fred Klopstock estimates that the leakage back to the United States is so rapid that the multiplier is about 1.05–1.09. Alexander Swoboda gives a value of about 2.00, which is close to the estimates of Boyden Lee. John Hewson and Eisuke Sakakibara find a range of 3–7, whereas John Makin has produced estimates from 10.31 to 18.45.[8] Clearly, the larger estimates must refer to deposits-to-reserve ratios rather than the Eurodollar multiplier and are incorrect as multiplier estimates.

8 These estimates are found in Boyden E. Lee, "The Eurodollar Multiplier," *Journal of Finance*, September 1973, pp. 867–74; John Hewson and Eisuke Sakakibara, "The Eurodollar Multiplier: A Portfolio Approach," *IMF Staff Papers*, July 1974, pp. 307–28; Fred H. Klopstock, "Money Creation in the Euro-Dollar Market: A Note on Professor Friedman's Views," *Monthly Review*, Federal Reserve Bank of New York, January 1970, pp. 12–15; John H. Makin, "Demand and Supply Functions for Stocks of Eurodollar Deposits: An Empirical Study," *Review of Economics and Statistics*, November 1972, pp. 381–91; and Alexander K. Swoboda, *The Eurodollar Market: An Interpretation*, Essays in International Finance, no. 64, Princeton University Press, Princeton, NJ, 1968.

MULTINATIONAL BANKING

The multinationalization of banking

Offices of foreign-owned banks are becoming commonplace in financial districts of larger cities and towns. In the United States, for example, 547 foreign banks had offices in 2004. US foreign bank assets in 2004 topped $1.3 trillion. Banks are competing in each others' markets for the share of deposits and loans. For example, as Figure 19.1 shows, foreign banks' share of US deposits is above 15 percent, while the share of assets is about 20 percent. Measured by loans to businesses, the presence of foreign banks is even more pronounced, with more than a quarter of such loans in the United States in 2001 coming from foreign banks (see Figure 19.2).

International banks are linked together in various formal and informal ways, from simply holding accounts with each other – correspondent accounts – to common ownership. As we shall see, the types of connections affect the nature of the business that the banks conduct.

Organizational features of multinational banking

Exhibit 19.1 describes the different forms of banking offices in the United States and their importance in the supply of financial capital. The various forms of banking organization are described in the following paragraphs.

Correspondent banking

An informal linkage between banks in different countries is set up when banks maintain correspondent accounts with each other. Large banks have correspondent relationships with banks in almost every country in which they do not have an office of their own. The purpose of maintaining foreign correspondents is to facilitate international payments and collections for customers. The term "correspondent" comes from the mail or cable communications that the banks used to use for

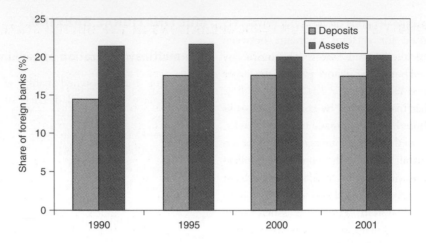

Figure 19.1 *Deposit and asset shares of foreign banks in the United States, 1990–2001*
Source: US Department of Commerce, Bureau of Census, *Statistical Abstract of the United States,* 2001.

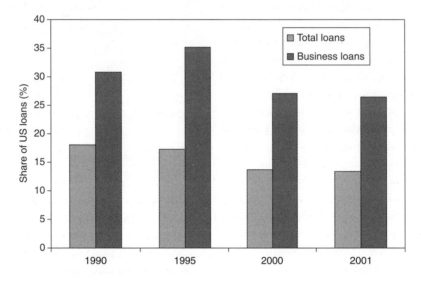

Figure 19.2 *Share of loans by foreign banks in the United States, 1990–2001*
Source: US Department of Commerce, Bureau of Census, *Statistical Abstract of the United States,* 2001.

settling customer accounts. Today, these communications have largely been replaced by SWIFT messages, and the settling between banks occurs via CHIPS or CLS.[9] For example, if Aviva wants to pay a Canadian supplier, it will ask its US bank, which will communicate with its Canadian correspondent bank via SWIFT. The Canadian bank credits the account of the Canadian firm, while Aviva's bank debits Aviva's account. The US and Canadian banks then settle through CHIPS, with the Canadian bank being credited with US dollars and Aviva's bank in the United States being debited the US dollars.

9 SWIFT, CHIPS, and CLS were discussed in Chapter 2. For more on how correspondent banking has been rationalized and reorganized through these message and bank-settlement systems see "On Correspondent Banking," *Euromoney,* December 1988, p. 115.

EXHIBIT 19.1 FOREIGN BANK OPERATIONS IN THE UNITED STATES

The following description of foreign bank operations in the United States, including their importance to the US financial system, is provided under the heading, "What is a Foreign Bank?" by the Conference of State Bank Supervisors.

Foreign banks most often come to the United States to provide services to U.S. subsidiaries of clients in their home countries. Once here, however, they provide a wide range of wholesale banking services to U.S. businesses and individuals. In fact, foreign banks make almost 40% of all loans to American businesses. As of December 31, 2002 state-licensed foreign banks held more than $1.15 trillion in assets, accounting for about 86% of all foreign bank assets in the United States. Consequently, foreign banks play a critical role in the economy and the U.S. banking systems.

Foreign banking organizations can acquire or establish freestanding banks or bank holding companies in the United States. These entities are regulated and supervised as domestic institutions. For most foreign banking organizations, however, it is more cost-effective and productive to operate as one of several other available structures: branches, agencies, loan production offices, representative offices, Edge Act or agreement corporations. Each structure has a different set of regulatory requirements and powers.

Branches and agencies are the most common structures for commercial lending by foreign banking organizations in the United States. Of the 547 foreign banks in America, 300 are branches or agencies. The major difference between these two types of banking offices is that branches may accept deposits, but agencies generally may not. Both structures can make and manage loans, conduct foreign exchange activities, and trade in securities and commercial paper. These offices may conduct most of the activities a domestic bank performs. The primary exception is that foreign branches and agencies may not accept deposits of less than $100,000 unless they had FDIC insurance before December 19, 1991 . . . The Federal Reserve serves as the federal regulator of state-licensed foreign bank branches and agencies, in a system similar to that for domestic banks.

Foreign banks may also establish representative offices, which have more limited powers than branches or agencies. Foreign banks often open representative offices as a first step to establish a presence in the United States. These offices serve as liaison between the parent bank and its clients and correspondent banks in the United States. They may develop relationships with prospective clients, but they cannot conduct any banking transactions themselves. Representative offices must register with the Federal Reserve, and may be licensed by the states as well.

Edge Act and agreement corporations are foreign bank offices chartered by the Federal Reserve (Edge Act) or the states (agreement corporations) to provide financing for international trade. Domestic banking organizations may also establish Edge Act or agreement corporations. These offices have a broader range of powers than other banking organizations, but all their activities must relate to international trade. Other structures available to foreign banks are commercial lending companies, licensed by New York State, and export trading companies.

To protect American consumers and the overall stability of the U.S. financial system, the states and the Federal banking agencies regulate and supervise foreign banking operations in the United States. The major Federal laws affecting foreign banks in the United States are the International Banking Act (IBA) of 1978 and the Foreign Bank Supervision Enhancement Act (FBSFA) of 1991. The Riegle–Neal Interstate Banking and Branching Efficiency Act of 1994 also addresses foreign banks' operations in the United States . . .

In short, foreign banks in the United States are valuable corporate citizens, and an essential part of the American financial system.

Source: "What is a Foreign Bank?" Conference of State Bank Supervisors, www.csbs.org/international/intl_foreign_bank.htm

Correspondent banking allows banks to help their customers who are doing business abroad, without having to maintain any personnel or offices overseas. This relationship is primarily for settling customer payments, but it can extend to providing limited credit for each other's customers and to setting up contacts between local businesspeople and the clients of the correspondent banks.

Resident representatives

In order to provide their customers with help from their own personnel on the spot in foreign countries, banks open overseas business offices called **representative offices**. These are not banking offices in the sense of accepting local deposits or providing loans. The primary purpose of these offices is to provide information about local business practices and conditions, including the creditworthiness of potential customers and the bank's clients. The resident representatives will keep in contact with local correspondent banks and provide help when needed. Representative offices are generally small; they have the appearance of an ordinary commercial office rather than a bank.

Bank agencies

A **bank agency** is like a full-fledged bank in every respect except that it does not handle small retail deposits. The agencies deal in the local money markets and in the foreign exchange markets, arrange loans for businesses, clear bank drafts and checks, and channel foreign funds into financial markets helping finance businesses and governments. Agencies are common in New York; for example, Canadian and European banks keep busy offices there, with perhaps several dozens of personnel dealing in the short-term credit markets and in foreign exchange. Agencies also often arrange

long-term loans for customers and act on behalf of the home office to keep it directly involved in the important foreign financial markets.

Foreign branches

Foreign branches are operating banks just like local banks, except that the directors and owners tend to reside elsewhere. Generally, foreign branches are subject to both local banking rules and the rules at home, but because they can benefit from loopholes, the extra tier of regulations is not necessarily onerous. The books of a foreign branch are incorporated with those of the parent bank, although the foreign branch will also maintain separate books for revealing separate performance, for tax purposes, and so on. The existence of foreign branches can mean very rapid check clearing for customers in different countries, because the debit and credit operations are internal and can be initiated by fax or electronic mail. This can offer a great advantage over the lengthy clearing that can occur via correspondents. The foreign branch also offers bank customers in small countries all the service and safety advantages of a large bank, which the local market might not be able to support.

There would probably be far more extensive foreign branch networks of the large international banks were it not for legal limitations imposed by local governments to protect local banks from foreign competition. Britain has traditionally been liberal in allowing foreign banks to operate and has gained in return from the reciprocal rules that are frequently offered. On the other hand, until the 1980 Canadian Bank Act was passed, the opening of foreign bank subsidiaries within Canada was prohibited, and branches of foreign banks are still restricted. The United States selectively allows foreign banks to operate. The regulation and supervision of foreign banks within the United States is provided for in the International Banking Act of 1978. This act allows the US Comptroller of the Currency to grant foreign banks a license to open branches (or agencies). The foreign banks can open wherever state banking laws allow them to. The banks are restricted to their declared "home state" and are subject to federally imposed reserve requirements when they are federally chartered.[10] They have access to services of the Federal Reserve and can borrow from its discount window. Since 1980, the foreign banks that accept retail deposits have been required to provide deposit insurance for customers. The foreign banks are relatively more important in providing commercial and industrial loans than in other investment activities.

Foreign subsidiaries and affiliates

A foreign branch is part of a parent organization that is incorporated elsewhere. A **foreign subsidiary** is a locally incorporated bank that happens to be owned either completely or partially by a foreign parent. Foreign subsidiaries do all types of banking, and it may be very difficult to distinguish them from an ordinary locally owned bank.

Foreign *subsidiaries* are controlled by foreign owners, even if the foreign ownership is partial. **Foreign affiliates** are similar to subsidiaries in being locally incorporated and so on, but they are joint ventures, and no individual foreign owner has control (even though a *group* of foreign owners might have control).

Consortium banks

Consortium banks are joint ventures of the larger commercial banks. They can involve a half dozen or more partners from numerous countries. They are primarily concerned with investment, arrange large loans, and underwrite stocks and bonds. Consortium banks are not concerned with taking deposits, and deal only with large corporations or perhaps governments. They will take equity positions — part ownership of an investment — as well as make loans, and they are frequently busy arranging takeovers and mergers.

Edge Act and agreement corporations

While US banks can participate in investment-bank consortia and may operate branches overseas, they cannot themselves have equity — direct ownership — in foreign banking subsidiaries. However, because of a 1919 amendment to the Federal Reserve Act initiated by Senator Walter Edge, US banks are able to establish subsidiaries for doing business "abroad." These subsidiaries, which are federally chartered, can have equity in foreign banks and are known as **Edge Act corporations**. They profit both from holding stock in subsidiaries overseas and by engaging in **investment banking** which involves borrowing and investing. Edge Act corporations engage in almost all the activities of banking: accepting deposits, making loans, exchanging currencies, selling government and corporate securities, and so on. They can invest in equity, while domestic banks are not allowed to.[11] A major impetus to the growth of Edge Act corporations has been that they enable a bank to open an office outside of its home state. The International Banking Act of 1978 allows *foreign* banks to open Edge Act corporations and accept deposits directly related to international transactions. There is no longer a rule that states that foreign-bank-owned Edge Act corporations will be permitted only if the directors of these corporations are US citizens. These changes in the International Banking Act were made to put foreign and US banks on a more equal footing.

---

10 Foreign as well as domestic banks can, however, operate outside their declared home states by establishing Edge Act subsidiaries. These are discussed later in this chapter.

11 In February 1988, the Federal Reserve Board made an exception when it allowed US banks to swap loans to governments of heavily indebted developing countries into equity investments. This was done to help the debtor countries and the US banks deal with the third-world debt crisis.

Agreement corporations are a little different from Edge Act corporations. The authority to establish agreement corporations dates from a 1916 amendment to the Federal Reserve Act. This allows banks that are members of the Federal Reserve System to enter into an agreement with that organization to engage in international banking. Agreement corporations, unlike Edge Act corporations, can be chartered by a state government, but they can only engage in international banking, not in general investment activities. There are very few agreement corporations.

US international banking facilities (IBFs)

We have already mentioned IBFs in connection with the Eurodollar market. Since 1981, US banks, Edge Act corporations, foreign commercial banks through branches and agencies in the United States, savings and loan associations, and mutual savings banks have been allowed by the Board of Governors of the Federal Reserve System to establish IBFs as adjunct operations.[12] The motive for this permission is to allow banks in the United States to participate in the lucrative offshore currency market. IBFs are not subject to domestic banking regulations, including reserve requirements and interest ceilings, and escape some local and state taxes. IBFs can accept deposits only from non-Americans and with a minimum size of $100,000. Withdrawals are also subject to a $100,000 minimum. Deposits cannot be withdrawn without at least 2 days' notice. However, overnight deposits can be offered to overseas banks, other IBFs, and the IBF's parent bank. Funds obtained by IBFs cannot be used domestically; they must be used overseas. To ensure that US-based companies and individuals satisfy this requirement, borrowers must sign a statement when they begin taking loans. Several hundred IBFs have been established, the majority in New York and California.

Why banking has become multinational

Through the opening of representative offices, agencies, and branches and through the acquisition or establishment of subsidiaries, banking has become a truly multinational enterprise. While reputation, regulation, and the other factors contributing to the multinationalization of business in general apply to banking, there are special factors that apply to banking alone. These include market information, borrower information, serving clients, custodial services, and regulation, all of which are discussed below.[13]

Market information

It might seem that with the rapid dissemination of information via modern subscription services such as Bloomberg, Reuters, Dow Jones Newswires, and Moneyline Telerate, which flash up prices and news developments on video screens at the speed of light, there is no need to have operations in expensive money centers such as London and New York. However, it is one thing to be plugged into the latest developments, but quite another to be able to interpret or even anticipate events. For being able to interpret what is happening and to get a sense of where markets are going there is nothing like having personnel on the spot in the big markets where important events are unfolding. For this reason we find a vast number of foreign banks with offices in the large money-market centers, especially London and New York. Many of these offices may not be profitable on their own, but by acting as eyes and ears for their parent banks, they improve the profitability of overall operations.

---

12 For more on IBFs see K. Alec Chrystal, "International Banking Facilities," *Review*, Federal Reserve Bank of St. Louis, April 1984, pp. 5–11.

13 For empirical evidence on the importance of some different factors for the evolution of multinational banking see Michael A. Goldberg, Robert W. Helsley, and Maurice D. Levi, "On the Development of International Financial Centers," *The Annals of Regional Science*, February 1988, pp. 81–94. For the evolution of the structure of international banking see Robert L. Heinkel and Maurice D. Levi, "The Structure of International Banking," *Journal of International Money and Finance*, June 1992, pp. 251–72.

Borrower information

When making loans abroad, banks could in theory take the word of a foreign bank such as a correspondent about the financial stability of a borrower, or send bank personnel to the borrower's country and review the borrower's finances on the spot. It can, however, be cheaper and more efficient to maintain local offices to gather "street talk," not only at the time of making a loan, but afterwards when the borrower's circumstances may suddenly deteriorate.

The importance of reliable information about borrowers has played a significant role in banking history and, in particular, in the relative success of early family banking houses. For example, it was no accident that the Rothschild bank did so well in the nineteenth century, after the founder, Mayer Rothschild of Frankfurt, posted his sons in the capitals of Europe. Mayer Rothschild could trust the reports coming from his sons about the quality of sovereign borrowers in a way that banks without "in house" overseas representation could not. Thus, in competition with banks with less reliable information, family banking houses such as the Rothschilds, Warburgs, and others did extremely well. Indeed, we can meaningfully consider the family banking houses of Europe as the precursors of today's multinational banks, their success being based on the same factors.[14]

Serving clients

Profit-maximizing banks do not open overseas offices merely to provide services for clients. Usually, correspondents could do most of what an

14 The House of Rothschild in particular knew the value not just of information about borrowers, but also about events which could affect financial markets. For example, by using pigeons, runners, horsemen, and rowers, Nathan Rothschild, the London-based member of the Rothschild family, knew before others that the Duke of Wellington had defeated Napoleon in the battle fields of Waterloo in 1815. Rothschild capitalized on his superior information by *selling* British bonds. This triggered panic selling, because it was known that Rothschild would be the first in London to know the outcome of the battle. Rothschild profited by employing others to buy the heavily discounted bonds before word finally arrived that Wellington had won.

overseas office can do to serve customers. However, it may be better for a bank to serve its domestic customers in their foreign operations than to allow its customers to develop strong ties with foreign banks or competing domestic banks that do have overseas offices. Some overseas banking offices may therefore follow the trade of domestic clients for strategic reasons rather than to earn from the services provided to clients.

Of course, it may be that the services that are provided by overseas banking offices *are* profitable. For example, the handling of collections and payments for domestic clients engaged in foreign trade can be lucrative and serve as reason for having an office, such as a representative office, in a country in which important clients are doing business. Indeed, for many banks the fees from services provided to customers that are connected to international trade have become an increasingly important component of their earnings. For example, the sale of letters of credit, the discounting of bills of exchange, the provision of collection services, and the conversion of currencies have become increasingly important in comparison with accepting deposits and making loans.

Custodial services

One fee-for-service activity of multinational banks that was mentioned in Chapter 15 is the provision of custodial services. These services are provided to clients who invest in securities overseas. As we have seen, global custodians take possession of foreign securities for safekeeping, collect dividends or offer up coupons, and handle stock splits, rights issues, tax reclamation, and so on. The custodians are typically banks. It is clear that custodial services require that banks have overseas offices, that is, that they be multinational.

Avoiding regulations

In the list of reasons why banks have become so multinational we should not overlook the role of regulations. As we saw in our discussion of the evolution of the offshore currency market, banks have frequently moved abroad to avoid reserve requirements, deposit insurance, onerous reporting requirements, corporate taxes, interest-rate ceilings, and other hindrances to their operations. For example, many US banks opened offices in London and in tax-havens to avoid US regulations and taxes. Similarly, many Japanese banks have opened offices in New York and London to avoid domestic restrictions and to exploit special opportunities. Indeed, over the years, the activities which are open to foreign banks have become increasingly similar to those open to domestic banks. This is made clear in Table 19.2, which shows by the similarity of the "yes" and "no" entries for functions in different centers that, with a few exceptions, there is little discrimination

Table 19.2 Activities open to different institutions in different centers

Activity	Location[a]	Permitted to[b]					
		US Bank Holding Co.	Japanese City Bank	UK Clearing Bank	US Securities Firm	Japanese Securities Firm	UK Merchant Bank
Banking	NY	Yes	Yes	Yes	S	S	S
License	LO	Yes	Yes	Yes	Yes	Yes	Yes
	TO	Yes	Yes	Yes	No	No	No
Dealing in	NY	No	No	No	Yes	Yes	Yes
corporate	LO	Yes	Yes	Yes	Yes	Yes	Yes
securities	TO	S	No	S	Yes	Yes	Yes
Foreign-	NY	Yes	Yes	Yes	Yes	Yes	Yes
exchange	LO	Yes	Yes	Yes	Yes	Yes	Yes
dealing	TO	Yes	Yes	Yes	No	No	No
Dealing in	NY	Yes	Yes	Yes	Yes	Yes	Yes
US treasuries	LO	Yes	Yes	Yes	Yes	Yes	Yes
	TO	No	No	No	Yes	Yes	Yes
Dealing in	NY	No	No	No	Yes	Yes	Yes
UK gilts	LO	Yes	Yes	Yes	Yes	Yes	Yes
	TO	No	No	No	Yes	Yes	Yes
Dealing in	NY	No	No	No	Yes	Yes	Yes
Japanese	LO	Yes	Yes	Yes	Yes	Yes	Yes
government bonds	TO	Yes	Yes	Yes	Yes	Yes	Yes
Trust bank	NY	Yes	Yes	Yes	S	S	S
	LO	Yes	Yes	Yes	Yes	Yes	Yes
	TO	Yes	No	Yes	No	No	No
Account at	NY	Yes	Yes	Yes	S	S	S
the central	LO	Yes	Yes	Yes	Yes	Yes	Yes
bank	TO	Yes	Yes	Yes	Yes	Yes	Yes

Notes
a NY = New York; LO = London; TO = Tokyo.
b Yes = full license permitted; No = not generally permitted; S = permitted only through special-purpose companies, such as a 50-percent-owned affiliate or a "near bank."

Source: E. Gerald Corrigan, "A Perspective on the Globalization of Financial Markets and Institutions," *Quarterly Review,* Federal Reserve Bank of New York, Spring 1987, pp. 1–9.

between foreign and domestic banks in the important financial centers – New York, London, and Tokyo.

While overseas offices may make banks more profitable by avoiding domestic regulations, at the same time they make banks and the banking industry more vulnerable and subject to crisis through "contagion." It is worthwhile considering this as well as other problems that can accompany the multinationalization of banking.

The problems of multinational banking

"Deregulation wars"

Banking can be risky business. Evidence of the risk of multinational banking has been provided by a string of failures and other crises including the failure of Franklin National Bank and Bankhaus Herstatt; major losses by the Union Bank of Switzerland, Westdeutsche Landesbank, Lloyds International, Anglo Irish Bank, and Barings; the upheaval at the Banco Ambrosiano; and the banking crisis of the 1980s, which occurred after Mexico, Brazil, Argentina, and over 20 other borrowers announced they were unable to meet scheduled repayments on their debts.

The major cause of the risk of multinational banking is also a major cause of the development of multinational banking. In particular, the opening of overseas offices to avoid domestic regulations such as reserve requirements, reporting of asset positions, and payment for deposit insurance has at the same time made banks more vulnerable to deposit withdrawals. Furthermore, the acceptance of default and other risks from overseas lending has made banks' domestic depositors subject to greater risks. While there has been some easing of anxiety of depositors in the twenty-first century, it is worthwhile considering why the problem developed.

Banking provides a country with jobs and prestige. Consequently, each country has an incentive to make its regulations just a little more liberal than other countries' and thereby attract banks from other locations. For example, if London can be a little less regulated than New York, it can gain at

New York's expense. Then, if the Cayman Islands, Bermuda, the Netherlands Antilles, or Liechtenstein can be less regulated than London, they can gain at London's expense. The attractiveness of banking in this way can draw more and more countries into competitive deregulation, with special advantages being offered by Cyprus, Jersey, Guernsey, Malta, Madeira, Gibraltar, Monaco, the Isle of Man, and other new entrants. Traditional centers like London and New York may be forced to respond to avoid losing their niche. Indeed, there was a wave of financial deregulations in the 1990s that left more than a few regulators feeling extremely uneasy.

One approach to help prevent "deregulation wars" is international cooperation. Some efforts have been made in this regard. For example, the **Basle Committee** was established after the Herstatt and Franklin bank failures for the purpose of "better co-ordination of the surveillance exercised by national authorities over the international banking system . . . " This committee has had some success in sharing information on banks and their subsidiaries so that national regulators can learn more quickly about difficulties occurring outside the country that could adversely affect bank safety at home. For example, for the situation of a subsidiary experiencing serious loan losses, the 1975 and 1983 **Concordat Agreements** among the Basle Committee members provide a procedure for relaying this information to the parent bank's regulators.

With the world's financial system so intricately connected and with deregulations having taken on a competitive element, those responsible for overseeing the international banking system sounded the alarm and swung into action. The leading role was taken by the Bank for International Settlements (BIS), which set new global standards for bank safety.[15] The most important step was the establishment of a recommended capital requirement of 8 percent, meaning that banks should maintain a net worth, or equity, of at least 8 percent of deposits and other liabilities. While banks in many countries

---

15 The Bank for International Settlements is discussed in Chapter 23. See especially Exhibit 23.4.

EXHIBIT 19.2   DERIVATIVES: DIFFERENTIATING THE HYPERBOLE

Debate over the potential benefits and dangers of the explosive growth in derivatives trading has been raging without any resolution. Nothing high-lighted the debate more than the dramatic events surrounding the financial crisis that followed the los-ses of Long-Term Capital Asset Management, LTCM, which led to investigations by the United States General Accounting Office and other international bodies.

Do banks that buy and sell currency or interest futures and options put themselves, their depositors, and even taxpayers at risk, or are they reducing risk for themselves and everybody else by hedging their business exposures? As the great British economist John Maynard Keynes is reported to have said: "If you lose a thousand pounds you have a problem. If you lose a million pounds the bank has a problem." We might extend this to say that if you lose a billion pounds, we all have a problem. Do the banks or do we even all have a problem, or are derivatives as David Mullins, a former Vice President of the US Federal Reserve said, "one of the most dramatic success stories in modern economic history?"

There is no doubt that derivatives can reduce risk, with futures, currency options and other instruments well designed to eliminate or at least greatly reduce dangers from involvement in foreign exchange. However, this is a complex matter, and the instru-ments themselves can be complex. They also link many different markets, with potential spillover between them. One of the dangers is so-called counter-party risk whereby failure of one party to cover losses could have a domino effect as others counting on payment from the failed party find themselves in turn unable to pay their creditors.

Regulation is difficult in the derivatives markets, and it is hard to do anything without knowing the exposures faced by the different parties, especially the banks. At the very least we can expect greater reporting requirements and higher capital adequacy standards.

Source: Based in part on "Long-Term Capital Management: Regulators Need to Focus Greater Attention on Systemic Risk," Report of the United States General Accounting Office, October 29, 1999, and "A Survey of International Banking," *The Economist*, April 30, 1994, p. 40.

were at or above this capital standard at the time it was recommended, other banks, especially in Japan, were below it. This required banks with inadequate capital to issue shares and/or reduce their liabilities in order to move toward the new BIS standard.

Derivatives trading

One problem which has occupied the attention of the BIS and the G-8 members is the increased activity of banks in the **derivatives markets**.[16] The concern is the risk that some banks face that is not reflected in traditional measures of bank safety, such as the reserve-deposit and capital-deposit

16 We refer to the G-8, consisting of the G-7 plus Russia which has been given a seat at the periodic G-7 finance ministers' meeting. The Group of Seven, G-7, is the United States, Britain, Japan, Germany, France, Italy, and Canada.

ratios. Concern over bank trading in derivatives reached crisis proportions after the massive losses of Barings from trading in Japanese stock market index futures by a 28-year-old trader at the bank's Singapore office. (Losses, revealed in 1995, ex-ceeded $1 billion.) Losses at Anglo-Irish, a bank in Baltimore, were also due to losses in derivatives trading. While it is true that trading derivatives such as currency and interest-rate futures and options can be risky, as Exhibit 19.2 points out, derivatives can be used to *reduce* risk as well as to *take* risk. It all depends on other business exposures that a com-pany faces. This is what makes the issue of deriva-tives so difficult for regulators to resolve. The matter is still a burning issue for policymakers, and we can expect further changes in standards in the future, especially in the requirements for disclosure of derivative positions of banks.

SUMMARY

1   Eurodollars are US-dollar bank deposits held outside the United States. Included within the Eurodollar market are the Asiadollar market and other markets outside Europe.

2   Offshore currencies are bank deposits held outside the home countries of the currencies.

3   Offshore currency markets allow investors and borrowers to choose among different currencies of denomination at the same location.

4   The commonly held view is that Eurodollars came into existence initially as the result of the preferences of Soviet holders of dollar balances. For safety and ideological reasons, they preferred to hold their dollars in Europe. Perhaps more important were the US Federal Reserve System regulations on maximum levels of interest rates on deposits, and on holding reserves. These regulations encouraged a flow of dollars to Europe. The borrowing of these dollars was stimulated by credit and capital-flow restrictions in the United States.

5   The convenience of holding deposits in and negotiating loans with local banks, as well as the lower spreads on offshore currencies from the absence of severe regulation, resulted in the later expansion of Eurodollars and other offshore currencies.

6   Offshore currencies result in potential multiple expansions of bank deposits. The size of the multiplier depends on the speed with which funds leak to a currency's home market.

7   Banks can do business abroad via holding deposits with foreign banks, called correspondents. They can also post representatives abroad to help clients. If they wish even greater involvement overseas, they can consider opening an agency, which does not solicit deposits, open a foreign branch, or buy or establish a subsidiary. Banks can venture abroad as part of a consortium. In the United States, banks can establish an Edge Act subsidiary to invest in foreign subsidiary banks or otherwise invest outside the home state or abroad, or they can establish an international banking facility.

8   Banks are among the most multinational of firms. The benefits of being multinational include more timely and meaningful information on financial markets and events, better information on borrower quality, keeping domestic clients from using other banks when doing business overseas, earning fees from custodial and other services, and avoiding onerous regulations.

9   The opening of overseas offices to avoid domestic regulations on required reserves, on reporting assets, and on paying deposit insurance premiums may have increased the riskiness of banks. That is, the major factors making banks multinational are also the major factors contributing to their riskiness.

10   Countries have to some extent competed with each other by progressively deregulating banking. Banking regulators have tended to match the deregulations of other countries to make their countries attractive to banks, but as a result, banking has become more risky.

REVIEW QUESTIONS

1 What is a Eurodollar?
2 What is an offshore currency?
3 How did the US Federal Reserve contribute to the supply of Eurodollar deposits?
4 What contributed to the demand for Eurodollar loans?
5 Did US trade deficits contribute to the growth of Eurodollars?
6 What is meant by "LIBOR?"
7 Why do banks trade Eurodollar futures?
8 What is the Eurodollar multiplier?
9 How do leakages of dollars back to the United States affect the size of the Eurodollar multiplier?
10 Why do banks have correspondent relationships with other banks?
11 How does a foreign bank agency differ from a branch?
12 Why have some banks set up Edge Act corporations?
13 What is an IBF?
14 In what ways has information contributed to the multinationalization of the banking industry?

ASSIGNMENT PROBLEMS

1 Since a person can open an offshore sterling account with dollars – by converting the dollars into pounds – or open a dollar account with sterling, what yield differences can exist between different (forward-hedged) offshore currency deposits?
2 Why do you think Eurodollars are the major offshore currency? Does it have to do with the amount of business transacted in US dollars?
3 Given the relatively extensive use of dollars in denominating sales contracts in international trade, are Eurodollar multipliers likely to be larger than multipliers for other offshore currencies? (*Hint*: Recall that the value of a multiplier has to do with the speed with which funds return to their home.)
4 a   What is the Eurodollar creation from a deposit of $2 million when the offshore banks maintain a 5 percent reserve? Assume that the $2 million is deposited in a London office of Barclays Bank, which makes a loan to British Holdings Ltd, which uses the funds to pay for goods from British Auto Ltd, which in turn places the proceeds in Citibank in London. Assume that Citibank uses its extra dollars to make a loan to Aviva Corporation, which uses the dollars back in the United States.
   b   Recompute the change in Eurodollars in 4a assuming instead that a 10 percent reserve-deposit ratio is maintained.
   c   Recompute the change in Eurodollars in 4a with the 5 percent reserve ratio, assuming that five banks are involved before leakage occurs.
   d   What do you think is more important in affecting the size of the Eurodollar multiplier – the size of reserve ratio or the time before a leakage occurs?

5 Give a reason (or reasons) why each of the following might open a Eurodollar account

   a   The government of Iran

   b   A US private citizen

   c   A Canadian university professor

   d   A European-based corporation

   e   A US-based corporation.

6 Does it make any difference to the individual bank that makes a loan whether the loaned funds will leak to the United States? In other words, does the individual bank lose the funds no matter who borrows the dollars?

7 What is the difference between a foreign branch, a foreign subsidiary, a foreign affiliate, and a foreign agency? Which type(s) of foreign banking will make banks multinational?

8 If the object of US banks moving overseas had been purely to help customers, could they have used only correspondent relationships and representative offices? Why then do you believe they have opened branches and purchased subsidiaries?

9 In what way does Table 19.2 suggest little discrimination against foreign financial firms? Can you find any apparent examples of discrimination?

10 Empirical evidence suggests that banks tend to locate near importers rather than exporters. What do you think is responsible for this?

BIBLIOGRAPHY

Aliber, Robert Z., "International Banking: A Survey," *Journal of Money, Credit and Banking*, Part 2, November 1984, pp. 661–78.

Baker, James C. and M. Gerald Bradford, *American Banks Abroad, Edge Act Companies and Multinational Banking*, Frederick A. Praeger, New York, 1974.

Bhattacharya, Anindya, *The Asian Dollar Market*, Frederick A. Praeger, New York, 1977.

Corrigan, E. Gerald, "Coping with Globally Integrated Financial Markets," *Quarterly Review*, Federal Reserve Bank of New York, Winter 1987, pp. 1–5.

Debs, Richard A., "International Banking," *Monthly Review*, Federal Reserve Bank of New York, June 1975, pp. 122–9.

Dufey, Gunter and Giddy, Ian, *The International Money Market*, Prentice-Hall, Englewood Cliffs, NJ, 1978.

Einzig, Paul A., *The Euro-Dollar System*, 5th edn, St. Martin's Press, New York, 1973.

Freedman, Charles, "A Model of the Eurodollar Market," *Journal of Monetary Economics*, April 1977, pp. 139–61.

Friedman, Milton, "The Euro-Dollar Market: Some First Principles," *Morgan Guarantee Survey*, October 1969, pp. 4–44.

Goldberg, Michael A., Robert W. Helsley, and Maurice D. Levi, "On the Development of International Financial Centers," The *Annals of Regional Science*, February 1988, pp. 81–94.

Heinkel, Robert L. and Maurice D. Levi, "The Structure of International Banking," *Journal of International Money and Finance*, June 1992, pp. 251–72.

Henning, Charles N., William Pigott, and Robert H. Scott, *International Financial Management*, McGraw-Hill, New York, 1977.

Klopstock, Fred H., "Money Creation in the Euro-Dollar Market: A Note on Professor Friedman's Views," *Monthly Review*, Federal Reserve Bank of New York, January 1970, pp. 12–15.

Lees, Francis A., *International Banking and Finance*, John Wiley & Sons, New York, 1974.

McKenzie, George W., The *Economics of the Euro-Currency System*, John Wiley & Sons, New York, 1976.

McKinnon, Ronald I., *The Offshore Currency Market*, Essays in International Finance, no. 125, Princeton University Press, Princeton, NJ, 1977.

Ricks, David A. and Arpan, Jeffrey S. "Foreign Banking in the United States," *Business Horizons*, February 1976, pp. 84–7.

Robinson, Stuart W., Jr, *Multinational Banking*, A. W. Sijthoff International, Leiden, The Netherlands, 1972.

Chapter 20

Instruments and institutions of international trade

In war as in love, to bring matters to a close, you must get close together.

Napoleon

EXTRA DIMENSIONS OF INTERNATIONAL TRADE

In ordinary domestic commercial transactions, there are reasonably simple, well-prescribed means of recourse in the event of nonpayment or other causes of disagreement between parties. For example, the courts can be used to reclaim goods when buyers refuse to pay or are unable to pay. The situation is substantially more complex with international commercial transactions, which by necessity involve more than one legal jurisdiction. In addition, a seller might not receive payment, not because the buyer does not want to pay, but because, for example, the buyer's country has an insurrection, revolution, war, or civil unrest and decides to make its currency inconvertible into foreign exchange. In order to handle these and other difficulties faced in international transactions, a number of practices and institutional arrangements have been developed, and these are explained in this chapter.

In addition to different practices and institutions for ensuring payment and delivery in international versus domestic trade, national and international institutions have been established to finance and monitor international trade. This chapter will describe the roles of these institutions as well as

explain practices such as forfaiting and countertrade that are unique to the international arena.

INTERNATIONAL TRADE INVOLVING LETTERS OF CREDIT: AN OVERVIEW OF A TYPICAL TRANSACTION

In order to give a general introductory overview of the documentation and procedures of international trade, let us suppose that after considering costs of alternative suppliers of cloth, Aviva has decided to buy cloth from the British denim manufacturer British Cotton Mills Ltd. An order is placed for 1 million yards at £4 per yard, with Aviva to receive the shipment in 10 months, and pay 2 months after delivery.

Assume that after having made the agreement with British Cotton Mills, Aviva goes to its bank, Citibank, N.A., in New York and buys forward (12 months ahead) the £4 million. Assume that at the same time Aviva requests a **letter of credit**, which is frequently referred to as an **L/C**, or simply as a **credit**.[1] An example of a letter of credit

---

1 If Aviva frequently does business with British Cotton Mills, or if Aviva has had problems paying in the past, a different procedure is likely to be used. This is described later in the chapter.

application and agreement issued by Citibank, N.A., in New York is shown in Figure 20.1.[2] The letter of credit is a guarantee by Aviva's bank that if all the relevant documents are presented in exact conformity with the terms of the letter of credit, the British exporter will be paid. Aviva Corporation will have to pay Citibank, N.A., a fee for the letter of credit. Citibank will issue the letter only if it is satisfied with the creditworthiness of Aviva Corporation. If it is unsure, it will require some collateral.

A copy of the letter of credit will be sent to Citibank, N.A., in London. That bank will inform the British exporter's bank, Britbank Ltd., which will in turn inform British Cotton Mills of the credit advice. In our example, Citibank is both the "opening bank" and the "paying bank," as shown by the "drawn on" entry in the letter, while Britbank is the "advising bank." On receiving the letter of credit advice, British Cotton Mills Ltd. can begin producing the denim cloth, confident that even if Aviva Corporation is unable to pay, payment will nevertheless be forthcoming from Citibank, N.A. The actual payment will be made by means of a **draft** (also called a **bill of exchange**), and this will be drawn up by the exporter or the exporter's bank after receipt of the letter of credit. The draft stipulates that payment is to be made to the exporter at the exporter's bank, and therefore it is different from conventional checks, which are drawn up by those making the payment rather than by those who are to receive payment.

The draft corresponding to the letter of credit in Figure 20.1 is shown in Figure 20.2a. It was drawn up by the exporter, British Cotton Mills Ltd., and specifies that £4,000,000 is to be paid at the exporter's bank, Britbank. This is a **time** or **usance** draft, because the exporter, British Cotton Mills, is allowing a 60-day credit period.[3] The draft will be sent directly or via Britbank Ltd. to Citibank, N.A., in London, and that bank will **accept** the draft if the draft and other relevant documents that are presented to the bank are in exact conformity with the letter of credit. If the draft is stamped and signed by an officer of Citibank, it becomes a **banker's acceptance**. A banker's acceptance looks like the specimen in Figure 20.2b.[4]

British Cotton Mills Ltd. can sell the accepted draft at a discount which reflects the interest cost of the money advanced but not any risk associated with payment by Aviva Corporation because the draft has been guaranteed. The draft is sold in the banker's acceptance market at a discount related to the quality of the accepting bank, Citibank. Since the draft is in pounds, it will be discounted at a pound rate of interest and will probably be sold in the London money market. Alternatively, instead of selling the draft, British Cotton Mills Ltd. can wait until payment is made to Britbank Ltd. and its account with the bank is credited. This will occur on June 30 – 2 months after the date on which the draft was accepted (April 30) and a year after the date of the sales contract.

Citibank in London will forward the documents to New York. Citibank in New York will require payment from Aviva Corporation on June 30 of the dollar amount in the forward contract agreed to in the previous year for the purchase of £4 million. At the same time that Aviva's account is debited by Citibank in New York, Citibank will give the documents to Aviva. The New York and London offices of Citibank will then settle their accounts with each other. British Cotton Mills will have been paid via Britbank; Aviva will have paid Citibank in New York; Citibank in New York will have paid Citibank in London; and Citibank in London will

---

2 The format of the letter of credit application and agreement shown in Figure 20.1 follows the standard recommended by the International Chamber of Commerce. The letter in Figure 20.1 was kindly provided by Citibank, N.A. Examples of letters of credit and other documents can be found in *An Introduction to Letters of Credit*, Citibank, New York 1991. The letter of credit we have presented is for a straightforward situation.

3 The maturity of a time or usance draft is also sometimes referred to as its **tenor**.

4 Citibank in London is the accepting bank because the draft is in pounds. If the draft were denominated in dollars, it would be accepted by Citibank in New York.

Application and Agreement For Documentary Letter of Credit

Citibank, N.A. 111 Wall Street North American Trade Finance	16th Floor, New York, N.Y. 10005 Credit Number:

Advising Bank (Name and Address) Britbank Ltd, 1 Floor Street, London, England	Applicant (Name and Address) Aviva (Denim Clothing) Corp. New York, New York

Beneficiary (Name and Address) British Cotton Mills Ltd. London, England	Amount (Four Million British (in specific currency of Credit) pounds sterling) L4,000,000
	Expiry Date and Place (for negotiation) June 30, (next year)

Subject to the following terms and conditions, please issue your Irrevocable Letter of Credit (hereinafter called the "Credit") to be available by the beneficiary's draft(s):

Drawn at ☐ Sight, ☒ __60__ Days Sight, ☐ _____ Days Date, ☐ other _____

Drawn on ☐ Citibank, N.A. New York, N.Y. for _____ % invoice cost.

Drawn on ☒ Citibank, N.A. London, England for _____ % invoice cost.
(Name and Address of paying bank if any).

Accompanied by the following documents which are indicated by an "X".

☒ Commercial Invoice(s) _____ original(s) and __2__ copies.

☒ Customs Invoice(s) _____ original(s) and __0__ copies.

☐ Insurance Policy and/or Certificate (to be effected by shipper, unless otherwise indicated below)

☐ Insurance to include: (list coverage) _____

☒ Transport Document: ☒ Marine, ☐ Multimodal, ☐ Air, ☐ Other (define) _____

issued in full set consigned: ☐ to, or ☐ to the order of __Citibank, N.A.__

marked Freight ☐ Collect or ☐ Paid and notify __Aviva Corporation, New York, New York__
Dated Latest: __June 20, (current year)__

☐ Other documents _____

Covering: Merchandise described in the invoice(s) as: (Brief Description) __1,000.000 yards of denim cloth__

Terms:
☐ FAS _____, ☐ FOB _____, ☒ CFR _____, ☐ CIF _____,
☐ CPT _____, ☐ CIP _____, ☐ Other _____

Shipment from __London, England__ to __New York, New York__

For Multimodal Transport Document only:
Place of Receipt/Taking in Charge _____ Place of Final Destination _____

Partial Shipment ☒ Permitted, ☐ Prohibited Transhipment ☒ Permitted, ☐ Prohibited

Draft(s) and documents must be presented to the negotiating or paying bank within __15__ days after the date of issuance of the Bill(s) of Lading or other shipping documents, but not later than the expiry date of the Credit.

☐ All banking charges other than issuing bank's charges are for account ☐ Beneficiary, ☐ Applicant.

☐ Negotiation fees are for account ☐ Beneficiary, ☐ Applicant.

☐ Discount charges are for account ☐ Beneficiary, ☐ Applicant.

☐ Acceptance fees are for account ☐ Beneficiary, ☐ Applicant.

☒ Insurance effected by the Applicant.

Attachments hereto impose additional terms and conditions on Applicant and/or Citibank and are incorporated into this Application and Agreement as if fully set forth herein.

Transmit the Credit through your correspondent, or directly to the beneficiary, or to: _____

_____, by ☐ Cable/Swift, ☐ Airmail, ☐ Courier Service, ☐ Pre-Advice by Cable/Swift.

All drafts and documents called for under the Credit are to be delivered by the negotiating or paying bank to Citibank, N.A., New York by Airmail in a single mailing.

Shipping documents for custom house entry are to be sent by you to _____

To induce the establishment of the Credit, Applicant agrees to the terms and conditions of the Agreement as set forth hereinafter

Figure 20.1 *Application and agreement for documentary letter of credit*

Source: Citibank N.A. Reproduced by permission.

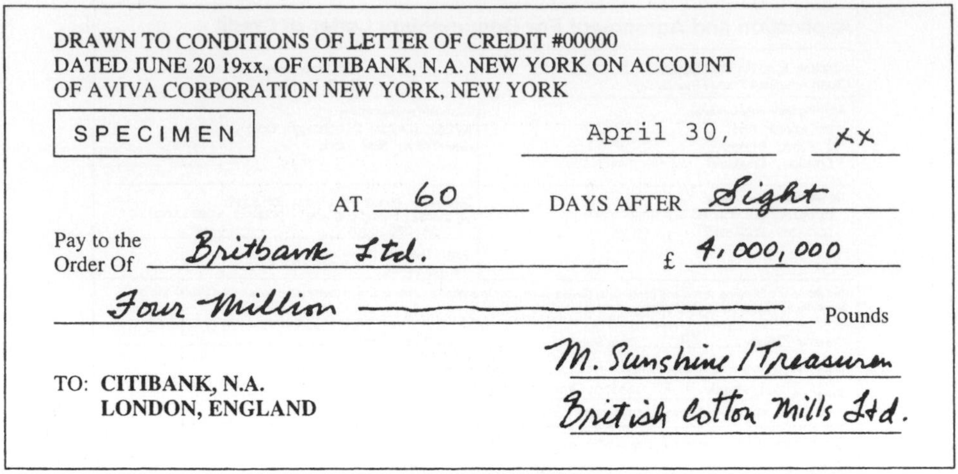

DRAWN TO CONDITIONS OF LETTER OF CREDIT #00000
DATED JUNE 20 19xx, OF CITIBANK, N.A. NEW YORK ON ACCOUNT
OF AVIVA CORPORATION NEW YORK, NEW YORK

SPECIMEN   April 30,   xx

                        AT 60 DAYS AFTER *Sight*

Pay to the
Order Of *Britbank Ltd.*   £ *4,000,000*

Four Million _____ Pounds

TO: CITIBANK, N.A.   *M. Sunshine / Treasurer*
     LONDON, ENGLAND   *British Cotton Mills Ltd.*

(a) Bank draft

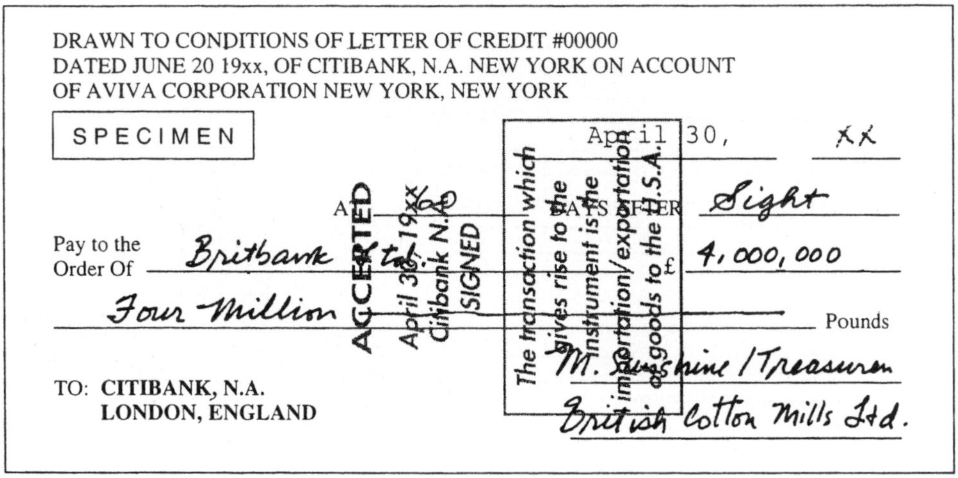

DRAWN TO CONDITIONS OF LETTER OF CREDIT #00000
DATED JUNE 20 19xx, OF CITIBANK, N.A. NEW YORK ON ACCOUNT
OF AVIVA CORPORATION NEW YORK, NEW YORK

SPECIMEN   April 30,   xx

                        AT   DAYS AFTER *Sight*

Pay to the
Order Of *Britbank Ltd.*   £ *4,000,000*

Four Million _____ Pounds

                   ACCEPTED April 30, 19xx / Citibank N.A. / SIGNED

                   The transaction which gives rise to the instrument is the importation/exportation of goods to the U.S.A.

TO: CITIBANK, N.A.   *M. Sunshine / Treasurer*
     LONDON, ENGLAND   *British Cotton Mills Ltd.*

(b) Banker's acceptance

Figure 20.2 *The draft and banker's acceptance*

Source: Citibank N.A. Reproduced by permission.

have paid Britbank. Aviva will have the papers to receive the cloth. The transaction is complete. The steps are summarized in the numbered sequence in Figure 20.3.

Because the letter of credit in Figure 20.1 requires that certain documents be presented, it is a **documentary credit**. This is shown at the top of the letter. The accompanying draft (Figure 20.2a) is referred to as a **documentary draft**. A **clean draft** does not require a letter of credit or other supporting documents and is used only when there is complete trust – for example, when goods are shipped between subsidiaries of the same multinational. If the documents are delivered upon the *acceptance* of a draft, the draft is an **acceptance draft**, and if the documents are delivered upon the *payment* of a draft, the draft is a **payment draft**.[5]

5 When payment is made upon the presentation of a draft, the draft is a sight draft. When payment is made after sight, the draft is a time draft (as in Figure 20.2a)

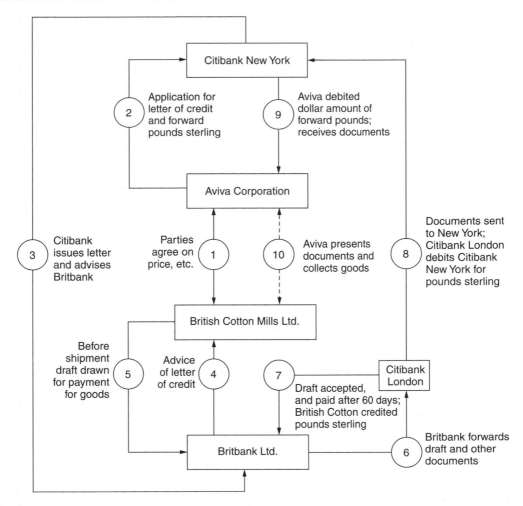

Figure 20.3 *The steps in international trade*

Source: Leonard A. Back, *Introduction to Commercial Letters of Credit*, Citicorp, New York, undated.

The most important document that is required before a bank will accept a draft is the **bill of lading**. The bill of lading, or **B/L**, is issued by the carrier and shows that the carrier has originated the shipment of merchandise. The B/L can serve as the title to the goods, which are owned by the exporter until payment is made. Then, via the participating banks, the bill of lading is sent to the importer to be used for claiming the merchandise. An **order bill of lading** is a bill which gives title to a stated party. It can be used by that party as collateral for loans.

When goods are sent by air, the equivalent of the bill of lading is called an **air waybill**. This serves the same purpose as a bill of lading, being required for release of the goods and transferring ownership from seller to shipper to final buyer. A logistical difficulty with air waybills is ensuring they reach buyers before the goods which are to be claimed. The waybill may accompany the goods, but for reasons of safety – to ensure the right party receives the goods – waybills are better sent separately. Today, waybills can also be sent electronically.

ALTERNATIVE PAYMENT AND GUARANTEEING PROCEDURES

Open-account and consignment sales

If Aviva and British Cotton Mills have been doing business with each other for many years and Aviva has established a reputation for prompt payment, the company may try to avoid the expense of a letter of credit, for which banks charge a fee according to the credit rating of the importer and the value of the credit. Instead, Aviva might ask British Cotton Mills if it can order cloth on an **open account** basis, whereby the value of cloth shipped is added to the account Aviva keeps at British Cotton Mills. An invoice might be sent at the end of each month when transactions are frequent, or after each shipment when they are infrequent, allowing Aviva to pay by buying a clean draft, or simply by writing a check on an account denominated in the invoice currency. This saves collection fees as well as the cost of the letter of credit.

In situations of trust, goods are sometimes supplied on a **consignment** basis. In this case, payment is not made until after the buyer has sold the goods, and in the meantime the goods remain the property of the supplier.

Cash in advance and confirmed credits

When there is little or no trust, as after a firm has developed a bad reputation for settling its accounts, perhaps having been late settling previous transactions with the supplier, payment may be required in advance. In this situation, cash is sent to the supplier's bank before the goods are shipped.

When an exporter's lack of trust concerns the importer's bank or the importer's government — perhaps the importer's bank is poorly capitalized, or perhaps the importer's government might freeze foreign exchange payments – and when the importer cannot pay cash in advance, the exporter can ensure payment by having a letter of credit guaranteed by a domestic bank. What usually happens in this situation is that the exporter asks the importer for a letter of credit, even though this

will be issued by a bank in the importer's country. The exporter then takes this letter to a bank at home and pays the domestic bank to guarantee, or **confirm**, the letter of credit. The result will be a foreign letter of credit with a domestic confirmation. The exporter will then be paid regardless of what happens to the importer's bank or in the importer's country. Nonpayment due to the failure of the importer's bank or action taken by the importer's government is the problem of the confirming bank and not the exporter, provided that the exporter has delivered the goods.

Export insurance

Letters of credit must be purchased by the importer, and while the cost is not high – usually a few percent at most if the importer's credit is good – obtaining the letter may be inconvenient, and will reduce the importer's remaining available credit for other purposes. For these reasons, an exporter may find that a sale may not occur if they insist on a letter of credit. Indeed, pressure from other exporters who are not requiring letters of credit frequently means exporters can assume that any talk of letters of credit will mean no sale. In such a case exporters can buy what can be considered an imperfect substitute for a letter of credit, namely **export credit insurance**. Credit insurance is arranged and paid for by the exporter and can cover a variety of risks.

It is possible to buy credit insurance against commercial risk only, or against both commercial and political risk. Insurance against both commercial and political risk serves rather like a confirmed letter of credit in that the exporter will be paid whether the importer pays or not, and whether the importer's country allows payment or not. Insurance against commercial risk alone serves rather like an unconfirmed letter of credit in that the exporter will not be paid if the importer's government prevents payment. However, there are some important differences between letters of credit and export credit insurance, which is why export insurance is only an imperfect substitute for an L/C. One of these differences is the presence of a deductible portion on insurance, whereas letters of credit typically cover 100 percent of credit.[6] The deductible means the exporter loses something if the importer does not pay. The uninsured portion of a credit is a contingent liability of the exporter. As with insurance in general, the deductible is a means of reducing **moral hazard**.[7] Clearly, the presence of a deductible makes credit insurance less desirable to exporters than confirmed letters of credit. So, of course, does the need to pay for credit insurance; the *importer* pays for a letter of credit, while the *exporter* has to pay for export credit insurance.[8]

Typically, there are two forms of export credit insurance. One form provides automatic coverage up to a stated limit on exporters' receivables from buyers whose credit the insurers have approved. This type of insurance is well suited to exporters who must quote commodity prices over the telephone and accept orders if the buyers agree to these prices. For example, exporters selling lumber or wheat can buy credit insurance which covers all sales to approved buyers. This type of credit insurance is variously called **continuous, whole-turnover**, or **rollover** insurance.

A second form of credit insurance covers only specific contracts and specific risks. For this, an exporter must apply for coverage of the specific export credit. For example, if a firm receives an order for six large passenger planes, the exporter will have to apply to the credit insurer and state the specifics of the sale. This type of insurance is usually called **specific commodities export credit insurance**.

---

6 The deductible may be 10 percent or more of the amount insured. There are also other differences between letters of credit and credit insurance when an exporter is unable to deliver goods, when goods are damaged or lost in transit, and so on: credit insurance typically provides broader coverage than a letter of credit.

7 Moral hazard involves changes in behavior after insurance has been provided. Specifically, insurance increases the chance of bad events covered by the insurance due to a lack of care.

8 For a more detailed treatment of the pros and cons of letters of credit and credit insurance see Dick Briggs and Burt Edwards, *Credit Insurance: How to Reduce the Risks of Trade Credit*, Woodhead-Faulkner, Cambridge, UK, 1988.

The rationale for government-provided credit insurance

Even though export credit insurance can be purchased from private-sector insurance companies such as the large British-based insurance company Trade Indemnity and the horizontally integrated trade facilitating company, Coface, most governments provide export credit insurance themselves, usually through an especially established agency. For example, in the United States export credit insurance can be purchased from the Export-Import Bank ("Ex-Im Bank"), in Britain from the Export Credits Guarantee Department, in Sweden from the Export Credits Guarantee Board, in China from the China Export and Credit Insurance Corporation, and in Canada from Export Development Canada. Since governments do not typically provide fire, life, disability, automobile, and accident insurance, it is worth asking why in the case of insurance of export credits it has become the norm for governments to arrange coverage. That is, why do governments step in to insure export credits rather than allow private insurance companies to provide the insurance at a competitively determined premium? Even apart from trying to subsidize exports because of the jobs and incomes they generate, there are "market failures" which might warrant government involvement. There are also arguments that the government may be able to provide the insurance more cheaply. Let us consider these arguments.

Natural economies of scale

Credit insurance requires the insurer to keep current on the situation in different countries and in different companies. For private insurance companies to assess risks they all need to maintain overseas offices around the world.[9] It might be that the market in each country could support only one

---

9 Alternatively, the insurance companies might buy information from a country-risk-evaluating company. However, the risk-evaluating company would need to maintain offices abroad if it were to be current on the situations in different countries.

credit insurer, resulting in a monopoly. Then the government might have to regulate the industry if it did not provide the credit insurance itself. That is, from the economies of scale insurers enjoy, credit insurance may be a **natural monopoly**. It is normal to either regulate the pricing of natural monopolies, or for governments to provide the product itself.

Economies of scope

Another reason why governments may be better suited to provide export credit insurance than private insurance companies is that a government insurer can provide a trade representative with a desk and staff within its existing embassies and consular offices. The addition of the trade office is relatively low cost given that the infrastructure is already in place. A further advantage comes from the ability of government to use political muscle and thereby reduce risk of nonpayment of trade credits. For example, if a borrower decided they are not going to pay foreign creditors, a government export credit agency might ask its government to threaten withdrawal of aid to the delinquent country. These are examples of **economies of scope**. Economies of scope are a result of the *range* of activities performed or products produced, not the level of activity or production. In this case, governments enjoy economies of scope by being in a variety of activities, ambassadorial duties, and foreign aid, in addition to providing export credit insurance.

Positive spillovers

A factor which supports official credit insurance against private credit insurance, and which applies to export financing as well as to export insurance, is that there may be benefits to other firms in the exporting country if one of that country's companies makes an export sale. For example, if a US engineering company wins a contract to supply machinery to China, there may be improved prospects for other US companies to sell to China. Perhaps an American company that services the product might win a long-term contract. This is

not uncommon with complex equipment such as commercial aircraft and central telecommunications equipment. That is, there may be **positive externalities** or spillovers that derive from an export contract. These positive externalities will not be considered by private export credit insurers in a competitive market, but a government agency can take them into account when deciding whether to provide export insurance or export financing. That is, export insurance and financing have elements of a **public good**, and as is generally the case for public goods, they will be underprovided by private profit-maximizing firms.

THE FINANCING OF INTERNATIONAL TRADE

Short-term financing: banker's acceptances

When an exporter gives credit to a foreign buyer by issuing a draft that is dated for settlement some time in the future, the draft itself can be used by the exporter for short-term financing. As explained earlier, when the draft is stamped "accepted" by a bank and signed by an officer of the bank, it becomes a banker's acceptance. The exporter can sell the banker's acceptance in the money market at a discount that is related to the riskiness of the accepting bank. If the exporter's draft is drawn without a letter of credit from the importer's bank, the draft is a **trade draft**. This can be sold in the money market, but because it is only a commercial rather than a bank obligation, the draft will face a higher discount than would a banker's acceptance. However, the exporter can pay a bank to accept the draft, and then sell this at a lower discount. The acceptance charge can be compared to the extra value received on the accepted draft, with the acceptance path being used only if this costs less than the extra value received for the accepted draft. All documents, including shipping documents, will normally be provided to the bank accepting the draft.

When an exporter draws up a time draft, the exporter is granting the importer credit which the

**EXHIBIT 20.1   JUST-IN-TIME INVENTORY SYSTEMS: TOO LATE
FOR THE MERCHANT OF VENICE**

The Merchant of Venice in Shakespeare's play with the same title faced a trade-financing problem. For merchants of his day, goods would arrive from afar in large loads, in fact shiploads. Paying immediately for imported goods was difficult because of the sheer size of the amount that would arrive by ship, perhaps once or twice in a year, and because sales from the large inventories occurred continually through the year. Financing was needed to bridge the gap between lumpy arrival and steady sales, that is, financing was needed for the inventory stocks that the nature of trade forced upon merchants.

A just-in-time inventory system, were this to have been possible in the merchant's Venice, would have avoided the trade-financing problem. If goods could have arrived at the same rate as they were sold to customers in the area, the cash flow from sales would have paid for the imports. Clearly, the nature of ships, which cannot be made small enough to deliver one day's worth of sales, prevented the use of just-in-time

inventories at that time, just as it does today. Better predictions of arrival of goods and of sales can reduce the required inventory levels, but they cannot eliminate inventories of imports and the need to finance them. However, instruments such as letters of credit have been developed to ensure payment, allowing trade to be based on more acceptable collateral than the merchant's pound of flesh. That is, if the Merchant of Venice had at his disposal a bank that could guarantee his credit for an L/C fee, he could have guaranteed his payment for imports with paper instead of blood. Late arrival of payment for the imported product would have forced the L/C-issuing bank to pay Shylock, lifting the merchant's burden but stealing Portia's poetic appeal for all-round compassion.

> The quality of mercy is not strain'd;
> It droppeth as the gentle rain from heaven
> Upon the place beneath. It is twice blest:
> It blesseth him that gives and him that takes.
> *The Merchant of Venice*, Act 4, Scene 1

exporter may finance by selling the signed draft. When an exporter draws up a sight rather than a time draft, the exporter is not granting credit to the importer; there is no delay in payment. Nevertheless, a banker's acceptance may be created in this situation. This will happen if the importer is in need of credit, and draws up a time draft in favor of a bank, signs the draft, and has it accepted by the bank. The banker will immediately pay the importer the discounted value of the draft. The bank will then either sell the draft or hold it for collection. An importer might take this step to finance goods purchased from abroad before they are sold.[10]

The time after sight on a banker's acceptance, whether created by the exporter or by the importer, is typically 30, 60, 90, or 180 days. Consequently,

bankers' acceptances are only a mechanism for short-term trade financing.

Forfaiting: a form of medium-term finance

Forfaiting explained

Forfaiting is a form of medium-term financing of international trade.[11] It involves the purchase by the forfaiting bank, of a series of promissory notes, typically due at 6-month intervals for 3–5 years, signed by an importer in favor of an exporter.[12]

---

10 These means of financing trade and providing payment guarantees are an alternative to historical procedures such as those used by the Merchant of Venice. See Exhibit 20.1.

11 In French it is called a *forfait*, and in German, *Forfutierung*.

12 Of course, the language of these promissory notes must be in accordance with legal requirements. These requirements are spelled out in the Geneva Convention of 1930, which has been signed by numerous countries, and the Bill of Exchange Act of 1882, which governs international trade practice in Britain.

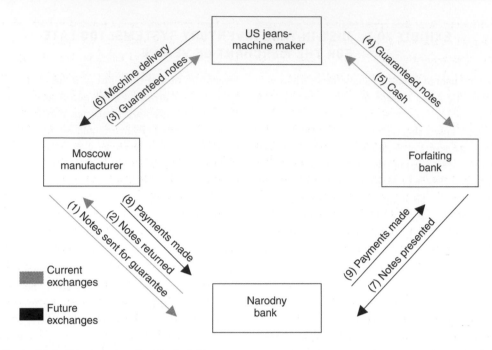

Figure 20.4 *The steps involved in forfaiting*

Notes
Forfaiting is a means of providing medium-term import credits. The importer prepares promissory notes that are guaranteed by a bank. These are sent to the exporter, who then sells them for cash to a forfaiting bank which may then sell the notes. The holder of the notes has no recourse to the exporter. The credit risk is entirely borne by the note holder.

These notes are frequently **avalled**, or guaranteed, by the importer's bank. The promissory notes are sold by the exporter to the forfaiting bank at a discount. The forfaiting bank pays the exporter immediately, allowing the exporter to finance the production and if necessary the transportation of the goods for export, and for the importer to pay later. The notes may be held by the forfaiting bank or they may be sold to an investor. The notes are presented for collection as they come due, without recourse to the exporter in whose favor the notes were originally drawn. This absence of recourse distinguishes the forfaiting of promissory notes from the discounting of trade drafts, for which the exporter is open to recourse in the case of non-payment.[13] All this can be summarized in the following short definition.

Forfaiting is medium-term non-recourse exporter-arranged financing of importers' credits.

The nature of forfaiting is also summarized in Figure 20.4. The figure shows what happens, and the order of events, when a US jeans-machine manufacturer sells its machines to a Russian jeans manufacturer. The lightly shaded arrows show the exchanges occurring at the time the export deal is made, while the dark arrows show subsequent settlements.

Some forfaiting banks hold the promissory notes themselves and collect payments as they come due. Others buy notes for investors who have expressed interest in taking up the high-yielding paper, and still others arrange forfaiting and then trade the notes in the secondary market.[14]

---

13 The lack of recourse explains the origin of the term "forfaiting"; the buyer of the promissory notes forfeits the right of recourse.

14 Forfaiting yields are relatively high because there is no recourse in the event the goods are not delivered, the importer does not pay, and so on.

The discount rates that apply to forfaiting depend on the terms of the notes, the currencies in which they are denominated, the credit ratings of the banks availing the notes, and the country risks of the importing entities. The spreads between forfaiting rates and offshore currency deposit rates, with which forfaiting rates move, are typically about one-and-a-half times the spreads between straight offshore currency loans and deposits.[15] The higher spreads reflect the lack of recourse and interest-rate risk; the typical 5-year term of forfaiting deals means forfaiters have difficulty matching credit maturities with the typically much shorter maturity offshore currency deposits and futures contracts. Although there have been some floating-rate agreements which have reduced interest-rate risk, fixed-interest-rate deals predominate.

Forfaiting banks have shown considerable flexibility and often quote rates over the telephone once they know the name of the importer or the avalling bank.[16] This allows exporters to quote their selling prices after working out what they will net from their sales after forfaiting discounts. Another advantage to the exporter is that because there is no recourse, the promissory notes are not carried on the exporter's books as a contingent liability. Yet another is that there is no need to arrange credit insurance. Of course, the advantage of forfaiting to importers is that they receive credit when it might not otherwise be offered or not be offered on the same terms.

The history of forfaiting

As with the introduction of Eurodollars, the development of forfaiting probably owes its origins, but not its subsequent popularity, to the difficulties faced in east-west trade. (We recall that it has been argued that the Eurodollar market started because the former Soviet Union wanted to hold US dollars, but not to hold them in the United States.) The practice of forfaiting dates back to the 1960s with the placing of orders by eastern-bloc Comecon countries for capital equipment and grain. Many of these orders were placed with German firms which were not in a position to supply trade credit themselves, or to arrange financing with banks or official lending agencies. That is, the exporters were unable to offer **supplier credits**, and they were unable to arrange **buyer credits** through lending institutions. Instead, they found banks which were willing to purchase the importers' promissory notes at a discount. One of the first banks to recognize the opportunity was Credit Suisse through its subsidiary Finance A.G. Zurich.[17] The original deals involved the sale of US grain to Germany, which resold the grain to eastern European countries. Forfaiting allowed the US exporters to be paid immediately and the eastern European buyers to receive medium-term trade credit.[18]

While originally viewed as "lending of last resort," forfaiting grew in popularity, spreading from Switzerland and Germany, where it began, to London, later to Scandinavia and the rest of Europe, and eventually to the United States. Forfaiting is still not as important as payment by traditional time or usance bills of exchange or credit from official export financing agencies, but it has nevertheless become a potential source of financing, especially for medium-term maturities.[19]

Financing by government export agencies

Because of the jobs and income that derive from a healthy export sector, it has become standard practice for governments around the world to help

---

15 See Donald Curtin, "The Unchartered $4 Billion World of Forfaiting," *Euromoney*, August 1980, pp. 62–70.

16 The forfaiter may charge a **commitment fee** for this service.

17 See Werner R. Rentzman and Thomas Teichman, "Forfaiting: An Alternative Technique for Export Financing," *Euromoney*, December 1975, pp. 58–63.

18 See Donald Curtin, op. cit.

19 As we have seen, time drafts typically provide only short-term financing. Clearly, time drafts are a form of supplier credit.

their exporters win contracts by offering export financing. This financing can be of short-, medium-, or long-term maturity, and takes a number of different forms.

A large part of official export financing takes the form of loan guarantees to exporters. For example, the US Export-Import Bank ("Ex-Im Bank") helps small businesses obtain working capital to finance exports. The bank does this by guaranteeing the principal and interest on working capital loans by commercial lenders to eligible US exporters. The funds can be used for producing the goods for export, buying raw materials, holding inventory, or marketing. The guarantees help companies raise supplier credits. Buyer credits, that is, loans or loan guarantees to the buyers of a country's exports, are also offered in many countries. For example, the Export Credits Guarantee Department offers buyer credits to purchasers of British exports, and Export Development Canada provides buyer credits to buyers of Canadian products.

Official export financing also takes the form of loans to domestic or foreign financial institutions, which in turn make loans to the importers. Sometimes only a portion of the funds required by the importer is made available to the financial institutions, the balance being provided by other lenders. In some countries, the export finance agency provides its component of the shared financing on a "first in, last out" basis. This means that the export agency commits its money before the private financial institution makes its contribution, and that the export agency gives the private financial institution the first claim on repayments. This and other financing practices have given rise to claims of hidden assistance and subsidies to exporters and to a number of disputes. Accusations that financing constitutes a subsidy have been especially common over interest rates charged on buyer credits. Some countries have tried to hide their subsidies by offering **mixed credits**, which are a combination of export credits at market interest rates and what the export agencies call "foreign aid." That is, some export agencies say that they are able to offer very low interest rates on export credits as a result

of contributions by their countries' development aid agencies.[20]

It is not uncommon for official export agencies to offer guarantees to banks in the exporter's country if the banks offer buyer credits. This substantially reduces the risk to the banks, thereby reducing the interest rates they charge. In the United States, the Ex-Im Bank guarantees export credits that are offered by the **Private Export Funding Corporation (PEFCO)**. PEFCO is a private lending organization that was started in 1970 by a group of commercial banks and large export manufacturers. PEFCO raises its funds through the sale of the foreign repayment obligations which it has arranged and which have been guaranteed by the Ex-Im Bank. PEFCO also sells secured notes on the securities market.

The need for export financing, the need for special trade documents, such as letters of credit and trade drafts, and the need for export insurance, are all greatly reduced or eliminated when international trade takes the form of countertrade. There are different variants to countertrade, and it is well worth considering what these variants are and why countertrade occurs.

COUNTERTRADE

The various forms of countertrade

Countertrade involves a reciprocal agreement for the exchange of goods or services. The parties involved may be firms or governments, and the reciprocal agreements can take a number of forms including the following.

Barter

The simplest form of countertrade involves the direct exchange of goods or services from one

---

20 The bickering over interest rates on export credits was reduced in 1983 when the OECD countries agreed to link interest rates to a weighted average of government-bond yields and to all charge the same rate. See *International Letter*, no. 515, Federal Reserve Bank of Chicago, December 16, 1983.

country for the goods or services of another. No money changes hands, so that there is no need for letters of credit or drafts. Furthermore, since the goods or services are exchanged at the same time, there is no need for trade financing or credit insurance. An example of a barter deal was the trading of the Polish soccer star Kazimierz Deyna for photocopiers and French lingerie.[21]

Counterpurchase

Barter requires a "double coincidence of wants" in that the two parties in the transaction must each want what the other party has to provide, and want it at the same time and in the same amount. Because such a coincidence is unlikely, a form of counter-trade called **counterpurchase** is substantially more common than barter. With counterpurchase the seller agrees with the buyer either to

1   make purchases from a company nominated by the buyer (the buyer then settles up with the company it has nominated) or
2   take products from the buyer in the future (i.e. the seller accepts credits in terms of products).

Counterpurchase can also involve a combination of these two possibilities. That is, the seller agrees to receive products at a future date from a company nominated by the buyer.

Counterpurchase frequently involves only partial compensation with products, and the balance in cash. These types of countertrade deals are called **compensation agreements**.

Industrial offset

A large portion of countertrade involves reciprocal agreements to buy materials or components from the buying company or country. For example, an aircraft manufacturer might agree to buy engines or navigation equipment from a buyer of its aircraft.

The components may not be only for the aircraft sold to the company or country. For example, a military aircraft manufacturer might agree to buy engines for all its planes from a foreign producer if the engine manufacturer's country agrees to buy a substantial number of its aircraft.

Buyback

This form of countertrade is common with capital equipment used in mining and manufacturing. In a **buyback agreement** the seller of the capital equipment agrees to buy the products made with the equipment it supplies. For example, the maker of mining equipment might agree to buy the output of the mine for a given period, perhaps 10 or 15 years. This is a guarantee to the equipment buyer that it can pay for the capital equipment whatever happens to the price of what it produces, provided, of course, it can ensure continued production. When the equipment buyer pays partly in terms of its product and partly in cash, then, as in the case of other counterpurchase agreements of this kind, the arrangement is called a compensation agreement.

Switch trading

Switch trading occurs when the importer has received credit for selling something to another country at a previous time and this credit cannot be converted into financial payment, but has to be used for purchases in the country where the credit is held. The owner of the credit switches title to its credit to the company or country from which it is making a purchase. For example, a British firm might have a credit in Poland for manufacturing equipment it has delivered. If a firm finds a product in France that it wishes to purchase, the British firm might pay the French firm with its Polish credit. The French firm might agree to this if it wishes to buy something from Poland. Because it is difficult for the various parties to locate each other for a switch deal, most of them are arranged by brokers. Many of these brokers are based in Austria. The reason Austria plays such a large role is that it sits between

21 See *Euromoney*, September 1988, p. 54.

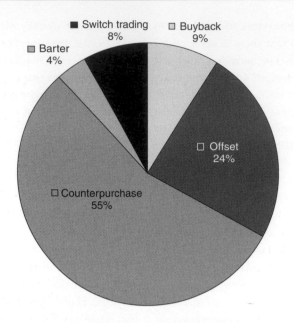

Figure 20.5 *The different forms of countertrade*

Source: Willis A. Bussard, in Christopher M. Korth (ed.), *International Countertrade*, Quorum Books, New York, 1987, p. 18.

east and west Europe, and in the past many of the deals were between the two sides of Europe.

The relative importance of the different forms of countertrade that we have described is shown in Figure 20.5. The figure shows clearly that counterpurchase is the dominant form and that barter is relatively unimportant.

Before leaving a description of the forms of countertrade we might mention that in the 1980s, in response to the deepening third-world debt crisis, some countries began to substitute commodities for debt payments. For example, in 1985 Peru repaid part of its foreign debt with broiler chickens, shoes, and a variety of other products. Mexico also tried to arrange an oil-for-debt swap. These arrangements are a form of countertrade in that they circumvent the use of convertible currencies.

Reasons why countertrade occurs

Given that countertrade has at some time or other been estimated to have constituted up to 10 or 20 percent of world trade, we might ask why

trading agreements that are so difficult to arrange have assumed such importance.[22] That is, why have so many firms and countries chosen not to sell their products for a convertible currency and use the convertible currency to pay for what they bought?

A common reason for circumventing the use of a convertible currency and instead practicing countertrade is that a buyer in the countertrade does not have access to convertible currency. It is no accident that countertrade occurs where at least one party cannot obtain convertible currency to make payments for imports. If one party cannot pay with convertible currency, then it must pay with goods, which is barter; with other companies' goods, which is counterpurchase; with credits, which could be a switch trade or a counterpurchase; and so on. Many LDCs (less-developed countries), restrict access to convertible currency, and therefore

22 See the surveys of countertrade summarized in Christopher Korth (ed.), *International Countertrade*, Quorum, New York, 1987.

many of the countertrades that occur involve an LDC.[23]

Countertrade is also encouraged when prices are kept artificially high or low. For example, if the official OPEC oil price is above the market price, an oil seller might arrange a countertrade in which the oil is implicitly valued at the market price. The alternative of selling the oil at market price and using the proceeds for purchases is more likely to cause anger among other members of the cartel. More generally, countertrade allows goods to be exchanged internationally in specific transactions at relative prices which reflect genuine market values, while allowing non-market prices to be charged domestically. That is, countertrade is a way of circumventing problems caused by mispriced goods or currencies.[24]

It has been argued that countertrade can promote exports. Rolf Mirus and Bernard Yeung have suggested that countertrade transactions constitute a sale of domestic goods for a "bundle" consisting of foreign goods plus marketing services.[25] The foreign firm will not "shirk" in its marketing effort because it stands to benefit fully; it takes ownership of the goods. The alternative of finding an independent firm to market the product on behalf of the producer offers a weaker incentive to work hard. By aligning the marketing firm's interest with that of the exporter, it is possible that exports are larger than they would have been otherwise.[26]

With many countries abandoning restrictions on currencies, especially former eastern European countries, the need for countertrade has been reduced. However, it has not been eliminated.

THE INSTITUTIONS REGULATING INTERNATIONAL TRADE

A glance along the shelves at the vast range of goods we purchase from abroad, and a moment's reflection on the number of jobs which depend on export sales, should amply convince us that international trade is vital to our well-being and that protectionism could do more to harm that well-being than almost any other development. Recognition of the potential damage that protectionism can bring has resulted in a number of post-Second World War institutional arrangements designed to reduce protectionism and allow us to more fully exploit the benefits of trade. We shall quickly review the more important of these institutional arrangements in concluding our discussion of the organization of international trade. The two most important arrangements involve the regulation of the conduct of trade by the **World Trade Organization (WTO)** (and formerly by the General Agreement on Tariffs and Trade, GATT), and by the establishment of **free-trade areas**.

The World Trade Organization and GATT

The World Trade Organization, which began operation in 1995 and which has reached 146 members, was created to replace the General Agreement on Tariffs and Trade. The WTO differs from GATT in that

1 the WTO is a chartered trade *organization*, not just a secretariat as was GATT;

2 the WTO has enhanced coverage vis-à-vis GATT. Most important, the WTO covers services, including trade-related aspects of intellectual property rights (TRIPs);

3 the WTO has a more compelling dispute settlement function than GATT because agreement cannot be blocked by a failure to achieve consensus.

23 See Rolf Mirus and Bernard Yeung, "Countertrade and Foreign Exchange Shortages: A Preliminary Investigation," *Weltwirtschaftliches Archiv*. 123, 3, 1987, pp. 535–44.

24 A denial of access to foreign currency can be considered a mispricing, in this case of the exchange rate; implicitly, the price of foreign currency is infinite if it cannot be purchased at any exchange rate.

25 Rolf Mirus and Bernard Yeung, "Economic Incentives for Countertrade," *Journal of International Business Studies*, Fall 1986, pp. 27–39.

26 See Jean-Francis Hennart, "The Transaction-Cost Rationale for Countertrade," *Journal of Law, Economics and Organization*, Spring 1989, pp. 127–53.

However, despite these differences, the WTO continues the work of GATT to limit harmful trade practices, just as the IMF is designed to limit harmful financial practices such as competitive devaluations.[27] In its role as trade regulator, GATT had some notable successes in reducing the level of damaging trade practices.

The two central principles of GATT were

1   trade relations could not be discriminatory;
2   export subsidies were not permitted.

The nondiscriminatory principle was effected via the **most favored nation** clause, which disallowed offering better trade treatment to any country than was given to other GATT signatories. This meant that all GATT members were treated in the same way as the most favored nation was treated. An exception was made to allow free-trade areas, or **customs unions**, to exist, whereby members of the area or union could *all* be treated more favorably than nonmembers. The prohibition on export subsidies meant that no benefits could be offered to domestic producers which would give them an advantage in foreign markets. Again, an exception was made, this time for agricultural products. Where subsidies were shown to exist outside agriculture, countries were permitted to apply discriminatory tariffs to counteract trade subsidies; these are referred to as **countervailing tariffs.**

GATT managed to broker some general reductions in tariffs under the so-called **Kennedy-**, **Tokyo-**, and **Uruguay rounds**. Completed in 1994, the Uruguay round represented major progress in dealing with services and various non-tariff trade barriers. The success of the WTO and its predecessor GATT can be measured by the fact that compared to the situation before them, developed-country tariffs have fallen from an average of approximately 40 percent to just 4 percent. Also, the proportion of industrial products entering developed countries duty-free has

more than doubled, increasing from 20 percent to 43 percent.[28]

Along with the reduction or even complete elimination of import tariffs achieved by GATT and the WTO has came an agreement to eventually eliminate hundreds of billions of dollars of subsidies provided to farmers in the world's richest countries, notably the United State and the European Union. The landmark agreement to do this came in August 2004 at WTO meetings in Geneva, with the purpose being to help poor nations whose farmers were unable to compete in world markets. In return, developing nations agreed to open their markets to manufactured goods. The hotly debated trade reform governing agricultural products came after failure to reach agreement on subsidies at a meeting in Cancún, Mexico in 2003. The meetings in Geneva and Cancún were both part of the so-called Doha Round of trade discussions by the WTO, launched in 2001.

Free-trade areas and customs unions

A **free-trade agreement** is in some ways the lowest level of economic integration.[29] While tariffs are removed on trade among members, each nation retains the freedom to set its own tariffs and other trade restrictions to outsiders. The North American Free Trade Agreement (NAFTA) has this characteristic. The next level of economic integration is a **customs union**. Customs unions have no tariffs among members, as in a free-trade agreement, but in addition have common tariffs for outsiders. The **European Union (EU)** has been a customs union since January 1993. A customs union has operational advantages because outside goods can be traded freely between members once the tariffs

---

27 The IMF is discussed in Chapter 23.

28 See Don Macnamara, "Peter Sutherland's GATT," *Acumen*, September/October 1994, pp. 18–24.

29 While not multilateral in nature, free-trade zones, which are sometimes called *foreign trade zones* and which have been an important element of China's economic reforms, are a step below free-trade agreements. Exhibit 20.2 discusses the economics of free-trade zones in the US context.

EXHIBIT 20.2 US FREE-TRADE ZONES

The United States has had free-trade zones (FTZs), also called "foreign-trade zones," since 1934. However, little use was made of them until the 1980s, which is the same time that other nations from Britain to China opened such zones within their borders. As the excerpt below explains, while the motivation for FTZs is to improve international trading competitiveness, the benefits of FTZs are largely financial, stemming from less money being tied up in customs duties, defective products, and so on.

Foreign trade zones (FTZ) are areas located within U.S. boundaries, but outside of its customs territory. Foreign goods can be imported duty-free into an FTZ and then either re-exported without duties or formally imported into the U.S. market accompanied by payment of U.S. import duty.

Foreign trade zones consist of two types of zones: general purpose zones and subzones. In practice, general purpose zones and subzones are used for different activities. The general purpose zone is created before any of its subzones and is normally located at a port of entry such as a shipping port, border crossing, or airport. A general purpose zone usually consists of a distribution facility or industrial park.

Space is leased in a manner similar to any other industrial park or shared warehousing facility. Activities in general purpose zones typically consist of inspecting, storing, repackaging, and distributing merchandise, and destroying defective merchandise, prior to re-export. For example, the Miami FTZ acts as a distribution center for European and Asian companies exporting into South America and the Caribbean. Manufacturing activities take place in only a few general purpose zones.

Subzones are areas that are physically separate from the general purpose zone but are legally and administratively attached. Subzones allow new or existing facilities that are located outside of the general purpose zone to take advantage of FTZ benefits. For example, subzones allow space-intensive facilities, such as assembly plants, to become part of an FTZ without using expensive port space. A subzone is used by a single company and is typically created around a manufacturing plant.

FTZs potentially provide firms with a wide array of benefits. Firms can repackage or assemble imported merchandise along with domestic components for re-export without having to pay a customs duty on the imported components. This benefit makes it competitive for exporters to operate within U.S. boundaries and was the original goal of the FTZs. However, many firms have found it to be more convenient and cost effective to avoid duties on re-exported goods by alternative means such as bonded warehouses or duty drawback programs, which return tariffs on re-exported goods.

Another benefit of FTZs is that custom duties and taxes on goods for domestic consumption are not paid until the merchandise leaves a foreign trade zone and enters U.S. customs territory. In fact, while in a zone, merchandise is not subject to taxes of any kind. Furthermore, defective imports can be discarded before tariffs are paid, so that tariffs are not paid on unusable products. In practice, the deferral of both tariffs and domestic taxes until the imported merchandise leaves the trade zone is the major benefit enjoyed by current users of general purpose zones. Most of these establishments are repackaging and distribution centers.

A third benefit of FTZs is that firms may keep merchandise in a zone indefinitely. This allows firms to weather periods of poor sales without paying import duties and to defer import quotas. If import quotas have been met for the year, the merchandise can be stored in the FTZ until the next year so that it will not be included in the current year's quota.

Source: David Weiss, "Foreign Trade Zones: Growth Amid Controversy," *Chicago Fed Letter*, Federal Reserve Bank of Chicago, no. 48, August 1991.

have been collected for the goods to enter the union via any member of the union. The level of integration above the customs union involves zero tariffs between members, common tariffs to outsiders, and the integration of trade policy, fiscal policy, monetary policy, and perhaps even political policy to outside bodies. Such economic and political integration within the European Union is the goal of the **Maastricht Treaty**.

Since its establishment in the 1950s, the European Union has expanded in stages from the original six members to 25 members after the admission of ten additional countries on May 1, 2004. Trade being an important component of economic activity within and between these nations, the EU is the largest customs union that exists. As a customs union, companies operating outside the EU have to face competition from firms inside the EU that sometimes have favorable terms within the union. For example, US-manufactured cars selling in Britain face tariffs, whereas German-, Italian-, and French-made cars do not.

The United States, which has traditionally been a staunch supporter of freer trade even if its rhetoric has sometimes been sharper than its actions, made its own entry into trading agreements when, in January 1989, it signed the Free Trade Agreement (FTA) with Canada. This agreement was then superseded in January 1994 by the **North American Free Trade Agreement (NAFTA)** between Canada, Mexico and the United States.

Although often overlooked, the fact is that US trade with Canada is larger than US trade with Japan, Germany, or any other single nation, and indeed, US–Canadian trade is the largest bilateral trading relationship on Earth. US–Mexican trade is not far behind, and has been growing at a rapid rate. The comprehensive and detailed arrangements of the NAFTA therefore mean that each country gains improved access to its largest foreign markets. In addition, each country obtains greater freedom to invest in the other. For the United States, one of the most important features of the NAFTA is Canada's agreement to give US energy producers and consumers the same treatment given to Canadians. The NAFTA operates within the rules of the WTO. Procedures have been put in place to resolve disputes, with the United States retaining its right to levy countervailing tariffs when it believes US industry is being damaged by unfair trading practices.

NAFTA provides a market of almost 400 million people. It was agreed to reduce tariffs over a 15-year period to create a borderless trading area, at least as far as tariffs and other explicit trade restrictions are concerned. Fear of job losses and environmental damage hindered acceptance of the NAFTA in the United States even though at the agreement's inception the United States enjoyed a large trade surplus with Mexico, and even though many people felt that if Mexico were a signatory of the NAFTA, Mexico's environmental standards could be more easily raised than if the country were left outside the agreement. Subsequent supplementary arrangements concerning the environment as well as labor standards in Mexico have been designed to increase acceptance of the NAFTA in the United States and Canada.

With trading agreements existing in North America, Europe, and Asia (in the form of the Association of South East Asian Nations, ASEAN), some people have come to fear the consequences of a world that is divided into a limited number of trading blocs. The pattern of localized freer trading arrangements with unchanged or even increased protectionism against outsiders does not correspond to the principles envisioned by those who established GATT and its successor, the WTO. The danger is that the large trading blocs have constituencies which would prefer restricted trade. The bigger the bloc, the more types of constituencies that are present, and the less they need to trade with outsiders. Big trading blocs could therefore ultimately threaten globally free trade.

SUMMARY

1   Special procedures have evolved for dealing with the extra risks of international trade, and national and international institutions have been established to finance and regulate international trade.

2   Before shipping goods to foreign buyers many exporters require buyers to provide a letter of credit from a reputable bank. This is a guarantee that the exporter will be paid if the goods are supplied in good order.

3   Payment is made by a bill of exchange, or draft, which is sent by the exporter to the importer or to the importer's bank. The importer or the importer's bank signs the draft. If the draft is payable on presentation, it is a sight draft. If it is payable at a future date, it is a time draft.

4   The shipper gives the exporter a bill of lading, the original copy of which is required for collection of the goods. The bill of lading is forwarded to the importer for the goods to be released.

5   When an exporter is confident an importer will pay, goods may be sold on an open account, and a bill presented after shipment. When an exporter suspects that an importer may not pay, cash may be demanded before shipment occurs.

6   When an exporter lacks trust in the importer's bank or country, the exporter can have the importer's letter of credit confirmed. A confirmed letter of credit is one way of avoiding country risk.

7   Export credit insurance is an alternative to letters of credit for avoiding commercial and/or country risks. Export insurance, however, typically involves a deductible portion of coverage and differs from letters of credit in other ways that are sometimes important.

8   Credit insurance may be a natural monopoly, and be more effectively offered by an official rather than a private institution, because a government may have more success avoiding nonpayment and because a government may consider positive spillovers of trade deals.

9   Official export financing agencies often provide direct buyer credits, as well as guarantees on credits to buyers granted by domestic or foreign financial institutions.

10   When an exporter's time draft is accepted by a bank, the resulting accepted draft is called a banker's acceptance.

11   Banker's acceptances are a means of short-term trade financing, typically up to 6 months. Forfaiting is a means of medium-term trade financing, with a typical term of 5 years.

12   Forfaiting involves the sale by an exporter of promissory notes issued by an importer and usually avalled by the importer's bank. The forfaiter has no recourse to the exporter in the event that, for whatever reason, the importer does not pay.

13   Forfaiting is a particularly useful means of financing the sale of capital goods. The exporter is paid immediately, while the importer can make payments out of revenue generated by the products of the capital goods.

14 Some international trade is countertrade. This may involve barter, an agreement to purchase products at a later date or from a designated supplier, an agreement to provide parts or to buy goods produced with capital equipment that has been supplied, or an agreement to switch credits for future product purchases.

15 Countertrade is motivated by foreign exchange controls and mispricing of products, and often involves less developed countries.

16 The conduct of international trade is governed by the World Trade Organization (WTO), which has succeeded GATT. Members of the WTO agree to have nondiscriminatory tariffs by accepting the "most favored nation" principle, and they agree to not subsidize exports.

17 The WTO offers exceptions to its tariff policy. These exceptions are to permit the establishment of free-trade areas and customs unions and to exempt agriculture from the prohibition on export subsidies.

18 The trend towards the establishment of trading blocs could threaten globally free trade by raising barriers between the blocs.

REVIEW QUESTIONS

1   What purpose is served by a letter of credit?
2   What purpose is served by a bill of exchange?
3   How does a time draft differ from a sight draft?
4   What is a banker's acceptance?
5   What is a "clean draft"?
6   What purpose is served by a bill of lading or air waybill?
7   Why might a company have a letter of credit confirmed?
8   Are letters of credit and export credit insurance perfect substitutes?
9   List the market failures that support government export credit insurance.
10 What is forfeited with forfaiting?
11 What forms does countertrade take?
12 Why does countertrade occur?
13 How does the WTO differ from its predecessor, the GATT?
14 What is the difference between a free-trade agreement and a customs union?

ASSIGNMENT PROBLEMS

1   Why are letters of credit less often used in domestic trade?
2   Why does the exporter provide the importer with the check for payment that the importer signs, rather than just allow the importer to send a check?
3   Why are banks willing to accept time drafts, making them bills of exchange, and why do importers and exporters arrange for banks to accept drafts?

4 Are cash terms likely when an importer can arrange a letter of credit?

5 Why is export credit insurance typically offered by government agencies?

6 Why do you think promissory notes used in forfaiting deals are avalled by the importer's bank?

7 What is the similarity between an aval and an acceptance?

8 Is forfaiting a form of factoring?

9 What form of trade financing is an exporter likely to seek first, and how would the choice depend on the export deal?

10 Why is counterpurchase so much more common than barter in countertrade?

11 How can a customs union or common market such as the EU hurt a US exporter?

12 Under what conditions might the emergence of a limited number of free-trade blocs lower standards of living?

BIBLIOGRAPHY

Citibank, *An Introduction to Letters of Credit*, Citibank, New York, 1991.

Harrington, J.A., *Specifics on Commercial Letters of Credit and Bankers' Acceptances*, Scott Printing Corp., Jersey City, NJ, 1974.

Hennart, Jean Francis, "Some Empirical Dimensions of Countertrade," *Journal of International Business Studies*, Summer 1990, pp. 243–70.

Korth, Christopher (ed.), *International Countertrade*, Quorum, New York, 1987.

Krugman, Paul R. and Maurice Obstfeld, *International Economics: Theory and Policy*, Chapter 9, Scott-Foresman, Glenview, IL, 1988.

Lecraw, Donald, "The Management of Counter trade: Factors Influencing Success," *Journal of International Business Studies*, Spring 1989, pp. 41–60.

Rentzmann, Werner F. and Thomas Teichman, "Forfaiting: An Alternative Technique of Export Financing," *Euromoney*, December 1975, pp. 58–63.

Sodersten, Bo, *International Economics*, 2nd edn, Chapter 17, Macmillan, London, 1980.

Watson, Alasdair, *Finance of International Trade*, Institute of Bankers, London, 1976.

Part VII

The international macroeconomic environment: theories and practices

Chapter 6 in Part II considered the determination of exchange rates when they are flexible, meaning that they are determined by the forces of private supply and demand. The supplies and demands were the result of imports and exports that appear in the balance of payments on current account, and hence were *flows*.

In Part VII we consider alternative theories of exchange rates that are based on *stocks* of currencies and demands to hold these stocks. These theories are explained in Chapter 21, where we begin with the monetary theory of exchange rates. This theory is based on the requirement that the demands and supplies of currencies must be in equilibrium. This leads to reasonable predictions such as the following: an increase in the supply of Country A's currency relative to the demand for A's currency, by more than the increase in supply of B's currency relative to the demand for B's currency, will cause A's currency to depreciate vis-à-vis B's currency. We show that while this prediction of the monetary theory sounds reasonable, predictions of the theory concerning economic growth and interest rates are different from the predictions of the flow supply and demand theory in Chapter 6. We also explain the portfolio-balance theory that considers a wider range of assets than the monetary theory, and the so-called "asset approach." The asset approach emphasizes the forward-looking nature of financial markets and in this way provides an explanation of why exchange rates may deviate from *current* PPP levels.

Chapter 22 moves from consideration of flexible exchange rates to a discussion of fixed-exchange-rate systems including the classical gold standard that lasted into the twentieth century, the Bretton Woods System roughly spanning the period 1944–73, the European Monetary System operating between 1972 and 1993, and the cooperative system operated by the Group of Seven, G-7 – now expanded to provide Russia with an observer's seat – since the mid-1980s. The focus is both on the mechanics of these systems of fixed exchange rates, and on how imbalances in private currency supplies and demands were corrected. The mechanisms for correcting imbalances of currency supplies and demands with fixed-exchange-rate systems are compared with the balance of payments adjustment mechanism under flexible exchange rates. Indeed, the chapter includes an account of the many arguments used in favor of or against fixed and flexible exchange rates.

Armed with an understanding of the different ways the international financial system can be organized, and with an appreciation of the pros and cons of the different systems, we are able to consider why international financial history has weaved the path it has. We describe the flaws in the classical gold standard, the Bretton Woods System and the European Monetary System that eventually brought about the collapse of each. This historical review of the international financial system brings us to the present time, including an account of the creation of the European common currency, the euro, which became fully operational at the opening of the twenty-first century. We show that the advantages of dealing with a single currency in terms of a reduction in the costs and risks of international trade, are offset by losses in monetary independence of member countries: a common currency means a common monetary policy. The size of the downside of sharing a common monetary policy is shown to depend upon how synchronized are member countries' business cycles, and on the mobility of factors of production between member countries. We also examine some of the problems the international financial system has had to cope with, from recycling "petrodollars," to foreign exchange reserve shortages, to widely different inflation and employment experiences, to massive debts of developing nations, to the contemporary problems of trade imbalances and shifting economic power. We shall see how international institutions such as the International Monetary Fund (IMF) and World Bank have been devised and adapted to deal with these problems.

Part VII is designed to provide readers with a wider understanding of the ever-changing international financial environment in which corporate and individual decisions must be made. The twists and turns of the twentieth century, from gold, to Bretton Woods, to flexible rates, to cooperative intervention, to the euro, tell us that if anything is predictable, it is that change in the international financial system can be counted on continuing into the future. Only by considering where we have been, and analyzing how previous international financial systems have worked, can we understand whatever new and untried systems we might some day face. A limited attempt is made to look into the future to see what today's burning, global issues might imply for the future path of the international financial system.

Chapter 21

Asset-based theories of exchange rates

We first survey the plot, then draw the model ...
Then must we rate the cost of the erection;
Which if we find outweighs ability,
What do we then but draw anew the model ...

William Shakespeare
Henry IV

STOCK VERSUS FLOW THEORIES OF EXCHANGE RATES

The supply-and-demand view of exchange rates in Chapter 6 considered *flows* of currencies – amounts per period of time. An alternative way of viewing exchange-rate determination is in terms of the *stocks* of currencies relative to the willingness of people to hold these stocks. Several variants of stock-based theories of exchange rates have been developed in recent years, where these theories differ primarily in the range of different assets that are considered, and in how quickly product prices can adjust to changes in exchange rates. We begin with the simplest stock-based model which considers only the stocks of different countries' monies versus the demands for these monies, and which assumes all price adjustments are instantaneous. This "monetary approach to exchange rates" is extended to the "asset approach" by considering how expectations about future prices can affect current exchange rates. The asset approach is followed by a more complete model which considers equilibrium in different countries' bond markets as well as their money markets. The chapter concludes with a discussion of models which extend the stock-based theories in order to explain exchange-rate volatility, where volatility takes the form of exchange-rate "overshooting": exchange rates can initially go too far, and then move back to equilibrium. The overshooting is the result of some product prices responding slowly to exchange rates.

THE MONETARY THEORY OF EXCHANGE RATES

Intuitive view

The fundamental idea of the monetary theory of exchange rates is that a change in the demand relative to the supply of one currency versus another will change the exchange rate. Consider, for example, US dollars versus euros, and think of the supply of a currency as the money supply.[1] We have

---

1 Money supply is the sum of coins, paper currency, and bank deposits. Inclusion of different types of bank deposits results in different definitions of the money supply, but for simplicity you can think of checking accounts only, providing what is generally called money supply, M1.

a demand for dollars, largely by Americans who use dollars for everyday purchases, and a demand for euros by Europeans who make their payments in their own currency, the euro.[2] We also have money supplies of these two currencies. Suppose the **European Central Bank**, the **ECB**, increases the supply of euros relative to the demand for euros by more than the proportion in which the US Federal Reserve increases the supply of dollars relative to the demand for dollars. What do you think will happen to the exchange rate? According to the monetary theory of exchange rates, *ceteris paribus*, the euro will fall in value relative to the US dollar. What occurs is that the relatively rapid expansion of the euro supply versus the demand to hold the euro – this being relative to the dollar – causes inflation in the Euro zone, making the euro worth less in terms of buying power. This is what is behind the fall in foreign exchange value of the euro in this supply expanding circumstance.

A currency will increase in value if the demand for it were to increase, relative to its supply, by more than happens to demand versus supply in another currency. For example, if the demand for euros were to increase versus the euro supply by more than the demand for dollars increased versus the dollar supply, the euro would go up in value in terms of dollars. Anything which can change the amount of a nation's money that people want to hold would have an effect on exchange rates through affecting demand versus supply of one country's currency versus another. Money demand is affected by economic growth: fast growing economies have growing demands for money for transactions purposes. In this way economic growth, *ceteris paribus*, can contribute to an appreciation of a country's currency. The demand for money also depends on interest rates, since they affect the opportunity cost of holding money: high interest rates on bonds

decrease the amount of money people want to hold. Money demand could also be affected by the price level in a country and other factors including political and economic concerns about the future. In this way economic growth, interest rates, price levels, political uncertainty, and other matters influence exchange rates through affecting money demand, just as do relative changes in countries' money supplies.

Formal view

As the preceding discussion would suggest, central to the monetary theory of exchange rates are equations specifying the demand for money in each country. Among other influences, one of the most important factors affecting the demand for money is the price level. If, for example, the prices of everything in a country were to double, *ceteris paribus*, the amount of money people would want to hold, that is, demand, would also double. If morning coffee, the newspaper, bus tickets, lunch, and so on were to suddenly cost twice as much, people would want to head off to work or school in the morning with approximately twice as much money in their wallets or pocket books as before the price increase occurred. We are assuming that the only thing which has changed is the price level. This *ceteris paribus* assumption means that we are holding all other things constant, such as real incomes and wealth, so people are not poorer because of higher prices: constant real incomes and wealth mean that nominal incomes and wealth increase at the same rate as prices.

If the demand for money varies by the same proportion as the price level, then we can think in terms of the "real demand for money." For example, if a 10 percent price level increase causes a 10 percent increase in money demand, we would have the same *real* money demand, where the real money demand for the US dollar and the pound can be written as M_{US}/P_{US} and M_{UK}/P_{UK} respectively. (Division of any nominal variable by the price level converts it into a real variable. For example, dividing the nominal GDP, usually written as Y, by

---

2 Some of the demand for US dollars is actually by foreigners who like the dollar. This raises the demand for dollars and, *ceteris paribus*, raises the foreign exchange value of the dollar. For simplicity of exposition at this point, we ignore foreign demand for a nation's currency.

the price level, P, gives the real GDP, usually written as $Q = Y/P$.)

Equations (21.1) and (21.2) show respectively the real demands for money in two countries, the United States and United Kingdom:

$$\frac{M_{US}}{P_{US}} = Q_{US}^{\alpha} r_{US}^{-\beta} \qquad (21.1)$$

$$\frac{M_{UK}}{P_{UK}} = Q_{UK}^{\alpha} r_{UK}^{-\beta} \qquad (21.2)$$

The real money demands are on the left-hand sides of the equations, being the nominal amounts demanded divided by the respective price levels. The first term on the right-hand side of each equation shows that the real demand for money in each country depends on the country's real GDP, respectively shown as Q_{US} and Q_{UK}. This is because the real GDP equals the real amount of goods and services people buy, and the more goods and services people buy, the more money they need to have for making purchases. The extent that the real quantity of money demanded varies with the real GDP is shown to depend on α. If, for example, $\alpha = 1$, then the real demand for money goes up and down by the same amount as the GDP: if the real GDP goes up 10 percent, real money demand also goes up 10 percent. If $\alpha > 1$ the real demand for money goes up by more than the real GDP, and if $\alpha < 1$ the real demand for money goes up by less than real GDP.[3] For simplicity we assume the value of α is the same in the two countries.

Equations (21.1) and (21.2) also show that the quantity of money demanded in each country declines as that country's nominal (or market) interest rate increases. This is because the opportunity cost of holding money (cash) rather than buying bonds or some other interest-bearing asset is the nominal interest that would otherwise be earned.

The assumption that the real demand for each country's money depends on real income and interest rates only in that particular country implicitly assumes that different countries' monies are not substitutable. The alternative assumption, that different countries' monies are substitutable, would mean, for example, that the British view US dollars as satisfying their demand for money: perhaps they can use these dollars in some circumstances to make payments. We could accommodate this situation by making the demand for US dollars in equation (21.1) a function of British economic variables as well as the US variables. Such an extension of the monetary theory would be helpful to explain why, for example, the US money supply could grow relatively fast without causing a US dollar depreciation: the demand for US dollars could keep pace with the supply if foreigners are also demanding the extra dollars. **Dollarization**, which refers to the growing use of the US dollar as the *de facto* international money during the last part of the twentieth century, could in this way explain the value of the dollar against many currencies during this period. A reduced demand for dollars by foreigners switching to alternative currencies starting in late 2003 could explain the subsequent drop in the dollar.

The monetary approach to exchange rates assumes that people adjust their money holdings until the quantity of money demanded equals the quantity of money supplied. The way this occurs is as follows. If, for example, the supply of money exceeds the demand for money, the public attempts to spend the excess supply of money by buying goods and bonds. Of course, money does not disappear when it is spent, but rather ends up in somebody else's hands – or more precisely, in somebody else's bank account. However, an attempt to get rid of money does restore equilibrium between money supply and demand. This occurs because the buying of goods causes an increase in the price level, and the buying of bonds causes higher bond prices, which in turn mean lower interest rates. The higher price level and lower interest rates increase the quantity of money demanded: higher prices mean people need more money to make their normal

---

3 The parameter α is the real income elasticity of the real demand for money. When this exceeds 1.0 we say that money is a "luxury," and when it is less than 1.0 we say that money is a "necessity." Empirical evidence suggests that the income elasticity of money demand is close to 1.0.

purchases, and lower interest rates reduce the opportunity cost of holding money, thereby raising the quantity of money demanded. The process continues until the demand for money has risen to match the higher supply. Similarly, an excess demand for money causes reductions in spending on goods and bonds as the public tries to restore their money holdings to desired amounts: by not spending they hope to have some money left from their income to add to their money holdings. The lack of spending on goods and bonds lowers prices and raises interest rates – due to lower bond prices – and the lower prices of goods and higher interest rates reduce the quantity of money demanded. This continues until money demand has been reduced sufficiently to match the lowered money supply.

If it seems odd that money demand adjusts to equal money supply, think of what would happen if helicopters flew overhead dropping money on everybody. This would not make countries richer. What it would do, since people had chosen the amount of the wealth to hold as money before the helicopters came, is cause an excess supply of money. With people holding "too much money," they would attempt to restore balance by either spending the money – increasing prices – or by investing it, raising bond prices, that is lowering interest rates. The higher prices of goods would increase the demand for money. Lower interest rates would also raise the demand for money because it would reduce the opportunity cost of holding it. The price increase and interest decrease would eventually raise money demand so that people want to hold the money that was dropped by the helicopters.

If the money demand equals the money supply, as we have just argued, then we can interpret M_{US} and M_{UK} as the two countries' money supplies as well as their money demands. If we also rearrange equations (21.1) and (21.2) to put the money supplies on the right-hand sides, we have

$$P_{US} = M_{US}Q_{US}^{-\alpha}r_{US}^{\beta} \qquad (21.3)$$

$$P_{UK} = M_{UK}Q_{UK}^{-\alpha}r_{UK}^{\beta} \qquad (21.4)$$

Remember that M_{US} and M_{UK} and are to be interpreted as money supplies. Equations (21.3) and (21.4) show that, *ceteris paribus*, price levels in the two countries vary in proportion with the countries' money supplies. Prices also vary inversely with real GDP, and in the same direction as nominal interest rates.

According to the monetary theory of exchange rates, the ratio of prices in two countries is related to the exchange rate between the two countries' currencies. In particular, in the context of the United States and the United Kingdom, the monetary theory assumes the PPP principle in static form as described in Chapter 7, namely that

$$S(\$/\pounds) = \frac{P_{US}}{P_{UK}} \qquad (21.5)$$

Substituting equations (21.3) and (21.4) into equation (21.5) we find

$$S(\$/\pounds) = \frac{M_{US}}{M_{UK}} \left(\frac{Q_{UK}}{Q_{US}}\right)^{\alpha} \left(\frac{r_{US}}{r_{UK}}\right)^{\beta} \qquad (21.6)$$

Equation (21.6) captures the essential features of the monetary approach to exchange rates.

An examination of equation (21.6) shows that the first and most distinctive implication of the monetary approach is that the US dollar value of the pound, $S(\$/\pounds)$, increases if, *ceteris paribus*, the US money supply increases more than the British money supply. The reason is that if the US money supply is rising faster than the British money supply, US inflation will be higher than British inflation, so that according to the PPP principle, the dollar must fall vis-à-vis the pound.

The second prediction of the monetary approach characterized by equation (21.6) is that, *ceteris paribus*, the value of the pound increases if the British real GDP increases faster than the US real GDP. This occurs because a higher real GDP means a higher quantity of money demanded. This is seen in equations (21.1) and (21.2). For a given supply of money, a higher quantity of money demanded means an excess demand for money. When there is an excess demand for money people reduce their spending on goods and services in an effort to add to their money holdings. It is not possible for people collectively to add to the nominal amount of money they collectively hold: the money supply is determined by the central bank in conjunction with the commercial banks, not the general public. However, the effort to add to money holdings by spending less lowers the price level, which does increase the *real* money supply.[4] According to the PPP principle as in equation (21.5), a lower price level means an appreciation of the exchange rate, which in this case of more rapid real GDP growth in Britain than the United States means an appreciation of the pound.

The prediction that faster real economic growth causes currency appreciation is different from what might be predicted from the flow supply and demand view of exchange rates in Chapter 6. The flow theory we explained in Chapter 6 might be interpreted as suggesting that faster growth of real GDP would lead to faster growth of spending, including the purchase of imports. Higher imports would increase the supply of currency in the foreign exchange markets and cause a depreciation of the exchange rate. Monetarists argue that the simple flow supply-and-demand models overlook the link between the goods and services market on the one hand, and the financial market on the other, that is, the link between GDP and the demand for money. The prediction of the monetary approach, that currency appreciation is associated with faster economic growth, tends to be supported by the data.

Another prediction of the monetary approach is that, *ceteris paribus*, the higher is the US interest rate relative to the British interest rate, the higher is the US dollar value of the pound. In terms of

equation (21.6), the higher is r_{US}, the higher is $S(\$/\pounds)$ because β is positive. It follows that an unexpected jump in a country's nominal interest rate will cause its currency to depreciate. The reason for this prediction of the monetary approach is that the higher is a country's nominal interest rate, the lower is the real quantity of money demanded: a high interest rate means a high opportunity cost of holding money. For a given money supply, a lower quantity of money demanded means an excess supply of money. This leads to an increase in the price level as people spend the money they do not wish to hold. The PPP condition, equation (21.5), shows that if the US price level increases, the US dollar loses value against the pound. Therefore, we reach the conclusion that the higher is the US interest rate relative to the British interest rate, the lower is the value of the dollar. Flow theories of exchange rates such as that outlined in Chapter 6 and conventional wisdom suggest otherwise, predicting that higher US interest rates – or more precisely US dollar interest rates – will increase the demand for US interest-bearing securities, thereby increasing the demand for dollars and the value of the dollar.[5]

A prediction of the monetary approach with which many economists will agree concerns the effect of expected inflation on the exchange rate. It is generally accepted that, *ceteris paribus*, higher expected inflation leads to higher nominal interest rates.[6] We have just

---

4 As well as buying fewer goods, people may attempt to add to their money holdings by selling bonds. This lowers bond prices and raises their yields. This reduces the demand for money because lower bond yields mean a lower opportunity cost of holding money. This helps eliminate the excess demand for money, along with lower prices. The simple monetary approach focuses on the price level rather than bond yields, while the more sophisticated theories, such as the overshooting theory explained later, consider both.

5 The evidence supports the prediction of the flow theory in that appreciations (depreciations) of the dollar are empirically associated with increases (decreases) in US nominal interest rates. See Brad Cornell and Alan C. Shapiro, "Interest Rates and Exchange Rates: Some New Empirical Results," *Journal of International Money and Finance*, December 1985, pp. 431–42, and Gikas A. Hardouvelis, "Economic News, Exchange Rates and Interest Rates," *Journal of International Money and Finance*, March 1988, pp, 23–35.

6 For the theory behind expected inflation and interest rates see Maurice D. Levi and John H. Makin, "Anticipated Inflation and Interest Rates: Further Interpretation of Findings on the Fisher Equation," *American Economic Review*, December 1978, pp. 801–12. For the empirical evidence, see Maurice D. Levi and John H. Makin, "Fisher, Phillips, Friedman and the Measured Impact of Inflation on Interest," *Journal of Finance*, March 1979, pp. 35–52.

473

seen that a relatively higher nominal interest rate causes a currency to depreciate. Therefore, the monetary approach predicts that relatively higher expected inflation causes depreciation. Because higher expected inflation suggests a future depreciation via the PPP condition (a higher future price level means a lower future currency value), what the monetary approach tells us is that the effect occurs immediately rather than later: we do not have to wait for the expected inflation to occur. The idea that expected future events are reflected immediately in spot exchange rates is an important ingredient of the **asset approach to exchange rates** considered in the next section.

The interest rate that represents the opportunity cost of holding money is the nominal interest rate, not the real rate: money is a contractual asset that has the same nominal value whatever the inflation rate, so what is given up by holding money is the nominal interest rate. The nominal interest rate is equal to the real rate plus the anticipated rate of inflation. Large swings in nominal interest rates are likely to be more the result of changes in anticipated inflation than they are the result of variations in real interest rates. Hence high nominal interest rates are likely to reflect high expected inflation which in turn is likely to mean a depreciation in the future via PPP. This conforms with the prediction of the monetary theory of exchange rates, that high interest rates are associated with a currency depreciation. The asset approach tells us this happens immediately. What we find is that it is important to distinguish between real and nominal interest rates when considering implications for exchange rates. Relatively high real interest rates are likely to be associated with currency appreciations while relatively high nominal interest rates are likely to be associated with currency depreciations.

Before leaving the monetary approach it is worth recalling that while the money demand equations (21.1) and (21.2) show each country's money demand depending on the country's own economic conditions, this is not necessarily the case. In particular, the demand for the US dollar could well depend on economic conditions in other countries due to the widespread use of the dollar for transactions and savings. This is an aspect of dollarization mentioned earlier. This means that rapid growth in world trade and overall economic conditions, and especially in countries where the US dollar is held in high regard as a "safe haven," could lead to an appreciation of the US dollar. The strength of the US dollar in the 1990s might be traced to the world economic growth of that decade and the rapid economic progress of China, Russia, and other economies where US dollars were widely held by ordinary citizens.

THE ASSET APPROACH TO EXCHANGE RATES

Exchange rates are relative prices of two assets: monies. The current value of an asset depends on what that asset is expected to be worth in the future. For example, the more valuable a stock is expected to be worth, the more it is worth now. Similarly, the more a currency is expected to be worth in the future, the more it is worth now. It follows that today's exchange rate depends on the expected future exchange rate. In turn, the expected future exchange rate depends on what is expected to happen to all the factors mentioned so far as affecting currency demands or supplies.

The asset approach to exchange rates, which has been articulated most clearly by Michael Mussa, looks at the current spot exchange rate as a reflection of the market's best evaluation of what is likely to happen to the exchange rate in the future.[7] All relevant available information about the future is incorporated into the current spot rate. Because new information is random, and could as easily be

7 Michael Mussa, "A Model of Exchange Rate Dynamics," *Journal of Political Economy*, February 1982, pp. 74–104. This paper follows an earlier statement of the asset approach in Jacob A. Frenkel and Michael L. Mussa, "The Efficiency of Foreign Exchange Markets and Measures of Turbulence," *American Economic Review*, Papers and Proceedings, May 1980, pp. 374–81.

good or bad news for one currency versus the other, the time path of the exchange rate should contain a random component. This random component fluctuates around the expected change in exchange rate. The expected change can reflect the implications of PPP – with more rapid inflation than elsewhere implying depreciation – or any other influence on exchange rates that is reflected in asset supplies or demands or in the balance-of-payments accounts.

The asset approach holds implications for the effect of fiscal policy as well as monetary policy. For example, it predicts that high fiscal deficits can result in an immediate depreciation. This would happen if the fiscal deficit caused people to expect future expansion of the money supply as the government allowed money to expand in the course of making interest payments on its growing debt. Higher future money supply implies higher future prices, and according to the PPP principle, this implies a future depreciation. The future depreciation translates into an immediate depreciation via the forward looking nature of the asset approach.

The predictions of the asset approach concerning the effect of a fiscal deficit are different from those that arise from the flow theory based on currency supplies and demands in the balance-of-payments account. In particular, suppose a country has a growing fiscal deficit, but that savings in that country and other demands for funds by businesses and consumers are given. The growing fiscal deficit therefore means more capital imports or smaller exports. The capital imports represent a demand for the currency of the country with the fiscal deficit. The bigger the deficit, *ceteris paribus*, the higher the capital imports and hence the higher the demand for the currency. *Ceteris paribus*, this should cause the currency to appreciate. We find the somewhat surprising conclusion that a fiscal deficit can cause a country's currency to strengthen in value. However, this is likely to be a temporary phenomenon as borrowing from abroad might mean a current demand for the country's currency, but it also means a future supply. This is because interest payments on the debt mean a supply of currency on

the current account. Indeed, the asset approach might suggest the deficit has a muted immediate effect at best because people will look forward and impute some present value to the future interest payments.

The asset approach offers an explanation for departures from PPP. Because expectations about the future are relevant to the current exchange rate, there is no necessity for the spot exchange rate to ensure PPP at every moment. For example, if a country is expected to experience rapid future inflation, poor trade performance, or something else leading to future depreciation, the current exchange rate of that country's currency is likely to be below its PPP value. However, because the expected future exchange rate could be based on a tendency for PPP to be restored, the asset approach is not inconsistent with PPP as a long-run tendency. Nor, therefore, is the asset approach necessarily inconsistent with the long-run implications of the monetary approach.

THE PORTFOLIO-BALANCE APPROACH TO EXCHANGE RATES

The simple monetary approach to exchange rates assumes that people want to hold their own-country's currency but not the foreign country's currency.[8] The **portfolio-balance approach** recognizes that people might want to hold *both* monies, although they are likely to hold relatively more of one money, their own. The portfolio-balance approach to exchange rates makes the same argument for bonds. That is, it assumes that people demand domestic and foreign bonds or, more generally, that people prefer diversified portfolios of securities. Furthermore, the portfolio-balance approach also recognizes that supplies and demands for monies and bonds must be in equilibrium or balance, that is, all financial markets must

---

8 We mentioned earlier that the monetary approach can be adapted to consider foreign demand for a country's currency, as has been the case for the US dollar.

clear.[9] (The fact that the approach is based on diversification of portfolios and has a requirement that markets balance explains its name, the portfolio-balance approach.)

In the monetary approach each country's bond market is assumed to clear, whatever happens to the supply of or demand for any country's bonds. This assumption is implicit in the absence of equations for bond supplies and demands, and in the absence of any conditions for bond markets to clear; without there being conditions showing when the bond markets clear, by implication they are assumed to always clear. It is possible to rationalize this assumption of the monetary approach if it is argued that one country's bonds are perfectly substitutable for another country's bonds. This is because then, if the supply of one country's bonds is increased, the extra bonds will be held by residents or foreigners substituting these for other countries' bonds they currently hold. Changes in the supply of just one country's bonds are of such insignificance in the context of the entire world market for bonds that the global demand for bonds equals the global supply without any noticeable effect on interest rates or exchange rates.

When we add bond demand equations and equilibrium conditions for bond demands to equal bond supplies for each country's bonds, as we do in the portfolio-balance approach, the implications are different from the monetary approach. In particular, we find effects of bond supplies and demands on exchange rates and interest rates as well as effects of money supply and money demand.

In order to illustrate the consequences of bond supplies and bond demands for interest rates

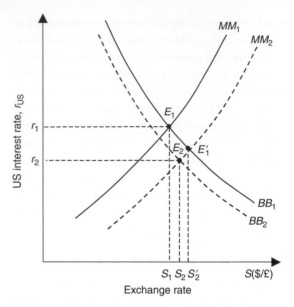

Figure 21.1 *The portfolio-balance theory: effect of open-market operations*

Notes
MM_1 represents initial equilibrium in the US money market. The line slopes upwards because higher r_{US} reduces money demand, while higher $S(\$/£)$ increases money demand via increasing wealth due to an increase in the dollar value of British bonds and currency. BB_1 represents initial equilibrium in the US bonds, market. The line slopes down because lower r_{US} reduces demand for US bonds, while a higher $S(\$/£)$ raises demand for US bonds by increasing wealth via making British bonds and currency more valuable in dollars. When the US money supply increases via the Fed's buying of bonds, MM_1 shifts to the right to MM_2, and BB_1 shifts to the left to BB_2. Both movements reduce r_{US}; compare E_2 to E_1. Note that the bond supply reduction reduces the depreciation of the dollar; compare E_2 to E_1' where the latter is the equilibrium when the money supply is increased without the Fed buying bonds.

and exchange rates we can use the diagrammatic representation of the portfolio-balance theory in Figure 21.1. The figure shows the US interest rate, r_{US}, on the vertical axis, and the exchange rate, $S(\$/£)$, on the horizontal axis, where a movement to the right along the horizontal axis is a depreciation of the dollar/appreciation of the pound.

The curve labeled MM_1 represents all of the interest rate/exchange rate combinations consistent with initial equilibrium in the US money market; along MM_1 the demand to hold US money equals the US money supply. MM_1 assumes a given, initial

9 Therefore, the portfolio-balance model consists of demand and supply equations for money and bonds in all countries, as well as equations setting money and bond demands equal to supplies. We do not need to write down these equations in order to appreciate the essential features of the approach. However, for a comprehensive treatment of the approach see Pentti J. K. Kouri and Michael E. Porter, "International Capital Flows and Portfolio Equilibrium," *Journal of Political Economy*, May/June, 1974, pp. 443–67.

money supply. MM_1 slopes upward because a higher US interest rate reduces the quantity of money that people demand; higher interest rates increase the opportunity cost of holding money. Because the supply of money is assumed constant, a lower quantity of money demanded represents an excess supply of money if nothing else is changed. However, by increasing $S(\$/\pounds)$ as r_{US} increases, the value of Americans' holdings of British bonds is increased; the pound values of British bonds and money held by Americans translate into more US dollars. That is, a higher value of $S(\$/\pounds)$ increases the wealth of Americans via an increase in the dollar value of their holdings of British bonds and money. Higher wealth increases the demand for US money; money is a component of wealth, and *ceteris paribus*, as wealth increases the demand for money increases. The higher demand for US money from a higher $S(\$/\pounds)$ offsets the lower quantity of US money demanded from a higher, r_{US}, so the demand for money can remain equal to the unchanged money supply. Therefore, the US money market can remain in equilibrium if $S(\$/\pounds)$ increases as r_{US} increases, meaning an upward-sloping line, MM_1, the line along which US money supply and demand are in equilibrium.

The line BB_1 represents all of the interest rate/exchange-rate combinations consistent with initial equilibrium in the US bond market, which is where the demand to hold US bonds equals the bond supply. The line slopes downwards because, *ceteris paribus*, as r_{US} decreases the fraction of wealth Americans want in US bonds decreases: lower returns on US bonds makes them less attractive than British bonds or holding money. However, the BB_1 line takes the US bond supply as given, so with Americans wanting less US bonds there is disequilibrium: US bond supply exceeds demand. Equilibrium can be maintained if the demand for US bonds can be increased to offset the lower demand at lower values of r_{US}. In order to achieve this, it is necessary to have an increased value of $S(\$/\pounds)$ which increases the US dollar value of US-held British bonds and money; the pounds translate into more US dollars. This makes Americans richer,

which among other things increases their demand for US bonds. Therefore, in order to maintain US bond market equilibrium it is necessary to increase $S(\$/\pounds)$ as r_{US} is decreased, which means a downward-sloping line BB_1: recall that the BB_1 line is the combination of the variables on the two axes maintaining bond market equilibrium.

The diagrammatic framework in Figure 21.1 can show how the implications of the portfolio-balance theory differ from those of the monetary theory. Consider, for example, the effect of an increase in the US money supply, M_{US}, brought about by open-market operations. The money supply is expanded by the Fed buying bonds in the open market, thereby reducing the supply of bonds available to the US public.[10] The monetary approach summarized by equation (21.6) predicts, *ceteris paribus*, that an increase in M_{US} will cause a depreciation of the US dollar by the same percentage as M_{US} increases. The portfolio-balance theory recognizes that in addition to the direct effect of the money supply, there is also an effect of the excess demand for bonds caused by the central bank's purchase of bonds, since as we have said, the supply of bonds available to the public is reduced.

In terms of Figure 21.1, the increase in M_{US} shifts the money market equilibrium line from MM_1 to MM_2. This follows because at a given r_{US} on the initial money market equilibrium line MM_1, there is an excess supply of money after the US money supply has been increased. This excess supply can be reduced by a lower r_{US}, which increases the quantity of money demanded via a lower opportunity cost. This means a downward shift from MM_1 to MM_2; equilibrium occurs everywhere at a lower r_{US}. The excess supply of money could also be reduced by an increase in $S(\$/\pounds)$ which increases Americans' wealth; British bonds and money are more valuable when translated into

10 In an open-market operation to expand the US money supply, the Fed buys Treasury bills and bonds in the open market, paying by crediting bill and bond sellers' accounts at the Fed. When spent, the sellers' deposits at the Fed become commercial bank reserves, permitting more bank loans and thus an expansion of the money supply.

US dollars with more dollars to the pound. The higher American wealth increases Americans' demands for money, especially their own. This means a rightward shift from MM_1 to MM_2. Whichever way we view the shift of MM – as downward or as rightward – the MM_1 curve has shifted to MM_2. The intersection of MM_2 with BB_1 is at a lower US interest rate and a depreciated value of the dollar: compare E_1' with E_1 in Figure 21.1, where we see that E_1' is at a higher value of $S(\$/£)$. However, this is not yet the new equilibrium because we have not yet accounted for the effect of the reduced supply of bonds available to the US public brought about by the Fed's open-market purchase of bonds used to increase the money supply.

Fewer US bonds in the hands of Americans, meaning a smaller US bond supply, also means an excess demand for US bonds. This can be prevented if r_{US} is lower or if $S(\$/£)$ is lower. (A lower US interest rate reduces the quantity of US bonds demanded, helping match the reduced bond supply. Similarly, less of Americans' wealth in British bonds caused by a lower $S(\$/£)$ helps achieve the preferred relative increase in US versus British bond holdings.) Whether it be via r_{US} being reduced or via $S(\$/£)$ being reduced, the effect of the reduced supply of US bonds is to shift BB_1 down and to the left to BB_2: the new equilibrium points corresponding to each previous equilibrium point is at a lower r_{US} or at a lower $S(\$/£)$. With the shift of MM_1 to MM_2 and of BB_1 to BB_2 we see what the portfolio-balance theory predicts. Specifically, an increase in the US money supply causes less of a depreciation of the dollar when the bond supply is reduced, as it is with open-market operations, than when the money supply is increased but the bond supply is not reduced; compare E_2, where BB_2 intersects MM_2, with E_1', which is the equilibrium with constant bond supply.[11] That is, unlike the monetary approach, the portfolio-balance approach predicts that the effect of changes in money supplies on exchange rates depends on *how* money supplies are changed. Also,

we no longer have a depreciation in the same proportion as the relative growth in the money supply as indicated by the monetary theory in equation (21.6).

As a second example of the predictions of the monetary theory versus the prediction of the portfolio-balance theory, consider the effect of a higher US real GDP. Equation (21.6) shows that the monetary theory predicts an appreciation of the US dollar by proportion α. The effect of higher US real GDP via the portfolio-balance theory is shown in Figure 21.2. The figure shows that MM_1 has shifted to MM_2. (The higher income increases the demand for money which can be offset by a higher r_{US} or lower wealth. The latter is achieved by a reduction in $S(\$/£)$ making British bonds and money less

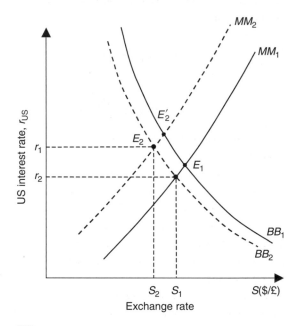

Figure 21.2 *Real income growth and the portfolio-balance theory*

Notes
Higher US income increases the demand for money in the United States and shifts MM_1 to MM_2; money equilibrium can be maintained via higher, r_{US}, reducing the quantity of money demanded, or via lower $S(\$/£)$, reducing wealth from a lower dollar value of British bonds and currency. Higher US income also increases savings and the demand for US versus British bonds. This causes BB_1 to shift left to BB_2; lower r_{US} and $S(\$/£)$ reduce the demand for US bonds. The new equilibrium from income growth involves an appreciated dollar.

---

11 In Figure 21.1 we assume that the effect of the shift in MM dominates the shift of BB so that the dollar depreciates.

valuable in Americans' portfolios.) Higher income also increases Americans' savings and thereby Americans' demands for US bonds relative to British bonds; Americans prefer US bonds to British bonds. A balance with the fixed supply of US bonds can be achieved via a lower r_{US} – shifting BB_1 down to BB_2 – or via a lower $S(\$/£)$, shifting BB_1 left to BB_2. Figure 21.2 shows that the leftward shift of MM_1 to MM_2 and of BB_1 to BB_2 both cause an appreciation of the US dollar.[12] This is the same qualitative conclusion as following from the monetary theory. However, we see that the exchange-rate appreciation is the result of adjustments in both the money and bond markets, and therefore is larger than the exchange-rate appreciation occurring only via the money market; compare E_2 with E_2', where E_2 is the equilibrium with adjustments in the money *and* bond markets.

THEORIES OF EXCHANGE-RATE VOLATILITY

The Dornbusch sticky-price theory[13]

In the monetary approach presented earlier, we assumed that the PPP condition holds for the overall price level; P_{US} and P_{UK} in equation (21.5) are the prices of baskets containing *all* goods and services. If this assumption about PPP is relaxed, the monetary approach can generate exchange-rate **overshooting**, which occurs when exchange rates go beyond their new equilibrium level before returning to it.

Let us suppose that PPP holds for internationally traded goods but not for products that are not traded internationally, such as land and many services. Let us suppose prices of nontraded goods are

"sticky," that is, they move slowly toward their new equilibrium after a disturbance. On the other hand, countries that are price takers pay the world price for internationally traded goods multiplied by their exchange rate, and so we can assume that prices of these goods are flexible, changing as the country's exchange rate changes. In these circumstances, if the exchange rate falls in proportion to the percentage increase in a country's money supply, as suggested by the monetary approach, there still remains an excess supply of money. This is because prices of traded goods increase in proportion to the country's money supply because they move directly with the exchange rate as given by equation (21.6), but prices of nontraded goods increase only slowly. Therefore, the overall price level increases less than the money supply, leaving the demand for money lower than the supply: recall that the demand for money increases in the same proportion as the *overall* price level. Eventually, the excess supply of money is eliminated via rising prices of nontraded goods, but in the interim the excess supply of money causes increased spending on goods and bonds.

The theory of overshooting exchange rates concentrates on the effect of the increased spending on bonds, arguing that this causes higher bond prices and, consequently, lower interest rates. If a country's interest rates are lower than rates in other countries, capital leaves the country until the country's currency is low enough that it is expected to appreciate by the extent to which its interest rate is below that of other countries.[14] In order for the currency to be expected to appreciate, the exchange rate must overshoot, going lower than its eventual equilibrium level. This means that prices of traded goods, which move with the exchange rate, increase by even more than the increase in the money supply, thereby augmenting the increase in the price index.

---

12 In Figure 21.2 we assume the shift in *MM* dominates *BB* so that at F_2 are higher than at F_1

13 More complete accounts of the Dornbusch sticky-price theory can be found in Rudiger Dornbusch, "Expectations and Exchange Rate Dynamics," *Journal of Political Economy*, December 1976, pp. 1161–76, and in Rudiger Dornbusch, *Open Economy Macroeconomics*, 2nd edn, Basic Books, New York, 1988.

14 This is because as we saw in Chapter 8, the return from investing in a country consists of two components: the interest rate, and the change in the value of the country's currency between the time of the investment and maturity. Therefore, an expected appreciation of a country's currency compensates for lower interest rates in that country.

This increases the demand for money, as does the low interest rate, helping to maintain the equality of supply and demand for money in the short run.

In the long run, prices of nontraded goods increase in the same proportion as the increase in the money supply: they increase slowly due to their stickiness, but do eventually catch up. This means that, in the long run, the exchange rate needs to depreciate only in the same proportion as the increase in the money supply. Therefore, after overshooting beyond the new (lower) long-run equilibrium level, the exchange rate appreciates back to its new equilibrium. This appreciation reduces prices of traded goods, so that in the end, prices of traded and nontraded goods have both increased in the same proportion as the money supply. Therefore, the overshooting is temporary, lasting only as long as the prices of nontraded goods lag behind the increase in the money supply. Furthermore, the appreciation of the currency back to equilibrium is consistent with the temporary reduction in the interest rate: the expected appreciation actually occurs.

Figure 21.3 illustrates the overshooting we have described. The ray from the origin in the top right-hand quadrant shows the PPP principle for a given level of British prices. The line reflects the PPP condition, $P_{US} = S(\$/£) \cdot P_{UK}$. The upward-sloping line shows that for a given P_{UK}, higher US prices are associated with a dollar depreciation of the same proportion; a higher $S(\$/£)$ is a dollar depreciation.

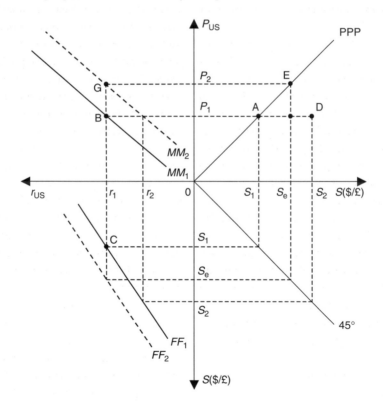

Figure 21.3 *Exchange-rate overshooting*

Notes
With the initial US money supply the equilibrium price level is P_1 and the exchange rate is S_1. An increase in the money supply shifts the money market equilibrium line from MM_1 to MM_2, and at the sticky price P_1, r_{US} falls to r_2 and the dollar depreciates from S_1 to S_2. As prices increase, the equilibrium P_{US} and $S(\$/£)$ move to E. At E the price level is, P_2, and r_{US} returns to r_1. The higher price level shifts FF_1 to FF_2; higher US prices must be offset by a depreciated dollar. The new exchange rate is S_e which is on the PPP line at price P_2.

The downward-sloping line MM_1 in the top left-hand quadrant represents initial equilibrium in the US money market for a given money supply. Higher prices increase the demand for money, and this is offset by an increase in the interest rate which reduces the quantity of money demanded by increasing the opportunity cost of holding it. The line FF_1 in the bottom left-hand quadrant represents initial equilibrium in the foreign exchange market. It shows a higher US interest rate associated with a dollar appreciation. (A higher r_{US} attracts capital and improves the capital account. For balance in the foreign exchange market, we need to offset this by a more expensive US dollar which worsens the current account. Hence, equilibrium in foreign exchange requires that dollar appreciation be associated with a higher interest rate.) FF_1 is drawn for the US price level P_1.[15]

Suppose that the US money supply is initially such that for a given British price level, the US is at point A on the PPP line, with price level P_1 and exchange rate S_1. Drawing a horizontal line from point A to point B on MM_1 shows the associated interest rate, r_1, where the US money market is in equilibrium: recall that along MM_1 US money demand equals money supply. Next, drawing a line from B on MM_1 down to C on the FF_1 line gives the spot rate S_1 on the vertical axis where the foreign exchange market is in equilibrium: the line FF_1 shows the combinations of interest rate and exchange rate providing foreign exchange market equilibrium. The 45-degree line in the bottom right-hand quadrant allows us to trace the spot rate over to the horizontal axis, where we have S_1, the initial spot rate, consistent with the initial US price level P_1; the 45-degree line simply allows us to transfer the vertical axis to the horizontal axis. Now let us consider what happens after an increase in the US money supply.

An increase in the US money supply shifts MM_1 to MM_2; to induce people to demand the extra money it is necessary to have a higher P_{US} or lower r_{US}. If prices are sticky at P_1, the new equilibrium interest rate is r_2, given off MM_2 at P_1. The line FF_1, which is drawn for price level P_1, shows the new spot rate S_2 associated with r_2. This spot rate is shown also on the horizontal axis; we transfer axes via the 45-degree line. With the current sticky price level P_1, and the spot rate S_2, we are at point D in the top-right quadrant, where point D is below the PPP line. This is a temporary disequilibrium, with the US dollar undervalued relative to PPP: there are more dollars per pound than for PPP.

Eventually prices of nontraded goods begin to increase. We can show that a new equilibrium is eventually attained at E. This is because at E the price level is P_2, and the US interest rate, given off MM_2 at point G is r_1. With prices higher at P_2, the foreign exchange market equilibrium line shifts from FF_1 to FF_2. (Higher prices would cause a current account deficit unless there was a depreciation of the dollar. Therefore, as the price level increases, foreign exchange market equilibrium requires a higher value of $S(\$/\£)$, which means a downward shift from FF_1 to FF_2, where FF_2 is the foreign exchange market equilibrium line at US price level P_2.) At r_1 and with FF_2 the spot rate is S_e. When S_e is transferred to the horizontal axis via the 45-degree line, the value of S_e and P_2 coincide at E, the new equilibrium exchange rate and price level satisfying PPP, with this being at the new, higher US money supply.

Figure 21.3 shows the spot rate going from S_1 to S_2 to S_e, an overshooting of the eventual equilibrium S_e. The US dollar appreciation from S_2 to S_e occurs after the interest rate has temporarily declined to r_2, with the expected appreciation of the dollar compensating for the lower r_{US}. As the appreciation ceases – the equilibrium value S_e is attained – r_{US} moves to its initial level, r_1; there is no reason for the interest rate to change when the stock of money changes to a new level and then remains constant because inflation should return to zero. We should recall that the overshooting of the exchange rate is

---

15 The 45-degree line in the bottom right-hand quadrant is simply to move between the goods market equilibrium in the upper right-hand quadrant and the foreign exchange market equilibrium in the bottom left-hand quadrant.

caused by some prices being sticky, in this case those of the nontraded goods. Exchange-rate volatility that has occurred has heightened interest in this overshooting theory, with Dornbusch's theory having been cited by the *The Economist* as one of the ten most influential economics papers of the twentieth century.[16]

Varying elasticities

As we saw in Chapter 6, if the demand for imports is inelastic in the short run, then depreciation can increase the value of imports; import prices increase by more than the quantity of imports declines, so that the value (price × quantity) of imports increases. This means that the amount of a country's currency supplied can increase with a depreciation. If the demand for the currency does not increase by as much as the supply because export demand is also very inelastic in the short run, a depreciation causes an excess supply of the currency. An excess supply means further depreciation. Therefore, while inelasticities persist there is depreciation, further excess supply, further depreciation, and so on. However, eventually, as elasticities of import demand and export supply increase, stability returns to the exchange rate. Therefore, it is possible for exchange rates to overshoot.

A particular variant of the varying elasticities explanation of overshooting that has been advanced by Steven Magee is that previously agreed-upon export contracts make demand and supply elasticities effectively zero in the short run.[17] For example, if a given, contracted quantity of wheat is purchased by Britain at a contracted US dollar price, then a depreciation of the pound increases pound payments for the wheat in proportion to the depreciation, causing an excess supply of pounds and further depreciation. What happens is that the British demand for imports has an elasticity of zero during the contract period. Only when the contract expires can the quantity purchased decline as a result of the higher pound price. In the interim, the exchange rate can overshoot.

Stock adjustment and flow fluctuations

Overshooting of exchange rates can also be explained by arguments akin to those of the **accelerator model**.[18] Let us do this with the help of an example.

Suppose British investors save £10 billion each year and divide it evenly between British and US investments. Suppose that they have accumulated £100 billion of investments in each country from their investments during previous years, but that suddenly, perhaps because of the election of a popular US president or an unpopular British Prime Minister, British investors decide to increase their US investments from 50 to 60 percent of their portfolios.

After their portfolios have been adjusted, the British will purchase £6 billion of US investment (60 percent of their annual savings of £10 billion) and therefore £6 billion of US dollars per year to pay for this investment. However, in order to readjust their accumulated portfolios, the British must purchase another £20 billion of US investments and the necessary US dollars; with £100 billion in each country, having 60 percent of the portfolio in US assets requires having £120 billion of US assets, and hence the extra $20 billion. If the readjustment of the accumulated portfolios occurs during one year, the path of the annual British demand for dollars goes from £5 billion during the year before the adjustment to £26 billion during the readjustment year, and then back to £6 billion per year after adjustment. Therefore, the demand for dollars is

16 "Why Exchange Rates Change," *The Economist*, Schools Brief, November 24, 1984, pp. 66–7.

17 Steven Magee, "Contracting and Spurious Deviations from Purchasing Power Parity," in Jacob A. Frenkel and Harry G. Johnson (eds), *The Economics of Exchange Rates: Selected Readings*, Addison-Wesley, Reading, MA, 1978.

18 The accelerator model offers an explanation of the business cycle – an overshooting of the GDP – based on assuming the stock of capital is proportional to the GDP. As GDP is rising investment is positive. When GDP stops rising investment drops to zero. This decline in investment causes a decline in GDP. The consequence is swings in GDP.

abnormally high during the period in which accumulated portfolios are being readjusted, and this can cause the value of the US dollar to overshoot. The basic reason is that accumulated portfolios are large relative to annual additions to portfolios, that is, stocks are large relative to flows.[19]

A reason why large shifts in desired portfolios might occur is that some forms of money do not pay interest. Normally, interest rates increase to make up for expected depreciations, so that investors do not switch assets because they anticipate a depreciation. Without interest being paid on money, this compensation is not possible. Consequently, large adjustments between different countries' monies can occur, causing large flow demands and exchange-rate overshooting.[20]

Other theories of overshooting

We have by no means exhausted the theories of overshooting. For example, Jeffery Frankel and Kenneth Froot have offered a theory of "speculative bubbles" in exchange rates, based on changes in the amount of attention currency managers pay to chartists, who extrapolate recent trends, and fundamentalists, who consider the fundamentals such as long-run adherence of exchange rates to PPP.[21] Frankel and Froot argue that portfolio managers attach more weight to the predictions of the group of forecasters that has been more accurate in the recent past. If chartists happen to be correct for a while possibly just by chance, their predictions are followed, making their predictions correct, causing even greater attention to be paid to them, and so on. Because the chartists' predictions are self-reinforcing, it is only when exchange rates have become completely out of line with fundamentals that the chartists are likely to falter, making portfolio managers switch their attention to the advice of fundamentalists. When this shift in attention occurs, exchange rates move back from their disequilibrium levels. Eventually, even if just by chance, the chartists are likely to be more correct than the fundamentalists, which with self-realizing effects, causes another bout of overshooting exchange rates.

SUMMARY

1. Several theories of exchange rates have been advanced which are based on the stocks of countries' monies versus the demands to hold these monies.

2. Asset-based theories differ according to the assets they consider, and whether they involve rational expectations of the future.

3. The monetary approach to exchange rates is based on the need for money supplies and money demands to be equal, where money demands depend on price levels, real GDPs and interest rates, and money supplies are determined by banks, especially the central bank.

---

19 This explanation for exchange-rate overshooting has been advanced by Robert M. Dunn, Jr, *The Many Disappointments of Flexible Exchange Rates*, Essays in International Finance, 154, Princeton University, Princeton, NJ, December 1983.

20 For variants of this explanation of volatility of exchange rates see Lance Girton and Donald Roper, "Theory and Implication of Currency Substitution," *Journal of Money, Credit, and Banking*, February 1981, pp. 12–30, and Ronald I. McKinnon, "Currency Substitution and Instability in the World Dollar Market," *American Economic Review*, June 1982, pp. 302–33.

21 Jeffrey A. Frankel and Kenneth A. Froot, "The Dollar as an Irrational Speculative Bubble: A Tale of Fundamentalists and Chartists," *National Bureau of Economic Research*, working paper 959, 1988. For an earlier model of overshooting based on different market players see Richard G. Harris and Douglas D. Purvis, "Diverse Information and Market Efficiency in a Monetary Model of Exchange Rates," *Economic Journal*, December 1981, pp. 829–47.

4   The monetary approach predicts an exchange rate will depreciate by the excess of money supply versus demand in one country over another. It also predicts that faster growth of real GDP will cause an appreciation, and that higher interest rates and expected inflation will cause a depreciation.

5   The asset approach to exchange rates suggests that the current exchange rate depends on the expected future exchange rate. Since the expected future rate can depend on expected inflation or anything appearing in the balance-of-payments accounts or affecting asset supplies and demands, the asset approach is consistent with other theories of exchange rates.

6   The portfolio-balance approach assumes different countries' bonds are not perfect substitutes. As a result, changes in preferences for bonds of one country over another, or changes in bond supplies, can affect exchange rates.

7   If prices are sticky, exchange rates may overshoot their equilibrium. Other explanations of exchange-rate overshooting include elasticities of import demand and export supply that vary over time, and portfolio readjustment causing jumps in currency supplies or demands during the readjustment period.

REVIEW QUESTIONS

1   What are the essential components of the monetary theory of exchange rates?

2   What does the monetary theory of exchange rates assume about the substitutability of different countries' monies and bonds?

3   What does the monetary theory of exchange rates imply for
   a   Relatively rapid growth in a country's money supply?
   b   Relatively rapid growth in a country's national income?
   c   An increase in a country's interest rates versus interest rates in another country?

4   Does the asset approach to exchange rates consider expectations about future exchange rates?

5   What does the portfolio-balance approach to exchange rates assume about the substitutability of different countries' monies and bonds?

6   What is meant by exchange-rate overshooting?

7   What does the Dornbusch overshooting theory assume about the speed of adjustment of different prices?

8   What happens in the Dornbusch overshooting theory to interest rates after exchange rates have overshot their eventual equilibrium?

ASSIGNMENT PROBLEMS

1   Why does the monetary approach imply that higher *expected* inflation causes a currency to depreciate?

2   Suppose that

$$M_{US} = \$500 \text{ billion}$$
$$M_{Can} = C\$50 \text{ billion}$$
$$Q_{US} = \$7,000 \text{ billion}$$
$$Q_{Can} = C\$600 \text{ billion}$$
$$\alpha = 1$$
$$\beta = 0$$

and that PPP holds. What exchange rate is implied by the monetary theory of exchange rates?

3   Assume in the previous question that all magnitudes are unchanged except the Canadian money supply which increases from C\$50 billion to C\$55 billion. What happens to the implied exchange rate, and how does this compare to the percentage change in the Canadian money supply?

4   Assume that all data in Question 2 are unchanged except the US GDP, Q_{US}, which increases from \$7,000 billion to \$7,700 billion? What happens to the exchange rate, and how does this compare in magnitude to the change in US GDP?

5   What does the asset approach imply about the ability to make money by speculating in foreign exchange?

6   How can the asset approach explain deviations from PPP based on current price indexes?

7   What are the principal differences and similarities between the monetary and portfolio-balance approaches to exchange rates?

8   What is the crucial assumption required for exchange-rate overshooting in the Dornbusch model? Do you think this assumption is valid?

9   Why does the foreign exchange equilibrium line *FF* move downwards in Figure 21.3 when there is an increase in the US price level?

10 How does the portfolio-balance approach differ in its predictions of the effect of a money supply expansion via open-market operations and a money supply expansion via a reduction in reserve requirements? Use a figure such as Figure 21.1 to reach your conclusions.

11 Is the long-run equilibrium of Dornbusch's overshooting theory consistent with the monetary theory of exchange rates?

12 Why does the interest rate return to its initial level in the Dornbusch overshooting theory after an increase in the stock of money to a new level?

BIBLIOGRAPHY

Bilson, John F.O., "The Monetary Approach to the Exchange Rate: Some Empirical Evidence," *Staff Papers,* International Monetary Fund, March 1978, pp. 48–75.

Chen, Chau-Nan, Ching-Chong Lai, and Tien-Wang Tsaur, "The Loanable Funds Theory and the Dynamics of Exchange Rates: The Mundell Model Revisited," *Journal of International Money and Finance,* June 1988, pp. 221–9.

Dooley, Michael P. and Peter Isard, "The Portfolio Balance Model of Exchange Rates," *International Finance Discussion Papers*, Board of Governors of the Federal Reserve, no. 141, May 1979.

Dornbusch, Rudiger, "Expectations and Exchange Rate Dynamics," *Journal of Political Economy*, December 1976, pp. 1161–76.

——, *Open Economy Macroeconomics*, 2nd edn, Basic Books, New York, 1988.

The Economist, "Why Exchange Rates Change," Schools Brief, November 24, 1984, pp. 66–7.

Hooper, Peter and John Morton, "Fluctuations in the Dollar: A Model of Nominal and Real Exchange Rate Determination," *Journal of International Money and Finance*, April 1982, pp. 39–56.

Stultz, René M., "Currency Preferences, Purchasing Power Risks and the Determination of Exchange Rates in an Optimizing Model," *Journal of Money, Credit and Banking*, August 1984, pp. 302–16.

Chapter 22

Alternative systems of exchange rates

As science joins with technology to reduce man's ignorance and appease his wants at appalling speed, human institutions lag behind, the victim of memory, convention and obsolete education in man's life cycle. We see the consequences of this lag...at the nerve center of national sovereignties; international economic arrangements.

Robert Mundell

When exchange rates are flexible, as they were assumed to be in Chapters 6 and 21, they are determined by the forces of market supply and demand. When exchange rates are fixed, they are determined by governments or government-controlled authorities such as central banks which provide residual supply and demand to prevent rates from changing.

During the last two centuries, several methods have been employed for fixing exchange rates. Our purpose in this chapter is to describe the main fixed exchange-rate systems that have been in effect at various times since the early nineteenth century, not to provide a history of international financial arrangements, but rather to explain how the different systems involved mechanisms which automatically helped correct deficits and surpluses in the balance of payments. This is a function that is performed by exchange rates themselves when they are free to adjust. We shall also see that international financial arrangements change through time, usually in response to deficiencies in the adjustment processes. Fixing one problem often highlights new ones which in turn need to be addressed. This suggests that while at this time the predominant

exchange-rate system is one of flexible exchange rates, there is no guarantee that things will remain this way, and furthermore, many countries even today persist in fixing rates. Some important countries, such as China, have limited convertibility of their currencies into foreign exchange, and with permitted conversions being done at a fixed rate.[1] Understanding how the international financial system has evolved and the variations that persist in this system is important for acquiring a comprehensive understanding of the international business environment.

One automatic balance-of-payments adjustment mechanism which has received particularly close attention is that involving the price level. We shall explain the so-called **automatic price-adjustment mechanism** in the context of the classical gold standard.[2]

---

1 China has to decide first whether to make the yuan freely convertible into foreign currencies, and second, if it is made convertible, whether to convert at an official fixed exchange rate or at a market determined exchange rate.

2 Two other adjustment mechanisms, one involving national income and the other interest rates, are explained in Appendix A in this chapter.

THE CLASSICAL GOLD-STANDARD SYSTEM

The gold standard and arbitrage

The essential feature of the gold standard is that each country stands ready to convert its paper or **fiat money** into gold at a fixed price.[3] This fixing of the price of gold fixes exchange rates between currencies. For example, if the US Federal Reserve agrees to buy and sell gold at $400/oz., and the Bank of England agrees to buy and sell gold at £250/oz., the exchange rate between the pound and dollar in the form of paper currency or bank deposits will be $1.6/£ ($400 ÷ £250). If the exchange rate is not $1.6/£, the foreign exchange market will not balance because it will be used for converting one currency into the other, but not vice versa. For example, if the exchange rate in the foreign exchange market is $1.50/£, the market will be used for converting dollars into pounds, but not for converting pounds into dollars. This is because it is cheaper for people converting pounds into dollars to buy gold from the Bank of England with pounds (one pound buys 1/250 oz. of gold at £250/oz.), ship the gold to the US, and sell it to the Federal Reserve for dollars; for 1/250 oz. the Fed pays $1.60 ($400/oz. × 1/250 oz.). This round-about exchange gives more dollars per pound to those converting pounds into dollars, than the $1.50/£ received in the foreign exchange market. However, people converting dollars into pounds pay $1.50/£ on the foreign exchange market versus $1.60/£ via buying, shipping, and selling gold. (Each pound requires selling 1/250 oz. of gold to the Bank of England. To buy 1/250 oz. of gold from the Federal Reserve costs $400 × 1/250 = $1.60.)

Since people are converting dollars into pounds, but not pounds into dollars at the exchange rate of $1.50/£ there is a demand for pounds on the foreign exchange market, but no supply of pounds. This excess demand for pounds will increase the price of the pound to $1.60/£. Similarly, if we begin with an exchange rate of $1.70/£, the foreign exchange market will be used by people converting pounds into dollars, but not by people converting dollars into pounds; the latter group will instead buy gold from the US Fed with dollars, ship the gold to Britain, and sell the gold for pounds. With people selling pounds and not buying pounds, the dollar value of the pound will fall from $1.70/£ until it reaches $1.60/£. That is, if the price of gold is $400/oz. in the US and £250/oz. in Britain, the equilibrium exchange rate on the foreign exchange market is $1.60/£.

We have based our argument on one-way arbitrage, that is, by considering people who plan to exchange currencies and are looking for the cheaper of two methods: exchange via the foreign exchange market, or exchange via buying, shipping, and selling gold. This is the type of arbitrage we considered when discussing cross exchange rates in Chapter 2 and covered interest parity in Chapter 8. An alternative way of reaching the same conclusion is with round-trip arbitrage, which involves showing that if the exchange rate in our example is not $1.60/£, people can profit by buying gold with domestic money, shipping the gold to the other country, selling the gold for foreign currency, and then selling the foreign currency for domestic money. This is a round trip, starting and ending with domestic currency. When there are no transaction costs, one-way and round-trip arbitrage produce the same result. However, when it is costly to exchange currencies as well as costly to ship, buy, and sell gold, round-trip arbitrage implies an unrealistically large possible range in the exchange rate. Appendix B derives the possible range in exchange rates based on the correct, one-way arbitrage argument. The end points of the possible exchange rate range are called **gold points**. Exchange rates must be between these points.

Price adjustment and the gold standard

Different exchange-rate systems involve different mechanisms for adjusting to imbalances in international payments and receipts. One of these

---

3 Fiat money is money whose face or stated value is greater than its intrinsic value. Its value comes from the edict, or fiat, that it must be accepted in discharge of financial obligations.

mechanisms involves changes in the price level. The price-level adjustment mechanism under the gold standard is known as the **price-specie automatic-adjustment mechanism**, where "specie" is just another word for precious metal. This mechanism was described as early as 1752.[4] In order to explain the mechanism, let us continue to assume that gold is $400/oz. in the US and £250/oz. in Britain and that the resulting exchange rate is $1.60/£. Let us also assume that Britain buys more goods and services from the United States than the United States buys from Britain, that is, Britain has a trade deficit with the United States. The price-specie adjustment mechanism explains how the British deficit and the US surplus are automatically corrected.

With Britain buying more goods and services from the United States than the United States is buying from Britain, there is an excess supply of pounds; more pounds are supplied by residents of Britain than are demanded by residents of the United States. With flexible exchange rates this would reduce the value of the pound below $1.60/£, but with a gold standard this will not happen because nobody will sell pounds in the foreign exchange market for less than $1.60. Rather, as soon as the pound dips even slightly below $1.60, people will sell pounds to the Bank of England in return for gold, ship the gold to the US, and sell the gold to the Federal Reserve for dollars. This gives people $1.60 for each pound. Therefore, the result of the British balance-of-payments deficit is the movement of gold from the Bank of England to the US Federal Reserve.

An alternative way of reaching this conclusion is to assume that while all domestic transactions are settled with paper money, international transactions are settled in gold. Therefore, if Britain buys more goods and services from the United States than the United States buys from Britain, more gold leaves Britain than arrives in Britain, with the reverse being the case for the United States.

Whatever way we view it, we have gold leaving the deficit country, Britain, and arriving in the surplus country, the United States.

The movement of gold from the deficit country, Britain, to the surplus country, the United States, has effects on both countries' money supplies. This is because in standing ready to exchange gold for paper money at a fixed price, central banks have to make sure they have sufficient gold on hand for those who wish to exchange paper money into gold. Prudent banking requires that a minimum ratio of gold reserves to paper money be held, and indeed, this used to be mandated in many countries, including the United States where a minimum gold reserve equal to 25 percent of circulating currency used to be required. The maintenance of a minimum reserve ratio means that as the Bank of England loses gold it needs to reduce the amount of its paper money in circulation. At the same time, the increase in the Federal Reserve's gold reserves allows it to put more paper money into circulation.

In fact, the changes in paper money in circulation occur automatically as people buy and sell gold for international settlement. The British take paper currency to the Bank of England when buying gold. This reduces the amount of paper pounds in circulation. At the same time Americans take gold to the Fed and receive paper money in return. In other words, as a result of the British trade deficit and US trade surplus the British money supply shrinks and the US money supply expands. In the minds of the eighteenth-century classical economists who described the working of the gold standard, the fall in the money supply in the deficit country would cause a fall in the country's price level. At the same time, the increase in the money supply in the surplus country (in the two-country world we are describing, one country's deficit is the other country's surplus) would cause an increase in the country's price level. The link between the money supply and prices the classical economists had in mind was the **quantity theory of money**. This theory predicts that prices change in proportion to changes in the money supply. With prices falling in the deficit country, Britain, and increasing in the

---

4 David Hume, "Of the Balance of Trade," in *Essays on Money, Political Discourses*, London, 1752, reprinted in Richard Cooper, *International Finance*, Penguin, Baltimore, MD, 1969.

surplus country, the United States, there is a decline in British prices versus US prices. The relatively cheaper British goods makes British exports more competitive in the United States, helping them increase. At the same time, US goods in Britain become less competitive than Britain's own import substitutes, so that British imports decline.[5] With British exports increasing and imports decreasing, Britain's deficit declines. Indeed, until the deficit has been completely eliminated there will be an excess supply of pounds, a sale of pounds to the Bank of England, a shipment of gold to the US, a decrease in the British money supply, an increase in the US money supply, lower British prices, higher US prices, increasing competitiveness of British products at home and abroad, and a continued reduction in the British trade deficit.

The price-specie adjustment mechanism works not only via changes in relative prices *between* countries, but also via changes in relative prices *within* each country. In the deficit country, for example, the prices of nontraded goods will decline, but the prices of goods which enter international trade will remain unchanged. This is because prices of traded goods are determined by world supply and demand, not by local market conditions. The fall in the relative price of nontraded versus traded goods in the deficit country will encourage local consumers to switch from traded to nontraded goods. At the same time, local producers will find it relatively more profitable to produce traded goods. The switch in consumer spending will free more tradable goods to be available for exports and at the same time producers will produce more tradable goods. These effects will be reinforced by developments in the surplus countries: the prices of nontraded goods in these countries will rise relative to the prices of traded goods, switching consumers toward traded goods and producers away from them. Altogether, we

shall find exports of the deficit country increasing and imports decreasing, thereby improving the trade balance.[6]

Unfortunately for the effectiveness of the price-specie automatic-adjustment mechanism of the gold standard, governments were often tempted to abandon reserve ratios between gold and paper money when the maintenance of those ratios ran counter to other objectives. If a deficit is not allowed to reduce the money supply because, for example, the government thinks this will raise interest rates or unemployment to intolerable levels, the price-adjustment process cannot work to correct the trade deficit. If, at the same time, surplus countries with rising gold reserves do not allow their money supplies to grow from surpluses because, for example, of a fear of inflation, then both causes of a relative price adjustment between countries are lost; we lose lower prices in the deficit country and higher prices in the surplus country. The policy of not allowing a change in reserves to change the supply of money is known as **sterilization** or **neutralization policy**. As goals of full employment became common in the twentieth century, many countries abandoned their effort to maintain reserve ratios and focused on their domestic economic problems.

As a result of neutralization, the gold standard was not allowed to work. This is perhaps the most powerful criticism of the system. But that does not explain whether it *could have* worked. Some economists, most notably Robert Triffin, have said that it could not work.[7] Central to this view is the notion that prices are rigid downward (a feature of Keynesian economics) and that therefore trade

---

5 However, we showed in Chapter 6 that, even if Britain buys a smaller *quantity* of imports from the United States because US goods become more expensive, there could be an increase in the *value* of imports. This would occur if the British demand for imports were inelastic.

6 For an account of this and other fixed-exchange-rate adjustment systems, see Rudiger Dornbusch, *Open Economy Macroeconomics*, 2nd edn, Basic Books, New York, 1988, or Leland Yeager, *International Money Relations: Theory, History, and Policy*, 2nd edn, Chapter 5, Harper & Row, New York 1976.

7 Robert Triffin, "The Myth and Realities of the So-called Gold Standard," *The Evolution of the International Monetary System: Historical Reappraisal and Future Perspective*, Princeton University Press, Princeton, NJ, 1964; reprinted in Richard Cooper, *International Finance*, Penguin, Baltimore, MD, 1969.

deficits from gold outflows cannot be self correcting via the automatic price-specie adjustment mechanism. Critics of the gold standard support this with evidence on the parallel movement of prices in surplus and deficit countries, rather than the reverse price movement implied by the gold standard.

It is true that without a decline in *absolute* prices, improving a trade deficit is made more difficult. However, it is *relative* prices which are relevant (including those of nontraded versus traded goods *within* each country), and relative prices could decline if surplus countries' prices rose to a greater extent than those of deficit countries. If, therefore, prices are flexible upward and surplus countries' prices rise faster than those of deficit countries, we still have an automatic price-adjustment mechanism, although it is weaker than the mechanism that might have existed if absolute prices could fall. The other common criticism of the gold standard – that gold flows were frequently sterilized – is a valid criticism, but it is as much a criticism of the government for not allowing the gold standard to operate as it is of the gold standard itself.

A number of twentieth-century economists and politicians have favored a return to the gold standard. What appeals to the proponents of this system is the discipline that the gold standard placed on the expansion of the money supply and the check that this therefore placed on inflation.[8] The economists who prefer a return to the gold standard include Jacques Rueff and Michael Heilperin.[9]

---

8 In the nineteenth century, rather than favoring the gold standard because it kept inflation under control, there were many who opposed it on the grounds it was deflationary. As Exhibit 22.1 explains, the political debate over ending the gold standard and replacing it with a **bimetallic standard** was sufficiently intense to inspire the writing of a famous allegorical children's classic, *The Wonderful Wizard of Oz*.

9 See Jacques Rueff, "Gold Exchange Standard: A Danger to the West," *The Times* (London), June 27–29, 1961, reprinted in Herbert G. Grubel (ed.), *International Monetary Reform: Plans and Issues*, Stanford University Press, Palo Alto, CA, 1963, and Michael Heilperin, "The Case for Going Back to Gold," *Fortune*, September 1962, also reprinted in Grubel, ibid.

The politicians include the late French President Charles de Gaulle and former New York Congressman Jack Kemp. A return to the gold standard, or some standard based on gold, would make exchange-rate forecasting a relatively straightforward task. The exchange rate in normal times would vary within the gold points which are set by the buying or selling prices of gold at the central banks and by the cost of shipping gold from country to country. Larger changes in exchange rates would occur when countries changed the price of their currency in terms of gold, and this would be a reasonably predictable event. Countries that were running out of gold reserves would be forced to raise the price of gold, while countries which were gaining reserves might lower it.

THE BRETTON WOODS AND DOLLAR STANDARDS

The mechanics of the Bretton Woods system

With a gold standard, exchange rates, or at least their ranges of potential variation, are determined indirectly via the conversion price of each currency vis-à-vis gold. When the gold standard came to an end with the depression of 1929–33 – after temporary abandonment during the First World War – the exchange-rate system which eventually replaced it in 1944 offered direct determination of exchange rates vis-à-vis the US dollar. The system adopted in 1944 is called the **gold-exchange standard**. It is also called the **Bretton Woods system** after the town in New Hampshire at which its outlines were worked out. This direct method of determining exchange rates allowed movement in exchange rates between **support points**. Support points were the exchange rates at which foreign central banks purchased or sold their currency for US dollars to ensure that the exchange rate did not move beyond these points. In return for foreign central banks fixing, or **pegging**, their currencies to the US dollar, the United States fixed the price of

EXHIBIT 22.1   THE WONDERFUL WIZARD OF OZ: A MONETARY ALLEGORY

L. Frank Baum, author of the fanciful children's tale *The Wonderful Wizard of Oz*, first published in 1890, may well have received his inspiration at the Democratic convention in Chicago in 1896. It was at this convention that Presidential candidate William Jennings Bryan brought the cheering delegates to their feet with his rousing "Cross of Gold" speech. Declaring "Thou shalt not crucify mankind upon a cross of gold," Bryan campaigned on the promise to rid the US of the gold standard by adding silver to the money base at a fixed ratio of seventy ounces of silver per ounce of gold. The motive was to expand the US money supply which had grown far slower than national output since 1850, causing deflation of approximately 50 percent in the second half of the nineteenth century. This deflation had hit grain prices particularly badly, affecting Kansas and its neighboring states, which is where the story of the Wonderful Wizard begins.

The Wonderful Wizard of Oz opens in Kansas, the center of the "free silver" movement, where a cyclone, a metaphor for the discontent that swept the depressed US prairie states, carries Dorothy and her dog Toto to the Land of Oz. The abbreviation oz is, of course, a form of writing "ounce," as in, gold costing $400/oz, and Toto happens to connect to the "Teetotalers," the Prohibition Party which gave its support to the silver forces in return for support on liquor prohibition. Dorothy is informed by the Munchkins who inhabit Oz that her landing has killed the Wicked Witch of the East — a reference to the Eastern establishment or President McKinley who supported the gold standard. In order to return to

Kansas, Dorothy is told to follow the Yellow Brick Road — a clear reference to the gold bricks in which official gold was held — and to take with her the Witch's silver slippers, the silver that Bryan's supporters wanted added to the money supply. (Hollywood later changed the silver slippers to ruby slippers in the movie version of Baum's work.)

On her way along the Yellow Brick Road Dorothy first encounters the Scarecrow who represents the agricultural workers who supported moving from the gold standard to a gold–silver based bimetallic standard. Then she meets the Tin Woodsman who represents the industrial unions that joined the movement to end the gold standard. The Cowardly Lion who tags along is Presidential candidate Bryan himself — whose dedication to reaching the Emerald City becomes as much in doubt as Bryan's commitment to end the US attachment to gold. Numerous other references to gold and silver line the road the strange foursome — Dorothy, the Scarecrow, the Tin Woodsman, and the Cowardly Lion — follow, including the golden plate capping the pot of courage, the gold buckle that threatened to lock them up for ever, and the gold-handled axe with a blade that glistened like silver. The Wicked Witch of the West grabs one of the silver slippers; divided, the silver forces would not reach their goal. It was to be several years after *The Wonderful Wizard of Oz* was published before the gold standard was finally abandoned.

Source: Hugh Rockoff, "'The Wizard of Oz' as a Monetary Allegory," *Journal of Political Economy*, August 1990, pp. 739–60.

---

the US dollar to gold. Therefore, the gold-exchange standard involved

1   the United States being willing to exchange US dollars for gold at an official price;
2   other countries being willing to exchange their currencies for dollars around an official, or **parity**, exchange rate.

We shall deal with the history of the international financial system in the next chapter, but we can note that the ability to convert foreign *privately* held gold to dollars by the United States lasted until 1968, and the ability to convert foreign *officially* held gold lasted until 1971. With only the second part of the gold-exchange standard remaining in effect after 1968 — that part involving the exchange of foreign currencies for dollars – the fixed exchange system from 1968 until the end of the Bretton Woods system in 1973 is best described as a **dollar standard**.

Under the gold-exchange standard and the dollar standard, countries which pegged their exchange rates to the US dollar were required to keep the actual rate within 1 percent of the selected parity value. In order to ensure that the exchange vis-à-vis the dollar remained within the required 1 percent of official parity, it was necessary for central banks to intervene whenever free-market forces would have created an exchange rate that was outside the range. This intervention took the form of buying and selling the local currency for US dollars at the upper and lower support points around the official par value. The support points meant adding to or reducing central-bank official reserves whenever the uncontrolled exchange rate would have moved beyond the official limits. We can illustrate the way these fixed exchange standards operated by using a diagram.

Suppose that the Bank of England has decided, as it did from 1949 to 1967, to peg the value of the pound at a central value of $2.80. The upper and lower support points that the bank must maintain are $2.8280/£ and $2.7720/£. These are shown on the vertical axis of Figure 22.1, which gives the spot price of pounds in terms of dollars. The horizontal axis gives the quantity of pounds, and so the diagram has the price and quantity axes familiar from the theory of supply and demand. We have added to the diagram conventionally sloping supply and demand curves for pounds drawn against the price of pounds (measured in dollars). We have drawn the initial private demand curve for pounds, $D_1(£)$, intersecting the private supply curve of pounds, $S(£)$, within the 1 percent range allowed under the gold-exchange and dollar standards.

Suppose that for some exogenous reason there is an increase in demand for British exports. This might, for example, be because of a general economic expansion outside of Britain, a change in taste towards British goods, or the discovery of more oil and gas in the North Sea. This will shift the private demand curve for pounds to the right, from $D_1(£)$ to $D_2(£)$, and the private demand for pounds will

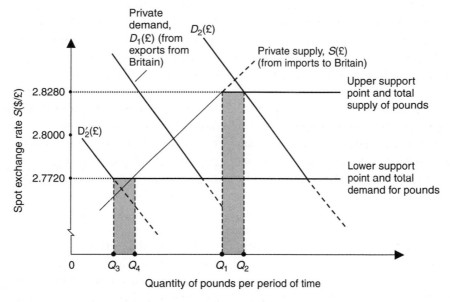

Figure 22.1 *The workings of the gold-exchange and dollar standards*

Notes
The Bank of England stood ready to buy pounds at the lower support point and sell pounds at the upper support point.
This made the demand curve for pounds perfectly elastic at the lower support point and the supply curve of pounds perfectly elastic at the upper support point, ensuring that the exchange rate was never outside the allowable range.

then intersect the private supply curve at an exchange rate above the allowed ceiling. In order to prevent this, the Bank of England must, according to the gold-exchange and dollar standards, intervene at the upper support point of $2.8280/£ and supply, in exchange for dollars, the pounds necessary to keep the rate from moving above this level. In terms of Figure 22.1, the Bank of England will supply Q_1Q_2 pounds for dollars. This, with the private supply of OQ_1 pounds and the demand curve of $D_2(£)$, would leave the exchange rate at $2.8280. Because the Bank of England will supply whatever number of pounds is required at the upper support point, the total supply curve of pounds becomes flat at this point, like the heavily drawn line in Figure 22.1. This is a feature of the gold-exchange and dollar standards; the total supply curve of the local currency – consisting of private and official supply – becomes perfectly elastic at the upper support point.

While the Bank of England supplies Q_1Q_2 pounds in Figure 22.1, it will be buying Q_1Q_2 times 2.8280 of US dollars, which is the shaded area above Q_1Q_2. The amount Q_1Q_2 is the gain in the Bank of England's foreign exchange reserves (its balance-of-payments surplus) valued in terms of pounds, and the shaded area above Q_1Q_2 is the gain in foreign exchange reserves, valued in terms of dollars.

Suppose that instead of rising to $D_2(£)$, the demand for pounds falls to $D_2'(£)$ as a result of, perhaps, a general slowdown in economic activity outside of Britain or a decline in prices Britain receives for its oil exports. According to private supply and demand, the price of the pound will fall below the lower support point, and to prevent this from happening, the Bank of England has to enter the market and purchase pounds. It will purchase Q_3Q_4 pounds with $2.7720 \times Q_3Q_4$ US dollars. The dollar amount is given by the shaded area above Q_3Q_4; it represents the decline in dollar reserves of the Bank of England. It is hence the deficit in the balance of payments, measured in terms of US dollars. Because the Bank of England must demand whatever number of pounds is not wanted by private buyers, the total demand for pounds that

includes both private and official demand is horizontal at the lower support point, $2.7720/£. This is another feature of the gold-exchange and dollar standards: the total demand curve for local currencies becomes perfectly elastic at the lower support point.

Price adjustment under the gold-exchange and dollar standards

To explain the price-level adjustment mechanism of the gold-exchange and dollar standards, we refer to Figure 22.2. Suppose that after starting with $S_1(£)$ and $D_1(£)$ and a privately determined exchange rate within the allowed range, there is an increase in private demand for pounds to $D_2(£)$. As before, the Bank of England will be required to supply Q_1Q_2 pounds. These pounds will increase the money supply in Britain; this occurs as the Bank of England sells pounds for dollars. If we again assume that prices vary with the money supply, the increase in the number of pounds in circulation will raise British prices. At each exchange rate on our vertical axis, this will lower the competitiveness of British goods. Exports will fall, assuming the demand for exports is elastic so that quantity declines more than export prices increase, and imports will increase. The decline in British exports will mean a lower demand for pounds. Therefore, the demand curve for pounds will move to the left. We assume that it moves to $D_2'(£)$. The increase in British imports will mean a larger supply of pounds to the foreign exchange market, and so the private supply curve moves to the right. We move it to $S_2(£)$. With the demand and supply curves at $D_2'(£)$ and $S_2(£)$, the privately determined exchange rate will return to the allowed range.

We find that intervention by a central bank affects the supply of money, local prices, and exports and imports and thus restores equilibrium between private supply and demand. Of course, if there is sterilization of the balance-of-payments surplus or deficit and the money supply is not allowed to change, the price-level adjustment mechanism will not work. Sterilization will result

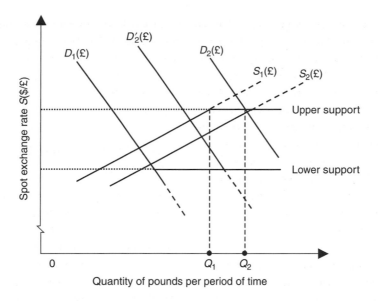

Figure 22.2 *The price-level adjustment mechanism of the gold-exchange and dollar standards*

Notes
If the demand for pounds moves to $D_2(£)$ and the quantity of pounds demanded exceeds the quantity supplied at the upper support point, the Bank of England must sell pounds in exchange for dollars. *Ceteris paribus,* this increases the British money supply and prices. Higher prices make British exports decline, shifting the demand curve for pounds back toward $D_2'(£)$. Higher prices also increase imports into Britain, and the currency demand supply curve shifts from $S_1(£)$ towards $S_2(£)$. Shifts in currency demand and supply curves move equilibrium exchange rates toward their allowable limits.

in a continued change in foreign exchange reserves and a need to eventually revise the parity exchange rate. This makes exchange-rate forecasting a potentially highly rewarding activity since the need to change the parity value becomes clearly apparent in foreign exchange reserve statistics. It is worthwhile to consider how exchange-rate forecasting can be done.

We have already noted that when exchange rates are determined on a gold standard, changes in exchange rates will follow large changes in gold reserves. For example, countries which are losing reserves will eventually be forced to raise the price of gold in terms of their own currency. This means a fall in the foreign exchange value of the currency. To take an example, if Britain were losing gold and raised its gold price from £250/oz. to £300/oz. while the US price remained fixed at $400/oz., the exchange rate would change from

$$S(\$/£) = \frac{\$400/oz.}{£250/oz.} = \$1.60/£$$

to

$$S(\$/£) = \frac{\$400/oz.}{300/oz.} = \$1.33/£$$

This is a devaluation of the pound.

By keeping track of gold reserves, a speculator could see when a central bank was under pressure to raise the price of gold, that is, to devalue. The exact date would be difficult to predict, but actions based on such an assumption would be unlikely to result in losses. A country that is losing reserves might manage not to devalue, but it certainly would not revalue, that is, raise the value of its currency by reducing the official price of gold. This means that a speculator would discover either she was correct and a devaluation did occur, or that the exchange rate remained as before. Thus, there is an opportunity for a one-way bet, and the worst that is likely to happen is that no speculative gain will be made. Indeed, widespread speculation that a devaluation will occur is likely to make it occur. Speculation

495

against a currency causes the central bank to buy its own currency, reducing foreign exchange reserves, thereby making devaluation appear even more likely. For example, prior to the devaluations of the Mexican peso in December 1994, speculators had decided that a peso devaluation was imminent. They therefore sold pesos, and the Mexican authorities were required to purchase them at the lower support point. The pesos were purchased with US dollars and hence the Mexican reserves were lowered. Eventually, reserves were so much reduced that the Mexican government was forced to devalue. The speculators' beliefs were vindicated. In a sense, their expectations were self fulfilling.

The need to reduce the value of a currency in a country experiencing deficits and declining reserves depends on the ability of the central bank to borrow additional reserves. There are arrangements between central banks for exchanging currency reserves, and procedures for borrowing from international institutions such as the International Monetary Fund (which is discussed in Chapter 23). The borrowing arrangements include **central-bank swaps**. Central-bank swaps involve, for example, the US government making US dollars available to the Bank of Canada when Canadian foreign exchange reserves are low. The Bank of Canada temporarily swaps these US dollars for Canadian dollars. The swap is reversed later, according to the original agreement. Often the swap is reversed only after a number of years to allow the borrowing country to correct its balance of payments. Central banks also frequently borrow from private banks. The Bank of Canada, for example, borrowed heavily from both Canadian and US commercial banks during the early- and mid-1980s despite the fact that the exchange rate was supposed to be flexible. The ability of central banks to borrow from other central banks, from private banks, and from international institutions makes the forecasting of exchange rates more difficult; revisions of par values can be delayed many years.

Another factor adding to the difficulty of forecasting changes in "fixed" rates is the difference in the need to react to surpluses and deficits.

Countries that are facing a deficit and losing reserves will ultimately be forced to devalue because their reserves and ability to borrow will eventually be gone. On the other hand, the countries enjoying surpluses will be under little pressure to revalue their currencies and may instead allow reserves to keep growing. This represents one of the major problems with the gold-exchange and dollar standards, namely that the responsibility for adjustment, whether this be via a change in the exchange rate or via an automatic change in money supplies and prices, falls on deficit countries more heavily than on surplus countries. This problem of asymmetric need for adjustment between deficit and surplus countries under the Bretton Woods system is one of the major differences between this fixed-exchange-rate system and the European Monetary System.

THE EUROPEAN MONETARY SYSTEM (EMS)

The structure of the EMS

At the same time as the Bretton Woods system was collapsing, a new fixed-exchange-rate system was emerging among the European Community (EC) countries. This new system began in 1972 as **the snake**, which was designed to keep the EC countries' exchange rates within a narrower band than had been adopted as part of a last minute attempt to salvage the dollar standard. The snake involved exchange rates being maintained within 1 and 1/8 percent of either side of selected par values, compared to $2\frac{1}{4}$-percent deviations allowed as part of a revision to the dollar standard in 1971. The snake was so-called after the shape of the time path of EC countries' exchange rates "wiggling" within the wider band allowed for other exchange rates. The snake, with some refinements including a widening of the band to $2\frac{1}{4}$ percent deviations, became the **Exchange Rate Mechanism (ERM)** of the **European Monetary System (EMS)** in 1979.

A central feature of the ERM was a **grid** that placed an upper and lower limit on the possible exchange rates between each pair of member currencies. The grid took the form of a matrix showing for each pair of currencies the par value as well as the highest and lowest permitted exchange rates, these being $2\frac{1}{4}$ percent above and below the par rates. That is, the matrix which listed the currencies across the columns and down the rows, had three exchange rates in each element: the par value, an upper limit, and a lower limit. If an exchange rate was at either limit, *both* countries were supposed to intervene. For example, if the Belgian franc was at its lower support point vis-à-vis the German mark, the Belgian authorities were required to buy Belgian francs *and* the German authorities were also supposed to buy francs. The fact that the Germans were also supposed to buy francs made the ERM fundamentally different from the Bretton Woods system. As we have seen, under Bretton Woods, if, for example, the pound was at its lower support point, Britain was required to buy pounds with dollars, but the United States was not required to cooperate by buying pounds too. Under the ERM, Germany was supposed to buy francs, which meant selling Deutschemarks, if the mark was at its upper limit against the Belgian franc, whether or not Germany liked the implications of the increasing money supply the sale of Deutschemarks brought about.

Partly because of the no-fault nature of the ERM, a **divergence indicator** was designed to identify if, for example, the Belgian franc was at its lower support point vis-à-vis the Deutschemark because of overly expansive Belgian monetary policy or overly restrictive German monetary policy. The divergence indicator was based on the value of the **European Currency Unit (ECU)**.[10]

The ECU was an artificial unit defined as a weighted average of each of the EC currencies. Each EMS country was required to maintain its exchange rate within a specified range of the ECU, as well as within a specific range vis-à-vis the other individual EMS currencies. This served to indicate which country was at fault when a currency approached a limit vis-à-vis another currency, because the country

at fault would also be close to its limit vis-à-vis the ECU. For example, if it was inflationary Belgian policy that forced the Belgian franc down vis-à-vis the German mark, the Belgian franc was also likely to be low against other currencies, and hence against the ECU. The country that was at fault was required to take corrective action or explain to other EMS members why it should not. Par values were to be realigned only as a last resort, although this happened on several occasions.

The ECU served an additional role in denominating loans among the EMS countries. For example, if Belgium borrowed from Holland to defend its exchange rate vis-à-vis the Dutch guilder or against the ECU, the loan could be denominated in ECUs. Private loans could also be denominated in ECUs. This reduced foreign exchange risk to the borrower and lender because the value of the ECU was likely to be more stable than the value of individual currencies; the ECU was like a portfolio of currencies, and as such, offered some diversification benefits. The ECU was also used to denominate loans made by the **European Monetary Co-operation Fund**, or **EMCF**. The EMCF made short-term and medium-term readjustment loans to EMS members out of a pool of funds at the **Bank For International Settlements** located in Basle, Switzerland. These lending arrangements as well as other detailed aspects of the EMS are dealt with in Exhibit 22.2.

The EMS ran into trouble during 1992. Britain was in severe recession with unemployment rates higher than at any other time since the Great Depression, 1929–33. Despite the recession, inflation had been relatively high, certainly vis-à-vis inflation in Germany during the several years prior to 1992. Italy was also experiencing recession and high inflation. These conditions in Britain and Italy occurred while Germany was experiencing its costly reunification. This required unprecedented offshore borrowing, and this in turn put German interest rates up; the need to attract capital meant German rates were above those in, for example, the Unites States – a stark reversal of traditional interest rate differentials. The high German interest rates put upward pressure on the Deutschemark, forcing

10 The acronym of the European Currency Unit, ECU, or *écu*, is the name of a silver coin that once circulated in France.

497

EXHIBIT 22.2 ALPHABET SOUP: ERM, EMS, ECU, AND ALL THAT

The European Monetary System was an attempt to improve upon Bretton Woods, keeping some of its features and adding new ones where necessary. The following article succinctly summarizes the important similarities and differences.

Like Bretton Woods, the EMS was based on a set of fixed parties called the Exchange Rate Mechanism (ERM). Each country was to establish a central parity of its currency in terms of ECU, the official unit of account. The ECU consisted of a basket containing a set number of units of each currency. As the value of currencies varied, the weights of each country in the basket would change. A parity grid of all bilateral rates could then be derived from the ratio of members' central rates. Again, like Bretton Woods, each currency was bounded by a set of margins of 2.25 percent on either side of parity, creating a total band of 4.5 percent (for Italy, and later the United Kingdom, when it joined the ERM in 1990, the margin was set at 6 percent on either side of parity). The monetary authorities of both the depreciating and appreciating countries were required to intervene when a currency hit one of the margins. Countries were also allowed, but not required, to undertake intramarginal intervention. The indicator of divergences, which measured each currency's average deviation from the central parity, was devised as a signal for the monetary authorities to take policy actions to strengthen or weaken their currencies. It was supposed to work symmetrically. Intervention and adjustment was to be financed under a complicated set of arrangements. These arrangements were designed to overcome the weaknesses of the IMF during Bretton Woods. The very short-term financing facility (VSTF) was to provide credibility to the bilateral parties by ensuring unlimited financing for marginal intervention. It provided automatic unlimited lines of credit from the creditor to the debtor members. The short-term monetary support (STMS) was designed to provide short-term finance for temporary balance of payments disequilibrium. The medium-term financial assistance (MTFA) would provide longer-term support.

Unlike Bretton Woods, where members (other than the United States) could effectively decide to unilaterally alter their parities, changes in central parities were to be decided collectively. Finally, like Bretton Woods, members could (and did) impose capital controls.

Source: Michael D. Bordo, "The Gold Standard, Bretton Woods and Other Monetary Regimes: A Historical Appraisal," *Review,* Federal Reserve Bank of St. Louis, March/April 1993, p. 180.

Britain and Italy to raise interest rates if they were to keep their exchange rates within the EMS limits. Speculators doubted they would do this, and sold British pounds and Italian lire hoping to gain from eventual devaluation. Germany refused to make any major concession by lowering interest rates, eventually forcing Britain and Italy to withdraw from the EMS in September 1992.

The European currency crisis of 1992 was matched in the following summer by a run on the French franc that eventually brought about a collapse of the EMS in August 1993. Only Germany and Holland decided to keep their currencies closely linked. The others agreed to a 15 percent deviation either side of EMS agreed par values. With a 30-percent range of variation, in effect the EMS fixed-rate era was over. Nevertheless, the European Community ministers continued to cling to the **Maastricht Agreement** which committed the Community members to a **common currency**. A common currency would mean truly fixed rates, because with all European member countries using the same currency, exchange rates could never change. Also, as we shall see, all countries sharing the common currency would have a common monetary policy.

Price adjustment under the EMS

Our explanation of the price-level adjustment mechanism of the gold-exchange and Bretton Woods system applies also to the EMS, with the one major difference that with the EMS, both countries' money supplies were influenced by official intervention. For example, if the Belgian franc was at its lower support point versus the Deutschemark, the Belgian money supply declined and the German money supply increased. *Ceteris paribus*, this reduced the Belgian price level and increased the German price level. This improved Belgium's trade in comparison with Germany's because of the lowering of Belgian versus German prices. Because prices in both countries contributed to the automatic adjustment, rather than one country as with the Bretton Woods system, the EMS price-adjustment mechanism was in principle relatively more effective. Furthermore, the requirement that both countries intervene helped overcome the problem of asymmetric needs for adjustment, a problem that detrimentally affected the functioning of Bretton Woods.

The EMS did allow for realignment of central values of the parity grid, and indeed there were several realignments. Forecasting when realignment would occur was made difficult by the cooperation built into the EMS in terms of joint foreign exchange market intervention, intercountry short-term lending, and loans from the EMCF. Nevertheless, as with the gold-exchange and dollar standards, it became evident to speculators when a currency urgently needed to be realigned, not least because of the currency's value vis-à-vis the ECU. This meant that speculators could guess which way the realignment would go. Indeed, as we have explained, pressure from speculators eventually helped bring about the collapse of the EMS.

HYBRID SYSTEMS OF EXCHANGE RATES

Fixed and flexible exchange rates are only two alternatives defining the extremes of exchange-rate systems. In between these extremes are a number of other systems which have been practiced at various times.

Dirty float

Central banks sometimes intervene in the foreign exchange markets even when they have declared that exchange rates are flexible. For example, Canada, which practiced floating exchange rates throughout the 1950s and has floated its currency since 1970, frequently intervenes (via the Bank of Canada) to "maintain order" in the foreign exchange markets. The Canadian central bank's policy is to try to prevent sharp changes in its exchange rate, but to allow market forces to operate over the long run. The purpose of this policy is to reduce short-run exchange-rate uncertainty, but to nevertheless allow the exchange rate to reflect differential rates of inflation and other fundamental forces over the long run. The Bank of Canada combines foreign exchange market intervention with interest-rate policy to stabilize Canada's exchange rate. This model of a so-called **managed float** or **dirty float** is a compromise between fixed and flexible exchange rates, and has been adopted by numerous countries at some time or other. Examples include Mexico, Singapore, Japan, Sweden, and Australia.[11]

Wider band

Another compromise between fixed and flexible exchange rates was tried for a very short while after December 1971, when the International Monetary Fund members decided at a meeting at the Smithsonian Institution in Washington, DC, to allow the range of fluctuation of exchange rates to be $2\frac{1}{4}$ percent on either side of the official value. This gave a $4\frac{1}{2}$-percent total range of variation before the central bank would intervene, compared with the

---

11 Those who favor exchange rate flexibility and who think intervention of any kind is a bad idea call it a dirty float. Those who think it is a good idea tend to call it a managed float.

2-percent range that existed from 1944 to 1971. The intention was to reduce the uncertainty about future exchange rates and at the same time allow more adjustment. The wider the band, the closer the system came to being a flexible-rate system.

The **wider band** was not tried by many of the major countries. Canada had opted for a floating rate before the Smithsonian meeting, and Britain and the other major European countries floated their currencies (some of which remained fixed to each other) shortly afterwards.[12]

Crawling peg

The **crawling peg** is an automatic system for revising the par or central value – the value around which the rate can fluctuate. This system can be combined with a wider band. The crawling peg requires the central bank to intervene whenever the exchange rate approaches a support point. However, the central value, around which the support points are set, is periodically revised according to the average exchange rate over the previous weeks or months, or perhaps according to inflation vis-à-vis an anchor currency. If the rate tends to remain at or near, for example, the lower support point, the new central value will be revised downwards. In this way the rate can drift up or down gradually, giving some degree of certainty without completely frustrating long-term fundamental trends.

Figure 22.3 illustrates a crawling peg. Starting at time t_0, intervention points are defined which are above and below a middle or par exchange rate. The intervention points are shown by parallel lines. If the actual exchange rate hovers at the lower end of its allowed range, then at the next setting of the intervention points the middle value is set at the average actual value during the previous period. If the actual exchange rate moves to the lower end of the new allowable trading range, the intervention points are again lowered at the next setting of these points. In this way the exchange rate can drift

12 For more on the wider band see John Williamson, "Surveys in Applied Economics: International Liquidity," *Economic Journal*, September 1973, pp. 685–746.

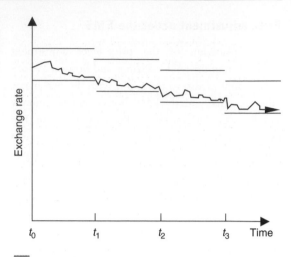

Figure 22.3 *Crawling peg*

Notes
Under a crawling-peg system, the support points are periodically revised according to a formula typically based on economic fundamentals such as inflation differentials, or according to past behavior of the exchange rate within its permissible band.

according to fundamental forces such as inflation rates and terms of trade, but importers and exporters can be reasonably sure about exchange rates applying to short-term foreign-currency receivables and payables.

An alternative way of readjusting the band within which a currency can trade is according to the recent rate of inflation. For example, the central value of the band vis-à-vis the US dollar could be changed by the country's inflation rate minus the US inflation rate. This keeps exchange rates moving directly according to economic fundamentals over long periods of time, but keeps them predictable in the short term. A crawling peg can also be based on balance-of-trade statistics or changes in the size of external debt. Most examples of crawling pegs have involved countries experiencing very rapid inflation. Several South American countries have at some time tried a crawling peg.

Mixed fixed and flexible rates

Another compromise between fixed and flexible exchange rates that has been tried is to have fixed exchange rates for some transactions, such as those on the current account of the balance of payments, but to have flexible rates for other transactions, such as those on the capital account. This division of systems would be motivated by a desire not to exert influence over international trade, but to maintain control over capital flows. Such a dual exchange-rate system was practiced by Belgium, which had a commercial exchange rate for imports and exports of goods and services, and a financial exchange rate for trading in financial assets. The commercial exchange rate was fixed, and the financial exchange rate was flexible. Only authorized banks were permitted to trade in the commercial market, while the financial market was open to all participants. The two tiers of the foreign exchange market were separated by a prohibition on buying foreign exchange in one market and selling it in the other.

Britain operated with two exchange rates for more than a quarter century while functioning under the Exchange Control Act of 1947. This act was designed to restrict capital outflows and required those making foreign investments to buy foreign currency from a **currency pool**. Funds in the pool came only from sales of securities trading in a currency or from occasional authorized additions. As a result the size of the pool of each currency was determined by the value of investments when the pool was established, subsequent realized gains on the value of investments, and special authorized additions. Exchange rates for investment funds from the pool were flexible and traded at a premium over exchange rates for noninvestment transactions. The exchange rates for other transactions were fixed over most of the years the currency-pool system was in effect.

Numerous other mixed exchange-rate systems have been tried, such as different exchange rates for imports versus exports, different exchange rates for different categories of imports, and so on, but these other systems are combinations of different fixed rates, not mixtures of fixed and flexible rates. Those interested in the other types of arrangements can consult the *Annual Report on Exchange Arrangements and Restrictions*, published by the International Monetary Fund.

Cooperative intervention in disorderly markets

After a period of considerable volatility in exchange rates, involving a substantial appreciation of the US dollar from its 1980 level and an equally sharp fall after 1985, a new compromise exchange-rate system was agreed to at an economic summit held in Paris at the Louvre Museum in 1987. This agreement, which became known as the **Louvre Accord**, represented a shift from a completely flexible exchange-rate system to a dirty float in which the leading industrial powers would cooperate.

The Louvre Accord followed the **Plaza Agreement** of 1985 – named after the Plaza Hotel in New York where it was worked out – in which the United States accepted the need to intervene in the foreign exchange markets during unstable times. The other leading industrial powers had recognized this need somewhat earlier, but knew that intervention would not work without close cooperation, given the very large size of private speculative capital flows. The Plaza Agreement was later confirmed at the 1986 Tokyo economic summit and reconfirmed at other economic summits, most notably the 1987 meeting in Paris that resulted in the Louvre Accord. These meetings took place against a background of immense exchange-rate instability, and resulted in a new compromise between completely flexible and completely fixed exchange rates. The meetings up to and including the 1986 Tokyo summit involved the United States, Japan, United Kingdom, West Germany, and France – the so-called Group of Five, or G-5. Subsequent meetings were expanded to include Canada – the US's largest trading partner – and Italy, and became known as the **G-7 summits**. Even more recently Russia has had observer status. The system that has emerged is not unlike Canada's approach of flexibility with intervention to achieve orderly markets, but because it involves cooperation, it is a little different from the Canadian dirty float.

The international financial system that emerged from the Louvre Accord can be characterized as a floating-exchange-rate system within **target**

zones that are periodically revised, but where the intervention levels are not precisely specified. The acceptable ranges of fluctuation have to be deduced from official communiqués released after summit meetings, or from statements by senior officials of the nations involved. For example, it might be stated after a G-7 meeting that the leaders are satisfied with exchange rates in their recent trading range. Alternatively, after a substantial movement of exchange rates, the governor of a central bank or a treasury official might say she believes the dollar is too low or too high, and that if the markets do not adjust there could be intervention. Market participants react to these statements according to how credible they believe them to be, and, for example, buy currencies the authorities say are too cheap. This can help reduce the need for intervention and has been described as "talking" exchange rates in the desired direction.

TARGET ZONES

The fixed exchange rate and compromise systems that have been described in this chapter can be characterized as involving, at least in part, a target zone for the exchange rate. For example, the zone in the gold-exchange standard was a 2-percent band around parity, in the EMS it was a $4\frac{1}{2}$ percent band, and so on. Having a credible target zone, which is one that private foreign exchange market participants believe is a government commitment, can help keep exchange rates *within* the declared zone – not at the outer limits – even if governments never actually intervene in the markets. Indeed, even if there is a less-than-total commitment to a declared target zone, the presence of the zone can be self-realizing. These conclusions have been reached in research by Paul Krugman.[13]

13 See Paul R. Krugman, "Target Zones and Exchange Rate Dynamics," *Quarterly Journal of Economics*, August 1991, pp. 669–82, and the papers in Paul R. Krugman and Marcus Miller (eds), *Exchange Rate Targets and Currency Bands*, Cambridge University Press, New York, 1992. For a survey of target-band research, see Lars E.O. Svensson, "An Interpretation of Recent Research on Exchange Rate Target Zones," *Journal of Economic Perspectives*, Fall 1992, pp. 119–44.

The stabilizing role of target zones can be described with the help of Figure 22.4. The actual exchange rate, taken as $S(\$/£)$, is shown on the vertical axis, while economic fundamentals affecting exchange rates are shown on the horizontal axis. Krugman assumed the fundamentals to consist of factors outside the control of government which evolve randomly, plus a factor – Krugman uses the money supply – that is under government control. Indeed, Krugman assumed that by appropriate adjustments of the money supply the government could counter any realization of the random factors, keeping the combined effects of the fundamentals – random factors plus money supply – such that the exchange rate would remain within the target zone. Krugman further assumed that the money supply is changed only if the exchange rate is at the ceiling or floor of the target zone, and not in between. That is, exchange rate intervention occurs only at the margins, with the money supply increasing at the ceiling, declining at the floor, and otherwise being constant. (An increase in money supply would cause higher inflation or lower interest rates pushing the currency down, while a decrease would achieve reduced inflation or higher interest rates pushing the currency up.)

The line showing the combined effect of the fundamentals on $S(\$/£)$ is the straight upward-sloping broken line in Figure 22.4. However, it is assumed that by adjusting the money supply as necessary at the margins – the target zone ceiling and floor – so that the combined fundamentals are within the limits F_L and F_U, the exchange rate can be kept within the target zone S_L to S_U.

Krugman realized that as well as fundamentals, a further factor affecting current exchange rates through the actions of speculators is expectations about changes in exchange rates in the future. That is, actual current exchange rates depend on current fundamentals plus speculators' exchange rate expectations. Expectations of changes in the future exchange rate depend on how close the current exchange rate is to the intervention levels. Specifically, the closer the exchange rate is to the upper level, S_U, the more likely is intervention, in this case

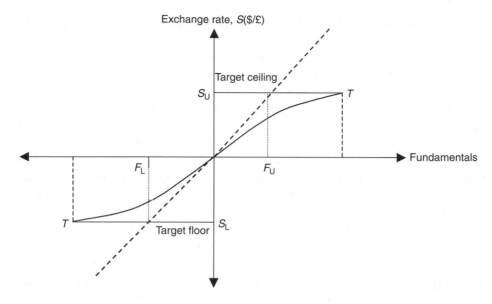

Figure 22.4 *Target zones for exchange rates*

Notes
The horizontal axis measures fundamentals, which consist of random uncontrolled factors, and the money supply, which is changed only at the target-zone edges to keep exchange rates within the zone. Exchange rates depend on fundamentals plus expectations about the future exchange rate. To the right of the midpoint along the horizontal axis there is expected pound depreciation – the probability of $S(\$/£)$ being pushed down is higher than the probability of $S(\$/£)$ increasing – and to the left of the midpoint there is expected pound appreciation. The combined effect of fundamentals and expectations is curve TT. This is tangential to the lines at the zone edges, implying no effect of fundamentals on exchange rates at the edges of target zones.

consisting of the Bank of England increasing the money supply to keep the pound from exceeding S_U. Similarly, the closer is $S(\$/£)$ to S_L, the more likely is a reduction in the British money supply to keep $S(\$/£)$ from moving below S_L. This means that as the exchange rate approaches S_U the probability of action to depreciate the pound makes the probability of depreciation exceed the probability of further appreciation. Therefore, there is an expected depreciation, where we use the term "expected" in the statistical sense: the probability-weighted outcomes that constitute the expected change in exchange rate are tilted toward an expected depreciation. As the exchange rate moves closer to S_L the reverse occurs, with the probability of official action to cause appreciation of the pound being relatively high. That is, to the right of the mid point on the horizontal axis of Figure 22.4 there is expected depreciation of the pound in the statistical sense, and along the left there is expected appreciation. Furthermore, the more we are to the right or left,

the greater is the expected pound depreciation or expected pound appreciation.

Recall that the actual exchange rate is the result of fundamentals plus exchange-rate expectations, where the latter is due to the actions of speculators. While *within* the target zone the fundamentals follow random patterns – intervention via money supply occurs only *at* the intervention points – the other component of exchange rate determination, the expectation of change in the exchange rate, pushes the rate to within the target zone. In terms of Figure 22.4, the effect of the combined fundamentals on their own (including the money supply) is for the exchange rate to follow the upward-sloping dashed line until the ceiling or floor is reached, and then to follow the horizontal lines at the ceiling or floor as the official intervention occurs. However, the other element of exchange-rate determination, namely the actions of speculators based on their expectations about exchange rates, works toward lowering current exchange rates to the right of the vertical axis in Figure 22.4, and to raising exchange rates to the left of the vertical axis. (Speculators sell pounds when their value is high, and buy when their value is low.) The aggregate effect of the two forces working together – the fundamentals and speculators – is the elongated S-shaped curve, *TT*. This curve is always flatter than the dashed line, and makes it clear that via speculators acting according to the prospect of intervention, the exchange rate follows a path *within* the target zone, even if the possible intervention does not occur. In some sense, stability is achieved without the government doing anything, other than *promising* to intervene if necessary.

There is a further conclusion to Krugman's model in addition to the "free stabilizing" conclusion we have just reached: it is free because it happens even when the government does nothing. The second conclusion is that at the edges of the target zone the exchange rate is insensitive to the random fundamentals. This conclusion follows by first noting that at the target zone edges the expected values on the horizontal axis which include the random fluctuations *and* the actions of the government are not continuous and random, but rather take "jumps." Specifically, at the moment the upper edge S_U is reached there is an upward jump in money supply, causing an expected negative change along the horizontal axis: the total fundamentals *include* the money supply. Similarly, the very moment S_L is reached there is a downward jump in the money supply, causing an expected positive change along the horizontal axis. While expected fundamentals themselves jump at the edges of the zone, the expected exchange rate cannot have jumps or there would be profit opportunities; jumps would allow one-way exchange-rate bets. It follows that if expectations of fundamentals jump at the target zone edges, but there is no corresponding jump in exchange rates at the target zone edges, then at the edges the fundamentals cannot be affecting exchange rates. This means that *TT* is horizontal and tangent to the target zone edges S_L and S_U; with *TT* horizontal, changes in the fundamentals have no effect on $S(\$/\pounds)$.

The preceding assumes that intervention always occurs at the target zone edges. While relaxation of the assumption that intervention always occurs does affect the preceding conclusions, there is still some stabilizing of exchange rates, even if intervention occurs only sometimes.[14]

In this account of the many possible compromises between truly fixed and truly flexible exchange rates and the way they work, we have given a rather patchy history of international finance. In order to provide a more systematic overview, in the next chapter we present a chronology of international financial developments during the twentieth century. This chronology has been deferred so that we would be equipped with an understanding of the systems and events we describe. Our chronology should serve to give a historical perspective on the international financial system, and demonstrate that the international financial system is not static, but something that continues to evolve. Possible directions of this evolution are also sketched in Chapter 23.

SUMMARY

1   A gold standard involves the settlement of international transactions in gold and the open offer to exchange domestic paper money for gold at a fixed official price. A deficit means an outflow of gold. The reduction in gold reserves reduces the local money supply and puts downward pressure on prices in the deficit country. The fall

14 See Krugman and Miller, op. cit.

in prices stimulates exports and lowers imports. In the surplus countries, the money supplies increase, raising prices in these countries. This causes a further reduction of relative prices in the deficit country. In addition, changes in relative prices of traded versus nontraded goods and services *within* each country help eliminate a deficit or surplus.

2   The price-specie adjustment mechanism can be frustrated by a neutralization policy. This policy severs the link between gold flows and money supplies, so that the automatic-adjustment mechanism is unable to function.

3   Critics of the gold standard argue that prices in surplus and deficit countries showed parallel movement rather than the reverse movement implied by the gold standard. Downward price rigidity could be responsible. However, an adjustment of relative prices will still occur if prices go up by more in surplus countries than in deficit countries. Another criticism of the gold standard is that governments did not allow it to work. This is as much a criticism of government as of the gold standard.

4   The gold-exchange standard required the US to fix its exchange rate to gold, and other countries to fix to gold or to the US dollar. This system operated from 1944 to 1968. From 1968 to 1973, the US dollar was not fixed to gold, but most other currencies were still fixed to the dollar. This was called a dollar standard. The entire period from 1944 to 1973 is the Bretton Woods era.

5   To maintain the fixed exchange rate in terms of the dollar, central banks must purchase or sell their local currency at the support points on either side of the parity value. If the free-market exchange rate would be above the upper support point, the central bank must sell its currency and purchase dollars. This raises official reserves and means a surplus in the balance of payments. It also raises the supply of money. At the lower support point, the central bank must purchase its currency with dollars, which reduces official reserves and results in a deficit in the balance of payments. It also lowers the money supply. Therefore, under fixed exchange rates, surpluses raise money supplies and deficits lower money supplies.

6   Because deficit countries which run out of foreign exchange reserves are eventually forced to devalue, it is possible to identify which currencies face devaluation. The need to revalue is less urgent than the need to devalue, making the timing of forecasts of revaluations more difficult than devaluations.

7   The European Monetary System (EMS) was a fixed-exchange-rate system in which countries cooperated to maintain exchange rates. Exchange rates were fixed within limits set by a parity grid, which involved an upper and lower point for each exchange rate. Exchange rates were also maintained within limits vis-à-vis the European Currency Unit, ECU. This helped identify which country was at fault for any difficulties in maintaining exchange rates. With both deficit and surplus countries being supposed to intervene under the EMS, it was intended that the burden of adjustment would be shared.

8   Alternatives to fixed-rate systems and flexible-rate systems include a fixed rate with a wide band, a crawling peg, fixed rates for some transactions and flexible rates for others, and a dirty float with intervention to maintain orderly markets. These combine attributes of both fixed-rate systems and flexible-rate systems.

9   The credible announcement of target zones helps to keep exchange rates within the zones.

10 At the edges of target zones, fundamentals have no effect on exchange rates.

REVIEW QUESTIONS

1   What is the essential feature of the gold standard concerning the exchange of paper money into gold?
2   What are the "gold points?"
3   What does the price-specie automatic-adjustment mechanism assume about the connection between the gold reserves of a country and that country's trade balance?
4   What does the price-specie adjustment mechanism assume about the connection between the trade balance and a country's money supply?
5   How are the money supply and prices linked according to the price-specie adjustment mechanism?
6   What is sterilization or neutralization policy in the context of the functioning of the gold standard?
7   What is meant by support points in the Bretton Woods system?
8   What is the difference between the dollar standard and the gold-exchange standard?
9   If a country increases its official price of gold, *ceteris paribus*, does that constitute a devaluation or revaluation of its currency?
10 Why might speculation be profitable in a gold-standard system?
11 What is a central-bank swap?
12 What exchange-rate system evolved from the snake?
13 What is the European Currency Unit?
14 To what type of exchange-rate system did the Maastricht Agreement commit participating European Community member countries?
15 What is a dirty float?
16 What is a crawling peg?
17 What was the Louvre Accord?
18 According to target zone research, does the establishment of a target zone for exchange rates increase or decrease the range within which exchange rates typically fluctuate?

ASSIGNMENT PROBLEMS

1   Assume the following gold prices have been declared by the central banks:
    a   Bank of England £300
    b   Federal Reserve System $475
    c   European Central Bank €500
    d   Reserve Bank of Australia A$700
    e   Bank of Canada C$600.
    Calculate all possible exchange rates between the currencies.
2   What assumptions have you made in Question 1?
3   How can government objectives such as the maintenance of full employment hinder the functioning of the gold standard?

4 Why might historical patterns of prices show parallel movements between deficit and surplus countries? Could gold discoveries and common movements in national incomes cause this?

5 Use Figure 22.2 to show the effect of a fall in demand for British goods in terms of (a) the balance of payments measured in terms of pounds and (b) the balance of payments measured in terms of US dollars. Show also the movements of curves that the deficit and associated contraction in the money supply will create in restoring equilibrium.

6 Why can speculators make profits with less risk under fixed rates? From whom do they make their profits?

7 Why do we observe deficits or surpluses under "flexible" rates? Does this tell us something of the management of the rates?

8 Do you think that the collapse of the Bretton Woods system would have been less likely had surplus countries expanded their economies to ease the burden of adjustment on the countries with deficits?

9 Why have central bankers frequently intervened in the foreign exchange market under a system of flexible exchange rates? If they have managed to smooth out fluctuations, have they made profits for their citizens?

10 Does a crawling peg system lend itself to profitable speculation?

BIBLIOGRAPHY

Barro, Robert J., "Money and the Price Level Under the Gold Standard," *Economic Journal*, March 1979, pp. 13–33.

Belongia, Michael T., "Prospects for International Policy Coordination: Some Lessons for the EMS," *Review*, Federal Reserve Bank of St. Louis, July/August 1988, pp. 19–27.

Bordo, Michael D., "The Gold Standard, Bretton Woods, and Other Monetary Regimes: A Historical Appraisal," *Review*, Federal Reserve Bank of St. Louis, March/April 1993, pp. 123–87.

Dornbusch, Rudiger, *Open Economy Macroeconomics*, 2nd edn, Basic Books, New York, 1988.

Harberler, Gottfried, *Money in the International Economy*, Harvard University Press, Cambridge, MA, 1965.

Hume, David, "Of the Balance of Trade," in *Essays on Money*, Political Discourses, London, 1752.

Krugman, Paul R. and Marcus Miller (eds), *Exchange Rate Targets and Currency Bands*, Cambridge University Press, New York, 1992.

Meltzer, Allan H., "U.S. Policy in the Bretton Woods Era," *Review*, Federal Reserve Bank of St. Louis, May/June 1991, pp. 54–83.

Mills, Terence C. and Geoffrey E. Wood, "Does the Exchange Rate Regime Affect the Economy," *Review*, Federal Reserve Bank of St. Louis, July/August 1993, pp. 3–20.

Rockoff, Hugh, "Some Evidence on the Real Price of Gold, its Costs of Production, and Commodity Prices," in Michael D. Bordo and Anna J. Schwartz, (eds), *A Retrospective on the Classical Gold Standard, 1821–1931*, University of Chicago Press, Chicago, IL, 1904, pp. 613–44.

——, "The Wizard of Oz as a Monetary Allegory," *Journal of Political Economy*, August 1990, pp. 739–60.

Solomon, Robert, *The International Monetary System, 1945–81*, Harper & Row, New York, 1982.

Svensson, Lars E.O., "An Interpretation of Recent Research on Exchange Rate Target Zones," *Journal of Economic Perspectives*, Fall 1992, pp. 119–44.

APPENDIX A

Other fixed-exchange-rate automatic-adjustment mechanisms

National income

The price-level adjustment mechanism requires flexibility of prices in order to operate. The macroeconomic revolution marked by the publication of *The General Theory of Employment, Interest and Money* by John Maynard Keynes, while focusing on a closed economy, spilled over into international finance and introduced an alternative adjustment mechanism that works if price flexibility does not exist.[15] This mechanism, popularized by the followers of Keynes, involves automatic adjustment via changes in national income. Like the price-level adjustment mechanism, the Keynesian income adjustment mechanism operates on the current account. The most straightforward way of describing Keynesian adjustment is to employ a Keynesian income-expenditure model and show how variations in national income work to correct incipient balance-of-payments surpluses and deficits.

A straightforward model which will reveal the important features of income adjustment consists of the following equations:

$$Y \equiv C + I_0 + (Ex_0 - Im) \tag{22A.1}$$

$$C = C_0 + cY \tag{22A.2}$$

$$Im = Im_0 + mY \tag{22A.3}$$

In these equations, Y is the national income, or GDP, C is aggregate consumption of goods and services, I_0 is the given amount of aggregate investment or capital formation, Ex_0 is the given amount of exports, and Im is imports.

The national-income accounting identity is given by equation (22A.1), where, because it is not relevant for our purposes, we have omitted government spending. The GDP, Y, is the total value of *domestically produced* goods and services. Because it is difficult for government statisticians to separate consumption and investment of domestic goods from consumption and investment of imported goods, especially when domestic goods have imported components, C and I refer to the *total* consumption and investment of goods and services. That is, C and I *include* imported products as well as domestically produced products. In addition, exports, Ex_0, include re-exports, that is, items from abroad that are resold after reprocessing or are used as inputs in exported products. Because Y refers to domestic production only, as the relevant output/income of a nation, and because C, I_0, and Ex_0 include imports, we must subtract imports, Im, to ensure the national income accounting identity (22A.1). This is the most convenient approach from the viewpoint of a national-income statistician, because records of imports exist with customs agents, and records of consumption and investment reveal total amounts and do not show imported components separated from domestic components.

Equation (22A.2) is the **consumption function**. The intercept, C_0, is the part of consumption that does not depend on income. The effect of national income on consumption is given by the **marginal propensity to consume**, c, which will be between zero and unity. Since C represents all consumption, it includes imports (Im), where the import equation itself is equation (22A.3). We assume that investment and exports are exogenous, or at least exogenous in relation to national income in the economy we are examining.

In order to discover how automatic adjustment via national income works, we can begin with an intuitive explanation. Suppose the balance of payments is initially in balance and that there is an exogenous increase in

15 John Maynard Keynes, *The General Theory of Employment, Interest and Money*, Macmillan, London, 1936.

exports, *Ex*. This means an increase in national income via equation (22A.1), which itself indirectly further increases income via the extra induced consumption in equation (22A.2). The higher national income will increase imports via equation (22A.3). We find that the initial increase in exports that moved the balance of payments into surplus will induce an increase in imports, which will tend to offset the effect of exports on the balance of trade. This is an automatic adjustment working via income. It is not apparent from our intuitive explanation that this adjustment, while tending to restore balance, will not be complete. We can see this by employing our model.

If we substitute equations (22A.2) and (22A.3) into the national-income accounting identity, equation (22A.1), we obtain

$$Y = C_0 + cY + I_0 + Ex_0 - Im_0 - mY \tag{22A.4}$$

By gathering terms, we can write Y as a function of exogenous terms

$$Y = \frac{1}{1 - c + m}(C_0 + I_0 + Ex_0 - Im_0) \tag{22A.5}$$

The factor $1/(1 - c + m)$ is the **multiplier**. We can note that the larger the **marginal propensity to import**, m, the smaller will be the multiplier. The multiplier depends on the leakages from the circular flow of income, and by having imports, we add a leakage abroad, m, to the leakage into savings given by the marginal propensity to save, $(1 - c)$. The more leakages we have, the smaller the increase in income from any exogenous shock.

Let us allow exports to increase exogenously from Ex_0 to $Ex_0 + \Delta Ex$ and the corresponding increase in GDP to be from Y to $(Y + \Delta Y)$. We can therefore write

$$Y + \Delta Y = \frac{1}{1 - c + m}(C_0 + I_0 + Ex_0 + \Delta Ex - Im_0) \tag{22A.6}$$

Subtracting each side of equation (22A.5) from equation (22A.6), we have

$$\Delta Y = \frac{1}{1 - c + m}\Delta Ex \tag{22A.7}$$

The value of ΔY in equation (22A.7) gives the effect on national income of an exogenous change in exports. To find the induced effect on imports of this change in national income, we can use ΔY from equation (22A.7) in the import equation (22A.3). Putting equation (22A.3) in terms of the new level of imports, $Im + \Delta Im$, after an increase in income to $Y + \Delta Y$, we have

$$Im + \Delta Im = Im_0 + m(Y + \Delta Y) \tag{22A.8}$$

Subtracting equation (22A.3) from equation (22A.8) on both sides gives

$$\Delta Im = m\Delta Y \tag{22A.9}$$

and substituting ΔY from equation (22A.7) in equation (22A.9) gives

$$\Delta Im = \frac{m}{1 - c + m}\Delta Ex \tag{22A.10}$$

Equation (22A.10) tells us that the automatic adjustment working via national income will raise imports by $m/(1 - c + m)$ times the initial increase in exports. The value of $m/(1 - c + m)$ is, however, below unity. This follows because the marginal propensity to consume, c, is below unity, that is, $c < 1$, so that $(1 - c) > 0$. We hence have m divided by itself *plus* the positive number $(1 - c)$. When a number is divided by a total larger than itself, the result is below unity. For example, if $c = 0.8$ and $m = 0.2$, imports will increase by only half of any exogenous increase in exports. If $c = 0.4$ and $m = 0.2$, the offset is only a quarter. What we have is an adjustment process via national income that is not complete. While an exogenous change in exports will change imports in the same direction, imports will change by less than the initial change in exports, and so initial effects persist.

Income and income adjustment are relevant to the financial manager who is trying to forecast movements in exchange rates. If a country's national income is growing more rapidly than that of others *as a result of growth in exports*, then the country's foreign exchange reserves will increase, and eventually the currency will probably increase in value. Induced increases in imports resulting from export growth will only partially dampen the growth of reserves and the need to eventually revalue the currency. When a nation's income is growing from a growth in consumption (C_0), then foreign exchange reserves will shrink, and eventually the foreign exchange value of the currency will have to be reduced. The growth in income will raise imports but not exports, since exports are determined by the incomes of *other* nations.

There is an additional force, also working via changes in national income, which will help complete the automatic-adjustment process. This force is induced changes in the money supply, which in turn affects interest rates, the rate of investment, national income, and imports. The process works as follows. If we start in balance and an exogenous increase in exports does not induce a sufficient rise in imports to offset the increase in exports, a trade surplus will remain. *Ceteris paribus*, under fixed exchange rates this will require the central bank to supply its currency to prevent its exchange rate from appreciating. This means an increase in the money supply. A money-supply increase tends to lower the interest rates. Lower interest rates stimulate investment, I, which will in turn both directly and indirectly work towards raising the national income, Y. Higher income will raise imports, Im, via equation (22A.3) and thereby help close the trade imbalance.

The force that we have just described involves a lowering of interest rates working via capital investment, income, imports, and the current account. In addition, interest rates have an effect on capital flows and the capital account.

Interest rates

The automatic **interest-rate adjustment mechanism** relies on the effect of the balance of payments on the money supply. We have seen that if the effects are not sterilized, a balance-of-payments deficit will reduce the money supply and a surplus will increase it. With a gold standard this occurs because a deficit means a gold outflow and a shrinking money supply, and a surplus means a gold inflow and an increasing money supply. In the gold-exchange and dollar standards, and in the EMS, the money supply also declines after deficits and increases after surpluses. In these cases the money supply changes because of intervention in the foreign exchange market. A deficit requires the local monetary authority to purchase its currency to keep the value up. Thus, money is withdrawn from circulation. Similarly, a surplus requires the central bank to sell its currency and hence increase the money supply. With this we can explain the interest-rate adjustment mechanism which works via the capital account.

The interest-rate adjustment mechanism via the capital account involves the following. If a deficit occurs, it will reduce the money supply and raise the interest rate.[16] The deficit means surpluses elsewhere; therefore, the money supplies of other countries will be rising, which will reduce their interest rates. For both reasons there is a rise in interest differentials in favor of the deficit country. This will make investment (in securities, and so on) in that country appear relatively more attractive. The resultant inflows on the capital account should improve the balance of payments, thereby correcting the original deficit.

Because capital flows are highly responsive to interest-rate differentials when capital can flow without restriction, the interest-rate adjustment mechanism working via the capital account is likely to be the most effective

---

16 The interest rate will not increase as a result of a reduction in the money supply if there is a **liquidity trap**, which occurs if the demand for money is perfectly elastic. If they have ever existed, liquidity traps are probably limited to serious recessions and will not hinder the interest-rate adjustment process in normal times.

mechanism in the short run. However, it is necessary that adjustment eventually occur via prices or national income and the current account. This is because capital inflows must be serviced. That is, there will be payments of interest which will appear as a debit in the invisibles part of the current account as income imports. This means that in the future, the current-account deficit will increase.

APPENDIX B

Gold points

Gold points are the extreme values between which the exchange rate can vary in a gold-standard world. The width of the zone defined by the extreme values within which exchange rates can vary is determined by the cost of exchanging currencies in the foreign exchange market and the cost of shipping gold between central banks. The gold points arising from the gold standard allowed exchange rates to vary within a zone of approximately 1 or 2 percent of the middle value. This idea of a zone was carried into the Bretton Woods system and the European Monetary System. We hence obtain a historical perspective by a study of gold-point determination.

Suppose that the US Federal Reserve and the Bank of England both offer to exchange their paper money for gold at fixed prices. Let us define these prices as follows.

$P_G^{US}(\text{ask})$ = Federal Reserve selling price of gold, in dollars
$P_G^{US}(\text{bid})$ = Federal Reserve buying price of gold, in dollars
$P_G^{UK}(\text{ask})$ = Bank of England selling price of gold, in pounds
$P_G^{UK}(\text{bid})$ = Bank of England buying price of gold, in pounds

Let us also define c_G as the cost of shipping gold between the United States and the United Kingdom. We can think of c_G as the fraction of the total value of gold shipped between the United States and the United Kingdom that is paid for shipping the gold. For example, $c_G = 0.01$ if shipping costs are 1 percent of the value of the cargo. Finally, let us define the bid and ask exchange rates as in the text, namely

$S(\$/bid£)$ is the number of dollars received from the sale of pounds in the foreign exchange market, and $S(\$/ask£)$ is the number of dollars required to buy pounds in the foreign exchange market.

Consider first a person wanting to buy dollars with pounds. For each pound, that person will receive $S(\$/bid£)$ dollars in the foreign exchange market. Alternatively, he or she can use their pounds to buy gold from the Bank of England, ship the gold to the United States, and sell it to the Federal Reserve for dollars. The number of dollars received per pound this way is calculated as follows.

Each pound buys $1/P_G^{UK}$ (ask) oz. of gold from the Bank of England. Shipping this to the United States involves a cost of c_G/oz. so that after shipping

$$\frac{1}{P_G^{UK}} \cdot (1 - c_G) \text{ oz.}$$

arrive in the United States. This can be sold to the Federal Reserve for

$$\$\frac{P_G^{US}(\text{bid})}{P_G^{UK}(\text{ask})} \cdot (1 - c_G) \tag{22B.1}$$

The value in equation (22B.1) is the number of dollars received for one pound via buying, shipping, and selling gold. Since we are going from pounds to dollars and not back again, the choice between this and exchanging via the foreign exchange market involves one-way arbitrage.

People buying dollars with pounds will use the foreign exchange market if they receive at least as many dollars for their pounds in that market as via one-way arbitrage. That is, for the exchange market to be used it is necessary that

$$S(\$/bid£) \geq \frac{P_G^{US}(bid)}{P_G^{UK}(ask)} \cdot (1 - c_G) \qquad (22B.2)$$

The amount on the right-hand side of equation (8A.12) is the **lower gold point**, and it is the minimum exchange rate for dollars to pounds in the foreign exchange market in a gold-standard world.

A person who wants to buy pounds for dollars could do this via the foreign exchange market and pay $S(\$/ask£)$ for each pound or alternatively, could use one-way arbitrage and use dollars to buy gold from the Federal Reserve, ship the gold, and sell it to the Bank of England. If this person chooses to use one-way arbitrage, the number of dollars he or she will pay per pound is calculated as follows.

Each pound requires selling to the Bank of England $1/P_G^{UK}$ (bid) oz. of gold. In order to have this amount of gold in Britain it is necessary to buy in the United States

$$\frac{1}{P_G^{UK}(bid)} \cdot \frac{1}{(1 - c_G)} \text{ ounces} \qquad (22B.3)$$

because only $(1 - c_G)$ of gold that is purchased remains after shipping costs. The amount that must be paid to the Federal Reserve for the amount of gold in equation (22B.3) is

$$\$ \frac{P_G^{US}(ask)}{P_G^{UK}(bid)} \cdot \frac{1}{(1 - c_G)} \qquad (22B.4)$$

The value in equation (22B.4) is the number of dollars that must be paid for one pound via buying, shipping, and selling gold.

People buying pounds with dollars will use the foreign exchange market rather than one-way arbitrage if they pay no more dollars via the foreign exchange market than via one-way arbitrage, that is, if

$$S(\$/ask£) \leq \frac{P_G^{US}(ask)}{P_G^{UK}(bid)} \cdot \frac{1}{(1 - c_G)} \qquad (22B.5)$$

The amount of the right-hand side of equation (22B.5) is the **upper gold point**, and it is the maximum exchange rate of dollars for pounds if the foreign exchange market is to be used. We find that when each central bank offers to buy and sell its currency for gold, a range of values will be established in the foreign exchange market within which the exchange rate can vary. The bid and ask exchange rates can vary between the limits of $S(\$/bid£)$ in (22A.12) and $S(\$/ask£)$ in (22B.5). No exchange-rate quotation at which transactions occur can lie outside this range. That is, the exchange rate in the foreign exchange market must be in the range

$$\frac{P_G^{US}(bid)}{P_G^{UK}(ask)} \cdot (1 - c_G) \leq S(\$/£) \leq \frac{P_G^{US}(ask)}{P_G^{UK}(bid)} \cdot \frac{1}{(1 - c_G)} \qquad (22B.6)$$

where $S(\$/£)$ stands for the exchange rate, whether it be a bid rate or an ask rate. For example, if the gold prices of the central banks are

$$P_G^{US}(\text{ask}) = \$402$$
$$P_G^{US}(\text{bid}) = \$400$$
$$P_G^{UK}(\text{ask}) = £251$$
$$P_G^{UK}(\text{bid}) = £250$$

and $c_G = 0.01$, the exchange rate must be in the range

$$1.58 \leq S(\$/£) \leq 1.62$$

The ends of the range are the gold points; in this case the gold points are $\$1.58/£$ and $\$1.62/£$. We find that the gold points result from both the bid-ask spreads on gold prices charged or paid by the central banks, and the cost of shipping gold between the two countries.

Chapter 23

The international financial system: past, present, and future

> And Jesus entered the Temple of God and drove out all who sold and bought in the temple, and he overturned the tables of the money-changers . . . He said to them, "It is written, 'My House shall be called a house of prayer', but you make it a den of robbers."
>
> Mathew 21:12

In this chapter we follow a time line of the international financial system as it functioned from the latter half of the nineteenth century until today. This takes us on a journey through the four principal types of financial system we have experienced: gold standard; Bretton Woods standard; flexible exchange rates; and cooperative intervention. Our travels take us through some remarkable territory, including the radical experiment of the creation of a new currency shared by many nations – the euro. Many crises on different continents, in Asia, Central and South America, are visited along the way.

After the historical tour, we extend the time line into the future by looking at the problems the international financial system faces, and how these are likely to affect the evolution of international financial arrangements. We focus on the mounting debt of some key economic players, and shifting economic power from the industrial leaders of the twentieth century to a broader base of successful trading nations. We also review the pros and cons of alternative arrangements for determining exchange rates. By analyzing the advantages and disadvantages of fixed and flexible exchange rates

we are forced to conclude that despite extensive experimentation with different international financial arrangements during this century, there is no obvious, dominant solution. Instead, different countries are likely to prefer different arrangements depending on their circumstances.

THE PAST

The classical gold standard, 1870–1914

For almost half a century before the First World War of 1914–18, the international financial system ran according to the rules of the classical gold standard. The success of this system has been traced to the credible commitment represented by the unconditional guarantee to convert paper money for gold at a fixed price. As we have seen in the preceding chapter, such a commitment is the essential element of the classical gold standard. Few if any doubted the willingness of governments to continue to exchange gold for fiat money, even after temporary suspensions during periods of war. Not only did participating countries such as the United States and France gain the confidence of others, but everybody could count on Britain to do whatever was necessary to underwrite the system.[1]

The criticality of credibility to the success of a rule-based system such as the gold standard has been cast in modern **game theory** terms, following the successful application of game theory to domestic monetary policy.[2] The key insight is that without rules and a credible commitment to maintain a stable price level, governments can be counted on saying they intend fighting inflation to induce people to lend to them at low interest rates, and then afterwards to abandon their promise. The government-induced inflation, *if* unexpected, reduces the government's real borrowing costs; interest rates which reflect anticipated inflation would not compensate for realized inflation. However, with rational expectations, it is not possible for governments to play this game successfully. Lenders know that the government will misrepresent its intentions, pursuing inflationary policy despite its promises. This drives the economy to an inefficient equilibrium – one in which the public expects the government to defect (i.e. to cheat) by inflating, the government knows that the public expects this, and does indeed cheat. Therefore, interest rates are high to reflect the expected, and actual, inflation. This is a so-called **Nash equilibrium**: expectations are consistent and ultimately vindicated, and each "player" chooses the best available action given these expectations. All this follows if governments take no costly steps to gain credibility.

Knowing how the "game" unravels when there is nothing to constrain government behavior, it becomes optimal for the government to agree to a constraint on its behavior. The promise to convert fiat money for gold is just such a constraint and **signal** of its sincerity. In this way gold serves as a **nominal anchor** – a credible commitment to a stable value of fiat money. The public reasons that the government would not agree to a fixed price of gold – or a fixed price of currency versus the US dollar under the Bretton Woods system – if it intended defecting. The government knows this and indeed, does not want to defect, instead preferring to keep inflation low even after it has borrowed. In this way the government keeps interest rates low; low inflationary expectations mean low nominal interest rates.[3]

Flexible rates and controls, 1914–44

The credibility that the gold standard brought to government policy was eroded somewhat by the First World War which began in 1914. As is usual in wartime, governments imposed currency controls and abandoned the commitment to convert their paper currencies into gold. Immediately after the First World War ended in 1918, rather than return to gold, there was a period of flexible exchange rates that lasted until 1926, during which time many countries suffered from hyperinflation. The gold standard was eventually readopted in 1926 in an effort to bring inflation under control and to help cure a number of other economic ills such as sweeping protectionism, competitive devaluation, and so on. However, for the gold standard to retain credibility, it is necessary that deficit countries allow the influence of deficits on their gold reserves to slow monetary growth. It is also necessary that surplus countries allow their increased gold reserves to

1 See, for example, Alberto Giovannini, "Bretton Woods and its Precursors: Rules versus Discretion in the History of International Monetary Regimes," in Michael D. Bordo and Barry Eichengreen(eds), *A Retrospective on the Bretton Woods System*, University of Chicago Press, Chicago, IL, 1993, pp. 109–55, and Michael D. Bordo, "The Gold Standard, Bretton Woods and Other Monetary Regimes: A Historical Appraisal," in *Review*, Federal Reserve Bank of St. Louis, March/April 1993, pp. 123–99.

2 See Finn E. Kydland and Edward C. Prescott, "Rules Rather than Discretion: The Inconsistency of Optimal Plans," *Journal of Political Economy*, June 1977, pp. 473–91, and Robert J. Barro and David B. Gordon, "Rules, Discretion and Reputation in a Model of Monetary Policy," *Journal of Monetary Economics*, July 1983, pp. 101–21.

3 See Michael D. Bordo and Finn E. Kydland, "The Gold Standard as a Rule," *National Bureau of Economic Research*, Working Paper 3367, May 1990, and G. de Kock and Vittorio U. Grilli, "Endogenous Exchange Rate Regime Switches," *National Bureau of Economic Research*, Working Paper 3066, August 1989.

liberalize their monetary policies. After the First World War, the burden of both types of adjustment was considered so great that there was reluctance to behave in this way. Many countries began to manipulate exchange rates for their own domestic objectives. For example, the French devalued the franc in 1926 to stimulate their economy, and the undervalued currency contributed to problems for Britain and the pound sterling. Then in 1928, the French government decided to accept only gold and no more foreign exchange. When in 1931 the French decided that they would not accept any more pounds sterling and also that they would exchange their existing sterling holdings for gold, there was little Britain could do other than make sterling inconvertible into gold. This they did in 1931. With the ability to exchange currencies for gold being the central feature of the gold standard, and with Britain having been the nucleus of the gold standard, this marked the end of the era. Indeed, when other countries found their holdings of pounds no longer convertible, they followed Britain. By 1934 only the US dollar could be exchanged for gold.

Since a full recovery from the Great Depression of 1929–33 did not take place until the onset of the Second World War the conditions for a formal reorganization of the international financial order were not present. The Depression had provided an environment in which self-interested **beggar-thy-neighbor** policies – competitive devaluations and increased tariff protection – followed the model established earlier by France. Since no long-lasting effective devaluations were possible and the great interruption of world trade eliminated the gains from international trade, such an environment hindered global economic growth: all countries cannot simultaneously devalue by raising gold prices, with collective action doing nothing more than devaluing money by causing inflation. When the war replaced the Depression, no cooperation was possible. It was not until July of 1944 that, with victory imminent in Europe, the representatives of the United States, Great Britain, and other allied powers met at the Mount Washington Hotel in Bretton Woods, New Hampshire to hammer out a new international financial order to replace the failed gold standard.

Bretton Woods and the International Monetary Fund (IMF), 1944–73

Of paramount importance to the representatives at the 1944 meeting in Bretton Woods was the prevention of another breakdown of the international financial order, such as the one which followed the peace after the First World War. From 1918 until well into the 1920s the world had witnessed a rise in protectionism on a grand scale to protect jobs for those returning from the war, competitive devaluations designed for the same effect, and massive hyperinflation as the inability to raise conventional taxes led to use of the hidden tax of inflation: inflation shifts buying power from the holders of money, whose holdings buy less, to the issuers of money, the central banks. A system was required that would keep countries from changing exchange rates to obtain a trading advantage and to limit inflationary policy. This meant that some sort of control on rate changes was needed, as well as a reserve base for deficit countries. The reserves were to be provided via an institution created for this purpose. The International Monetary Fund (IMF) was established to collect and allocate reserves in order to implement the **Articles of Agreement** signed in Bretton Woods.[4]

The Articles of Agreement required member countries (of which there were 184 as of May 2004) to

1 promote international monetary cooperation
2 facilitate the growth of trade
3 promote exchange-rate stability
4 establish a system of multilateral payments
5 create a reserve base.

The reserves were contributed by the member countries according to a quota system (since then

4 Exhibit 23.1 describes the competing views that had to be resolved before agreement was reached.

EXHIBIT 23.1   SEEING THE FOREST THROUGH THE TREES: THE BRETTON WOODS VISION

The two principal plans presented to the delegates at the Bretton Wood Conference in July 1944 were those of Britain, proposed by Lord John Maynard Keynes, and of the United States, proposed by Harry Dexter White. Representatives from 44 countries or authorities were determined to work together to "win the peace," and it is a remarkable testimony to their resolve that an agreement was reached that overcame the self-interest of countries; representatives agreed to forgo a measure of economic sovereignty for the common good. The following excerpt describes the two plans which dominated discussion.

The planning that led to Bretton Woods aimed to prevent the chaos of the interwar period. The perceived ills to be prevented included (1) floating exchange rates that were condemned as subject to destabilizing speculation; (2) a gold exchange standard that was vulnerable to problems of adjustment, liquidity and confidence, which enforced the international transmission of deflation in the early 1930s; and (3) the resort to beggar-thy-neighbor devaluations, trade restrictions, exchange controls and bilateralism after 1933. To prevent these ills, the case for an adjustable-peg system was made by Keynes, White, Nurkse and others. The new system would combine the favorable features of the fixed exchange rate gold standard – stability of exchange rates – and of the flexible exchange rate standard – monetary and fiscal independence.

Both Keynes, leading the British negotiating team at Bretton Woods, and White, leading the American team at Bretton Woods, planned an adjustable-peg system to be coordinated by an international monetary agency. The Keynes plan gave the International Currency Union substantially more reserves and power than the United Nations Stabilization Fund proposed by White, but both institutions would have had considerable control over the domestic financial policy of the members.

The British plan contained more domestic policy autonomy than did the U.S. plan, whereas the American plan put more emphasis on exchange rate stability. Neither architect was in favor of a rule-based system. The British were most concerned with preventing the deflation of the 1930s, which they attributed to the constraint of the gold standard rule and to deflationary U.S. monetary policies. Thus they wanted an expansionary system.

The American plan was closer to the gold standard rule in that it stressed the fixity of exchange rates. It did not explicitly mention the importance of rules as a credible commitment mechanism, but there were to be strict regulations on the linkage between UNITAS (the proposed international reserve account) and gold. Members, in the event of a fundamental disequilibrium, could change their parities only with approval from a three-quarters majority of all members of the Fund.

The Articles of Agreement of the International Monetary Fund incorporated elements of both the Keynes and White plans, although in the end, U.S. concerns predominated. The main points of the articles were: the creation of the par value system; multilateral payments; the use of the fund's resources; its powers; and its organization.

Source: Michael D. Bordo, "The Gold Standard, Bretton Woods and Other Monetary Regimes: A Historical Appraisal," *Review,* Federal Reserve Bank of St. Louis, March/April 1993, pp. 163–64.

many times revised) based on the national income and importance of trade in different countries. Of the original contribution, 25 percent was in gold – the so-called **gold tranche** position – and the remaining 75 percent was in the country's own currency. A country was allowed to borrow up to its gold-tranche contribution without IMF approval and an additional 100 percent of its total contribution in four steps, each with additional stringent conditions established by the IMF. These conditions were designed to ensure that correct-ive macroeconomic policy actions would be taken. The lending facilities have been expanded over the years. Standby arrangements were intro-duced in 1952, enabling a country to have funds appropriated ahead of the need so that currencies would be less open to attack during the IMF's deliberation of whether help would be made avail-able. Other extensions of the IMF's lending ability have taken place over the years to deal with urgent circumstances such as rising oil prices and rising interest rates on mounting debts. These extensions in lending ability were supplemented by the 1980 decision allowing the IMF to borrow in the private capital market when necessary, and the extension of borrowing authority in the 1990 **General Arrangements to Borrow** which allows the IMF to lend to nonmembers. The scope of the IMF's power to lend was further expanded in 1993, when new facilities to assist in exchange-rate stabilization were made available.

As we have seen, the most important feature of the Bretton Woods Agreement was the decision to have the US dollar freely convertible into gold and to have the values of other currencies fixed in US dollars. The exchange rates were to be maintained within 1 percent on either side of the official parity, with intervention required at the support points. This required the United States to maintain a reserve of gold, and other countries to maintain a reserve of US dollars. Because the initially selec-ted exchange rates could have been incorrect for balance-of-payments equilibrium, each country was allowed a revision of up to 10 percent within a year of the initial selection of the exchange rate. In this basic form the system survived until 1971.

The central place of the US dollar was viewed by John Maynard Keynes as a potential weakness. Keynes preferred an international settlement sys-tem based on a new currency unit, the **bancor**. However, the idea was rejected, and it was not until the 1960s that the inevitable collapse of the Bretton Woods arrangement was recognized by

a Yale economist, Robert Triffin.[5] According to the **Triffin paradox**, in order for the stock of world reserves to grow along with world trade, the pro-vider of reserves, the United States, had to run balance-of-payments deficits. These deficits were viewed by Triffin as the means by which other countries could accumulate dollar reserves. Although the US deficits were needed, the more they occurred, the more the holders of dollars doubted the ability of the United States to convert dollars into gold at the agreed price.

Among the more skeptical holders of dollars was France, which began in 1962 to exchange dollars for gold despite the objection of the United States. Not only were the French doubtful about the future value of the dollar, but they also objected to the pivotal role of the United States in the Bretton Woods system. Part of this distaste for a powerful United States was political, and part was based on the seigniorage gains that France believed accrued to the United States by virtue of the US role as the world's banker. **Seigniorage** is the profit from "printing" money and depends on the ability to have people hold your currency or other assets at a noncompetitive yield. Every government which issues legal-tender currency can ensure that it is held by its own citizens, even if it offers no yield at all. For example, US citizens will hold Federal Reserve notes and give up goods or services for them, even though the paper the notes are printed on costs very little to provide. The United States was in a special position because its role as the leading provider of foreign exchange reserves meant that it could ensure that foreign central banks as well as US citizens would hold US dollars.

In reality, most reserves of foreign central banks were and are kept in securities such as treasury bills which earn their holders interest. If the interest that is paid on the reserve assets is a competitive yield, then the seigniorage gains to the United States from foreigners holding US dollar assets is small. Indeed, with sufficient competition from (1) alternative

5 Robert Triffin, *Gold and the Dollar Crisis*, Yale University Press, New Haven, CT, 1960.

reserves of different currencies and (2) alternative dollar investments in the United States, seigniorage gains would be competed away.[6] Nevertheless, the French continued to convert their dollar holdings into gold. This led other countries to worry about whether the United States would have sufficient gold to support the US dollar after the French had finished selling their dollars: under a fractional reserve standard, gold reserves are only a fraction of dollars held.

By 1968, the run on gold was of such a scale that at a March meeting in Washington, DC, a two-tier gold-pricing system was established. While the official US price of gold was to remain at $35/oz., the private-market price of gold was to be allowed to find its own level.

After repeated financial crises, including a devaluation of the pound from $2.80/£ to $2.40/£ in 1967, some relief came in 1970 with the allocation of **Special Drawing Rights (SDRs)**.[7] The SDRs are book entries that are credited to the accounts of IMF member countries according to their established quotas. They can be used to meet payments imbalances, and they provide a net addition to the stock of reserves without the need for any country to run deficits or mine gold. From 1970 to 1972, approximately $9.4 billion worth of SDRs (or paper gold as they were sometimes called) were created. However, there was no further allocation until January 1, 1979, when SDR 4 billion was created. Similar amounts were created on January 1, 1980, and on January 1, 1981, bringing the total to over SDR 20 billion. No allocations of SDRs have occurred since 1981. A country can draw on its SDRs as long as it maintains an average of more than 30 percent of its cumulative allocation, and

a country is required to accept up to three times its total allocation. Interest is paid to those who hold SDRs and by those who draw down their SDRs, with the rate based on an average of money-market interest rates on dollars, pounds, euros, and yen.

The SDR was originally set equal in value to the gold content of a US dollar in 1969, that is, 0.888571 grams or 1/35 oz. The value was later revised, first being based on a weighted basket of 16 currencies, and subsequently being simplified to five currencies. The currency basket and the weights are revised every 5 years according to the importance of each country in international trade. The value of the SDR is quoted daily.

If the SDR had arrived earlier, it might have prevented or postponed the collapse of the Bretton Woods system, but by 1971, the fall was imminent. After only two major revisions of exchange rates in the 1950s and 1960s – the floating of the Canadian dollar during the 1950s and the devaluation of sterling in 1967 – events suddenly began to rapidly unfold. On August 15, 1971, the United States responded to a huge trade deficit by making the dollar inconvertible into gold. A 10-percent surcharge was placed on imports, and a program of wage and price controls was introduced. Many of the major currencies were allowed to float against the dollar, and by the end of 1971 most had appreciated, with the German mark and the Japanese yen both up 12 percent. The dollar had begun a decade of decline.

On August 15, 1971, the United States made it clear that it was no longer content to support a system based on the US dollar. The costs of being a reserve-currency country were perceived as having begun to exceed any benefits in terms of seigniorage. The ten largest countries were called together for a meeting at the Smithsonian Institution in Washington, DC. As a result of the **Smithsonian Agreement**, the United States raised the price of gold to $38 oz. (i.e. devalued the dollar). Each of the other countries in return revalued its currency by up to 10 percent. The band around the new official parity values was increased from 1 percent to $2\frac{1}{4}$ percent on either side, but several EEC

---

6 For an account and estimates of seigniorage gains, see the papers in Robert Mundell and Alexander Swoboda (eds), *Monetary Problems of the International Economy*, University of Chicago Press, Chicago, Il , 1969.

7 See Fritz Machlup, *Remaking the International Monetary System: The Rio Agreement and Beyond*, Johns Hopkins Press, Baltimore, MD, 1968, for the background to the creation of SDRs. For more recent developments see http://www.imf.org/external/np/exr/facts/sdr.htm

countries kept their own exchange rates within a narrower range of each other while jointly allowing the $4\frac{1}{2}$-percent band vis-à-vis the dollar. As we have seen, the "snake," as the European fixed-exchange-rate system was called, became, with some minor revisions, the Exchange Rate Mechanism (ERM) of the European Monetary System (EMS) in 1979.

The dollar devaluation was insufficient to restore stability to the system. US inflation had become a serious problem: see Exhibit 23.2. By 1973 the dollar was under heavy selling pressure even at its devalued or depreciated rates, and in February 1973, the price of gold was raised 11 percent, from $38 to $42.22 oz. By the next month most major currencies were floating. This was the unsteady state of the international financial system as it approached the oil crisis of the fall of 1973.

The flexible-exchange-rate period, 1973–85

The rapid increase in oil prices after the oil embargo worked to the advantage of the US dollar. Since the United States was relatively self-sufficient in oil at that time, the US dollar was able to weather the worst of the storm. The strength of the dollar allowed the United States to remove controls on capital outflows in January 1974. This opened the way for large-scale US lending to companies and countries in need – and came just in time. The practice of paying for oil in US dollars meant that the buyers needed dollars and that the sellers – principally the members of the Organization of Petroleum Exporting Countries (OPEC) – needed to invest their dollar earnings. And so the United States began to recycle petrodollars, taking them in from OPEC countries and then lending them to oil buyers.

It was not until 1976, at a meeting in Jamaica, that the system that had begun to emerge in 1971 was approved, with ratification coming later, in April 1978. Flexible exchange rates, already extensively used, were deemed to be acceptable to IMF members, and central banks were permitted to intervene and manage their floats to prevent undue volatility. Gold was officially demonetized, and half of the IMF's gold holdings returned to the members. The other half was sold, and the proceeds were to be used to help poor nations. Individual countries were allowed to sell their gold holdings, and the IMF and some other countries began sales. IMF sales were completed by May of 1980.

The Presidential election of 1980 and the subsequent adoption of **supply-side economics** by the Reagan Administration was followed by a period of growing US fiscal and balance-of-trade deficits. Nevertheless, the US dollar experienced a substantial appreciation, further adding to the US trade deficit. This took place against the backdrop of the worsening third-world debt crisis which was aggravated by the high-flying dollar; since most of the debt was denominated in dollars, it was more expensive for the debtor nations such as Brazil, Mexico, Poland, and Venezuela to acquire dollars to meet debt service payments. Adding to the difficulties of the debtor nations was a general disinflation which was particularly severe for resource exports, including oil, that were the source of much of their revenue. Furthermore, because they had to meet debt payments, the debtors could not reduce oil and other resource production as they would normally do at low prices. Indeed, some debtor nations had to increase production to make up for lower prices, and this put even more downward pressure on their export prices. That is, declining oil and other prices caused producers to produce more to meet debt payments, further lowering resource prices, thereby causing a further increase in output, and so on. While the third-world debt crisis which accompanied this resource deflation overlaps the period of flexible rates and the subsequent cooperative intervention period, it is worth singling out the debt crisis years because the crisis helped transform international financial arrangements.

The third-world debt crisis, 1982–89

The background

The high interest rates on loans to developing nations, and the rapid economic growth some of these countries had enjoyed in the 1970s, led

EXHIBIT 23.2   BRETTON WOODS FACES THE AXE

Inflation is a hidden tax; it reduces the value of fixed face-value assets such as currency. The United States resorted to the inflation tax to fight the unpopular Vietnam War, knowing that more explicit taxes, such as those on sales or incomes, would not be received favorably by the American public. The inflation tax was applied via accelerated growth in the money supply. The resulting inflation was "shipped" via the Bretton Woods system in the following way: US inflation with fixed exchange rates caused US trade deficits and corresponding trade surpluses elsewhere. In order to prevent appreciation of exchange rates in the surplus countries, their central banks were forced to increase the supplies of their currencies. This caused inflation among the US trading partners. The following explains how the inflation brought down the quarter-century old Bretton Woods system after a brief period, 1971–73, with a dollar standard.

After the establishment of the two-tier arrangement, the world monetary system was on a *de facto* dollar standard. The system became increasingly unstable until it collapsed with the closing of the gold window in August 1971. The collapse of a system beset by the fatal flaws of the gold exchange standard and the adjustable peg was triggered by an acceleration in world inflation, in large part the consequence of an earlier acceleration of inflation in the United States. Before 1968, the U.S. inflation rate was below that of the GNP weighted inflation rate of the Group of Seven countries excluding the United States. It began accelerating in 1964, with a pause in 1966–67. The increase in inflation in the United States and the rest of the world was closely related to an increase in money growth and in money growth relative to the growth of real output . . .

The key transmission mechanism of inflation was the classical price specie flow mechanism augmented by capital flows. The Bretton Woods system collapsed because of the lagged effects of U.S. expansionary monetary policy. As the dollar reserves of Germany, Japan and other countries accumulated in the late 1960s and early 1970s, it became increasingly more difficult to sterilize them. This fostered domestic monetary expansion and inflation. In addition, world inflation was aggravated by expansionary monetary and fiscal policies in the rest of the Group of Seven countries, as their governments adopted full employment stabilization policies. The only alternative to importing U.S. inflation was to float – the route taken by all countries in 1973.

The U.S. decision to suspend gold convertibility ended a key aspect of the Bretton Woods system. The remaining part of the system – the adjustable peg – disappeared 19 months later.

The Bretton Woods system collapsed for three basic reasons. First, two major flaws undermined the system. One flaw was the gold exchange standard, which placed the United States under threat of a convertibility crisis. In reaction it pursued policies that in the end made adjustment more difficult.

The second flaw was the adjustable peg. Because the costs of discrete changes in parities were deemed high, in the face of growing capital mobility, the system evolved into a reluctant fixed exchange rate system without an effective adjustment mechanism. Finally, U.S. monetary policy was inappropriate for a key currency. After 1965, the United States, by inflating, followed an inappropriate policy for a key currency country. Though the acceleration of inflation was low by the standards of the following decade, when superimposed on the cumulation of low inflation since World War II, it was sufficient to trigger a speculative attack on the world's monetary gold stock in 1968, leading to the collapse of the Gold Pool. Once the regime had evolved into a *de facto* dollar standard, the obligation of the

> United States was to maintain price stability. Instead, it conducted an inflationary policy, which ultimately destroyed the system.
>
> *Source:* Michael D. Bordo, "The Gold Standard, Bretton Woods and Other Monetary Regimes: A Historical Appraisal," *Review,* Federal Reserve Bank of St. Louis, March/April 1993, pp. 175–78.

even some of the most conservative banks from industrialized countries to make substantial fractions of their loans to developing countries. For example, for the largest 15 US banks, developing-country loans at the outset of 1982 amounted to 7.9 percent of their assets and 150 percent of their capital. This meant that default on all these loans would place the banks in technical insolvency. However, since many of the loans were made to governments or guaranteed by governments – so-called **sovereign loans** – few bankers seemed aware that defaults were possible. A commonly voiced opinion was that "countries don't go bankrupt, only companies go bankrupt." What was overlooked by the bankers in their complacency was that countries can go bankrupt *in terms of US dollars,* and the vast majority of third-world debt was denominated in US dollars. Clearly, if countries borrowed in their own currencies they could always repay debts; they have unlimited power to "print" their currencies. Of course, bankers would have been very wary of loans denominated in the borrowers' currencies, knowing that on repayment the currencies they received would probably have little value. It is worth noting that if the debtor nations had issued bonds rather than arranged bank loans, the inability to pay would have meant outright default, not **rescheduling**. For example, in a similar international debt crisis of the 1930s involving bonds, defaults occurred on the majority of foreign-issued US dollar bonds.[8]

The debt crisis first became obvious when in August 1982, Mexico announced it could not meet scheduled repayments on its almost $100 billion of external debt. Within one year of that announcement, 47 debtor nations were negotiating with their creditors and international organizations such as the IMF and World Bank to reschedule payments. The negotiations involved possible changes in magnitude, maturity, and currency composition of debt. Talk of a "debtors, cartel" and default by debtors was matched against the threat of denial of future credits by the creditor banks and their governments. This was the background to the intense bargaining between debtors and creditors which stretched on throughout the 1980s. The creditors knew that debtors would repudiate if the value of repudiated debt exceeded the present value of the cost of repudiation in the form of denied access to future credit.[9]

The causes

Numerous factors combined to make the crisis as severe as it was. Taking developments in no particular order, we can cite the following:

1   In the two years 1979 and 1980 there was a 27-percent decline in commodity prices, and a recession began in developing and developed nations alike. This meant that export revenues of debtor nations which depended on commodity exports were plunging, and yet it was from these export revenues that they had to service debts. The loans had been sought and granted based on an expectation of increasing

8 See Barry Eichengreen, "Resolving Debt Crises: An Historical Perspective," *National Bureau of Economic Research*, Working Paper 2555, April 1988.

9 The problem of creditor–debtor bargaining clearly fits in the paradigm of non cooperative game theory, and indeed, the debt crisis spawned numerous papers in this vein. See, for example, Jonathan Eaton and Mark Gersovitz, "Debt with Potential Repudiation: Theoretical and Empirical Analysis," *Review of Economic Studies*, April 1981, pp. 289–309.

commodity prices and export revenues, and yet the very opposite occurred.

2   The debts were denominated in US dollars, and in 1980 the US dollar began a spectacular climb that by 1985 had almost doubled its value against the other major currencies. Bankers and borrowers had not anticipated this surge in the dollar.

3   Interest rates experienced an unprecedented increase after a switch to anti-inflationary monetary policy in October 1979, with the US prime rate topping 20 percent. This made the payment of interest difficult for many borrowers, and the repayment of principal just about impossible.

4   A substantial component of borrowed funds had not been devoted to investment which would have generated income to help service debts. Rather, much of the debt had been used to subsidize consumption. Furthermore, due to political pressures it was difficult to remove these subsidies, and so borrowing continued. Many debtor nations were on a knife edge, risking riots or revolution if they reduced subsidies, but risking isolation from creditor nations if they maintained them. At the height of the debt crisis in the mid-1980s, visits by IMF officials to debtor nations to encourage reduced consumption-subsidization were frequently met with protests. In its efforts to force economic reorganization on debtors by making help contingent on a return to market forces, the IMF became a villain in the eyes of the poor in many developing nations.

The fear

The principal fear of officials was the consequence of bank failures brought about by outright defaults. This fear was based on the view that losses would exceed the capital of many banks, so that effects would not be limited to bank shareholders. Rather, losses would spill over to depositors. There could be runs on banks if governments did not bail them out by purchasing bad debts. Bank bailouts were viewed by many as inflationary.[10] Many argued, therefore, that the consequences of the debt crisis would be financial panic and runaway inflation.

The handling of the crisis

The fact that the 1980s ended without widespread bank failures and financial chaos reflects the step-by-step rescheduling that occurred, the almost two decades of economic growth, and a number of steps taken by international organizations and banks. Some of the more notable of the actions taken were extensions of stand-by credits by the key international financial institutions, rescheduling of payments over extended intervals, further private bank lending to avoid realizations showing on balance sheets, the forgiving of some old loans and reduced interest rates on other loans.

The experience with the third-world debt crisis shows how financially and economically interdependent we have become. Nations have come to recognize that failure of other countries' banks will spill over to their own banks, and economic setbacks among their customers will hurt their own firms that supply these customers. Through regular economic summits among national leaders, and through even more frequent contact among central bankers and other senior officials, countries have been cooperating. As with the physical environment, it has become recognized that the global good can no longer be achieved through independent, competitive action. The same conclusion emerges from considering the shift in thinking that prompted the Plaza Agreement in 1985.

---

10 This view is difficult to support if all that the governments did was prevent a collapse of their money supplies. In fact, failure of governments to prevent losses on deposits would almost certainly have been deflationary, as it was in the 1930s, and the maintenance of deposit levels, if done properly, should have been a neutral action.

523

Cooperative intervention: the Plaza Agreement era, 1985–

Throughout the run-up in the value of the dollar in the early 1980s, the US Administration repeatedly argued that the appreciating dollar was a sign of confidence in the US economy, and that the free market would take care of exchange rates if they were seriously out of line. However, many economists argued otherwise, saying that the soaring US dollar was the result of an exploding US fiscal deficit that was too large to be financed by bond sales to Americans. Instead, the fiscal deficit required borrowing from foreign savers such as those of Japan and Germany. Bond purchases by Japanese, German, and other foreign investors meant a demand for US dollars when paying for the bonds, and this pushed up the dollar's value. Furthermore, many economists argued that because a flexible exchange rate results in a balanced balance of payments, the capital inflow and resulting capital-account surplus required a matching current-account deficit, and this in turn was achieved by an overvalued US dollar that itself was the result of the demand for dollars to purchase US debt instruments.

As the US capital inflows and current-account deficits rose in tandem, the US response was to leave fiscal policy in place, and instead push the dollar down by foreign exchange market intervention. The decision to take this tack was made at a meeting in the Plaza Hotel in New York in 1985. The Plaza Agreement marks a turning point in that phase in the fortunes of the US dollar. During the following several years the US dollar lost its earlier gains in value against the other leading currencies, with the decline often very rapid. Despite this spectacular depreciation, the US trade balance worsened further.

With the plight of the dollar grabbing newspaper headlines, attention became focused on how to prevent the dollar falling further. Economic summits of the world's leaders were organized in which the volatility of exchange rates became a central issue. These summits culminated in the Louvre Accord reached in Paris in 1987, in which the G-7

industrial countries decided to cooperate on exchange-rate matters to achieve greater stability. This agreement marked a shift towards an orchestrated dirty, or managed, float. The reason for coordinating the management of the float was that the size of private capital flows had become so large that it had become difficult for the country whose currency was falling to muster sufficient exchange reserves to keep its exchange rate steady. However, since countries never run out of their own currencies, they can indefinitely prevent their exchange rates from increasing. Therefore, by agreeing to manage exchange rates cooperatively, it was felt that the authorities could keep them stable, even in the face of very heavy private speculation.

The agreement to intervene jointly in foreign exchange markets came in conjunction with an agreement for greater consultation and coordination of monetary and fiscal policy. This coordination was needed because, as indicated in Exhibit 23.2, when countries work to maintain exchange rates, inflation starting in one country can be shipped to the others. For example, there was fear that if the United States maintained its very expansionary monetary and fiscal policy, the US dollar would drop, forcing other countries to buy dollars and hence sell their currencies, thereby increasing their money supplies. Japan, West Germany, and the other G-7 countries were afraid the US fiscal deficit would eventually force the United States to expand its money supply, and therefore the agreement to cooperate with the United States was linked to US efforts to reduce its deficit.

The system that emerged from the Louvre Accord, which has been reaffirmed in subsequent economic summits, is one that is based on flexible exchange rates, but where the authorities periodically let it be known what trading ranges of exchange rates they believe are appropriate. Intervention is used to try to maintain orderly markets within stated target zone. However, as we showed in Chapter 22, the threat of intervention helps provide stability, because the closer are exchange rates to the limits of their target zones, the greater is the probability of official intervention. For example,

524

the more the dollar drops toward the bottom end of the target zone, the greater is the probability of official dollar buying, and this leads speculators to buy dollars before the intervention occurs. This helps keep the dollar within the target zone. Nevertheless, despite the prediction of target zones research that intervention would not have to occur, intervention has occurred on many occasions, including, for example, the extensive US dollar buying during the spring and summer of 1994. Despite the foreign exchange market intervention, the dollar fell to post war lows by April 1995, falling to just 80 Japanese yen. (In 1985, the dollar was worth more than 250 yen.) A further example of intervention that failed is the "peso crisis" of December 1994, when despite large peso purchases, the Mexican peso plunged almost 40 percent.

The Asian Financial Crisis, 1997–98

While the seriousness and pervasiveness of the Asian Financial Crisis did not become clear until the devaluation of the Thai baht in July 1997, the bankruptcies in the region and the global contagion that followed can be traced back at least to January 1997.[11] The first major event was the collapse of a large Korean chaebol, Hanbo Steel, under $6 billion of debt. This was shortly followed by the failure of the Thai company Somprasong to meet a foreign debt payment. Further debt overload problems quickly followed in Malaysia and the Philippines, with currencies coming under pressure as large companies in these countries were unable to pay their creditors, many of whom were large western banks. The final trigger for the full-fledged crisis was pulled on July 2, 1997, when Thailand devalued the baht. The rush to sell other regional currencies swept the area, with the meltdown reaching panic

proportions by the end of July 1997. One of the worst affected currencies was the Indonesian rupiah which, because of the economic importance of the country in overseas markets, spread contagion to South America, Russia, and other countries competing with Indonesian producers in export markets. The only currencies to weather the storm were the Hong Kong dollar, with the peg to the US dollar being maintained only by large run-ups in interest rates and support by the People's Bank of China, and the Chinese riminbi. The riminbi was helped by the fact that it was not freely tradable, denying speculators of something to sell.

The cause of the Asian financial crisis has been linked to a number of circumstances, and indeed, this may be a case where it was the confluence of many conditions which made the crisis so severe. Most commentators attribute the crisis to poorly regulated financial markets.[12] Unlike the third-world debt crisis which involved problems with sovereign debt, in Asia it was mainly private debt to companies, especially companies involved in major construction projects. Paradoxically, the construction projects themselves boosted economic growth and this served only to further the investment in projects and the willingness of banks to lend on these projects. Unfortunately, few lenders reflected on the scale of the accumulation of all the construction projects, and what this might mean for the return on each additional project. There is only so much room at any one time for successful construction projects. As the earliest ones were completed and remained unsold, other projects were halted mid-stream. In some cities in the region, decades of housing supply sat unfinished, with mega projects such as sports stadiums in limbo. Those blaming financial regulation blame those who should have seen the result of the separate private decision makers' over-supply problem. It is difficult to imagine what regulators could have been

---

11 For an exhaustive chronology of the Asian financial crisis, see "Chronology of the Asian Crisis and its Global Contagion" compiled by the Stern School of Business from *Reuters*, *Wall Street Journal*, *New York Times*, *CNNfn*, *Financial Times*, *Bloomberg* and other sources, at http://www.stern.nyu.edu/globalmacro/AsiaChronology1.html

12 For a commentary on the possible causes of the Asian financial crisis see http://www.twnside.org.sg/title/back-cn.htm

expected to do, other, perhaps, than those granting development permits for construction projects.

An alternative although not mutually exclusive cause of the crisis is **cronyism** or nepotism. This involves the favoring of friends' or family members' projects in the allocation of financing or development licences. When fund or licence allocation is based on the market, those with the projects with highest expected marginal returns are the ones likely to attract the financing or receive the licences. Any other allocation is likely to result in a lower expected return: the selection of projects will be sub-optimal. While the return is lower with fund allocation according to cronyism or nepotism, the cost of funds is not reduced if capital is being raised in global financial markets. With the same cost of funds, and lower expected returns, failure is more likely.

There were also external forces at work in the Asian crisis. One of these was the pegging of many of the troubled currencies to the US dollar. The strong dollar at the time of the crisis negatively impacted profitability of export industries. A further factor was the glut of products produced by the Asian economies. This glut in consumer electronics, sporting goods, clothing, houseware, and so on has been good for consumers who have enjoyed deflation in a large range of products from the region. However, it has made it difficult to service debt payments. We can think of what has happened as a paradox of composition. Any one country, such as Korea or Thailand, had they expanded production of these products on their own, could have sold the products without lowering prices. The problem is that very many countries at the same time expanded production, along with other nations from Eastern Europe to the Americas. The result of their collective success at producing consumer products has been to lower their prices. That is, these countries have worsened their own terms of trade – their export prices versus import prices – by their own success. Indeed, we can think of them as victims of their success.

Our list of factors behind the Asian crisis has not included the role of currency speculators. Blame in,

at times, extreme, vitriolic language has been aimed at speculators such as George Soros by the Malaysian Prime Minister, Mahathir Mohammed. We save our discussion of speculation until later when we shall argue that speculation is unlikely to be destabilizing, at least in a flexible-exchange-rate environment. The fixed rates of the currencies in the region might, however, have been very much to blame for the financial crisis.

The Argentine Banking Crisis, 2000–02

After decades of poor fiscal and monetary management and periods of rapid inflation, Argentina decided to adopt an exchange-rate system that had worked well for Honk Kong and other generally small economies, namely a currency board. The board began its work on April 1, 1991, with the peso pegged to the US dollar at one peso to the US dollar. It was hoped that this would herald a new era of stability for Argentina, a country blessed with abundant natural resources and an educated population. As we shall see, the actual result was almost unprecedented instability.

Calling the Argentine exchange rate arrangement a currency board stretches the meaning of the term because some of the elements behind such a system were not present. It has been suggested that a successful currency board needs to possess at least three features. First, the currency must be freely convertible into the anchor currency, in this case the peso versus the US dollar. Second, the conversion rate must be fixed. Finally, in order for the convertibility to be guaranteed at the official exchange rate, the country's money must be fully backed with hard currency.[13] Only in this way can holders of the currency feel confident in their ability to convert into the anchor currency at the stated price.[14] At some time or other during 1991–2002

---

13 These are also key conditions for a successful gold standard, where the anchor is gold.

14 This list of key characteristics of a currency board are provided in Steve Hanke and Kurt Schuler, "What Went Wrong in Argentina?" *Central Banking*, 12, 3, 2002.

when the currency board existed, some or all of these elements were absent.

Perhaps the most important of the key conditions for a successful currency board that was missing in the case of Argentina was the absence of backing with hard foreign currency. Instead, the charter of the board allowed it to hold domestic assets such as Argentine government securities. The excess of money creation over the backing is called the **fiduciary issue**, and at times this reached 20 percent. The currency board also made loans to banks, particularly during the Mexican peso crisis when bank deposits were withdrawn. In this way the board was involved in monetary policy, something that exceeds the foreign exchange role that is normally the focus of a successful board.

An external factor that contributed to the eventual demise of the Argentine currency board experiment was the large fiscal deficit that the country suffered.[15] In an effort to deal with the deficit the government raised income taxes in 2000, and applied a tax on financial transactions. These efforts did not work, but instead may have contributed to a worsening recession that in turn contributed to the fiscal deficit. By early 2001 there was a flood of money leaving the country, to which the government responded by raising interest rates to over 50 percent. This made the fiscal deficit even worse by increasing debt service costs, and with money still leaving the country despite the high returns offered on pesos, the conversion into dollars was suspended.

A second external factor, one that is common to all fixed exchange-rate regimes, and especially to ones that involve great rigidity, was the global strengthening of the anchor currency, the US dollar. The rise in the dollar was the result of circumstances in the United States, but yet Argentina's currency, by necessity, also rose along with the dollar vis-à-vis the world's major currency.

The stronger the dollar became the weaker became the Argentine economy as sales declined in its traditional export markets. By the end of 2001 the country was forced to shift to a new policy, initially one with dual exchange rates, a regime that involved a lowered exchange rate for exports. This did not work, and so in January 2002 the country adopted a floating exchange rate. The economic crisis, that had banks close their doors other than for short periods each week, and with only tiny money withdrawals allowed when they were open, was severe. An economy cannot function without a medium of exchange, and with banks closed and bills going unpaid, the economy sank into a depression.

The introduction of the euro: completed 2002

The news about international financial developments is not always about serious financial crises, with nations on the brink of collapse. One development which can be viewed in a positive light, certainly by those favoring economic integration as a means of economic and political harmony, is the establishment of the euro.

The idea of the euro can be traced back at least to the Delors Report of 1989. Jacques Delors, who was President of the European Commission, introduced a three-stage plan. Stage 1, which began on July 1, 1991, removed all controls on the movement of capital within the European Union. Stage 2, which began on January 1, 1994, involved establishment of the European Monetary Institute which coordinated the separate national central banks in an effort to steer the Union towards a common currency. The last step, Stage 3, began in January 1999, and involved the establishment of "irrevocably fixed exchange rates." At first the euro was used in credit and banking statements and for electronic transfers, with the euro amounts showing on invoices, receipts, and so on, but the old monies were still in use for cash settlements. However, by 2002, the old monies had been entirely withdrawn, and the euro was in widespread

15 For a discussion of the factors contributing to the failure of the board, see "Argentina's Currency Board: Lessons for Asia," *Economic Letter*, Federal Reserve Bank of San Francisco, August 23, 2002.

EXHIBIT 23.3   THE COST OF CHANGE: CONVERSION TO THE EURO

Estimates of the cost of switching from the previous collection of a dozen different currencies to the new European common currency, the euro, vary, but generally placed this cost in US dollar terms as somewhere in the region of $20 billion to $50 billion. Compared to the size of the new Euro-zone's economy, this is of the order of one half of 1 percent to 1 percent of the area's combined GDP.

One of the main costs was producing 50 billion new coins and 14.5 billion new notes, and exchanging this for the old coins and notes. On top of the cost of changing the money that people carry around with them were the costs faced by commercial banks. This has been estimated as 20–50 percent of the total cost, consisting of changing operational banking systems and information technology. All vending machines also had to be reconfigured, a total of approximately 3.5 million of them. Storefront currency exchanges also felt the cost. A very large number of these, measured in the tens of thousands, went out of business. Some foreign currencies are still changed into and out of euros – US dollars, pounds etc. – but there is no longer a need to change money when traveling through the bulk of the European continent.

A cost that is difficult to compute is the re-writing of financial and other business contracts. Leases, mortgages, pensions, wage agreements, long-term supply contracts, wills, corporate bonds, and so on all had to be re-written in terms of the new money. This involved no small change. Old documents such as bond certificates had to be replaced with new certificates, and care taken to ensure all the replaced contracts were duly destroyed. The dangers of accidental or even criminal duplications of contracts were very real.

The potential benefits are probably as large, or larger, than the costs. No more visits to the bank when traveling over a very large continent, just as it has been for Americans traveling in the United States. No more uncertainties about the cost when ordering or selling goods to another Euro-zone member. A retiree from one country can retire in another and simply move their money to a new bank. The pension checks are in the same money wherever they are cashed.

With all the costs incurred, this now represents a major barrier to any reversal of the change to the euro. It would costs at least as much to go back as has now been borne in creating this brand new money. Of course there are costs and disadvantages of a common currency. Most importantly, monetary policy is the same everywhere irrespective of the economic circumstances. However, it would take remarkable circumstances to image a reversal of this unprecedented experiment.

Source: In part based on estimates in a CNN special item at http://edition.cnn.com/SPECIALS/2001/euro/stories/euro.costs/

use, making it much easier and cheaper to travel and do business throughout the Euro-zone.

The withdrawal of a dozen European currencies and replacement with a single, common currency was not a simple enterprise. For one thing it cost up to 1 percent of a year's GDP, and this estimate does not include all the pre-existing private contracts, financial and otherwise, that had to be re-written.[16] Another complication was the establishment of the conversion rates for the pre-existing currencies into the euro. This job was given to the General Council of the European Central Bank, ECB, which was established in 1998. After reviewing price levels and other pertinent factors, the conversion rates were established in January 1999. The rates were the following number of units of currency per euro.

- 40.3399 Belgian franc
- 340.750 Greek drachma
- 6.55957 French franc
- 1936.27 Italian lira

16 Exhibit 23.3 reviews some of the conversion costs.

- 2.20371 Dutch guilder
- 200.482 Portuguese escudo
- 1.95583 Deutsche mark
- 166.386 Spanish peseta
- 0.787564 Irish punt
- 40.3399 Luxembourg franc
- 13.7603 Austrian schilling
- 5.94573 Finnish markka.

Establishing proper values is very important, because if a country overprices its currency it would make the country uncompetitive initially, and to underprice the currency would damage the wealth of the country's citizens: they would receive inadequate amounts of euros in their bank accounts in exchange for their old money.

The euro has important implications for the conduct of monetary policy, with the single currency meaning that monetary policy is "one size fits all." The damage done by such a limitation of monetary policy depends on issues such as the mobility of factors of production and the convergence of economic conditions in the member countries. However, this is not the best place to deal with these matters. They are better discussed under the topic of the pros and cons of fixed versus flexible exchange rates later in this chapter. As should be evident, adopting a common currency such as the euro is the adoption of a fixed exchange rate, with no chance to ever turn back.

THE PRESENT

If anything is clear from our description of key events in the history of the international financial system, it is that it evolves in response to the environment it serves. For example, the shift from the gold standard to the standard adopted at Bretton Woods came in response to the beggar-thy-neighbor and protectionist exchange-rate policies of the Great Depression and Second World War. In reaction to these competitive devaluations, the system that was chosen was characterized by extreme rigidity of exchange rates. With the oil shock of the

late 1960s and early 1970s, the rigidity of Bretton Woods could not provide the adjustment needed between oil-using and oil-producing nations, and so there followed after 1973 a period of exchange-rate flexibility. With the increasing financial and economic interdependence spawned by financial deregulation and the growth in trade, and with massive structural imbalances of trade and fiscal deficits, the unfettered flexibility of the 1970s and early 1980s was replaced by the more cooperative arrangements of the Plaza Agreement, 1985, and Louvre Accord, 1987. The obvious question with important implications for the future conduct of international business is: where do we go from here? Since the direction we take is again likely to be a response to current conditions, the answer requires that we identify the problems faced today. These include

1 shifting global economic importance of countries and regions
2 growing trade imbalances associated with the shift in economic importance
3 increasing environmental concerns relating to international financial and trade flows
4 need to select an appropriate degree of exchange-rate flexibility.

Let us consider each matter, and how it might influence the future.

THE FUTURE

Shifting global economic importance

At the end of the Second World War, the United States was the dominant economic power of the free world, and it is therefore little surprise that the international financial system adopted at Bretton Woods in July 1944 was in large measure the US plan, with the US dollar playing a central role. As would be predicted by an application of game theory, in situations involving an overwhelmingly dominant player, solutions invariably unravel according to the dominant player's preferences.

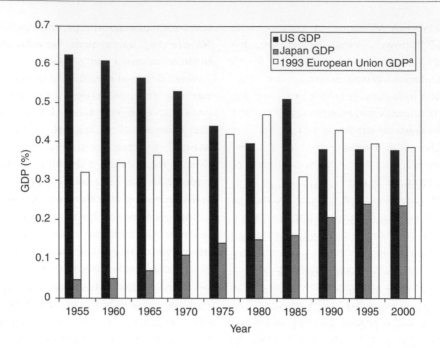

Figure 23.1 *Post-war changes in economic importance*

Notes

The size of the US economy substantially exceeded that of Japan and Europe combined until the early 1960s. By the twenty-first century the European economy, based on the same countries as in earlier years, had grown larger than the US economy. If decisions on international financial matters are based on economic importance, Japan has similar influence as the United States and Europe, because by forming a coalition with either entity, it can effect the balance of economic power.

a All data for EU based on the 12 members as of December 31, 1993.

Source: International Monetary Fund Yearbook, 1993, plus Energy Information Administration, Washington DC, http://www.eia.doe.gov/emeu/iea/tableb2.html

The "golden rule" is that "he who has the gold makes the rules," and in 1944 the United States held the majority of the free world's official gold reserves, approximately 75 percent of the total. Therefore, the United States was the only country in a position to fix its currency to gold.

The economic hegemony enjoyed by the United States at the end of the Second World War has been eroded by the phenomenal economic performance of South East Asian countries, most particularly the Peoples' Republic of China, Japan, and the "four tigers," Hong Kong, Singapore, Taiwan, and South Korea, and also by the growing strength of an increasingly integrated Europe. The European Union with its 25 members between the Baltic and the Mediterranean, and Aegean and Atlantic, is considerably larger than the United States in combined

GDP and population. The change in the balance of economic power is clear from Figure 23.1. What the figure reveals is that today there is a much more even sharing of economic power between the United States, Europe, and Japan.[17] This means that we can no longer predict important economic changes, such as in the organization of the international financial system, simply by studying the preferences of any one country. In any situation involving three players who can form coalitions, outcomes are difficult to predict. [The G-7 can be thought of as three groups: North America (United States plus Canada), Europe (Germany, Britain, France, and Italy) and Japan.] Indeed, if we associate

17 We focus on GDP, not trade. China would warrant inclusion were we to base importance on trade.

power with economic output, a country with 20 percent of the power, roughly Japan's share, has equal power to the other two players – North America and Europe with 40 percent of the countries' combined outputs. This is because by forming a coalition with either larger economic unit, the small country holds the balance of power. So what can we say about the likely evolution of the international financial and economic system in the face of this changed economic reality?

One clear consequence of the new balance of power is a need for each party to consult with the others. No single power can take the chance of triggering actions by the other two. This recognition of the need to cooperate has manifested itself in the G-7 summits, in the cooperative exchange-rate intervention policy of the Plaza Agreement and Louvre Accord, in the frequent meetings of leading central bankers under the aegis of the Bank for International Settlements – see Exhibit 23.4 – in the renewed attention paid to tariff negotiations, and in numerous matters involving taxation, interest rates, and other policies. It seems likely that with

increasing financial and economic interdependence, the evolving international financial system will involve even closer cooperation.

One of the consequences of the more even sharing of economic power is the potential emergence of three trading blocs of currencies, a dollar bloc based on the Americas, a yen or perhaps eventually a yuan bloc centered around Japanese or Chinese trade, and a euro bloc centered on the European Union. The pattern of international trade shows increasing regionalism with associated risks of increased protectionism. Indeed, the larger the regional trading blocs become, the greater is the danger of rising trade protectionism. This is because the blocs believe there is less to lose from trade restriction, and because in larger trading areas, more industrial constituencies are represented which have an interest in keeping competition for their own products more restricted. For example, without Spain and Portugal in the EU the lobby to restrict citrus fruits into the European market was weaker than when these citrus producers joined the EU.

EXHIBIT 23.4   THE BANK FOR INTERNATIONAL SETTLEMENTS

The Bank for International Settlements (BIS) is the world's oldest international financial institution. The following account of the BIS, excerpted from a description by the Federal Reserve Bank of New York, highlights the important work that has been done and is being done by the "Central Bankers' Bank."

Established in 1930 in Basel, Switzerland, the Bank for International Settlements (BIS) is a bank for central banks. It takes deposits from, and provides a wide range of services to, central banks, and through them, to the international financial system. The BIS also provides a forum for international monetary cooperation, consultation, and information exchange among central bankers; conducts monetary, economic, and financial research, and acts as an agent or trustee for international financial settlements.

Organizational Structure
As of March 2000, the BIS had 49 shareholding central banks from around the world. As of March 2000, the Bank's assets were $145 billion, including $5.8 billion of its own funds...

Board of Directors
The BIS Board of Directors elects a chairman from among its members and appoints the president of the Bank. There are three types of Board members: ex officio, appointed, and elected.

The ex officio members are the heads of the central banks of Belgium, France, Germany, Italy, the United Kingdom, and the United States. Appointed directors, who are from those six countries, hold office for three years and are eligible for reappointment...

Basel Capital Accord

In 1988, the Basel Committee on Banking Supervision developed the Basel Accord, which sets minimum capital standards for internationally active banks. The Committee believed that the framework would strengthen the soundness and stability of the international banking system by encouraging international banking organizations to increase their capital positions. Furthermore, the Committee believed that a standard approach applied to banks in different countries would reduce competitive inequalities...

In June 1999, the Basel Committee on Banking Supervision proposed a new capital adequacy framework to replace the current Basel Accord. The proposed framework focuses on three "pillars": (1) minimum capital requirements, (2) supervisory review, and (3) market discipline. Together, the changes to the current Accord are designed to differentiate degrees of risk more accurately and to improve the risk management practices of banks. Also, the Committee is seeking to expand capital requirements beyond credit and market risks to include interest rate and operational risks...

Center for Economic, Financial, and Monetary Research

The Monetary and Economic Department of the BIS conducts research and market analysis. For example, the BIS and central banks compile and analyze data on developments in international banking and financial markets. They collect data on activity in international securities markets, foreign exchange, and over-the-counter derivatives markets...

Financial Operations

The BIS offers a wide range of banking services to assist central banks in managing their external reserves. About 120 central banks and international financial institutions have deposits with the BIS. As of March 1999, currency deposits totaled $112 billion dollars, or about seven percent of world foreign exchange reserves. Most of these funds are in the form of investments with large commercial banks and purchases of short-term government securities. The BIS also conducts foreign exchange and gold operations for its customers...

Agency and Trustee Functions

The BIS assists in the execution of international financial agreements as trustee or fiscal agent. From 1986 to 1998, for example, the BIS was an agent for the European Currency Unit (ECU) Clearing and Settlement System...

Source: Bank for International Settlements, Fedpoints 22, Federal Reserve Bank of New York, 2004.

Trade imbalances

While there have always been imbalances of trade, there has been a growing concern since the mid-1980s that trade imbalances have become larger and more persistent. For example, Figure 23.2 shows the overall imbalances of trade for the United States and Japan. It shows growing US trade deficits with persistent, although diminishing, trade surpluses in Japan. Nothing seems to stop the trade imbalances in the world's two largest economies. All the automatic-adjustment mechanisms we have described, whether they involves exchange rates, price levels, incomes or interest rates, seem incapable of narrowing the imbalances of trade.

Even when countries have balanced trade overall, bilateral surpluses and deficits are bound to exist. A surplus a country enjoys with one nation or region may be offset by a deficit with another nation or region. For example, the United States might have a deficit with Japan and China and an offsetting surplus with South America. Similarly,

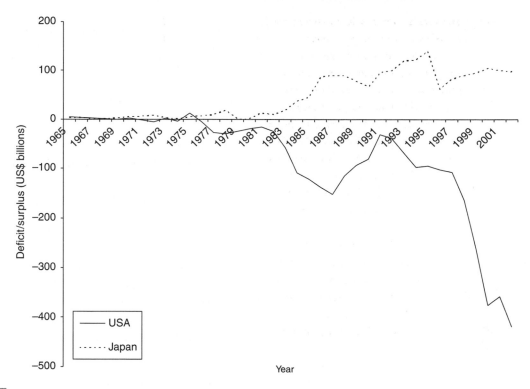

Figure 23.2 *US and Japanese trade balances, 1965–2002*

Notes
The US trade deficit has grown larger over the years while Japan's trade surplus has persisted. In terms of the Absorption Principle, the United States is living above its means while Japan is living below its means.

Source: United States Bureau of the Census, Washington DC, 2004, and *Statistical Handbook of Japan,* Bureau of the Ministry of Public Management. Tokyo, 2003.

Japan's surplus with the United States could offset a deficit with South America or countries supplying oil. All countries could, at least in principle, have balanced trade. Nevertheless, substantial attention has been paid to particular bilateral imbalances, particularly those between the United States and Japan and the United States and China.[18] Figure 23.3 shows that the bilateral imbalance with Japan has persisted while that with China has grown very rapidly. The imbalances have been an irritant in US–Japan and US–China relations. The danger is that even though bilateral imbalances are inevitable, if they are perceived to result from

18 See, for example, Alison Butler, "Trade Imbalances and Economic Theory: The Case for a U.S.-Japan Trade Deficit," *Review*, Federal Reserve Bank of St. Louis, March/April 1991, pp. 16-31.

unfair trade practices they can prompt trade actions that interfere with the international flow of goods and services.

Environmental damage and international finance

While the natural environment and international finance might appear to be unconnected, the two matters come together around the actions of an important international financial institution, the **World Bank**. Also known as the **International Bank for Reconstruction and Development,** the World Bank has been assisting developing nations since its creation out of the Bretton Woods agreement of 1944. Today, the World Bank raises about $20 billion per year that goes into helping

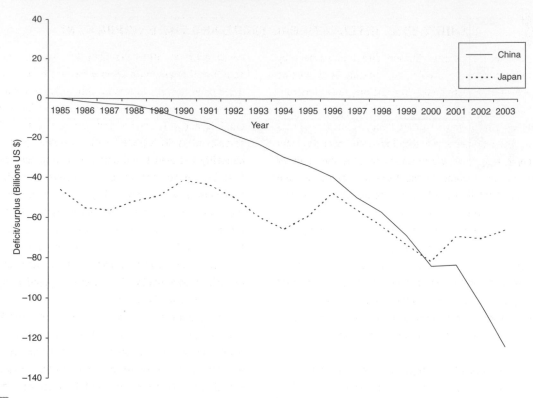

Figure 23.3 US bilateral trade balance with China and Japan, 1985–2003

Notes
In less than 20 years the US trade deficit with China has gone from close to zero to in excess of $100 billion. Indeed, by 2000 the US trade deficit with China exceeded the US trade deficit with Japan.

Source: US Bureau of the Census, Washington DC, http://www.census.gov/foreign-trade/balance/c5700[/c5880].html

finance activities in poor countries. They also provide policy advice and technical assistance. Despite several attempts to incorporate environmental considerations into World Bank lending policies, it has been argued that the Bank has contributed to environmental and social damage on a massive scale. By funding dams that have flooded prime agricultural lands and ancient villages, and financing highways into forests that have provided access to miners and farmers who have plundered the tropical rain forests, the Bank has been accused of assisting widespread global environmental destruction.[19]

For example, in a 1993 internal review it was found that over 37 percent of recently evaluated projects did not even meet the Bank's own social and environmental performance goals.[20] With increasing concern over the environment we can expect mounting pressure on international institutions and national governments to have "greener" lending and/or trading practices. For example, embargoes could be placed on nonrenewable resources, just as they have been on ivory and endangered animals. While thus far action against countries has been limited mostly to public-interest organizations, the stage is set for wider actions, some of which is likely to involve official agencies.

19 For a scathing attack on World Bank lending practices, see Bruce Rich, *Mortgaging the Earth*, Beacon Press, Boston, MA, 1994. See, however, Exhibit 23.5 which argues that international trade has, if anything, been good for the environment.

20 See Emily T. Smith "Is the World Bank a World Menace?" *Business Week*, March 21, 1994.

EXHIBIT 23.5   INTERNATIONAL TRADE AND THE ENVIRONMENT

The desire to attract foreign direct investment by multinationals for their job creating and income generating effects could, in principle, lower environmental standards. That is, there could be a "race to the bottom." On the other hand, if multinationals improve incomes where they invest and operate, local people may have a propensity to consume some of their extra income in the form of cleaner air and water. That is, the effect of the activities of multinational corporations could contribute to a cleaner or to a dirtier environment. The following paragraphs provide a summary of one study that has tried to determine how globalization in the form of international trade and investment has impacted on countries' air quality. Contrary to what is commonly believed, it would appear from the study that globalization has, if anything, been beneficial for the environment.

Opponents of globalization claim that international trade harms the environment. They believe that in open economies a "race to the bottom" in environmental standards will result from governments' fears that enhanced environmental regulation will hurt their international competitiveness. In "Is Trade Good or Bad for the Environment: Sorting out the Causality"... Jeffrey Frankel and Andrew Rose examine the environmental effects of openness to trade in a statistical cross-section of countries in 1995. They find that the impact of trade on at least three kinds of air pollution appears to be, if anything, beneficial, not adverse, for a given level of income. Openness, measured as the ratio of trade to income, appears to reduce air pollution. The level of significance is high for Sulfur Dioxide (SO_2), and moderate for Particulate Matter and Nitrogen Oxides (NO_x).

Correlations need not prove causation. The observed correlation between trade and pollution could arise in other ways. It is possible that countries that are more democratic tend to be both more open to trade and more responsive to environmental concerns. Also, higher levels of income can interact with trade and the environment in all sorts of ways. This paper tries to disentangle the causality between trade and the environment by first testing for the effect of openness on the environment while controlling for income. Then the authors focus on exogenous variation in trade attributable to geography (for example, distance from major trading partners), and on variation in income per capita attributable to standard growth determinants (for example population, investment and education).

How could trade be good for the environment? Trade allows countries to attain more of what they want, including environmental protection (the authors call this proposition the gains-from-trade hypothesis). Trade might lead to international pressures to increase environmental standards, or to beneficial technology and managerial innovations. Multinational corporations tend to bring clean state-of-the-art production technologies from higher-standard countries of origin to host countries where such standards are not yet known. Furthermore, trade economists believe that openness to trade encourages continual innovation both in technology and in management practice; such innovation likely will be applied to environmental concerns as well as to pure economic goals. In other words, Frankel and Rose suggest, environmental improvements may well accompany globalization.

Source: "Is Trade Good or Bad for the Environment?" a summary of Jeffrey Frankel and Andrew Rose, Working Paper No. 9201, National Bureau of Economic Research, Cambridge, MA, in *The NBER Digest,* November 2002.

DEGREE OF EXCHANGE-RATE FLEXIBILITY: FIXED VERSUS FLEXIBLE EXCHANGE RATES

During the last century the pendulum has swung back and forth between fixed and flexible exchange rates. Rather than end this chapter by speculating on the next experiment in international financial arrangements, let us list the pros and cons of flexible versus fixed exchange rates. The arguments we list seem likely to circulate continuously as debate continues over the "ideal" system. It should become clear from the arguments we present that either system has its weaknesses. The reader can reach her or his own judgment on whether we will move towards more or less exchange-rate flexibility from our current managed, or dirty float system. First, let us consider the arguments favoring flexible exchange rates.

Arguments favoring flexible exchange rates[21]

Better adjustment

One of the most important arguments for flexible exchange rates is that they provide a less painful adjustment mechanism to trade imbalances than do fixed exchange rates. For example, an incipient deficit with flexible exchange rates will merely cause a decline in the foreign exchange value of the currency, rather than require a recession to reduce income or prices as fixed exchange rates would. We should note, however, that the decline in the value of a nation's currency still cures a trade deficit by reducing real (price-level-adjusted) income and wages. A country's products can become more competitive either by a reduction of local-currency prices or by a reduction in the

foreign exchange value of its currency. For political and social reasons it may be impractical to reduce local-currency wages, so instead it may be necessary to reduce the international value of the country's currency.

We can see how a currency devaluation or depreciation reduces real wages in two ways. First, it means more expensive imports and domestically-produced tradable goods, which raises the cost of living and thereby reduces the buying power of given local wages. Second, when the wages or incomes of the workers in different countries are ranked in terms of a common currency, the fall in the value of a currency will mean that wages and incomes in that country fall vis-à-vis those in other countries. It should hence be clear that a decline in the value of a currency via flexible exchange rates is an alternative to a relative decline in local-currency wages and prices to correct payments deficits. The preference for flexible exchange rates on the grounds of better adjustment is based on the potential for averting adverse worker reaction by only indirectly reducing real wages.

Better confidence

It is claimed as a corollary to better adjustment that if flexible exchange rates prevent a country from having large persistent deficits, then there will be more confidence in the country and the international financial system. More confidence means fewer attempts by individuals or central banks to readjust currency portfolios, and this gives rise to calmer foreign exchange markets.

Better liquidity

Flexible exchange rates do not require central banks to hold foreign exchange reserves, since there is no need to intervene in the foreign exchange market. This means that the problem of having insufficient liquidity (international foreign exchange reserves) does not exist with truly flexible rates, and competitive devaluations aimed at securing a larger

---

21 The classic case for flexible exchange rates has been made by Milton Friedman in "The Case for Flexible Exchange Rates," in *Essays in Positive Economics*, University of Chicago Press, Chicago, IL, 1953, and by Egon Sohmen in *Flexible Exchange Rates: Theory and Controversy*, University of Chicago Press, Chicago, IL, 1969.

share of an inadequate total stock of reserves should not take place.

Gains from freer trade

When deficits occur with fixed exchange rates, tariffs and restrictions on the free flow of goods and capital invariably abound. If, by maintaining external balance, flexible rates avoid the need for these regulations which are costly to enforce, then the gains from trade and international investment can be enjoyed.

Avoiding the so-called "peso problem"

During the 1980s and 1990s, Mexico fought to keep the peso fixed to the US dollar despite widespread opinion that it would eventually be forced to devalue. To discourage investors from withdrawing funds from Mexico to avoid losses when the devaluation eventually occurred, the Mexican government had to maintain high interest rates. These high rates were the indirect consequence of fixed exchange rates and stifled investment and job creation. Interest rates had to be kept high as long as a necessary devaluation was deferred. After the devaluation happened, interest rates could return to normal if the devaluation was successful in restoring an appropriate exchange rate. In such a circumstance further devaluation would be unlikely. Because of the situation where it was identified, the problem of high interest rates due to the possibility of a devaluation with fixed exchange rates has become known as the **peso problem.**

Increased independence of economic policy: optimum currency areas

Maintaining a fixed exchange rate can force a country to follow the same economic policy as its trading partners. For example, as we have seen, if the United States allows a rapid growth in the money supply, this will tend to push up US prices and lower interest rates (in the short run), the former causing a deficit or deterioration in the current account and the latter causing a deficit or deterioration in the capital account. If the Canadian dollar is fixed to the US dollar, the deficit in the United States will most likely mean a surplus in Canada. This will put upward pressure on the Canadian dollar, forcing the Bank of Canada to sell Canadian dollars to maintain the fixed exchange rate, and hence increase the Canadian money supply. We see that due to fixed exchange rates an increase in the US money supply causes an increase in the Canadian money supply. However, if exchange rates are flexible, all that will happen is that the value of the US dollar will depreciate against the Canadian dollar.[22]

The advantage of flexible rates in allowing independent policy action has been put in a different and intriguing way in the so-called **optimum-currency-area argument**, developed by Robert Mundell and Ronald McKinnon.[23] A **currency area** is an area within which exchange rates *are* fixed. An optimum currency area is an area within which exchange rates *should be* fixed. We can explain what constitutes an optimum currency area by considering the consequences of the adoption of the euro by twelve of the European Union countries. We can begin by asking what would happen if one of the euro countries – let us consider Italy for the purpose of discussion – suffers a fall in demand for its exports with resultant high unemployment,

---

22 For more on the theory and evidence of the linkage between the United States and other countries' money supplies under fixed and flexible exchange rates see Richard G. Sheehan, "Does U.S. Money Growth Determine Money Growth in Other Nations?" *Review*, Federal Reserve Bank of St. Louis, January 1987, pp. 5–14. For an alternative view, see Edgar L. Feige and James M. Johannes, "Was the United States Responsible for Worldwide Inflation under the Regime of Fixed Exchange Rates?" *Kyklos*, 1982, pp. 263–77.

23 See Robert Mundell, "A Theory of Optimum Currency Areas," *American Economic Review*, September 1961, pp. 657–65, and Ronald McKinnon, "Optimum Currency Areas," *American Economic Review*, September 1963, pp. 717–25. See also Harry Johnson and Alexander Swoboda (eds), *Madrid Conference on Optimum Currency Areas*, Harvard University Press, Cambridge, MA, 1973.

while the economies of the remainder of the Euro-zone countries continue to grow.

In order to use monetary policy to offset the fall in demand and ease the unemployment in Italy, the monetary authorities would need to expand the money supply. With the common currency, this can only be done by the European Central Bank which would raise the Euro-zone's money supply. This would involve the risk of inflation in the Euro-zone economies with full employment. We see that Italy cannot have an independent monetary policy with a common currency. If, however, Italy had still had its own currency, then the money supply could have been expanded to take care of Italy's unique problem. Moreover, even if the discretionary monetary policy action were not taken, having a separate currency with a flexible foreign exchange value would have meant that this adjustment would have been achieved automatically; the fall in demand for Italian exports would have lowered the external value of the Italian lira, and the lower value would then have stimulated export sales. In addition, a lower lira encourages investors to build plants in Italy and take advantage of the cheap Italian wages vis-à-vis wages elsewhere.

The optimum-currency-area argument can be taken further. Why not have a separate currency with a flexible exchange rate just for northern Italy? Then a fall in the demand for manufactured goods, produced largely in the north of Italy, would cause a fall in the value of this hypothetical northern Italian currency, stimulating other industries to locate in the same region. A separate currency would also allow discretionary policies to solve the economic difficulties specific to the region. And if northern Italy, then why not Milan, or even parts of Milan? Extending the argument to the United States, why shouldn't there be a separate northeastern dollar or a separate northwestern dollar? Then if, for example, there is a fall in the demand for the lumber of the northwest, the northwestern dollar can decline in value, and other industries would be encouraged to move to the northwest. But what limits this?

We can begin our answer by saying that there is no need to have a separate northwestern dollar if the people in the northwest are prepared to move to where opportunities are plentiful so that unemployment does not occur. We need a separate currency for areas from which factors of production cannot move or prefer not to move. This prompted Robert Mundell to argue that the optimum currency area is the "**region**." A region is defined as an area within which factors of production are mobile and from which they are immobile. Mundell argued that if currency areas are smaller than existing countries, then there is considerable inconvenience in converting currencies, and there is exchange-rate risk in local business activity. This risk might be difficult to avoid with forward contracts and the other usual risk-reducing devices because the currency area is too small to support forward, futures and options markets. That is, the optimum currency area, like so many other things, is limited by the size of the market. In addition, thin currency markets can experience monopolistic speculation whereby powerful interests might try to manipulate prices. Mundell therefore limited the optimum currency area to something larger than a nation. This makes the problem one of asking which countries should have a common currency, or alternatively, truly fixed exchange rates.

Another factor affecting the extent of an optimum currency area is the degree to which economic activity is correlated throughout the area. For example, if all of the European Union countries followed the same business cycle, they could all have a common currency without having locally specific problems from rigid exchange rates. They would all need easier or tighter monetary policy, or higher or lower exchange rates, at the same time, meaning little or no conflicts on preferences for economic policy.

Britain opted out of the first round of euro adoption, even though the country met the criteria established in the Maastricht Agreement which was designed to make countries converge in the sizes of their debts and deficits, and in their inflation rates. (Without similar conditions in these key dimensions it would be very difficult or impossible to operate a common currency.) One reason is obviously history, with great nostalgia for the pound, which in the nineteenth century was the monarch of the world's monies. Another is the design to remain sovereign. But in terms of the optimum currency area argument, this decision could rationally be based on a lack of factor mobility across the English Channel, and the absence of a high correlation of Britain's business cycle with that of the Continent of Europe. Some countries that did join the euro also viewed mobility as lacking due to language and cultural barriers. They also doubted the correlation that would be needed for success. However, there was a feeling that taking the brave step of adopting the common currency could itself bring about the necessary conditions. That is, with a common currency people are more likely to be mobile, changing jobs across national borders. The different economies would also be more likely to move together in their business cycles.

Finally, it should be mentioned that transfers between areas can reduce the harmful effects of fixed exchange rates. Money can be paid to areas suffering from a high currency caused by strong demand elsewhere in the area.[24]

The notion that the minimum feasible size of a currency area is limited by the greater risk and inconvenience of smaller areas is closely related to one of the leading arguments against flexible exchange rates: that they cause uncertainty and inhibit international trade. Let us begin with this in our discussion of the negative side of the flexible-exchange-rate argument.

Arguments against flexible exchange rates

Flexible rates cause uncertainty and inhibit international trade and investment

It is claimed by proponents of fixed exchange rates that if exporters and importers are uncertain about the future exchange rate, they are more likely to stick to local markets. This means less enjoyment of the advantages of international trade and of overseas investments, and it is a burden on everyone. To counter this argument, a believer in a flexible system can say the following:

1   Flexible rates do not necessarily fluctuate wildly, and fixed rates do change – often dramatically.[25] There have been numerous well-publicized occasions when so-called fixed exchange rates have been changed by 25 percent or more. Many changes have taken place in the fixed value of British pounds, Israeli shekels, French francs, and Mexican pesos. In addition, there have been periods of relative stability of flexible exchange rates. For example, the Canadian dollar varied within a range of about 2 percent for a large part of the 1970s.

2   Even if flexible exchange rates are more volatile than fixed exchange rates, there are several inexpensive ways of avoiding or reducing uncertainty due to unexpected changes in them. For example, exporters can sell foreign-currency receivables forward, and importers can buy foreign-currency payables forward. Uncertainty can also be reduced with futures contracts, currency options, and swaps. Furthermore, the cost of these uncertainty-reducing techniques is typically small.[26]

Flexible rates cause destabilizing speculation

As mentioned earlier in this chapter in the context of the highly charged volley of statements exchanged between George Soros and Prime Minister Muhathir of Malaysia during the Asian financial

---

24 Transfers between US states have helped the United States maintain a common currency. See Jeffrey Sachs and Xavier Sala-i-Martin, "Fiscal Federalism and Optimum Currency Areas: Evidence for Europe from the United States," *National Bureau of Economic Research*, Working Paper 3855, 1991.

25 Occasionally, proponents of fixed exchange rates refer to flexible rates as "fluctuating exchange rates." There is no such thing as a *system* of fluctuating rates.

26 There are, however, limits on the ability to hedge exchange-rate risk, especially when tendering on overseas contracts. Such matters are discussed in Chapter 12.

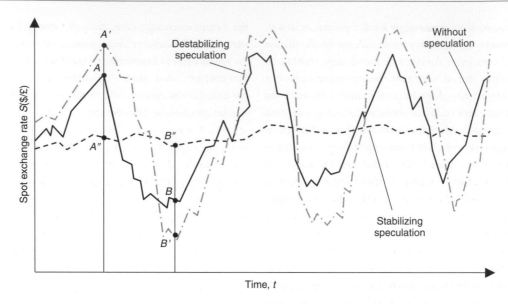

Figure 23.4 *Stabilizing and destabilizing currency speculation*

Notes
Destabilizing speculation occurs if variations in exchange rates are larger than they would otherwise be without speculation. Profitable speculation involving buying low and selling high should, however, reduce variability.

crisis, there are people who believe that speculators cause wide swings in exchange rates. These swings are attributed to the movement of "hot money." This expression is used because of the lightning speed at which money can move in response to news items. There are two counterarguments that can be made:

1 To be destabilizing, speculators as a whole will have to make losses. The argument goes like this. To cause destabilization, speculators as a whole must buy a currency when the price is high to make it go higher than it would have gone, and sell when it is low to make it go lower than it would have gone. In this way the variations in exchange rates will be higher than they would otherwise have been, as is illustrated in Figure 23.4. If the rate without speculation would have followed the path shown, then for speculators to make the rate vary by more than this, speculators as a whole must be buying pounds when $S(\$/£)$ is at A, making $S(\$/£)$ rise to A'; speculators must sell when $S(\$/£)$ is at B, making $S(\$/£)$ fall

to B'; and so on. But this means buying high and selling low, which is a sure recipe for losses. If speculators as a whole are to make a profit, they must sell pounds when $S(\$/£)$ is at A, forcing $S(\$/£)$ toward A'', and buy pounds when $S(\$/£)$ is at B, forcing $S(\$/£)$ toward B''.[27] In this way speculators dampen variations in exchange rates and stabilize the market.[28]

2 Speculation with fixed exchange rates *is* destabilizing, and it can be profitable too. When a

27 The fact that speculators as a whole lose money does not mean all speculators lose.

28 It has been argued that if there is an imperfect signal that demand for a currency will be high in the next period, speculators may buy the currency even though they know the signal may not be correct. Then, if there is not another high-demand signal next period, speculators might sell their currency holdings, pushing the exchange rate lower than it would have gone. This is claimed to be destabilizing and, it is argued, may also be profitable. See Oliver D. Hart and David M. Kreps, "Price Destabilizing Speculation," *Journal of Political Economy*, October 1986, pp. 927–52. For other special circumstances for which it is claimed that destabilizing speculation can be profitable see Robert M. Stern, *The Balance of Payments*, Aldine, Chicago, IL, 1973.

country is running out of foreign exchange reserves, its currency is likely to be under selling pressure, with the exchange rate at its lower support point. When speculators see this, they will sell the currency. Under fixed rates the central bank will purchase the currency sold by the speculators at the lower support price and use up foreign exchange reserves. This will make the shortage of reserves even worse, causing other holders of the troubled currency to sell. This will further lower foreign exchange reserves and eventually force the central bank to reset the rate at a lower level. This is highly destabilizing speculation. It is also profitable for the speculators who make money at the expense of the central bank, and thereby indirectly at the expense of taxpayers. This is because the central bank is buying before the price of the currency falls.

With fixed exchange rates speculators know in which direction an exchange rate will move, if it is to move. For example, when the pound sterling was pegged to the Deutschemark within the EMS during the early 1990s, a *revaluation* of the pound versus the mark was exceedingly unlikely. By selling pounds the worst that could have happened to a speculator was that the pound would not fall in value. If there was to be a change in the exchange rate it would be a pound devaluation, and if that happened, the speculator who shorted the pound would profit. And so fixed-rate speculation is destabilizing, and because it provides one-way bets, may be profitable for speculators (and costly for central banks and taxpayers).

Flexible rates will not work for small open economies

An argument against flexible exchange rates for currencies of small, open economies such as Hong Kong has been made by a number of economists, including Robert Mundell. The argument begins by noting that a depreciation or devaluation of currency will help the balance of trade if it reduces

the relative prices of locally produced goods and services. However, a depreciation or devaluation will raise prices of tradable goods. This will increase the cost of living, which in turn will put upward pressure on wages. If, for example, a 1-percent depreciation or devaluation raises a country's price level by 1 percent, then if real wages are maintained nominal wages must rise by the amount of depreciation or devaluation. If wages rise 1 percent when the currency falls by 1 percent, the effects are offsetting, and changes in exchange rates, whether in flexible or pegged values, will be ineffective. In such a case the country may as well fix the value of its currency to the currency of the country with which it trades most extensively.

Flexible rates are inflationary

Rigid adherence to the gold standard involved a constraint on monetary authorities. They had to keep their money supplies and inflation under control. It is claimed by proponents of fixed rates that the Bretton Woods and dollar standards also involved discipline, since inflation would eventually force devaluation. This, it is said, motivated the central bank to keep inflation under control. On the other hand, according to this argument, flexible exchange rates allow inflation to occur without any eventual crisis. Therefore, there is less reason for governments to combat inflation.

It has alternatively been argued that flexible exchange rates have an inherent inflationary bias because depreciations increase prices of traded goods, but appreciations do not cause parallel reductions in prices. This argument is based on a **ratchet effect** that is avoided with fixed rates; with fixed rates there are fewer changes in exchange rates to be subject to a ratchet. However, the empirical evidence does not support the existence of a ratchet.[29] Economists who believe that prices are

29 Morris Goldstein, "Downward Price Inflexibility, Ratchet Effect and the Inflationary Impact of Import Price Changes," *Staff Papers*, International Monetary Fund, November 1976, pp. 509–44.

related to the money supply are not surprised. This is because they believe that higher and higher price levels resulting from fluctuations in exchange rates would cause an excess demand for money that would reduce spending unless the higher prices were **accommodated** by the central bank expanding the money supply in line with higher prices.

Flexible rates are unstable because of small trade elasticities

If import demand or export supply elasticities are small, the foreign exchange market may be unstable in the sense that small disturbances to exchange rates can grow into large disturbances.[30] Instability is possible because, for example, a depreciation can increase the value of imports by increasing import prices more than it decreases the quantity of imports. A depreciation can therefore increase the currency supply more than it increases the value of exports and currency demand. Consequently, depreciation can cause an excess supply of currency, further depreciation, and so on. If this is the case, and other factors influencing currency supply and demand such as speculation do not limit the movements in exchange rates once they begin, the government might wish to limit exchange-rate movements itself by fixing exchange rates. Of course, then the country must depend on the potentially painful price-level, income, and interest-rate adjustment mechanisms of fixed exchange rates.

Flexible rates can cause structural unemployment

After the discovery and development of vast supplies of natural gas off the Dutch coast, the Dutch guilder appreciated substantially. This made traditional Dutch exports expensive, causing

unemployment in these industries. The gas industry is far less labor intensive than the traditional Dutch export industries making it difficult for the displaced workers to find alternative employment. This problem of structural unemployment due to exchange rate changes has become known as the **Dutch disease**.[31]

We can see that there are valid arguments on both sides of the ledger for fixed and flexible exchange rates. For one thing, the appropriate exchange rate depends on the size of a country. A small country is likely to have low import elasticities of demand for imports because the possibilities of import substitution are very limited: a small country is likely to have few industries in its industrial mix, so when foreign goods become more expensive after depreciation, there are limited domestic substitutes. Low import demand elasticities, as we have explained, contribute to unstable foreign exchange markets. In addition, a small economy is likely to experience inflation after devaluation, undoing the trade improvement that normally accompanies currency depreciation. This explains why most small, open countries have fixed exchange rates to the currency of their major trading partner. In Europe, for example, several of the smaller states that are not in the Euro-zone have fixed their exchange rates to the euro.

As far as the international financial system as a whole is concerned, in the absence of any approach that dominates in every dimension, we can expect it to evolve in response to circumstances. Rising trade imbalances could push the system towards flexibility while increased volatility from political events could push the system in the other direction. The compromise of the Louvre Accord in place since 1987 might continue to serve us well, but judging from the shifting systems of the twentieth century, further change seems likely.

31 It has been argued that Britain suffered from the Dutch disease too. See K. Alec Chrystal, "Dutch Disease of Monetarist Medicine? The British Economy under Mrs. Thatcher," *Review,* Federal Reserve Bank of St. Louis, May 1984, pp. 27–37.

30 This was shown in Chapter 6.

SUMMARY

1 The classical gold standard was in effect for the half century before the First World War, and again during 1926–31. The guarantees by governments to convert paper money to gold provided a credible commitment that inflationary policy would not be pursued.

2 The 1930s were marked by "beggar-thy-neighbor" policies of competitive devaluations. During the Second World War there were controls on currency convertibility.

3 The Bretton Woods system of 1944 was a response to the conditions between the wars. Exchange rates were fixed to gold or the US dollar, and the International Monetary Fund, IMF, was established to administer the system.

4 The IMF still functions after having gone through many changes, but the Bretton Woods system ended in 1973 when many major countries moved to flexible exchange rates. It has been argued that the collapse of the gold-exchange standard was inevitable because growing reserves required continuing US deficits that reduced the acceptability of US dollars as reserves.

5 Exchange rates were flexible from 1973 to 1985, with only infrequent interventions by central banks to maintain order. After September 1985 and the Plaza Agreement action was taken to force down the dollar, and a dirty-float period began.

6 An agreement to coordinate foreign exchange market intervention and domestic economic policies was reached in Paris in 1987. This became known as the Louvre Accord, and marked a change to cooperative intervention by the G-7 within imprecisely specified target zones.

7 The third-world debt crisis reached a head in the early 1980s, when several Latin American borrowers were unable to meet scheduled payments. The causes of the crisis included worsening terms of trade of debtor nations, a rapid appreciation of the US dollar, high interest rates, and the use of debt for subsidizing consumption rather than for investment.

8 The much-feared bank failures due to the debt crisis did not occur because international institutions and private banks cooperated to provide credits. This cooperation was necessary to prevent panic in an interdependent financial and economic environment.

9 The Asian financial crisis was due to poor financial regulation, worsening terms of trade and cronyism that resulted in poor project selection. The Argentine financial crisis was due to inadequate backing of the currency board.

10 The global balance of economic power has shifted from US dominance to a more even distribution of power between Europe, Japan, and the United States. Stability requires cooperation among these economic powers, helped by periodic economic summit meetings.

11 Trade imbalances have widened and been persistent since the 1980s raising the danger of protectionist policies.

12 Environmental consequences of trade in, for example, lumber from rainforests, and of large-scale projects financed by the World Bank, have become, and are likely to remain, major issues in the international financial system.

13 Arguments *for* flexible rates include better adjustment to payments imbalances, better confidence, more adequate foreign exchange reserves, and increased economic policy independence.

14 The case *against* flexible exchange rates includes the argument that they cause uncertainty and thereby inhibit international trade. Counterarguments are that fixed rates, as they have worked in practice, have also been uncertain, and that forward, futures and options contracts allow exporters and importers to avoid exchange risk at a low cost.

15 Another argument against flexible rates is that they allow destabilizing speculation. However, this requires that speculators incur losses, and in any case, speculation with fixed rates is destabilizing as well as profitable.

16 A valid argument against flexible rates is that they will not work for small economies because wages are likely to be forced up along with prices of imports, offsetting the effect of depreciation, and that import demand elasticities are likely to be small due to lack of import substitution possibilities. Another argument is that flexible rates are inflationary.

17 An optimum currency area is an area within which exchange rates ought to be fixed. The optimum-currency-area argument provides an alternative viewpoint with regard to the debate on fixed versus flexible exchange rates.

18 Having many small currency areas improves automatic adjustment and allows local monetary policy to be tailored to local needs. However, it adds to uncertainty and introduces costs of exchanging currencies in local trade. The optimum currency area is the region, which is the area within which there is factor mobility. It is generally claimed that this area is at least as large as a country.

REVIEW QUESTIONS

1 What role did commitment play in the successful functioning of the gold standard?
2 What events helped shape the Bretton Woods system?
3 How did the International Monetary Fund, IMF, help implement the Bretton Woods system?
4 What are Special Drawing Rights?
5 What is meant by "seigniorage?"
6 What is a "sovereign loan," and what error did some bankers make when considering the risk of such loans?
7 What factors contributed to the third-world debt crisis?
8 How has economic power shifted in recent years?
9 What type of bank is the Bank for International Settlements?
10 What type of bank is the International Bank for Reconstruction and Development, or World Bank?
11 What is the "peso problem?"
12 What is an "optimum currency area?"
13 What counterarguments can be made to the claim that flexible rates contribute to uncertainty and thereby inhibit trade?
14 What is the "Dutch disease?"

ASSIGNMENT PROBLEMS

1 How can government objectives such as the maintenance of full employment hinder the functioning of the gold standard? Would adjustment via income or via interest rates be inhibited in the same way?

2 Why might historical patterns of prices show parallel movements between deficit and surplus countries? Could gold discoveries and common movements in national incomes cause this?

3 In what ways did Bretton Woods require countries to sacrifice economic sovereignty for the public good?

4 Why can speculators make profits with less risk under fixed rates? From whom do they make their profits?

5 Assume that you are going to poll the following groups:
   a. Central Bankers
   b. Business executives
   c. Consumers

   How do you think each group would weigh the arguments for and against flexible rates? What does each group have to gain or lose from more flexibility?

6 Why do we observe deficits or surpluses under "flexible" rates? Does this tell us something of the management of the rates?

7 Should Appalachia have its own currency? Under what conditions should the Hong Kong dollar be pegged to the Chinese yuan rather than the US dollar?

8 Will *re*valuations or appreciations work for small, open economies? Why is there asymmetry in the effect of revaluation and devaluation?

9 Do you think that the collapse of the Bretton Woods system would have been less likely had surplus countries expanded their economies to ease the burden of adjustment on the countries with deficits?

10 How would you go about trying to estimate the seigniorage gains to the United States? (*Hint:* They depend on the quantity of US dollars held abroad, the competitive rate of interest that would be paid on these, and the actual rate of interest paid.)

11 Why do you think some European countries maintained pegged exchange rates after the collapse of the Bretton Woods system? Relate your answer to optimum currency areas?

12 Do you think that coastal China and western China should have separate currencies?

13 Do you think North America should adopt a common currency?

14 Why have central bankers frequently intervened in the foreign exchange market under a system of flexible exchange rates? If they have managed to smooth out fluctuations, have they made profits for their citizens?

15 Which argument for fixed exchange rates do you think would be most compelling for Fiji? (*Hint:* Fiji's major "export" is tourism, and most manufacturers and other consumer goods are imported.)

16 Do you think that problems might arise out of a difficulty for Americans to accept a relative decline in economic power? What form might these problems take?

BIBLIOGRAPHY

Alogoskoufis, George S., "Monetary Accommodation, Exchange Rate Regimes and Inflation Persistence," *Economic Journal,* May 1992, pp. 461–80.

Archer, Clive, *International Organisations,* Routledge, London, 2001.

Bardo, Michael D., "The Gold Standard, Bretton Woods and Other Monetary Regimes: A Historical Appraisal,"*Review,* Federal Reserve Bank of St. Louis, March/April 1993, pp. 123–99.

—— and Barry Eichengreen (eds), *A Retrospective on the Bretton Woods International Monetary System,* University of Chicago Press, Chicago, IL, 1993.

Bayoumi, Tamin and Barry Eichengreen, "Shocking Aspects of European Monetary Unification," *National Bureau of Economic Research,* Working Paper 3949, January 1992.

Berg, Andrew, and Eduardo Borensztein, *Full Dollarization: The Pros and Cons,* Economic Issues No. 24, International Monetary Fund, Washington, DC, December 2000.

Black, Stanley W., "International Monetary Institutions," *New Palgrove Dictionary of Economics,* Macmillan, London, 1987 pp. 665–73.

Drysdale, Peter (ed.), *Reform and Recovery in East Asia,* Routledge, London, 2000.

Dunn, Robert M. Jr and John H. Mutti, *International Economics,* 5th edn, Routledge, London, 2000.

Feldstein, Martin, "The Case Against EMU," *The Economist,* June 13, 1992, pp. 19–22.

Friedman, Milton, "The Case for Flexibility Exchange Rates," in *Essays in Positive Economics,* University of Chicago Press, Chicago, IL, 1953.

Giavazzi, Francesco and Marc Pagano, "The Advantage of Tying One's Hands: EMS Discipline and Central Bank Credibility," *European Economic Review,* June 1988, pp. 1055–75.

Grubel, Herbert G., *International Economics,* Richard D. Irwin, Homewood, IL, 1977.

Heller, H. Robert, *International Monetary Economics,* Prentice-Hall, Englewood Cliffs, NJ, 1974.

Johnson, Harry G., "The Case for Flexible Exchange Rates, 1969," in George N. Halm (ed.), *Approaches to Greater Flexibility of Exchange Rates: The Burgenstock Papers,* Princeton University Press, Princeton, NJ, 1970; reprinted in Robert E. Baldwin and J. David Richardson, *International Trade and Finance: Readings,* Little-Brown, Boston, MA, 1974.

McKinnon, Ronald I., "Optimum Currency Areas," *American Economic Review,* September 1963, pp. 717–24.

—— "The Rules of the Game: International Money in Historical Perspective," *Journal of Economic Literature,* March 1993, pp. 1–44.

Mundell, Robert A., *International Economics,* chapter 12, Macmillan, New York, 1968.

Schardax, Franz, "An Early Warning Model for Currency Crises in Central and Eastern Europe," Unpublished Thesis, Donau University, Krems, Austria, 2002.

Sohmen, Egon, *Flexible Exchange Rates: Theory and Controversy,* rev. edn, University of Chicago Press, Chicago, IL, 1969.

Willett, Thomas D. and Edward Tower, "The Concept of Optimum Currency Areas and the Choice Between Fixed and Flexible Exchange Rates," in George N. Halm (ed.), *Approaches to Greater Flexibility of Exchange Rates: The Burgenstock Papers,* Princeton University Press, Princeton, NJ, 1970.

Yeager, Leland B., *International Monetary Relations: Theory, History and Policy,* 2nd edn, Harper & Row, New York, 1976.

Glossary

80–20 subsidiary   A specially established wholly owned company used to raise capital for a US-based corporation. The subsidiary must earn 80 percent or more of its income abroad. Up to 20 percent of income may be earned in the United States. 80–20 subsidiaries do not need to withhold tax (see **withholding tax**) and therefore are useful for raising funds from foreigners who would not receive full credit for tax withheld.

absolute advantage   A country has an absolute advantage in products it can produce at lower cost than other countries. See **comparative advantage**.

absolute form of the purchasing-power-parity condition   The form of the **purchasing-power-parity principle** stated in terms of *levels* of prices and *levels* of exchange rates, rather than in terms of inflation and changes in exchange rates. See **relative form of the purchasing-power-parity principle**.

absorption approach   Interpretation of the **balance of trade** in terms of the value of goods and services produced and the value of goods and services "absorbed" by consumption, investment, or the government. The absorption approach views the **balance of payments** from the perspective of the **national-income accounting identity**.

accelerator model   Theory which links the demand for capital goods to the level of GDP, and hence the rate of investment in capital goods to the growth rate of the GDP.

accept   Willingness of a bank to guarantee a **draft** for payment of goods and services.

acceptance draft   Check or **draft** for which documents such as the **bill of lading** are delivered upon acceptance of the draft by the payee's bank. See **clean draft**, **documentary draft**, and **payment draft**.

accommodation   Situation in which a central bank expands the money supply to prevent a reduction in spending after a jump in the price level, thereby supporting the higher price level.

accounting exposure   The amount of **foreign exchange exposure** reflected in a company's financial statements.

adjusted present value (APV)   A technique for capital budgeting that is similar to **net present value** but which considers difficult matters, if necessary, after dealing with easy-to-handle matters.

administered prices   Prices set by firms, often for internal purposes or to reduce taxes, not by the market. See **arm's-length pricing**.

agency cost   The cost that may be faced by shareholders, and perhaps also by the economy at large, when managers do not own the companies they manage. The cost occurs when managers pursue their own interests instead of the interests of shareholders.

agglomeration economies   Mutual benefits firms enjoy from being in the same location.

agreement corporation   A means for a US-based bank to engage in international banking. Can be established with permission of the Federal Reserve Board or a state government.

air waybill   The document issued by a carrier showing details of the merchandise being transported by air. See **bill of lading**.

American Depository Receipts (ADRs)   Claims issued against foreign shares and traded in the over-the-counter market. ADRs are used so that the foreign shares can trade in their home market but nevertheless be sold in the United States.

American options   Options contracts that can be exercised on any date up to and including the maturity date of the option. See **European options**.

appreciation   An increase in the foreign exchange value of a currency when exchange rates are **flexible**. See **depreciation**, **devaluation**, and **revaluation**.

arbitrage   Simultaneously buying and selling for the purpose of profiting from price differences.

arbitrager   A person or institution engaging in **arbitrage**.

arbitrage profit   The profit from simultaneously buying and selling the same item.

arm's-length pricing   Prices set according to proper market values. See **administered prices** and **transfer prices**.

Articles of Agreement (Bretton Woods)   The principles signed at the Bretton Woods conference which helped define the **Bretton Woods system**.

Asian Crisis, 1997–98   Starting with the Thai bhat, several Asian currencies fell precipitously after debt payments were missed. The crisis has been attributed to poor financial regulation, cronyism, and worsening terms of trade. The spread of crisis conditions from country to country has been called **contagion**.

ask rate   The price at which a bank or broker is willing to sell. See **bid rate**.

asset approach to exchange rates   A theory which emphasizes that monies are assets and therefore have values according to what market participants think the monies will be worth in the future.

Association of South East Asian Nations (ASEAN)   The economic membership organization between countries of South East Asia working towards tariff reductions and easier access of members to each others' markets. The ASEAN is less formalized and covers a narrower range of concerns than does the **European Union** or the **North American Free Trade Agreement**.

at-the-money option   An option with a **strike price** or **exercise price** equal to the current market price of the underlying asset. For example, an option on spot pounds is "at the money" if the US dollar strike price equals the US dollar spot value of the pound. See **in-the-money options** and **out-of-the-money options**.

autarky   Having no trade relations with other countries.

autocorrelation   The situation in which successive regression errors are systematically related, indicating, for example, that relevant variables may be missing from a **regression equation**. Also called **serial correlation**, autocorrelation causes a bias towards finding that included variables are significant.

automatic price-adjustment mechanism   The built-in way that deficits and surpluses in the **balance-of-payments account** are self-correcting via changes in countries' price levels, with the price-level changes caused by changes in money supplies. Money supplies are changed by central-bank responses to **balance-of-payments surpluses** and **deficits**. See **price-specie automatic adjustment mechanism**.

avalled   Guaranteed **time drafts** provided by an importer's bank in association with **forfaiting**.

balance-of-payments account   A statistical record of the flow of payments into and out of a country during an interval of time. Provides a record of the sources of supply of and demand for a country's currency.

balance-of-payments on capital account   The difference between the value of a country's assets *sold to* nonresidents and the value of assets *bought from* nonresidents during an interval of time.

balance-of-payments on current account   The **balance on goods**, **services**, and **income**, plus net **unilateral** transfers.

balance-of-payments deficit   Usually applied to the decline in a country's foreign exchange reserves.

balance-of-payments surplus   Usually applied to the increase in a country's foreign exchange reserves.

balance of trade   A commonly used abbreviation for the balance **on (merchandise) trade**, and equal to **merchandise exports** minus **merchandise imports**.

balance-of-trade deficit   The extent to which the value of **merchandise imports** exceeds the value of **merchandise exports** during an interval of time. See **balance-of-trade surplus** and **balance on (merchandise) trade**.

balance-of-trade surplus   The extent to which the value of **merchandise exports** exceeds the value of **merchandise imports** during an interval of time. See **balance-of-trade deficit** and **balance on (merchandise) trade**.

balance on goods, services, and income   The difference between the value of exports of merchandise, services, and investment income *received from* abroad and the value of imports of merchandise, services, and investment income *paid* abroad.

balance on (merchandise) trade   The difference between the value of **merchandise exports** and the value of **merchandise imports** during an interval of time.

bancor   Name given by John Maynard Keynes to a proposed form of international money which was to be used for international settlements.

bank agency   A bank's operation in a foreign country which is like a full-fledged bank except that it does not handle retail deposits.

bank draft   A check issued by a bank promising to pay the stated amount of a currency. See **draft** and **time draft**.

banker's acceptance   A **time draft** which has been guaranteed by a bank stamping it as **accepted** so that the draft can be sold at a bank-related discount rate, not at a rate related to the risk of the issuer of the draft.

Bank for International Settlements (BIS)   An organization of central bankers and bank regulators, located in Basle, Switzerland. The BIS is a "bank for central banks" and serves as a forum for central bankers to discuss international banking regulatory standards and coordinate central-bank policies.

bank note   The paper currency of a nation, such as the US "greenback" or Bank of England paper money. Bank notes are frequently referred to as "cash."

bank-note wholesaler   A company that buys currency in the form of **bank notes** from banks or currency dealers and sells the notes to other banks or currency dealers, usually in the home country of the currency.

Basle Committee   A bank-safety surveillance organization which provides information to bank regulators about the financial condition of banks and their subsidiaries.

bearer shares   Equities which are not registered in an owner's name. This is the form of many equities sold in the **Euroequity** market.

549

beggar-thy-neighbor policy Policy of **devaluation** that attempts to help exporters and create jobs but which hurts other countries whose exports compete with those of the devaluing country. Therefore, the policy shifts unemployment to other countries.

bid rate The price which a bank or broker is willing to pay. See **ask rate**.

bilateral trade Trade between two nations.

bill of exchange A check used for payment between countries, that is, an intercountry form of **bank draft**.

bill of lading (B/L) Document issued by a shipper (or carrier) to show the details of merchandise that is to be transported. The bill of lading can serve as title to the merchandise and is needed to obtain the merchandise when it arrives at its destination.

bimetallic standard An exchange rate system in which exchange rates are faced by central banks exchanging their currencies for either of two precious metals, gold or silver.

blocked funds Funds that cannot be **repatriated**.

borrowing capacity The amount of debt a company feels it can carry on a new project, where the debt provides a tax shield.

branch A foreign office of a bank or other company that is domestically incorporated and integrated with domestic operations. See **foreign (bank) branch**.

Bretton Woods system The procedure for fixing exchange rates and managing the international financial system, worked out in Bretton Woods, New Hampshire, in 1944. The system involved fixing foreign currencies to the US dollar, and the US dollar to gold. The Bretton Woods system was in effect until the early 1970s. Also called the **gold-exchange standard**.

brokers Agents who help arrange the trading of currencies between banks by assembling buy and sell orders and showing the **inside spread**, which is the lowest selling **(ask)** rate and highest buying **(bid)** rate.

buyback agreements countertrade Where the seller of equipment agrees to buy some or all of the products made with the equipment.

buyer credits Loans to buyers, especially importers, from banks. See **supplier credits**.

call option Gives the buyer the right, but not the obligation, to buy an asset such as a foreign currency at the stated **strike price** or **exercise price**. See **put option**.

calling (margin) Situation in which a bank or broker demands that additional funds be placed in a **margin** account.

canton Local area in Switzerland which collects taxes from residents and provides services.

capital asset pricing model (CAPM) An economic model which gives the equilibrium expected return on an asset or a portfolio of assets in terms of the risk-free interest rate and a risk premium representing the **systematic risk** of the asset or asset portfolio.

capital budgeting A technique for deciding whether to incur capital expenditures such as building a new plant or purchasing equipment.

capital gains tax A tax paid on the increase in value of an asset between its purchase and sale.

capital market line The line tracing the expected returns and risks associated with different combinations of a risk-free asset (treasury bills) and the market portfolio (the portfolio of all securities existing in the market).

capital rationing When it is not possible to pursue all investments which add value to a company so that choices must be made among alternatives.

capital structure The amount of debt versus equity in a firm's financing.

Cartagena Agreement, 1969 A free-trade agreement among South American countries.

central-bank swaps   Arrangements between central banks for exchanging currency reserves to assist in supporting a country's exchange rate, where reserve exchanges are reversed later.

certificate of deposit (CD)   A negotiable claim against a deposit at a bank.

chaebol   Consortium of Korean companies.

CHIPS   See **Clearing House Interbank Payments System**.

clean draft   A check providing payment without the need to present any other documents.

clearing corporation   A corporation that pairs orders to buy futures or options contracts with orders to sell, and which guarantees all resulting two-sided contracts.

clearing house   An institution at which banks keep funds that can be moved from one bank's account to another bank's account in order to settle interbank transactions.

Clearing House Interbank Payments System (CHIPS)   The **clearing house** used to settle interbank transactions which arise from foreign exchange purchases and sales settled in US dollars. CHIPS is located in New York and is owned by its members.

closed economy   An economy without trade of goods or capital with other nations. The assumption of a closed economy is used as a means of simplifying economic models.

clusters   Geographical areas that contain related and supporting industries.

coefficient of variation   A statistical measure of volatility consisting of the standard deviation divided by the mean. Can be used to compare the volatility of exchange rates in different time periods.

cointegration techniques   Statistical procedures involving the comparison of the path followed by the difference between two economic variables over time and the paths followed by the variables themselves.

commercial drafts   Post-dated checks issued by companies for sale in order to provide financing. They are sold at a discount in the **money market**.

commitment fee   A charge by a **forfaiting** bank for quoting a rate for accepting (buying) payments from an exporter.

commodity arbitragers   Those who attempt to profit from differences in prices in different locations, buying commodities where they are cheap and selling them where they are more expensive. Their actions help bring about the **law of one price**.

common currency   Situation, as in the United States, where the same currency is used everywhere. The **European Union** has adopted a common currency; the euro.

comparative advantage   A relative efficiency in producing something, indicated by having a lower opportunity cost of one product versus another product that occurs in some other country. Countries gain from international trade by producing products for which they have a comparative advantage. See **absolute advantage**.

compensation agreement countertrade   In which some payment is in cash.

competitive advantage   A term coined by Michael Porter to reflect the edge a country enjoys from dynamic factors affecting international competitiveness. Factors contributing to a **competitive advantage** include well-motivated managers, discriminating and demanding consumers, and the existence of service and other supportive industries, as well as the necessary factor endowments.

composite currency unit   A unit formed by combining a number of different currencies. Examples are **Special Drawing Rights** and the **European Currency Unit**. Composite currency units are also called **currency baskets** and **currency cocktails**.

concessionary financing   Below market interest rates provided to companies for selecting a particular location. The low interest rates are used as an inducement to attract companies to a particular area.

Concordat Agreements   1975 and 1983 agreements for host countries to provide information to a parent bank's home regulators when an overseas subsidiary of the parent bank is experiencing serious loan losses.

confirm (letter of credit)   Occurs when an exporter obtains a guarantee from a local bank of a **letter of credit** issued by a foreign bank.

confiscation   The seizure of assets without compensation. See **expropriation**.

consignment sales   The basis of payment whereby the producer is paid by an intermediary only after the intermediary has sold the goods.

consortium banks   Joint ventures of large banks.

constant returns to scale   The situation where average cost of production remains the same when all factors of production are varied in amount to produce more or less of a product. For this to occur, output must change in the same proportion as the inputs employed, and input prices must remain constant. **See increasing returns to scale**.

consumption function   A relationship between consumption and the value of national income. See **marginal propensity to consume**.

contagion   The spread of financial crisis from country to country.

continuous (export) insurance   Insurance of credits granted by exporters where exporters do not have to inform the insurer of each credit that is to be insured. Also called **whole turnover** and **rollover** insurance.

continuous linked settlement   A procedure for banks to settle accounts between themselves that credits and debits accounts simultaneously. It is designed to reduce the chance of risk in the financial system.

continuous market   A market in which quotations of prices are continuously available.

contractual assets or cash flows   Assets or cash flows with a fixed face value. See **noncontractual assets** and **contractual liabilities**.

contractual liabilities   Payment obligations with a fixed face value. See **contractual assets** or **cash flows**, and **noncontractual assets**.

cooperative intervention   Situations whereby **G-7** central banks work together to stabilize exchange rates. Agreement to cooperate reached in the **Plaza Agreement**, 1985, and effected after the **Louvre Accord**, 1987.

corporate governance   The structure in the corporate control system, particularly as it relates to the integrity of the system of ownership and control.

correspondents   Banks which maintain accounts with each other against which checks can be drawn on behalf of customers.

counterpurchase countertrade   In which the return exchange is delayed, or in which some other party is nominated to receive the return exchange.

countertrade   A reciprocal agreement for the exchange of goods or services.

countervailing tariffs   Taxes applied to offset measures that other countries have taken to make their goods artificially cheap, such as **export subsidies** or **dumping**.

country risk   Uncertainty surrounding payment from abroad or assets held abroad due to the possibility of war, revolution, asset seizure, or other similar political, social, or economic event. See **political risk** and **sovereign risk**.

cover   To take steps to isolate assets, liabilities, or income streams from the consequences of changes in exchange rates. See **hedge**.

covered interest arbitrage   Borrowing and investing with **foreign exchange exposure hedged** in order to profit from differences in yields/borrowing costs on securities denominated in different currencies.

covered interest-parity condition   The situation whereby, *ceteris paribus*, interest rates on different currencies are equal when exchange-rate risk has been eliminated by the use of forward exchange contracts.

covered interest-parity principle   An aspect of the **law of one price** that occurs in financial markets, namely, that if **foreign exchange exposure** is **covered** by a **forward contract**, yields and borrowing costs are the same irrespective of the currency of investment or borrowing. Takes the form of a mathematical condition that the difference between interest rates on different currency-denominated securities equals the **forward premium** or **discount** between the currencies.

covered margin   The advantage, if any, from engaging in **covered interest arbitrage**.

covered yield   The return on an investment when the foreign exchange risk has been **hedged**.

crawling peg   An automatic system for revising the **parity** (par) exchange rate, typically basing the par value on recent experience of the actual exchange rate within its **support points**. The crawling peg allows exchange rates to move towards equilibrium levels in the long run while reducing fluctuations in the short run.

credit   Short form of **letter of credit**.

credit swap   An exchange of currencies between a bank and a firm, with the exchange reversed at a later date. See **parallel loan**.

cronyism   Favoritism in the allocation of projects or financing. Said to be a possible factor in the **Asian Crisis, 1997–98**.

cross forwards   A **forward contract** between two currencies, neither of which is the US dollar.

cross (exchange) rate   An exchange rate between two currencies, neither of which is the US dollar.

currency area   An area, consisting of a country or set of countries, in which exchange rates are fixed.

currency basket   A unit of measurement for international transactions formed by combining a number of different currencies, such as **Special Drawing Rights** and the **European Currency Unit**. Also called a **composite currency unit** and a **currency cocktail**.

currency center   The central location where a **multinational corporation** manages cash flows.

currency cocktail   A unit of measurement for international transactions formed from a combination of different currencies, such as **Special Drawing Rights** and the **European Currency Unit**. Also called a **composite currency unit** and a **currency basket**.

currency futures   Standardized contracts for the purchase or sale of foreign currencies that trade like conventional commodity futures on the floor of a futures exchange. Unlike **forward contracts**, currency futures are for standardized amounts, they trade for a limited number of **maturity dates**, and gains or losses are settled every day between the contract holder and the futures exchange. See **marking to market**.

currency option   A contract which gives the buyer the opportunity, but not the obligation, to buy or sell at a pre-agreed price, the **strike price** or **exercise price**.

currency per US dollar   The method of quoting exchange rates as the amount of foreign currency per US dollar. See **US dollar equivalent** and **European terms**.

currency pool   In Britain after the Exchange Control Act of 1947, those wishing to make foreign investments were required to buy foreign currency out of a pool of currencies. The amount in the pool was limited by the British government.

customs union　An association between countries in which **tariffs** are low or zero between members of the association, and in which all members impose common tariff levels on outsiders. See **free-trade area**.

debtors' cartel　Title given to a feared collusion of debtor countries collectively refusing to repay loans.

debt-service exports　Investment income earned from abroad during an interval of time. See **debt-service imports**.

debt-service imports　Investment income paid to nonresidents during an interval of time. See **debt-service exports**.

decentralized, continuous, open-bid, double-auction market　The organizational form of the **interbank market** for foreign exchange. See **decentralized market**, **open-bid market** and **double-auction market**.

decentralized market　A market which does not have a centralized location but which instead involves buyers and sellers linked by telephone or similar means.

defect　To opt for a noncooperative action, usually involving cheating.

deposit ratio　The ratio of bank deposits to bank reserves.

depreciation　A decline in the foreign exchange value of a currency when exchange rates are **flexible**. See **appreciation**, **devaluation**, and **revaluation**.

derivative　A financial asset such as a futures or options contract, the value of which is derived from the claim it makes against some underlying asset, such as a foreign currency.

derivatives markets　Markets in which assets whose values derive from underlying securities are traded. Examples are options and future markets.

Deutschemark (DM)　The former currency of the united Germany, before being replaced by the **euro**.

devaluation　A decline in the foreign exchange value of a currency on **fixed exchange rates**. It occurs when the **parity** rate is set at a lower level. See **appreciation**, **depreciation**, and **revaluation**.

direct investment　Short version of **foreign direct investment**, which is overseas investment where the investor has a measure of control. For accounting purposes, control is defined as holding 10 percent or more of a company's voting shares.

direct taxes　Taxes, such as income taxes, paid directly by the persons or companies taxed. See **indirect tax**.

dirty float　Occurs when governments attempt to influence exchange rates which are otherwise **flexible** and allowed to float. Also called a **managed float**.

discount rate　The percentage interest rate used for converting future incomes and costs into current, or present, values. Usually set equal to the opportunity cost of funds, which is what shareholders could otherwise earn on an alternative investment of equal risk.

divergence indicator　A mechanism based on the **European Currency Unit** for determining which country is at fault for a currency being at the upper or lower support of its permissible range within the **Exchange Rate Mechanism** of the **European Monetary System**.

divest　Selling off past investments.

documentary credit　A credit guarantee which requires that certain documents be presented before settlement. **Letters of credit** are documentary credits.

documentary draft　A check providing payment subject to certain documents being presented and usually associated with a **documentary credit**. See **acceptance draft**, **clean draft**, and **payment draft**.

dollarization   The increased role of the US dollar outside the United States, with the dollar being used to settle transactions. When the dollar replaces another country's currency for all transactions it is **full dollarization**. The term is also sometimes used to refer to the adoption of another country's currency when this is not the US dollar. For example, some countries in eastern Europe use the **euro**.

dollar standard   The exchange-rate system in effect during 1968–73 when foreign currencies were fixed to the US dollar as they were with the **Bretton Woods system**, but the US dollar was no longer freely convertible into gold.

domestic international-sales corporation (DISC)   A device for encouraging US firms to export by offering low corporate income tax rates. Since 1984, DISCs have largely been replaced by **foreign sales corporations**.

domestic reporting currency   The currency in which a firm reports its income and in which it produces its financial statements. Usually the currency of the country in which a corporation's head office is located.

Dornbusch sticky-price theory   Explanation advanced by Rudiger Dornbusch as to why exchange rates might **overshoot**. The theory emphasizes that because some goods' prices change slowly, exchange rates must overadjust to keep the demands and supplies of monies in balance throughout the adjustment process.

double-auction market   A market in which the participants on both sides of a transaction could be either buyers or sellers. For example, when two banks are in contact with each other about trading currency, both banks may show prices at which they are willing to buy or sell.

double-entry bookkeeping   Accounting procedure in which every debit is matched by a credit elsewhere in the account.

draft   A check used for payment, also called a **bill of exchange** when the payment is between countries.

dumping   Selling goods or services abroad at a lower price than at home. Done to attract customers away from local producers.

Durbin–Watson statistic (D–W)   A statistical measure indicating whether **serial correlation** is present in a **regression equation**.

Dutch disease   Problem associated with **flexible exchange rates** and originally identified after the discovery of natural gas off the Dutch coast, and the associated appreciation of the Dutch guilder. The increase in the value of the guilder hurt traditional Dutch exporters and employment in the traditional industries.

dynamic capital structure   Systematic changes in the amount of debt versus equity in a firm's ideal **capital structure** over time in response to changed circumstances of the firm.

EC   See **European Community**.

economic exposure   A more complete title for **exposure**, with the word "economic" added to distinguish true *economic* effects of exchange rates from effects which appear in financial statements. Effects in financial statements involve **accounting exposure**.

economic risk   An alternative title for **exchange-rate risk**, with the word "economic" added to distinguish true *economic* risk from risk that might be evident upon evaluation of financial statements.

economy of scope   Cost savings associated with the range of items being produced.

Edge Act corporations   A means by which US banks can engage in overseas **investment banking**.

EEC   See **European Economic Community**.

efficient market   A market in which prices reflect available information. See **weak-form efficiency**, **semi-strong-form efficiency**, and **strong-form efficiency**.

efficient markets form of the purchasing-power-parity principle The statement of the **purchasing-power-parity principle** in terms of *expected* inflation in two countries and the *expected* change in the exchange rate between their currencies. Also called **the expectations form of the purchasing-power-parity principle**.

efficient portfolio A collection of assets, the amounts of which are designed to have maximum expected return for a given volatility, or minimum volatility for a given expected return.

envelope (of efficient portfolios) The upward-sloping part of the curve giving the best combinations of expected return and risk that can be achieved with different portfolios.

equity home bias puzzle The strong tendency of people to hold a disproportionate fraction of their equity portfolio in their own country's companies. It is a puzzle because the bias occurs even when there are no obvious barriers to foreign investment.

escrow account An account which a bank holds at a **clearing house** for settling interbank transactions.

EU See **European Union**.

euro The new common currency used by many countries in the **European Union**, and which has completely replaced the countries' previous currencies.

Eurobond A bond denominated in a currency that is not that of the country in which it is issued; often sold in several countries simultaneously. See **foreign bond** and **Eurodollar bond**.

Eurocurrency deposits Deposits at financial institutions denominated in currencies other than those of the countries in which the deposits are located. A generalization of **Eurodollar deposits**.

Eurocurrency multiplier The multiple by which **Eurocurrency deposits** increase from an original increase in foreign exchange reserves.

Eurodollar bond A US-dollar-denominated bond sold outside of the United States. A particular type of **Eurobond**.

Eurodollar deposit A US-dollar-denominated bank deposit at a financial institution located outside the United States. See **Eurocurrency deposits**.

Eurodollar market The market outside of the United States in which US-dollar-denominated loans are made and in which US dollars are deposited in financial institutions.

Eurodollars A commonly used abbreviation for funds held in the form of **Eurodollar deposits**.

Euroequity (issues) Shares sold simultaneously in two or more countries' stock markets.

European Central Bank The central bank of the **European Union** countries.

European Community (EC) The successor of the **European Economic Community** and predecessor of the **European Union**.

European Currency Unit (ECU) An artificial unit defined as a weighted average of each of the **European Monetary System** currencies and used as a **divergence indicator** as well as for denominating loans.

European Economic Community (EEC) The association of European countries which limited its activities largely to economic matters, mainly tariffs and trade conditions, and which became the **European Community** and eventually the **European Union** as its domain of interest expanded beyond economic concerns.

European Monetary Cooperation Fund (EMCF) A central pool of money and source of help, advice, and policy coordination for the members of the **European Monetary System**.

European Monetary System (EMS) The procedure involving the **Exchange Rate Mechanism** for fixing exchange rates among the **European Union** countries. The EMS was intended to be a precursor to a **common currency**.

European options   Options contracts that can be exercised only on the maturity date of the option and not before this date. See **American options**.

European terms   The quotation of exchange rates as the amount of foreign currency per US dollar. See **US dollar equivalent** and **currency per US dollar**.

European Union (EU)   The association of countries formerly called **the European Community (EC)**, and prior to that known as the **European Economic Community (EEC)**. The EEC became the EC when the issues handled in common moved from solely economic matters to social and political matters. The EC became the EU when common **tariff** levels were applied by all members to outside countries. The EU is a **customs union**.

Eurosterling bond   A British-pound-denominated bond sold outside of Britain.

even-dated contracts   Standard-length forward contracts with, for example, 3-month maturity, 1-year maturity, etc.

event study   A statistical approach examining the situation before, after, and at the same time something happens. The purpose is to check if conditions are normal or unusual surrounding the event.

Exchange Rate Mechanism (ERM)   The procedure used for fixing exchange rates within the **European Monetary System** from 1979 to 1993. The ERM involved establishing a grid which provided upper and lower **support points** for each member's currency versus each other member's currency. When an exchange rate between two currencies approached a support point, the central banks of both countries were required to take action. Assistance to maintain exchange rates was also available from the **European Monetary Cooperation Fund**.

exchange-rate risk   The variance of the domestic-currency value of an asset or liability attributable to unanticipated changes in exchange rates.

excise tax   Another word for a **tariff**. A tax on imports, usually based on value, *ad valorem* or on weight.

exercise price   The price at which an options contract buyer has the right to purchase or sell. See **strike price** and **currency option**.

expectations form of the purchasing-power-parity principle   The form of the **purchasing-power-parity principle** stated in terms of the *expected* inflation in two countries and the *expected* change in exchange rate between the countries' currencies. Also called the **efficient markets form of the purchasing-power-parity principle**.

Export Credit Insurance   Insurance coverage providing compensation to exporters in the event they are not paid for products they have delivered.

Export-Import (Ex-Im) Bank   US export promotion agency which guarantees loans by private banks to US exporting firms.

export insurance   Guarantee of payment to an exporter when credit has been extended to a foreign buyer.

export subsidy   An action designed to make a country's exports artificially inexpensive.

exposure   A commonly used abbreviation for **foreign exchange exposure**.

exposure line   A plot of the systematic relationship between changes in values of assets or liabilities and unanticipated changes in exchange rates.

expropriation   The seizure of assets with compensation. See **confiscation**.

FAS 8   The now-abandoned reporting system of the US Financial Accounting Standard Board which required companies to show all foreign exchange **translation** gains or losses in the current-period income statement. Replaced by **FAS 52**.

FAS 52   The reporting system of the US Financial Accounting Standards Board which replaced **FAS 8** and which allows companies to include foreign exchange **translation** gains and losses in a separate shareholder-equity account. This reduces income volatility and allows income tax to be deferred on translation gains.

FASB   Financial Accounting Standards Board that helps to establish and improve standards of financial accounting and reporting.

Fedwire   A way of making payments or transferring money very quickly in the United States, which avoids the usual delays of debiting and crediting accounts.

fiat money   Money, the acceptability of which is required by an order or edict of government. Paper money is fiat money.

filter   A selection rule for decision making.

financial engineering   A technique that uses **payoff profiles** to show the consequences of different financial strategies. The profiles can be combined to show the outcomes of different strategies.

financial structure   Composition of capital raised by a firm – for example, the mix between debt and equity.

Fisher equation   An equation which states that interest rates observed in the market consist of the **real interest rate** plus the expected rate of inflation.

Fisher-open condition   The mathematical condition that **real interest rates** are equal in different countries.

fixed asset   As asset such as real estate or plant and equipment. Fixed assets are often called **real assets**.

fixed exchange rates   A system of exchange-rate determination in which governments try to maintain exchange rates at selected official levels. See **flexible exchange rates**, **floating exchange rates**, and **pegged exchange rates**.

flat   The situation where the forward exchange rate equals the **spot exchange rate**.

flexible exchange rates   A system of exchange rates in which exchange rates are determined by the forces of supply and demand without any interference by governments or official bodies. See **fixed exchange rates**, **floating exchange rates**, and **pegged exchange rates**.

floating exchange rates   Another way of referring to **flexible exchange rates**.

flow   Value per period of time. See **stock**.

foreign (bank) affiliate   Similar to a **foreign (bank) subsidiary** in being locally incorporated and managed, but a foreign (bank) affiliate is a joint venture in which no individual owner has control.

foreign (bank) branch   A bank similar to local banks in appearance and operations except that incorporation and ownership are in the parent bank's country. Operations of foreign branches are integrated with those of the parent bank.

foreign (bank) subsidiary   Locally incorporated bank owned completely or partially by a foreign parent.

foreign bond   A bond sold by a foreign issuer and denominated in the currency of the country of issue. For example, a US-dollar-denominated bond of a Canadian firm issued in the United States is a foreign bond. See **Eurobond**.

foreign direct investment (FDI)   Investment in a foreign country in which the investor has a measure of control of the investment, usually taken as holding 10 percent or more of voting shares of a public company. See **direct investment**.

foreign exchange exposure   The sensitivity of changes in the real domestic-currency value of assets or liabilities to unanticipated changes in exchange rates. Exposure can be measured by the slope of a **regression equation** which relates changes in values of assets or liabilities to unanticipated changes in exchange rates.

foreign exchange market (forex)   The market in which foreign currencies are traded.

foreign-pay bond   A bond denominated in a foreign currency.

foreign resident withholding tax   A tax applied to nonresidents at the source of their earnings. See **withholding tax credit**.

foreign sales corporation (FSC)   A device made available in 1984 for promoting US exports by offering low corporate tax rates to companies primarily engaged in exporting. Replaced **domestic international-sales corporations**.

foreign-trade income   The income of a **foreign sales corporation** that is subject to a preferred tax rate.

forex   A contraction of "foreign exchange."

forfaiting   A form of medium-term nonrecourse export financing. Involves a series of **avalled** time drafts.

forward bias   A systematic difference between the **forward exchange** rate and the expected future **spot exchange** rate.

forward discount   The situation when the price of a currency for forward delivery is lower than the current spot exchange rate. It indicates that the market expects the currency to fall in value in the future. Countries with currencies which trade at a forward discount tend to have relatively high interest rates to compensate for the expected loss of holding the currency. See **forward premium**.

forward (exchange) contract   An agreement to exchange currencies at a specified exchange rate on a future date. See **outright forward contract**.

forward exchange market   The market within which forward exchange contracts are traded. The participants are primarily banks.

forward exchange rate   The rate that is contracted today for the exchange of currencies at a specified date in the future. See **forward contract**.

forward-forward swap   Purchase/sale of a currency offset by a subsequent sale/purchase of the same currency, where both transactions are forward transactions.

forward premium   The extent that the forward price of a currency exceeds the spot price. See **forward discount**.

Four Tigers   The rapid-growth economies of South East Asia: Hong Kong, Singapore, Taiwan, and South Korea.

free-trade agreement   An official agreement between countries that their goods move between themselves without tariffs or quotas. See **free-trade area**.

free-trade area   An area within which trade between members is not subject to **tariffs** or **quotas**. However, member countries can have their own tariff levels against outsiders. On the other hand a **customs union** has free trade between members and common tariffs to outsiders. This means that in a free-trade area foreign goods cannot move freely between members, whereas in a customs union they can.

free-trade zone   An area within a country in which import tariffs are not paid. Often used as a device for reexporting products.

full dollarization   The complete adoption of the US dollar in place of a county's own currency.

functional currency   The primary currency in which a subsidiary operates. This is the currency in which a subsidiary reports its income; such reporting may involve translating foreign-currency amounts into the functional currency. US parent companies convert functional currency magnitudes into US dollars.

futures contract   A standardized agreement to buy or sell a given amount of a commodity or financial asset, including currencies, at a given date in the future.

futures exchange   The exchange where futures contracts are traded.

futures option   An option to buy a **futures contract** at a stated price. See **spot option**.

G-7   See **Group of Seven**.

game theory   The paradigm that views actions in terms of each player's or agent's expectation about the actions of other players or agents.

GATT   See **General Agreement on Tariffs and Trade**.

General Agreement on Tariffs and Trade (GATT)   A multicountry framework dating back to the 1940s to restrict tariffs and other impediments to international trade. Replaced by the **World Trade Organization** in 1995.

General Arrangements to Borrow   1990 extension of the **International Monetary Fund's** lending authority to permit loans to nonmember countries.

global custodians   Financial firms, typically banks, which hold and handle transactions involving securities on behalf of overseas owners of these securities.

globalization   The movement from local, **segmented** markets to multinational, **integrated** markets.

gold-exchange standard   Also known as the **Bretton Woods system**, the gold-exchange standard involved fixing exchange rates of foreign currencies to the US dollar, and the US dollar to gold. The gold-exchange standard was in effect from 1944 to 1968, after which time it became the **dollar standard**.

gold points   The upper and lower limits on the range within which exchange rates can move when currencies are fixed to gold. The size of the range within the gold points depends on the costs of shipping gold and of exchanging currencies for gold. See **lower gold point** and **upper gold point**.

gold standard   The system of fixing exchange rates between currencies by fixing the price of the currencies to gold. The gold standard lasted well into the twentieth century.

gold tranche   The part of the original contributions that countries made to the **International Monetary Fund (IMF)** that took the form of gold and against which IMF members could borrow without conditions.

grid   The matrix of upper and lower **support points** of the exchange rates among the **European Monetary System** currencies.

Group of Seven (G-7)   Consists of government leaders from the United States, Japan, Germany, Britain, France, Canada, and Italy. Holds "summit" meetings at least once each year to discuss economic matters of mutual interest. Russian leaders are invited as observers, resulting in reference to group G-8.

hedge   The action of reducing or eliminating effects from, for example, changes in exchange rates. See **cover**.

hedged yield   The yield on a foreign investment after foreign exchange risk has been removed.

home-country bias   Holding a disproportionately large fraction of domestic assets vis-à-vis an efficiently diversified international asset portfolio.

hot money   Short-term funds which move easily between countries or currencies in response to small changes in interest rates.

IMF   See **International Monetary Fund**.

imperfect competition   The situation in which there are a large number of firms with free entry into and out of an industry but different firms' products are not exactly the same.

import duty   A tax or **tariff** on imported products.

import quota   A limit on the quantity of a good that can be imported.

import substitutes   Goods or services produced at home that may be purchased instead of similar foreign goods or services.

increasing returns to scale   The situation where average cost of production decreases when inputs of all factors of production are increased to produce more of a product. For this to occur, output must increase by a greater proportion than the inputs employed. See **constant returns to scale**.

indirect barriers   Factors, such as difficulties in obtaining information on foreign firms, that cause capital markets to be **segmented**.

indirect tax   A tax which is ultimately paid by somebody other than the person or firm being taxed. For example, a sales tax is remitted by a firm, but if the tax is fully added to the amount paid by the consumer, it is actually paid by the consumer, not the firm.

industrial offset countertrade   Involving reciprocal agreements to buy materials or components from the buying company or country.

inflation risk   The result of uncertainty in the buying power of an asset in the future due to uncertainty about the future price level.

inside spread   The lowest selling (**ask**) price and the highest buying (**bid**) price on the books of a broker. These are the best prices available, constituting the smallest difference between buying and selling prices.

integrated international capital market   Situation when the connection between countries' capital markets is seamless. Occurs when markets are not **segmented**.

interbank   Between banks. Term used to distinguish the part of the foreign exchange market in which banks deal directly with each other from the part involving **brokers**.

interbank market   The currency market in which banks trade with each other over the telephone or via other electronic means. Central banks as well as commercial banks trade currencies in the interbank market.

interest arbitrage   Simultaneously borrowing and lending for the purpose of gaining from **(covered)** interest rate differences.

interest-rate adjustment mechanism   Automatic tendency for deficits and surpluses in the **balance-of-payments account** to be self-correcting under **fixed exchange rates**, and operating via changes in interest rates. For example, deficits cause declines in money supplies, higher interest rates, and improvements in the **balance of payments on capital account and the balance of payments on current account**.

internal rate of return   The **discount rate** that makes the **net present value** equal zero.

International Bank for Reconstruction and Development (IBRD)   Also known as the **World Bank**, the IBRD assists developing nations by granting loans and providing economic advice. Origin dates to the start of the **Bretton Woods system**.

international banking facilities (IBFs)   Adjunct operations of US banks which raise funds and make loans outside the United States but which operate in the United States without having to meet normal regulatory requirements of US banks.

international capital asset pricing model (ICAPM)   An extension of the **capital asset pricing model** to the international context.

International Development Agency (IDA)   An organization (affiliated with the **World Bank**) that provides very long-term loans at a zero interest rate to poor countries.

International Finance Corporation (IFC)   An organization (affiliated with the **World Bank**) that provides loans for private investments and sometimes takes equity positions along with private-sector partners.

International Monetary Fund (IMF)   Membership organization of over 180 countries, originally established as part of the **Bretton Woods system** in 1944. The IMF holds foreign exchange reserves of members, makes loans, provides assistance and advice, and serves as a forum for discussion of important international financial issues.

international-investment-position account   The record of a country's foreign assets and its liabilities to nonresidents.

in-the-money option   An option which, if exercised immediately, would provide the holder of the option with some value. For example, a **call** option on **spot** pounds is "in the money" if the spot value of the pound is above the **strike price**. See **intrinsic value**, **out-of-the-money option**, and **at-the-money option**.

intrinsic value   The extent to which an option is **in the money** See **time value**.

investment banks   Institutions which raise funds in capital markets and then provide financing, often in the form of equity. **Edge Act corporations** are established by US commercial banks to engage in investment banking.

invisibles   Service imports and exports including tourism, royalties, licences, consulting fees, and business services.

J-curve (effect)   The path of the **balance of trade** over time after a change in exchange rates. The path of the balance of trade after a devaluation may have the appearance of the letter J.

joint venture   Shared ownership of an investment, instituted because of need for a large amount of capital or to reduce the risk of **confiscation** or **expropriation**.

keiretsu   Consortium of Japanese companies.

Kennedy round   General tariff reductions arranged by the **General Agreement on Tariffs and Trade** in the 1960s.

law of one price   The rule resulting from actions of **arbitragers** that a given item will cost the same everywhere, whether this be a commodity or a financial asset. The law of one price means that prices of the same item in different currencies reflect the exchange rates between the currencies. See **covered interest-parity condition** and **purchasing-power-parity principle**.

leading and lagging   The practice of **netting** receivables and payables over a period of time forward, called leading, and backward, called lagging.

"leaning against the wind"   The practice of some central banks to try to reduce fluctuations in the value of their currency by raising interest rates to prevent depreciations and lowering interest rates to prevent appreciations.

letter of credit (L/C)   An irrevocable guarantee from a bank that a seller's credit to a buyer will be honored provided the seller fulfils her or his part of a specified agreement, such as the delivery of goods on time and in good condition. Also called a **credit**.

limit orders   Orders given to brokers to buy or sell limited, specified amounts of currency at specified prices on behalf of clients.

liquidity preference   The value asset holders attach to being able to cash in assets cheaply and at a predictable value. Liquidity preference may induce investors to hold domestic- currency assets instead of hedged foreign-currency assets.

liquidity trap   Situation where increasing the money supply does not reduce interest rates.

London Interbank Offer Rate (LIBOR)   Interest rate charged on interbank loans in London. The average of rates charged by large, London banks on a given currency is often used as the basis for adjusting interest rates on floating-rate loans.

long   Having agreed to buy more of a currency than one has agreed to sell. Alternatively, holding more of a currency than is needed. See **short**, **long position**, and **short position**.

long exposure   Situation when, for example, a company or individual gains when the foreign exchange value of a currency increases. See **short exposure**.

long position   Having contracted to buy a currency on the **forward market** or on a **futures exchange**. See **long**, **short**, **short position**.

Louvre Accord   An agreement reached at the Louvre Museum in Paris in 1987 for the leading industrial powers to cooperate in stabilizing exchange rates. The Louvre Accord followed the **Plaza Agreement**, which accepted the need to periodically intervene in foreign exchange markets.

lower gold point   The lowest possible value of an exchange rate when currencies are fixed to gold. See **gold points** and **upper gold point**.

Maastricht Agreement   An agreement between **European Union** countries, signed in Maastricht, Holland, to work towards common economic, social, and political policies, including achievement of a **common currency**.

maintenance level   The minimum amount in a margin account below which the account must be supplemented by buyers and sellers of **futures** or options contracts.

managed float Flexible-exchange-rate   System in which central banks occasionally intervene in the foreign exchange markets to prevent extreme changes in exchange rates. Also called a **dirty float**.

margin   Money posted at a brokerage house, bank, or clearing corporation to help ensure that contracts are honored.

marginal efficiency of investment   The rate of return enjoyed on an additional, or incremental, investment. It is the return from increasing the amount of capital formation during a given interval by a small amount.

marginal propensity to consume   The percent of extra, or incremental, income spent on consumption, representing the slope of the **consumption function**.

marginal propensity to import   The percentage of extra, or incremental, income spent on imports.

marginal utility   The increase in utility, or satisfaction, from a small, incremental increase in the rate of consumption.

market-makers   Agents who continuously stand ready to buy and to sell assets, including currencies.

marking to market   Adjustment of margin accounts to reflect daily changes in the values of contracts against which **margins** are held.

marking-to-marking risk   Risk from variability in interest rates on funds in a **margin** account. Risk is due to a possible difference between funds in a margin account and the gain or loss on an asset or liability.

Marshall–Lerner condition   The requirement concerning the elasticities of demand for imports and exports in order for foreign exchange markets to be stable. Named after the co-discoverers of the condition, Alfred Marshall and Abba Lerner.

maturity date   The date of expiry of a bond, option, or forward contract.

Mercantilists   Adherents to the view that the objective of international trade is to earn gold and run balance-of-trade surpluses. Mercantilism was popular from the sixteenth century to the eighteenth century.

merchandise exports   Sales of tangible items to foreign buyers.

merchandise imports   Purchases of tangible items from abroad.

merchandise trade   Imports and exports of tangible items, as distinct from services.

mixed credits   A procedure used to calculate an interest rate for credit provided to an importer, where the interest rate is an average of rates on different credit sources.

monetary theory of exchange rates   The theory that bases the value of a country's currency in foreign exchange markets on the supply of that currency (money supply) relative to the demand to hold the currency (money demand).

money market   The market in which short-term borrowing and investment occur (with "short term" usually meaning less than one year).

moral hazard   The tendency of people to behave in ways that are in their self interest and against the interest of others. Used in the context of insurance, where people are less careful after they insure.

most favored nation (clause)   The clause in the **General Agreement on Tariffs and Trade** which disallowed offering better trade terms to any country than those terms given to the most favored country.

multicurrency bond   A bond which gives the owner repayment in two or more currencies. Also called a **currency cocktail** bond. See **unit-of-account** bond.

multinational corporation   A company which has made **direct investments** overseas and which thereby has operations in many countries.

multiple regression equation   The fitted relationship between three or more variables. See **regression equation**.

multiplier   The change in the national income relative to the size of the underlying, original cause of this change.

NAFTA   See **North American Free Trade Agreement**.

Nash equilibrium   The situation in **game theory** where expectations of different players are consistent and where the expectations are borne out.

national-income accounting identity   A statement of national income divided into four components: consumption, investment, government spending, and exports minus imports.

natural monopoly   A situation in which a supplier faces a declining average cost over a very large range of output relative to market demand, and thereby becomes the sole supplier of a good or service.

negative externalities   Adverse effects of others of an activity.

net present value (NPV)   The income from a capital project minus the cost of the project stated in terms of the current (or present) value of the income and project cost. A technique for **capital budgeting**. See **adjusted present value** and **internal rate of return**.

netting   Calculating the overall situation for payables and receivables in a currency that faces a firm. Amounts to be paid are subtracted from amounts to be received so that **hedging** can be limited to the net amount of the currency coming in or going out. See **leading and lagging**.

neutralization policy   A policy of not allowing changes in foreign exchange reserves to affect a country's money supply, frustrating the **automatic price-adjustment mechanism**. Also called **sterilization policy**.

nominal anchor   Something linked to the money supply, such as gold, which serves to maintain a stable price level.

nominal interest rate   The interest rate observed in the market. See **real interest rate**.

noncontractual assets   Assets without a fixed face value, such as real estate or equities. See **contractual assets** and **contractual liabilities**.

noncontractual liabilities   Liabilities without a fixed face value.

nondeliverable forward contracts   **Forward exchange** agreements where only the difference between the forward price and the realized price is settled in a deeply traded currency. These types of contracts are used when currency delivery is difficult.

nontariff trade barriers   Restrictions on imports, such as size restrictions and red tape, that interfere with international trade. Nontariff barriers are often less obvious but just as harmful as explicit import restrictions such as tariffs and quotas.

North American Free Trade Agreement (NAFTA)   The 1993 treaty between the United States, Canada, and Mexico containing provisions for the reduction or elimination of trade barriers between the countries. In late 1994, Chile signed its intent to join the NAFTA.

OECD   See **Organization for Economic Cooperation and Development**.

offer rate   Price or exchange rate at which there is a willingness to sell. Also called **ask rate**.

offshore currencies   Bank deposits which are denominated in a currency different from that of the country in which the deposits are held. A generalization of **Eurodollar deposits**.

one-way arbitrage   The process of choosing the best way to exchange one currency for another or choosing the best currency in which to invest or borrow. See **arbitrage**, **round-trip arbitrage**, and **triangular arbitrage**.

open account (sales)   The basis of sales where the amount due is added to the buyer's account, and the balance owed is settled periodically. A payment method used when the seller trusts the buyer's credit.

open-bid market   A market in which participants quote both buying (**bid**) and selling (**ask**) prices.

open economy   An economy with trade of goods and capital with other nations. See **closed economy**.

open interest   The number of outstanding two-sided futures or options contracts at any given time.

operating exposure   The sensitivity of changes in the real domestic-currency value of operating incomes to unanticipated changes in exchange rates. Also called **residual foreign exchange exposure**.

operating risk   Related to the volatility of real domestic-currency operating incomes due to unanticipated changes in exchange rates. Usually measured by the variance in operating incomes from unanticipated changes in exchange rates.

optimum currency area   An area within which exchange rates *should* be fixed. Coverage of area depends on the mobility of factors of production and the similarity of the economies of component countries. See **region**.

option premium   The amount paid per unit of foreign currency, when buying an options contract.

order bill of lading   A **bill of lading** which gives title (ownership) of goods that are being shipped to a stated party and which may be used as collateral against loans.

Organization for Economic Cooperation and Development (OECD)   A Paris-based government-level organization providing information and advice on the economies of its 24 member nations, which include the United States and most of Western Europe.

out-of-the-money option   An option which, if exercised immediately, would not provide the holder with any value. For example, a **call option** on **spot** pounds is "out of the money" if the spot value of the pound is below the **strike price**. See **in-the-money option** and **at-the-money option**.

outright forward contract   An agreement to exchange currencies at an agreed exchange rate at a future date. See **swap**.

Overseas Private Investment Corporation (OPIC)   Insures US private investments in developing nations.

overshooting of exchange rates   The situation whereby exchange-rate changes are larger in the short run than in the long run. Occurs when exchange rates go beyond their eventual equilibrium level. See **Dornbusch sticky-price theory**.

over-the-counter (OTC) option   An option sold by a bank to a customers as opposed to the type of standardized option that trades on an options exchange.

parallel loan   An exchange of funds between firms in different countries, with the exchange reversed at a later date. See **credit swap**.

parity (exchange rate)   The officially determined exchange rate under fixed exchange rates.

payback period   The length of time before the capital cost of an investment project has been recovered.

payment draft   Check or **draft** for which documents such as the **bill of lading** are delivered upon payment of the draft by the payee's bank. See **acceptance draft** and **clean draft**.

payoff profile   A plot of the gains or losses on an asset against unexpected changes in price. For example, a forward exchange contract payoff profile shows the gains or losses on the forward contract against unexpected changes in the spot exchange rate.

pegged exchange rates   Another term for **fixed exchange rates**, which are rates set by governments at selected, official levels.

perfectly competitive market   A market in which there are so many buyers and sellers that each buyer and seller can take the price of a given, homogeneous product as given. Also involves free entry and exit of new firms and perfect information on prices.

perfectly substitutable (monies)   The situation in which people are equally prepared to hold one country's currency as to hold that of another country.

permanent   A change in an economic variable that persists, such as a long-lasting increase in income or an exchange rate. See **transitory**.

peso problem   Problem of having high interest rates when there is a possibility of a **devaluation**, with interest rates remaining high while the devaluation is delayed.

Plaza Agreement   An agreement among the **G-7** leaders reached at the Plaza Hotel in New York in 1985 that accepted the need to intervene in foreign exchange markets. Led to the **Louvre Accord** of 1987 which involved cooperative intervention.

point   The last digit in traditional exchange rate quotations.

political risk   Uncertainty surrounding payment from abroad or assets held abroad because of political events. A special case of **country risk**, which includes economic and socially based uncertainty as well as political uncertainty.

pooling   The practice of holding (and managing) cash in a single location.

portfolio-balance approach to exchange rates   A theory basing exchange rates on the supply of and demand for money and bonds. The situation for money/bond supply and demand in one country versus another country determines the exchange rate between the two countries currencies. People are assumed to hold both countries' money and bonds but prefer to hold their own. Exchange rates are such that all money and bonds are held.

portfolio investment   Investment in bonds, and in equities where the investor's holding is too small to provide effective control.

positive externalities   Benefits or cost savings enjoyed by others which are in addition to benefits or cost savings of those taking an action.

price-specie automatic-adjustment mechanism   The built-in way that deficits and surpluses are self-correcting via movements of precious metals between countries and consequent changes in money supplies and price levels. The **gold standard** is said to exhibit the price-specie automatic-adjustment mechanism.

Private Export Funding Corporation (PEFCO)   A private US organization providing loans to US exporters.

probability distribution   The relationship between possible outcomes and their probability of occurrence.

product life-cycle hypothesis   Theory that companies follow a similar evolutionary path, going from domestic to multinational orientation.

public good   Something that nonpayers cannot be excluded from enjoying.

purchasing-power-parity (PPP) principle   The idea that exchange rates are determined by the amounts of different currencies required to purchase a representative bundle of goods.

pure exchange gain   That part of the overall gain from trade which arises from the exchange of products without any specialization of production.

put–call (forward) parity   A procedure for pricing European options based on **arbitrage**.

put option   A put option gives the buyer the right to sell an asset such as a foreign currency at the stated **strike price** or **exercise price**. See **call option**.

quantity theory of money   The view that inflation is caused by money supply growth being in excess of the growth rate of output.

quasi-centralized market   A market in which brokers in several different locations help to facilitate transactions.

quasi-centralized, continuous limit-book, single-auction market   A market in which brokers in several locations take **limit orders** and show the resulting **inside spread** occurring at any time to prospective clients.

quota (import)   A restriction on the quantity of a good that can be imported.

ratchet effect   Effect attributed to **flexible exchange rates** concerning the impact they have on inflation. The ratchet refers to jumps in prices from **depreciations** without fully offsetting declines in prices during **appreciations**.

rational forecasts   Forecasts which are on average correct and which do not reveal persistent errors.

real asset   An asset such as real estate for which the market price tends to go up and down with inflation. Sometimes called **fixed assets**.

real change in exchange rates   A change that produces a difference between the overall rate of return on domestic versus foreign assets/liabilities or in the profitability of export-oriented, import-using, or import-competing firms.

real interest rate   The **nominal interest rate** minus expected inflation.

reference currency   The official currency of measurement of values of assets, liabilities, or operating incomes.

regime   A period during which a particular policy, for example, towards regulating exchange rates, is in effect.

region   Term used by Robert Mundell to describe an **optimum currency area**, being an area within which factors of production are mobile and from which they are not mobile.

regression coefficient   An estimate of the magnitude of the impact of a variable on some other variable. An element of a **regression equation**.

regression equation   A statistically calculated relationship between two or more variables. See **multiple regression equation**.

regression error   The difference between the actual value of a variable and the value predicted from a **regression equation**.

relative (or **dynamic**) **form of the purchasing-power-parity principle**   The form of the **purchasing-power-parity principle** stated in terms of inflation and changes in exchange rates: a country's currency depreciates by the excess of its inflation over that of another country. See **absolute form of the purchasing-power-parity condition** (or **principle**).

567

relative-price risk Risk due to the possibility of changes in the price of an individual asset vis-à-vis asset prices in general.

repatriation Bringing funds home from abroad.

representative (bank) office An office maintained by a bank in a foreign country to facilitate contact with local banks and businesses and to provide services for clients.

rescheduling Arranging for delay in the repayment of interest or principal on loans. Occurred frequently during the **third-world debt crisis**.

residual foreign exchange exposure Another term for **operating exposure** which reflects the difficulty companies have hedging their operating exposure.

revaluation An increase in the foreign exchange value of a currency on fixed exchange rates. It occurs when the parity rate is set at a higher level. See **appreciation**, **depreciation**, and **devaluation**.

reversion to the mean A tendency for above and below average values of variables to eventually move back to their average when they deviate from the average.

risk premium (forward) The difference between the **forward exchange rate** and the expected future **spot foreign exchange** rate.

rollover (swap) A **swap** where the purchase/sale and subsequent sale/purchase of a currency are separated by 1 business day.

rollover export insurance Where sellers do not have to inform the insurer of each credit that is to be insured. Also called **continuous** and **whole-turnover** insurance.

round-trip (triangular) arbitrage Borrowing in one currency, lending in another, and then selling the second currency back into the first so as to end up back in the first currency. See **arbitrage**, **one-way arbitrage**, and **triangular arbitrage**.

scenario approach The consideration of how exchange rates might impact a company by calculating what would happen to key magnitudes from different possible increases and decreases of exchange rates.

segmented international capital market Situation where different countries' capital markets are not **integrated** because of implicit or explicit factors inhibiting the free movement of capital between the countries.

seigniorage The profit from creating money. Said to have occurred from the need for countries to hold US dollar foreign exchange reserves under the **Bretton Woods system**.

semi-strong-form efficiency The situation where all publicly available information is reflected in market prices. See **efficient market**, **weak-form efficiency**, and **strong-form efficiency**.

serial correlation A situation in which successive **regression errors** are systematically related, indicating, for example, that relevant variables may be missing from a **regression equation**. Also called **autocorrelation**.

short Having agreed to sell more of a currency than one has agreed to purchase. Alternately, holding less of a currency than is needed. See **long**, **long position**, and **short position**.

short exposure Situation where, for example, a company or individual faces a loss when the foreign exchange value of a currency increases. See **long exposure**.

short position Having contracted to sell a currency on the forward market or on a futures exchange.

sight draft A draft payable not on some stated future date, as with a **time draft**, but rather payable on presentation to the issuing bank. It can be cashed immediately.

signal An action which indicates credibility to others. Credibility is usually achieved by taking an action which is costly and which therefore would not be taken unless the agent was in the situation implied by the signal.

single-auction market   A market where the agent being approached, but not the person making the approach, quotes buying and selling prices.

Smithsonian Agreement   Agreement of **International Monetary Fund** members reached in December 1971 to raise the US dollar price of gold and to create a **wider band** within which exchange rates could **float** before central bank intervention.

snake   The **fixed-exchange-rate system** designed to keep the **European Community** (EC) countries' exchange rates with a narrower band vis-à-vis each other's currencies rather than vis-à-vis non-EC currencies, such as the US dollar.

Society for Worldwide International Financial Telecommunications (SWIFT)   Satellite-based international communications system for the exchange of information between banks, used, for example, to convey instructions for the transfer of deposits.

sourcing   A **hedging** technique involving the invoicing of input prices and other cost items in the currency of sales.

sovereign loans   Loans to governments or guaranteed by governments.

sovereign risk   Uncertainty involving loans to foreign governments or government agencies.

Special Drawing Rights (SDRs)   Reserves at, and created by, the **International Monetary Fund** (IMF) and allocated by making ledger entries in countries' accounts at the IMF. Used for meeting imbalances in the balance of payments and assisting developing nations.

specific (commodities) export credit insurance   **Export insurance** for a particular stated item.

speculation   Taking an **exposed** position, consciously or unconsciously.

spot exchange rate   The exchange rate between two currencies where the exchange is to occur "immediately," meaning usually the next business day or after 2 business days.

spot foreign exchange market   The market in which currencies are traded and where delivery is "immediate," meaning usually the next business day or after 2 business days.

spot option   An option to buy or sell **spot exchange**. See **futures option**.

spread   The difference between the buying (**bid**) and selling (**ask**) prices of a currency, or the difference between borrowing and lending interest rates.

stationary   The situation where the process, or statistical model, generating data is not changing over time.

statistical discrepancy   The adjustment required to balance the balance-of-payments account due to errors in the measurement of items included in the account.

sterilization policy   A policy of not allowing changes in foreign exchange reserves to affect a country's money supply, frustrating the **automatic price-adjustment mechanism**. Also called **neutralization policy**.

sterling   Another name for the British pound, written as £.

stock   Value or quantity at a point in time. See **flow**.

straddle   The purchase of a **put option** and a **call option** at the same **strike price**. Used as a means of speculating on high volatility.

strike price   The price at which an option can be exercised. For example, the exchange rate at which a **call option** buyer can purchase a foreign currency. See **currency option** and **exercise price**.

strong-form efficiency   The situation where all information, including that available to insiders, is reflected in market prices. See **efficient market**, **weak-form efficiency**, and **semi-strong-form efficiency**.

subsidiary   A foreign operation that is incorporated in the foreign country but owned by a parent company.

supplier credits   Financing provided by the seller, usually by issuing **time drafts**.

569

supply-side economics An economic philosophy popular after the 1980 US presidential election, based on the view that production (supply) in the economy would be increased by lower tax rates.

support points The upper and lower limits of an exchange rate band at which central banks step in to prevent the exchange rate from going outside the band. Central banks buy at the lower support point and sell at the upper support point in a **fixed-exchange-rate** system.

swap (currency) A sale/purchase of a currency combined with an offsetting purchase/sale for a later time, or borrowing and lending in the same currency. The initial purchase/sale might be a **spot** transaction, with the offsetting sale/purchase being a **forward** transaction. This is a spot-forward swap. However there are also **forward-forward swaps** involving offsetting purchases and sales where all transactions occur in the future. See **outright forward contract, swap-in**, and **swap-out**.

swap-in Term used to indicate the currency being purchased and subsequently sold in a **swap** transaction. See **swap-out**.

swap-out Term used to indicate the currency being sold and subsequently bought back in a **swap** transaction. See **swap-in**.

swap points The number of **points** to be added to or subtracted from the spot exchange rate in order to calculate the **forward exchange rate**.

SWIFT See **Society for Worldwide International Financial Telecommunications**.

switch trading countertrade Where a title to a credit is transferred to another party.

symbiotic relationship Connection of mutual benefit, for example, between firms which move together into a foreign market.

systematic relationship Situation where two variables change in more or less predictable ways vis-à-vis each other. For example, if on average dollar values of assets go up with the foreign exchange value of the dollar, there is a (positive) systematic relationship.

systematic risk The part of risk that cannot be diversified away.

target zone The range within which an exchange rate is to be kept.

tariff A tax on imports. See **excise tax**.

tax arbitrage Attempt to profit from pricing or interest rate situations due to the existence of taxes. For example, borrowing in one currency and investing in another currency which is at a **forward premium**. This can be profitable when forward (exchange) premiums face a low **capital gains tax** rate.

tax haven A country with low tax rates that attracts companies or individuals fleeing higher tax rates elsewhere.

tax shield Tax saving due to the deductibility of interest payments from income subject to tax.

technical forecasts Forecasts of a variable based on the pattern of past values of the variable.

temporal distinction Different accounting treatment of operating income and expenses than of **fixed assets** and liabilities.

tenor The maturity of a **time draft** or **usance draft**.

term structure The pattern of interest rates or forward rates of different maturities. How the rates on average vary with maturity.

terms of trade The price of exports in terms of imports determining the amount of imports a country can receive per unit of exports. An improvement in terms of trade occurs when a country can obtain more imports per unit of its exports.

thinness A market is thin when the volume of transaction is low, that is, when transactions are relatively infrequent.

third-world debt crisis Serious concern in financial markets during 1982–89 that developing nations would be unable to meet scheduled payments on loans from developed-country-based banks. See **rescheduling**.

tick The minimum price change on a futures or options contract.

time draft A check, or **draft**, payable at a future date and used as a form of credit. Also called a **usance draft**.

time value The part of an **option premium** that comes from the possibility that an option might have higher intrinsic value in the future than at the moment.

Tokyo round General tariff reductions arranged by the **General Agreement on Tariffs and Trade** in the 1970s.

tradable inputs Inputs that are traded internationally or could be traded internationally.

trade draft An exporter's **draft** that is drawn without an importer's **letter of credit** and which is therefore a commercial rather than a bank obligation.

trading pit The floor of an exchange where traders callout prices and make transactions.

transaction cost The amount paid in brokerage or similar charges when making a transaction. On currencies, transaction costs are represented by the **spread** between the **bid** and **ask** exchange rates.

transaction exposure The sensitivity of changes in realized domestic-currency values of assets or liabilities when assets or liabilities are liquidated with respect to unanticipated changes in exchange rates.

transaction risk The uncertainty of realized domestic-currency asset or liability values when the assets or liabilities are liquidated due to unanticipated changes in exchange rates.

transfer prices Prices used for goods and services moving within a **multinational corporation** from one division to another. Rules typically require that transfer prices be **arm's-length prices**.

transitory A change in an economic variable that is short-lived, such as a once-and-for-all increase in income or an exchange rate. See **permanent**.

translated value The value of an asset, liability, or income after it has been converted into another currency. For example, the value of a foreign-currency asset converted into the owner's domestic currency.

translation Conversion of the value of an asset, liability, or income from one currency to another.

translation exposure The sensitivity of changes in real domestic-currency asset or liability values appearing in financial statements with respect to unanticipated changes in exchange rates.

translation risk The uncertainty appearing in financial statements due to unanticipated changes in exchange rates.

transnational alliance Separately owned corporations from different countries working in cooperation for such purposes as research and development or marketing.

triangular arbitrage Simultaneously buying and selling for the purpose of profiting from differences between **cross rates** and direct exchange rates vis-à-vis the US dollar. Such arbitrage involves three currencies and transactions.

Triffin Paradox Problem that for the Bretton Woods system to succeed the United States must run a trade deficit to provide dollars, but by running deficits the system would eventually collapse.

US dollar equivalent The quotation of the price of a currency in terms of its value in US dollars. See **European terms** and **currency per US dollar**.

US official reserve assets Liquid foreign assets held by the US Federal Reserve or Department of the Treasury. Includes gold, foreign currencies, and short-term investments.

uncovered interest-parity condition The situation, analogous to the **covered interest-parity condition**, in which **foreign exchange exposure** is not **covered** with **a forward (exchange) contract**. Takes the form of a mathematical condition that the difference between interest rates on different currency-denominated securities equals the expected rate of change of the exchange rate between the two currencies.

unilateral transfers   Payments from one country to another in the form of gifts and foreign aid.

unit-of-account bond   A bond making payments based on pre-established **fixed exchange rates**.

upper gold point   The highest possible value of an exchange rate when currencies are fixed to gold. See **gold points** and **lower gold point**.

Uruguay round   General tariff reductions agreed to in 1994 resulting from many years of negotiation centered in Uruguay and under the auspices the **General Agreement on Tariffs and Trade**.

usance draft   Another term for a **time draft**. A check payable at a future date and used as a form of **supplier credit**.

value-added tax (VAT)   A tax on the difference between the amount received from the sale of an item and the cost of acquiring or making it.

value date   The date on which currency is to be received. See **maturity date**.

vector auto regression   A statistical technique which selects variables and combinations of variables for inclusion in a **regression equation** according to how strong a statistical relationship they provide.

waybill (air)   Another term for **bill of lading**, used particularly for goods being transported by air cargo or courier.

weak-form efficiency   The situation when information only on historical prices or returns on a particular asset are reflected in market prices. See **efficient market**, **semi-strong-form efficiency**, and **strong-form efficiency**.

weighted average cost of capital   The per annum cost of funds raised via debt (bank borrowing, bonds) and equity (selling shares), where the two items are weighted by their relative importance.

whole turnover insurance   **Export insurance** where sellers do not have to inform the insurer of each credit that is to be insured. Also called **continuous** and **rollover** insurance.

wider band   A compromise between fixed and flexible exchange rates which allows exchange rates to fluctuate by a relatively large amount on either side of an official value. Tried during 1971–73 after approval by **International Monetary Fund** members as part of the **Smithsonian Agreement**.

wire transfer   The movement of money with instructions being sent by electronic means, such as via **SWIFT**.

withholding tax   A tax applied to nonresidents at the source of their earnings. See **withholding tax credit**.

withholding tax credit   Allowance made for taxes withheld by foreign governments in order to avoid double taxation.

World Bank   Also known as the **International Bank for Reconstruction and Development**, the World Bank assists developing nations by granting loans and providing economic advice. Origin dates back to the early 1940s.

World Trade Organization (WTO)   The World Trade Organization took over from the **General Agreement on Tariffs and Trade** in 1995. The WTO's objective is to expand international trade and resolve trade disputes.

writer (option)   The person selling an option, who must stand ready to buy (when selling a **put option**) or to sell (when selling a **call option**).

Yankee bond   A bond denominated in US dollars, issued in the United States by foreign banks and corporations.

Name index

Subject index